*Feasting on the Gospels
John, Volume 2*

Editorial Board

A Feasting on the Word™ Commentary

Feasting on the Gospels

John, Volume 2
Chapters 10–21

CYNTHIA A. JARVIS and E. ELIZABETH JOHNSON

General Editors

WJK WESTMINSTER
JOHN KNOX PRESS
LOUISVILLE • KENTUCKY

First edition
Published by Westminster John Knox Press
Louisville, Kentucky

15 16 17 18 19 20 21 22 23 24—10 9 8 7 6 5 4 3 2 1

Book design by Drew Stevens
Cover design by Dilu Nicholas

Library of Congress Cataloging-in-Publication Data

Feasting on the gospels—John : a feasting on the WordTM commentary / Cynthia A. Jarvis and E. Elizabeth Johnson, general editors. — First edition.
    volumes cm
  Includes index.
  Contents: Volume 1. chapters 1–9 — Volume 2. chapters 10–21.
  ISBN 978-0-664-23553-6 (v. 1 : hbk. : alk. paper) — ISBN 978-0-664-26036-1 (v. 1 : pbk. : alk. paper) —
ISBN 978-0-664-23554-3 (v. 2 : hbk. : alk. paper) — ISBN 978-0-664-26037-8 (v. 2 : pbk. : alk. paper)   1. Bible. John—
Commentaries.   I. Jarvis, Cynthia A.   II. Johnson, E. Elizabeth.
  BS2615.53.F43 2015
  226.5'077—dc23

                                                                                    2014031603

PRINTED IN THE UNITED STATES OF AMERICA

♾ The paper used in this publication meets the minimum requirements of the American National Standard for Information Sciences—Permanence of Paper for Printed Library Materials, ANSI Z39.48-1992.

Contents

Publisher's Note

Feasting on the Gospels is a seven-volume series that follows in the proud tradition of *Feasting on the Word: Preaching the Revised Common Lectionary.* Whereas *Feasting on the Word* provided commentary on only the texts in the lectionary, *Feasting on the Gospels* will cover every passage of the four Gospels. *Feasting on the Gospels* retains the popular approach of *Feasting on the Word* by providing four perspectives on each passage—theological, pastoral, exegetical, and homiletical—to stimulate and inspire preaching, teaching, and discipleship.

Westminster John Knox Press is grateful to the members of the large *Feasting* family who have given so much of themselves to bring this new series to life. General editors Cynthia A. Jarvis and E. Elizabeth Johnson stepped from their service on the editorial board of *Feasting on the Word* to the editorship of *Feasting on the Gospels* without missing a beat. Their commitment, energy, and unflagging enthusiasm made this work possible. The project manager, Joan Murchison, and project compiler, Mary Lynn Darden, continued their remarkable work, bringing thousands of pieces and hundreds of authors together seamlessly.

The editorial board did enormous work under grueling deadlines and did it with excellence and good humor. The hundreds of writers who participated—scholars, preachers, and teachers—gave much of themselves to help create this bountiful feast. David Bartlett and Barbara Brown Taylor took the time and care to help conceive this new project even as they were finishing their excellent work as general editors of *Feasting on the Word*.

Finally, we are again indebted to Columbia Theological Seminary for their partnership. As they did with *Feasting on the Word*, they provided many resources and personnel to help make this series possible. We are grateful in particular to seminary President Stephen Hayner and Dean of Faculty and Executive Vice President Deborah Mullen. It is with joy that we welcome you to this feast, in hopes that it will nourish you as you proclaim the Word to all of God's people.

Westminster John Knox Press

Series Introduction

At their best, people who write about Scripture are conversation partners. They enter the dialogue between the biblical text and the preacher or teacher or interested Christian and add perspectives gained from experience and disciplined attention. They contribute literary, historical, linguistic, and theological insights gathered over the millennia to the reader's first impressions of what is going on in a text. This conversation is essential if the reading of Scripture is to be fruitful in the church. It keeps reading the Bible from being an exercise in individual projection or uncritical assumption. That said, people who comment on the Bible should never become authorities. While a writer may indeed know more about the text than the reader does, he or she nevertheless writes from a particular perspective shaped by culture, ethnicity, gender, education, and theological tradition. In this regard, the writer of a commentary is no different from the writers and readers of Scripture.

The model for this series on the Gospels is the lectionary-based resource *Feasting on the Word* (Westminster John Knox Press, 2008–2011), now widely used by ministers as they prepare to preach. As central as the task of preaching is to the health of congregations, Scripture is the Word that calls the whole community of faith into being and sends out those addressed as witnesses to the Word in the world. Whether read devotionally by those gathered to pray or critically by others gathered to study, the Bible functions in a myriad of ways to undergird, support, and nurture the Christian life of individuals and communities. Those are the reasons that Westminster John Knox Press has taken the next step in the *Feasting* project to offer *Feasting on the Gospels*, a series in the style of *Feasting on the Word* with two major differences. First, all four Gospels are considered in their entirety, a *lectio continua* of sorts that leaves out nothing. Second, while *Feasting on the Word* is addressed specifically to preachers, *Feasting on the Gospels* is addressed to all who want to deepen their understanding of the Gospels—Bible study leaders and class members, seasoned preachers and seminarians, believers and skeptics.

The advantage of *Feasting on the Gospels* is that the reader encounters multiple perspectives on each text—not only the theological, exegetical, pastoral, and homiletical emphases that shape the essays but also the ecumenical, social, ethnic, and cultural perspectives of the authors. Unlike a single-author commentary, which sustains a particular view of a given interpreter throughout, *Feasting on the Gospels* offers readers a broad conversation that engages the text from many angles. In a church as diverse as the twenty-first-century church is, such deliberate engagement with many voices is imperative and, we hope, provocative.

A few observations about the particular challenges posed by the Gospels are in order here. The Gospels were written in a time when fledgling Christian communities—probably in their second generation—were just beginning to negotiate their relationships with Judaism (within which they were conceived and born), a community that was itself in the process of redefinition after the destruction of the Second Temple in 70 CE. Some of that negotiation was marked by great tension and sometimes outright hostility. The temptation for Christian readers to read anti-Semitism into texts that portray intra-Jewish conflict has beset the church almost from its beginnings. Our editors have been particularly mindful of this when dealing with essays on texts where the temptation to speak contemptuously of Jews and Judaism might threaten faithful interpretation. In these two volumes on John, readers will also find a helpful essay by Jaime Clark-Soles, a member of the editorial board and a Johannine scholar, about the troublesome language of "the Jews" in the Fourth Gospel and how faithful interpreters might deal with it.

A second observation involves the New Testament manuscript tradition. In *Feasting on the Gospels* we identify and comment on significant manuscript variants such as Mark 16:9–20 and John 7:53–8:11, something we did not have to contend with in *Feasting on the Word*. We identify those variant readings the way the NRSV does, except that we talk about "other ancient manuscripts" rather than the "other ancient authorities" of the NRSV notes.

The twelve members of our editorial board come from a broad swath of American Christianity: they are members or ministers of Presbyterian, Baptist,

United Church of Christ, Roman Catholic, and Disciples of Christ churches. Some of them are academics who serve on the faculties of theological schools; others are clergy serving congregations. All of them are extraordinarily hardworking, thoughtful, and perceptive readers of Scripture, of the church, and of the world. The writers whose work comprises these volumes represent an even wider cross-section of the church, most of them from North America, but a significant number from around the world, particularly the global South.

We could not have undertaken this work without the imagination, advice, and support of David Dobson, Editorial Director at Westminster John Knox Press, and his colleagues Don McKim, Marianne Blickenstaff, Michele Blum, and Julie Tonini. We are deeply grateful to David L. Bartlett and Barbara Brown Taylor, our mentors in the *Feasting on the Word* project, who continued to offer hands-on

assistance with *Feasting on the Gospels*. We thank President Stephen A. Hayner and Dean Deborah F. Mullen of Columbia Theological Seminary and the congregation of The Presbyterian Church of Chestnut Hill in Philadelphia, Pennsylvania, who made possible our participation in the project. Joan Murchison, who as Project Manager kept all of us and our thousands of essays in order and enforced deadlines with great good humor, is once again the beloved Hammer. Mary Lynn Darden, our compiler, who corralled not only the essays but also information about their authors and editors, brought all the bits and pieces together into the books you see now.

To the preachers, teachers, Bible study leaders, and church members who will read the Gospels with us, we wish you happy feasting.

Cynthia A. Jarvis
E. Elizabeth Johnson

"The Jews" in the Fourth Gospel
Jaime Clark-Soles

The Problem of Translation

John's Gospel refers seventy-one times in sixty-seven verses to *hoi Ioudaioi*.[1] The phrase appears in every single chapter of John except the Farewell Discourse (chaps. 14–17) and chapter 21. The NRSV usually translates this phrase "the Jews," although the phrase resists facile translation, because it does not mean the same thing each time it occurs. Numerous scholars have suggested various meanings for *hoi Ioudaioi* in the different instances in John, and these have been considered and categorized by Urban von Wahlde.[2]

"The Jews." First, the "national" sense refers to religious, cultural, or political aspects of people. When an event occurs in the time frame described as a festival of *hoi Ioudaioi*, it may be fine to translate it as "the Jews," because indeed the Festival of Sukkot (Booths or Tabernacles), for example, is a Jewish occasion, not a pagan one. Additionally, when Jesus declares to the Samaritan woman that "salvation is from the Jews" (4:22), he invokes the whole ethno-socio-religious history of God's covenant with Abraham and Sarah, Isaac and Rebekah, and Jacob and Rachel and Leah. This usage is ethically neutral and merely descriptive. Von Wahlde includes the following passages in this category: 2:6, 13; 3:1; 4:9a, 9b, 22; 5:1; 6:4; 7:2; 11:55; 18:20, 35; 19:21a, 40, 42.

"The Judeans." Sometimes, though, it is better to translate *hoi Ioudaioi* as "the Judeans." Von Wahlde calls this the "regional" sense. If one changes the Greek I to an English J (as we do with Jesus' name), one can practically hear the word "Judea." At times the term is used to designate those who are geographically connected to Judea. This usage also is ethically neutral and merely descriptive and can be found in the following verses: 3:22, 25; 11:18, 19, 31, 33, 36, 45, 54; 12:9, 11, 18; 19:20.

Here is where it begins to get complicated, though, because it is clear that Jesus comes into conflict with the leaders of his own tradition, whose symbolic (and literal) seat of power was located in Jerusalem, which, of course, is in Judea. As the three-year ministry of Jesus is narrated, notice that Galilee is a safe haven of sorts for Jesus, whereas each time that he goes to Jerusalem (or even contemplates it), ominous music begins to play in the background. In 1:19 we read: "This is the testimony given by John when *hoi Ioudaioi* sent priests and Levites from Jerusalem to ask him, 'Who are you?'" One might argue that this should be translated as "the Judeans," since the party comes from Judea.

"The Religious Authorities." The example from 1:19, however, raises another translation possibility. It is not everyone in Judea who sends priests and Levites; it is patently the religious authorities. The same is true in 7:13, and in both cases it would be best to translate *hoi Ioudaioi* as "the religious authorities." They are not the only religious leaders, though, as even 1:19 makes clear with the mention of priests and Levites. There are also high priests, rulers, and Pharisees. This brings us to von Wahlde's third category, which he designates the "Johannine use" of the word; most instances of the phrase *hoi Ioudaioi* fall into this category, so it is worth explicating, if briefly.

First, in these instances, the term does not have the national meaning, since these "Jews" are distinguished from other characters in the narrative who are also Jewish in the national sense. In other words, taken in a literal ethnic or religious sense, it makes no sense to translate these instances as "the Jews," because that does not distinguish them from anyone else in the Gospel: apart from the centurion and Pilate, everyone in the narrative is Jewish (even the Greeks in chap. 12 may be Greek Jews), both those who believe in Jesus and those who do not. Second, this usage is characterized by hostility toward Jesus. Passages that depict hostile or skeptical religious authorities include 1:19; 2:18, 22; 5:10, 15, 16, 18; 7:13, 15; 9:18, 22a, 22b; 18:12, 14, 36; 19:38; 20:19. Third, in these instances, the authorities labeled "the Jews" think and act en masse: "they represent a single undifferentiated reaction."[3] This use includes 2:18, 22; 7:33; 7:35.

1. John 1:19; 2:6, 13, 18, 20; 3:1, 22, 25; 4:9 (twice); 22; 5:1, 10, 15, 16, 18; 6:4, 41, 52; 7:1, 2, 11, 13, 15, 35; 8:22, 31, 48, 52, 57; 9:18, 22 (twice); 10:19, 24, 31, 33; 11:8, 19, 31, 33, 36, 45, 54, 55; 12:9, 11; 13:33; 18:12, 14, 20, 31, 33, 35, 36, 38, 39; 19:3, 7, 12, 14, 19, 20, 21 (three times), 31, 38, 40, 42; 20:19.

2. Urban von Wahlde, "The Johannine 'Jews': A Critical Survey," *New Testament Studies* 28 (1982): 33–60; "'The Jews' in the Gospel of John: Fifteen Years of Research (1983–1998)," *Ephemerides Theologicae Lovanienses* 76 (2000): 30–55. See also Joshua D. Garroway, "*Ioudaios*," in *The Jewish Annotated New Testament*, ed. Amy-Jill Levine and Marc Z. Brettler (New York: Oxford University Press, 2011), 524–26.

3. Von Wahlde, "The Johannine 'Jews,'" 47.

Religious authorities or the common people? Another issue that always arises in the debate about *hoi Ioudaioi* in John is that, after one has moved through the national and regional meanings (which are ethically neutral) and has extracted the passages that refer rather clearly to religious authorities, one still has a batch of verses to address. With those, it is less clear whether the author has in view the religious authorities or the common people. This becomes even further complicated because sometimes the author blurs the line between *hoi Ioudaioi* and the "world" (*kosmos*). The "world" is another complex character in John's Gospel, sometimes believing and sometimes not. "He was in the world, and the world came into being through him; yet the world did not know him" (1:10). Some interpreters conflate "the [unbelieving] Jews" with "the [unbelieving] world." Such a move is not helpful.

For our purposes, one of which includes reading the New Testament ethically, trying to determine which instances might refer to the common people instead of the authorities is not productive and can, in fact, lead to a reasoning that results in a seemingly "partial" anti-Semitism: "Well, it is not Jews per se who are to be maligned, but just their leaders; or maybe just the Jews who did not accept Jesus; or maybe just the Jews who do not accept him now." Faulty logic quickly becomes deadly logic. That said, with respect to the "debatable" instances, von Wahlde argues that, with two exceptions (6:41, 52), they likely refer still to "the religious authorities" rather than "the common people." These are 7:1, 11; 8:22, 48, 52, 57; 10:24, 31, 33; 11:8; 13:33; 18:31, 38; 19:7, 12, 14, 31.

We have now accounted for all of the occurrences of *hoi Ioudaioi* and shown the variety of meanings and the problems in attempting a reasonable translation in each instance. Two further observations should be made. First, because John's passion narrative has been a particularly thorny text with respect to Christian anti-Semitism, it may be worth noting that even there varieties in meaning inhere. The "Johannine sense" of *hoi Ioudaioi* appears in the following, according to von Wahlde: 18:12, 14, 31, 36; 19:12, 14, 31. The following use one or another of the other senses discussed earlier: 18:20, 33, 35, 39; 19:3, 19, 20, 21a, 21b, 21c, 40, 42.

Untranslated. Second, regarding the meaning of the seventy-one occurrences of *hoi Ioudaioi*, there is actually a surprising level of general agreement among scholars about the "Johannine uses." The

following seven, however, remain the most contested: 3:25; 8:31; 10:19; 11:54; 18:20; 19:20, 21. So riddled with difficulties is this translation issue that many scholars simply leave the phrase untranslated in those cases. Several authors of the essays in these volumes have made precisely that choice.

The Importance of Context

The Fourth Gospel evinces numerous tensions within itself, obvious literary seams, responses that do not answer the question posed, and so on. There are apparent strata, and scholars posit a lengthy and complicated composition history. Let us take a moment to sort out at least three of these strata chronologically.

1. Jesus of Nazareth is born, conducts his ministry, and dies at the hands of the Roman governor Pontius Pilate in about 30 CE.
2. Post-Easter, Jesus' disciples preach publicly about Jesus' identity, words, and deeds.
3. These oral traditions are committed to writing and eventually are drawn together into the narrative we know as the Gospel of John. Tension with the parent tradition remains high as the community discerns its identity vis-à-vis that tradition.
4. Sometime after the composition of the Fourth Gospel, the Epistles of John are penned, reflecting a later stage of the community. The issues now center on internal church conflict among the leaders, apostasy, and docetic Christology.

At the time of Jesus, the temple in Jerusalem is still standing, and numerous varieties of Judaism exist. The power of the Sadducees is temple-based; thus, when the temple is destroyed in 70, they fade from power. The Zealots, Sicarii, and the Fourth Philosophy are nationalists who oppose Roman occupation and favor civil war. The Essenes are a reformist, ascetic sect residing primarily at Qumran near the Dead Sea. The nationalists and the Essenes are decimated by the Roman army in the war of 66–70. The Pharisees are Torah-based teachers whose power derives from their ability to interpret the law—kind of a cross between lawyers and Bible scholars. When the temple is destroyed, they are the ones best positioned to assume leadership. The destruction of the temple effectively ends the period known as Second Temple Judaism and makes way for rabbinic Judaism, the kinds of Judaism that perdure to this day.

The original Johannine community consisted of Jews who worshiped in synagogues with their fellow Jews; they were Christian Jews because they believed that Jesus was the Messiah. Claiming that "the" or "a" Messiah had come was certainly not foreign to first- and second-century varieties of Judaism. John of Gischala in the first century and Simon Bar Kochba in the second were declared Messiahs. This was not grounds for dismissal from the Jewish community. So what happened? It is impossible to say with certainty, but clearly the Johannine community began to experience conflict with its parent tradition. The author of the Fourth Gospel claims that the members who made up John's community were put out of the synagogue, *aposynagōgos* (a word unknown in early Jewish or Christian literature apart from John 9:22; 12:42; 16:2), due to their high Christology, perhaps even confessing Jesus as God. It is clear that a full confession of the identity of Jesus as defined by John led to extremely painful conflict between the parent tradition and the sect that formed as a result of their expulsion from the synagogue.

According to J. Louis Martyn,[4] John can be read as a two-level drama. First, there is the story of the historical Jesus, what happened "back then." Second, there is the reality that the Johannine community is experiencing near the end of the first century, sixty to seventy years after Jesus' death and twenty to thirty years after the temple has been destroyed; the Pharisees (not the Sadducees) are in power, and the synagogue (not the temple) is the seat of power for the religious authorities. The story of the Johannine community living in the late first century gets retrojected onto the story of Jesus and the first disciples.

For example, when one is reading in chapter 9 the story of the blind man being persecuted and put out of the synagogue, unsupported by his parents, one should imagine a Johannine Christian who is openly professing faith in Christ and being persecuted by members of the parent tradition. The story is anachronistic, because the Pharisees and the synagogue were not such centers of power in Jesus' own day; the Sanhedrin and temple were. It is also anachronistic because no one could give a confession of Jesus as Lord (as the blind man does), Son of God, God (as Thomas does), Messiah, Son of Man, and more until *after* the passion, resurrection,

sending of the Paraclete, and return of Jesus to God. In other words, the story could not have happened historically the way it is narrated. One should therefore be careful about making historical assumptions based on texts that have a different rhetorical aim. Certainly the text caricatures anyone who opposes Jesus, the hero of the narrative. The Pharisees are not excused from the Fourth Evangelist's lampooning.

While certain aspects of this reconstruction have recently been contested,[5] important conclusions and warnings can nevertheless be drawn from it. First, the Fourth Gospel reflects an intra-Jewish debate, not a debate between "Christians" and "Jews"; they are all Jews. This is the way sects develop. The Johannine community makes sense of itself as a Jewish community in categories drawn from the Hebrew Bible and Jewish markers of all kinds. Remembering this is crucial when reading this text. Those who choose to ignore the concrete social setting of the New Testament will find it easy to justify anti-Semitism by drawing on John. His violent, seething language about "the Jews" has been used and still is used to charge Jews with all sorts of wickedness.

Second, remember that the Gospel is a story and follows narrative conventions, including characters drawn for symbolic purposes, conflict that the hero must overcome, and so on. It is not a historical rendering, and it takes great poetic license in its depiction of history. Interpreters will be able to understand that only when they learn about the historical context from historical sources that, happily, scholars have provided in abundance.

The Insidious Problem of Anti-Semitism

Easter has always been a potentially dangerous time for Jews, as Christians accuse them of being guilty of deicide, of being Christ-killers, and, thanks to John 8, of being murderous children of the devil. In a post-Shoah world, it is ethically incumbent upon all Christians, especially those who preach and teach, to address and to battle anti-Semitism. There are at least three ways that the Gospel of John may fuel anti-Semitism. We have already addressed the first problem: the repeated use of the phrase *hoi Ioudaioi* in primarily pejorative ways.

The second problem is Johannine dualism. It begins already in chapter 1, where "grace and law"

---

4. J. Louis Martyn, *History and Theology in the Fourth Gospel, Revised and Expanded*, New Testament Library (Louisville, KY: Westminster John Knox Press, 2003).

5. See the work of Adele Reinhartz, for example: *Befriending the Beloved Disciple: A Jewish Reading of the Gospel of John* (New York/London: Bloomsbury Academic, 2002); and "John," in *The Jewish Annotated New Testament*, 152–96.

and "Jesus and Moses" are presented as opposites: "From his fullness we have all received, grace upon grace. The law indeed was given through Moses; grace and truth came through Jesus Christ" (1:16–17). Other dualistic categories include light and darkness, truth and falsehood, life and death, God the Father and Satan the father, above and below, not of this world and of this world. Jesus and the disciples are associated with all of the good categories; "the Jews" are primarily associated with the negative trait in each pair.

This contributes to a third problem that arises in the Fourth Gospel: the use of typology in a way that leads to Christian supersessionism.[6] Jesus is depicted as like, but superior to, numerous Old Testament figures, including Moses (chaps. 1, 5, 6), Jacob (1:51; chap. 4), Abraham (chap. 8), and Woman Wisdom herself. Jewish symbols and rituals now find their fulfilled meaning only in Jesus: his incarnation is a tabernacle (1:14); his body is now the temple (chap. 2); he is the bread from heaven celebrated in the Passover; he is the Passover lamb (which is why he dies a day earlier in John than in the Synoptics); he is the King of the Jews. He has fulfilled or replaced everything worthwhile in Judaism. In this way, John may be accused of being anti-Jewish, if not anti-Semitic. Helpful is the following from the Jewish Johannine scholar Adele Reinhartz:

It must be emphasized that the Gospel is not anti-Semitic in a racial sense, as it is not one's origins that are decisive but one's beliefs. Nevertheless, it has been used to promote anti-Semitism. Most damaging has been John 8:44, in which Jesus declares that the Jews have the devil as their father. . . . While John's difficult rhetoric should not be facilely dismissed, it can be understood as part of the author's process of self-definition, of distinguishing the followers of Jesus from the synagogue and so from Jews and Judaism. This distancing may have been particularly important if the ethnic composition of the Johannine community included Jews, Samaritans, and Gentiles. This approach does not excuse the Gospel's rhetoric, but it may make it possible for readers to understand the narrative's place in the process by which Christianity became a separate religion, to appreciate the beauty of its language, and to recognize the spiritual power that it continues to have in the lives of many of its Christian readers.[7]

The authors and editors of the two John volumes of *Feasting on the Gospels* have worked diligently to bear such convictions in mind as they worked through this rich and complex Gospel to offer preachers, teachers, Bible study leaders, and interested Christian readers guidance through the thicket of language and images that historically have divided Christians from Jews and frequently resulted in Christian violence against Jews.

---

6. Supersessionism is a theological claim that Christianity supersedes or replaces Judaism in God's plan of redemption. Sometimes it is called fulfillment or replacement theology.

7. Reinhartz, "John," 156.

Feasting on the Gospels
John, Volume 2

John 10:1–6

¹"Very truly, I tell you, anyone who does not enter the sheepfold by the gate but climbs in by another way is a thief and a bandit. ²The one who enters by the gate is the shepherd of the sheep. ³The gatekeeper opens the gate for him, and the sheep hear his voice. He calls his own sheep by name and leads them out. ⁴When he has brought out all his own, he goes ahead of them, and the sheep follow him because they know his voice. ⁵They will not follow a stranger, but they will run from him because they do not know the voice of strangers." ⁶Jesus used this figure of speech with them, but they did not understand what he was saying to them.

Theological Perspective

This passage comes immediately after the story of the healing of a blind man. The blind man claims in awe that Jesus must be sent from God to do the things he has done. The Pharisees are challenging the claims that Jesus is from God, though, because of the lack of external markers—for example, he came from Galilee and not from Bethlehem—and because he heals on the Sabbath. In other words, they believe that Jesus cannot be from God because he does not bear the expected indications of being the Messiah.

In answer to them, Jesus describes a scene that should have been very familiar to them, the common practice of shepherds who enclose their sheep in a communal pen for safety. In the Palestine of the day, shepherds often secured their sheep communally, several flocks to a sheep pen. There was a gate or an opening to the pen that was guarded to prevent sheep from escaping or strangers from entering. Legitimate shepherds have access through the gate, but those who come in otherwise, Jesus asserts, do so only in order to steal or destroy the sheep.

A different metaphor is possibly more familiar to today's urban person: the electronic car entry key, which I will call the "clicker." When my car is parked, for example, in a parking lot, I usually lock it. When I click my car key, it sends out an electronic signal, calling my car as it is parked among a hundred more

Pastoral Perspective

A computer-savvy young adult might recast this text in terms of a prohibition against "hacking" one's way into Christian leadership. There are no "backdoor" entrances or gaming "workarounds" for genuine leadership or participation in Christian community. Like a well-constructed video game, congregations and small groups thrive because they are patterned on a set of commitments and practices embedded in the fabric of communal life. Friends and foes are recognized by their adherence to interactive conventions defined by these shared understandings and behaviors. A true leader is made known to the community by the ways in which that person genuinely embodies the community's core commitments.

Of course, just as gamers may differ in their interpretation of what "matters" in a successful quest to conquer evil, Christians often disagree about what constitutes a core belief or practice. Is a belief in the literal resurrection of Jesus essential to Christian faith? Is the ability to forgive terrorists who place bombs at marathon finish lines a necessary trait of Christian discipleship? Are certain positions on social issues (e.g., same-sex marriage, fair trade, enemy combatants) ethically more Christian than other perspectives? Many Christian communities avoid taking a communal stand on such issues precisely because they know their members are of many

Exegetical Perspective

Sheep and shepherding were common parts of life in antiquity. As a result, they enter the biblical texts both in references to actual herds of livestock and metaphorically as an expression about the leadership of a group of people. Both biblical and nonbiblical sources attest to the shepherd as a conventional metaphor for a leader or king. In the Old Testament, David's role as a shepherd becomes a qualification to fight Goliath (1 Sam. 17:34–35), and he is later identified as a shepherd of God's people (e.g., Ezek. 34:23). God is also imagined as a shepherd (e.g., Ps. 23).

John's language, however, brings specific elements of the biblical background into focus. The parable addresses the question of rightful leadership. Thieves and bandits attempt to sneak into the sheepfold, though the gate is opened only for the legitimate shepherd (vv. 1–3). Although there were many elements of shepherding that were familiar to his readers, John centers in on the metaphor of the shepherd as leader of a group of people.

Ezekiel 34 uses the shepherding metaphor in a similar way and thus may provide a helpful comparison. Ezekiel also uses shepherding as a metaphor for leadership of God's people, and indicates a conflict over the leadership of the sheep. Through the prophet, God accuses the shepherds of Israel of feeding themselves and not tending the sheep (Ezek.

Homiletical Perspective

John's Gospel invests heavily in the theological framework by which we are to understand who Jesus is. Jesus is the Logos made flesh, the light of the world, the one from above, the one of the Spirit, the one human who is also of another realm. So how are we to understand this one of us who is from somewhere else and so clearly different? How are we to understand ourselves in relationship to him? The preceding narrative builds foundations for understanding through the metaphor of sight and the condition of sin. Those who think they see on their own are blind with sin, and those who are humble enough to know they are blind may see when touched by Jesus. Those who encounter Jesus in humility and faith are free to see.

This parable presents a detailed pastoral scene illustrating how we might consider Jesus and ourselves. A shepherd comes to a sheepfold, and when he calls the sheep through the gate to pasture, they recognize his voice and follow. The characters are connected by voice and sound. The previous passage engaged the sense of sight; John's Gospel also engages the sense of taste ("I am the bread of life," 6:35, 48), and the current passage engages the sense of hearing. John's Gospel gives us the impression that all these senses build on each other and suggests that knowing God will take all our senses.

Theological Perspective

cars, and my car responds by locking or unlocking itself (or by beeping in panic if I press a different button). My car, out of the many in the parking lot, recognizes the particular signal from my clicker. It does not recognize any other signal from other car clickers. This relationship was manufactured in the factory, or coded in along the way.

In *The Little Prince*, by Antoine de Saint-Exupéry, the narrator crashes his plane in a desert. There he meets a young prince from a tiny distant planet who has found his way there as well. This planet has three volcanoes and a single rose, which the young prince has carefully tended and protected. In the little prince's adventures in the desert on earth he meets a fox. The fox asks the young outlander to tame it. The fox explains to the little prince that the process of taming is what forms a friendship and makes each one unique to the other. The parties wait for each other, slowly get used to the other's presence, and "waste time" with each other. They develop rituals and routines familiar to the other, and over time they come to expect each other and miss each other if one is gone. The fox offers, "You become responsible forever for what you have tamed," and "One sees clearly only with the heart. Anything essential is invisible to the eyes."[1]

This story about a fox and boy points out the difference between the relationship of a sheep to its shepherd and that of my car to my car key. Unlike car and car key, sheep and shepherd are not born recognizing each other; this must be cultivated over time. When the shepherd calls out his own sheep by name and they follow him, the process is one of mutual recognition, because the shepherd has tamed the sheep. The shepherd has tamed the sheep by "wasting" time with them. They have become unique to each other. The sheep recognize the shepherd's as the only voice they will follow, and he is responsible to them. Unfortunately, my car and I do not have the same relationship. Anyone, including a thief or robber, can click my clicker, insert the key, and drive it off. We are not unique to each other. I have not wasted time with my car, taming it and teaching it to answer my clicks. It simply does it out of a factory-installed blind obedience.

Similarly, with living beings, there is a difference between responding in mutual relationship and responding out of blind obedience. Blind obedience is demanded when one has positional authority only.

1. Antoine de Saint-Exupéry, *The Little Prince*, trans. Richard Howard (New York: Harcourt, Inc., 1943), 63–64.

Pastoral Perspective

minds. The voice of wisdom appears to have no single recognizable tone to which a unified Christian community can respond.

This text, then, challenges congregations to explore the boundaries of their communal faith and identify the gateway through which they encourage wisdom to enter. As part of a global community, Christians reside in a sheepfold populated with the followers of many shepherds. They participate in yoga-based exercise classes and learn meditation techniques in therapy that provide soft introductions to Eastern religious traditions. They relax to television shows and cinema films that depict a variety of moral perspectives as equally viable options. They listen to music that depicts God metaphorically as smoking on street corners ("You Found Me"), steering an out-of-control car ("Jesus, Take the Wheel"), and catching a train out of town ("American Pie").[1] They tune in (or out) televangelists, celebrities, and pundits who claim to know the truth with a capital T. These are the voices they bring with them to church on Sunday, where they try for an hour to make sense of being Christian in the twenty-first century amid so many different possibilities for meaning-making.

It is perhaps both blessing and curse that contemporary believers are not particularly sheepish in their curiosity about otherness. While this interest may not be explicitly religious, the obsession with quasi-reality shows such as *Duck Dynasty*, *Here Comes Honey Boo Boo*, and *Survivor* suggests that voyeuristic engagement with strangers is an amusing pastime for millions of people. It is not hard to imagine that the advice of Long Island Medium Theresa Caputo might more readily come to mind in a time of crisis than a pastor's recent sermon.[2] Whether these voices represent divinely inspired wisdom or the misleading words of thieves and bandits is a complex question for Christians who recognize that God works in and through cultural contexts as well as in contradiction to cultural values.

What guidance, then, might a pastor provide to aid parishioners in distinguishing between the voice of a genuine Christian shepherd and the clamoring noise of pretenders whose attempts to sneak into prominence endanger Christian faith? One option is to encourage the congregation to name the criteria by which they assess different kinds of advice

1. The Fray, "You Found Me" (Sony BMG, 2008, CD); Carrie Underwood, "Jesus, Take the Wheel" (19 Recordings Limited, 2005, CD); Don McLean, "American Pie" (United Artists, 1971, record).
2. *Duck Dynasty* (A&E, 2013); *Here Comes Honey Boo Boo* (TLC, 2013); *Survivor* (CBS, 2013); *Long Island Medium* (TLC, 2013).

34:1–4). God intends to rescue the sheep, first as shepherd (Ezek. 34:11–16), and then through a shepherd like David (Ezek. 34:23–24). Like Ezekiel, John 10:1–6 uses the shepherding metaphor to evoke a conflict over human leadership of God's people.

John's metaphors are often read in ways that separate them from their literary context. When read as a conflict over leadership, the parable of the Shepherd becomes an integral part of the literary context of John 9–10. Metaphors like the bread of John 6:35 and the shepherd of John 10:11 float free from their original contexts and make their way into Christian art and liturgy as freestanding images. Although there is nothing wrong with this way of reading, interpreting the metaphors as a part of the narrative can reintroduce meanings that have been ignored.

John 10:1–6 continues a conversation that begins at the end of chapter 9. Jesus engages the Pharisees who have opposed his healing of the man born blind. He challenges their understanding of the healing as evidence of their "blindness" (9:39–41). The shepherd parable extends that discussion by suggesting that Jesus is the rightful leader of the sheep and that the Pharisees are thieves and bandits.

The later part of chapter 10 continues the question of legitimate leadership with a slightly different focus. After this conversation ends in 10:18, the people are divided about Jesus' teachings. He indicates that those who accept his words are the sheep who "hear [his] voice" (vv. 4, 27). Those who do not believe "do not belong to my sheep" (10:26). Here the question is not whether Jesus is the leader, but who will follow him. Those who recognize Jesus' leadership "belong to [his] sheep" (10:26).

The stories that precede and follow chapter 10 illustrate the idea of belonging to Jesus' flock and hearing his voice. In the healing of the blind man, Jesus rejects the interpretation of the blind man as a sinner and instead instructs him to wash (9:7). The blind man follows Jesus' instructions and is healed (9:7). Later in the chapter, when Jesus identifies himself (9:37), the man responds with belief (9:38). Like Jesus' sheep, the blind man hears and follows.

The example of Lazarus in chapter 11 also fits the role of the sheep from the parable. Jesus' command, "Lazarus, come out!" (11:43), parallels the language of 10:3: "He calls his own sheep by name and leads them out." The blind man and Lazarus are examples of sheep who know the voice of their shepherd.

The thieves and bandits of 10:1 are false alternatives to the shepherd. They attempt to enter the sheepfold without going through the gate. The

The parable's characterization of shepherd and sheep as a metaphor for the Savior and the people speaks to some of our deepest spiritual yearnings. A shepherd was a common image for a leader, an authority and guide for the people to follow. This metaphor of the shepherd, particularly as characterized, addresses deep human longings for connection with the Divine. The shepherd who calls is heard and known by the sheep. The sheep are called by name and led out to pastures of bounty. The shepherd and sheep are related and familiar, even intimate. The sheep trust this familiar shepherd and follow him. To be known intimately by God, and to be called by name, to be cared for, and to trust God as familiar—these are some of the deepest human longings. The preacher should find ways for these words and images to speak an assuring word to those yearnings in the hearts of hearers.

One path between this text and a hearer's heart is to explore the "voice" of the Savior and what it might mean to hear and recognize it. Concepts like "calling" or "election," which are common in the church's vernacular, can be alienating to those who do not understand what it means or feel as though they have never experienced the voice of the Divine in their lives. Is the Savior's voice something you hear in your head, like the voice of a friend, or is it merely a feeling?

The experience of hearing an unexpected but familiar friend call your name to get your attention could help illustrate the visual and aural imagery of the passage. The experience of sensing that a grieving friend needs a visit could extend the imagery of the passage to include the calls from God we feel. Everyday examples of divine voices calling to you or someone you know would be well invested in helping this imagery come alive.

The parable claims that when the voice of someone other than the shepherd calls, the sheep run away, and do not follow the stranger. Inner voices of temptation and feelings like revenge, the destructive callings that should not be followed, might be contrasted with the kind of voices that are God's. In addition to the simple construction of good and bad voices, the preacher could also explore the ways that Jesus and this metaphor might appear strange to some. Following Jesus with a faith community and experiencing the blessings of self-giving together can help the voice of Jesus become more familiar and trustworthy.

While this surface space of the parable has plenty to explore, we should also be sure to explore the

John 10:1–6

Theological Perspective

It is demanded instantly, not cultivated over time. Although sometimes touted as a virtue, it arises out of fear of the consequences of disobedience. Blind obedience is the antithesis of taming and building trust. Demanding blind obedience, for whatever reason, would be stealing and robbing the personhood—the free will, love, and trust—of the other person.

When Jesus describes a mutual relationship that arises out of time wasted and trust earned, he is claiming that authority from God comes of the heart, not by external position or pedigree. As a shepherd tames his sheep, faith and trust are earned and not stolen. The sheep follow the shepherd willingly, because the shepherd has consistently provided protection and pasture for them. Similarly, godly leaders must be authentic, transparent, and caring; authority and respect must be earned and not demanded or bullied.

The Pharisees do not accept Jesus, because his claims to be from God are not supported by external markers. John points out that Jesus' claims to be from God instead arise from his relationship with his people: his healings and miracles in their service. It is Jesus' message—of the good news of God's love and salvation—that proves he is from God.

Why do the Pharisees not understand the metaphor? Surely it is not because they do not know shepherds. Perhaps they can recognize or acknowledge God only if God comes in ways they expect, namely, tradition and the external markers of authority. They are not looking with the heart.

Similarly, I wonder what my blind spots are. Where are the evidences of life in God that I cannot see because they come from sources I do not expect? What am I not looking at with my heart?

SHARON M. TAN

Pastoral Perspective

and ask whether and how those criteria are linked to Scripture and tradition. These are the means by which Jesus believed that Christian sheep would know their shepherd: through the stories of God's interaction with God's people from the creation of the world through the exodus out of Egypt, the governance of kings and the challenges of prophets, the bravery of Esther and the judges, the earnest efforts and mistakes of the disciples, the witness of the early church, and the history of the church's ministry and mission throughout time.

In the context of the Gospel of John, Jesus' hearers would have relied primarily on the Hebrew Scriptures and their knowledge of Jesus' life and teaching. Contemporary Christians have access not only to those resources but also to the reflections of theologians who have struggled for centuries with the question of how one recognizes the voice of God and hears God's call to move out of the fold and into the world as witnesses to the good news of Christ's presence.

Listeners may take comfort in the Gospel writer's acknowledgment that the task of recognizing and following Christ was as daunting for early believers as it is today. When Jesus tried to explain the difference between his message and that of messianic imposters, those questioning him "did not understand what he was saying to them" (v. 6). Part of this confusion stemmed from the difference between what Jesus' listeners expected in a spiritual leader and what they heard and saw in his teaching and life. Additional uncertainty may have arisen from the listeners' inability to think metaphorically and theologically when what they wanted was a straightforward description of a divine plan for religious ascendency.

They were not eager to enter "a school for the Lord's service" (to quote from the sixth-century monastic Rule of Benedict[3]) in order to learn what it means to follow Christ. Instead, they hoped Jesus would offer them a declaration of the truth that might guide them on a failsafe quest to vanquish evil in the world and establish the God of Abraham and Sarah as the one true God. As any dedicated gamer can attest, a really good and meaningful quest is never that simple or straightforward. The joy is in the discovery and development of new skills of discernment and the honing of practical abilities that give deeper meaning to human experience and hope.

KAREN-MARIE YUST

---

3. Available at http://www.documentacatholicaomnia.eu/03d/0480-0547,_Benedictus_Nursinus,_Regola,_EN.pdf ; accessed April 5, 2014.

gatekeeper opens the gate for the shepherd of the sheep, validating his identity as shepherd and distinguishing him from the thieves and bandits (vv. 2–3). The appearance of the gatekeeper as an actor in verse 3 corresponds to what Jesus says elsewhere about his Father: "Just as the Father has life in himself, so he has granted the Son also to have life in himself; and he has given him authority to execute judgment, because he is the Son of Man" (5:26–27). As the Father grants authority to the Son, so the gatekeeper opens the gate for the shepherd and authorizes his leadership.

Unlike the thieves, the "strangers" of verse 5 do not pose a direct threat to the sheep. They illustrate the sheep's knowledge of their shepherd's voice. The sheep will not follow everyone. They will run from strangers, but they know the voice of their shepherd and follow him.

Listeners respond to Jesus' parable with misunderstanding (v. 6). A similar response often follows Jesus' parables in the other Gospels. For example, in Mark 4, Jesus teaches the parable of the Sower to a large crowd (Mark 4:1–9), but explains it only in private to his disciples (Mark 4:10–20). In John 10, the audience Jesus addresses includes the Pharisees he has accused of blindness and sin (9:39–41). Their inability to understand does not seem to be a result of Jesus' mysterious nature but their own refusal to see him for what he is.

As in Mark, Jesus goes on to explain the parable. There are two notable differences, though. First, the audience in John does not change. Jesus' explanation is addressed to all those who hear and misunderstand the parable. Second, Jesus gives two distinct explanations of the parable. Although interpreters emphasize the second, where Jesus identifies himself as the good shepherd (10:11), the intervening verses give an alternative way to understand the parable, with Jesus as the gate for the sheep. The layers of meaning John offers to readers are a distinctive feature of the Gospel. They offer a wealth of resources to help readers think about Jesus' identity and come to understand him better.

SUSAN E. HYLEN

deeper rungs of the parable. We get a clue that there is more to the parable when we learn the Pharisees did not understand.

The parable can be understood fully only with the succeeding two pericopes, because as soon as we have explored the parable with Jesus as shepherd, verse 7 turns this shepherding framework on its side. "I am the gate," Jesus says. This unexpected interpretation of the parable reshuffles our understanding of it, and begs us to look at other angles of meaning. As both shepherd and gate, Jesus leads the sheep to a safe place and at the same time provides the entrance into that safe place.

This parable's simplest and most accessible construction speaks to deep yearnings inside, like hearing and seeing our help and guide. Sometimes we rush to read into parables only that for which our spirits yearn. We have to take care that our basic assumptions, images, and vocabularies do not limit our understanding of Jesus. Deeper exploration suggests that Jesus, the one from above, is not merely the Savior we hope or imagine. He may be more than a voice whispering to us, or a stranger speaking to us, or a feeling of passion. This parable invites us to consider that Jesus, the one from above, is not only a voice but also a way, a way out of captivity and narrow space into spacious and fertile ground. Perhaps Jesus, the one from above, is a way that can be pointed out to us by guiding voices who know where to find him.

To know Jesus through the use of parables in the Gospel of John takes work and asks something of us. Leading sermon hearers on this parable's journey into the deep end of the pool will communicate its methodology and draw them closer to John's gospel truth.

DAVID LOWER

John 10:7–10

Theological Perspective

After Jesus realizes that the Pharisees do not understand his general metaphor about shepherds and sheep, thieves and robbers, he becomes more specific. He likens himself to the gate to salvation and life in the fullest, or abundant life. Here Jesus links salvation with life in its fullest; this is not a metaphysical or afterlife event, but involves life in the present, in body, soul, and spirit.

As the gate protects the sheep from intruders who steal and rob, so it also opens the way to pasture. Salvation and life in its fullest involve both protection and provision. It is more than mere physical survival or living in quiet desperation. Life in its fullest involves body, soul, and spirit. It is living with security, sufficiency, meaning, and self-determination—in other words, human flourishing.

The United States proclaims in its Declaration of Independence that its citizens have the rights to "life, liberty, and the pursuit of happiness." The United Nations declares a list of rights humans have by virtue of being human, including the right to freedom of conscience. Christian tradition upholds the norms of love and justice (defined variously) as necessary to the Christian ethical life. The good news Jesus proclaims is that God is concerned about human flourishing.

I suggest that human rights, if appropriately contextualized, are one way of expressing and

Pastoral Perspective

Advertisers suggest that salvation and abundant life are available through the many products devised for consumer comfort and convenience. An award-winning commercial depicts a statuesque woman in white strutting past cake- and muffin-mix boxes to the beat of fashion runway music while a narrator declares that she will dominate the school bake sale after purchasing her ingredients from a specific local chain store. The parting shot of the woman crushing an egg with one hand while holding a whisk like a scepter suggests that bake-sale dominance is a highly satisfying goal for modern mothers, who are delighted that the store chain can deliver this triumphant achievement. A multitude of advertisements for beauty products offer a similar message of salvation—in these cases, from aging or presumably less-than-favorable genetic endowments—and equate the use of the right wrinkle cream, mascara, or lipstick with self-acceptance and social power.

Men navigate their own maze of identity-defining messages. They are urged to drive the right car, drink the right beer, and ask their doctor about the right medications to ensure sexual prowess. A tongue-in-cheek car commercial suggests that purchasing one of their vehicles can overcome the masculine shortcoming of athletic ineptitude, allowing a father to make up for teaching his son the wrong way to

Feasting on the Gospels

Exegetical Perspective

Jesus' parable about the shepherd and the sheep (10:1–5) requires explanation (10:6). Although the controversy with the Pharisees (9:39–41) has prepared the reader for Jesus' identification of himself as the shepherd of the parable, this is not what happens. Jesus will later identify himself as "the good shepherd" (10:11). First, he creates a different relationship between himself and the parable, one that is unexpected and more difficult to understand. Although the metaphor of the good shepherd is well known to Christians and often depicted in art, the metaphor of the gate is less often explored.

Modern readers often skip over the content of these verses about the gate by combining the gate metaphor with the shepherd metaphor. Many interpreters assert that shepherds in antiquity lay down across the gate of the sheepfold as a way of protecting their sheep. Because of this, Jesus' words "I am the gate" simply indicate another of his roles as shepherd. However, there is scant evidence for the phenomenon of the shepherd as gate. Usually the equation of the shepherd and gate is made without offering evidence. The only support for the argument I have ever encountered made reference to a 1943 encounter with modern Bedouins.[1]

1. John Van Ess, *Meet the Arab* (New York: John Day Co., 1943).

Homiletical Perspective

Building on the pastoral parable in the previous passage, Jesus explains that he is the gate for the sheep. This revelation surprises our presuppositions about the parable, in which a shepherd comes to a sheepfold to call and lead the sheep to pasture through the gate. We anticipated in the previous passage, as the Jewish hearers would have, that Jesus is the shepherd in the parable, calling by name the sheep who recognize his voice. Jesus challenges those expectations, though, and claims the role not of a character but of an inanimate architectural passage. John's Gospel continually challenges assumptions about God and salvation. These assumptions are those of the disciples, the Pharisees, or perhaps even the readers, and this teaching functions as such a challenge. The reign of God is at hand, and it is likely different from what you imagine or expect.

Jesus is the gate to the sheepfold, giving preachers an opportunity to reflect on the image of the gate and ways it might help us understand the Savior. The gate is part of the protection and order provided by the pen, and the particular part that can be opened to let in or let out. The gate is the passage through which sheep must enter and leave the sheepfold. The gate is the way by which sheep pass to go beyond a narrow and confined existence—a gateway to liberation. The gate is also the way by which sheep pass

Theological Perspective

institutionalizing love and justice in the world today. There are two components to human rights, very similar to what the gate provides the sheep: protection and provision. Negative rights are rights that protect an individual from unjust restraint and oppression, for example, freedom of conscience, freedom of religion, and freedom from unwarranted restraint. They basically guarantee an individual freedom from unnecessary governmental interference. Positive rights are those that guarantee more than simple freedom from government oppression; they provide the right to a good in the community, for example, food, health care, and education.

Negative and positive rights exist in tension with each other in a world of limited resources, as the provision of positive rights to a group in a community may require the contribution of the resources from individuals not from that group. In the United States, individual and negative rights are emphasized, although it and many other nations also promise some positive rights to their citizens. Life in its fullest, or human flourishing, must consist of a combination of both positive and negative rights. The particular combination of rights and their specific contours must grow out of the history of a particular community.

A number of Christian ethicists agree that justice is a precondition to love; only when one's relationship is based on justice can one say that one loves as well. On the other hand, it is also true that the desire for and the goal of love can be the impetus for justice. For example, if we believe that God created and loves the world, we work toward justice in the world. It is in both justice and love that shalom is present.

Seeking justice and one of its expressions, human rights, is a deeply Christian endeavor. In seeking justice and human rights, though, we must not impose our cultural biases on others. That would be antithetical to human flourishing; it would be to steal and rob communities of their religious and cultural traditions by imposing a Western point of view. There exists a delicate balance and a difficult tension between the concerns of an individual's human rights if they conflict (or appear to conflict) with a group's claims to self-determination and authorship of their culture. To find the delicate balance, one must work from within the culture, that is, with a shepherd who knows his or her sheep and whom the sheep follow and trust.

This leads us to a discussion of the gate. When Jesus said he was the gate, did he also imply that he was the only gate? Some would look to claims like

Pastoral Perspective

throw a baseball by passing down a great family car. Average-looking husbands are reminded that they lack the power of a pictured star in a yogurt advertisement and learn that they can control women's bodies and affections with the application of a certain body spray.

Advertisers even attempt to shape children's ideas of abundant life with the intertwining of juvenile entertainment, product placement, and fast-food-meal tie-ins. Animated film releases are linked with the campaigns of fast-food chains designed to incite children's desires for an entire collection of cheap plastic toys. Television characters decorate children's clothing, subtly conveying that life is best when shared with a commercial alter ego outlined on one's body. Popular children's books generate heavily marketed product lines. Parents are left wondering: if I refuse to participate in a certain fad when everyone else is doing it, will my children's Christmas memories be a little less joyous?

The danger in the rampant commercialization of abundant life is not so much in the particular value (or lack thereof) of a specific product being marketed, but in the insidious ways in which advertising campaigns steal a person's ability to discern what is necessary for a fruitful life and what is extraneous. Advertisers kill an individual's sense of self-worth and uniqueness in the eyes of God by promoting excessive regard for the approval of others and competition for the most stuff, rather than promoting good living as collaboration with each other.

Christians throughout the ages have struggled to discern the role that possessions can and should play in faithful living. The passage at hand does not directly address this issue. What it does offer is some cautionary advice for contemporary Christians who wish to take up this question anew. This text suggests that there are "thieves and bandits" (v. 8) who pretend to have the best interests of good people at heart, but really want only "to steal and kill and destroy" (v. 10). Thus, Christians need to embrace spiritual practices that will enable them to identify and resist commercial messages that undermine their primary identity as children of God and disciples of Christ. These practices should also encourage them to wonder about the nature of life with God and the ways in which one measures abundance on a divine scale.

One critical spiritual practice for discernment is attentiveness. First, Christians need to pay attention to the number of commercial messages to which they are exposed daily and the common themes embedded in those advertisements. With researchers

Although this solution has been appealing to many, it is problematic, because it substitutes the role of the shepherd in verses 11–18 for what is actually said about the gate in verses 7–10. Here the gate is the point of authorized entry for the shepherd, and a way for sheep to access the pasture. Neither of these ideas matches what Jesus will say about the shepherd (10:11–18). They are specific to the role of Jesus as gate.

The equation of shepherd and gate is compelling because it allows the reader to solve the "problem" of John's use of two metaphors for Jesus. In the parable, the gate and the shepherd are discrete entities with different functions, yet John asserts that Jesus is both gate and shepherd. This dual relationship to the parable seems less problematic when viewed in the context of the Gospel as a whole. John uses many metaphors to characterize Jesus: Word, bread, vine, and many more. No one metaphor completely captures who Jesus is. Each one illumines some aspect of Jesus' identity. The gate and shepherd metaphors should be read in this way. Each one articulates a piece of John's understanding of who Jesus is. Because of this, the reader may stand to gain something by considering the gate metaphor on its own terms.

Following on the heels of the parable, Jesus' words "I am the gate for the sheep" identify him with the gate of verses 1–6. There, the gate has a specific function. It is the place of authorized entry. Entry through the gate identifies the shepherd and distinguishes him from the thieves and bandits (10:1–2). The gate is not presented as a conscious actor but is opened by the gatekeeper for the shepherd. The shepherd leads the sheep out (10:3) through the gate.

To understand Jesus' function as gate in this sense, it may help to remember the context of this teaching. Jesus' parable follows the healing of the man born blind and continues the discussion Jesus was having with the Pharisees about their own blindness. In 9:39 Jesus said of himself, "I came into this world for judgment so that those who do not see may see, and those who do see may become blind." Jesus' presence becomes a moment of judgment through which it becomes possible to see the blindness of the Pharisees.

This function is similar to the role of the gate. The gate makes clear who the shepherd is and who the thieves and bandits are. It is a means by which the sheep come to see the thieves and bandits for what they really are.

Like the gate that is opened by the gatekeeper (10:3), Jesus' role in judgment is not an active one.

to find abundant green pastures. The gate provides protection and order, as well as liberation and abundance. These qualities are the essence of a pen's gate, and are worth exploring as essential to the purpose and function of Jesus the Christ.

The gate metaphor, however, presents potential problems to be mindful of in theological interpretation. Gates separate those from the outside from those on the inside, and the image has historically been used to promote Christian exclusivity and exceptionalism. The gate imagery has been used to divide people: Christians from non-Christians, "right" Christians from other Christians, masters from slaves, straight people from gay people. A good reading of this passage reveals that the gate does not function to separate sheep from other sheep, but to lead sheep in and out of the sheepfold, so that they will be protected and fed.

The gate becomes the way to distinguish between the shepherd who leads sheep to fertile ground and the thieves who steal and kill. In the context of John, this seems to be an explicit reference to the Pharisees who refused to believe in Jesus (7:48), cast out the man born blind who believed in him (9:34), and would seek to destroy him (11:53). The gate is the way to abundant life, and anyone leading a different way is taking away that life and its abundance. Those who use the gate of Jesus as a divide by which to separate people can be understood as the kind of bandits about which Jesus warns. Exploring what this gate says about Jesus, and what it does not say about Jesus, are two important homiletical opportunities offered by the text.

Jesus says, "I am the gate." The gate is a natural and fruitful place in which to look for the parable's teaching, but we should also not overlook the significance of his use of the declaration "I am." The words "I am" have a theological history, of course, and a context in the Gospel of John worth drawing upon. In Exodus, God reveals God's name to Moses as "I AM WHO I AM" (the translation of YHWH in Exod. 3:14). God also makes self-declarations in Isaiah using "I am": "I am the LORD, and there is no other" (Isa. 45:5a), "I am He; I am the first, and I am the last" (Isa. 48:12b). These words "I am" of Jesus draw on Jewish theological tradition; in using them, Jesus identifies himself with God.

Jesus identifies himself with God, but as a human being teaching these parables in person. So when he teaches with "I am," he is not referring only to his abstract or metaphorical or theological self; he is referring to himself in the flesh, the one standing before those being taught.

John 10:7–10

Theological Perspective

this (and also Jesus' somewhat larger claim to be the way, the truth, and the life, 14:6) and understand them to be claims of exclusivity. They understand that faith in Jesus, even possibly cognitive assent to a certain doctrine about Jesus, is the only way to salvation and heaven.

Despite appearances, is Jesus' claim to be the gate also inevitably a claim to be the only gate? Here lie the limitations of language and logic. Although "unique" and "only" have meanings in common, we understand them somewhat differently. "Only" is a subset of "unique," but "unique" does not necessarily mean "only." In fact, to say someone is unique implies that there are others, but this one is different in a way in which no other is different. Thus, if Jesus is a unique gate, this does not necessarily mean he is the only gate; there are also other gates, but they are different from this one. In the story of *The Little Prince* by Antoine de Saint-Exupéry, taming someone or something makes that someone unique to you. It is the taming relationship that makes one unique. However, that someone (be it a fox, or a rose, or a boy with golden hair) may be one of hundreds and thousands of others foxes, roses, or boys with golden hair.[1]

I rather think that Jesus meant that instead of being a thief or robber, a gate to a futile and meaningless life, he is the gate to a full life. He is claiming that the kingdom or reign of God is good news, not bad news. Jesus is saying that through him we can experience God's richness and fullness. That means he is unique. He comes to bring life, unlike those who come to take it away; but this does not mean that there are not other gates that also bring life and fullness.

What are your needs? What keeps you from flourishing? What keeps you from working toward human flourishing everywhere? One way we can flourish is to work toward the flourishing of others; it is in giving that we receive.

SHARON M. TAN

Pastoral Perspective

estimating that individuals view or hear as many as five thousand messages each day, paying attention could quickly become a full-time job! What matters here is not a comprehensive attentiveness but an increasing awareness of the pervasive and corrosive nature of commercial influences. Second, Christians need to pay attention to God's voice as a counterpoint to the negative aspects of advertising. Such attentiveness can occur when individuals, families, and congregations deliberately separate themselves from the noisiness of everyday life and spend time in the set apart "pastures" (v. 9) of personal and communal prayer, contemplation, and worship.

Alongside attentiveness, Christians need to cultivate self-reflection. Commercial messages affect a person's self-image and desires. Thus, individuals and families need to explore the ways in which their sense of self as beloved children of God may have been compromised by persistent messages of falling short, not of God's glory (see Rom. 3:23), but of the unholy expectations of a commercialized society. When these expectations translate into personal desires, they become like "thorns" that "choke the word" (Mark 4:19) and leave Christians feeling parched and empty of divine grace. A regular habit of self-reflection can unmask the unhelpful clutter of the interior life and lead those who are willing to greener pastures via Christ, who is the gateway to abundant living.

Adding the virtue of perseverance to the skills of attentiveness and self-reflection increases the likelihood that Christians will learn how to resist the deadly messages of rampant commercialization. Advertising exposure will remain a part of human life, but those who long to follow the Good Shepherd can become like "the sheep [who] did not listen to them" (v. 8). Such resistance, however, does not develop overnight; persons must pay attention day after day to the ways in which their lives are misshapen by commercialization, redirect their primary attentive to God's alternative desires for their well-being, and welcome the respite of God's pasture in the midst of thorny fields. In this way they will "have life, and have it abundantly" (v. 10).

KAREN-MARIE YUST

1. Antoine de Saint Exupéry, *The Little Prince*, trans. Richard Howard (New York: Harcourt, Inc., 1943), 59, 63.

Exegetical Perspective

John's language circles around the nature of Jesus' role in judgment. Jesus indicates repeatedly that he came not to judge but to save (e.g., 3:17; 12:47). Nevertheless, Jesus' presence brings about judgment or discernment of what is right. His exact role remains fuzzy: "You judge by human standards; I judge no one. Yet even if I do judge, my judgment is valid; for it is not I alone who judge, but I and the Father who sent me" (8:15–16). Likewise, the gate metaphor of chapter 10 leaves undefined the precise nature of Jesus' role in judgment. The gate is inanimate. It cannot be said to act as an agent, yet it distinguishes between the shepherd and the thieves: "The one who enters by the gate is the shepherd of the sheep" (10:2). As the gate, Jesus' presence identifies the false leaders of the sheep.

Verses 7–10 add another role that was not mentioned in the parable: "Whoever enters by me will be saved, and will come in and go out and find pasture" (v. 9). John's more familiar term for being "saved" is having "eternal life" (3:16). "Life" is mentioned explicitly here as a function of the gate: "I came that they may have life, and have it abundantly" (v. 10). John does not confine "eternal life" to a heavenly afterlife (cf. Matt. 25:46), but consistently sees "life" as a present gift Jesus offers to believers. The verb in the phrase "that they may have life" is present subjunctive. The present tense indicates that it is an ongoing gift; the subjunctive indicates contingency. In this case, life is contingent on Jesus' having come: "I came that they may have life." The abundant life Jesus offers refers to a quality of life believers experience now. The life of faith participates in the abundance of God, to whom all things belong.

The gate is therefore a portal to abundant life. It is not a one-time exit to life (as it would be if John were speaking only of the afterlife). Instead, the sheep "come in and go out and find pasture" (v. 9). The gate offers protection from those who would kill and destroy (v. 10) and access to the abundant pasture God provides for the flock.

SUSAN E. HYLEN

Homiletical Perspective

This basic move reinforces the notion that Jesus the gate is a way through, as the parable suggests, not a way to separate. This gate is a distinctive person from above who comes to bring bread and light and water and life. This gate is not doctrine or dogma or religion, but a particular person with a particular purpose and way, who is inviting us out into the great and fertile land. The passage through the fold is associated not just with God, but with the fullness of humanity that we come to know in Jesus. The person Jesus is not owned by anyone, and thus may not be used as exclusionary or exceptional, despite the way the religion created in his name so often gets presented. The words "I am" associate the Savior with the person Jesus, whose humanity unites and includes all.

The Gospel of John offers six other instances in which Jesus teaches about himself using the "I am" construction: "I am the bread of life" (6:35), "the light of the world" (8:12), "the good shepherd" (10:11), "the resurrection and the life" (11:25), "the way, and the truth, and the life" (14:6), and "the true vine" (15:1). Each of these instances associates the name of God with particular images or characteristics that express the saving relationship of Jesus to the world. These other associations could be drawn upon to highlight our understanding of Jesus as the gate to so much more.

The gate to the sheepfold is a metaphor for salvation. Whoever enters by me—the fully human and fully divine Jesus, not a messenger, doctrine, or dogma—will come in and go out and find pasture, and have life abundantly. Jesus embodies God's life given for the world. We are humans too, like Jesus, and therefore have access to this life he offers us. If we follow the way he revealed to us, and believe in the truth proclaimed to us, we share in the inspired life that is eternal.

DAVID LOWER

John 10:11–18

¹¹"I am the good shepherd. The good shepherd lays down his life for the sheep. ¹²The hired hand, who is not the shepherd and does not own the sheep, sees the wolf coming and leaves the sheep and runs away—and the wolf snatches them and scatters them. ¹³The hired hand runs away because a hired hand does not care for the sheep. ¹⁴I am the good shepherd. I know my own and my own know me, ¹⁵just as the Father knows me and I know the Father. And I lay down my life for the sheep. ¹⁶I have other sheep that do not belong to this fold. I must bring them also, and they will listen to my voice. So there will be one flock, one shepherd. ¹⁷For this reason the Father loves me, because I lay down my life in order to take it up again. ¹⁸No one takes it from me, but I lay it down of my own accord. I have power to lay it down, and I have power to take it up again. I have received this command from my Father."

Theological Perspective

Jesus again changes the metaphor for himself. Now, instead of the gate, he says he is "the good shepherd." This he contrasts with hired hands who have no responsibility for the sheep. Rather, a good shepherd is one who lays down his life for the sheep. He knows the sheep and is known by the sheep.

There have been centuries of discussion of Jesus as the good shepherd, and countless explanations of what a shepherd does for her sheep. Here, I want to focus on the concept of Jesus as good.

To say someone is good can mean two things. First, the term "good" can mean "technical proficiency," to qualify the task of a person. In this case, "good" is a synonym for "effective," "efficient," or "accurate." To say that someone is good is to say that someone produces a good product. For example, to say someone is a good electrician, or carpenter, or dentist generally means that the person knows what she is doing, and does his or her work well and efficiently. This use of "good" does not have to describe that person in his or her other capacities, for example, as parent, child, or lover.

Second, the term "good" can be a description of the character of the person herself and the relationships that emerge out of that character. Here, the term "good" can be understood to mean that the person is a good person who lives a good life and

Pastoral Perspective

When the news media report a natural disaster or terrorist attack, they frequently focus on the heroic actions of first responders and volunteers who rush into these crises despite the danger, rather than avoiding or running away from them. Iconic photos of a firefighter's helmet amid the Twin Towers rubble after 9/11, a runner tending a man who lost his legs in the Boston marathon bombing, and rescuers quickly clearing patients from a nursing home when a fertilizer plant exploded in West, Texas, circulate on the Web and grace the front pages of newspapers. In light of these images, viewers are invited to wonder: if I had been there, would I have run to help, or run for cover? Despite the assurances of officials that seeking safety is the most rational response to disasters, many people hope they would be moved to help others, rather than to seek only to save themselves.

In this text, Jesus is a first responder. When his sheep are threatened, he rushes to the sheepfold to rescue them, without regard for the potential loss of his own life. He knows without a doubt that the power to make decisions about how he uses his own life lies in his hands. Even though he did not initiate the threat to the people he comes to save, he chooses to insert himself into the situation because he believes his actions can make a difference in the outcome. Remaining on the sidelines is an option, but

Exegetical Perspective

In verse 11, Jesus identifies himself with the shepherd of the parable (10:1–6). As in the parable, Jesus is a shepherd who knows his sheep (10:3, 14) and whose sheep recognize his voice (10:3–4, 16). Just as the gate metaphor of verses 7–10 introduced new information about the gate, though, so also the good shepherd metaphor elaborates on the role of the shepherd from the parable.

Instead of thieves and bandits, Jesus' words in verses 12–13 contrast the shepherd with the "hired hand." Unlike the thieves, the hired hand has a valid relationship with the sheep; however, the hired hand does not put himself at risk to protect the sheep. He "sees the wolf coming and leaves the sheep and runs away" (v. 12).

In contrast to the hired hand, the shepherd is now described as one who "lays down his life for the sheep" (v. 11; cf. 15, 17, 18). Throughout John's Gospel, the author has assumed that the reader knows the end of Jesus' story (e.g., 2:22). Jesus will die and rise again. When readers hear Jesus speak of "laying down his life," they rightly associate these words with his crucifixion.

With Jesus' death in mind, the last verses of the passage anticipate the way John will portray Jesus as being fully in control of the events of his death. He knows what will happen beforehand (13:1, 21, 38).

Homiletical Perspective

Jesus' self-declaration, "I am the good shepherd," comes in the context of a parable using pastoral imagery to describe the Savior. In the parable, a shepherd comes to a sheepfold to lead the sheep to pasture through the gate. This parable itself is followed by two teachings. First, Jesus interprets himself in the parable: "I am the gate." Second, in this text, Jesus interprets himself again: "I am the good shepherd." So this text comes as part of the sequence of the pastoral parable, and should be understood in its context as an additional teaching. Preaching on this passage should capture the revealing descriptions in it as part of an expansive discourse about the identity and nature of Jesus.

In the preceding pericope, Jesus has just interpreted the pastoral parable by saying, "I am the gate for the sheep" (10:7). The inanimate image of the gate has character in its shape and function, as protection when closed and passage when open. Then, with the words, "I am the good shepherd," Jesus shifts within the pastoral paradigm from an architectural feature to a person. This shepherd, in the parable itself, comes to the gate and calls to the sheep with a voice they recognize and follow.

When Jesus makes these "I am" statements, they are loaded with significance. In saying "I am," Jesus is identifying himself with the God of Moses, whose

Theological Perspective

has a consistent pattern of acting toward the common good, and this extends to the quality of her relationships. This second understanding of the term is embedded in a host of cultural meanings: what is good in one culture may not be (as) good in another. For example, assertiveness, honesty, and independence are more highly valued in North American cultures than in some other cultures, where perhaps values such as cooperation, discretion, and loyalty may be more highly prized.

Generally, in describing a person in a relational capacity (for example, as a good teacher, mother, or father), one needs to have both types of good in mind. A person who is seen as a good father or mother (or shepherd, for that matter) must be a person who consistently responds with an orientation toward the good and is proficient at the technical tasks of fathering or mothering (or shepherding).

What is a good person? A good person not only does good deeds; she does them habitually. Virtues are habits of excellence that arise out of doing something for intrinsic reward, or for their own sake. For example, a courageous person becomes a courageous person out of a habitual practice of the good, not for fame, glory, or monetary reward. The four cardinal or governing human virtues are (1) prudence or wisdom directing one toward the good, (2) temperance or self-control, (3) justice or right relationships, and (4) courage or appropriate risk taking. A whole host of other virtues includes the simpler ones of kindness, honesty, mercy, and so on. The three traditional theological virtues—faith, hope, and love—arise not from human nature but only from God through grace.

In his novel *How to Be Good*, Nick Hornby describes a physician who is sure she is a "good person," in spite of her marital infidelity, because, after all, she is a doctor, and doctors "help others."[7] She is confronted, though, with how good she actually is or is not when her husband, after a spiritual conversion experience, starts to work against homelessness in the neighborhood and influences her children to give their possessions away. How good does one have to be to be good enough?

In this passage in John, there are several specific answers to this question. First, there is the notion of self-sacrifice traditionally linked with agapic love. The good shepherd is the kind of shepherd who willingly lays down his life for his sheep. Likewise, the good person links his welfare to those he is responsible for, even prioritizing their welfare over

7. Nick Hornby, *How to Be Good* (New York: Riverhead, 2002), 60, 222.

Pastoral Perspective

not one he wishes to exercise. He intercedes because he has the power and the will to do so.

Typical Christians appreciate that Jesus was willing to give his life for the salvation of humanity. They laud the heroic efforts of others when those actions are publicized. They hope there will be a hero handy, should they ever find themselves in need of saving. If they are honest with themselves, they also hope that they will not find themselves in the position of choosing between self-preservation and heroic intervention at the risk of their own lives.

Contemporary Western Christians tend to think of faith as a personal matter. As persons who value individual spirituality more highly than membership in religious institutions, they focus most of their energy on bettering the self. When it comes to taking care of the community, they assume that pastors are responsible for the well-being of congregations, that politicians and social-service providers are the caretakers of cities and towns, and that principals and teachers stand as safeguards for schoolchildren. Mission and outreach projects often occur within the protective bubble of hands-off monetary gifts or programmed responses in which "the other" comes into a space regulated by the care providers. Apart from familial ties that might evoke extraordinary protectiveness in a time of crisis, most Christians do not seek out opportunities to lay down their lives for others.

This reluctance to risk self-sacrifice for the greater good poses a dilemma for those who would become like Christ. It is not enough to embrace the promise of abundant life; one must also acknowledge that abundance brings with it a responsibility to care about the well-being of all God's people. A Christian cannot act like a "hired hand" (vv. 12–13) who flees when the community is in need. Christians are called to "put on Christ" (see Rom. 13:14), not only in good times but also in times of crisis; to become imitators of the Good Shepherd who know and claim all those in need as their own. The "command" (v. 18) that Jesus acknowledges remains in force: "We know love by this, that he laid down his life for us— and we ought to lay down our lives for one another" (1 John 3:16). Indeed, the writer of the Gospel of John also underscores this point a few chapters later, stating, "No one has greater love than this, to lay down one's life for one's friends" (15:13).

How do good people cultivate the courage to step up rather than step away? One approach is to practice extravagant hospitality during times of ease, so that reaching out to the other is second nature when trouble strikes. Instead of ignoring those asking

Although Judas is said to betray Jesus by handing him over to the authorities, John has Jesus identify himself at his arrest (18:5). Furthermore, it is Jesus who "hands over" his spirit on the cross (19:30). All these features of John's passion narrative resonate with what Jesus says here: "No one takes [my life] from me, but I lay it down of my own accord." Finally, just as John has long indicated that Jesus' death will also involve his exaltation (3:14) or glorification (12:16), so also Jesus has power to lay down his life and to take it up again (10:18). The way John understands Jesus' death and resurrection shapes the language of these verses and the shepherd's role in laying down his life.

Although Jesus' death plays an important and culminating role in the Gospel, John's notion of Jesus' "laying down his life" is not limited to his death. It describes much of Jesus' activity throughout the Gospel. This can be seen more clearly when the Greek words are translated "to risk one's life" instead of "to lay down one's life." Although laying down one's life connotes death, risk suggests the possibility of death. The shepherd is defined by his willingness to risk, not only by his death. This translation choice is a good option for three reasons.

First, "to risk my life" is a more common meaning of the Greek phrase *tēn psychēn mou tithēmi* (10:15). The phrase, which occurs a number of times in the Greek versions of the Old Testament, is often translated "to take one's life in one's hands." For example, Jephthah says to the men of Ephraim, "When I saw that you would not deliver me, I took my life in my hand, and crossed over against the Ammonites, and the LORD gave them into my hand. Why then have you come up to me this day, to fight against me?" (Judg. 12:3; cf. 1 Sam. 19:5; 28:21). In its broader use, the Greek phrase that John employs communicates the notion of risking one's life, but does not necessitate death.

Second, to translate the shepherd as "risking his life" makes sense in the context of shepherding. When David recounts his bravery as a shepherd protecting his father's sheep, he points to his readiness to risk on behalf of others: "But David said to Saul, 'Your servant used to keep sheep for his father; and whenever a lion or a bear came, and took a lamb from the flock, I went after it and struck it down, rescuing the lamb from its mouth; and if it turned against me, I would catch it by the jaw, strike it down, and kill it'" (1 Sam. 17:34–35). David draws on the idea of a shepherd as protector to characterize his actions. Similarly, when Jesus says

very name is I AM. Using this construction, Jesus pronounces himself related to God and committed to God's purposes and work. By attaching "I am" to a metaphor, Jesus is saying he is of God and has a certain nature described by the image that follows.

The image with which Jesus identifies himself as the Son of God is the good shepherd. These particular and distinctive qualities make him good. The shepherd's role is to lead, guide, feed, protect, and seek lost sheep. Jesus is the good shepherd, one who is favorable, noble, and exemplary. The goodness of the shepherd is described as knowing and being known by the sheep, gathering the scattered sheep, and laying one's life down for the sheep.

The goodness of the shepherd can be understood in contrast to other shepherds, mere hired hands, who are invested in themselves and their own provision and security. The difference between the hired hand and the good shepherd includes both motivation and will. The hired hand cares ultimately for himself, while the good shepherd cares ultimately for the sheep. The hired hand is there to do a job; the good shepherd is there to protect, nurture, and deliver the sheep at all costs. The good shepherd cares for the sheep so much that no sacrifice is too great.

This passage is primarily about salvation. Therefore, the preacher may choose to explore salvation in these helpful constructs. How many human constructions and worldly forces work upon us, but ultimately care only about themselves? How many things in which we put our trust—celebrities, corporations, governments—prioritize themselves and their own preservation over ours? These things all have their place, but not as shepherds. The sheep must trust that their shepherd has their needs and security in mind above all else. Examples like a loving parent, supportive mentor, or loyal AA sponsor can help illustrate the virtues of the good shepherd.

Jesus is the good shepherd invested not in himself but in the sheep. What does it mean to be loved by a God whose ultimate priority is all us sheep? God's good priority of us can be a difficult notion to trust, especially when we suffer or despair for the world. However, the preacher of this gospel word might find ways to illustrate that nothing can separate us from the love of God or that empowerment comes with being forgiven and set free to live rightly.

The preacher might also challenge the congregation with leading faith questions. Have you experienced the saving, liberating knowledge that you are known, sought, and cared for so deeply that God would give God's own life so that you might

John 10:11–18

Theological Perspective

his own. This goodness goes beyond technical competence and excellence, requiring the character traits of love, courage, prudence, and self-determination. It is extremely important to note that love as sacrifice is not something that can be demanded by someone else; in fact, to demand one give herself in self-sacrifice would be to eviscerate its virtue and turn love into fear. By definition, self-sacrifice must never be coerced, but freely given out of a sense of autonomy or self-government.

Second, the good shepherd knows her sheep and is known by her sheep; in other words, the good shepherd is accessible to her sheep. The good person is attentive to those around her, and lives without fear of being known and with nothing to hide. She gives of her person and meets the relational and emotional needs of her charges. One's love for another must outweigh the risks of being known and the fear of rejection. This is a character trait enabling one to live in community, and involves at the very least honesty, patience, justice, and humility.

We now turn to Jesus' mention of the other sheep not of this sheep pen. Jesus speaks of bringing them along, and uniting the flock under him. Most commentators believe that Jesus is referring here to Gentiles. Since Gentiles comprise most of Christianity today, my question is whether we can now assume that this task has been accomplished. If so, is there no more to learn from this passage? Are there yet more sheep that belong to Jesus? Perhaps one could imagine as the other sheep those who currently are yet unknown and unfamiliar to those who consider themselves within the fold. Perhaps there are sheep belonging to Jesus that even we today do not know of. Jesus' claim is that those that follow him are his, even if they are not ours.

SHARON M. TAN

Pastoral Perspective

for money on street corners, Christians can smile and nod in a sign of respect for the humanity of all people and offer to buy a meal or provide a blanket on a cold day. Rather than volunteering just a few times a year at a soup kitchen or food pantry, followers of Christ can serve once a week and include a smile and conversation with their provision of bodily sustenance. In place of outbursts about the annoyance of "panhandlers," Christians can advocate for increases in social services for those with mental illnesses, who make up a disproportionate percentage of persons who are homeless. Courageous believers can offer General Education Degree (GED) classes for those who are incarcerated in city jails, provide English for Speakers of Other Languages (ESL) instruction for recent immigrants, or sponsor the relocation of refugees from war-torn regions. Wherever Christians encounter persons who make them uncomfortable, there is an opportunity to engage in forms of hospitality that help believers practice choosing the role of good shepherds.

Good shepherd wannabes can also spend time getting to know the original Good Shepherd better. Jesus points out that "my own know me" (v. 14). In the busyness of contemporary life, many Christians find it difficult to spend quality time with God outside of corporate worship. Classical spiritual practices such as practicing the presence of God, in which believers identify a given signal from among the sights or sounds of an ordinary day and pause briefly to acknowledge that God is present, and contemplative silence, in which adherents sit quietly and clear their minds of any distractions so that God may dwell companionably with them, are time-tested approaches to knowing God. Breath prayers, in which Christians repeat a preselected word or phrase (e.g., "shalom," "Christ, have mercy") in order to lose themselves in the presence of God, and Taizé singing, which is essentially a sung version of a breath prayer, are also effective means to get to know God better.

KAREN-MARIE YUST

that the shepherd "risks his life," the hearer might well assume that the shepherd is useful to the sheep when he is alive. Shepherding puts him in a position of danger, but a good shepherd defends the sheep successfully.

Finally, the notion of the shepherd's "risking his life" makes sense in context, because John often characterizes Jesus as undertaking tasks that put him at risk. Jesus' enemies are first identified as seeking to kill him in 5:18. Later he declines to go to Jerusalem because his "time has not yet come" (7:6), and the desire of the authorities to arrest or kill Jesus is apparent in 7:25, 30, and 32. Nevertheless Jesus does go up to the festival and teaches openly (7:14, 28, 37–38). His teaching occasions an acrimonious exchange (8:31–59) that ends in an attempt to stone him. Jesus goes out from the temple (8:59) and encounters the blind man (9:1), whose healing subsequently occasions the current discussion with the Pharisees (9:40–10:18).

Following the teaching about the good shepherd, Jesus continues to risk his life. His teaching that "the Father and I are one" (10:30) results in another attempt to stone him (10:31), and they try to arrest him again in 10:39. Because of this, the disciples' fear for Jesus' life in chapter 11 makes a good deal of sense. They discourage him from returning to save Lazarus (11:8, 12). Jesus does return, though, and it is the widespread faith of the Jews following the raising of Lazarus that leads directly to the plot to kill Jesus (11:45–53). Jesus risks his life for the sake of his sheep.

As shepherd, Jesus' role is not simply to die, but to risk his life on behalf of his sheep. He continues to teach and heal, even after his teaching and healing bring threats to his life. John understands Jesus' death as consistent with his life. His death results from the risk that Jesus takes out of love for his sheep.

SUSAN E. HYLEN

have yours fully? Have you come to understand that God loves your neighbors and strangers just the same? If accepted, such knowledge should breed humility, gratitude, trust, openheartedness, and other-mindedness.

If God's saving love is like this, there are ethical and ecclesiastical implications for following such a God as has been made known in Jesus. If we understand the church as the body of Christ in the world, then how can the church function like the good shepherd? How can the church prioritize others, not itself, and not rest until all are gathered in the knowledge of God's saving love? This passage invites an exciting opportunity for a preacher and congregation to discern new ministries of care outside the church walls, focusing (as a good shepherd would) on those who are marginalized and those who cannot find the gate.

How can the church lay down its life for the sake of others, particularly the marginalized and the lost? Is the church willing to pay an ultimate and dear price to be true to God's command to love, serve, and give? How might we commit ourselves to approaching the kind of goodness made known to us by the good shepherd? The good shepherd would serve as a powerful theological and ethical reflection for a church focusing on stewardship and mission in ways that engage deeply and take risks.

The return for the shepherd and those who follow him is not sacrificial death but new life. Jesus says, "I lay down my life in order to take life up again [in a new way]" (v. 17). Jesus claims there is power in giving one's life, because God is in on this way of being. This was commanded of the good shepherd, Jesus, and it is similarly commanded of us as his body in the world. This allusion to the forthcoming death and resurrection of Jesus, before they happen in the Gospel story, invites us to engage deeply what it means to be "good." The good shepherd—characterized by giving, selflessness, risk-taking for others—invites us to take on such a character and to trust the good God who has inspired the way.

DAVID LOWER

John 10:19–30

[19]Again the Jews* were divided because of these words. [20]Many of them were saying, "He has a demon and is out of his mind. Why listen to him?" [21]Others were saying, "These are not the words of one who has a demon. Can a demon open the eyes of the blind?"

[22]At that time the festival of the Dedication took place in Jerusalem. It was winter, [23]and Jesus was walking in the temple, in the portico of Solomon. [24]So the Jews gathered around him and said to him, "How long will you keep us in suspense? If you are the Messiah, tell us plainly." [25]Jesus answered, "I have told you, and you do not believe. The works that I do in my Father's name testify to me; [26]but you do not believe, because you do not belong to my sheep. [27]My sheep hear my voice. I know them, and they follow me. [28]I give them eternal life, and they will never perish. No one will snatch them out of my hand. [29]What my Father has given me is greater than all else, and no one can snatch it out of the Father's hand. [30]The Father and I are one."

Theological Perspective

Often this section's meaning hinges on Jesus' words, "The Father and I are one" (v. 30). The result is a focus on Christology or reflection on the messianic character of Jesus Christ. Echoes of questions from fourth- and fifth-century church councils resound in the passage: Is Jesus the incarnate Logos, the divine Word made flesh? Is Jesus of one nature, *ousia*, with God the Father? Is Jesus, rather, simply God in human form?

While the Fourth Gospel introduces Jesus as the Logos, and while many consider it the most spiritual Gospel, we must not dismiss the humanity of Jesus— the one made flesh—in its narrative. John's narrated theology does not move above social concerns, but through them. It is within this theology that Jesus as the good shepherd and God as the loving parent make sense.

When we arrive at this section, we are already in the thick of Jesus' last public discourse. He has healed a blind man with saliva and mud, prompting the Pharisees immediately to depict him as a huckster. Now the religious leadership attempts to identify Jesus as a threat, the personification of a demonic power. By the time the narrative arrives at the unity declaration at verse 30, Jesus has become such a dangerous threat that lethal violence begins to spill into the story.

*See "'The Jews' in the Fourth Gospel" on pp. xi–xiv.

Pastoral Perspective

This story reflects a time when the words of Jesus stirred up controversy. His comments about being the good shepherd, laying down his life for the sheep, and having the power to take it up again received a mixed response. Some thought that he was "out of his mind" (v. 20) and not worth listening to, while others were inclined to listen because of the blind man he had recently healed. They decided to ask him, "If you are the Messiah, tell us plainly" (v. 24). Jesus' response begins with, "I have told you" (v. 25). He continues, "The works that I do . . . testify to me" (v. 25).

Jesus basically says, "Take a look at my life; take a look at my actions. My behavior shows you who I am." This response reminds me of a lesson I learned as a chaplain-in-training through the Association for Clinical Pastoral Education. With supervision, I was providing pastoral care in a psychiatric hospital for a patient who talked with the staff and me very convincingly about his desire to reconcile with his wife. He seemed full of regret for his past bad behavior and expressed strong resolve to "do better." His words were convincing, not just to me as a beginning chaplain but also to seasoned professionals, yet during every home visit he created trouble and chaos. Then, when he returned to the hospital, he continued to talk to the hospital personnel with seemingly

Feasting on the Gospels

Exegetical Perspective

This pericope follows directly on the heels of Jesus' good shepherd discourse in 10:1–18 and divides neatly into two parts: 10:19–21, which describes the response to that discourse, and 10:22–30, which describes ongoing interactions between Jesus and the Jewish authorities regarding Jesus' identity. Taken as a whole, this passage points to a critical issue within the Fourth Gospel: the identity of Jesus and his relationship to the Father. It emphasizes their unity of purpose in works, especially in the task of protecting Jesus' followers.

John 10:19–21. This dialogue comes as a direct result of the good shepherd discourse (10:1–18): a schism (*schisma*) occurs "because of these words" that Jesus has just spoken (v. 19). Jesus has just made some remarkable christological claims in verses 1–18. His words demand a response; some will respond negatively, and some will respond favorably.

Who are these "Jews" who are divided over Jesus' words in verse 19? Within the larger narrative context, "the Jews" who argue with one another here are members of the group of Pharisees last mentioned explicitly in 9:40. They are members of the same group of Jewish authorities in Jerusalem who interrogated the man born blind in chapter 9. Here the group is divided in their response to Jesus, much as

Homiletical Perspective

This text is so chock-full of homiletic challenges! It resembles a very delicately woven gold chain that has (over time) become kinked with knots. The only way to begin reclaiming the necklace's beauty—and that of this text—is by a slow, gingerly untying of each knot.

One of the most problematic knots tangling up this text is the narrator's repeated use of the phrase "the Jews," often in a pejorative sense or, as is the case in this text, in reference to those in a combative encounter with Jesus. "The Jews" is used seventy times in the Gospel attributed to John (sixteen in the Synoptic Gospels). Scholars try to alleviate the anti-Jewishness of John by employing several methods. The first underscores that the author of John's Gospel, as well as the participants (including Jesus), were Jews. Another posits that the Gospel was written to influence—rather than offend and isolate—Jews. A third reading emphasizes that any interpretation of the term "the Jews" within John must be contextualized; after the destruction of the temple, disputes escalated within and among the Jewish communities, including the controversy over the messiahship of Jesus.

In terms of homiletical method, a good, solid teaching sermon provides an excellent strategy for untangling the pejorative use of the phrase "the Jews." In a teaching sermon the preacher can set as a goal the reinterpretation (or reappropriation) of

Theological Perspective

Why this escalation? What kind of threat has Jesus become? Although some are undecided about the origin of his authority, the idea that Jesus is God's anointed representative apparently falls beyond the imagination of his interlocutors. To them, Jesus is a divider, deceiver, and blasphemer. In this section the narrator takes great care to answer the first two concerns, concerns the Johannine community surely dealt with in their expulsion from the synagogue. Much is at stake for "the Jews" and the "Christ-followers."

Is Jesus a divider? While the Synoptic Gospels frequently portray the entrance of the reign of God using the language of division, John does not participate in that message. This Gospel speaks for a community questioning the meaning of estrangement and division.

One of the most interesting elements of the good shepherd metaphor is the predator/prey relationship. It was a dynamic central to first-century people's surviving natural and imperial threats. Its theological and social meanings interact to convey both a vividly spiritual and a decidedly social message. Wolves and thieves threaten the sheepfold, while Jesus, empowered by the Father, protects it. The message could not be clearer. Jesus is no threat to the community; human power is.

Then is Jesus a deceiver? In *Jesus and the Disinherited* Howard Thurman writes about deception of the sort that prey animals use to hide from their predators. It is an ancient practice of defense of the weak against the strong. It is often considered a legitimate response by victims to the real and continuous threat of the oppressor. Deception seeks to level the playing field and flatten power by ambushing it with lies. It often ignores ethical and spiritual implications. The penalty of deception, though, is to become deception, Thurman says. Jesus embodies sincerity, not hypocrisy. With Jesus we learn sincerity is no simple defense by the weak against the strong, but an encounter between human beings.[1]

In this passage many seek to discredit and dishonor Jesus. They charge him with demon possession. In that world, demons or unclean spirits threatened the order of things. They deceived and distorted human agency. Perhaps this explains Jesus' statement, "I lay down my life in order to take it up again. No one takes it from me, but I lay it down of my own accord" (10:17–18). He testifies here to his own sanity and agency. Only God's anointed could fulfill the responsibility contained in the symbolic

1. Howard Thurman, *Jesus and the Disinherited* (Boston: Beacon Press: 1976), 65–73.

Pastoral Perspective

believable regret and resolve. This cycle continued. We were stuck, and his situation was getting worse rather than better.

My supervisor, a wise old chaplain, said to me, "Listen to his actions rather than his words. Talk with him about his behavior, not his intentions." The next time the patient talked with me about loving his wife and wanting to reconcile, I said, "Your behavior says something different." After he protested, I said something like, "This is what you did at the last home visit. . . . Let's listen to your behavior. . . . What does it say about what you want in your relationship with your wife?" Finally, he was able to be honest with himself and me, and then we were able to make progress toward healing and reconciliation. Helping him to be honest, rather than accepting his excuses, was the turning point of the pastoral relationship. In the language of the passage, I was asking him this question: "What do the works that you do testify about who you are?" (v. 25). Exploring that question led to additional inquiries: "Who do you want to be?" "Who were you created to be?" Exploring these powerful questions was a huge step forward that invited him to realize that actions demonstrate character and intentions.

Listening to the behavior of the people to whom we minister can have important implications for the life and ministry of a congregation. For example, many congregations struggle with finding the best ways to minister when people ask the church for financial help. Followers of Jesus often want to provide financial help for people who need it. At the same time, some folks worry about doing harm by providing money that people might use to hurt themselves, such as with drugs or alcohol.

Listening to the behavior of the group as a whole tells us that some people who are given money will use it for good and some will use it for ill. Knowing how to assist people who need help without doing harm to others is difficult. Many churches have responded to this dilemma by offering tangible help like food, clothing, and bus tickets or by supporting social service agencies that assess need and provide resources.

Jesus' saying, "The works that I do . . . testify to me" (v. 25), suggests another solution: consider the actions and behaviors of the individual who is requesting help. This approach involves taking the time and energy to get to know a person well enough to see his or her actions and behaviors. It also includes listening to the person's behavior and recognizing when intentions and behavior differ.

they were split in their response to the healing of the blind man (9:16).

The respondents fall into two groups: those who think that Jesus is possessed by a demon and is "raving" (*mainetai*, v. 20), and those who find his words plausible, based on the healing in chapter 9. The suggestion by the first group that Jesus "has a demon" recalls a similar claim made in 8:48. This insult seems only fair, as Jesus has just suggested that the Jewish leaders are "thieves" and "robbers" (10:8); they are merely returning Jesus' insults in kind. Jesus is neither possessed nor stark raving mad, however; he speaks truth (1:14, 17; 14:6) and has the "words of eternal life" (6:68). He will ultimately prove the truth of his words by laying down his life and taking it back up again (10:18).

The second group finds Jesus' words in 10:1–18 credible, based on the healing of the blind man. After all, miracles in the Fourth Gospel are "signs" that reveal Jesus' identity (2:11) and promote belief (2:23). Thus, verses 19–21 signal that the healing miracle and the good shepherd discourse ought to be read and interpreted in light of each other.

One more note on this brief section: many interpreters have come to believe that the Johannine community was engaged in a bitter dispute with synagogues and "the Jews" at the end of the first century. This text reminds us that the response to Jesus' ministry among Jewish persons was never homogeneous. Likewise, the relationship between the Johannine community and their fellow Jews toward the end of the first century CE was likely very complex and not characterized solely by conflict.

John 10:22–30. This section falls within a larger discrete unit (10:22–39) in the Gospel. An introduction establishes the setting in verses 22–23 and is followed by two exchanges that deal with claims about Jesus' identity. Both exchanges begin with a question or accusation from the Jewish leaders (vv. 24, 33), entail lengthy responses from Jesus (vv. 25–30, 34–38), and provoke hostile reactions (vv. 31, 39).

While verse 22 indicates that time has passed and it is now winter, there is significant continuity between this passage and what immediately precedes it. Jesus is still in Jerusalem and his interrogators are apparently still members of the Pharisees. The note that this encounter takes place during the festival of Dedication is quite significant. Also known as Hanukkah, this festival commemorates the rededication of the Jerusalem temple in the second century BCE. The Seleucid ruler Antiochus IV Epiphanes

a problematic biblical text or of a social issue. The anti-Jewishness in the Gospel of John provides a perfect homiletical occasion for both textual and social reappropriation!

Such a teaching sermon might begin with the remarkably underpreached fact that Jesus was a Jew and came as a prophet, calling Jews to the prophetic strand of their heritage: to care for the widow, the orphan, the sojourner in their midst. This divided the Jews. They could not agree on whether to stand with or against their fellow Jew, Jesus.

The second move of the teaching sermon could note that regardless of how sensible the use of the term "the Jews" may have been within its Johannine context (see above), the term has since proven negatively influential, historically speaking, with Christians blaming Jews for the death of Christ. Early church father John Chrysostom, for example, preached in his *Eight Homilies against the Jews*, "The Jews have no excuse left to them. . . . [they are] condemned, shameless, and obstinate." He warned against "the evil gatherings of the Jews and their synagogues [as] robbers' dens and dwellings of demons." "This is my strongest reason for hating Jews . . . and the synagogue. . . . the Jews stubbornly fight against God."[1] Anti-Jewish rants like Chrysostom's have influenced countless Christians from the first century right through to today.

Roman Catholics on Good Friday used to pray for the "perfidious Jews" in the Roman Rite. When Pope Pius XII was asked by the chief rabbi of Rome to remove the word "perfidious" from the prayer for the Jews, Pius declined, explaining that the adjective "perfidious," which is ordinarily defined as "deliberately treacherous" or "deceitful," actually meant "incredulous" in the context of Catholic prayers.[2] The prayer was not altered until 1959, during the pontificate of John XXIII.

Protestant reformer and theologian Martin Luther argued in his tract *The Jews and Their Lies* that Jewish synagogues and schools should be burned, their homes "destroyed," their prayer books and Talmudic writings taken, their rabbis forbidden to teach "on pain of loss of life and limb," that safe conduct on highways be "abolished for Jews," that "all cash and treasure of silver and gold be taken from them," and that a "flail, an ax, a hoe, a spade, a distaff, or a spindle

1. Paul W. Harkins, trans., *St. John Chrysostom: Discourses against Judaizing Christians*, in *Fathers of the Church* 68 (Washington, DC: Catholic University of America Press, 2010), 145, 148.

2. Robert G. Weisbord and Wallace P. Sillanpoa, *The Chief Rabbi, the Pope, and the Holocaust: An Era in Vatican-Jewish Relations* (New Brunswick, NJ: Transaction, 1992), 171.

Theological Perspective

reference to the feast of Dedication (v. 22) and the historic purification of the temple. Feeling compressed by the weight of the moment, they demand a sincere, clear, and public answer from Jesus: "Are you the Messiah?" they ask.

Identifying the presence of God is often an epistemological, theological, social, and spiritual riddle. Human limitations often keep God's presence at bay for a time, as Gustavo Gutiérrez remarks, though. The experience of God begins the life of discipleship; theology comes afterward.[2] The Fourth Gospel is replete with experiences of encounter with God through the pre- and postpassion Christ. Here too, Jesus attempts in this encounter to include even those who suppress the light of the world. He understands the dilemma developing before him with the Jewish leaders. His response is one of complete sincerity, but not of conformity.

Jesus answers, "The Father and I are one" (hen, v. 30). Christological reflection might suggest that "one" (hen) speaks to the divinity of Jesus, comporting with later church doctrine. Certainly this emphasis can be found in the Fourth Gospel's theological concerns. Since the adjective is neuter rather than masculine, however, divine partnership—perhaps more than divine personhood—is the revelation here. Either way, Jesus continues the posture of an unheard-of intimacy with God. Likewise, he opens the door for a fuller and more complete encounter with God for both the characters in and the readers of the story.

Several theological points stand out in the exchange between Jesus and the religious leaders. The points are vitally important for the hope of the Johannine community and creation. First, God is indwelling the world, not deceiving it, through Jesus the Christ. God is forming a new community rather than destroying the known one. Second, God is revealing God's self through Jesus the Christ, not revealing something else or someone other.

The church has often divided Christology into theologies that are "from above" and those that are "from below." This distinction frequently leads to division, especially when one view of Jesus (the spiritual) is privileged over another (the social). Might instead a thick notion of divine collaboration, as seen in this passage, balance out the idea of the "communication" between Christ's natures found in the early christological doctrine, the *communicatio idiomatum*, the communication of attributes?

ANDY WATTS

Pastoral Perspective

This information can help ministers and congregations determine the best way to assist the person to become who he or she was created to be.

"What does your behavior tell us about who you are?" is a good question to ask ourselves when we are getting to know an individual and preparing to minister with him or her. Another illuminating question is, "What is needed for you to demonstrate the image of God that is within you?" These questions can help a minister or congregation come to an in-depth understanding of a person's character and needs, which can then shed light on how appropriately to respond to her or his real needs. Asking, "What kind of actions would the person you are called to be choose to take?" can lead to a plan for spiritual, mental, emotional, and physical growth.

The church as a long-term community seeking to receive and offer Christlike love is uniquely suited to provide this kind of care with individuals. Listening carefully to the behavior of people to whom we minister can revolutionize the congregation's ministry. When we avoid the mistake of accepting excuses rather than inviting honesty and change, the church can become a dynamic, spirited community filled with the energies of love and transformation.

Finally, listening to our own behavior helps us become more effective followers of Christ. Learning to pay attention to our own actions, rather than excusing bad behavior because we have good intentions, will open our eyes to the ways that we do not love and trust God, other people, or ourselves. Comparing our actions with Jesus' actions and seeking to align our behavior with his behavior will enable us to grow toward greater love and trust of God, other people, and ourselves. May we grow toward such Christlike love that we, like him, understand the actions of ourselves and other people through the simple, clear, and confident knowledge, "The works that I do . . . testify to me" (v. 25).

DENISE MCLAIN MASSEY

---

2. Gustavo Gutiérrez, *We Drink from Our Own Wells: The Spiritual Journey of a People* (Maryknoll, NY: Orbis Books, 2001), 35–37, 52–54.

Exegetical Perspective

had desecrated the temple in 167 BCE by sacrificing to Zeus on a pagan altar inside the temple. This event provoked the successful Maccabean campaign that freed Jerusalem from the grip of the Seleucids and permitted the rededication of the temple. Thus, within the context of the festival, the request from the Jewish authorities in verse 24 for Jesus to tell them "plainly" if he is the Messiah has political overtones: is Jesus the one who will liberate the Jewish nation from Roman imperial rule?

While there is some ambiguity concerning the intent of the question in verse 24, it is likely sarcastic and hostile, since members of the Jewish authorities have been trying to kill Jesus since 5:18. Regardless, this is the one place in the Fourth Gospel where Jesus is asked directly if he is the Messiah. His response in verses 25–30 indicates that his identity has been made "plainly clear" through his words and his works, even if he has not openly said, "I am the Messiah" (4:25, 29; 11:27).

Jesus' response to his interrogators in verses 25–30 echoes many of the claims he has made in previous speeches. The works that he does in the Father's name testify to his origin and unity with God, yet many are unable to believe (5:31–47). It is only Jesus' "sheep" who know his voice, follow him, receive eternal life, and remain securely in his grasp (10:1–18).

The unity of work that Jesus and the Father share is noteworthy in verses 28–29: they both hold the "sheep" securely in their hands, so that no one can "snatch" (*harpazō*) them away (10:12). Jesus' radical statement in 10:30 that "the Father and I are one" should not necessarily be read through a Trinitarian lens. The Greek word for "one" (*hen*) is neuter, and thus refers to their unity in work, much as verses 28–29 suggest (cf. 5:19). Still, this is enough to incite the Jewish authorities in verse 31 to pick up stones to kill him. That Jesus calls God his Father and claims to share in his work and power amounts to blasphemy for his antagonists (cf. 5:18).

ARTHUR M. WRIGHT JR.

Homiletical Perspective

[be placed] into the hands of the Jews . . . Letting them earn their bread in the sweat of their noses."[3]

Clearly and tragically, there was in pre–Nazi era Europe a pervasive anti-Jewishness within both Roman Catholic and Reformed prayers and pulpits. It should come as no surprise to us that Christians of all denominations cooperated with the Nazi Holocaust (though with tremendous exceptions like Dietrich Bonhoeffer) and further that Nazis reproduced and widely distributed Christian anti-Semitic writings, blaming the Jewish race solely and collectively for killing the Son of God. Christian participation in the Holocaust provides all the more reason and justification for ensuring that always, whenever we now preach on texts such as John 10:19–30, we testify against the pejorative use of "the Jews" in the Gospel attributed to John.

A third move in this teaching sermon might critically engage the historical evidence that suggests (in contradistinction to John's interpretation of the events surrounding Jesus' crucifixion) that "the Jews" in fact could not have been responsible for Jesus' death. Caiaphas's complicity in bringing Jesus to trial was not so much a result of Caiaphas's being Jewish as of his being so closely allied to the Roman power structure that he understood Jesus as a political threat. Although it remains incontestable that Jesus had been a troublesome, harsh critic of the religious authorities and was seen as a subversive, only the Roman Empire had the authority to carry out executions.

The teaching sermon's conclusion can reach beyond this specific Johannine text toward the overarching theological aim of the Fourth Gospel, namely, Jesus' call that we love one another as he has loved us, as Christians extending now that love to include our forebears: the Jews.

KAY LYNN NORTHCUTT

---

3. Martin Luther, *The Jews and Their Lies*, in *Luther's Works*, vol. 47, *The Christian in Society 4*, ed. Franklin Sherman (Philadelphia: Fortress Press, 1971), 268–93.

John 10:31–39

³¹The Jews* took up stones again to stone him. ³²Jesus replied, "I have shown you many good works from the Father. For which of these are you going to stone me?" ³³The Jews answered, "It is not for a good work that we are going to stone you, but for blasphemy, because you, though only a human being, are making yourself God." ³⁴Jesus answered, "Is it not written in your law, 'I said, you are gods'? ³⁵If those to whom the word of God came were called 'gods'—and the scripture cannot be annulled—³⁶can you say that the one whom the Father has sanctified and sent into the world is blaspheming because I said, 'I am God's Son'? ³⁷If I am not doing the works of my Father, then do not believe me. ³⁸But if I do them, even though you do not believe me, believe the works, so that you may know and understand that the Father is in me and I am in the Father." ³⁹Then they tried to arrest him again, but he escaped from their hands.

Theological Perspective

This passage continues to display the unity of Jesus and God in unparalleled ways. The Fourth Gospel has portrayed Jesus as the bread of life, the Son of God, and the light of the world. Here the focal point is the substance of that relationship. It provides an exclamation point to the question of the origin of Jesus' authority and power.

The early part of this section brings to mind the tension felt by early Christians concerning the fruits of their witness. It is a tension that most likely existed in the Johannine community, a community expelled from the synagogue. Subsequently, for these early Christians, their rejection carried theological implications. One implication concerned redemption: the rejection of the prophet is a rejection of God. Another concerned sanctification: the rejected prophet's identity is called into question.

Scholars believe the teaching on the unforgivable sin in Matthew 12:31 represents this tradition. Those who speak against the Son of Man will be forgiven, but those who speak against the Holy Spirit will not. In other words, the unforgivable sin denies God as doer of God's own works. In the passage at hand we encounter a similar issue. Though the unforgivable

* See "'The Jews' in the Fourth Gospel" on pp. xi–xiv.

Pastoral Perspective

The larger context of this passage in which Jesus talks about his good works is his healing of the man born blind (9:1–41). The immediate context is Jesus' thoughtful comment, "The Father and I are one" (10:30). After saying that his good works demonstrate who he is, Jesus names his oneness with God. As a result, his own people take up rocks and prepare to stone him. While being threatened as a result of his claim of union with God, he asks them what actions they find objectionable. Jesus' question indicates that he considers his relationship with God and his actions to be intimately intertwined. He sees action on behalf of others and oneness with God as two sides of the same coin. In other words, he believes that justice and contemplative spirituality are intimately intertwined. In this section of John, Jesus' actions and his relationship with God are discussed in an alternating, close, and interdependent manner—much like the ebb and flow of the ocean.

Oneness with God lead to his actions of justice, which reveal God's love and care for people. These actions then lead Jesus to recognize and claim his oneness with God and to invite people to believe. Many individuals and churches seem to prefer one side of this coin to the other. Worship, Bible study, programming, mission trips, quiet times, and other spiritual practices can become unbalanced when we

Feasting on the Gospels

Exegetical Perspective

John 10:31–39 continues one of the major themes of the Fourth Gospel that was also prominent in 10:19–30: Jesus' identity and his relationship to the Father. This passage, which presents another hostile encounter between Jesus and the Jewish authorities, emphasizes Jesus' identity as God's Son. He has been sanctified and sent into the world as the Father's representative, embodying God's presence and fulfilling God's works.

John 10:31–33. This passage picks up right where the previous pericope (10:19–30) left off within the narrative. In spite of the NRSV's decision to start a new paragraph with verse 31, this verse more properly belongs with verses 22–30, as the attempt to stone Jesus in verse 31 comes as a direct response to Jesus' comments in verses 25–30. Jesus has uttered statements that the Jewish religious leaders consider blasphemous, which warrants stoning (cf. Lev. 24:16). This violent reaction should come as no surprise to readers; this is the second time within the Gospel that Jewish authorities have picked up stones to kill Jesus (8:59), and the evangelist has indicated on several occasions that they intend to put him to death (5:18; 7:1, 19; 8:37, 40).

Before the Jewish authorities have a chance to follow through with the stoning, Jesus responds. His

Homiletical Perspective

As the portrayal of Jews as Christ killers is often traced to the Fourth Gospel's use of the phrase "the Jews," this specific text, in which "the Jews" are casting about for stones to throw at Jesus, provides an excellent opportunity for the preacher to untangle a problematic historical knot. Biblical scholar Phyllis Trible calls such dangerous texts—and their terrible legacy—"texts of terror."[1] It is important to preach them in order to remind ourselves not only that we ourselves are capable of scapegoating virtually anyone (individually and collectively) but also that we must work against our human need to blame. The problem then is how to preach about "the Jews," who are presented in this text as argumentative, threatening, and all too eager to pick up a stone to (eventually) hurl toward Jesus.

The first move in such a sermon could remind the congregation that whomever history judges to be great leaders, teachers, scientists, and miracle workers are inevitably misunderstood (or misjudged) within their era. Persons like Nelson Mandela, the women of Seneca Falls, and Martin Luther King Jr.— along with their activities, writings, and thoughts— were seen as "dangerous texts" by the cultures to

1. Phyllis Trible, *Texts of Terror: Literary-Feminist Readings of Biblical Narratives* (Philadelphia: Fortress Press, 1984).

Theological Perspective

Pastoral Perspective

sin does not appear in John, the basic sentiment behind Jesus' response contains its echoes (v. 32). The religious leaders charge Jesus with demon possession. His works are not from God. Jesus, however, makes it clear his works are from "the Father" and not from himself. It is as if he warns, "Be careful about what you say about me, my works, and in whose name I do them. You are imperiling yourselves."

Jesus earlier asserted that he and "the Father" are united in their works (*hen*, v. 30). He now links his works to God using the same adjective found in the image of the good shepherd: "good." His works extend from God because they are good works (*erga . . . kala*, v. 32). He and they represent God. Their good quality signifies their origin and substance. We are reminded of the theological weight that "good" carries in Jesus' interaction with the rich man in Mark 10:18: "Why do you call me good? No one is good but God alone."

"Good" (*kalos*) is an adjective whose ancient Greek and Jewish meanings are found in the Fourth Gospel. In Greek philosophy the idea of the good represented that form of higher being desired by the soul. It was a beautiful goodness. It pointed to intellectual activity that contained political, social, ethical, and spiritual implications. Plotinus in the third century CE expanded it to mean moral beauty.[1]

While in the Old Testament the Greek understanding of "good" is found in reference to the person of God more than to human persons, it often includes human moral activity. In the Septuagint, the Greek translation of the Old Testament, *kalos* not only describes the goodness of creation in Genesis but also signifies what is morally good, as spoken by prophets like Micah. It speaks of the quality of the relationship between the God of the covenant and the community of the covenant. Subsequently, the meaning of *kalos* is broader than "pleasant," "right," "favored," "obedient," or "useful." It reverberates with God's beauty and goodness, yet it is not a quality inherent in any human social construction crafted by human making.[2] What is good is God present in the world, both transcendently and immanently. Humans cannot make this kind of good under their own power, but receive it as a gift and participate in it. Jesus, however, has performed this good in his works.

1. Georg Bertram, *kalos*, in *Theological Dictionary of the New Testament*, ed. Gerhard Kittel, trans. Geoffrey W. Bromiley (Grand Rapids: Eerdmans, 1965), 3:542–43.
2. D. Stephen Long, *The Goodness of God* (Grand Rapids: Brazos Press, 2001), 24.

focus too much on either our action or our union with God.

Action without contemplation can become dry, dull, shame-bound, filled with the expectations of others, and dictated by our own tyrannical consciences. Our actions too easily become attempts to earn God's love, rather than responses to God's extravagant love. Individuals and congregations can become addicted to activity, busyness, and adrenaline. Without the fuel of oneness with God, individuals and churches can become burned out through drawing too heavily upon their own means, rather than depending upon spiritual resources. Without the common and clear purpose that oneness with God provides, Christian groups and congregations can become fractured and conflicted as they seek to take action drawing only from their own resources. Trying to solve the problems of too many or wrongly motivated actions with more action only makes the problems worse.

Likewise, contemplation without action can become rote and stale, filled with unrealistic expectations from ourselves and other people. It can become an attempt to earn or prove God's love, rather than a confident and joyful resting in God's love. Contemplation without action can degenerate into attempts to manipulate God or to treat God as our servant. This imbalance can lead to viewing God as a kind of cosmic bellhop who fulfills our commands of "bring me this; give me that." Contemplation without action in response can lead to our feeling overfull, something like the experience of being stuffed yet unsatisfied. When we binge on more contemplation, we make the problem worse. Trying with more contemplation to cure the problems caused by excessive contemplation only intensifies the problems.

On the other hand, when our actions become the overflow of our oneness with God, and when we nurture our oneness with God through intentional actions, the picture becomes very different. We do what we do—actions and contemplative practices—as a result of God's love for us and others, not as an attempt to earn or prove God's love. Our actions and our contemplation become characterized by our feelings of ease, joy, clarity, and love. At times, other people will value and appreciate our spirituality and behaviors, just as some people expressed their gratitude to Jesus in the passages leading up to this one. At other times, people may take offense, mildly or strongly, for a variety of reasons. This passage tells of people taking such strong offense at Jesus that they start gathering rocks to stone him. Jesus' response again shows his emphasis on behavior and action: "I

retort in verse 32 is severely ironic and skewers the Jewish religious leaders. He has done "good works" among them, including two healing miracles in Jerusalem, yet both were met with a hostile response (5:1–20; 9:1–41). The Jewish authorities are simply incapable of understanding this because they do not belong to his sheep (10:26) and are blind (9:39–40). They respond to Jesus by clarifying that they do not actually want to kill him because of "good works." Their opposition to Jesus comes primarily as a result of his remarkable claims about his identity, which they declare blasphemous (v. 33).

The accusation in verse 33 is the first and only official charge of blasphemy in the entire Gospel, although it is implied in 8:59. Though there is scarce evidence in Jewish literature of this period regarding what legally constituted blasphemy, it is clear that here they are uneasy with Jesus' claim of unity with God. They mistakenly insist that Jesus is "making" himself out to be equal with God (5:18). Ironically, within the narrative of the Fourth Gospel, Jesus is not "making" himself anything more than he is. He truly is equal to God (1:1).

John 10:34–39. Jesus responds in verse 34 to the Jewish leaders' accusation by quoting Psalm 82:6: "I said, you are gods." By quoting one line of the psalm, Jesus evokes its entirety, which served in its historical context as a rebuke to unjust judges. Since judgment belonged to God (Deut. 1:17), judges were those who were responsible for enacting God's justice among the people. Standing before a judge was regarded as standing before God (e.g., Exod. 22:9). Jesus' argument against the blasphemy charge in verses 34–36, which may seem like poor exegesis by today's standards, is in line with typical rabbinical interpretive techniques of his time. If judges were called gods in Scripture, Jesus reasons, then how can the Jewish leaders accuse him of blasphemy if he merely calls himself God's Son? The reference to Psalm 82:6 is especially fitting because Jesus functions as judge in the Fourth Gospel; the Father has "given him authority to execute judgment" as the Son of Man (5:27). The mention of "those to whom the word of God came" (v. 35) is ironic, because in the Fourth Gospel, Jesus is the Word of God (1:1, 14).

Note that in verse 34 "law" is broadly conceived, as it does not refer strictly to the Pentateuch but to the larger corpus of Jewish Scriptures. Further, while Jesus says, "Your law," he is in no way rejecting it as his own Scripture. Instead, by claiming that "the scripture cannot be annulled" (v. 35), he is claiming

which they spoke. When Galileo posited that the earth rotated around the sun (directly challenging the church's position), he was not only excommunicated; his safety and well-being were threatened.

Without intending it, makers of history—like those who have opposed apartheid, worked for women's rights and civil rights, and made scientific discoveries that altered the normative worldview—become lightning rods for their causes, a new, more inclusive normal. Such persons upset the balance of what is perceived to be normal. They are inevitably considered to be dangerous. Unfounded and unprovable accusations are hurled at them, from "madman" to "communist" to "uppity." When Martin Luther King Jr. was alive and leading the civil rights movement, all the fathers on my block—my very Caucasian, lower-middle-class block—believed him to be a "Communist troublemaker." They wanted him silenced.

The second move in the sermon could remind the congregation that, paradoxically, the "oppressed" whom great leaders are hoping to liberate often view their liberators—along with the establishment—as dangerous. There were South Africans who disagreed vehemently with the African National Congress, along with its leaders such as Nelson Mandela. Women who were against suffrage protested vehemently against the suffragists. At the height of Martin Luther King Jr.'s influence, with the majority of his support from the church, there were Christians from both white and black churches who were among his most bitter, angry opponents.

Jesus was Jewish, and he came to reform his own Jewish tradition, to call it back into its greatness. This divided Jews. They could not agree on how to stand on the matter of Jesus. We are not surprised. North American Christians could not agree about how to stand on the matter of Martin Luther King Jr. and his war against poverty. Other North American Christians could not agree about civil rights reform. Earlier North American Christians could not agree about women's suffrage.

We are not surprised that the first-century Jewish community was divided in its response to Jesus. What is surprising is that as preachers we have failed, on the whole, to explain, document, and underscore the Jewishness of Jesus and to acknowledge that in John's Gospel there is a profound disagreement—even violent at times—over who this Jesus was and what he meant to their tradition. The best way to approach preaching this dangerous text would be to imagine your Jewish friends sitting among your parishioners as you preach.

John 10:31–39

Theological Perspective

The idea that Jesus could claim such a status draws the hostility of the Jewish leaders.[3] The Pharisees purport to be the agents of good and, as such, associate their authority with God (v. 33). Yet Jesus brazenly associates himself with God, fueling the charge that he is "making himself God" (5:18). In response, Jesus invokes the Psalms, not only to explain the commonality of his claim but also to democratize the goodness of God's actions. The implication is this: to refuse to accept the sanctifying work of God in Jesus or in others who do God's work is itself blasphemy. Jesus says frankly, "If I am not doing the works of my Father, then do not believe me" (v. 37). Here we encounter an argument found in the Synoptics: "Whoever is not with me is against me" (Matt. 12:30; Luke 11:23).

The last few verses of this section offer possibilities for reconciliation on several levels. In each case, it is the teachings and practices of the Jewish establishment that need reconciliation with God's reality. It begins by knowing the palpable presence of God in this moment. If "the Jews" cannot overcome the affront to their expectations of Messiah, then they can surely believe the works. If they can manage this move, then they might gain knowledge of God and Jesus. Knowledge in the Gospel of John, as commentaries explain, is not a cognitive category, but a category of relationship. Here we find indications that for some, faith is not possible without works.

Reconciliation is elusive for both the religious leaders confronting Jesus and the Johannine community. Even as Jesus acknowledges the reality of cognitive and spiritual dissonance, he makes room for a relationship with the Father. As in the postresurrection encounter with Peter in chapter 21, Jesus makes a concession for love's sake. He understands the lure that the goodness of humanity's own making has for God's people. Especially powerful is the self-made account of goodness found in human institutions. Jesus points to effective common-ground values—Scripture and works—to initiate the reconciliation that is his larger work. At the end of this passage, however, the dissonance appears too great. The socioreligious commitments leave the religious leaders inimical to Jesus.

ANDY WATTS

Pastoral Perspective

have shown you many good works from the Father. For which of these are you going to stone me?" (v. 32).

They say, "For blasphemy, because you, though only a human being, are making yourself God" (v. 33). Jesus' answer implies that he does not see oneness with God as something that is unique to him; rather, he sees union with God as available to human beings who have received the word of God. He reminds them of the line in Psalm 82, "You are gods" (v. 34). He goes on to make the point that if Scripture says, "You are gods," in reference to those who have received the word of God, then Jesus, whom God had "sanctified and sent" (v. 36), cannot be accused of blasphemy for claiming to be the Son of God.

Jesus seems to be emphasizing that union with God is both true for him and available to human beings. It must be noted that "You are gods" in Psalm 82 is quickly followed by an important line, "You shall die like mortals and fall like any prince" (Ps. 82:7). These verses seem to be a poetic expression of one of the great mysteries of human life: it may be said that we are gods who die and who fall. The psalmist was not proclaiming that union with God would prevent death or falling from power. He might have been saying that the image of God and our relationship with God remain with us even as we make bad decisions, experience falls, or die.

Likewise, in this Gospel passage, Jesus seems to suggest that union with God can undergird and inform all of our actions, just as oneness with God is at the heart of his actions. He describes union with God as a type of indwelling, saying that God is in him and that he is in God. Ordering our lives so that we are aware that we live in God and that God lives in us might result in our feeling more serenity, grace, acceptance, and love. Our actions might then reflect the serenity, grace, acceptance, and love of God. May we experience these fruits of our union with God.

DENISE MCLAIN MASSEY

---

3. Rudolf Bultmann, *The Gospel of John: A Commentary*, trans. George Beasley-Murray (Philadelphia: Westminster Press, 1971), 388.

the ongoing authority and validity of the Jewish Scriptures as his own.

Jesus' statement in verse 36 that he is "the one whom the Father has sanctified" resonates within the setting of this passage during the festival of Dedication (10:22). The festival recalls the rededication and sanctification of the altar within the Jerusalem temple in 164 BCE, following its desecration by Antiochus IV Epiphanes. Just as God has been revealed in the temple, God is now revealed through the one who is sanctified and sent into the world: Jesus (cf. 6:69; 17:19).

Jesus concludes his rebuttal in verses 37–38 by appealing once again to his works as evidence of his origin and identity in the Father (5:36; 10:25, 32). His works have been a part of his revelatory mission from the beginning and are intended to promote belief in those who witness them (cf. 5:36). His declaration that "the Father is in me and I am in the Father" (v. 38) speaks powerfully to the mutual indwelling and intimacy that Jesus and the Father share, a theme prominent throughout the Gospel (1:1, 18; 10:15, 30; 14:9–11; 17:21–23).

This is the second time that Jesus has made a dramatic claim of unity with God during the festival of Dedication. Like the first claim, that "the Father and I are one" (v. 30), this profound christological declaration also elicits a violent response from his antagonists. They attempt to "arrest" or "seize" him (the Greek word *piazō* can mean either), most likely in order to follow through on their plan to stone him (v. 31; cf. 11:8). Faced with capture, however, Jesus escapes effortlessly from the Jewish authorities' hands. From the theological standpoint of the Fourth Gospel, Jesus cannot be captured, because his hour has not yet arrived (7:30; 8:20). When it does arrive, Jesus will go willingly to his capture and death (12:23–27; 18:1–12).

ARTHUR M. WRIGHT JR.

Sadly, I did not know or love—or even meet—a Jew until I was an eighteen-year-old undergraduate and my roommate was a Reformed Jew. It was woefully late in life for me. It was not until Linda told me that she was Reformed that I learned the difference between the Orthodox and Reformed Jewish traditions in the United States. It was not until Linda invited me to Rosh Hashanah services that, as the shofar sounded and the cantor began to sing a psalm, I understood for the first time what the Judeo-Christian label actually meant. It meant that the early Jesus movement really was Jewish and that the Psalms really were and are Jewish. My own roots really were Jewish. I was stunned at how at home I felt in a synagogue—and even more stunned by my lack of curiosity and engagement with Judaism prior to entering university.

A Jewish friend I currently enjoy dinner conversations with is a rabbi. She is one of two women rabbis in my hometown. She is the Reformed rabbi, and her colleague is Orthodox. I asked Rabbi Mary if, while she was in seminary, the curriculum there included studying Christian texts, such as the Fourth Gospel, that have negatively shaped Christian preconceptions of Judaism. In her six years of study, Rabbi Mary remembered one class in which they glanced at anti-Jewish texts throughout history. I asked her advice regarding preaching this text and John's troubling use of the term "the Jews." Rabbi Mary smiled and said, "There isn't any such thing as 'the Jews.' Saying 'the Jews' is as silly as saying 'the Christians.' Jews disagree on virtually everything from theology to worship liturgy to the color of the carpet in the synagogue—just like Christians." Then she added, "What I would like to hear as a Jew regarding this John text is that the Jews were divided in their response to Jesus. Most Jews simply didn't know what to make of Jesus."

The conclusion of this sermon could invite the congregation to attend a Friday evening synagogue service in your town or neighboring city, along with the hope that the congregation would begin not only an interfaith dialogue but also interfaith engagement.

KAY LYNN NORTHCUTT

John 10:40–42

⁴⁰He went away again across the Jordan to the place where John had been baptizing earlier, and he remained there. ⁴¹Many came to him, and they were saying, "John performed no sign, but everything that John said about this man was true." ⁴²And many believed in him there.

Theological Perspective

In the closing verses of chapter 10, Jesus heads east across the Jordan River to the place where his public ministry began. It was there John the Baptist identified him as the lamb of God (1:29, 36). Most likely the trip provided much needed rest after months of tension. This was a place of restoration. It was a place of peace and identity confirmation for Jesus.

Exegetes have considered this short passage an interlude. For some it represents a small pause before Jesus continues his ministry of signs. For others, it appears to be a more significant narrative break that prepares the reader for Jesus' hour, which arrives at 12:23 and culminates in his death. Several commentaries highlight this passage as a return to origins. It is the site of a first encounter with John the Baptist, the first witness to Jesus. It is theological punctuation for others, a testimony that "many believed" (v. 42).

Understanding the ultimate purpose and structure of the Fourth Gospel cannot be reduced to one interpretation. John's author, having just brought us through dialogues full of high Christology, invites a breath. The east bank of the Jordan River invites the reader to a fresh look at Jesus, as well as to preparing for difficult events ahead. It provides a theological rest stop for Jesus and for the reader. It also makes room for a brief return to the Jewish roots of the salvation found in Jesus.

Pastoral Perspective

This brief passage describes a transitional time in Jesus' life. As such, it can suggest some wisdom for us in the transitional times in our own lives. Jesus had healed a blind man on the Sabbath (chap. 9) and then answered a question about whether he was the Messiah by saying that his good works testify to who he is (10:31–39). He had claimed that his good works were done because of his oneness with God. After Jesus had claimed to be the Son of God, the leaders had tried to arrest him because they viewed this statement as blasphemy. Paradoxically, the disbelief and challenges of his own people seemed to catalyze Jesus' recognition of his oneness with God.

In this passage, Jesus is running for his life after having been called crazy, accused of being possessed by a demon, and threatened by his people's belief that he deserved to die. Do you identify with Jesus in any way here? Are you facing challenges from without? Does someone think you are crazy because you have followed God's leadership in some area of your life? Has your view of yourself begun to change? Do you feel such oneness with God that you wonder at the audacity of your dreams and what you are feeling called to do and be in this world?

On the other hand, you may not feel at one with God at all. You may have no idea what oneness with God means. Perhaps your transition is related to the

Exegetical Perspective

These final verses of John 10 serve as a major turning point within the narrative of the Fourth Gospel. Jesus retreats in verse 40 from a hostile encounter with the Jewish authorities in Jerusalem (10:22–39) and will not face them again until the passion narrative. His public ministry effectively comes to an end as he returns to the other side of the Jordan River, where his ministry began (1:28). Jesus' public ministry commenced with the proclamation of John the Baptist along the banks of the river (1:29), and in 10:41 John's testimony once again sparks belief in Jesus. Jesus' public ministry is thus bookended by John's testimony, which is mentioned here for the last time in the Gospel.

Whereas the Jewish authorities in Jerusalem were unable to grasp the radical nature of Jesus' identity on the basis of his works (10:22–39), verses 40–42 present "many" coming to belief in Jesus on the basis of John's testimony. Their statement in verse 41, that "John performed no sign, but everything that John said about this man was true," is introduced by an imperfect tense verb in Greek, translated as "they were saying" (*elegon*). Here the imperfect tense suggests repetitive action; the people are chattering enthusiastically with one another about Jesus' presence. Verse 41 also draws a clear line between the ministries of John and Jesus. John's spoken words

Homiletical Perspective

Three years into my first pastorate, frustrated with my lackluster growth as a Christian, I identified what I thought was the most remarkable Christian in my congregation and asked her if I could interview her. "Elizabeth," I said, "you are the kind of Christian I've always wished that I could be, and I was wondering if you could tell me how exactly you became as you are." Without a second's hesitation she enthusiastically retorted, "My baptism really took!" She went on, "You know Willis and I fell in love during the Great Depression. I was a waitress, supported my mom, dad, and five siblings on my meager earnings, and Willis kept showing up at the café counter, asking for a coffee refill. We waited seven years to be married—as each of us was the only one in our families, respectively, with jobs.

"When finally we married, Willis took a job working steel in Ohio. Anyway, Willis and I decided we wanted to get baptized for Christmas. The only problem was the Disciples church didn't have a baptistery; so, as was the custom, the Disciples borrowed the Baptists'. The temperature that morning was hovering right at zero, and as I pressed my toes onto the first step of the baptistery, I saw something shiny. I looked closer, and then pressed my toe down against the shine—and the entire baptistery was covered with a thin sheet of ice! Yes," she said, smiling

Theological Perspective

On the east bank Jesus returns to a place of encounter and identity and exile and community. Here we see the Gospel of John working its subtle ecclesiology in and out of a layered narrative. While scholars propose various reasons for the Fourth Gospel—including a defense of Jesus, evangelizing Gentiles, and converting Jews—the rest stop in the narrative points to a different reason.[1] The believing community needs reinforcing and affirmation. It longs to hear again the words of new creation.

Encounter and Identity. At this point in the story a return occurs. The Johannine community is invited to return to other places of encounter with God experienced by their ancestors. The east bank could be Bethel, where Abraham memorialized his call as the first of the true vine. It could be the burning bush, where Moses shook with fear as he met the great I AM. It could be the hard ground of Peniel, where Jacob wrestled the angel of God to receive a name to be a light for the nations. It could be the wilderness moment, where the Hebrews first learned to trust the liberating God, where they received the sustaining bread of life. It could be the moment of Jesus' first anointing, where he understood he was the resurrection and the life.

It could be all of these symbols, for the east bank of the Jordan represents reassurance to the Johannine community. It serves as a reminder they are the sheepfold following the shepherd of God. Amidst the social disruptions created by exclusion from the synagogue, spiritual confusion has set in. Here we must remember the parallels between Jesus and the Johannine community. Judaism as they know it is reacting to a dissonant message. Time to recollect.

Exile and Community. That Jesus is on the east bank carries ecclesiological significance. The east bank is foreign territory in proximity to Jerusalem. Politically, it may provide refuge from the Jerusalem establishment. Theologically, it recalls Ezekiel's vision of the glory of God leaving the temple and moving eastward toward Babylon to be with God's people in exile (Ezek. 10:18).

Exile would have been a multilayered life world for the Johannine community. Separated from Jerusalem, expelled from the local synagogue, and threatened by rising animosities toward Christians, the community hungers for the bread of life. The east

1. Luke T. Johnson, *The Writings of the New Testament: An Interpretation* (Philadelphia: Fortress Press, 1986), 472.

Pastoral Perspective

feeling of being bored because you have been playing it safe and small. You may be scared of what will happen if you truly follow this Christ. To take even a small step in that direction may feel frightening. Your transition may be about growing toward oneness with God, remembering that love casts out fear (1 John 4:18). Another's transition may be about addressing the results of union with God. In either case, Jesus' experience in this transitional time can be helpful for you.

As he was dealing with challenges from without and an expanding view of his life's purpose within, what did Jesus do? Where did he go? Verse 40 gives the answer: "He went away again across the Jordan to the place where John had been baptizing earlier, and he remained there." Jesus went back to his spiritual roots. He returned to where he had lived before, to where his journey had begun, and to where he had first recognized his call. Perhaps he was moving to a place far from the influence of the people who wanted to kill him.

The phrasing of verse 40 is striking. He went to the place "where John had been baptizing earlier." The passage does not say, "to the place where Jesus had first been baptized." The emphasis is on John, the one who had publicly recognized Jesus' life purpose. Jesus reconnects with his spiritual community, his spiritual ancestors. John had known who Jesus was, even before Jesus had openly, verbally claimed it for himself. Before he baptized Jesus, John had said of Jesus, "Here is the Lamb of God who takes away the sin of the world!" (1:29, 36). According to Luke, John had known Jesus his entire life. In fact, the first encounter between them occurred when they were both in the womb. John while in Elizabeth's womb leaped in recognition of Jesus in Mary's womb (Luke 1:41). Jesus returned to the place where his mother and relatives knew intimately of his union with God.

Here, Jesus would have encountered cousins, elders, ancestors, old friends, mentors, and other people who knew who he was. He returned to a place where he had been known, called, and loved. These are the people and places to which we must return when life becomes too much for us. We must remember who we are and where we came from. We can draw strength from our baptism and from our spiritual family.

This place Jesus went also would have undoubtedly contained people who had been detractors. There would have been some unpleasant memories, but the fact that the Gospel writer describes it as "the place where John had first baptized" seems to imply

witnessed to Jesus, but only Jesus performed signs that revealed his identity (2:23; 3:2; 6:2).

John the Baptist "Decreases" within the Narrative. It is quite possible that the "many" who come to Jesus are actually followers of John the Baptist. John has presumably been put into prison (3:24) by this time and may have even been killed, although the Fourth Gospel does not narrate either of these events (cf. Mark 6:14–29; Matt. 14:1–12; Luke 9:7–9). This is a reasonable assumption, as John is no longer baptizing here (v. 40).

Curiously, each successive appearance of John the Baptist within the Fourth Gospel has been shorter than the last (1:19–36; 3:22–30; 5:33–35; 10:40–41). John himself declared that "[Jesus] must increase, but I must decrease" (3:30), and his presence in the text quite literally diminishes with each subsequent mention. Is it possible that the author of the Fourth Gospel has cleverly crafted the narrative in a manner so that it reflects this idea? Some commentators have argued that, in the late first century, the Johannine community was in conflict with a number of external groups, including followers of John the Baptist.[1] If this is true, then John's testimony about Jesus serves as a technique to bolster faith in Jesus vis-à-vis John. John's voice gradually fades out of the narrative, to the point where he himself is physically absent, while others continue his testimony about Jesus within the text (v. 41).

Nevertheless, John has served an integral role with his powerful testimony to Jesus through the first half of the Gospel. John is, after all, the "friend of the bridegroom" who points the "bride" toward Jesus, the bridegroom (3:29). He was the first to identify Jesus within the narrative, declaring him "the Lamb of God" (1:29, 36) and "the Son of God" (1:34). John's disciples are among the first in the Fourth Gospel to follow Jesus (1:37), and though Jesus found rejection among the Jewish authorities in Jerusalem (10:22–39), he still receives a favorable welcome among those who knew and followed John the Baptist (vv. 40–42).

Remaining and Abiding. The text says that Jesus "remains" (*emeinen*, v. 40) on the other side of the Jordan for an unspecified amount of time. The Greek verbal root translated here as "remained" (*menō*) is theologically significant throughout the Fourth

and laughing, "my baptism really took! Willis and I thought our teeth would never stop chattering that Sunday afternoon!"

That Christmas baptism was the defining moment in Elizabeth's life, a moment to which she returned again and again, particularly in times of trial and challenge. Jesus too did precisely that in this reading from John. He crossed the Jordan to return to the place where John had been preaching and baptizing, because Jesus wanted—and needed—to remember his own baptism.

According to John 1:28 this place was "Bethany beyond the Jordan," not to be confused with the Bethany near Jerusalem, where Lazarus, Martha, and Mary lived. The Bethany where John had been baptized was a double ford across the river, approximately six miles north of the Dead Sea at the point traditionally assumed to have been where the Israelites under Joshua had crossed into the promised land (Josh. 3:1–17). It was also allegedly the place where Elijah had ascended into heaven in a fiery chariot and Elisha had taken up Elijah's prophetic mantle (2 Kgs. 2:1–15). John had undoubtedly chosen the site of his ministry carefully. What better place could there have been for all Jews to remember that they were God's chosen people, and for a particular Jew, Jesus, to come to recognize that he had been chosen in a special way to be God's anointed?

This sermon's first move could emphasize that wherever and however we were baptized (as an infant, as an adult, at a font, in a baptistery, in a livestock tank, or in a river), remembering our baptism—even if it is remembering what we have been told about our infant baptism—helps us to bring to the forefront of our consciousness that we have a special relationship with and calling from God, just as Jesus did. Such remembering is important particularly, but not exclusively, in difficult times such as Jesus was experiencing in this text. Remembering our baptism brings us back to focus on who we are and whose we are.

In the Fourth Gospel, John the Baptist is the primary human being who understands who Jesus truly is. John's testimony was based on what he himself had experienced at Jesus' baptism: the Spirit descending on Jesus and a voice declaring Jesus to be God's chosen one. No wonder that John 10, a chapter recounting the division among "the Jews" regarding Jesus' messiahship and an attempt first to stone and then to arrest him, concludes with Jesus returning to the very place of his own baptism by John. Remembering his baptism not only helped Jesus personally

1. E.g., Raymond E. Brown, *The Community of the Beloved Disciple: The Life, Loves, and Hates of an Individual Church in New Testament Times* (New York: Paulist Press, 1979), 69–71.

John 10:40–42

Theological Perspective

bank of the Jordan steps the reader backward from the pain endured as a Jesus follower to the hope found in God's presence in this one called Jesus. They are reassured their community is one of Jesus' good works, and therefore one of God's good works. Though exiled from the synagogue, they are included in God's story ongoing since the call of Abraham.

Jeremiah's words to those in exile in Babylon resonate in the background of the Jordan River moment: "My people have been lost sheep; their shepherds have led them astray, turning them away on the mountains; from mountain to hill they have gone, they have forgotten their fold" (Jer. 50:6).

The return of Jesus to the place of his calling on the banks of the Jordan reminds them: the Good Shepherd is alive in Syria, Turkey, or wherever the Johannine community is living in exile. This flock has chosen to abide in Jesus; here, says John's author, is a moment to remember.

A troubling reality confronts this community. Is their suffering necessary and redemptive? While Jesus alluded to the hatred of the world for those who follow him, his embodiment of palpable hope— of rivers of living water—has sustained their belief. This is the question addressed by Dietrich Bonhoeffer in *The Cost of Discipleship*. There we are told, "When Christ calls a man, he bids him come and die."[2] For Bonhoeffer, the presence of the cross presents to the believer costly grace. Exile and abundant life are mutually inclusive of one another.

Bonhoeffer's attitudes toward suffering and discipleship, gained from his own costly experience, would have been too familiar to the Johannine community. The Fourth Gospel anticipates much of this view. It also conceives of discipleship in terms of safeguarding the humanity of Jesus' followers. It maintains a theo-ethical support for health as a sign of Christian commitment.[3] Discipleship is life-giving.

On to the east bank of the Jordan Jesus goes, and to there the narrator returns audiences then and now, to remember the life-giving presence of God in the community.

ANDY WATTS

Pastoral Perspective

that it was a reminder of Jesus' own baptism and the teachings of John about Jesus.

Jesus lived for a while in the place where his spirituality had been recognized and nurtured. It appears that after claiming oneness with God and experiencing his people's fear and anger, he gave himself some time to integrate this new knowledge and its consequences. He went back to a place where he could be in relationship with others who were also following the leadership of God. Jesus could have been tempted to act as though he had to face his problems alone. Instead he sought companionship from those who had previously recognized his gifts and calling.

Jesus lived there for a while. What happened? Many "came to him" (v. 41). His oneness with God, even while retreating and returning, attracted them. He did not set out to make being the Messiah happen. He lived as who he was, and people sought him out. Many "believed in him" (v. 42), after they recognized that "everything that John said about this man was true" (v. 41). The people had heard John's words, and then they saw the truth for themselves.

Jesus' instinct to seek community and help while dealing with conflict and disbelief enabled people to believe in him. Seeking help, solace, and community, as well as returning to where he was known and loved, fulfilled the next step in his journey to become who he was.

The same can be true for us, if we allow it. Our transitional times call for us to seek support from those who have known, nurtured, and recognized our calling by returning to our spiritual home.

DENISE MCLAIN MASSEY

---

2. Dietrich Bonhoeffer, *The Cost of Discipleship* (London: SCM, 1948), 89.
3. Anthony Pinn, "Dietrich Bonhoeffer on Discipleship," in *Beyond the Pale: Reading Ethics from the Margins*, ed. Stacey M. Floyd-Thomas and Miguel A. De La Torre (Louisville, KY: Westminster John Knox Press, 2011), 142.

Gospel. Often rendered in English as "dwelling" or "abiding," the verb is employed by the author of the Gospel to describe the intimate relationship between Jesus and God (14:10). It indicates a similar relationship between Jesus and believers: Jesus abides in believers, just as they abide in him (15:4). Likewise, the Holy Spirit abides in believers (14:17). Believers are also urged to abide in Jesus' words (8:31) and in his love (15:10). Following Jesus' encounter with the Samaritan woman in 4:1–39, Jesus "stays" (*emeinen*) with the Samaritans for two days (4:40). As a result of his "staying" with them, many come to believe in him and declare that he is "the Savior of the world" (4:41–42). Likewise, because Jesus "remains there" on the other side of the Jordan (v. 40) for a period of time, many come to believe in him (v. 42). "Abiding" is not a mundane activity in the Fourth Gospel. It suggests a profound closeness and deep intimacy that is life-giving to those involved.

Theological Significance of the Narrative Movement. Though unnamed in this text, the place that Jesus retreats to is Bethany, in the region of Perea, "the place where John had been baptizing earlier" (v. 40; cf. 1:28). This is not the same Bethany in which Lazarus, Mary, and Martha live in 11:1, which is close to Jerusalem in the region of Judea. Jesus travels in verse 40 from Jerusalem to the Perean Bethany. He then travels from the Perean Bethany to the Judean one in chapter 11 in order to be with Lazarus's mourning sisters. This travel—from Jerusalem in Judea, to Bethany in Perea, then back to Judea—advances one of the major theological motifs of the Gospel, that Jesus goes willingly to his own death in obedience to the Father (10:17–18). The Jewish authorities have just attempted to kill him in 10:31, but he is able to escape their clutches (10:39) because it is not yet his "hour" to die (7:30; 8:20). In 11:7–8, Jesus chooses of his own accord to return to the hostile Judean region, with full knowledge that he will die there (12:23–28).

ARTHUR M. WRIGHT JR.

to relive the defining moment of his messianic identity and mission; it also helped others to remember John's testimony about Jesus.

The sermon's second move could underscore that remembering our baptism includes remembering that the baptism ritual itself, while it may be intensely personal, is also a communal event, occurring within the context of a community of faith. The public aspects of baptism affect people other than the person being baptized. Perhaps this is seen most clearly in churches that primarily practice infant baptism, where parents and godparents and congregations make formal promises to educate and nurture the child in the faith. Baptisms themselves are community faith events with the whole congregation participating. How wonderful it would be to reinstate the practice of the early church as recorded in the second-century *Teaching of the Twelve Apostles*, that both the baptizer and baptized ought to fast before the baptism, as well as any others who care to do so (*Didache* 7)! It takes an entire congregation to help us live into our baptism, which, while it occurs in a moment of time, is also a lifelong process.

The third move of this sermon could propose that helping baptisms "to take" can be a cherished, sought-after, and worked-toward hope of the congregation. Last Easter the children in my congregation who had made the decision to be baptized were baptized outdoors in a tank, a huge livestock tank filled with water. When we first built our church and ran short of funds before completing the building, the baptistery was eliminated. It was cold last Easter in Oklahoma—the wind whipping across the prairie—and I recruited "warmers" who stood next to the tank with warmed blankets—ready to receive the newly baptized and warm them up! Outdoor baptisms, on the Oklahoma prairie, the congregation gathered beaming around the tank. I am thinking these are baptisms that will take. Clearly, Jesus' did.

KAY LYNN NORTHCUTT

John 11:1–6

¹Now a certain man was ill, Lazarus of Bethany, the village of Mary and her sister Martha. ²Mary was the one who anointed the Lord with perfume and wiped his feet with her hair; her brother Lazarus was ill. ³So the sisters sent a message to Jesus, "Lord, he whom you love is ill." ⁴But when Jesus heard it, he said, "This illness does not lead to death; rather it is for God's glory, so that the Son of God may be glorified through it." ⁵Accordingly, though Jesus loved Martha and her sister and Lazarus, ⁶after having heard that Lazarus was ill, he stayed two days longer in the place where he was.

Theological Perspective

The gospel that is offered to us in Jesus Christ is about a life of relationships. The core of the gospel, as John understands it, is that God in love comes to us to restore us to God's life. Jesus' earthly life embodies such love, a life-giving love. His love calls us back to love God. In Christ we are invited to participate in the inner life of God, to partake in God's love and to commune with God. Jesus' relationship with the family at Bethany—the family of Martha, Mary, and Lazarus—is illustrative of how God in Christ relates to us and how we as God's children are invited to relate to God.

Friendship as the Essence of Jesus' Relationship to the World. Jesus nourished a very special relationship with Martha, Mary, and Lazarus. It is evident from the text that Jesus loved the family (vv. 3, 5). The family too loved Jesus. Bethany is the place where Jesus resided when he visited Jerusalem and received hospitality from this family. Mary was to anoint Jesus later, as he headed to Jerusalem for the last time. Jesus' ministry was sustained by the support of such families. Brown reasons, "If Bethany was Jesus' lodging place when he came to Jerusalem (and this is attested in the Synoptic tradition), then it is not too unreasonable to suggest that it was at this home that he stayed and that its occupants

Pastoral Perspective

Mary and Martha languish in worry and grief for their brother. Jesus delays in responding to their summons. The reader or listener identifies with the problem of spiritual expectation in the midst of mundane life unfolding in time.

Speaking with a young professional, I learned that he had emerged from a very dark place. For a couple of years he had been caught in an extremely difficult situation at work and could not see a way out. He said that whenever he came to church, he took to focusing on the lines of Scripture inscribed high on the chancel wall. Above an image of John the Baptist is the passage: "Let not your hearts be troubled" (14:1 KJV). Above Moses' picture are two short phrases: "Wait on the Lord. Be of good courage." He said those sentiments became his mantra. Over time they seemed the only prayer he had.

I shared with him that some years ago, not many years after I first came to the church, I also discovered the power in those sentiments. Finding myself in a dark time, I discovered that if I sat up in the balcony at certain hours during the day, the light coming in from the back window would faintly illuminate those phrases, and they held my heart.

My young friend said he learned about patience and waiting during these last couple of years. He learned something important about his relationship

Feasting on the Gospels

Exegetical Perspective

The narrative of the raising of Lazarus in John 11:1–44 is one of the more colorful, theologically rich stories in all of Scripture. The initial verses in this unit (vv. 1–6) highlight the faithfulness of Mary and Martha, the promise of a hopeful ending, and the contrast between the timetable of Jesus and what his followers seek. As the last miracle account in John, this narrative prefigures the passion account of later chapters and reflects the prominent role of women in the Gospel.

In terms of flow, the unit opens by citing the serious nature of Lazarus's condition and his connection to Mary and Martha (v. 1). Yet the details in the subsequent verse are puzzling: "Mary was the one who anointed the Lord with perfume and wiped his feet with her hair; her brother Lazarus was ill" (v. 2). The problem here is that the description of Mary washing Jesus' feet does not appear until the following chapter (12:3). This is actually the first mention of Mary and Martha in John. Consequently, this verse could be an editorial insertion that links this story with what follows in chapter 12. Perhaps there were common traditions surrounding Mary and Martha, and the biblical writer assumes knowledge of them.

Jesus declares that a miraculous reversal will take place for Lazarus: "This illness does not lead to death; rather it is for God's glory, so that the Son

Homiletical Perspective

The opening verses of this chapter set the stage for what is to follow by weaving together several ideas for our consideration. The story begins with assurances and remembrances of love. We are introduced to a family of three siblings in the village of Bethany—Mary, Martha, and Lazarus—whose close relationship with Jesus is based on mutual love. Jesus "loved Martha and her sister and Lazarus" (v. 5). The sisters treasure this love and give expression to it in their message to Jesus about their brother: "Lord, he whom you love is ill" (v. 3). We are reminded that Mary is held in blessed memory as the one who anointed Jesus with perfume and wiped his feet with her hair (v. 2; 12:3). This was an act of extravagance that reflected Mary's love and devotion to Jesus. Their mutual love is publicly displayed toward the end of the story in a sequence of events. First, Mary knelt at the feet of Jesus and wept (11:32); second, Jesus wept (11:35); and third, those who witnessed his tears remarked on his love: "See how he loved him!" (11:36). We also share in this love as we love one another: "Just as I have loved you, you also should love one another" (13:34).

This narrative points us to a grave concern triggered by an illness. It is the illness of a certain man named Lazarus (v. 1); illness of a brother (v. 2); illness of the one whom Jesus loved (v. 3); illness that

John 11:1–6

Theological Perspective

were truly his close friends."[1] It was a relationship of mutual love, care, and support. The church and the ministry of the community of Jesus would not have been possible without such homes. They loved Jesus! They were the midwives of the emerging Jesus movement.

To characterize Jesus' love for the family, the Gospel writer uses the verbs *philein* (v. 3) and *agapan* (v. 5), both of which mean "love." Brown suggests that there seems to be no great difference between them, since *agapan* is "a parenthetical insertion to assure the reader that Jesus' failure to go to Lazarus (v. 6) does not reflect indifference."[2] If these words could be used interchangeably—the way in which the Gospel writer uses them—such usage collapses the conceptual hierarchy that is built in Christian popular imagination of four forms of love, namely, *agapē* (self-giving love), *philia* (friendship), *eros* (sexual love), and *storgē* (affections).[3] *Agapē*, the love that is there at the heart of God, embodies itself in *philia* (friendship). Without *philia*, *agapē* remains an abstract idea. It has to embody itself in a relationship. Friendship is one such embodiment. Jesus invites his followers into a relationship of friendship.

Later, as Jesus sups in the upper room, he tells his disciples that he no longer calls them servants but friends (15:14–15). In a world of teeming hostilities Jesus brings in God's reign of love as human communities are formed in friendship. Jesus' relationship to Martha, Mary, and Lazarus is a symbolic representation of the reconfigured relationship in the redeemed community. It is not a patronizing love, but a participatory love, wherein the persons are configured as equals who bring in their gifts for the well-being of each other. While the family in Bethany sustains Jesus' ministry, Jesus is looked up to and expected to bring healing when it is needed. It is a community of friends who celebrate love through their hospitality, serve each other in reverence, and participate in each other's afflictions in solidarity. Healing happens in such practices of friendship. In such relationships human predicaments are dealt with and well-being is restored.

A Perspective on Illness and Death. When the sisters at Bethany send a word to Jesus that Lazarus whom he loves is ill, Jesus responds by saying, "This illness does not lead to death; rather it is for God's glory,

1. Raymond E. Brown, *The Gospel according to John I–XII*, AB 29 (Garden City, NY: Doubleday, 1966), 431.
2. Ibid., 423.
3. The concept was first articulated by C. S. Lewis in *The Four Loves* (New York: Harcourt Brace, 1960).

Pastoral Perspective

with God and about his life. Though he did not elaborate on the point, he had suffered over these years. Not suffering on the scale of a terrible tragedy, but suffering, nevertheless, of some potency, linked to his sense of identity and purpose, his freedom and future. He felt trapped, and he chose to work at "waiting on the Lord" over an extended period of time. He chose to sweat it out with God, praying that his troubled heart could find courage to endure the waiting.

His experience does not reek of high drama, but it is redolent of authentic spiritual pilgrimage. Over lunch my young friend told me about a portion of his journey. We did not set it up that way. After ordering our meals I did not say, "So, tell me about your spiritual pilgrimage." That is what he did, though, and I shared some of mine. I was struck by certain similarities, even though we were separated by two decades, occupying very different moments in our lives.

Of course the similarities extend beyond just the two of us. If any two readers of these words scheduled a luncheon, somewhere between the entrée and coffee the conversation might swerve onto the road of spiritual pilgrimage, and if there was openness and a modicum of transparent bravery, they would each likely reveal something the other would recognize, something that also pertained to suffering and waiting and trusting. It might even resonate with a variation on the theme of having been trapped, caught, stuck in a dark place at some time, maybe for a long time.

My lunch mate told me his wait was over. His life situation had resolved for now. A new day dawned. He was no longer trapped. The earth's rotation left the darkness behind for the time being. He credited his waiting and praying, counting on God's enduring presence despite the lack of felt evidence. On this side of it, he said, he had learned about trust. I believed him. Surely the learning was now deeply a part of him; experience gleaned in extra decades suggested he would need it again, and then at least once more after that, for that is the nature of long journeys.

Everyone has her or his story to tell about the map they have been drawing, about the adventures, calamities, wrong turns, dead ends, setbacks, losses, filling stations, and guides that have occupied their days. At any given moment the sense of forward momentum can feel interrupted, accompanied by a sense of holy absence—God missing in action.

We know from verse 21 ahead that Martha and Mary have been "waiting on the Lord," that is,

of God may be glorified through it" (v. 4). Rather than ending in death (*thanatos*), Jesus' actions with Lazarus demonstrate the power of the Son of God to shine in the midst of adversity. The same principle is at work in the resurrection account involving Jesus himself. Suffering and physical death become opportunities for the glory of God to become manifest (12:23–24; 13:31; 21:19). In this respect, the episode involving Lazarus prefigures the passion story that lies at the heart of the Gospel and underscores the ability of God, working through Jesus, to transcend the limits of human mortality.

The most difficult aspect of this passage occurs in the following verses, when Jesus announces his itinerary. The Gospel writer explains Jesus' love for these two women and for Lazarus (v. 5), but says Jesus does not leave immediately from his current location: "After having heard that Lazarus was ill, he stayed two days longer in the place where he was" (v. 6). How does one reconcile the commitment of Jesus to this family with his decision to remain in his current location? The fact that Jesus will utilize suffering to highlight the glory of God means that there is no rush. He knows that even if Lazarus's condition worsens to the point of death, this will allow a dramatic reversal to occur. His decision to remain in Perea (10:40) for two more days may appear to be a callous response, but this is not the case. The biblical writer is careful to emphasize Jesus' devotion to the family (vv. 5, 36), and the delay of two days assures that Jesus performs the miracle in a manner that foreshadows the events of John 19–20.

The unhurried nature of the journey furthermore suggests not only that all things are possible with God but that the anxious pleas of the followers do not always correlate with the divine plan. This response underscores the idea that Jesus' schedule does not necessarily conform to what his followers seek. A similar delay occurs in Jesus' response to his mother in the account of the wedding at Cana (2:4). Perhaps he had additional tasks in Perea, and it is also probable that Lazarus was already dead by the time the message reached Jesus. His decision to delay does not reflect disregard for this faithful family, but a desire to glorify God according to a different timetable.

The two women play a more prominent role in John than in Luke (Luke 10:38–42). Mary and Martha interact with Jesus throughout John 11, and in verse 3 they are the ones who send word about the condition of their brother. Their message is plaintive and brief: a follower of Jesus, their sibling, is in grave condition,

is for God's glory (v. 4); and illness to which Jesus will respond in his own time (v. 6). The illness is not identified; so this story may easily resonate with any family or community with a loved one who is suffering from illness. We may also recall our own experiences of illness and our desire to be surrounded by love and care. In this story, love provides the framework for an encounter with illness and its consequences, and love serves as the premise for inviting Jesus to be with the family in their time of distress.

The story is designed so that we do not linger in the place of illness or engage in a conversation about finding a cure. Even in the message from the sisters to Jesus, there is no explicit request. We are not invited to speculate on the nature of the illness or to suggest an appropriate mode of healing. We are not given a formula or a rubric to use in the design of our own rituals when our loved ones are ill. Rather, Jesus uses the occasion to invite those around him to see that his words and actions reveal divine love and life. The love that Jesus has for this family flows from his work of revealing divine love to the world. His love for them is superseded by his work of making God known, however. Jesus chooses this moment to make explicit that his response will be less about Lazarus and more about the glory of God. The disciples were not to be overwhelmed by whether Lazarus would die or recover; rather, they were to believe that in Jesus the glory of God would be revealed (v. 4).

We may all have different ways of imagining the glory of God, such as the warmth and radiance of light that causes our faces to shine as we are transfigured (Exod. 34:30, 33–35; Luke 9:29–31) or a presence that surrounds us like a cloud (1 Kgs. 8:10–11; Luke 9:34–35) and transports us to a place of rapture and overwhelming peace, joy, or worship. In this Gospel story, the glory of God is revealed in God's love and life-giving work in the world. Jesus participates so intimately in divine love that in him we see the nature and character of God; above all, through him we have access to the divine life (3:16). Jesus invites us to believe that he is one with God and shares in God's love and glory. He is glorified in every moment, word, or action that reveals God at work in and through him (12:28). Beyond his daily ministry, the Gospel indicates that Jesus will be glorified when he enters into that decisive hour to reveal God through his death, resurrection, and exaltation (12:16, 23). His actions in this story will be the opening act in a divine drama that will culminate in his own death.

John 11:1–6

Theological Perspective

so that the Son of God may be glorified through it" (v. 4). The writer has a theological intention when he selectively incorporates various signs into his Gospel. The christological implication of Lazarus's being raised from death is that Jesus is the giver of life, and in him the resurrection of the dead is assured to humanity. It is to suggest that illness and death will not have the final word, but life in God can be mediated through such experiences. It is particularly so in John's Gospel. The hour of glory for Jesus is his cross and resurrection, from which life in all its fullness flows. The resurrection of Lazarus is symbolic of the promise that is offered to the world in Christ, that the world in the end shares God's life. In the end what happens to Lazarus is for God's glory, the eternal presence of the Divine. In Christ we are invited into such life. His death and resurrection mediate that life.

While this story is symbolic of God's promise to the world in Christ, it also could be symbolic of the destiny of Jesus. By placing this narrative right before the passion narrative, the Gospel writer perhaps suggests that this illness and death are symbolic of Jesus' impending death and resurrection. In that case, the event of the glorification of Jesus does not lie in the popularity that he would receive after this event, but the cross where he would be lifted up. Christ is revealed to us not in the sites of seeming glory but in the sites of suffering. It is in Bethany (an Aramaic name that means "house of affliction") that the glory is revealed, the presence of God is experienced. It is here in Bethany that what began as Jesus' relationship to a brother and his sisters becomes the ultimate revelation of God's divine relationship to and work on behalf of humankind.

JOSEPH PRABHAKAR DAYAM

Pastoral Perspective

desperately waiting for Jesus. Mary loved him so much that she anointed his feet with her tears and perfumed oil and dried them with her hair. Their holy love for one another was much in evidence; but now she, along with her sister, had to wait through the calamity of their brother's death. "Where were you, Jesus?!" we hear ringing in our minds as he arrives at last in Bethany. We hear this ringing as much for our own recognition of his absence as for their experience in the story line.

John provides an explanation for Jesus' dawdling: God's glory will be made manifest in his delay. In other words, Lazarus will yet live again, pointing to Jesus' identity. From the existential human perspective, that can seem a glib, two-dimensional construct. In the meantime love, trust, and patience are on trial; so too human expectation of divine delivery of services.

For the purposes of writing an account of the mystery of Jesus Christ, John's presentation stresses resurrection power. In the moment, however, Martha and Mary must wait. Their waiting is as instructive to us as Jesus' eventual appearance. This is instructive in the sense that even these beloved disciples cannot snap their fingers expectantly and have their wish fulfilled after the manner of their desire. They must wait on the Lord and be of good courage. We suspect that in the meantime their hearts are troubled.

As this reflection suggests, this passage requires a pastoral touch for helping readers understand the multilayered texture combining fact, experience, mystery, and faith. Lazarus will be raised as evidence of resurrection life; but even for Lazarus, life in the flesh will remain a temporary condition. Undergirding our entire life pilgrimage are lessons about waiting and trusting that, through faith in God, all things cohere at last. In the meantime, life as it is in all of its glory and peril is treasured as a remarkable and astonishing gift.

STEPHEN P. BAUMAN

and he should come quickly to perform a miracle. The devotion of the women to Jesus is noteworthy here. While their brother Lazarus has a passive role by virtue of his crippling illness, the faith of Mary and Martha and their willingness to ask Jesus for assistance drive the story. Their belief in his healing power and commitment to discipleship are hallmarks of Johannine piety. This piety occurs in the service of a greater purpose, the revival of their brother.

Along with their faith, the assertive manner in which they proceed is a salient feature of John 11. The emotional response of Mary and Martha to their brother's condition is one of the more vivid aspects of the story. These followers challenge Jesus later in the narrative (11:21, 32, 39), and it is noteworthy that the initial request comes from the two sisters, rather than another family member or elder in Bethany. Interpreters of this passage have often focused on the connection between the revival of Lazarus and what follows in the Gospel. The grief of Mary and Martha pervades the entire chapter, and their interactions with Jesus demonstrate not only the life-giving power of the Son of God but also the mournful nature of the scene and their willingness to seek assistance. Few if any events are more traumatic than the death of a sibling, and Mary and Martha channel their grief in effective and forceful ways. The careful reader should note the prominence of their sentiments in shaping the story: the exchanges among Mary, Martha, and Jesus are heartbreaking, although ultimately hopeful. The initiative of Mary and Martha allows the reader to witness some of the more human exchanges in the Gospel of John.

SAMUEL L. ADAMS

Jesus' disciples had been with him at the wedding in Cana when he performed his first sign. Through this action, Jesus revealed his glory and his disciples believed in him (2:11). The two actions of revealing and believing are closely linked (11:40). Must we believe so that we may see the glory of God, or do we see God revealed and therefore believe? What we do know is that belief goes beyond rational and informed approval of Jesus' words or actions, beyond acknowledging the divine life in him, to receiving and participating in that divine life (5:24). From this perspective, belief seems to refer to a dynamic relationship like the life-giving vitality of a vine: "As the Father has loved me, so I have loved you; abide in my love" (15:9). As disciples, we are invited into a life-giving relationship in which God is revealed in Jesus, we participate in the divine life, and we bear fruit by which God is glorified (15:5, 8).

The continuous cycle of believing and revealing is ongoing; it never ends. Jesus reveals his glory at the wedding in Cana, and his disciples believe (2:11). Yet again, his glory will be revealed in the life of his friend Lazarus so that his disciples may believe (11:15a). We too are invited to see God revealed in Jesus and come to believe (11:27). Ultimately, we too participate in and share the witness of the Gospel story: "And the Word became flesh and lived among us, and we have seen his glory, the glory as of the Father's only Son, full of grace and truth" (1:14).

LINCOLN E. GALLOWAY

John 11:7–16

⁷Then after this he said to the disciples, "Let us go to Judea again." ⁸The disciples said to him, "Rabbi, the Jews* were just now trying to stone you, and are you going there again?" ⁹Jesus answered, "Are there not twelve hours of daylight? Those who walk during the day do not stumble, because they see the light of this world. ¹⁰But those who walk at night stumble, because the light is not in them." ¹¹After saying this, he told them, "Our friend Lazarus has fallen asleep, but I am going there to awaken him." ¹²The disciples said to him, "Lord, if he has fallen asleep, he will be all right." ¹³Jesus, however, had been speaking about his death, but they thought that he was referring merely to sleep. ¹⁴Then Jesus told them plainly, "Lazarus is dead. ¹⁵For your sake I am glad I was not there, so that you may believe. But let us go to him." ¹⁶Thomas, who was called the Twin, said to his fellow disciples, "Let us also go, that we may die with him."

Theological Perspective

The controversy about Jesus' claim that he is the Son of God leads to the attempts by his detractors to arrest him. Going up to Bethany involves the risk of being arrested and a possible stoning. Jesus and his disciples are well aware of this risk. Nevertheless, Jesus proposes that they go to Bethany to be with Lazarus's family at the moment of crisis. Jesus through his reference to "twelve hours of daylight" and "walk during the day" (v. 9) suggests that his calling involves the way of the cross. If Jesus is God's love embodied, it is natural that Jesus responds to the need of his friend's family, even though it involves risking his life. It involves participation in the pain of those whom he loves and who love him.

Jesus' response, "Our friend Lazarus has fallen asleep, but I am going there to awaken him" (v. 11b), does not trivialize the misery of death in the experience of the dying and the bereaved. We see in the succeeding section that Jesus weeps at the death of Lazarus and the bereavement of his sisters. Jesus is well aware of the agony of dying and the agony of being left behind. He resolutely sets his face toward Bethany to show his oneness with the suffering family, to share their tears, and thereby to bring about life. This is what is involved in Christ's pitching his

_{* See "'The Jews' in the Fourth Gospel" on pp. xi–xiv.}

Pastoral Perspective

This passage speaks of travel, walking, and going. Jesus and the disciples are on the move. Verse 7 begins with Jesus saying, "Let us go." and verse 16 concludes with Thomas exclaiming, "Let us also go, that we may die with him."

One of the most durable ways to think about the spiritual project is likening it to a journey. Preachers routinely endorse the concept of spiritual journey when addressing the essential nature of our time on earth. This is often trivialized in popular culture. It can seem quite esoteric in the mouths of all kinds of spiritual seekers and cynics alike. Spiritual journey is hard to beat, though, as a concept for understanding how we make meaning in our lives. Journey-form spirituality is a powerful means for understanding the pastoral project. It emphasizes the reality that our spiritual and religious understandings are not static, but emergent, evolving, maturing over time. As we walk through our days, we have the opportunity to participate in becoming what was intended in the first place, the way an acorn holds the promise of a mighty oak.

The concept of spiritual journey has movement and directionality. It is a way of framing our existence. Choosing consciously to "travel" through life makes the claim that our lives have meaning and that an element of our time on earth is discovering

Exegetical Perspective

This passage from John continues the narrative of the raising of Lazarus (11:1–44), as Jesus and his followers journey to Bethany and discuss the health of this ailing man. Principal concerns in this section include worry about Jesus' safety upon returning to Judea and whether Lazarus is merely resting or has died. The capacity of the Son of God to perform miracles—typically called "signs" in John (e.g., 11:47)—and the faith that such acts can instill among Jesus' followers are larger themes.

The first section of this unit (vv. 7–10) addresses the plan to return to Judea from Jesus' current location (Perea, last mentioned in 10:40). The disciples warn him that his life could be in danger (see 10:31–32), but Jesus replies, somewhat cryptically, that he has on his side a power that his aggressors do not. He declares, "Those who walk during the day do not stumble, because they see the light of this world" (v. 9). Those who walk at night lack this advantage, "because the light is not in them" (v. 10). This response highlights sharper vision during the day, but the underlying theological assertion relates to walking in "the light of this world," which is a way of referring to Jesus and his ministry (1:1–14; 8:12; 9:5). This statement does not promise immunity from all dangers; rather, it speaks to the disciples' need to persevere in their

Homiletical Perspective

In this portion of the story we are reminded that Jesus operates on his own time in matters of both life and death (13:1). Having received news of Lazarus's illness, Jesus chooses to remain where he is for another two days. The Gospel is quite clear that Jesus' work of revealing God has its own time frame. Jesus indicates this to his mother at the wedding in Cana when he says, "My hour has not yet come" (2:4), and to his brothers when they advise him to perform his works openly (7:6). In the life of Jesus we come to understand that there is a time to reveal the glory of God, and even a time to die. Human events do not determine the hour of Jesus' ministry, death, or glorification. The Gospel story reveals this principle as the ministry of Jesus unfolds. "Then they tried to arrest him, but no one laid hands on him, because his hour had not yet come" (7:30; cf. 8:20). In Jesus' hour he reveals God through signs, he gives life to the dead, and he lays down his life for his friends (15:13).

After two days, Jesus announces his decision to go back to Judea. We recall that Jesus has just escaped from those who try to stone him (10:31) and also to arrest him (10:39). This mission is fraught with danger, and the disciples make this clear to Jesus (11:8). In Jesus' response we may note four things: loaded theological discourse, figurative speech, plain speech,

John 11:7–16

Theological Perspective

tent with and among us (the verb the NRSV translates "lived" in 1:14 comes from the word for "tent").

Incarnation of the Son in Christ is not a visitation but an intimate and intrinsic engagement with the world, an active solidarity with the suffering. It is to embrace both the beauty and the agony of the world. In Jesus, the second person in the triune life of God plunges into the depths of human misery, the abyss of darkness, and unveils the presence of God. It is precisely in the sites where God is seemingly absent that God manifests Godself. God's life-giving engagement transforms death into slumber. The Chalcedonian affirmation that Christ is one with humans is not merely an indication that Jesus is human, but that he is God's elect for and in humans. Jesus participates in the predicament of the world and through his resurrection offers us hope of our participation in God's life. Christ is Immanuel, God with us.

Jesus suggests that he is glad that the death of Lazarus has happened, since what awaits the disciples at Bethany is a revelatory moment. They will witness God's presence in Jesus and be confirmed in their faith that he is the one who is to come, the one in whom God's reign of compassion and God's life of love are symbolically given to them. In him a new possibility is opened up for the world: its participation in God's life. The disciples are going to witness it. Jesus' gladness is not over the death of Lazarus, for that is unthinkable for the kind of person he manifested himself to be. His gladness arises out of the anticipation of what God is going to do in and through him at Bethany: the unleashing of God's life.

The disciples' journey to Bethany is suggestive of what life in Christ involves. As Jesus sets his face toward Bethany and goes toward it, the disciples follow him. They too are aware of the impending danger. They object to it, saying, "Rabbi, the Jews were just now trying to stone you, and are you going there again?" (v. 8). Thomas reiterates this objection when he says, "Let us also go, that we may die with him" (v. 16). The journey to Bethany involves participation not only in a revelatory moment of God's life-giving power but also in the cross. Thomas and the rest of the disciples are reluctant, yet they go with him.

A commitment to the way of the cross is often a reluctant commitment. It is reluctant since the cross should not happen; and suffering in itself is not desirable. Yet it calls for a commitment, since the world of crosses is the world's reality. Such a world, characterized by suffering, can be transformed only by active engagement with that world. Christian

Pastoral Perspective

who we actually are and where we might actually be headed. Understanding setbacks and failures and various sufferings as aspects of the journey helps us account for them. These do not stand outside what life is supposed to be about, but are instead an intrinsic element of our life dynamic.

Paul likened his life project to a journey of sorts, like a runner in a race. He wrote, "Not that I have already obtained [the prize] or have already reached the goal; but I press on to make it my own, because Christ Jesus has made me his own. Beloved, . . . this one thing I do: forgetting what lies behind and straining forward to what lies ahead, I press on toward the goal for the prize of the heavenly call" (Phil. 3:12–14).

There is in this a sense that our days are lived in the meantime, on the path straining forward within a world rich with spiritual metaphor. Paul runs the race because of what he refers to as a heavenly call. He knows who he is, and he can strain forward with confident expectation of one day completing the journey. Compellingly, he writes this from a prison cell; even as a prisoner, he lives in great freedom and joy, because he knows who he is and where he is headed.

Some years ago my teenage son wished to extend a church-sponsored work trip in Ghana, West Africa; he had grown enamored of finding Timbuktu. I helped him work out the details of his adventure and then prayed hard when he left the team at the airport. As his travel progressed, I became aware of an important component of my son's willingness to take this adventure. I also came to realize that for all of his initial ignorance of what might befall him during his trip, his willingness to take the risk was in part due to an unconscious yet certain knowledge of who he was, where he was from, and even where he was ultimately going. He was going home. In other words, he was tethered to a secure anchor. The tether was as real as iron, but invisible to the naked eye. Now this small journey fits into my son's larger life journey. He still knows who he is and where he is headed. He is headed home, like all of us. In the meantime his and our days are filled with the opportunity to choose to become what was intended in the first place.

The concept of spiritual journey is found in every level of our passage from John. Jesus and his friends are traveling to Judea. In many preceding chapters and verses Jesus is on the go, traveling from place to place. In this case, he is on his way to a dramatic encounter with friends Martha and Mary and their brother Lazarus. In a larger sense, however, he is on

commitment to Jesus and to follow him, even to perilous locations.

The most difficult element in verses 7–10 is the mention of "the Jews" as the group who might harm Jesus: "Rabbi, the Jews were just now trying to stone you, and are you going there again?" (v. 8). References to "the Jews" (*hoi Ioudaioi*) in John have generated much controversy over the centuries, including many erroneous and blanket assumptions about Jesus' opponents, sometimes leading to anti-Semitism. In a great many cases—including this question by the disciples in verse 8—"the Jews" is not a religious designation but, rather, a geographic one. These "Jews" are simply some of the Judeans living in and around Jerusalem. The disciples are referring to specific opponents of Jesus, rather than some collective group of Jews (note that certain Jews come to console Mary and Martha in v. 19). Careful deliberation over each occurrence of this term in John is necessary, because the Gospel writer does not usually add nuance to his use of "the Jews." It is also important to note that Jesus and his disciples considered themselves to be Jewish (followers of Jesus were seen as a Jewish sect), and therefore conclusions about "the Jews" in the Gospel have to be measured against the specific context of each passage.

These verses describing the journey (vv. 7–10) are somewhat tangential to the Lazarus story and could indicate a later insertion into the narrative. There is no mention of Lazarus, but only concerns over what might befall the disciples in Judea. The purpose of the return is presumably to assist Lazarus, but we get no indication of such a reason until verse 11.

The next section (vv. 11–16) addresses the health of Lazarus. The back-and-forth between Jesus and the disciples clarifies the nature of his condition. The disciples claim that if Lazarus is merely sleeping, he will ultimately recover (v. 12). Jesus explains the real situation: "Then Jesus told them plainly, 'Lazarus is dead'" (v. 14). The Greek verb Jesus uses initially in verse 11 is *koimaomai* ("has fallen asleep"), which can mean either to "sleep" or to "die." The interchangeability of terms for sleeping and dying is a common occurrence in modern English expressions (cf. death as the big sleep), and many ancient Greek and Hebrew terms reflect the same dual usage. The disciples' assumption that Lazarus is merely resting underscores their lack of full perspective on the situation and gives Jesus an opportunity to perform a miracle. The inability of his closest followers to discern the true scope of Jesus' powers is a

and unspoken communication. In the first instance (vv. 9–10), as Jesus notes that there are twelve hours of the day, he appears to be reminding his disciples that his time and theirs are in the hands of the one who laid the foundation of the earth and who knows where light dwells and where darkness resides (cf. Job 38:4–7, 19).

The reference to the hours of the day allows us to recall that Jesus also speaks in terms of his own hour. There is a time for God's presence to be made visible in Jesus, a time of eschatological fulfillment (4:21, 23), and a time for death and resurrection (5:25, 28). The conversation becomes more explicitly theological when Jesus turns the light and darkness of the daily chronological cycle into teaching about himself. The disciples have heard Jesus teach that he is the light of the world: "Whoever follows me will never walk in darkness but will have the light of life" (8:12; cf. 9:5). They are reminded of what their decision to follow Jesus really entails. His time and hour is now theirs as well.

Jesus then communicates through a word play. He says, "Our friend Lazarus has fallen asleep, but I am going there to awaken him" (v. 11). Jesus uses sleep as a euphemism for death and awakening for resurrection. It was not uncommon for Jesus to speak using figurative language. "I have said these things to you in figures of speech. The hour is coming when I will no longer speak to you in figures, but will tell you plainly of the Father" (16:25). In our congregational life, we are reminded that our teaching, preaching, and liturgy are expressed in language that may sometimes be figurative and complex and may at other times be plain. There are times when we stand with Nicodemus as we understand and misunderstand what Jesus is teaching when he speaks of wind/spirit and of being born again/from above (3:3, 7–8). In this story, the disciples misunderstand Jesus' speech. They are quite likely questioning the soundness of undertaking very risky travel just to awaken a sleeping friend.

At this point Jesus chooses to speak plainly. He is probably well known for his use of figurative speech in his teaching (10:6). On a previous occasion, while Jesus was in the temple in Jerusalem, some people had insisted that he speak plainly about being the Messiah (10:24). Jesus responded that he had done so in both word and works, but they had refused to believe (10:25). We are reminded that the works of Jesus represented "plain speech," that he had come from above, and that the divine life was revealed in and through him. Here in this story, Jesus in plain

John 11:7–16

Theological Perspective

discipleship calls for a participation in the suffering of the world. It involves embracing the cross so as to bring to an end our human tendency to erect crosses. It is not to romanticize human suffering, but to be realistic about the human condition, that our world is an agonizing world and that it groans for redemption. Christ's mission is to engage with the suffering world and to redeem it from its suffering.

Christ's suffering is redemptive suffering. It is not suffering as an end itself, but suffering for the world so as to redeem it from its suffering. Though reluctantly, the disciples go with Jesus to Bethany as a mark of their commitment to him. They cannot see the horizon beyond his death, but for Christ there is a horizon beyond suffering and death. His horizon becomes the disciples' participation in the life-giving presence of God. Jesus is delighted by what is ahead, the promise of life.

The way of the cross is agonizing, since it involves participation in human suffering. It is a delight too, since such participation ushers in God's life-giving presence. Jesus' journey to Bethany is suggestive of the mission of Christ. It is the mission to participate in the pain of the world and to transform it, with the world's participation in the life of God as its horizon. Jesus as God's Word to the world unveils to the world who God is. God is the one who intensely and intimately accompanies the world in its suffering and brings to the world God's own life. Christian discipleship is a journey to Bethany: participation in the pain of Christ and the delight in God's life that awaits us.

JOSEPH PRABHAKAR DAYAM

Pastoral Perspective

his way to Jerusalem and an even greater culmination. We know what awaits him there; he does too. He knows his ministry is coming to a climactic moment in the season of Passover, which, tellingly, is an annual recounting of a journey out of Egypt as the Hebrew people find their way home.

In one sense, Jesus' journey to Jerusalem is archetypal, a grand prototype of the journey everyone travels. He journeys to a certain death. On our most sober days we know this is true for us as well. We understand how our time is bounded by our being born and having to die. Indeed, the more conscious and embracing we are of this fact, the more capable we become of attaining spiritual maturity, the better we are at living in the meantime, the better we can pray, Lord, "help us to live as those who are prepared to die. And when our days here are accomplished enable us to die as those who go forth to live, so that living or dying our life may be in you."[1]

Jesus and his friends are on their way to Judea. Thomas seems to understand the stakes with a steely resolve, but we know he still has miles to go before he sleeps, and doubt will overwhelm his conviction of this moment—yet one more bend in the road on his way home. For now, he knows who he is and where he is headed. He is tethered by a secure anchor. That this will be tested ahead does not diminish the importance of his conviction today. Lazarus will live again for a while, until he finds his way home at last, and Thomas will have a role in his journey. Both will come to know how Jesus was at the very heart of the matter.

STEPHEN P. BAUMAN

---

1. "Complete Funeral Service for a Person of Faith," *The United Methodist Hymnal* (Nashville: United Methodist Publishing House, 1989), 871.

characteristic feature in Mark, but it also appears at several points in John.

The miracle has two primary goals in this narrative: to bring the disciples to a deeper faith (cf. 2:11) and to manifest the glory of God through the Son of Man (v. 4). The capacity of Jesus to perform a resurrection act will instill in his followers a more profound faith (11:45), and the fear it creates among the chief priests and Pharisees (11:46–53) will lead to the passion events later in the Gospel.

The final exchange in this section involves Thomas, who also plays a prominent role in the resurrection account (20:24–28). Thomas gets the last word of this unit: "Thomas, who was called the Twin, said to his fellow disciples, 'Let us also go, that we may die with him'" (v. 16). His verbal willingness to offer his life in this regard is admirable, but Jesus later proclaims that his closest followers will abandon him, including Thomas (16:31–32). Despite the fact that he will perform this amazing miracle with Lazarus, Jesus will face his own trying hour without the company of Thomas and the other disciples. Thomas comes to full acceptance and loyalty only after he sees the marks in Jesus' hands and side at the end of the Gospel (20:27–28). Despite noble intentions, Thomas demonstrates the human fallibility of us all with his declaration of loyalty here in chapter 11 and his eventual skepticism.

This section of the Lazarus miracle advances the narrative in significant ways, primarily demonstrating the resolve of Jesus to reveal the glory of God, even at the risk of his own safety and life. These verses also display the disciples' misunderstanding and tendency to be many steps behind the thought process and plans of their teacher, whose march to the tomb of Lazarus is a prelude to his own solitary journey at the end of the Gospel.

SAMUEL L. ADAMS

speech tells his disciples that Lazarus is dead. However, even plain speech can be confusing and disconcerting. Had Jesus not said concerning Lazarus, "This illness does not lead to death" (11:4)? On that occasion was Jesus speaking plainly or figuratively? In any event, it was now plain that death had become a very present reality. Plain speech meant that death was certain, and the disciples were about to embark on a futile mission. Lazarus was dead, and the disciples were on a journey to join him (v. 15b).

In the final movement, there is much that is unspoken as Jesus says to his disciples: "For your sake I am glad I was not there, so that you may believe" (v. 15a). Sometimes the Gospel writer helps the reader understand what is going on in the story (v. 13). Here, though, we are not told that Jesus is speaking of the outpouring of love that they will witness in Bethany. Nor are we reminded that Jesus will perform a sign in which many will see the glory of God (11:4, 40). Indeed, the disciples do not know that theirs is an unspoken invitation to witness the gift of life (v. 16). They will affirm that the work of Jesus belongs to the daylight.

What is unspoken at this point is that the disciples are in the presence of life as the story turns from sickness and death to resurrection and life, and the glory of God. Jesus' words are life, his actions bring forth life, and he is indeed the resurrection and the life (11:25). Like the disciples, we too are invited to recognize that when we follow Jesus, we are being invited into life.

LINCOLN E. GALLOWAY

John 11:17–27

¹⁷When Jesus arrived, he found that Lazarus had already been in the tomb four days. ¹⁸Now Bethany was near Jerusalem, some two miles away, ¹⁹and many of the Jews* had come to Martha and Mary to console them about their brother. ²⁰When Martha heard that Jesus was coming, she went and met him, while Mary stayed at home. ²¹Martha said to Jesus, "Lord, if you had been here, my brother would not have died. ²²But even now I know that God will give you whatever you ask of him." ²³Jesus said to her, "Your brother will rise again." ²⁴Martha said to him, "I know that he will rise again in the resurrection on the last day." ²⁵Jesus said to her, "I am the resurrection and the life. Those who believe in me, even though they die, will live, ²⁶and everyone who lives and believes in me will never die. Do you believe this? ²⁷She said to him, "Yes, Lord, I believe that you are the Messiah, the Son of God, the one coming into the world."

Theological Perspective

Like the other miracles in the Gospel of John, the story of the raising of Lazarus functions as a concrete sign that points to a more abstract and comprehensive theological truth. This particular miracle is uniquely significant, for it is the culmination of a crescendo of signs, surpassed only by Jesus' own death and resurrection. In fact, the raising of Lazarus prefigures Jesus' own death, and actually triggers the events that eventuate in his crucifixion. While the various meanings of the miracles in the Gospel of John are not totally obscure, they are elusive, for they strive to express truths that transcend ordinary language. Consequently, Jesus usually delivers a discourse to partially clarify their meanings. Here Jesus' dialogue with Martha takes the place of an explanatory discourse, and this evocative conversation actually precedes the miracle. The normal order of sign and explanation is reversed. Here it is the miraculous action, Lazarus's resurrection, that serves to clarify Jesus' somewhat cryptic remarks to Martha.

The impact of this literary inversion is to put the reader in the position of Martha, someone who is struggling to understand an exceedingly mysterious teaching. What does Jesus mean by "I am the resurrection and the life," and what does he mean

* See "'The Jews' in the Fourth Gospel" on pp. xi–xiv.

Pastoral Perspective

Death enfolds the story of Lazarus—and not only death itself, but with it, layers of pain. As this section opens, we have already felt the weight of it: the poignancy of intimate friendship, recalling Mary's anointing of Jesus (11:2); the hard choice of competing priorities, as Jesus lingers "for God's glory," even though the friend he loves is ill (11:4); Jesus' own mortality, as he risks death if he returns to Bethany (11:8); the cumulative power of fear, and the loyal leadership of Thomas, daring to die with Jesus (11:16). Now, as we accompany Jesus to the home of his friend, we can feel the burden of mortality accumulate, its heartache and loss multiplying in ways all too familiar to many of us.

First, any hope lingering prior to this verse is now extinguished. Anyone who has heard a loved one's terminal diagnosis knows how tenaciously we can try to cling to hope, a desperate life preserver that keeps the heart from sinking into an ocean of despair. Maybe the doctor is wrong. Maybe my brother will get better. Maybe my wife will beat the odds. Maybe my child will respond to treatment. Then it becomes clear: death wins, and hope is not only pointless; it is cruel. As we discover not only that Lazarus has died but that he has been entombed for four days, hope is lost. Three days of death meant what we experience today standing

Feasting on the Gospels

Exegetical Perspective

Death leaves little room for niceties and disingenuous exchanges. The face of mortality has the power to reveal our truest nature. This Gospel passage prefigures the rite of the Christian wake. Rather than skipping ahead to Lazarus's joyous resurrection, readers should take the opportunity to acquaint themselves with those persons in mourning. Through the death of Lazarus, the evangelist lays bare a notion of holy camaraderie (*philadelphia*) and knowledge (*gnōsis*) of Jesus Christ.

Holy Camaraderie. The evangelist describes the wake as a solemn social affair. That "many Jews" (*Ioudaiōn*) tended to the bereaving sisters suggests at minimum a religious dimension to the gathering, but the author gives little detail as to what rituals this may have entailed. We do know, however, that in addition to the Jews' soothing words (*paramytheomai*, "to exhort or speak soothing words") in verse 19, Jesus and Martha have a deep theological exchange. Suffice it to say that those gathered shared enough of a worldview to reasonably discuss the meaning of death (vv. 21–27). Mary and Martha's consolation was more than just pleasantries; it was a sacred trust. Death may have tested the family's bonds, but the occasion tightened those of the sisters' community with holy camaraderie.

Homiletical Perspective

When Jesus arrived in Bethany to find Lazarus dead, Martha's words to him could be interpreted as angry criticism of the Galilean. When the account is read this way, Martha seemed to be accusing Jesus of allowing her brother to die: "Lord, if you had been here, my brother would not have died" (v. 21). Since Martha and Mary sent messengers to Jesus telling him that their brother was critically ill and Jesus did not respond, Martha's anger would have been understandable. Martha had every right to assume that Jesus had ignored her message, deeming other work to be more important.

When coupled with Martha's words that followed her apparent complaint, however, another interpretation may better reflect her feelings. After stating the impact of Jesus' absence, she continued, "But even now I know that God will give you whatever you ask of him" (v. 22). Considering her words to Jesus in their totality, we can view Martha as either acknowledging that her brother's death could have been avoided, had Jesus responded to her message in a timely manner, or continuing to believe that Jesus could bring her brother back to life and health. Using the latter interpretation, we have a passage that can be used pastorally and homiletically to encourage the faithful never to give up on God.

John 11:17–27

51

Theological Perspective

by asserting that those who die shall live and those who believe shall never die? The reader does not yet know the outcome of the story, any more than Martha does. This prolongs the ambiguity, forcing the reader to wrestle with Jesus' words. The reader must wait until the miracle to grasp more fully what Jesus' cryptic declarations mean.

Martha, with whom the reader is invited to identify, functions as a model of faith seeking understanding. Like all of us, she is troubled that Jesus has not prevented a loved one's death. In the same way we all wonder why God allows bad things to happen. In spite of her uncertainties, she trusts that God can somehow act restoratively through Jesus. Her faith is too circumscribed, though, for she is insufficiently aware of the profundity and magnitude of God's life-giving intentions. In response to Jesus' assertion that Lazarus will rise again, she professes an eschatological belief, not uncommon in her religious culture, that Lazarus will be raised on the last day. In the drama that is about to unfold, Jesus does more than put his imprimatur on traditional eschatological teachings.

As John Calvin observed, Martha's response about a future resurrection is spiritually timid, for she hopes for something less than the abundant new life available right now through Christ.[1] For Martha, as for all of us, Jesus' deeds serve to stretch standard convictions and introduce new spiritual vistas. The meaning of his words, which could have been constricted by a conventional interpretation of resurrected life, is opened up by an action that challenges ordinary conceptualities.

Seen from this perspective, Jesus' dialogue with Martha is not primarily about a future eschatological restoration, but about a way of living amid the nitty-gritty specificities of earthly existence. The episode happens not in another dimension, but in a particular geographic location. Bethany is named, and its distance from Jerusalem is reported. The story also has a temporal location: it occurs neither after history nor beyond time. Rather, it unfolds in the earthly time known to all of us, as the reference to its occurrence four days after Lazarus's death emphasizes.

The actual miracle amplifies and elucidates Jesus' remark, "I am the resurrection and the life" (v. 25). The episode is not just an extraordinary tale about the resuscitation of an individual, nor is it primarily a testimony to Jesus' willingness to intervene in the

1. John Calvin, *Calvin's Commentaries: The Gospel according to St. John 11–21*, trans. T. H. L. Parker, ed. David Torrance and Thomas Torrance (Grand Rapids: Eerdmans, 1961), 7–10.

Pastoral Perspective

beside a hospital bed, watching the lines go flat on the heart monitor.

Next, with Martha, we ask, "What if?" anyway—perhaps out of magical thinking, perhaps out of anger or guilt. Martha, who leaves her comforters, greets Jesus demanding, "Lord, if you had been here, my brother would not have died" (v. 21). We can appreciate the lure of revisiting the past that led up to our loss, the pull of rehearsing the possibilities before death came, replaying the days and nights before our worst fear came to pass. What if? What if I had insisted on a visit to the doctor? What if she had tried the experimental drug? What if we had had the money to afford the best care possible? What if our friends had prayed harder? In the face of death, the longing for "if only" can consume the living. In Martha's case, the very one who could have intervened now stands before her, judged for his abdication.

Nevertheless, a breath of faith may sometimes accompany our grief, as it does for Martha as she professes, "Even now I know that God will give you whatever you ask" (v. 22). It is hard to know the mood behind her statement. Out of our own experience we know that such a prayer might mean "in spite of my loss, I have faith"; it might convey "if I believe hard enough, maybe God will bless me"; it might include "I have no energy left, but you, my friend, can carry my prayers for me." The very ambiguity of Martha's whispered prayer offers room for our own tentative faith.

Jesus' promise, "Your brother will rise again" (v. 23), sets the stage for a key question for the nature of a newborn hope for Martha, and for us: What does it mean that our loved ones will be raised? Does it mean, as Martha professes, that our loved ones will be resurrected at the eschaton? Jesus' response itself is fodder for myriad interpretations: "I am the resurrection and the life. Those who believe in me, even though they die, will live, and everyone who lives and believes in me will never die" (vv. 25–26a). These are seemingly mutually exclusive scenarios. Which is it? That those who believe will die and live again? That those who believe will never die? Perhaps Jesus' perplexing answer points to a different possibility: that all who have faith will find life, in this world and the next.

What is the nature of this life-yielding faith? What does Jesus mean when he uses the verb *pisteuō*, translated in most English Bibles as "believe"? Is it that we must believe in Jesus as a cognitive assent or profession, without which we will have no life, now or in the life to come? Is it that we

The characters' physical arrangement also conveys the facets of communal life. The wake takes place in the village of Bethany, fifteen stadia (about two miles) east of Jerusalem. This provides a sense that the Jews who had immediately attended to the sisters may have come not only from inside the village but also perhaps from the surrounding region of Judea. John 11:31 explicitly notes that Jesus' arrival followed that of other Jews, but this can be intimated from our selection, given that Jesus and his disciples arrived four days after Lazarus had been entombed (v. 17). Jesus' late arrival reiterates the reserve with which he holds Lazarus's death. While others stood by the sisters, Jesus took two days before departing for the village of Bethany (11:6). This is not to say that Jesus did not care for Lazarus or Mary or Martha—for verse 5 notes the opposite—but it dramatizes the perspectives presented in verse 4: "But when Jesus heard [of Lazarus's illness], he said, 'This illness does not lead to death; rather it is for God's glory, so that the Son of God may be glorified through it.'"

Lazarus's fate prompts a "gut check" for the characters in our passage. The death of the brother subjects the sisters to suffering (hence those who rushed to their side), but Jesus' distance affords him the privilege of place to concern himself more with the glorification of God and God's Son. The wake forces the community to make sense of their own humanity (anthropology) and all that they associate with the Divine (theology).

Knowledge of Jesus Christ. As modern readers, we are accustomed to seeking out the canonical forest at the expense of the textual trees. Works like the Fourth Gospel advance specific perspectives held by specific communities. Jesus' conversation with Martha (vv. 20–27) presents a particular school of thought in early Christianity. The writer hopes that by reading this good news, Christians will better come to understand Jesus as the Son of God and believe in his salvific agenda of raising the dead. Though now a familiar refrain, competing interpretations of the good news were not uncommon in the late-first and early-second centuries. Thus the evangelist is not simply reporting, but arguing about what to believe.

Here again the author uses geography to make a statement, this time about the transcendence of Jesus Christ. Recall that Jesus first learned of Lazarus's illness and death in the place where John had been baptizing (10:40). In 1:28, the author locates this at "Bethany across the Jordan." The Bethany near

At some point, many of us become angry with God when our petitions for divine intervention are not answered as we hoped. We pray for an end to a war or for a cancer within us to be removed. When our prayers go unanswered, the war continues, or the cancer spreads, we are left to ask, "God, did you hear me and reject my request, or are you just too busy elsewhere and unable to attend to my problems?" Whether we decide that God is busy or that God is ignoring us, we usually conclude that God has failed us. We think the opportunity for our prayers to be answered has ended.

A parishioner came to her pastor and protested, "I am very angry with God. I have been praying for a job so I can support my kids, but every job interview ends up with nothing. God has abandoned not only me but my children as well!" With her unflappable faith in the power of God, Martha is a remarkable, positive role model for people such as this unemployed woman. Like the jobless mother, Martha did not receive what she wanted—her brother being saved from death. Even when faced with the worst possible scenario, Lazarus's death, Martha continued to believe that God could accomplish that for which she prayed. Can the woman looking for a job do the same? Can she continue to believe in the power of God, even when her prayers seem to be unanswered? Can we?

In a conflict as seemingly intractable as the struggle between Israel and the Palestinians, it is easy to lose hope that peace is possible. The Palestinians suffer under the weight of the occupation, subjected to random searches, and some farmers are cut off from vineyards their ancestors worked. The Israelis suffer from constant threats to their very existence, surrounded by some dangerous neighbors who have threatened to wipe Israel off the face of the earth. Given such unrelenting hostility, who dares to dream of peace among these peoples? In the Middle East today, it would seem that the possibility of peace is buried in a tomb in Israel-Palestine as surely as Lazarus was buried in his tomb. The faithful know, however, that peace is still a possibility and work to realize it.

Hope for peace and justice flows from the faith we witness in Martha, a faith that knows nothing is over until God declares it over. When others saw only the finality of Lazarus's death, Martha continued to have faith in the possibility of life. When others thought God had abandoned them, Martha knew that God was still present and at work in Jesus.

Jesus responded to Martha's faith with the affirmation that nothing and no one could stop what

Theological Perspective

lives of grieving friends. Rather, this dialogue-sign pattern suggests that Jesus is the power of a resurrected life that can begin right now for everyone. Human existence, not just Lazarus's demise and the bereavement of his family, is the object of Jesus' revitalizing agency. By identifying Jesus as Lord, Messiah, and Son of God, Martha confesses a hope for the promised restoration of all things. The world should not be construed as a tomb with a rock blocking the exit. The shadow of death that has poisoned and stunted human life is not the ultimate reality.

In Jesus, the bonds of death are snapped and human existence is restored to life. The eschatological promise is actualized now. The triumph of resurrected life is already happening. This resurrected life is not restricted to just one side of the boundary dividing earthly life and death. The ordinary biological dichotomization of alive/dead is undermined by Jesus' assertion that, paradoxically, those who die will live, and those who are alive will not die. Faith in Christ makes possible abundant life, a life that possesses a perduring quality that can transcend death in the present.

It is significant that Jesus identifies himself as this resurrected life, rather than as the mere conduit or catalyst of new life. Jesus himself is the divine life that has come into the world, making resurrected life a current possibility. The reader is prodded to speculate that somehow identification with Jesus' life is itself the spiritual regeneration that transcends earthly endings. This sets the stage for the theme developed by John that participation in Christ, and Christ's Spirit indwelling the believer, is the presence of a life that death cannot destroy.

The dialogue highlights Jesus' probing question concerning Martha's faith. Martha confesses that Jesus is the Messiah and the Son of God coming into the world. The resurrection of Lazarus has not yet occurred, though, so the content of Martha's faith remains undetermined. The narrative situates the reader in the position of Martha. We are left to wonder what this resurrected life really is. Jesus' words and Martha's confession do not define it. Whatever it is, it is not simply future postmortem existence. Even the raising of Lazarus does not definitively settle the issue of the meaning of resurrected life. The reader must continue to struggle with the question of what it means to identify with Jesus and to participate in his eternal life.

LEE C. BARRETT

Pastoral Perspective

are invited to "trust" Jesus, another translation, in a relational affirmation, to lean on him when we have no strength left of our own? Is it that we are to "place confidence in" Jesus, still another translation, as the one who does battle on our behalf, whose courage then inspires our own? Is it to "entrust oneself" to Jesus, yet a fourth possibility, in the legal sense of relinquishing custody of one's life to another's wise stewardship and protection? In a theological debate, such questions bear exploring. In a pastoral setting, though, the very breadth of possibilities creates a generous ambiguity. The nature of Jesus' interaction with Martha is, after all, not one of rabbinic or scribal disputation, but one of friendship and compassion.

At the close of these verses, Jesus asks Martha—and all of us who look on—"Do you believe/trust this?" (v. 26b). In this question, Jesus shifts the focus from Lazarus's fate to Martha's own well-being. In the end, the question of resurrection and indeed, life's purpose, is not for the one who has died but for those who are still living.[1] As with all of us who grieve the loss of people we love, Martha is faced with the question of how she will continue to live. Jesus' question is not so much a catechetical test as it is an invitation: his hand outstretched to raise us from the ground of grief. As we answer, may we be able to reach for such enduring hope: "Yes, Lord, I believe—I trust—I place my confidence in you," as Christ continues to come into the most heartbroken places of our world (v. 27).

CHRISTINE CHAKOIAN

---

1. The meaning of the resurrection—and its import to the living—was much in play in Jesus' age. Cf. Mark 12:27 and Luke 20:38, when Jesus answers the Sadducees regarding the nature of the resurrection: "He is God not of the dead, but of the living."

Exegetical Perspective

Jerusalem (v. 18), the setting for the figurative wake, does not appear to be the same as the site of baptism. Otherwise Jesus would not have needed to call the disciples to return with him to Judea in 11:7. They would have already been within the province.

Nothing in the archaeological record indicates the existence of a Bethany outside of Judea, but the most convincing scholarly arguments understand the riverside locations to be a creative rendering of a nearby region called Batanea.[1] In the Hebrew Bible, it is known as Bashan, which the Septuagint (Num. 32:32–33; Deut. 3:8; 4:47) and Josephus (*Jewish Antiquities* 8.37) describe as "across the Jordan" (*peran tou Iordanou*). Unlike the tense religious climate of Herod Antipas's Judea, Batanea enjoyed the rule of the more religiously tolerant tetrarch, Herod Philip. According to this theory, Jesus would retreat across the Jordan when met with hostility in Jerusalem (e.g., 10:39–40). This interpretation best fits with the historical literature available to scholars and helps explain how Jesus could leave the one Bethany for Judea.

The relationship between the two Bethanys is also thematic. In Bethany across the Jordan, we witness John the Baptist testifying to Jesus as the Son of God who baptizes with the Holy Spirit (1:33–34). Similarly, in the village of Bethany, Martha testifies to what the reader should now know, that Jesus is "the Messiah, the Son of God, the one coming into the world" (v. 27). At both Bethanys, the evangelist presents an understanding of Jesus' divine nature.

Conclusion. The final identifier, "the one coming into the world," draws attention to the motif of Christ's coming from afar. Recall that shortly after we learn of the Word becoming flesh, Jesus first walks in Bethany across the Jordan; note that Jesus came from an entirely different region to be with Lazarus's sisters in the Judean village of Bethany. If we continue to think about the passage as a wake, we can begin to understand Jesus' exchange with Martha as a summary of who he is, the "resurrection and the life" (v. 25). In the context of the whole Gospel, the reader learns that Jesus is the one who conquers death and the one who can make people be born again or from above (3:3, 6). The selected passage helps advance the evangelist's notion of orthodoxy.

RICHARD NEWTON

Homiletical Perspective

God wants. "Even though they die, [they] will live" (v. 25b), said Jesus of those who believe in the power of God. Hitler attempted to exterminate the Jews. Nevertheless, to this day, the Jewish people thrive. Some marriages go through incredible trials and tribulations; in the end, though, love thrives in many marriages that seemed dead. Hurricanes devastate a coastal city such as New Orleans, but it is resurrected to new life. What God intends to live will live.

There is perhaps no aspect of our preaching more important than keeping the light of hope alive in a sometimes dark world. At the beginning of John's Gospel, the author proclaims, "the darkness did not overcome [the light]" (1:5). It is a major theme in his Gospel. Even with her brother buried in the darkness of a tomb, Martha refused to let the darkness of death overcome the light of hope.

In addition to being a remarkable role model for all with her tenacious faith, Martha also presents preachers with yet another powerful female role model in Scripture. Women throughout history have been inspired by Martha's persistent, consistent faith. In the 1970s at a downtown church in Washington, D.C., a small, elderly woman named Elinor Martin believed that her slowly dying congregation could live, even when many in the church's denomination were planning its burial. As she carried out the mundane, behind-the-scenes tasks of discipleship in her efforts to keep the church alive, Elinor was an incarnation of Martha's faith in God's ability to give you whatever you ask of God. Just as Martha's faith was vindicated when Lazarus was raised, so Elinor's hope was vindicated when the congregation emerged from its near-death experience and grew into an important force in Washington in the latter part of the twentieth century.

In his poem "Hope," Friedrich Schiller writes, "At the threshold of life hope leads us in."[1] Martha's hope led Jesus to Lazarus's tomb, whence her brother emerged to live again.

JOHN W. WIMBERLY JR.

---

1. For a more technical presentation of this argument and its implications, see Douglas Earl, "'(Bethany) Beyond the Jordan': The Significance of a Johannine Motif," *New Testament Studies* 55:3 (2009): 279–94.

1. *The Poems of Schiller*, trans. Edgar Alfred Bowring (orig. 1851; Charleston, SC: BiblioLife, 2010), 232.

John 11:28–37

28When she had said this, she went back and called her sister Mary, and told her privately, "The Teacher is here and is calling for you." 29And when she heard it, she got up quickly and went to him. 30Now Jesus had not yet come to the village, but was still at the place where Martha had met him. 31The Jews* who were with her in the house, consoling her, saw Mary get up quickly and go out. They followed her because they thought that she was going to the tomb to weep there. 32When Mary came where Jesus was and saw him, she knelt at his feet and said to him, "Lord, if you had been here, my brother would not have died." 33When Jesus saw her weeping, and the Jews who came with her also weeping, he was greatly disturbed in spirit and deeply moved. 34He said, "Where have you laid him?" They said to him, "Lord, come and see." 35Jesus began to weep. 36So the Jews said, "See how he loved him!" 37But some of them said, "Could not he who opened the eyes of the blind man have kept this man from dying?"

Theological Perspective

In some ways the structure of the story of Mary's interaction with Jesus parallels that of her sister Martha. The episode occurs in the same place as the earlier conversation with Martha, and both sisters plaintively say, "Lord, if you had been here, my brother would not have died" (vv. 21, 32b). These striking parallelisms make the divergences all the more significant. The two stories represent two different possible ways of responding to Jesus and the prospect of resurrected life.

While Martha actively goes to see Jesus, here Mary stays behind, and Jesus takes the initiative to summon her. Similarly, even today one individual may seem to initiate an encounter with Jesus, while another person may seem to be more responsive. The story of Martha ends in her confession of belief, while the story of Mary ends with her weeping. In the same way, contemporary persons may respond to the story of Jesus with inchoate trust or with confusion and residual anguish.

As the narratives unfold, these seeming differences are trivialized. In both cases, it is Jesus who is the motivating force in the interaction. Neither response to Jesus has any impact on the outcome that Lazarus is raised. In both instances, whether

Pastoral Perspective

What is the appropriate approach of faith in the face of death? Pastoral experience tells us that there is no single answer. This passage, like the section that precedes it, offers confirmation of what William James once called "the varieties of religious experience."[1]

At the start of the story, Jesus' friends Martha and Mary have sent word to Jesus alerting him to their brother Lazarus's grave illness. Rather than hasten to visit, Jesus has intentionally tarried with his disciples. When at last he comes to Bethany, Lazarus has already been entombed four days—long past the passage of time required for death to be confirmed. While still on the way, Jesus is confronted by Martha, who engages in "what ifs" and accuses Jesus of neglecting his friend in need. Their interaction ends on a very different note, though, with Jesus' presence evoking a surge of faithfulness and trust.

Now Martha returns to Mary, who lingers with their sympathizing friends at their family's home. The privacy that Martha accords her sister is touching, for we can well imagine the press of company that fills their house. Such privacy is all the more required for intimate friends, as is Mary's relationship with Jesus (11:2; 12:3), displayed in her gesture

---

1. William James, *The Varieties of Religious Experience: A Study in Human Nature. Being the Clifford Lectures on Natural Religion delivered at Edinburgh in 1901–1902* (London & Bombay: Longmans, Green, & Co., 1902).

* See "'The Jews' in the Fourth Gospel" on pp. xi–xiv.

Exegetical Perspective

For all of its abstract metaphors, the Gospel of John here bears witness to an intimate moment in the life of Jesus. The one on whom "the Spirit descend[ed] and remain[ed]" (1:33) is "disturbed in spirit" (v. 33). The one through whom "all things came into being" (1:3) is "deeply moved" (v. 33). "The Word [that] became flesh and lived among us" (1:14) sheds tears with the Jews in Bethany (v. 35). These and statements like them make for a complex portrait of the character of Christ.

As the characters in this passage approach Lazarus's tomb, the reader arrives at one of the most esteemed passages in the Christian Scriptures. While this Jesus has come to wake Lazarus from the dead, the evangelist intends to lay to rest some simplistic notions of what it means to be the Christ.

This passage presents a vision of Jesus that challenges those inside and outside of the text to rethink the appearance of the Savior and his salvation, what many Christians have historically referred to as doxology (cf. 1:14; *doxa*, meaning "glory" or "appearance," and *logos*, meaning "word" or "idea"). The selected passage elaborates on Martha's identification of Jesus in 11:27: what has this anointed (*christos*) Son of God come to do? John 11:28–37 shows us a Jesus who brings salvation via controversial teachings and intimate love.

Homiletical Perspective

In this passage, we encounter a man weeping. Indeed, it is none other than the Son of God who is weeping. The passage opens the door to sermons about why so many people, especially men, are afraid to show their emotions. Even in the twenty-first century, Americans and people in many other cultures send a lot of signals to men that they should not cry. Why? Are tears to be interpreted as a sign of weakness? Are they viewed as allowing our emotions to get the best of us? Is there not a sacred role for tears in God's creation?

As the story about Lazarus's death and resurrection continues, we find Mary at home with friends. Cultures around the world have developed ways of helping people spiritually and emotionally to process the death of a loved one. The Ewe people in Ghana have a ritual in which they literally surround the house of a grieving person to keep away visitors, believing that it is important for mourners to immerse themselves in the grief process—tears, anger, and all. Judaism has a similar practice in which a mourner stays alone with his or her grief. Following this time of weeping and lamentation, friends and family are invited to sit shiva with those who have suffered a loss. While we do not know for certain if this scene in John formally captures the family and friends of Lazarus sitting shiva, we do

Theological Perspective

they confess or cry, the restoration of Lazarus must be received by the sisters as an unanticipated gift. God's grace dominates the action, in spite of differences of individual agency and response. To reinforce this implication of the plot, it is emphasized that Mary's relation with the life-giving power of Jesus is based on the fact that she is called, not on her own innate spiritual prowess.

Perhaps even more strikingly, here Jesus' reaction to Mary is very different from his demeanor in his dialogue with Martha. In these verses there is no enigmatic conversation about the resurrection. Instead, Mary simply weeps, as does the crowd who has followed her. The display of grief occasions Jesus' own perturbation of spirit, and the prospect of seeing Lazarus's tomb provokes his own weeping.

Moreover, the response of human beings to Jesus is different in this episode. Instead of eliciting a confession of faith like Martha's, here Jesus' emotional behavior triggers questions in those who witness it. In fact, Jesus' weeping catalyzes two divergent assessments of him. One group sees nothing but human vulnerability in his weeping; the other faction suspects a failure of his allegedly supernatural power. The reader is positioned in this crowd of onlookers, wondering about the significance of Jesus' display of emotion and his failure to prevent Lazarus's death. Is Jesus a paragon of passive but ineffectual empathy, or does he simply fail to protect his friends? In times of tragedy, most of us probably consider both these options, but as the story later makes clear, neither construal of Jesus is adequate.

All of these factors in the narrative focus attention on the brutal reality of death much more strongly than had been the case in Jesus' dialogue with Martha. Mary grieves, the onlookers grieve, and Jesus shares their pain. It is the sight of the outpouring of anguish that causes Jesus to be "greatly disturbed in spirit and deeply moved" (v. 33). His question, "Where have you laid him?" (v. 34), shifts the focus to the tomb itself. The invitation, "Lord, come and see" (v. 34), the prospect of a face-to-face encounter with death, is the specific factor that elicits Jesus' tears. Ironically, Jesus is not exempt from the journey through the valley of the shadow of death, but confronts the full horror of human mortality. Of course "death" in this episode signals much more than the cessation of biological functions, for it points to the devastating impact of grief, fear, loss of hope, and failure of trust on human lives. Our hearts are a tomb, sealed by the anxiety and loss of hope to which all mortal flesh is heir.

Pastoral Perspective

of anointing and wiping his feet with her hair. As is often the case for those who mourn, the balance between privacy and company is rarely one's own choice. So it is that Mary will not be left alone; as she goes to meet Jesus, her consolers follow her.

Mary's encounter with Jesus replays the exact words of her sister: "If you had been here, my brother would not have died" (v. 32b). These words may well convey the regret of "what if" that many of us understand, the retrospection that reviews again and again alternative scenarios that might have brought about a different conclusion. In this setting, they also hold a painful accusation: if Jesus had just been there, his friend, their brother, would still be alive. Just as Martha has expressed her faith—"Even now I know that God will give you whatever you ask" (v. 22)—now Mary kneels at Jesus' feet, a posture of both appeal and humility, and as she kneels, she weeps.

Mary's tears and those of her comforters stir Jesus. If we presumed that "the Messiah, the Son of God, the one coming into the world" (v. 27), was to be invulnerable and remote, such a claim unravels in this moment. While the exegetical commentary might deal more closely with translation issues, suffice it to say that Jesus' response (*enebrimēsato tō pneumati* and *etaraxen heauton*, v. 33) conveys the deepest of emotions: "greatly disturbed," "indignant" and "troubled," "agitated."[2] The feelings beneath this response are left unsaid. Perhaps he feels anger at death itself, perhaps distress at the troubles inevitably to come, perhaps irritation at unbelief; perhaps he is moved by the impulse to weep with those who weep, and especially to weep with those he loves. For those who face their own grief and loss today, the breadth of possibility is not so much disturbing as it is permission giving.

Whatever the emotion inspiring his strong reaction, Jesus himself weeps on his way to Lazarus's tomb. The image of Jesus weeping provides comfort still to those whose tears overwhelm them. There is no sorrow that we bear that he himself has not felt, no strain of life that he has not borne. This tone is echoed later in the book of Hebrews: "For we do not have a high priest who is unable to sympathize with our weaknesses, but we have one who in every respect has been tested as we are, yet without sin. Let us therefore approach the throne of grace with

2. Gail O'Day argues against the NRSV and NIV translations of either phrase as "deeply moved." She notes: "The first verb (*embrimaomai*) connotes anger and indignation, not compassion. . . . The primary meaning of the second verb is 'agitated' or 'troubled' (*tarassō*) and is used here to underscore the intensity of Jesus' emotion" ("John," in Leander E. Keck, ed., *The New Interpreter's Bible* [Nashville: Abingdon Press, 1995], 9:690).

Salvation as Controversial Teaching. Familiarity with John 3:16 might lead modern readers to associate Jesus with a unifying disposition. However, "for God so loved the world" needs to be held in tension with the larger narrative setting of the Fourth Gospel and what it says about the social implications of Jesus' teachings. The evangelist communicates some of these through the members of the Jewish community who have gathered to mourn Lazarus. Here in this passage, the Gospel of John reiterates that although "we have all received, grace upon grace" (1:16), there are people who did not accept him. Jesus' own words and deeds sometimes serve as a source of division.

As many of us have experienced, wakes and funerals have a way of gathering a diverse group of people connected to each other in any number of ways. The same holds true here. Lazarus's sisters, Mary and Martha, grieve their brother. Many seem to have come to support them. Jesus, a family friend of sorts (11:2–5), has arrived to join them all. Their common purpose does not negate the differences between them, though. In fact, Lazarus's death and Jesus' response seem to draw out some of these differences. In verse 28, Martha shares news of Jesus' arrival with Mary in private, as opposed to with the whole group. It is as if they recognize what becomes clear to the reader in verses 36–37: some see Jesus favorably, while others question his abilities and motives. As we modern readers proceed through the text, we should not take for granted the level of contention that accompanied this Gospel in its ancient context.

Salvation as Love. Through the sisters' relationship with each other and Jesus, the evangelist goes to great lengths to present salvation as an opportunity to return God's love. Thus far, we have witnessed the sisters approach Jesus as their "Lord" and a family friend. In verse 28, though, they discuss Jesus as their "Teacher." Martha does not call him rabbi but, rather, uses the Greek term *didaskalos*. Generally, the evangelist uses the former (rabbi) in order to show Jesus as the beloved sage of disciples (e.g., 3:2, 20:16) and the latter (*didaskalos*) to relate Jesus as the arbiter of knowledge (e.g., 3:2; 8:4). The use of "teacher" in 11:28 is for the reader's benefit; it signals the coming of a teachable moment demanding out attention.

To begin, notice how Martha and Mary speak their mind to Jesus in the same terms: "Lord, if you had been here, my brother would not have died" (11:21, 32). Mary, however, does this from a vulnerable position at Jesus' feet. Rather than responding to her with

know that Mary is deep in grief and has allowed herself to be surrounded by family and friends.

When Martha informed Mary that Jesus had arrived, Mary got up to go and meet her spiritual leader. Finding Jesus, Mary echoed Martha's opinion that had Jesus been present, her brother would be alive. Jesus did not respond to Mary with words, as he did to Martha. On the contrary, he was initially silent. Faced with the grief of Lazarus's family and friends, John describes Jesus as "greatly disturbed," "moved," and weeping. Immersed in his own grief, Jesus asked, "Where is [Lazarus]?" The mourners invited Jesus to go to his tomb.

John notes that some people were moved by Jesus' tears. Others, however, wondered why Jesus allowed things to get to this point. They questioned why Jesus had not done something to keep Lazarus alive when that was still a possibility. "Could not he who opened the eyes of the blind man have kept this man from dying?" they complained (v. 37). For the third time in twenty verses, the point is made that Jesus could have stopped Lazarus from dying, had he come more quickly. Clearly the author of John's Gospel thought this question would linger on the lips of his readers for centuries to come and needed to be addressed.

Jesus' tears, however, suggest that the question is not whether or not he could have prevented Lazarus's death. Jesus' sadness and tears speak to his acceptance of death as an inevitable tragic part of the human experience. People are born. People die. Even if Jesus had arrived earlier and healed Lazarus, eventually the man would have died. Indeed, even after Lazarus was raised from the dead, at some point he died. When that happened, tears of grief once again filled the eyes of Lazarus's family. Death cannot be avoided.

Faced with death, injustice, cruelty, and suffering, Jesus teaches us that an initial, appropriate response is profound sadness. God does not expect or want us to view such painful realities stoically. They trigger soul-deep emotions. God expects us to cry, become angry, or feel depressed. These are important human feelings that need to be expressed.

Jesus' tears at the sight of Martha, Mary, and their friends grieving tell us that it is good to feel and express our emotions. Since our physical and emotional lives are inseparable, Jesus' tears also indicate that we should not attempt to hold our emotions in check, suppressing them within us.

A pastor noticed that one of his members was continually angry. The anger rarely expressed itself

Theological Perspective

Jesus' distraught response is particularly striking because this is the very same Jesus whom John typically presents as being the dominant force in every situation and as controlling the unfolding of events. For John, Jesus is the very Word of God who was with God from the beginning and does what he sees the Father doing. Here the eternal Word shares human desolation. The one who came from heaven cries like the rest of us. Karl Barth construed this passage as the premier manifestation of God's solidarity with suffering humanity, for Jesus looks death soberly in the face before he banishes it.[1] Jesus understands the apparent dominion that death holds over frightened and aching people.

As John Calvin explained, Jesus cries here because he encounters the general misery of the entire human race.[2] He is affected, not only by the death of a friend and the grief of loved ones but by all the woes that accompany mortality. Calvin concluded that when the Son of God put on flesh, he also voluntarily put on human feeling and experienced our infirmities. Jesus groans because the tyranny of death stands before his eyes. His response is not any stoic stony numbness. Rather, Calvin is quick to add, Jesus' grief is also not abject despair. It does not undermine Jesus' human trust in God, nor does it jeopardize the incarnation of the divine nature in him. God is so powerful that God can share in the limitations that afflict humanity without sacrificing God's ultimate sovereignty.

God's sovereignty over death, in the midst of genuine anguish, is evident in another dimension of the story. It is significant that Jesus proceeds to act without any confession of faith from Mary and without any demonstration of trust from the onlookers. The triumph over death is not contingent upon the potency of Mary's faith or the authenticity of anyone's religious experience. It is the agency of God, exercised by Jesus, which demonstrates the reality that we have been ordained for life, not death.

LEE C. BARRETT

Pastoral Perspective

boldness, so that we may receive mercy and find grace to help in time of need" (Heb. 4:15–16).

Even Jesus' tears are the cause of speculation among those who watch. Some of Mary and Martha's consoling friends are moved all the more by Jesus' weeping: "See how he loved him!" (v. 36). Yet others find themselves uttering the very sentiment that Lazarus's sisters shared. If Jesus had been there, Lazarus would not have died: "Could not he who opened the eyes of the blind man have kept this man from dying?" (v. 37).

For the third time, the problem of Jesus' absence—indeed, apparently willful absence—has been raised (11:21, 32, 37), although the text does not condemn Jesus' accusers. Instead, their exclamation is portrayed as a natural response to suffering and death, not only for scoffers but among those who love the Lord. The possibility that we might rail at Jesus and not be judged for it brings comfort still. Believers who endure hardship, and those who mourn the loss of those they love, still hurl this accusation at the Lord. If Jesus loves his friends so much, why is he not there to shield them from suffering and death? Where is Jesus when we need him now? Why does God let terrible things happen to good people, indeed, to followers of Jesus to whom he promised, "Everyone who lives and believes in me will never die" (v. 26)?

The answers will not be found in this text. Perhaps we are given a hint of them in the larger point the Gospel makes: even suffering itself—Lazarus's, Jesus', and perhaps even our own—might bring glory to God (11:4). If we are left still to wonder? In this Gospel, there is room for us too.[3]

CHRISTINE CHAKOIAN

1. Karl Barth, *Church Dogmatics*, ed. G. W. Bromiley and T. F. Torrance, trans. G. W. Bromiley (Edinburgh: T. & T. Clark, 1958), IV/2:227.
2. John Calvin, *Calvin's Commentaries: The Gospel according to St. John 11–21*, trans. T. H. L. Parker, ed. David Torrance and Thomas Torrance (Grand Rapids: Eerdmans, 1961), 10–13.

3. Cf. John 20:24–29, in Jesus' interaction with Thomas.

God talk or theology as he did with Martha, Jesus empathizes with Mary on a human level or anthropologically. These meetings with the sisters dramatize the crux of the evangelist's Gospel (i.e., 1:1–18).

Then Jesus observes the weeping around him and joins them in their tears. Just as Philip invited Nathanael (1:46) and the woman at the well called to her fellow Samaritans to witness Jesus' awesome power (4:29), those grieving bid Jesus to "come and see" the awful source of their misery, Lazarus's tomb (v. 34). What Martha receives through instruction, Mary receives in empathy, a rhetorical move that translates the evangelist's divisive teaching into loving good news. With these words, the evangelist challenges the reader, not to a decision whether or not to accept a hard teaching (6:60), but to the more gut-wrenching, soul-aching, high-stakes decision to return the love of the "Word [that] became flesh and lived among us" (1:14).

The controversial teachings of Jesus elicit two responses among the community. There are those who invite Jesus into the circle of the human condition. These persons recognize Jesus as having loved Lazarus (v. 36) and welcome him as a worthy companion in enduring the difficulties that it entails while maintaining the hope that he will save them. There are also those who keep Jesus at a distance, questioning his ways (v. 37). They do not deny Jesus as someone with power, but they remain suspicious of his agenda.

The evangelist presents these responses as an acknowledgment of how the audience might perceive the controversial message that is the Fourth Gospel. Some will take it as good news; others will dismiss it as ineffective. For those unconvinced by its message, the author hopes that they will continue to read on, in hopes that they will see its promise of bringing new life, as symbolized by the raising of Lazarus in the words to come. It might also suggest that the ideal Christian community should be faithful enough to envelop the devotee and the doubter alike. Salvation, according to the evangelist, is a plan that unfolds through the encouragement of a community.

RICHARD NEWTON

in loud outbursts. It was a simmering anger, just below the surface of this person's life. Others could feel it and were intimidated by it. Finally, the pastor decided to ask the man about his anger. "James, I may be wrong, but I sense a deep anger within you. Am I wrong?" The member began to cry. He cried for a long time before he was able to speak. Then, for over an hour he talked about his harsh father who had abused him physically, verbally, and emotionally. James had suppressed his anger about the abuse for decades, or so he thought. As James talked with his pastor, though, he realized that the anger was surfacing in many different ways, and others noticed it. His wife and kids had commented on it. Coworkers wondered about it. He always told those who noted his anger that they were misreading his emotions. The man's tears were the beginning of a process that led him to a therapist where he was able to unpack and ultimately defuse the anger that was controlling him.

Observing Mary, Martha, and Lazarus's friends in grief, Jesus cried. Being fully human, maybe he felt anger that death takes from us people we love. Perhaps he felt sadness that he too would soon have to die. Maybe he was even upset with himself, wondering if those asking why he had not come to see Lazarus earlier were correct. There is a multitude of reasons why Jesus may have cried as he saw Mary, Martha, and others mourning for Lazarus. The reasons for his tears are not as important as the fact that he allowed the tears to flow. He did not do what we are often told to do. He did not hold back tears, bottle up his emotions, or maintain self-control.

When we refuse to cry in the face of something that should prompt tears, what are we suppressing? What are we holding back that God wants to come out? Are we willing to grieve major losses in our lives? These are all questions raised by Jesus' tears in this precious story.

JOHN W. WIMBERLY JR.

John 11:38–44

38Then Jesus, again greatly disturbed, came to the tomb. It was a cave, and a stone was lying against it. 39Jesus said, "Take away the stone." Martha, the sister of the dead man, said to him, "Lord, already there is a stench because he has been dead four days." 40Jesus said to her, "Did I not tell you that if you believed, you would see the glory of God?" 41So they took away the stone. And Jesus looked upward and said, "Father, I thank you for having heard me. 42I knew that you always hear me, but I have said this for the sake of the crowd standing here, so that they may believe that you sent me." 43When he had said this, he cried with a loud voice, "Lazarus, come out!" 44The dead man came out, his hands and feet bound with strips of cloth, and his face wrapped in a cloth. Jesus said to them, "Unbind him, and let him go."

Theological Perspective

John presents the raising of Lazarus as the seventh, climactic sign revealing Jesus' identity. The passage offers rich possibilities for reflection.

All of us aspire to lives that matter. We want to be significant, to make a difference, to create a legacy. Yet overshadowing every human aspiration and achievement is the dark cloud of death, with its accompanying specters of anonymity and futility. Death erases our most important relationships and sweeps away our proudest achievements in its grim tide of forgetfulness and nonbeing. In response, human life becomes twisted and distorted by desperate attempts to escape or deny the futility that stands in the background of all our endeavors. We cling to idols that offer false promises of security; we seek escape in sensual and materialistic self-indulgence; we trample our neighbors in desperate attempts to feel worthy and substantial and more significant than the rest.

Jesus approaches the tomb of Lazarus greatly disturbed. The incarnate Word embraces the heart of the human dilemma, moved by compassion for our plight. This picture presents good news of a scope and intensity that is overwhelming when we begin to grasp it: the transcendent power and intelligence that formed the entire universe and sustains it in being takes an active interest in human existence. The

Pastoral Perspective

The story unfolds apace with intensity, since life is at stake. Jesus experiences profound empathy at the tomb of Lazarus, which propels a series of decisive actions that culminate in an exhortation that calls the man to life. The text boldly calls listeners to hear and believe, but what exactly do we need to hear and believe?

A central theme is the movement from death to life that occurs because of others' concerned activity. When we are individually "dead to the world," whether immobilized by fear, sunk in periods of lethargy or depression, or untethered from reality by anxiety-producing events, we often come back to ourselves because others care about and for us. We come into the fullness of who we are because of others who through care and compassion prod and pull us into new life. We cannot do it ourselves; we need help. Thus congregations serve a vital function, providing a space for holding, calling, and restoring members back to life when they are in the grips of despair, loss, and pain.

The moment of "Aha!" or transformation is usually comprised of many occurrences that coalesce into an identifiable action. Even when we desire to respond to Christ's call to life, we need the assistance of others to help remove death-dealing bondages, those negative stereotypes, constrictive

Exegetical Perspective

John 11:38–44 continues the story of Jesus and the family of Martha, Mary, and Lazarus. Jesus' sign and the various responses that it elicits form the hinge on which the Gospel turns. After the raising of Lazarus, the narrative will focus on events leading to the hour of Jesus' glorification. The evangelist is less concerned about the miracle itself (which is only briefly narrated) than about the reality to which it points. Hence the evangelist's use of the term signs (*sēmeia*) to refer to Jesus' miracles (2:11; 4:53–54). The Pharisees identify the raising of Lazarus as a sign in 11:47. The raising of Lazarus is meant to reveal the glory of God and elicit belief in Jesus and the God who sent him to bring eternal life (11:4, 25–26).

The passage opens with a reference to Jesus' emotions. The NRSV translation suggests that Jesus is "greatly disturbed" as he comes to the tomb, but this is a softening of the Greek verb *embrimaomai*, which refers to anger. The difficulty lies not in the meaning of the word, but rather in understanding the reason for Jesus' anger. The verb has already appeared in 11:33 in reference to Jesus' response to the weeping of Mary and her fellow Jews. For this reason, some interpreters argue that Jesus is angry at the lack of faith expressed by the Jews, and perhaps also by Mary. In this reading, Jesus' renewed anger in verse

Homiletical Perspective

This is not resurrection we are talking about here. This is madness or blinding light, a burning outrage.[1] This is crazy gospel. One simply cannot make up anything better than this, and it cannot be ignored because it is so familiar to our congregations. Some ask, "Do you think this really happened?" For many of us, our responses most likely include some measure of doubt. Perhaps the best homiletical essay on this text would simply be a bibliography with instructions to choose what resources you like with best wishes for a successful sermon.

The lectionary, of necessity, breaks this incredible story into three parts. Preachers, also of necessity, must often refer to the larger context. We are frequently faced with trying to make sense of a story within a story. I find it helpful to read the whole story as part of the weekly preparation. I read it aloud, repeatedly. I change how I read it each time. I try different voices: serious, silly, outrageous. I listen for the text to speak. In worship, it is sometimes effective to read the text as an ensemble performance, or to intersperse sections of the story throughout the worship service, shout it from the balcony, or set it to music (more on that below). The sermon will be found there, in the preparation

1. Reynolds Price, *Incarnation*, ed. Alfred Corn (New York: Viking, 1990), 39.

John 11:38–44

Theological Perspective

Creator and Lord of the entire cosmos here engages the deepest contradictions of human life through a fathomless compassion that is radically *on our side*. The passage invites us to reflect on what difference it makes, in dealing with daily joys and heartbreaks, to know that the entire scope of our lives, from birth to death and beyond, is the object of this compassionate divine interest. Such reflection might follow the logic of Romans 8:31: "If God is for us, who is against us?"

Jesus' prayer reveals that his action is not a solo initiative, but arises out of his communion in the Spirit with the One he calls Father. Jesus prays out loud in order to reveal that communion to his followers. Lazarus's emergence from the grave reveals God's intention that we become not just witnesses to this Trinitarian communion, but participants in its divine power and life. Passages like John 15:1–10 and 1 John 4:11–16 suggest how this participation in the life of the Trinity begins in the present life on this side of death.

Awareness of this participation calls into question conventional understandings of discipleship as grounded in willed obedience to external commands—simply following a set of rules. Such discipleship is often motivated by nagging and marked by a strong sense of guilt. In contrast, John paints a picture in which devotion to Jesus draws people into the life of God. Discipleship here involves believers joyfully saying yes to the divine love—and eventually eternal life—that appears among and within them as Christ through the Spirit draws them into his shared communion with the Father.

Jesus raises Lazarus from the dead with a personal word of command: "Lazarus, come out!" This pattern makes sense of Jesus' statement to Martha (11:25), "I am the resurrection and the life," because it shows the resurrection to be the work of Jesus himself. It also corresponds precisely to the picture of the universal resurrection presented in John 5:25–29, where the dead rise in response to hearing the voice of the Son of Man.

Note that Lazarus's resurrection falls short of this eschatological hope: Lazarus rises not to eternal life, but to a restored, earthly existence that will again know death. For this reason the raising of Lazarus functions as a sign rather than an inaugural instance of the final resurrection. The shape of this event, though, reveals the extent to which trust in Jesus and Christian hope for eternal life are one and the same thing.

This episode illumines the form Christian comfort takes in the face of death. Lazarus's resurrection

Pastoral Perspective

social patterns, and laws that keep Lazarus (or us) entombed. Jesus calls back to life the deadened one, the spiritual self that has forgotten who and what she or he is. The community of compassionate care must also spring into loving action with undue haste, since we cannot untie our bound selves alone.

Jesus shows us how to care, upending our cultural pretense that it is simply about "being nice" or making helpful suggestions. This is radically engaged care and compassion with bold and intentional direction: moving away blockages, calling forth life, and commanding the community to do its work. Jesus comes to the place of death, unrepelled by the stench, and models bodily and spiritual tending: moving toward rather than away from that which is difficult to experience. With heartfelt sensitivity, he calls the deadened to life in an emotionally connected but nonreactive way, while also beckoning the community to service.

Lazarus is the object of care and attention, a passive figure who himself never speaks, even though others speak about him and to him. His only response is to Jesus' exhortation. The subjects are the story's other named ones, including Jesus and Martha, and all of us who hear and believe. As listeners, we grow in awareness that the deeper reality made manifest in Jesus Christ is of the Holy One who stirs us to life, draws us to service, and calls the dead within and among us to stand up and walk out.

We are called to life, each one of us, but we cannot do it alone. Sometimes a pull or tug or push necessarily puts in motion a series of events that provides a new lease on life. Others may be laboring diligently and fully on our behalf, outside of our conscious knowing. The passage asserts theologically that we are not alone, even in the gravest of times in our lives, though this point may be lost on those who experience separation from communities of support.

Lazarus is dead to life, an unavoidable and unsettling truth. Any one of us could be in that place. Shifting life circumstances can unwittingly entomb us; they can also sensitively shape our perspective on and response to others in need. This is the case when others mobilize to bring about change. A prevalent and unfortunate assumption in Western capitalist cultures is that we create our own economic destinies. Prized is the notion of a "self-made" man or woman. Such false thinking spills over into our spiritual and religious thinking, creating the illusion that we can give life to ourselves. We never stand wholly apart from the communities and contexts that revive us, sustain us, and call us toward renewed life.

38 would be the result of the Jews' question in verse 37. It is true that verses 36–37 distinguish between a group that rightly recognizes the love that Jesus had for Lazarus and a group that questions why Jesus did not help his beloved friend. Both groups offer legitimate observations, though, and neither one necessarily indicates a lack of faith.

As for Jesus' anger in verse 33, it seems implausible that Jesus would be angry over expressions of grief in which he himself shares (v. 35)! It is also unlikely that the evangelist means to show the "human" side of Jesus. There is no need to demonstrate Jesus' humanity. It is asserted from the beginning of the Gospel in the language of the incarnation and assumed throughout the narrative. Perhaps it is best to take the image the evangelist offers at face value: Jesus is grieving and angry over the death of his beloved friend. In the Gospel of John, Jesus comes into the world as light and life. Now, coming to the place of death, confronted with the reality of death in the world, he is angry at the pain and grief that it causes.

At Jesus' command to remove the stone, Martha offers another reasoned observation. After four days in the tomb, the body of her brother will smell bad. In part, Martha's words function to confirm just how dead Lazarus is—there can be no dispute about the great sign that Jesus will perform. Again, although past commentators have been quick to accuse Martha of faithlessness, this seems unduly harsh. Earlier she offered the most full-bodied confession of faith in Jesus in the Gospel (11:27). At the most, we might view Martha's statement as a moment of ambiguity, when the narrative's frequent push for a yes-or-no statement of faith confronts the reality of human lives caught up in the pain and sorrow of death.

In any case, Martha's blunt comment provides the opportunity for Jesus to reiterate his teaching. Note that Jesus' reply does not offer a remonstration of Martha, but instead summarizes his teaching from verses 4, 15, and 25 for the Gospel's audience. Similarly, the prayer that Jesus offers in verses 41–42 is explicitly offered for those listening in. It is a public prayer, emphasizing once again that the point of what is to happen is that those present come to believe in God through the sign performed by Jesus.

At the climax of the story, when Jesus calls Lazarus out of the tomb, he symbolically enacts what he taught in 5:28–29, that "all who are in their graves will hear his voice and will come out," and what he asserted to Martha in 11:25: "I am the resurrection and the life." That said, it is important to understand

or perhaps even in the presentation. It will emerge from the sound of the story in your voice or in other voices. It will come forth like Lazarus in the speaking of the words, perhaps even in the moment of preaching, if we are open to it.

It is worth noting how different Lazarus's resuscitation is from Jesus' resurrection in all the Gospel accounts. Lazarus comes forth as a lurching, filthy, stinking corpse, still bound in his burial clothes. There is an excellent portrayal of this in the film version of *The Last Temptation of Christ*.[2] Resurrection in the Gospels is not that. Most notably among all the resurrection accounts in the Gospels, Jesus' friends and closest followers fail to recognize him at first. Something has happened to him. He has changed. Lazarus, on the other hand, has not changed. Everyone recognizes him as the dead man brought forth from his tomb. If he saw something while he was dead, experienced something during those four days, he does not say; we are not told. We are also not told how he feels about being dragged back into the land of the living. His only purpose here seems to be as an object for the demonstration of Jesus' power—the ultimate and final demonstration, as it turns out. Should we feel good about this? What sort of "life" is it to which Lazarus has returned? I once preached a sermon on this story that I called "Lazarus, Go Back!" in which I invited the congregation to imagine the story from Lazarus's perspective.

This may be the wildest story in all of Scripture: Jesus' delay after hearing that Lazarus had fallen ill; a perplexing, comic exchange with his disciples (11:7–16); the confusing pronouncements about resurrection, belief, dying and living again, living and never dying (11:17–27); Jesus being greatly disturbed, deeply moved; and the tumultuous climactic scene at the tomb. As a divinity student at Yale, for a Performance of Biblical Texts course, I set this whole story to music (guitar and voice). One revelation for me was how readily these scenes lent themselves to musical expressions of great diversity, always signs of a good story. For our present text (11:38–44), I worked out a 1950s doo-wop theme: "Lazarus come ou-ou-out, Lazarus come ou-out (shoo-bee-do-wah)," which I call "The Raising of Lazarus Chorus." We performed it in church a few times, with guitar, piano, and full choir singing and doing steps. In this way, I think we began to approach through sensory overload a level of outrageous speaking, hearing, and

2. *The Last Temptation of Christ*, dir. Martin Scorsese (1988, Universal Pictures; 2012 DVD).

Theological Perspective

demonstrates that life beyond the grave comes to us through Jesus himself, as his personal gift. Our hope for that life is therefore grounded not in abstract beliefs about immortality, but in Jesus' own presence with us. Between the ascension and second coming, we experience Christ's presence as the presence of his Spirit within the church. The fruits of the Holy Spirit in the life of the church are therefore the concrete signs of Christ's presence; Galatians 5:22 presents a representative list. The Lazarus story therefore helps believers claim the ordinary gifts of the Spirit like faith, hope, and love—signs of Jesus' presence—as tangible sources of hope for eternal life.

This connection between the gifts of the Spirit and the life-giving presence of Christ makes clear why Paul understands the Holy Spirit as a guarantee of our resurrection in Christ (2 Cor. 1:22; 5:5). It also resonates with the hope presented in Psalm 23: even when life takes believers through the valley of the shadow of death (NRSV "darkest valley"), we fear no evil, because God is with us. Such a connection is also reflected in Question 1 of the Heidelberg Catechism: "What is your only comfort in life and in death?" The answer begins: "That I am not my own, but belong—body and soul, in life and in death—to my faithful Savior, Jesus Christ."[1]

Verse 44 of the passage also has a significant history: the risen Lazarus stumbles out of the tomb still wrapped in burial cloths, which Jesus commands his disciples to remove. Christians through the ages have found in this vignette a picture of the church's life: Christ through baptism raises believers to new and righteous life, but sinful habits and temptations of the old life still encumber us and obscure our vision. Christ therefore entrusts to his disciples the task of unbinding each other from these remnants of the old life that persist in the aftermath of our redemption. This picture helpfully clarifies the respective roles of Christ and the church in believers' growth in grace. It also underscores the significance of the church's ministries of encouragement and mutual accountability, by which believers grow into the new life Christ has won for them.

P. MARK ACHTEMEIER

Pastoral Perspective

A stark experience of life ceasing occurred in a social situation where I was present. Standing before me talking was a man in his late thirties, intelligent and athletically fit. In the middle of a conversation, he suddenly slumped to the floor in full cardiac arrest. Fortunately, a trained paramedic came to assist, and very shortly thereafter a medical team arrived and restarted his heart. The man would not be alive today if others had not been present and called for life-giving assistance. He would have died if he had been alone, unable to revive himself. Such raw experience acts as a metaphor for the vital role of congregations and communities: bystanders become faithfully engaged participants in God's holy work.

In the film *Lars and the Real Girl*, the protagonist experiences many traumas that leave him wounded and fearful of connection with others. Deep emotional and psychological scars make friendships hard and romantic relationships nearly impossible. Through a number of steps, from a pretend and emotionally safe relationship with a doll to the development of a friendly and romantic relationship with a real woman, Lars blossoms and grows, but something in him also dies: his attachment to a life-sized doll named Bianca. The dying in him allows for reaching out and touching in authentic relationship. Lars trades a false love for a true one. Still, the process of letting go is not easy, and the community that surrounds Lars recognizes his loss as real, not imaginary, and provides support through his grief.

In one memorable scene, entitled "Outpouring of Love," flowers and cards appear at Lars's doorstep, and casseroles and other food fill the dining-room table. Lars sits slumped in the living room, looking grim and dejected. Ladies from the church sit in chairs around him with knitting projects in hand. One of them says, "That's what we do in tragedy. We come and sit." Sitting together in loving service is the congregational activity that calls Lars to life, even as it recognizes and honors his loss and grief.[1]

MICHAEL S. KOPPEL

---

1. Available at http://www.crcna.org/sites/default/files/HeidelbergCatechism.pdf; accessed January 6, 2014.

1. *Lars and the Real Girl*, dir. Craig Gillespie (2007, MGM; 2008 DVD).

Exegetical Perspective

what this resurrection life means to the Fourth Evangelist. In some ways, the story of the raising of Lazarus could be misleading, because this display of resuscitation after death taken literally is *not* likely what the author has in mind. To interpret the sign this way is to err in the direction of the literal rather than a symbolic understanding; such a literal understanding is represented by Nicodemus in 3:1–10 and the Samaritan woman in 4:7–15.

When the Johannine Jesus speaks of eternal life, it refers to life that is already available to believers in the present. It indicates a fullness of life and transcendent existence not possible for those who do not recognize Jesus as one sent from God (e.g., 3:14–16, 36; 4:14; 5:24; 6:47, 68–69; 10:28; 17:3).

To be sure, the idea of a future resurrection and judgment "on the last day" is also present in the Gospel (see 6:39–40, 44, 54; 12:48). The author does not dispense with this traditional idea altogether, but allows it to stand in tension with the overall emphasis on the fullness of life that believers already experience in the present through belief in Jesus. Chapter 11 deals with that tension directly: Martha expresses the traditional understanding in 11:24, and the Johannine Jesus symbolically demonstrates with Lazarus that resurrection life is available in the present to those who hear his voice. In other words, eternal life is not limited to a literal idea of resurrection after death or to a general resurrection on "the last day." Finally, given the symbolic nature of this sign, readers would be wise not to get sidetracked with the question, did this really happen? There is no way to confirm or deny the historical veracity of the tradition; in any case, the question does not affect the opportunity for life that the story offers.

COLLEEN M. CONWAY

Homiletical Perspective

experience that seemed fitting for the raucous story world in which we find ourselves here.

Sometimes in preaching it is precisely *not* the text's meaning that we ought to be trying to convey. In many instances, we cannot even say what the meaning of a text might be, and this after years of study and a week of focused preparation. The sacred word is mysterious and deep. Rabbinic tradition has for centuries identified multiple layers of meaning in the biblical texts. Many biblical texts have few, if any, relevant applications in our everyday lives, no matter how hard one tries to coax them out. The raising of Lazarus story, I suggest, has no relevant meaning and no practical applications for our day-to-day existence. There is no resurrection here, no lesson to be learned, no enduring truth for us to cling to as people of faith. Here Jesus yanks his friend Lazarus out of his tomb, out of his death, out into the glaring light and into his former life—and takes his sweet time getting around to it too—and the Gospel storyteller whom we call John makes a rousing good tale out of it. We have lost the art, in our modern times, of hearing a great story and taking the sound and experience of that story deep within ourselves, making it part of us, and becoming transformed by it in ways that have nothing to do with our rational selves.

What is it, exactly, that Jesus has done? Lazarus is raised/unbound/undressed/exposed. He stinks. Is forgiveness in order? Did something go wrong here? Now Jesus' enemies will seek his death. Now Lazarus will languish in his shadowy human form while being targeted for a second death. Now his sisters have gotten their wish. The crowd is divided. The disciples are nowhere to be seen. The hour is drawing near.

Behind all of this lurks the divine power and presence that permeates John's entire Gospel. Jesus calls out, the Holy is summoned, Lazarus comes forth, and the spine tingles at the thought of it.

BERT MARSHALL

John 11:45–54

⁴⁵Many of the Jews* therefore, who had come with Mary and had seen what Jesus did, believed in him. ⁴⁶But some of them went to the Pharisees and told them what he had done. ⁴⁷So the chief priests and the Pharisees called a meeting of the council, and said, "What are we to do? This man is performing many signs. ⁴⁸If we let him go on like this, everyone will believe in him, and the Romans will come and destroy both our holy place and our nation." ⁴⁹But one of them, Caiaphas, who was high priest that year, said to them, "You know nothing at all! ⁵⁰You do not understand that it is better for you to have one man die for the people than to have the whole nation destroyed." ⁵¹He did not say this on his own, but being high priest that year he prophesied that Jesus was about to die for the nation, ⁵²and not for the nation only, but to gather into one the dispersed children of God. ⁵³So from that day on they planned to put him to death.

⁵⁴Jesus therefore no longer walked about openly among the Jews, but went from there to a town called Ephraim in the region near the wilderness; and he remained there with the disciples.

Theological Perspective

"Many of the Jews . . . believed in him. But some of them went to the Pharisees" (vv. 45–46a). The varying responses to Jesus' raising of Lazarus illustrate one of the deep mysteries of divine grace. Christians through the centuries have marveled at how a single event or witness could produce diametrically opposed responses in different groups of people. This episode illustrates Jesus' teachings about the Spirit in 3:8: "The wind blows where it chooses, and you hear the sound of it, but you do not know where it comes from or where it goes. So it is with everyone who is born of the Spirit." Pondering this passage might prompt believers to be more humble and thankful for the gift of faith that they have received. Without the assistance of the Holy Spirit, our response to Jesus could be very different. Such recognition also increases compassion for nonbelievers, as people come to recognize that there, but for the grace of God, go I.

The passage also illumines the hazards of bypassing the witness of the Spirit and evaluating Jesus on the basis of external, worldly criteria. Instead of trusting the witness of their own eyes and hearts, the one group defers to the judgment of religious authorities. These authorities in turn subordinate

* See "'The Jews' in the Fourth Gospel" on pp. xi–xiv.

Pastoral Perspective

What are we to make of a death sentence for an innocent person? This question lurks and haunts people of faith, citizens both of a nation and of God's realm, who long for justice and peace to reign in the land. We want healing and restoration; we often know only pain and separation. Death promises to be the answer that will bring unity. Mostly, though, we are left with vexing questions that we hope will prompt reflection. What is it about human nature and life in community that drives us to kill one another, in reality and in imagination? What need drives this action?

Death becomes the solution when the root problem remains unclear. We can all too easily make hasty and ill-informed decisions based on anxiety and fear. Authoritative bodies take action to preserve the "in" group and seal off the threat from the "outside" person or group. Killing off the problem seemingly accomplishes this goal. If this action troubles us on some level, though, it is good news. It is better news if that event inspires us to action. People dedicated to living gospel truths steeped in faithful trust rather than instinctual reactivity must wrestle with difficult questions and, when necessary, respond boldly. Fissures within and between people need to be patched with care, to avoid having them develop into unbridgeable chasms.

Exegetical Perspective

The opening verse of this passage follows immediately on Jesus' command to unbind the resurrected Lazarus. The evangelist records no immediate reaction to the sign at the tomb, but instead opens with a report of a divided response among the Jews who had accompanied Mary to the tomb. While many of them come to belief, some report the event to the Pharisees (vv. 45–46). This is not the first time in the Gospel that such division has occurred (6:52, 66; 9:16; 10:19), and the theme will continue (12:37–43). From the opening prologue of the Gospel, the evangelist has indicated that such will be the case (1:10–13).

The author uses the phrase "the Jews" (*hoi Ioudaioi*) to refer to believers, those who report to the Pharisees, and those whom Jesus must avoid (vv. 45–46; 54). Although many times *hoi Ioudaioi* is used to designate representatives of unbelief, clearly that is not exclusively the case here.[1] Instead, the first reference to "the Jews" points to the success of Jesus' sign. Jesus prayed that his actions would lead the crowd to belief (11:42), and this is what occurred for some of the Jews who were there.

As a result of the report, the Pharisees and chief priests call a meeting of the ruling council, the

Homiletical Perspective

Many of you recognize this text as the source for one of the great scenes in the Lloyd Webber and Rice rock opera *Jesus Christ Superstar*. Caiaphas sings: "I see bad things arising / the crowds crown him king / which the Romans would ban / I see blood and destruction / Our elimination because of one man."[1] Not a bad sermon opener. The choir could sing the chorus parts, and soloists take Priest 3 and Annas. The preacher could continue with the Caiaphas solo.

It is unlikely that any of Jesus' followers or subsequent tellers of his story would have had access to a high-level council meeting of this nature. We are almost certainly dealing with an imaginative reconstruction of what probably seemed obvious at the time to everyone, and what may well have been the prevailing word on the street; that is, the council had met, decisions were made, rumors were spreading, and Jesus was now a marked man. Jesus apparently understood the implications of his actions too—from the raising of Lazarus to the anticipated reaction of the authorities. As a result, he went into hiding at Ephraim.

John the storyteller has a way of fleshing out these very earthy, human aspects of his story. For

---

1. For a brief introduction to the question of *hoi Ioudaioi* in the Fourth Gospel, see Adele Reinhartz, "Judaism in the Gospel of John," *Interpretation* (2009): 382–93, and the essay by Jaime Clark-Soles at the beginning of this volume.

1. Andrew Lloyd Webber and Timothy Miles Bindon Rice, "This Jesus Must Die," *Jesus Christ Superstar*, dir. by Norman Jewison (1973; Universal Pictures, 2012 DVD).

John 11:45–54

Theological Perspective

considerations of Jesus' actual miracle to worldly political calculations. The result is a disastrously misguided response to Jesus.

The text invites readers to ponder how attachments to worldly standards of judgment can cause believers to overlook Christ's work in the world. For example, expectations that God will provide material blessings of wealth, success, and protection from misfortune sometimes cause individuals to overlook God's actual blessings in times of crisis. Among churches, preoccupation with worldly measures of success—money and membership numbers— can lead smaller congregations to overlook the many remarkable ways Christ's love and blessing are present in their common life.

"If we let him go on like this . . . the Romans will come and destroy both our holy place and our nation" (v. 48). The Pharisees view Jesus' raising of Lazarus as a threat to political order and stability. This makes sense, because the credibility of coercive state action ultimately depends on the ability of authorities to wield the power of death. In the raising of Lazarus, Jesus demonstrates a power of God that is stronger than the power of death, and this demonstration is deeply troubling to all who have a stake in the status quo. Ironically, Caiaphas and the council respond by attempting to wield that same power of death that Jesus has called into question: they plot Jesus' execution. The futility of this course of action will be demonstrated in Jesus' resurrection, and later on in the witness of the Christian martyrs. God in Christ has broken the power of death, and with that victory the ultimacy of worldly rulers and empires has been cast down.

This text illumines our tendency to overlook God and make idols of earthly power and authority. One area where this happens is in our human quest for security. In our pursuit of absolute physical safety and security, Americans have entrusted vast amounts of money and power to worldly institutions like the military and the medical industry. Reflecting on this text might lead us to question whether the chimera of absolute worldly security is worth the cost we are paying in lives and treasure and freedoms. In the end, these efforts prove powerless to stave off the inevitability of death. The text challenges us to explore the different kind of security that comes with embracing Christ's victory over the power of death.

"He prophesied that Jesus was about to die for the nation" (v. 51b). Caiaphas serves as an unwitting prophet of Christ's redemption of the world. His words prefigure the grace-filled irony that Christ

Pastoral Perspective

We ought to contemplate and to rail against the injustice raised by this text. Only one man, Caiaphas, carries a voice of authority. Jesus, the one who is accused, does not speak, nor does anyone else speak on his behalf. How we situate ourselves in the story—as those who believe in Jesus or as those who turn him in—influences an interpretation of the unfolding events. Listeners of faith, no doubt, feel the gravity of the situation. The one who brings words of life and opens new possibilities faces condemnation and death. We confront a text in which Jesus is speechless, which in turn may render us as speechless as the disciples. Jesus stands powerless as people in authority decide his fate; however, we, like the disciples, face a choice to exercise power or not.

We are left hanging in suspense, and not in a good way. As witnesses to a developing tragedy, we feel the weight of powerlessness and culpability. We are simultaneously bystanders and participants in this unfolding drama, which carries real-life consequences. At times the lines blur between those who believe and those who do not, creating a group of those who simply are not sure what to make of the events. Neither ardent believers nor stark disbelievers, many observers identify themselves as people who seek to be faithful, yet feel conflicted and unsure. Those in this rich middle ground symbolize the space that is created when listening and hearing the testimony of the One who has been condemned for sharing life-giving words.

The themes of injustice and powerlessness unite in a contemporary rendering of this story. Innocent people are sometimes convicted of crimes they did not commit. Particularly compelling is the story of Kirk Noble Bloodsworth, the "first inmate in the nation to be sentenced to death and then exonerated by DNA" evidence.[1] A former Marine with no previous criminal record, he was convicted of the rape and murder of a nine-year-old girl after a woman called police saying that her neighbor Kirk looked like the man in the police sketch.[2] Mr. Bloodsworth spent nine years in prison and was finally freed after DNA testing proved he was not the killer. There have been "142 prisoners sentenced to death and then exonerated in the last 40 years, [and] just 18 were freed over DNA evidence."[3]

Many people of faith and congregations recognize that justice is not always served, even in systems

---

1. Scott Shane, "A Death Penalty Fight Comes Home," *The New York Times*, February 6, 2013, A-14.
2. Ibid.
3. Ibid.

Sanhedrin, to discuss the problem of Jesus and his signs. The exchange between the chief priest and the Pharisees offers a distinctive moment in the Gospel traditions where a rationale is offered for the plan to put Jesus to death. The problem is cast in political terms: given the Roman occupation of Palestine, having "everyone" believe in Jesus would constitute a threat to the temple ("holy place," v. 48 NRSV) and to the nation (the people of Israel). That no further explanation is given as to *why* this would be true, suggests that the author found the reasoning obvious. We could surmise that large crowds gathering around a charismatic figure (note the "everyone" of verse 48) would be viewed as a threat to the stability of the region.

Note that the author does not attribute to the leaders more malicious intent (which he does not hesitate to do with Judas in 12:6). The evangelist could have suggested, for example, what many commentators assume, namely, that the Jewish leaders, whose own limited power was tenuously held through their cooperation with Roman authorities, felt personally threatened by Jesus. Thus, they plot to kill him under the insincere rationale that his removal would help preserve the nation. Moody Smith is more on target with his observation that the evangelist "ascribes a motive that is not dishonorable or malicious; at worst it may be prudential and self-serving."[2]

We can go still further and note that from a postcolonial perspective—one that reads the Bible with an interest in discerning the effects of living under colonial occupation and/or imperial domination—Caiaphas's words offer a unique insight. It is the only place in the Gospel traditions where a perceived threat from Rome is voiced openly and the plot against Jesus is linked to the political reality of Roman domination. This is not to suggest that the council's reasoning should be taken as historically accurate, that is, that following Jesus *would* have led to the destruction of the nation. After all, the author and Gospel audience know that armed revolt against Rome led to the destruction of the temple.

Still, that the evangelist conceives of this reasoning as a plausible explanation for the plot against Jesus reveals the fearful attitude toward Rome that existed in his own time. Moreover, a postcolonial perspective points to the reality of "horizontal violence" that is reflected in the council's plan to put Jesus to death. Horizontal violence is directed internally

all the difficulties we may have with his theological discourses, John's story narratives are deep and rich. One reads this text and is immediately drawn into the tension beginning to settle in around these final days of Jesus' earthly life. The public and his followers are divided. The religious authorities are feeling threatened and are preparing to take action. Jesus is sufficiently concerned to stop appearing openly among the people. His disciples have become almost invisible. A volatile mix of anxiety, caution, and fear becomes the engine of the story's movement. Suddenly, contrary to the gist of his statements elsewhere in this Gospel, it seems that Jesus is no longer in complete control of his destiny.

It would require more space than is available here to discuss John's use of the term "the Jews" (*hoi Ioudaioi*).[2] Here, at least, he suggests that some of the Jews believed in Jesus after he raised Lazarus, and some did not. Those who did not went to the religious authorities to report a miraculous occurrence they had probably already heard about. For the purposes of preaching this text, I would suggest reminding congregations that Jesus, his disciples, their followers and supporters, and just about everyone else in the Gospel narratives are Jews. In spite of some excellent scholarly work in recent times, we really cannot explain the Fourth Gospel's relentless use of this term in contexts that are most often derogatory and have been, down through the ages, a source of murderous persecution by Christians against Jews. We certainly have the duty and the obligation to counter this perspective from the pulpit forcefully and unambiguously.

I suggest that we have no idea what John is referring to when he uses the phrase "the Jews." He may be alluding to an obscure sect or splinter group—known to him and his contemporaries but lost in the mists of history and unknowable by us—whom he blames for the events that led up to Jesus' death. Even here, we must also remember that this Gospel, more than the others, portrays Jesus as being overwhelmingly in complete control of his destiny, and therefore it seems strangely incongruous that John would be blaming this group—or any other group, for that matter—for something he repeatedly insists that Jesus himself was controlling all along. Is it possible for a storyteller/writer to be that unaware of such a glaring internal contradiction in his own story?

This of course points to a larger theological issue, and one that I believe ought to be preached from

---

2. D. Moody Smith, *John* (Nashville: Abingdon Press, 1999), 231.

2. See the essay by Jaime Clark-Soles at the beginning of this volume.

John 11:45–54

Theological Perspective

redeems the world precisely through the world's ultimate rejection of him on the cross. God uses the very actions of those who most oppose the divine purposes in order to bring those purposes to fruition! Caiaphas thus provides us a reassuring glimpse of God working in, through, and in spite of human error, ignorance, and rebellion. This episode provides a concrete illustration of the claim Paul makes in Romans 8:28: "We know that all things work together for good for those who love God, who are called according to his purpose." Caiaphas manages only to further God's purposes, despite his fervent opposition to Jesus.

Meditation on this passage can therefore help its hearers attain a surer grasp of the peace and confidence that come with knowing that God's plans are certain, and nothing in life or in death can finally separate us from God's love for us in Jesus Christ. The world feels like a much safer place when we know it is finally in the hands of a loving God whose purposes cannot be thwarted, even by the most ardent resistance. Readers might reflect on those places in their lives where they have been least confident about being aligned with God's will, or where they are most fearful about God's plans not coming to fruition. The enlistment of Caiaphas as God's unwitting prophet can provide a rich source of comfort and reassurance about our inability to bring God's plans to a standstill.

"Jesus therefore no longer walked about openly among the Jews, but went from there to a town called Ephraim" (v. 54a). Some theologians point out that Jesus continued to possess divine power and was fully capable of standing up to the authorities.[1] His withdrawal to Ephraim therefore provides an example to his disciples, suggesting that they should avoid unnecessary confrontations. Believers will of course hold fast to their confession when faced with direct challenges. Christians should not actively seek out conflicts in situations where they can be avoided, though, because doing so would provide occasion for those who persecute them to fall into greater sin. Loving one's enemy requires the avoidance of unnecessary confrontations. Jesus' example here might prompt reflection on contemporary church attitudes toward secular society. Are there times when today's Christians seek out unnecessary confrontations with secularists or other opponents?

P. MARK ACHTEMEIER

Pastoral Perspective

intended for justice. Rather than being discouraged by this reality, congregations can take up the practices of watchful vigilance and advocacy, for the death-dealing aspects of imprisonment are not limited to those who have been mistakenly sentenced to death. It also includes the many men and women who, because of systemic patterns of racism as well as economic and social deprivation, disproportionately experience imprisonment. Congregations and people of faith, empowered by their hearing and living of Jesus' story, can take up the cause of Jesus by advocating, in particular ways and in specific places, for systems of justice and peace. Communities can "gather into one" (v. 52) as they seek to unravel patterns that lead to plots that kill people. In so doing, they unite with Jesus in a mission of justice.

Congregations would do well to reframe Caiaphas's exclamation, "You know nothing at all!" (v. 49) into: "We know something." What congregations know and are called to embody for the world is prophetic life in Jesus Christ. As disciples, we are forgiven and freed to resist forces of death and to take up Jesus' ministry of restoring life to a world in need of mending. With Jesus, congregations create community for the marginalized and misunderstood, and for those who believe and those who are not sure.

Jesus forms community with friends as the threat of death looms. We imagine Jesus retreats "near the wilderness" (v. 54) with his disciples as a form of protection and revitalization. People and communities who have experienced the searing pain of marginalization know the need for retreat as a practice of soul renewal. Retreat creates space for self and others to gain clarity and to renew purpose while dwelling in God's Spirit. Creation of such space interrupts usual patterns within us and among us. Retreat has effects far beyond our rational knowing, as it gathers us back to ourselves, so that we can regain clarity of mind and purpose. Together with the disciples, Jesus rested until he found renewal, so that he could then move forward to the vast unknown.

MICHAEL S. KOPPEL

---

1. See Thomas Aquinas, *Catena Aurea*, John 11:54–57, http://www.catechetics online.com/CatenaAurea-John11.php; accessed February 25, 2014.

Feasting on the Gospels

across groups who are all under the oppression of a stronger power. Living under foreign domination creates social forces (competition for special privileges granted by the oppressor, frustration over a situation of powerlessness) that lead to misdirected fear and violence within groups. The deadly struggle between Jesus and his opponents in the Fourth Gospel may reflect this sort of horizontal violence.

The passage is notable also for its interpretation of the meaning of Jesus' death. The narrative aside in verses 51–52 explains that Caiaphas, in his role as high priest, unwittingly and ironically predicts the true significance of Jesus' death. Jesus will indeed die "on behalf of the nation" (*hyper tou ethnous*) and to gather in the dispersed children of God. While the nation again likely refers to the people of Israel, the dispersed children of God may refer to the gathering in of Gentiles that was part of the biblical tradition (Isa. 56:6–7; Zech. 14:16; and in the New Testament, Eph. 2:11–18). Supporting this interpretation is the Pharisees' proclamation in 12:19 that "the world" has gone after Jesus, followed by a report of some Greeks who come to the Passover festival to worship and want to see Jesus (12:20). When Jesus hears about it, he declares that the hour for his glorification/crucifixion has arrived. In John 12:32–33, Jesus speaks of his own death as a "lifting up" to draw all people to himself. Thus, in the Fourth Gospel, the salvific aspect of Jesus' death is focused on unifying the children of God into a relationship with God.

The passage concludes with the withdrawal of Jesus to Ephraim, a town northeast of Jerusalem. One should not take this as an act of fear. The Johannine Jesus mysteriously hides and appears across the narrative, suggesting that he is determining the course of events and will present himself when his hour has arrived (6:15; 7:8–10, 30; 8:59; 12:36). His withdrawal also sets the stage for the suspense that will open the next scene, where the speculation grows as to whether Jesus will appear at the Passover festival (vv. 55–56).

COLLEEN M. CONWAY

our pulpits: in light of Christianity's foundational claim that God, as Jesus, came to live among humans in human form, and had predetermined a path of suffering and death on our behalf, how can it be anyone's fault that he indeed suffered and died? In our text today, we see perhaps one of the more honest portrayals of John's struggle to make sense of all this. Many of "the Jews" believed in Jesus (v. 45), but "some of them went to the Pharisees and told them what he had done" (v. 46). We overhear what amounts to a political debate inside the council, a debate that takes into account some very real threats that are perceived by the authorities, and concludes with a decision that is chilling in its calculating pragmatism and its contemporary parallels.

Jesus *is* a threat. We have known it all along. In *The Gospel in Solentiname*, the Nicaraguan campesinos whose reflections are the substance of the book are talking about Lazarus and the revolutionary implications of Jesus' act of raising him. Ernesto Cardenal offers a poem by César Vallejo, in which a peasant revolutionary dies:

[And] a man came and said to him: "Don't die, I love you so much!" But the corpse stayed dead. And two men came and they said to him: "Don't leave us! Come back to life!" But the corpse stayed dead. And twenty people came, a hundred, a thousand, five hundred thousand crying: "So much love, with no power against death!" But the corpse stayed dead. Millions of people surrounded him, with a common plea: "Stay with us, brother!" But the corpse stayed dead. Then all the people on earth surrounded him; the sad, disturbed corpse saw them; he got up slowly, embraced the first person, and began to walk.[3]

BERT MARSHALL

---

3. César Vallejo, "Masses," quoted in Ernesto Cardenal, *The Gospel in Solentiname* (New York: Orbis Books, 1976), 514.

⁵⁵Now the Passover of the Jews* was near, and many went up from the country to Jerusalem before the Passover to purify themselves. ⁵⁶They were looking for Jesus and were asking one another as they stood in the temple, "What do you think? Surely he will not come to the festival, will he?" ⁵⁷Now the chief priests and the Pharisees had given orders that anyone who knew where Jesus was should let them know, so that they might arrest him.

¹²:¹Six days before the Passover Jesus came to Bethany, the home of Lazarus, whom he had raised from the dead. ²There they gave a dinner for him. Martha served, and Lazarus was one of those at the table with him. ³Mary took a pound of costly perfume made of pure nard, anointed Jesus' feet, and wiped them with her hair. The house was filled with the fragrance of the perfume. ⁴But Judas

Theological Perspective

"They were looking for Jesus and were asking one another . . . , 'What do you think? Surely he will not come to the festival, will he?'" (v. 56). In the face of potentially lethal opposition, attendees at the Passover festival sensibly assume that Jesus will keep a safe distance. Jesus surprises them, though, and his appearance draws large crowds. His words on the occasion of Mary's anointing make clear that his appearance in Jerusalem is not some calculated risk, born of the belief that he will successfully elude his enemies. Jesus travels to Jerusalem consciously accepting the death that he knows awaits him.

This passage invites reflection on how this same pattern plays out in the lives of Christians: circumstances of illness, tragedy, or personal failure often strike us as situations from which Christ's love is far removed. Yet how often does Jesus surprise us with his sustaining presence, precisely in the midst of our darkest times? His presence with us in such times is possible because he has chosen through the cross to enter into the darkness along with us. In our darkest moments many of us look upward, longing to see a divine hand reaching down from above to help us. What catches us off guard, however, is that the loving hand that reaches out to us comes not from above,

* See "'The Jews' in the Fourth Gospel" on pp. xi–xiv.

Pastoral Perspective

Worship serves as the focal point of Christian life, just as it does in this passage. Mary pours out precious perfume and the gift of herself in the ritual washing of Jesus' feet. The intimate act of love occurs at the home of Lazarus, whom Jesus called back to life. It is Mary, though, who becomes the true host of this event, sharing abundance from the heart. Love that flows from the heart often appears in unexpected forms, as this text so beautifully narrates. Mary has been touched and inwardly transformed in her relationship with Jesus. Her act of unbidden and unprompted generosity springs from her very being. She cannot help but be grateful for God's presence around and within her.

As Mary teaches us, devotion becomes service in and for life, not simply a means to safeguard against death. So often we can store up precious resources— whether material, spiritual, or emotional—with the intention to use them eventually, yet the activity of saving can itself consume our lives and limit the opportunity for the outpouring of gifts. Our inclination may be to hold back, in mindless fear that sharing the resources means losing them, unaware that some resources can become activated only through wholehearted offering. Why save for tomorrow what can be well used today? Mary's offering shows individuals and communities a faith-filled outpouring

Iscariot, one of his disciples (the one who was about to betray him), said, [5]"Why was this perfume not sold for three hundred denarii and the money given to the poor?" [6](He said this not because he cared about the poor, but because he was a thief; he kept the common purse and used to steal what was put into it.) [7]Jesus said, "Leave her alone. She bought it so that she might keep it for the day of my burial. [8]You always have the poor with you, but you do not always have me."

[9]When the great crowd of the Jews learned that he was there, they came not only because of Jesus but also to see Lazarus, whom he had raised from the dead. [10]So the chief priests planned to put Lazarus to death as well, [11]since it was on account of him that many of the Jews were deserting and were believing in Jesus.

Exegetical Perspective

With a setting "near" the Passover (11:55) and then "six days before the Passover" (12:1), the passage begins the countdown to the final days before the crucifixion/glorification of Jesus. The account of Mary's act of anointing in connection with Jesus' death and burial contributes to the overall structure of chapters 11–12 as a transition between the first half of the Gospel, focusing on the signs of Jesus, and the second half of the Gospel focusing on his glorification and return to the Father (see 13:1).

The story is framed with references to Lazarus, "whom Jesus raised from the dead" (12:1), which connect the anointing scene with Jesus' sign in Bethany. The passage opens with a focus on Jesus' opponents and the gathering crowd in Jerusalem. The crowd's speculation regarding Jesus' appearance increases the narrative tension. After relating the intimate scene in the house at Bethany, the passage will return again to the crowd and to Jesus' opposition. We will return to discussion of the narrative frame below and focus first on the Johannine use of the anointing story.

In shaping the scene, the author has adapted traditional material to his own narrative purposes. Both Mark 14:3–9//Matthew 26:6–13 and Luke 7:36–50 relate stories of an unnamed woman who performs an anointing as act of devotion toward Jesus. In

Homiletical Perspective

We have reached the turning point. At the halfway mark, John begins to tell the story of Jesus' final week. The raising of Lazarus has steeled everyone's resolve; the die is cast, there will be no more dialogue, no more discussions, no more signs and wonders. All the major players in the story have set themselves on a collision course that apparently cannot be altered, or at least one from which they all refuse to turn back. Divine inevitability requires human complicity in order to reach fulfillment, and at this point in the Gospel the cast of characters begins to assemble for the final act. Jesus, the religious authorities, Mary and Martha, Judas Iscariot, and the crowds are here; the others are waiting in the wings.

Questions abound in this pivotal section of John's Gospel. Why does this Gospel repeatedly single out and identify a particular group called "the Jews" (*hoi Ioudaioi*), when it is obvious that Jesus, his disciples, and most of the main actors in the story are also Jews? This makes no sense. The Passover of the Jews (v. 55) is also the Passover of Jesus, his disciples and followers, and countless others—their ancestors, their contemporaries, and their descendants down through the ages. Whether this was meant to be polemic, or is an indication that the writer is an uninformed outsider to Judaism, it is still unclear

John 11:55–12:11

but from directly alongside us in the darkness. That is what it means to have a crucified Savior who has chosen to embrace the depths of human darkness and suffering.

The dinner at Bethany also presents rich opportunities for reflection, with Judas and Mary representing different patterns of discipleship. Judas's mode of following Jesus has much to commend it, at least from an external standpoint. Judas's discipleship is practical, serious-minded, and deeply engaged with issues of social justice. His protest of Mary's action is grounded in a conviction reflected throughout the New Testament: authentic proclamation of the gospel necessarily involves good news for the poor. Is it too much of a stretch to see the godly aspirations of a great many contemporary congregations reflected here?

Unfortunately, Judas also reflects a kind of discipleship that appears to embrace Jesus *for the sake of* other higher, nobler causes. In a situation where there is a perceived tension between the competing goods of honoring Jesus and serving the needs of the poor, Judas makes clear where his highest loyalty stands. Though concern for the poor is admirable in itself, privileging any noble cause above loyalty to Jesus invites trouble.

What may have started as a noble intention in Judas has now been corrupted by sinful self-interest. Now the funds devoted to the help of the poor also serve the personal needs of Judas himself. We might imagine him justifying this "support" for his personal ministry on the grounds that he was, after all, the disciple most concerned with the needs of the poor. In the end, this "for-the-sake-of" discipleship degenerates from self-interest into active opposition to Jesus. Perhaps Judas traded information on Jesus' whereabouts for thirty pieces of silver in order to offset the lost support for the poor that Mary's extravagant gesture had incurred.

This passage provides opportunity to reflect on ways in which individuals, congregations, and denominations are tempted by "for-the-sake-of" patterns of discipleship. Are there pressures leading the church to give its highest allegiance to the maintenance of hallowed buildings, programs, budgets, structures, or ministries, with the result that Jesus becomes a mere instrumental means for generating the necessary funding and enthusiasm?

Mary's discipleship, by contrast, is of a wholly impractical and profligate sort. Judas's critique rings true: surely Mary could have found a more practical and measured stewardship of a year's wages than this

practice, a gesture of openness rather than of restraint. The perfume that Mary pours on Jesus' feet and wipes with her own hair is not just an act in isolation; it is an inclusive ritual with effects that pervade the home. This gesture of welcoming hospitality sweeps in all who recognize its dedicated sincerity.

In family and congregational life, we often can be surprised by generous love. One woman, a longtime member of her congregation, regularly attended worship at her church. She also participated actively in a spiritual retreat ministry, giving generously of her financial resources and providing sumptuous food. No one asked Roberta to provide any of these resources; it was simply what she did, an offering of love given from the heart. Some in the church worried that with her advancing age, these activities might be "too much" for her. Others even tried to dissuade her from bringing so much food to events, but all these efforts met with her refusals.

Another example comes from my family. My grandmother was never one to pray aloud in public. At the Thanksgiving dinner table the year she turned ninety, though, Grandma Vera offered to say the blessing. As everyone at the table bowed their heads, Grandma suddenly looked up and said, "I just want to say thanks for the food and I'm glad we're all here." It was a genuine expression of love that left us in tears. Such faith-filled outpourings as these mirror Mary's love-filled hospitality.

As counterpoint to generous devotion, ominous warnings of arrest and death infiltrate this passage. The chief priests and Pharisees plan to arrest Jesus (11:57) and to kill him as well as Lazarus (12:10). Beautiful worship practice occurs in a text and within a world rife with danger. Instead of searching for an escape or withdrawing into a privatized faith, healthy congregations accept this reality and the tensions produced as a source for spiritual growth and community action. Systemic forces that tear at the fabric of shalom community exist outside as well as inside the walls of churches and other religious organizations. Judas Iscariot symbolizes one who seemingly acts on behalf of the larger good, but is, in fact, one who serves his own interests.

We too may ponder the Judas question: "Why was this perfume not sold . . . and the money given to the poor?" (12:5). Caring for the poor is a noteworthy cause, but it seems that Judas has no intention of carrying out this form of service. Rather than a helpful point of reflection, his statement is a protest intended as a roadblock. Embedded in the objection is Judas's own manipulative self-interest, which can

Exegetical Perspective

Mark and Matthew, the setting is Bethany, not long before the Passover. In an unidentified location, an unnamed woman anoints Jesus' head with costly nard. The point of the story is similar to John's version. Some who are present scold the woman for wasting money; Jesus defends her, linking her act to preparing for his own impending death. In Luke, the anointing story again features an unnamed woman, who is identified as a "sinner." She approaches Jesus while he is dining as an invited guest at the house of Simon, a Pharisee. The woman stands behind him, weeping, and wets his feet with her tears. She then dries Jesus' feet with her hair and anoints them with perfume. The point of this anointing story is the woman's repentance: Jesus forgives her sin because of her act of love.

The Fourth Evangelist seems to have conflated both traditions and adapted them to his own purposes. In the Johannine version of the story, the unnamed woman becomes Mary of Bethany, while the anonymous "some" who protest against her in Mark (identified as disciples in Matt.) are identified singularly as Judas. In this way, John's version of the story draws a sharp contrast between two specific disciples of Jesus. Mary, as a faithful follower of Jesus, shows devotion to Jesus with an act of extravagance. Judas, on the other hand, is revealed as a duplicitous disciple, motivated by self-interest.

One effect of the evangelist's use of *both* traditions is the rather peculiar picture of Mary wiping off the expensive nard from Jesus' feet with her hair. In Luke's version, it makes sense to have a weeping woman wipe tears from his feet with her hair, but in the Fourth Gospel, the author has linked this intimate detail with the anointing of Jesus' feet with oil (an uncommon practice). It may be that the author is associating Mary's act of devotion with the foot-washing scene in the following chapter. The verb used for Mary's "wiping" of Jesus' feet (*ekmassō*) is the same verb that the evangelist uses to describe Jesus' act of wiping the disciples' feet in 13:5. It occurs nowhere else in the Fourth Gospel. In this sense, Mary demonstrates the type of intimate service that Jesus will teach his disciples to perform for each other (13:14–15).

Indeed, Mary emerges as the quintessential disciple—one whom Jesus defends for her anticipation of and preparation for his upcoming death and burial. The evangelist includes the detail also present in Mark's story: the value of the nard at three hundred denarii, which was equivalent of a year's wages for the typical worker (see Matt. 20:2). This, along with

Homiletical Perspective

as to why the storyteller fails to recognize such an obvious internal contradiction in his own story. This is an important opportunity for the preacher to confront Christian anti-Semitism from the pulpit, as well as some of its corresponding travesties, such as triumphalism and supersessionism.

Here, I believe, the preacher can and must confront these issues openly in the presence of our congregations, and say in no uncertain terms (a) that this aspect of the Fourth Gospel is not internally consistent, that is, separating Jews from Jews, with no apparent knowledge of their unity or of the diversity of religious practice within that unity; (b) that the alleged treachery of Judas Iscariot is also internally out of sync with a story line that insists upon Jesus' divine destiny and his absolute control over it; and (c) that these particular texts in this Gospel have contributed significantly to two thousand years of Christian discrimination, persecution, and unspeakable violence against our Jewish sisters and brothers. I know of no other way to think about it.

One might also ask, in the context of preaching, what Christianity might look like if we could permanently jettison those twin aspects of our identity—triumphalism and supersessionism—and move toward a theological grounding that does not depend upon winning the world-religion tournament. Indeed, what path might Christianity have taken, had the early Christians not felt compelled to blame "the Jews" for the death of Jesus? In the Synoptic tradition, the Passover is simply the Passover, and the crowds are just the crowds. Why does John add his murderous modifier? Does he believe that this somehow accentuates Jesus' eventual "victory" over his opponents?

It is surely tragic that Jesus' victory was not framed as a triumph over the Roman Empire, which ultimately failed to quiet him or to kill him, using the most horrifying means of torture and execution known to humanity at the time. The empire, in spite of the overwhelming power at its disposal, was also unable to silence Jesus' followers, nor did it succeed in crushing the movement that arose in his name. This will definitely preach in our time.

Meanwhile, Mary takes out a pound of expensive ointment, anoints Jesus' feet, wipes them with her hair, and in the process gets the whole house smelling of perfume, right at dinner time. She is utterly indifferent to everything I have addressed in this essay. She is unconcerned about Jesus' eternal destiny. She does not anoint him because she thinks he will win. She does not caress his feet with her hair

Theological Perspective

over-the-top extravagance poured out upon Jesus; yet Mary is the one Jesus commends.

It is difficult to justify Mary's action on practical grounds. In her defense, however, it is clear that Mary's love for Jesus echoes, in a small but significant way, the lavish impracticality of Jesus' own love for the world. This is no chance occasion that brings Jesus to dinner in Bethany, after all. The incarnate Son of God is here on his way to Jerusalem in order to give his life for the reconciliation of the world. The extravagance of Mary's offering is overshadowed and subsumed by the far greater extravagance of God's own offering in the cross of Christ.

Mary's example invites us to reflect on what genuine discipleship feels like. So much of contemporary church life is measured and practical, weighed down by a sense of duty, obligation, and coloring within the lines. What would happen if contemporary Christians let down their guard enough to allow the Holy Spirit occasionally to sweep aside their stodgy practicality? What would it look like if today's churches opened themselves up to a passionate love for Jesus that could lift them out of themselves into expressions of devotion that from a practical standpoint appear ill-advised or reckless? Are there examples of such devotion presently visible that we ought to celebrate? The stories of the saints of the church are full of appearances of such passionate, joyous, ecstatic, and wholly impractical expressions of love. "Something beautiful for God" was a phrase Mother Teresa of Calcutta used to describe it.[1]

We find Jesus urging just this sort of impractical discipleship in his encounter with the rich man in Mark 10:17–31: This young man is a devout believer who faithfully observes the commandments, yet something still compels him to seek out Jesus and inquire what he is missing. In response to his query, Jesus loves him and challenges him to embrace an extravagance of devotion he has never before considered: "Go, sell what you own, and give the money to the poor . . . ; then come, follow me" (Mark 10:21). Such texts invite hearers to reflect on the opportunity given by the Holy Spirit to move from a discipleship of dutiful, practical, measured obligation to joyous, passionate, extravagant, overflowing love for Jesus. Does possessing this opportunity sound like genuinely good news, and is it a gift we are willing to risk asking for?

P. MARK ACHTEMEIER

Pastoral Perspective

become a warning sign. People of faith and congregations can also begin to recognize our Judas tendencies: focusing on our institutional and personal interests to the exclusion of God's expansive vision. We would do well not to get caught in the trap of Judas's argument.

Jesus certainly does not, as evidenced by his response to leave Mary alone and to respect the choice she has made. "You always have the poor with you" (12:8a) is *not* a statement of *promise* but, rather, an *indictment* of people and systems that capitalize on those who are actually poor. Jesus' words provide criticism of the Judases in our midst, whose own poverty of heart and mind keeps in place systems of power that disadvantage the economically poor. "You will always have the poor with you" is a wake-up call to service.

Congregations need not be divided between loving devotion to God and service with the poor, whatever particular form that might take in any given community. One local judicatory's vision statement calls for the transformation of leaders for the transformation of the world. Such activity relies on the integration of head and heart, so that congregations and people of faith do not retreat into self-centered piety or engage in rigid social action.

Loving God with a full heart means that we serve one another and do not become trapped or immobilized by false either/or choices. Sometimes the call of the heart is to give fully without counting in advance the cost or the benefit to ourselves. Loving service as an act of faith is not about giving so that we may then get something in return. We might, though, listen to critical voices in our communities or even in our own heads as a gesture, not of deference, but of respect. We might wonder and vision together: how can faith be nurtured within and among us so that being in love with God and doing the deeds of love are united?

MICHAEL S. KOPPEL

---

1. Malcolm Muggeridge, *Something Beautiful for God: Mother Teresa of Calcutta* (repr.; New York: HarperOne, 2003), 125.

Exegetical Perspective

the reference to the aroma filling the house, draws attention to the extravagance of Mary's act.

In contrast to the positive presentation of Mary of Bethany, the Johannine version of the anointing story names Judas as the sole critic of Mary. It also identifies him as a thief who steals from the common funds that he keeps. Thus, while Judas's betrayal of Jesus is attributed to Satan or the devil, in this case, his basic character is impugned as well (see, similarly, the charge that Judas betrayed Jesus for money in Matt. 26:14–15). One effect of John's claim that Judas had no real concern for the poor is that readers may feel less concerned about what might otherwise seem a rather callous statement on the part of Jesus (12:8).

Following the scene in the house, the narrative shifts focus back to the large crowd that has gathered to see Jesus, but especially to see the resurrected Lazarus for themselves. This is the only place that we hear of the additional plan to kill Lazarus. One may view it as a dramatic addition, designed to highlight the villainy of Jesus' opponents. More interesting is the observation that many of the Jews were "deserting" (the Greek *hypagō* means "to depart"), presumably the synagogue community.

This statement certainly reflects dynamics at work in the late first century, rather than during Jesus' lifetime. There is no indication that Jesus ever called Jews away from the synagogue, and the Gospels report that his teaching was often in the context of the synagogue. Notably, although John 9:22; 12:42; 16:2 claim that Jesus-followers were in danger of being cast out of the synagogue community by the authorities, this verse suggests they were leaving on their own. Both verses point to the growing tension between the synagogue community and the Jesus-followers, which was increasing in the late first century.

COLLEEN M. CONWAY

Homiletical Perspective

because she knows about and believes two thousand years of unwritten theological doctrine. She is not there in the home she shares with Martha and Lazarus to receive either compensation or reward. In fact, at this particular moment, she may well fear Jesus' impending defeat at the hands of those who seek his life. That does not deter her from her mission of love and service, though. It is interesting to note the devotion of Jesus' followers in the Gospels—none of whom knows what will happen to him or what will be told about him or what councils centuries later will decide that we should believe about him. Jesus' community is not comprised of church members. There is no church.

What shall we say about Judas Iscariot, who for some curious reason has to be reintroduced at or near the beginning of the passion narratives in all four Gospels: "Judas Iscariot, one of his disciples (the one who was about to betray him)" (12:4)? We know who he is. He was introduced earlier in the Gospel. Matthew attributes the complaining about the cost of the perfume to Jesus' disciples. Mark simply states that "some who were there" (Mark 14:4) responded to this extravagance in anger. Neither of them names the woman. Luke omits the whole scene from his passion narrative. John, though, names Judas Iscariot as the one who speaks up in protest, and even includes an aside about Judas's character (he was a thief and used to steal from the common purse), and he names Mary as the woman who commits the radical act of anointing Jesus' feet and incurring the wrath of the men in the room.

One realizes at some point that none of these people really knows who Jesus is. They have traveled with him, eaten with him, witnessed signs and wonders, listened to his teachings, and somehow they have made it this far, all the way to the edge of a world about to be changed forever. They follow him, even though they do not know what will happen to him. Would you?

BERT MARSHALL

¹²The next day the great crowd that had come to the festival heard that Jesus was coming to Jerusalem. ¹³So they took branches of palm trees and went out to meet him, shouting,

"Hosanna!

Blessed is the one who comes in the name of the Lord—
    the King of Israel!"

¹⁴Jesus found a young donkey and sat on it; as it is written:
¹⁵ "Do not be afraid, daughter of Zion.
    Look, your king is coming,
        sitting on a donkey's colt!"

¹⁶His disciples did not understand these things at first; but when Jesus was glorified, then they remembered that these things had been written of him and had been done to him. ¹⁷So the crowd that had been with him when he called Lazarus out of the tomb and raised him from the dead continued to testify. ¹⁸It was also because they heard that he had performed this sign that the crowd went to meet him. ¹⁹The Pharisees then said to one another, "You see, you can do nothing. Look, the world has gone after him!"

Theological Perspective

Jesus enters Jerusalem with a jubilant crowd awaiting his arrival from Bethany. Many in this crowd that welcomed Jesus to Jerusalem had been with him when Jesus had raised Lazarus from the tomb in Bethany (v. 17). Others in the crowd had heard about this sign (v. 18). The sign had ignited their imaginations and hope for the coming of God's messianic kingdom. Even though Jesus is certainly at the center of this text, so is the crowd. The people play an important role in this passage through their witness to Jesus as king. It raises the question about the role of the people in mediating knowledge of God, and the relationship between God and the common people.

In this case, the people can be assumed to be the common folk of Israel. There is no mention that they belonged to any particular religious group or class of people. Indeed, because we see in the Gospels that people from all walks of life approached and followed Jesus, we can surmise that the crowd in Jerusalem included people from all economic, religious, and social groups within Israel.

The Roman Catholic Church has a concept that recognizes the knowledge of God that the people of faith have. It is called in Latin the *sensus fidelium*, which translates into English as "faithful intuition." The Roman Catholic theologian Orlando Espín uses another term for this concept in the title of his book,

Pastoral Perspective

Worship leaders planning a Palm Sunday service based on this account of the triumphal entry can easily justify two elements many congregants will already expect: palm leaves and exuberance. John's Gospel is the only one of the four to specify that the branches used in the procession were from the symbolic palm tree. John's is also the most obviously triumphal of the four accounts. Thus a Palm Sunday with this passage as its base can afford to be unabashedly festive. Although this narrative from John leads inevitably to the passion and death of Jesus, it does so while holding those events within the knowledge of Christ's resurrection and his glorified new life.

Unlike John, the Synoptic Gospels devote a great deal of the "triumphal" entry to the subplot of how the disciples found a suitable animal (or two). Luke and Matthew lead the upbeat procession straight to the temple, but "Palm Sunday" concludes for them with the surprising and troubling depiction of Jesus clearing out his Father's house. Mark's account is even more upsetting, perhaps, by being so anticlimactic: Jesus arrives in Jerusalem with great fanfare, but then simply looks around and heads out of town. As a result, the meaning and significance of Jesus' entry into Jerusalem is harder to discern from these accounts, and readers can be left with

Exegetical Perspective

The setting for this passage is Passover (11:55), the first of the three great pilgrimage festivals of the Jewish year. According to Exodus 23:14–17; 34:18 and Deuteronomy 16:1–17, all Jewish men were obliged to be present in Jerusalem to celebrate (1) Passover, held in the spring, commemorating the exodus; (2) Shavuot (Weeks, or Pentecost), held seven weeks after Passover, offering the first fruits of the crops; (3) Sukkot (Booths), the harvest festival held in autumn. The population of the city grew enormously during these festivals, with many people staying outside in tents.

The Triumphal Entry (vv. 13–15). Jesus is walking from Bethany, the home of Lazarus, Martha, and Mary, to Jerusalem, a journey of about three miles. The festival crowd in Jerusalem goes out to meet him as he approaches the city. The crowd in the city has heard much about him, especially about the raising of Lazarus (v. 18), concluding (we may assume) that this was the promised Messiah King.

The crowd greets Jesus with palm branches. In the Synoptics, people cut branches and throw the branches and their cloaks on the road before him, with no mention of palms (Mark 11:1–10; Matt. 21:1–9; Luke 19:29–38). The palm branches in John have special political meaning. In two passages describing the victories of the Maccabees over their

Homiletical Perspective

The narrative of Jesus' triumphal entry into Jerusalem has several features that are typical of the final redactor of John and to which the preacher must be attentive. In this Gospel, it is incarnation that saves the world, and the divine/human Jesus is always in charge. Thus, the order of events and their details have been adapted to fit the author's theological goals. Whereas in the Synoptics Jesus' passion begins with the triumphal entry into Jerusalem and subsequent expulsion of the money changers from the temple, early in this Gospel's account of Jesus' ministry he goes to the temple on the Passover and cleanses it (2:13–22). Moreover, he returns to Jerusalem on the occasion of other significant feasts. In this Gospel the event that leads to the Messiah's passion and triumphal entry is the raising of Lazarus. This author is interested in Christology, the role of Jesus: Jesus' triumphal entry into Jerusalem after the raising of Lazarus is a symbolic eschatological challenge, a sign of the sovereignty of Christ as conqueror of death and Lord of life.

Some scholars argue that here are two distinct stories being told simultaneously. Because the community for whom the author is writing has already been expelled from the synagogue, the events of the passion have been redacted to be meaningful in a new situation. The author is telling both the story of

John 12:12–19

Theological Perspective

The Faith of the People. The faith of the people exists as part of the larger tradition of the church. The tradition that is most commonly recognized is a written record of the decisions of church councils, popes, and other church leaders, the liturgy, and the writings of theologians. There is also the oral tradition in the church that exists within the life of the people of faith, sometimes referred to as popular religion, popular religiosity, or popular piety. Espín identifies popular religion as a cultural expression of the *sensus fidelium*. Espín adds: "Just as important as the written texts of Tradition (or, in fact, more important) is the living witness and faith of the Christian people."[1]

Of course, there exists the need to test the expressions of the *sensus fidelium* and popular religion to ascertain whether they are consistent with the Christian message. Expressions of popular religion need to be interpreted and tested to discern the extent to which they are coherent and in "fundamental agreement with other witnesses of revelation."[2] This discernment occurs in dialogue with Scripture, the documented tradition of the church, and the historical and sociological contexts within which popular religion occurs.

One aspect of popular religion among Latino evangelicals and Pentecostals is the testimony. It is common for there be a time in worship that allows individuals to give testimony to their faith. Although the testimony does not find any place in the documented liturgies throughout the church's tradition, it finds an important place in the tradition of Latino evangelicals, as well as other evangelicals and Pentecostals. The testimony, which Latinos inherited from the evangelical tradition of worship, offers to worshipers who often live in conditions of oppression and challenges to their dignity the opportunity to claim the sovereignty of God over all evil, and the lordship of Christ in the face of sinfulness.

In his essay "*Testimonios* and Popular Religion in Mainline North American Hispanic Protestantism," the Protestant theologian Luis Pedraja states that "the practice of *testimonios* also seems to be more prevalent in churches whose membership consists primarily of people in lower socioeconomic brackets. This would correlate with the practice of *testimonios* encountered in early Methodism, which appealed in large extent to the poor at that time."[3] Among Latino evangelicals and Pentecostals, though, economic

1. Orlando O. Espín, *The Faith of the People: Theological Reflections on Popular Catholicism* (Maryknoll, NY: Orbis Books, 1997), 64, 65.
2. Ibid., 66.
3. Luis G. Pedraja, *Teología: An Introduction to Hispanic Theology* (Nashville: Abingdon Press, 2004), 8.

Pastoral Perspective

the same confusion—and perhaps disappointment—that the expectant crowds of the story may have experienced.

John, on the other hand, focuses squarely on the entry into Jerusalem and includes details that serve only to affirm the event as a momentous occasion, a sign of Jesus' lordship, and a foreshadowing of his final victory. The context is the upcoming festival. The characters include a great crowd of happy people and—as a nice foil—a bunch of despondent Pharisees. Although the group of disciples does not necessarily understand what is transpiring in the moment, John assures us that they will come to realize soon enough the significance of these things. As with so many passages in John, the would-be mysterious sayings and doings of Jesus are revealed from the outset as portents of good news.

Perhaps most telling—and most useful for framing this passage at the beginning of Holy Week or any other week in the church year during which people will have died—is how John uniquely makes reference to the raising of Lazarus. Fittingly, Matthew and Mark preface the triumphal entry with a healing story, and Luke provides a parable. John, though, wants to remind his readers of another man called out from the tomb, and therefore of Jesus' preliminary defeat of death. The preceding verses (12:9–11) explain that the gathering crowds are particularly interested in this greatest of miracles; the reader also knows that Lazarus's resurrection is the chief concern for the chief priests. The great crowd of the festival in verse 12 gets intermingled with those who associate Jesus with Lazarus, and may be synonymous with those who "continued to testify" in verse 17 about Jesus' resurrecting power. In other words, the triumphal entry in John is when the centrality of Jesus' victory over death is widely revealed as the heart of the passion story. Even with darker days ahead, this vital point provides great hope.

Two things that arise from this text then are the reassurance of where the story is heading, and the exhortation to be a part of the victor's side. Liturgies, sermons, and Bible studies on this passage can prepare the congregation to enter Holy Week with heads held high, with foreknowledge that the one riding in on a donkey is without doubt the king of Israel, the promised Messiah, and the conqueror of the grave. Our problems are real, our sins are many, tomorrow's paper will be filled with bad news, and often things will get worse before they improve. None of that is denied in this narrative, but the final victory is assured.

Feasting on the Gospels

Gentile overlords, palm leaves are used as markers of victory and celebration (1 Macc. 13:51; 2 Macc. 10:7).

The crowd shouts words from Psalm 118:25–26 (a psalm traditionally sung at Passover): "Hosanna! Blessed is the one who comes in the name of the Lord—the King of Israel!" (v. 13b). The phrase "the King of Israel" is an addition to the words of the psalm. "Hosanna" means in both Hebrew and Aramaic, "Save (us), please!" and could be used both as a petition and as a joyous outcry, as seen here. They cheer Jesus and offer praise (Luke 19:37), as he is the one who may deliver Israel from the Romans ("Save us!").

In the psalm, "Blessed is the one who comes in the name of the Lord" refers to anyone and everyone who comes to Jerusalem to celebrate the feast. Over time, however, this phrase came to be used of the expected "Coming One," the Messiah (Matt. 11:3). The crowd uses the sentence to hail Jesus as the Messiah King.

The crowd adds to the quotation of the Coming One the title "the King of Israel." Each of the four Gospels specifies in its own way that the triumphal entry is to be understood as a declaration that Jesus is the King of Israel. In John, the issue is crucial and central to the meaning of the entire Gospel. In chapter 1, Nathanael declares that Jesus is the King of Israel (1:49), and Jesus answers, "You will see heaven opened and the angels of God ascending and descending upon the Son of Man" (1:51). In other words, he is not the traditional Davidic king. After the feeding of the five thousand, when the crowd tries to make Jesus king (6:15), he withdraws, because they want him to be the wrong kind of king. After the arrest of Jesus, Pilate asks Jesus, "Are you the King of the Jews?" and Jesus answers, "My kingdom is not from this world" (18:33, 36). Pilate later places an ironic inscription (as we are to understand it) over the cross of Jesus: "Jesus the Nazarene, the King of the Jews" (19:19).

So here Jesus, after being hailed as the Coming One, King of Israel, finds a young donkey and rides it (v. 14). In the Synoptics, Jesus instructs his disciples to get a young donkey ready for him before he begins his triumphal entry. In John, Jesus himself finds the donkey, only after being acclaimed as the Coming One. He does so to correct the misconceptions of the authorities and crowds, and to declare what kind of king he actually is.

To make this point, the Gospel writer adds an adjusted version of Zechariah 9:9, "Your king comes sitting on a donkey's colt." He does not come on a

the church about 100 CE and the story of Jesus about 30 CE. All "the world has gone after him!" (v. 19), but that world and his disciples (v. 16) misunderstand that story.

We are part of that world that has gone after him. Through the streets of David's city, whose pavement reverberated with shouts of "Hosanna" as he rode by beneath waving palms, we heard the sound of voices declaring the arrival of a savior; but it was a savior of our own design. When we proclaimed him to be all that we had longed for, we knew not what we said. Like Zechariah (9:9), who foretold this scene centuries ago, we heralded his coming. Proclaiming him king of Israel, we kept step to a victory march; but it was a procession whose destiny we did not comprehend. Still we misunderstand that kingdom. Still we mistake its coming. Still we know not what we do.

Six centuries after Zechariah, the crowds went out to meet him; but all too quickly their cry changed from "Blessed is the one who comes in the name of the Lord!" to the response of the chief priests and guards: "Crucify him!" (19:6, 15). Jesus, the chief cornerstone of the life we seek to build into a spiritual house our soul calls home, was and is derided, defiled, and denied. We think we can define him, and we put our trust in truths that we can grasp, in humanly made doctrines, in concepts we can circumscribe. He came to tell us not of limits, though, but of limitlessness, of a world whose reality passes by us like a breath.

We are no different from the people to whom Zechariah prophesied or those for whom Jesus gave symbolic expression to his authority, by his kingly entry into Jerusalem. We may pray to live in a world under his rule, but the kingdom of his dominion is not what the Israelites who sought peace in Zechariah's day anticipated. The kingdom of his dominion is not what Jesus' followers two thousand years ago sought. The kingdom of his dominion is not what we expect.

We still exalt the forms of kingship, not the content of his reign. We focus on the outline of the concept without perceiving its substance. We look for a crown, while we have been given a cross. We still do not understand that his is not a kingdom of fame and achievement. His is a realm of service and sacrifice. His is not a political victory. It is a promise of victorious, abundant life now. His action is less a claim concerning himself than it is a sign of the presence of God's kingdom.

In that kingdom there is no war, no injustice, no hunger. No terror at the names Afghanistan, Sierra

John 12:12–19

Theological Perspective

disenfranchisement is not their only significant condition. They also experience cultural, social, gender, and political marginalization. In most Latino evangelical congregations, women tend to give more testimonies than men, perhaps as a means of expressing their faith in God and demonstrating that, despite their marginalization because of their gender, God can reveal God's love and power through women also. We can point to the political and economic oppression the Jews experienced as vassals of the Roman Empire and the cultural oppression of Hellenism that they fought against as biblical parallels. Through their faithful intuition, they also were able to give testimony to their hope in Jesus Christ.

According to Pedraja, *testimonios* are not only accounts of miraculous healing by God; they are also accounts of God's divine accompaniment during times of suffering. He notes that divine accompaniment is a recurring theme of Latino/Latina *testimonios*.

Another important aspect of popular religion is that it is often, although not always, in tension with the institutional or official church. The history of Latinos in the Catholic Church is replete with popular expressions of faith that for many years, until recently, were viewed by officials of the church as corruptions of the true faith. Nevertheless, these expressions of popular religion, such as an intimate relation with Nuestra Señora de Guadalupe (Our Lady of Guadalupe), viewed by most Mexicans and Mexican Americans as a divine revelation of Mary in the form of an indigenous woman, are viewed by many as means of empowerment and resistance against oppressive structures.

The instance of the crowd recognizing the lordship of Jesus Christ in an intuitive way stands in stark contrast to the Jewish religious leaders. The Jewish leaders look with scorn upon the crowd's praise of Jesus, telling each other, "Look, the world has gone after him!" (v. 19). We see in this passage that God uses the humble, the oppressed, the vulnerable as the instruments of witness and revelation.

PAUL BARTON

Pastoral Perspective

While Lent can often be a drag, to be able to enter into the final stretch knowing that the end in sight will have a glorious result can provide a necessary second wind. Many churches may choose to blend Palm/Passion Sunday with a mix of happy "Hosannas" at the start and ominous warnings to follow, but this text in that case is not the one to use. Instead, John leads us to loud shouts of release and to fearless declarations of who the Christ really is.

This assurance encourages us to become an active part of the Palm Sunday crowd, and not just the one that recognizes the king of Israel and waves branches in the air. The crowd that shouts, "Hosanna!" in John continues to testify about Jesus' resurrecting power, even after the events of that day. For those who are convinced of Jesus' victory over death, anything less than exuberance and full commitment to the cause seem lacking. John knows all too well that another crowd will soon shout, "Crucify!" just as loudly (19:15); but as Raymond Brown points out, the Johannine literature's final depiction of a large crowd with palms is the one in chapter 7 of Revelation: the great multitude from every nation, seeing with their own eyes the victorious lamb who was slain.[1]

John's triumphal entry begins Holy Week with great pomp, and in doing so previews the joyous day that is still to come. As an Easter people, we look back on that first Palm Sunday with the outcome already known. We can therefore not only fully participate in a festive procession of palms; we can also give up our spot on the sidelines and join the winning side with confidence. Christ has won. Death has met its match. The worst is yet to occur as far as Holy Week is concerned, but the end result cannot be in doubt. If even the Pharisees could recognize way back then that "the world has gone after him," then what are we still waiting for today?

ALEXANDER WIMBERLY

---

1. Raymond E. Brown, *The Gospel according to John (I–XII): Introduction, Translation, and Notes*, Anchor Bible Commentary 29 (New York: Doubleday, 1966), 463.

chariot or (war) horse. Zechariah 9:9 actually reads, "humble and sitting on a donkey's colt," and then continues by declaring that he will "command peace to the nations" (Zech. 9:10). In addition, the author begins the quotation, "Do not be afraid, daughter of Zion." This language may (or may not) derive from Zephaniah 3:16 ("Do not be afraid, O Zion") or similar passages, and Jesus will soon reassure his disciples, "Let not your heart be troubled" (14:1, 27). In the immediate context of chapters 11–12, though, there is another reason to fear: The authorities argue that "if we let him go on like this, . . . the Romans will come and destroy both our holy place and our nation" (11:48). They see Jesus as a pretender to the warrior king idea who surely would lose in a war with Rome.

The Uncomprehending Disciples (v. 16). This is the second time in John that we are told directly that the disciples remembered and came to understand Jesus' words and deeds only after his resurrection (cf. 2:22). That his disciples did not understand Jesus during his earthly ministry is evident in several places (4:32–34; 10:6; 11:8; 13:7, 29; 14:5–10), as it is often in the Gospel of Mark (Mark 4:13; 6:52; 8:17–21; 9:32). What they do not understand here is that Jesus, the crowd-proclaimed king of Israel, is not the kind of Messiah king everyone expected, a misunderstanding that will be clearly stated in 12:34.

Two Crowds and the Effect of the Raising of Lazarus (vv. 17–18). Jesus had walked to Jerusalem from Bethany, accompanied by a crowd who had joined him there at Bethany, both to see Jesus and to marvel at Lazarus (12:9). Their reports were motivations for a second crowd in Jerusalem to come out to meet Jesus and proclaim him the Coming One. Verse 19 finds the Pharisees reiterating what had been said in 11:48 ("everyone will believe in him"). This underscores the point of this section: the growing—and to the authorities dangerous—popularity of Jesus.

G. J. RILEY

Leone, Sudan. No shame at the labels black, female, old. No fear for the loss of position, power, prestige. No, in his kingdom evil is overcome by devotion to others and self-denial. In his kingdom people are not valued for their physical appearance, social rank, ethnic origin, or intellectual capacity. They are valued because they are unique, and that uniqueness is of God. In his kingdom we would serve God in every person, giving to each of our selves and substance, and learning from each those things of which we know not. In his kingdom of service with others, we would experience love whose origin is God, knowledge of God that is life eternal, but his is a kingdom we often do not acknowledge.

It is the human condition to seek to control our own destiny, to order our universe, to avoid pain and suffering. At the expense of others, we protect ourselves. We do not know that what we are actually doing is denying death. It is into that denial of suffering and death, that reality of the human condition, that Jesus comes. The passion of Jesus brings tragedy and triumph, the past and the future, crashing in on the present.

Lazarus stood as a witness to the truth of life out of death, but now the Lord of life conquers death by dying. The self-emptying incarnation of Christ saves the world by accepting union with humanity, pointing away from himself to God. Jesus' passion proclaims that the power of evil will not be matched by an equal display of destroying power, but will be ultimately overcome, swallowed up in good. The hour has come permanently in which divine life in the present extends into the future with God.

JUDITH M. MCDANIEL

John 12:20–26

²⁰Now among those who went up to worship at the festival were some Greeks. ²¹They came to Philip, who was from Bethsaida in Galilee, and said to him, "Sir, we wish to see Jesus." ²²Philip went and told Andrew; then Andrew and Philip went and told Jesus. ²³Jesus answered them, "The hour has come for the Son of Man to be glorified. ²⁴Very truly, I tell you, unless a grain of wheat falls into the earth and dies, it remains just a single grain; but if it dies, it bears much fruit. ²⁵Those who love their life lose it, and those who hate their life in this world will keep it for eternal life. ²⁶Whoever serves me must follow me, and where I am, there will my servant be also. Whoever serves me, the Father will honor."

Theological Perspective

John juxtaposes the incredulity of the Pharisees in John 12:19 with the expression of belief that some Greeks have for Jesus in verse 20. Clearly, John wishes to send a message to his readers that the good news of Christ will come also to the Gentiles. These Greeks most likely were persons who had forsaken their various pagan religions and embraced Judaism, although they did not receive circumcision or practice all of the Mosaic laws. For this reason their worship at the Jerusalem temple was restricted to the court of the Gentiles.

The desire of some Greeks (Gentiles) to see Jesus raises an important question about the place that Gentiles have in God's covenant with Israel. The relationship between Jews and Gentiles has been an issue since the early days of Israel. In Genesis 12:1–3, God establishes God's covenant with Abraham, promising him not only that he will be blessed but also that he will be a blessing to the nations. So God's purpose in his election of Abraham is not only for the sake of Abraham and his descendants but also so that Israel might serve as an instrument of God's redemption for all nations.

The election of Israel for the sake of God's reconciliation with all nations is recounted again in different stages of Israel's history. Isaiah 49:6 prophesies that God will make Israel "as a light to the nations,

Pastoral Perspective

What do we really know about these Greeks who wish to see Jesus? Not much, but at least they seem to have good manners. Instead of rushing up to Jesus and accosting him, as some in the Gospels do, these seekers choose to operate through an intermediary. They approach Philip, who in turn seeks Andrew's assistance. This vignette begins, therefore, with a sense of reservation and containment, of protocol and procedure. When the action reaches Jesus, however, the one the Greeks seek responds to their request by releasing a proclamation that is both unsettling and empowering. His message breaks down barriers of exclusivity, but also challenges anyone who hears it.

To provide pastoral guidance, leaders will want to decide whether their audience considers itself on the outside, on the inside, or somewhere in between. For those who are looking in on Christianity with hesitation, there is much in this passage to encourage full participation within Christ's fold. Whether the "them" Jesus addresses are the Greeks or their emissaries is unclear, but the Son of Man clearly welcomes the outsiders' inclusion. Indeed, the initiative of these non-Jewish seekers accompanies—perhaps even triggers—"the hour" that has come. An expansive understanding of who is on the "inside" is therefore very much tied to Christ's glorification.

Exegetical Perspective

The Gospel of John may fairly be divided by this section, in which Jesus turns from ministering to the world to the final private training of his disciples and his journey to the cross. He has earlier said, "I have other sheep that do not belong to this fold. I must bring them also" (10:16). These other sheep are represented by the "Greeks" of verse 20. The term may mean people of Greek culture, or, as here, the term may be used more generally for people who were not Jewish, as a synonym for "Gentile," as in 7:35. Note Paul's opposing pair "neither Jew nor Greek" (Gal. 3:28; also 1 Cor. 1:22), as though that encompassed everyone in the world.

Of the twelve disciples, only Philip and Andrew have purely Greek names. "Philip" means "lover of horses," while "Andrew" is derived from the Greek word *andreia*, meaning "courage." Both are from Galilee (1:44), which is, according to Matthew 4:15 (quoting Isa. 9:1), "Galilee of the Gentiles," a district of Palestine that has long been majority non-Jewish. It may be that the Greeks mentioned here are also from Galilee and approach Andrew and Philip as fellow Galileans with familiar-sounding Greek names.

The Greeks wish not merely "to see" Jesus, but to meet him and speak with him, in the same sense of the word that Herod wants to "see" Jesus in Luke 23:8, or that Paul calls together the leading Jews "to

Homiletical Perspective

Verses of Scripture have layer upon layer of meaning, voices that speak from depths unknown to generations that are in a constant state of change. To interpret these voices requires methods that are diverse, yet true in different ways. The church has over the ages adopted various means to extract the import of these sacred writings: literal, allegorical, anagogical, tropological, historical, canonical, literary, form, redaction, rhetorical, and contextual criticism, to name just a few. The preacher as interpreter of the Gospel according to John must be able to distinguish each of those tools but also take into consideration the unique characteristics of this Gospel: signs, feasts celebrated in Jerusalem, misunderstanding, irony, characters as types, wisdom language, dual meanings, and realized eschatology, all evident in this passage. How is the preacher to focus?

One approach is to keep in mind that what is a vision of the future in the Synoptics is already present in this Gospel: the union of God and humanity. Jesus tells about his preexistence and unity with God throughout, and the structure of this Gospel reveals that unity. The Gospel is divided into two major sections: the Book of Signs and the Book of Glory. The signs speak a coded language with multiple layers of meaning. Verses 20–26 mark the end of the Book of

John 12:20–26

Theological Perspective

that my salvation may reach to the end of the earth."
Zechariah 2:11 states that many nations will join
themselves to Israel in the future. Clearly, God's
covenant with Israel serves as a platform for God's
larger purpose of restoring all of humanity to a right
relationship with God.

The early Christian church viewed itself as continuous with Israel. Since the first followers of Jesus
were Jews, they perceived Jesus to be the fulfillment
of the Old Testament prophecies. Paul lays out his
understanding of the relationship between Christians and non-Christian Jews most elaborately in
chapters 9–11 of Romans. In these chapters, Paul
also provides his response to the question of whether
Israel still has an inheritance in God's plan of salvation. Part of Paul's answer involves the notion of
the sovereignty of God. Because God is sovereign,
God's choice of persons and groups to include in his
covenant is not unjust. In Romans 9:15, Paul refers
to God's telling Moses: "I will have mercy on whom
I have mercy, and I will have compassion on whom I
have compassion." In Romans 11:17–21, Paul argues
that the church is grafted onto the tree of Israel. In
this way, he asserts that the early church participates
in the redemption history that God began with
Abraham and Israel.

The early church uses several other images that
convey its sense of connection with Israel. One of
the key images is that of the church as the people
of God. Just as God chose Israel to be an instrument of reconciliation with the world, God has now
expanded his covenant to include the Gentile Christians. The author of 1 Peter 2:10 tells his readers,
"Once you were not a people, but now you are God's
people; once you had not received mercy, but now
you have received mercy."

Another term that the early church used for itself
that connected it with Israel was the Greek word for
church, *ekklēsia*. *Ekklēsia* originally was used by the
Greeks to refer to an assembly of the community
to conduct civic affairs. The term began to be used
in the Septuagint (the Greek Old Testament) for
the "assembly" of Israel when it gathered at certain
moments in relation to God's covenant. By the time
of the early church, *ekklēsia* was understood to refer
to the assembly of God's chosen people.

The relationship between the Jews and the Gentiles
continued to be an issue for the first Christians after
Jesus' resurrection and ascension. Much of the book
of Acts deals with the incorporation of Gentiles into
God's covenant. In Acts 6:1–6, the apostles select
seven men to serve as deacons to serve the widows.

Pastoral Perspective

More than being another of John's messianic
signs, though, the widening recognition of Jesus as
the Son of Man has potential benefits for those in
the know. Giving one's life to Christ will bear much
fruit. Each grain of wheat can produce a large crop.
As the potent message of Jesus is being revealed as
a universal one, the benefits of membership within
this inclusive group are also made known: anyone
who chooses to serve Jesus will be honored by his
Father in heaven. What more could those Greeks
have wanted?

Nevertheless, the cost is great. This account
comes as part of the greater narrative focusing on
Jesus' death and victorious resurrection, but this particular passage makes it clear that any of us who are
welcomed within Christ's company must be prepared
to give up all we have. John will repeatedly allude to
the sacrifice of Christ, but our own self-giving is also
a part of the story. In order to bear its fruit, the grain
must die. Those who wish to gain eternal life must
lose their earthly ties. Those who come seeking Jesus
must be ready to follow him in service. Membership may have its privileges, but this is not a cushy
club. Moreover, as inspiring as it is for believers to
acknowledge that in Christ there is neither Jew nor
Greek, neither insider nor outsider, it can be a ter-
rifying experience for everyone involved when what
separates us disappears.

After all, taking on a new identity means saying
good-bye to another. When we welcome strangers,
we invite what is strange about them to come along
too. When outsiders are allowed in, what was familiar no longer is. At this point, the protocol and procedures we adhere to, the integral steps we take to
ease our way closer and closer to our goal, may seem
more comforting than restrictive, more pastoral than
prohibitive. Yet unless a grain of wheat falls into the
earth and dies, it remains just a single grain. Being
a servant of Christ, being a part of the church, is to
be in an honored position, but being one of his life-
giving grains means inevitably to fall to the earth.

As we can see, much of what is packed into these
seven verses is the interplay between the individual
and the communal, between the potential and the
actual, between Jesus' unique authority and his universal accessibility. It may make sense then to concentrate some attention on the passage's designated
intermediaries, Philip and Andrew. These are two
of Jesus' disciples who were, for whatever reason,
particularly approachable. Both appear earlier in the
narrative, and both in stories about invitation, with
calls to "come and see." Jesus had encouraged one

see and speak with" them (Acts 28:20). Jesus' "hour" has finally arrived (v. 23). We have been told earlier in the Gospel that "they tried to arrest him, but no one laid hands on him, because his hour had not yet come" (7:30), and that "no one arrested him, because his hour had not yet come" (8:20). Now that the Greeks have come, the "other sheep" of 10:16, the time for Jesus' death, resurrection, and return to the Father has arrived.

The enigmatic phrase "Son of Man" is used many times by Jesus to refer to himself, and is never used by others to address him. It has two opposite poles of meaning. It may refer to a mere and lowly human, as in Psalm 8:4: "What is man that thou art mindful of him, and the son of man that thou dost care for him?" (RSV). It may refer to the glorious "one like a son of man" of Daniel 7:13 (RSV), to whom Jesus refers during his trial in Mark 14:62.

"The Son of Man" in John, however, partakes of both meanings and is similar to the hero of the Christ hymn (Phil. 2:6–11), who was once in glory, became a lowly human being, and will one day return to glory (3:13; 6:62). As the Son of Man, Jesus once had the glory of the Father, is on his way to the cross, and will someday regain his previous glory (17:5, 24). The cross is a curse and a humiliation (Gal. 3:13), but in the irony of the Gospel of John, it is bravely accepted as the means to glorification (7:39; 12:16).

Jesus declares in verse 24 that "if [a grain of wheat] dies, it bears much fruit." There is no good parallel to this verse in either the Synoptics or the Old Testament. Closest is Paul's language in 1 Corinthians 15:36–37 and 42–44. John 15:1–8 presents a parable of the Vine and Branches with a similar point of bearing much fruit, but with no reference to the necessity of dying first. We have parables about the Sower, the Secretly Growing Seed, and the Mustard Seed in Mark 4, but again dying is not mentioned. The most influential mystery cult in the contemporary Greco-Roman world, however, the Eleusinian mysteries of Demeter, was based on a similar image and made a very similar point about death to life.

The traditional saying of Jesus, "Those who love their life lose it" (v. 25), has several parallels in the Synoptics (Mark 8:35; Matt. 10:39; 16:25; Luke 9:24; 17:33). The general reference is to cowardice and bravery on the battlefield, here transferred to brave fidelity to Jesus and the gospel. In the classical epic tradition, the courageous soldier who lost his life defending city and family won *kleos aphthiton*,

Signs and the fulfillment of verse 19: "The world has gone after him!"

The coming of the Greeks marks the coming of the hour, the hour of crucifixion, which is the hour of victory, when God's glory is brought to earth to be revealed only to believers. Verses 20–22 are a discourse whose single theme is the approaching passion and its significance. Verse 23 alerts the reader to the idea that the hour of glorification in death leads to life. Verses 24–26 are an insertion that interrupts the discourse with sayings commenting upon the meaning that Jesus' death and resurrection will have for humanity.

What these seven verses are telling us is that without the death of Christ, no worldwide gathering into the unity of the divine life would be possible. Our union with God is made possible by being with Jesus in the Father's love, for Jesus is the point of contact between heaven and earth. The future is present in Jesus. He is in heaven even as he is on earth. Eternal life and the kingdom of heaven have been merged. Eternal life is not about time. Eternal life is God's life. The kingdom/divine rule is being translated into life.

In *The Shaking of the Foundations* author Paul Tillich recalls a story told at the Nuremberg war-crimes trials. A number of escapees from Nazi gas chambers lived for a time in a cemetery in Wilna, Poland. One of the young women escapees gave birth in a grave, assisted by an eighty-year-old grave digger. Wrapped in a linen shroud, and hearing the first cries of this baby, the old man prayed, "Great God, hast Thou finally sent the Messiah to us? For who else than the Messiah Himself can be born in a grave?"[1]

God went the way of all flesh. His grave has been raided, though, and life has begun anew in him. The power of Christ's resurrection and its significance for us are linked to his sharing in our deaths.

God's love, seen in Jesus the Christ, has joined us and will join us wherever evil threatens to overtake us. Love came down, love divine, to join us in whatever pain or loss or sorrow might be ours. In the person of Jesus, God has made God's self available to humankind and all that humankind can do. Pouring himself out for the life of the world, Jesus makes heaven and earth one. There on the cross God is fully all in all: the true vine of which we are the branches (15:1–5); the good shepherd who searches for us until he finds us (10:1–16); the light of the world that the darkness cannot overcome (1:5). The

1. Paul Tillich, *The Shaking of the Foundations* (New York: Charles Scribner's Sons, 1948), 165.

John 12:20–26

Theological Perspective

This occurred due to tension between Hebrew and Hellenist Christians. It is significant that the apostles selected all Greek-speaking deacons, signaling an opening of God's covenant to persons beyond Israel. In Acts 8:26–39, the Ethiopian learns about the Christian faith from Philip and is baptized, signaling the extension of God's covenant to nations beyond Israel. In Acts 10, God's Spirit comes to both Cornelius and Peter to guide Peter into a new awareness of the relationship between Gentile and Jewish Christians. Peter learns through his visions and his encounter with Cornelius that even the things that humans consider profane are valued by God. In Acts 15:1–21, the apostles hold a council in Jerusalem to deliberate about how to incorporate Gentiles into their nascent Christian community, which has heretofore consisted exclusively of Jews. They recognize that the Gentiles have an equal part in the Christian community and commission Paul to be an apostle to the Gentiles.

In this passage, Jesus creates new terms by which persons may belong to the people of God. This makes it possible for persons of all backgrounds to participate in God's new covenant established through Jesus Christ. Rather than following a prescribed list of laws, what marks one as a member of the people of God is his or her desire to follow Jesus. Jesus sets forth the nature of such following: it consists of serving him and being willing to lose one's life in service to him. In the end, the terms for membership in the people of God require much greater sacrifice than the requirements set forth in the Old Testament covenant.

PAUL BARTON

Pastoral Perspective

of the earliest disciples, Andrew, by saying to him, "Come and see" (1:39); Philip used the same words when telling Nathanael about Jesus (1:46). "Come and see" can be used to entice those who are still somewhat hesitant to trust that what is just out of reach has greater worth than what is already known (the Samaritan woman invites the townspeople to do the same at 4:29).

As is evident from Philip and Andrew's subsequent success, a small investment can bring a great return. Philip and Andrew are therefore apostles of curiosity, of wondering, of rethinking and reimagining. The result of going through them to find meaning in this passage is to be led to a man who greatly rewards initiative, who demands a fundamental change in each one of us, and who invites us to become something far better than we were.

Much of church life is regimented by tradition, order, and good manners. As resistant as we rightly might be to rigid structures, protocols, and procedures, it would be difficult to function without them. Nevertheless, this passage reminds us that at the heart of Christianity is a bunch of unsettling truths: some things we are familiar with need to die, in order for new life to arise; the work of the Spirit will not be contained in set patterns; and anyone and everyone who wants to get involved should do so.

In the end, the blessing and honor of God come not to those who follow guidelines, but to those who give up their lives in service. That message is not just for the newly initiated, but for all who have been brought into Christ's circle. Church leaders who incorporate this passage into sermons or lessons will quickly find room to explore radical ideas and inspiring possibilities. They (we) will also find that Jesus' challenging response to those who earnestly seek him still prompts anxiety and reservation. Only by opening up the conversation, however, can we bring forth its great reward.

ALEXANDER WIMBERLY

"unwilting fame," the only equivalent in that era for eternal life.

The words for "serve" and "servant" (v. 26) come from the same root as our word "deacon." This verse is based on a fundamental aspect of Jesus' ministry, that he was the servant (Luke 22:27) who gave his life for his followers. Mark 10:45 reads, "the Son of Man came not to be served but to serve, and to give his life." In John, Jesus is the Good Shepherd who lays down his life for his sheep (10:11). Later he says, "No one has greater love than this, to lay down one's life for one's friends. You are my friends" (15:13–14). In chapter 13, Jesus washes the disciples' feet and tells them, "I have set you an example, that you also should do as I have done to you" (13:15).

The servant must follow Jesus. He is the Good Shepherd, "and the sheep follow him" (10:4), but this reference in John has further implications, as in Mark 8:34: "If any want to become my followers, let them deny themselves and take up their cross and follow me." Jesus warns the disciples of persecution to come: "An hour is coming when those who kill you will think that by doing so they are offering worship to God" (16:2).

The servant who follows will be with the master. In the Farewell Discourse, Jesus makes a similar promise: "I go and prepare a place for you. I will come again and will take you to myself, so that where I am, there you may be also" (14:3; cf. 14:18, 28).

Jesus twice refers to the approval or glory that comes from God (5:44; 12:43). Paul likewise speaks of the "commendation from God" (1 Cor. 4:5; cf. 2 Cor. 10:18) and "praise . . . from God" (Rom. 2:29).

G. J. RILEY

beginning and the end have been brought together. His end is our beginning.

His passion for us and with us, the proclamation that God has acted and will act, motivates and enables us. God has visited us to leave behind the materials necessary for fullness of life. All God seeks is recognition of that fullness and a sharing of its joy. What is needed on our part is awareness of the new life that is available to us. Education and resolutions will not satisfy this need, but only such disposition in our hearts and souls as will enable that new life of love, power, hope, virtue—which surround us on every side—to enter into our being. This disposition of heart and soul, this awareness is a discovery that each person must make for himself or herself: namely, the discovery that one cannot grasp for oneself what one really needs; rather, we have been showered with it, because God gives it to us. All that is needed is openness to that gift. All that is needed is the oblation Jesus made of himself on the cross. Should we be blessed by reflection and awareness, what then of the rest of our lives? If his end is our beginning, how shall we abandon life as a personal possession, in order to gain the life Christ offers?

Our beginning is the living of our lives with thanksgiving and praise for all the ways in which we have been graced. Because his love has obliterated our sin, we can live. No longer must we seek for the truth of our lives, for the Truth has come to us. God has taken the initiative to search us out and know us. With glorious, extravagant love God redeems us. Through Christ Jesus, despair is overcome by hope, weakness is swallowed up in strength, hatred is surrounded and finally conquered by love. His was a life of complete transparency to God, a life that entered into death but triumphed in glory. His was a life that is ours to share.

JUDITH M. MCDANIEL

John 12:27–36a

²⁷"Now my soul is troubled. And what should I say—'Father, save me from this hour'? No, it is for this reason that I have come to this hour. ²⁸Father, glorify your name." Then a voice came from heaven, "I have glorified it, and I will glorify it again." ²⁹The crowd standing there heard it and said that it was thunder. Others said, "An angel has spoken to him." ³⁰Jesus answered, "This voice has come for your sake, not for mine. ³¹Now is the judgment of this world; now the ruler of this world will be driven out. ³²And I, when I am lifted up from the earth, will draw all people to myself." ³³He said this to indicate the kind of death he was to die. ³⁴The crowd answered him, "We have heard from the law that the Messiah remains forever. How can you say that the Son of Man must be lifted up? Who is this Son of Man?" ³⁵Jesus said to them, "The light is with you for a little longer. Walk while you have the light, so that the darkness may not overtake you. If you walk in the darkness, you do not know where you are going. ³⁶While you have the light, believe in the light, so that you may become children of light."

Theological Perspective

The author of John recapitulates here the theme of light and darkness, first introduced in John 1:4–9 and then repeated in 3:19–21; 8:12; 9:5; 11:9–10. This theme of light and darkness has a close association with the battle between God and the forces of evil. In John 12:31, Jesus says, "Now is the judgment of the world; now the ruler of this world will be driven out." There are two themes to be examined in this passage. First, how have Christians interpreted the passage on Jesus as the light and his related admonition for his followers to walk in the light? Second, how should Christians engage in conflict with evil?

One common—and unfruitful—way of interpreting this text is to assume a privileged status for the followers of Jesus. Indeed, if Jesus calls us to walk as children of the light, it is easy to imagine ourselves as followers of Jesus reflecting the light of Christ in us in the midst of darkness. This light and darkness metaphor of John establishes an us-vs.-them duality that leads to a power imbalance between those who have the light and those who are in darkness. This was exemplified by the paternalistic theory and practice of missions in the nineteenth and twentieth centuries. Many missionaries viewed themselves as carriers of the light to the nations and to all those who were not part of the people of God and lived in

Pastoral Perspective

Among other things in this befuddling section of John are the references to darkness overtaking the light and the voice of the Father being mistaken for thunder. It is somewhat fitting, therefore, that readers would be left confused about what is actually being said. Lifted out of its context, this passage has the power to obscure more than to illumine. By looking widely at the Gospel's understanding of Jesus' imminent death and recognizing this passage as situated at the climax of his public ministry, the particular aspects of verses 27–36a become clearer and more useful for a congregation's life and witness. Above all, it encourages a continued discourse on the meaning of Christ's death and the choices readers now have in light of his final victory.

Perhaps the best place to begin a discussion about this passage is with the sentence that immediately follows it: "After Jesus had said this, he departed and hid from them" (12:36b). By looking back from here, we can see more clearly the import of the verses that come before. This is Jesus' final audience before the Passover. What occurs over the next several chapters will take place outside the public's view. Chapter 12 continues with John's commentary on Isaiah 53 and a summation of Jesus' teaching, but now the action moves away from the public square. As Jesus departs, John cleverly reinforces the idea of Jesus as the "light

Exegetical Perspective

This section of the Gospel further marks the purposeful turning to the cross that Jesus begins when he knows that his hour has finally come in 12:23. John 12:27 marks the one place in John that corresponds to the agony of the Garden of Gethsemane found in the Synoptics. Jesus may here be alluding to Psalm 6:3, but this is not a cry from the fear in his soul. He is troubled (after all, he knows he is about to be killed), but not that troubled. Jesus does enter the Garden of Gethsemane in 18:1, although the garden is not named. There is in that passage no praying that God "remove this cup from me" (Mark 14:36). Instead, Jesus declares, "Am I not to drink the cup that the Father has given me?" (18:11). Jesus enters the garden and Judas shows up with the soldiers. Jesus confronts them boldly and courageously, completely in control, and knocks them all to the ground with the words, "I am" (18:6), which reminds us of God's name in Exodus 3:14.

"And what should I say—'Father, save me from this hour'?" Jesus has just told everyone else that cowards who love their lives will lose them (12:25). He is not a coward. The hour is Jesus' "hour" that John has often mentioned (2:4; 7:30; 8:20; 12:23). It has finally come, because the Greeks (12:20), the "other sheep that do not belong to this fold" (10:16), have come to Jesus, fulfilling the goal "to gather into

Homiletical Perspective

The imagery of this passage brings to a climax the reality behind the signs the author has been giving the reader. Throughout the preceding chapters of the Book of Signs (chaps. 1–12), the author has written with double entendre, language capable of more than one interpretation, suggesting that human rationality is incapable of mastering divine knowledge. Divine things are not known only through the accumulation of information. They are known by intimacy with God. With these last words spoken during Jesus' public ministry, the preacher and congregation stand at the juncture of two cultures, two ways of looking at the cross and at the world. Our perception of what we thought was normal has been altered. Signs of light and life have come, and with them our perspective on reality has shifted. We hold in mind a cross, a means of death, and yet an instrument of life. How can two such contradictory perspectives be encompassed in one symbol?

This portion of Scripture is often called the Johannine Gethsemane. While Jesus' prayer expresses agony over what is in store, its elaboration also proclaims victory. His is a message of judgment and mercy, condemnation and compassion. The church has expressed the paradoxical nature of this passage by reading it, on the one hand, during Lent and during the solemn liturgies of Holy Week in

John 12:27–36a

Theological Perspective

darkness, meaning they were spiritually, morally, and culturally inferior to Christians.

Such a paternalistic stance led to practices of mission in which the missionary stood in a position of power, since he or she had the truth of Jesus Christ, and the receiving community stood in the position of vulnerability, since the members of the indigenous community did not know the gospel truth. The missionary had the responsibility to impart the gospel truth to the "heathens," so that they too could eventually become like the missionaries. This way of thinking led to a number of problems in the practice of mission for a few centuries. Not only did Christian missionaries view themselves as spiritually superior to the heathens, even the converted heathens, but they also considered themselves intellectually and culturally superior. This colonial mentality manifested itself as missionaries maintained supervisory authority over indigenous pastors and evangelists, and as missionaries maintained control of the financial decision making of the churches in mission settings.

The image of the light, of the light of the world or children of the light, needs to be tempered with humility and with a theology of the Holy Spirit. If we attend solely to Christology and neglect pneumatology, we place ourselves in Christ's position of healing and saving the world, when in fact we as the church are participants with God in God's saving activity in the world.[1] By including a pneumatological vision of our evangelistic work, we recognize that the Holy Spirit operates in the world in ways that transcend the people of God. We see this in the Old Testament with God's using Balaam to prevent Israel's enemy from harming God's people in Numbers 22–24. God uses Cyrus, the king of Persia, a non-Jew, as an instrument of his redemptive activity by facilitating the return of the Jews from Babylon to Palestine. These biblical examples challenge us to have a more expansive notion of the people of God. Adopting a pneumatological dimension in our sense of mission would go some way toward preventing a triumphalist stance and place greater emphasis on the way in which God is already at work in the world.

The battle between light and darkness, coupled with references such as the one in verse 31, in which Jesus announces that judgment has come and the ruler of this world is driven out, has been used to promote a militaristic approach to evangelism

1. Carlos F. Cardoza-Orlandi, *Mission: An Essential Guide* (Nashville: Abingdon Press, 2002), 45.

Pastoral Perspective

of the world" (cf. 1:4; 8:12; 9:5, etc.) and implicitly explains what Jesus means about the approaching darkness. The next few days will be hard. The light of the world will indeed go out. The struggle with the "ruler of this world" has reached its finale. Jesus is addressing the crowd before suiting up for battle. This is his closing statement, and in it he explains that the time has come to decide between the side of light and the side of darkness.

The hope that the crowd will ultimately make the right decision seems in jeopardy as the people debate what has occurred in verses 28–30. Was that thunder? Did an angel confer privately with Jesus? Jesus himself explains that the voice from heaven is not for his sake but for theirs—but this clarification only reveals the depths of the misunderstanding and the unlikelihood that the people will be able to comprehend the choice before them. Again, reading this passage with the conclusion of Christ's victory already known makes the crowd's uncertainty more tragic, but it also makes Jesus' challenge to modern readers more pointed: you know better, so what do you choose? In some ways, the confusing nature of this passage, with its questions of what and how and who, actually lends itself to a discussion about the greater matter at hand: why should we continue to walk in darkness when the light is available, the light we know will shine forever?

True, the return of the light is not explicitly foretold in these verses; instead, the darkness ominously closes in, and Jesus' hour has come. Even without John's usual reassurances, there is in this passage the promise that the Son of Man will be lifted up. Again, looking back from the end of verse 36 and keeping in mind John's overarching theme of Christ's ultimate victory help to illuminate this imagery. Jesus says these things and then hides himself away. He will not return into public view until he is "lifted up" as part of the passion narrative. The judgment of the world is imminent, but so is Christ's glorification. As the Son of Man is lifted up on the cross, lifted up from the grave, and lifted up from the earth, Isaiah's "light to the nations" will be seen. Connecting this passage specifically to the cross, the grave, and the ascension not only helps to explain its language; it provides the encouragement needed to face the harsher elements of the unfolding story.

Such forbearance is partly what distinguishes John's telling of Jesus' prayer of "agony." Many familiar episodes from the Synoptic texts are reworked in John so as to reinforce the evangelist's overall message. Here in John, instead of pleading that the

one the dispersed children of God" (11:52). It is the hour for Jesus to be glorified (12:23), that is, to be crucified, resurrected, and to return to his glory with the Father (17:5).

The author seems to know of the agony of Gethsemane recounted in the Synoptics and rejects such an idea. Jesus in John is always obedient to the Father's will (5:19, 30, et al.). The Father's will is to send his Son to die for humanity (3:16). Jesus cannot do otherwise, since he is the Father's Logos and emanation (1:1; 8:42). Therefore he did not need to make a choice to die and follow the Father's will on his last day alive (10:18). He was never afraid of anything at all, and he was never in danger of being abandoned on the cross (8:29; 16:32). Nevertheless, he is a real human being, and the prospect of being crucified is troubling. Yet he despises the alternative of cowardice, knowing that he was sent into the world for this purpose (cf. Heb. 12:2).

A voice from heaven is heard in verses 28–30. Twice in the tradition of the Synoptics a voice from God is heard: at the baptism of Jesus, the voice declares, "You are my beloved Son" (Mark 1:11), and at the transfiguration, Peter, James, and John are warned, "This is my beloved Son; listen to him!" (Mark 9:7). Neither event nor voice is found in John, while the voice here is found only in John. The voice is said to be for the benefit of the audience. Some think that the voice is thunder, while others think that it is an angelic voice. In either case, the voice or thunder serves to authenticate Jesus as being under divine favor, supported by angels in Jewish tradition, or confirmed by the thunder of Zeus among Gentiles.

The judgment on the ruler of this world is mentioned in verse 31. The "world" is a system of people and powers ruled by the devil (8:23, 44), the power of darkness (Luke 22:53). Jesus is the light whom the darkness does not comprehend or overcome (1:5), but whom the dark world hates (7:7) because he exposes its evil deeds (3:19–20). Neither Jesus nor his followers belong to the world (17:16), so the world also hates Jesus' followers (15:18–19). Jesus prays that the Father keep them from the evil one (17:15). The ruler has no power over Jesus (14:30), but will nevertheless use Judas to bring about the crucifixion (13:2, 27). Even so, Jesus reassures his followers: "Take courage; I have conquered the world!" (16:33).

The Gospel makes ironic use of ambiguous language in several places (e.g., 1:5: seize/comprehend; 3:3: born again/from above; 4:10: flowing water/living water; 12:23: glorified). The same is true with

preparation for Good Friday and, on the other, as the proper for the celebration of the joyous feast of the Holy Cross. Thus we are presented with two quite different observances centered upon one cross.

Over the centuries the cross has emerged from the minds of artists in strikingly different images. The representational art of Latin, Western Christianity regularly depicts the cross with the tortured body of the crucified still hanging on its beams. The iconography of Eastern Christianity often portrays an empty cross, representing released spiritual energy and resurrection. Both images are true, but they epitomize distinctive ways of looking at God's creation. They tell us there is not only more than one way to view the cross but also more than one way to view reality.

Some observe that the art of Western Christianity is rationalistic, focused on the definition and analysis of human experience in order to understand Christ. Eastern art, on the other hand, contemplates the person and work of Christ in order to understand humanity. In fact, we need both images even to begin to grasp the meaning of the cross.

How many times have you heard someone say when beset by misfortune, "I guess that is just my cross to bear in life"? That way of looking at life is a culture all its own, a culture that puts meaningless fate at the center of existence. In that culture, human experience determines reality. Is that perspective God's reality? Does that way of looking at the world and at the cross employ the mind of Christ Jesus?

Taking up one's cross does not mean bearing the burdens, tragedies, and heartaches life thrusts upon us. Taking up one's cross means willing obedience and self-emptying for the sake of God's kingdom. Taking up one's cross means redescribing reality from the perspective of God's vision. Taking up one's cross means professing that God is the center of existence and the source of grace for living.

To understand Christ's passion as a unit, the cross as a symbol of both death and life, consider the feast of the Holy Cross. Holy Cross Day is commemorated on September 14 because that is the date of the dedication of a fourth-century shrine. This shrine was built by Constantine on what was believed to be the site of Christ's crucifixion and resurrection. Pilgrims have come to that site since the first Easter, and evidence of their feelings of joy is available for any modern pilgrim to see. In the crypt of the Holy Sepulcher, the church built over Constantine's shrine, are the foundations of the nave of the fourth-century basilica. On the bedrock of one foundation stone is

John 12:27–36a

Theological Perspective

and mission. As one Hispanic pastor stated in my evangelism course, evangelism is a battle between the good news and evil. Evil is not cast out easily or with soft words and deeds. For evil to be cast out of people's lives, the gospel must be proclaimed with power. Such was this pastor's experience in his ministry with persons suffering from addictions and emotional and relational problems. It is important, though, to make the distinction between proclaiming the gospel forcefully and proclaiming it violently. Except for the one instance of Jesus overturning the tables of the money changers in the temple, Jesus did not make violence a part of his ministry. He did act powerfully many times, though, in driving out demons, healing the sick, and criticizing hypocritical interpretations of the law.

There is a fine line that needs to be drawn between proclaiming the gospel violently and forcefully. Many nineteenth-century and twentieth-century missionaries, in spite of their love for the people they evangelized, practiced a violent evangelism, to the extent that they required native converts to reject much of their culture in order to become Christian. It is still possible to be forceful in ministry without being violent.

For example, a group of indigenous Christians in Panama asked a missionary and his friends to pray for a sick woman, who had malaria, after they heard the missionary speak on the admonition in the book of James for the elders of the church to pray for the sick. The missionary and his companions felt uncertain about the ability of their prayers to achieve the sick woman's healing; not surprisingly, the woman did not get better after they prayed over her. Later, the Panamanian Christians prayed for the sick woman, deliberately without the missionaries, and she quickly became better. When one missionary asked why they were excluded from praying again with the indigenous Panamanians, the husband of the recovered wife responded that the missionaries were not invited because they did not believe, and only those who truly believed that their prayers could heal the woman should be present.[2] This incident shows that it is possible to engage the forces of evil forcefully but not violently.

PAUL BARTON

Pastoral Perspective

cup be taken from him, as the other Gospel writers report him doing in the garden, Jesus wonders rhetorically in the middle of a discourse whether he should want to be spared from "this hour," only to answer emphatically, "No!" There is no hesitation, no real question, no contrary will. Jesus' soul may be troubled, but his mind is made up. This is what he has been working toward, after all: the chance to glorify his Father's name.

Unlike the Jesus of the Synoptics, who has his prayer go unanswered, Jesus' galvanizing pep talk in John prompts an immediate response. "I have glorified [my name]," says the voice from heaven, "and I will glorify it again" (v. 28). As confused as the crowds are at the time, the modern reader, knowing the end of the story, can understand the meaning of this epiphany as Jesus himself does: what is about to take place must occur if the triumph of God is to be achieved.

Jesus' "hour" arrives in verses 27–36a, with the people around him and with readers today still unclear about what it all means. As is so often the case with John, though, the present moment makes sense only in light of what is promised to come. Reading this passage through the lens of the passion narrative helps us to see what would otherwise be obscured. As muddled and confused as these verses can seem, they nevertheless provide ample opportunity to explore larger concepts about what the death of Christ means, whether we ourselves are walking in the light, and what questions we as followers still have. Perhaps the greatest lesson from this text is that whatever current obstacles we face, whatever misunderstandings we still have, and whenever darkness threatens to take over, the best way to move forward is to start at the end—with the knowledge of God's victory in Christ—and to work back from there.

ALEXANDER WIMBERLY

2. Jonathan J. Bonk, *Missions and Money: Affluence as a Missionary Problem*, rev. and expanded (Maryknoll, NY: Orbis Books, 2007), 94–95.

"lifted up" in verses 32–33. The verb "lifted up" means to "raise something up," as Moses raised up the serpent on a pole in the wilderness (3:14), and to "exalt" someone who is humble (Matt. 23:12); here and in 8:28 it is used as a euphemism for "raise up on a cross, crucify."

Jesus will draw all people to himself, will fulfill the goal stated in 11:52, "to gather into one the dispersed children of God." One may imagine Jesus using a net, as do his disciples in 21:6, 11 (using the same verb). The Father is the one who draws people to Jesus in 6:44.

The people contrast their view of the Messiah with Jesus' use of the title Son of Man in verse 34. The traditional Jewish Messiah was supposed to be a conquering hero who defeated the enemies of Israel and "remained forever" as king of a restored and greatly enhanced Davidic kingdom. The Son of Man, on the contrary, is to be crucified. Jesus is therefore not the kind of Messiah that his hearers expect. As Paul tells us, the cross was a stumbling block for Jews (1 Cor. 1:23). A crucified man could not be the Messiah in the traditional understanding (Gal. 3:13), a fact that the Gospel of John faces here directly.

Light and darkness are major themes in John. In verses 35–36a, Jesus is the light that shines in the darkness, light that the darkness does not seize or understand (1:5). He tells his disciples to walk in light, that the darkness not seize them (same verb, 12:35). He is the light of the world (9:5), and those who follow him "will not walk in the darkness, but will have the light of life" (8:12). They are to believe in the light (12:46), and so become "children of light" (cf. Luke 16:8; 1 Thess. 5:5; Eph. 5:8).

G. J. RILEY

a carving dated somewhere between 135 and 330 CE. The carving pictures a sailboat with sails furled and an inscription that reads, "Lord, we have come." Those who carved that inscription came to that spot in order to arrive at the place of intimacy with Christ's passion, and the modern pilgrim is invited to do likewise.

Moving from Jerusalem north to England and the fourteenth century, we come upon Julian of Norwich, whose visions of Christ's passion are filled with joy. In her fourteenth revelation, Julian speaks of how our Mother Jesus carries us within him and brings us to spiritual birth. In Hebrew Scripture the word for the merciful, long-suffering love of God is derived from the word for womb. It is unlikely that Julian knew any Hebrew; yet it is as if she sees the cross as the womb by which Jesus gives us birth and life. His merciful, long-suffering love is self-emptying and fruitful and is the source of his promise to Julian: "I can make all things well, and I shall make all things well, and I will make all things well; and you will see yourself that every kind of thing will be well."[1] Julian did see for herself. She arrived at a state of intimacy with Christ's passion, and we are invited to do likewise.

On the cross was enthroned not evil but Love. Neither the "ruler of this world" (v. 31) nor meaninglessness is easily cast out. Serving at our culture's stress, even breakdown, points, we can minister at the points of greatest creativity and new life, for it was out of chaos that creation came. With a spirituality of engagement, we the church can claim the high ground of thoughtful, critical Christianity, viewing chaos and uncertainty as opportunities for God's grace to penetrate our reality.

With grace, we view creation from God's perspective. Enveloped in grace, preacher and congregation await the flowering of the tree of life with Christ's strength to bear our spirits up, knowing that there is no place we can go where Christ Jesus has not gone before. With joy, we proclaim Christ and him crucified as we lift high his holy cross.

JUDITH M. MCDANIEL

1. Julian of Norwich, *Showings*, trans. Edmund Colledge, OSA, and James Walsh, SJ (New York: Paulist Press, 1978), 229.

³⁶ᵇAfter Jesus had said this, he departed and hid from them. ³⁷Although he had performed so many signs in their presence, they did not believe in him. ³⁸This was to fulfill the word spoken by the prophet Isaiah:
"Lord, who has believed our message,
    and to whom has the arm of the Lord been revealed?"
³⁹And so they could not believe, because Isaiah also said,
⁴⁰ "He has blinded their eyes
    and hardened their heart,
  so that they might not look with their eyes,
    and understand with their heart and turn—
    and I would heal them."
⁴¹Isaiah said this because he saw his glory and spoke about him. ⁴²Nevertheless many, even of the authorities, believed in him. But because of the Pharisees they did not confess it, for fear that they would be put out of the synagogue; ⁴³for they loved human glory more than the glory that comes from God.

Theological Perspective

John 12:36b–50 constitutes the epilogue to the first part of this Gospel, and marks a transition to the passion narrative that is to follow. In this first passage, the evangelist reflects in his own voice on a major theological question facing the Johannine community: Why did so many of the children of Israel reject the signs and the teachings of Jesus? Why did so many who had heard the words of the prophets fail to see Jesus as Son of God and the promised Messiah? John provides two different responses to this puzzle, two different angles on the same situation, which together may help hearers ponder the relationship between God's activity in the world and real, flawed human activity.

Verses 38–40 provide the first answer to the question. People failed to believe because God "blinded their eyes and hardened their heart" (v. 40, quoting Isa. 6:10). That is, people's failure of faith is not simply their own fault or the fault of the messenger, but can be traced to God's own mysterious work. This sounds like bad news, because it attributes human faithlessness to God's prior decision. At its worst, such a view can contribute to passivity and despair. Who can have any hope, if God has already determined who is going to believe and who is not? Are we just playthings in the hands of a demonic god who intentionally keeps people from seeing the truth

Pastoral Perspective

There is a suburban prep school in Boston with a modern, eco-friendly gym featuring overhead lights controlled by motion detectors. Basketball practices at this gym tend to be lively affairs, since the lights remain on only by sustained action. Any significant lull results in a rapid loss of illumination, bulbs extinguishing like dominoes falling. Sessions in this gym yield strong results, because the threat of darkness has a way of focusing the mind. A similar kind of dynamic seems to be at play in our Johannine text.

One imagines that Jesus, nearing the end of his public ministry, sensed the coming darkness of Golgotha as a storm amassing ominously on the horizon. Like a fisherman studying dropping barometric pressure, Jesus must have felt in his bones that time was running out. What more could he say or do to sway the crowds gathering ever larger in Jerusalem for Passover? Despite a dazzling string of signs and wonders, including the miraculous calling forth of Lazarus, many remained moored to their skepticism. No doubt Christ's voice was tinged with urgency as he implored them, "Walk while you have the light, so that the darkness may not overtake you. . . . While you have the light, believe in the light, so that you may become children of light" (vv. 35–36). The cynical crowd appeared unmoved, provoking Jesus to do something odd. Whether out of frustration or simply

Exegetical Perspective

This scene functions in three ways: first, it concludes Jesus' public ministry; second, it concludes the Book of Signs (chaps. 1–12); finally, it presents a threefold summary and report of and rationale for Jesus' public ministry (12:36b–43) as a transition to the Farewell Discourse (chaps. 13–17). Verses 36b–43 provide a somber threefold series of summary reports (vv. 37, 39, and 41–43) on the impact and effect upon the crowds of the many signs and words of Jesus. Moreover, this scene's conclusions resemble the conclusions at the end of chapters 20 (vv. 30–31) and 21 (vv. 24–25). In 20:30–31, the author reflects on the signs (*sēmeia*) by indicating their effect on the belief of the intended audience. Overall, in this scene (12:36b–43), these summary reports on the effects of the signs portray a quite mixed and grim ministry effect; yet in the end (v. 43), the lack of success of the many signs and wonders results in a dismal outcome because signs alone are insufficient for sustaining the abundant life (*zōē*) of the one who believes on this level.

Setting the Scene (v. 36b). As a transition between the public ministry of Jesus and his final days, verse 36b marks a new scene from the Johannine Gethsemane and the end of Jesus' public ministry. The author does not clearly establish the temporal or spatial setting for this scene (vv. 36b–43). All the

Homiletical Perspective

If we consider that an essential theme in the Gospel of John is light in the darkness, with more than twenty references (eight in chaps. 11 and 12 alone) to Jesus as the light in a world of darkness, then it is significant that our text begins with Jesus departing and hiding from the public. Darkness is generally understood in John as unbelief in the message of God's love incarnate in Jesus Christ. In our passage, that incarnate light is being withdrawn from the world.

One might sense in the act of Jesus' withdrawal and hiding from the crowd a tone of sadness or frustration, behavior that can be understood as both emotional and prophetic. It is emotional in that it demonstrates Jesus confronting the end of his public ministry and the rejection by those who were both the object of both his primary mission and his deepest affection, his own people. It is prophetic in that the community of John (v. 40, referring to Isa. 6:9) understands rejection of Jesus and his message as a historic pattern of rejecting God's call. He seems particularly concerned that his disciples mature and endure in their faith even after his death.

Note that Isaiah attributes that darkness or faith-blindness to God's judgment and action (v. 40): "[God] has blinded their eyes . . . that they might not look with their eyes." The Gospel of John begins with hopefulness regarding the message of indomitable

John 12:36b–43

Theological Perspective

out of his or her own dark whimsy? Nevertheless, Isaiah, the writer of Exodus (e.g., Exod. 7:13; 9:12), and John all unite in this chorus: God hardens the hearts of certain people so that they do not follow God's ways.

The danger of this teaching lies in isolating it from its wider context. In Exodus, as in Isaiah and in John, the broader narratives trace God's saving activity—through the Red Sea, out of exile, by the cross and resurrection of Jesus. In each case, such saving work meets serious resistance, sometimes from other powers (Pharaoh) and sometimes from the people themselves (as in Isaiah and John). What the biblical writers seem to affirm with this "hardening of heart" language is that even such resistance is not outside the scope of God's covenant purposes. Despite appearances to the contrary, the "arm of the Lord" is at work even here. God's guidance of history is not thwarted by human failings; in some mysterious way, as with Joseph's brothers, what we mean for evil, God intends for good (Gen. 50:20).

Even with this positive interpretation, however, such a response to the question of why so many rejected Jesus remains incomplete. It is not enough simply to say that people did not believe because God hardened their hearts. There is also a human explanation, so John also gives a second answer to the perplexing question of why so many children of Israel failed to believe in Jesus: the twin motives of fear and idolatry. As verse 42 explains, some people did believe, but did not confess it, because of "fear that they would be put out of the synagogue." As John's audience seems to know all too well, some Jesus-following Jews were being kept out of synagogues by the time this Gospel was written. So for the first readers of John, confessing Jesus as Messiah could well lead to exclusion. This specific, historical fear is understandable. It draws attention to a more general theme that a reader of this passage might explore: the power of fear to control our lives, preventing faithful discipleship.[1] What do we fear and what prevents us from believing in the light?

Fear, according to John, keeps many from professing their faith openly, but the concluding verse of this passage illumines the deeper obstacle to faith: "for they loved human glory more than the glory that comes from God" (v. 43). Love of human glory—fame, good reputation, inclusion in

Pastoral Perspective

exhausted sadness, Jesus abruptly departed and "hid" from them. One minute he was there; the next he was gone, and the brilliant charisma was shrouded.

Our Gospel writer makes sense of this scene through the lens of his Jewish tradition, which characterizes unresponsiveness as an echo from long ago. John draws on the words of the prophet Isaiah, who himself hearkened back to the time of Pharaoh by calling such disbelief a hardening of the heart (v. 40). The Greek verb used here for hardening is *epōrōsen,* a derivative of *pōros,* a kind of marble, used figuratively to mean "insensible, as unperceptive as a rock." The word has also been translated variously as "calloused," "thick," and even "fat."

This pericope offers a resonant message for today. Have not our own hearts grown fat, made numb by an endless barrage of sensory overload and breaking news bulletins ricocheting throughout our information-drenched world? "Turning and turning in the widening gyre / The falcon cannot hear the falconer," wrote Yeats in "The Second Coming,"[1] describing a spiritual estrangement yet endemic today. Our eyes and ears and hearts are calloused from the scratching of words and images on all sides, and so we sit dully, as unmoved and unmoving as stones.

However, darkness may not be our greatest challenge in seeing Christ today—but, instead, too much light. It calls to mind the true story of Luna Island, a small spit of land at Niagara Falls. A modest sign marks the island as a favorite of tourists in the late nineteenth century, who flocked there to see the lunar rainbows which formed on cloudless full-moon evenings. Moonshine would evidently catch the mist of the mighty waterfalls and create actual rainbows in the night sky. Nowadays, the sign notes, there is just too much ambient artificial light, what scientists call "light pollution," to be able to see the moon bows anymore. Though the colorful wonder no doubt remains, our modern senses are unable to see it.

Jesus has a remedy: move. Walk in the light, so that you may become children of the light. Do *this,* so that you may become *that.* Transformation is the goal, and this requires something of us that is deeper than passive assent (see Jas. 2:18–20). Note the warning in verse 42: "Nevertheless many, even of the authorities, believed in him. But because of the Pharisees they did not *confess* it, for fear that they would be put out of the synagogue." "Confess," says *Webster's Dictionary,* means "to make known." It is

---

1. See Lynn Japinga, "Fear in the Reformed Tradition," in *Feminist and Womanist Essays in Reformed Dogmatics,* ed. Amy Plantinga Pauw and Serene Jones (Louisville, KY: Westminster John Knox Press, 2006), 1–18, for a perceptive discussion of the power of fear.

1. "The Second Coming," in William Butler Yeats, *Michael Robartes and the Dancer* (Churchtown, Dundrum, Ireland: The Chuala Press, 1920), 19.

reader knows is that Jesus departed and hid (*ekrybē*) himself from the crowds. Consequently, this scene sets the tone and setting of the mixed and dismal reports on Jesus' ministry. After the Johannine Gethsemane (12:27–36a), Jesus, due to disgust because of the shallow response to his signs, departs from the crowds and his disciples and hides himself in solitude both in this scene and in the following one (12:44–50). As mentioned above, the author does not provide temporal or spatial markers to set the tone of the scene; rather, this elusive maneuver of escaping the crowds and hiding himself causes the reader to reflect more intently on what follows to learn why Jesus displays such behavior.

Summary Report #1 (vv. 37–38). The narrator indicates the impact of Jesus' signs and wonders on the crowds (cf. 12:34). The crowds did not believe in Jesus, despite the signs that he performed in their presence or before their eyes, due to their spiritual blindness or darkness, as will be proposed in verses 39–40. This may indicate the reason that Jesus departed and hid himself from them; that is, the crowds did not respond to Jesus' words or signs because they rejected the light, and as a result they remained in the darkness—they were blind.

The author reports the fulfillment of Isaiah 53:1 and, later, Isaiah 6:10 (both cited verbatim from the Septuagint, LXX), which suggests in reverse order that although the mighty arm of God reveals mighty works in their presence (v. 38c), the result would be, "Who has believed our message?" (v. 38b). In the Old Testament, Isaiah cites this prophecy to introduce why part of Israel failed to believe in YHWH. Similarly, it is cited here as an apology regarding why some Jews did not believe, despite the mighty works and despite the words of Jesus; people still do not believe in God (Jesus). According to the author, Jesus' words and signs were rejected and people remained in a state of disbelief because of the prophet Isaiah's prediction.

Summary Report #2 (vv. 39–40). In this second summary report, the author makes it clear that the unbelief of the crowds could not be attributed to Jesus; it was because they refused to believe in him. Quoting Isaiah again (Isa. 6:10), the narrator indicates why the crowd was in a state of unbelief—God. This quotation from Isaiah is also employed in the Synoptic Gospels as the reason that Jesus spoke in parables (see Mark 4:12 and pars.); the Jewish authorities who sought to silence Jesus were not able

light: "the light shines in the darkness, and the darkness did not overcome it" (1:5). Now the light is being withdrawn. The preacher or teacher may want to invite the congregation to consider how they deal with failure or rejection in a ministry effort.

In verse 36a, which concludes the last public discourse of Jesus before his passion, the appeal to his beloved people ends with a plea for them to become "children of light," for according to the prophets (Isa. 9:2; 49:6) it is, and always has been, the mission of the chosen people to be a light to the world. Previously, in 12:20, there is a request by Greeks (Gentiles) to see Jesus. Jesus seems to resist distraction from the urgent purpose of his discourse, which is to deepen his disciples' faith. The coming of the Greeks marks an important transition in the Gospel of John, as Jesus' public ministry ends, and his final preparatory discourse and transitional work with his disciples begins.

Acceptance of his impending death seems to create an urgency in his focus upon those to whom he must entrust his mission. They must understand and fully embrace his message now before doubt or unbelief overtakes them (12:35). This is dramatically stated in 12:36a, where Jesus urges his disciples to believe in the light, now, before his death, so that they may become "children of light," inheritors of his witness. As inheritors they must testify to God's true light, "grace and truth" (1:14), a hope that is greater than the judgment of law (1:17) and that cannot be overcome by darkness or the world's disbelief (1:5).

Some scholars believe that the first-century (or later) Jewish Christian community of John's Gospel is at an important juncture in its ministry and corporate faith life.[1] As they experience rejection by those whom they love most, do they recall verse 37, which reads, "Although he had performed so many signs in their presence, they did not believe in him"? Perhaps the gift of this memory to the disciples and John's church is remembering that Jesus also experienced the pain of disbelief and rejection.

The teacher might invite her community to consider five aspects of the passage. First, how do we know when our work is done, and the unaided action of God begins? How do we let one form of ministry die, so that we may be more open to new, greater manifestations of God, or "glorification" of the good news? Is it possible to be faithful in retreating and temporarily disengaging, to discern what

---

1. Raymond E. Brown, *Introduction to the New Testament* (New York: Doubleday, 1997), 350–51, and John Marsh, *Saint John* (Philadelphia: Westminster Press, 1978), 469.

John 12:36b–43

Theological Perspective

a respectable community—is the real motivating force in the lives of those in this passage who do not confess faith in Jesus. Fear of being excluded, yes; but what drives such fear? The pleasure that comes from being respected, being part of a community that means something in society. That kind of glory means more than the strange, uncomfortable glory that Jesus reveals, which involves getting up on a cross to show the extent of God's self-giving love for the whole world. The searing light of God's glory manifest in the cross and resurrection is hard to love, and so we mostly settle for loving smaller, more manageable human glory.

The theological question raised in this passage regards providence, the doctrine of God's ongoing work in creation and human history. Classical Protestant theology of the seventeenth and eighteenth centuries helpfully described God's providence in three dimensions: as preservation (*conservatio*), accompaniment (*concursus*), and rule or government (*gubernatio*).[2] Seen together, these three dimensions enable us to appreciate the multiple ways in which God is at work beneath, beside, and beyond human activity, without rendering humans powerless. Two of these dimensions of providence are held in tension in this passage: accompaniment and government. The first answer affirms God's government: God is the one who blinds the eyes, so that people do not believe. Their unbelief is not a failure of God's promises, but a part of God's own plan to bring about salvation. The second answer affirms God's accompaniment: people fail to believe in Jesus, or fail to confess their faith, because of real human motivations. God moves in human history, not apart from creatures, but in and through creatures—even flawed, faithless human creatures. A teacher or preacher working with this passage may point out that the two answers given to the one question helpfully illuminate one another, affirming that even in human denial of Jesus, what people intend for evil, God intends for glory.

MARTHA MOORE-KEISH

Pastoral Perspective

an action. Eugene Peterson, in *The Message* translation, renders verses 42–43 this way: "On the other hand, a considerable number from the ranks of the leaders did believe. But because of the Pharisees, they didn't come out in the open with it."

What would it look like to "come out in the open" with our faith today? Can we name our fears in confessing our faith? What Pharisaic judgment are we so afraid of, what perceived loss or rejection are we trying to avoid? The word "evangelism" has fallen out of favor in many circles lately, perhaps because it smacks of an ill-fitting proselytizing in today's pluralistic world; but is there a way to recast evangelism? Might it be as simple as asking: What kind of "good news" is God speaking through each of our lives? In what ways are we embodying faith in Jesus? Have there been times when we felt moved to speak up passionately about something but refrained? What were the reasons we remained silent?

Lest any congregant imagine this text solely as a mandate for street preaching in the town square, it is helpful to note that *Webster's* provides a second definition for "confess": "to give evidence of." This recalls the words often attributed to Francis of Assisi: "Preach the gospel, and if necessary, use words." Confession is expansive enough to include not just proclamation but also a slow flowering of Christ love in our hearts, a faith nurtured by the steady attentiveness of discipleship.

This is the core of Christ's message in John 12: to believe in the light is to walk in the light. Despite our dulled senses, we must activate a faith that leads to transformation. Otherwise, like listlessly practicing basketball in a modern gym, our inertia will too soon be followed by lights abruptly shutting down, falling like dominoes, plunging us into the darkness of a hidden Jesus.

SUZANNE WOOLSTON BOSSERT

---

2. Karl Barth reworked these categories in *Church Dogmatics*, III/3, *The Doctrine of Creation* (Edinburgh: T. & T. Clark, 1961).

Exegetical Perspective

to understand the intended meaning of the parables. In John 12:40, the quotation from Isaiah serves a different function, which includes a rationale for the crowds' unbelief: God's blinding their eyes and hardening their hearts. Moreover, the inability to believe was not Jesus' doing, or the crowd's. Instead, here it was God who blinded their eyes and hardened their hearts, so that they could not believe in mere signs or words alone, lest they would be healed without authentic belief.

Summary Report #3 (vv. 41–43). The refusal of some Jewish authorities to believe because of fear of being expelled from the synagogue in the event of a public confession of belief in Jesus is ascribed to their preference for human approval over God's. (Nicodemus and Joseph of Arimathea, however, are Jewish authorities who do believe; see 3:1–12 and 19:38–42, respectively.) Consequently, some of the Jews and even some of the Pharisees lacked sufficient evidence for them to come to public belief. Nonetheless, this report seems to focus primarily on the few leaders who failed to respond publicly in faith for fear of being expelled from the synagogue.

Much has been written on this phenomenon of being expelled from the synagogue (*aposynagōgos*; 9:22; 12:42; and 16:2). The term is anachronistic, of course; it reflects the time period of the author's own community near the end of the first century, rather than the period of Jesus' earthly ministry. Before the destruction of the temple in 70 CE, the temple and Sadducees served as the center of power. After the destruction, the Pharisees are poised to assume leadership, as their power lay in interpretation of Torah, not the running of the temple. The notion of being removed from a synagogue refers to John's own time. The Johannine community seems to be enjoying some evangelistic success. The text portrays various levels of belief, though. Belief without signs is exemplary, on the one hand, while refusing to profess one's faith publicly, due to fear or the love of human acclaim rather than God's approval, represents the lowest level. As a result, Jesus' public ministry in John ends on a negative note.

LARRY D. GEORGE

Homiletical Perspective

God may do next? How may God "glorify" the good news, even in the midst of the death of current ministries?

Second, if the congregation is dealing with discouragement about perceived responses to its ministry and witness, how might the actions of Jesus in this passage suggest a time of withdrawal for renewal and discernment of what new thing God may be doing to "glorify" or "lift up" up the good news beyond the current efforts of ministries?

Third, verse 37 indicates that even after the "many signs in their presence," the community to which Jesus believed he was most called did not believe. A sermon might ask: How do we react when those about whom we care most (our youth, the unchurched, those with whom we share some deep affinity) reject the good news despite our efforts?

Fourth, John's community may be experiencing stress, much as did Jesus with his disciples. Perhaps some in John's community are fearful that their message may offend certain authorities or alienate close relationships. What are the circumstances or issues facing a congregation politically, socially, or morally for which there is risk when engaging the gospel? The teacher might encourage an individual or congregation to risk courageously in sharing their faith, even if they or their witness is not accepted. The life and message of persons like Dietrich Bonhoeffer, Martin Luther King Jr., and Dorothy Day may be helpful anecdotal and theological resources.

Finally, how might persons who have significant public office or status be encouraged when they are struggling with the choice between security or status and faith commitment? Jesus refers to such dilemmas of choice in verse 43: "for they loved human glory more than the glory that comes from God." If there are congregational members in public office or with other influence facing complicated choices, a pastoral prayer might be offered for them as part of worship (see, e.g., the "Prayer for those who Influence Public Opinion" in the *Book of Common Prayer*).[2]

NATHAN D. BAXTER

---

2. *Book of Common Prayer* (New York: Church Publishing, 1979), 827.

John 12:44–50

⁴⁴Then Jesus cried aloud: "Whoever believes in me believes not in me but in him who sent me. ⁴⁵And whoever sees me sees him who sent me. ⁴⁶I have come as light into the world, so that everyone who believes in me should not remain in the darkness. ⁴⁷I do not judge anyone who hears my words and does not keep them, for I came not to judge the world, but to save the world. ⁴⁸The one who rejects me and does not receive my word has a judge; on the last day the word that I have spoken will serve as judge, ⁴⁹for I have not spoken on my own, but the Father who sent me has himself given me a commandment about what to say and what to speak. ⁵⁰And I know that his commandment is eternal life. What I speak, therefore, I speak just as the Father has told me."

Theological Perspective

John 12:36b–50 constitutes the epilogue to the first part of this Gospel and marks a transition to the passion narrative that is to follow. In this second half of the epilogue, John shifts from the voice of the narrator to the voice of Jesus, who "cries aloud" a summary of key points of his teaching in the preceding eleven chapters: light and darkness, judgment and eternal life, and the inextricable relationship of Jesus to the one he calls Father. This essay will take up two of these theological themes: the relationship of Jesus to the Father and the tricky issue of final judgment.

In verse 44, Jesus points beyond himself to the one who sent him: "Whoever believes in me believes not in me but in him who sent me." He returns to this theme at the end of the passage, insisting that he speaks not on his own, but based on the words, the commandment, given to him by the Father (vv. 49–50). These affirmations raise a basic question, both for the early church and for contemporary Christians: How are we to understand the relationship between Jesus and "the one who sent [him]"? Does this verb "sent" mean that Jesus is a subordinate messenger from God the Father, and that we are to look, not at Jesus himself, but at the source of his life and his teaching? Is he, rather, directing our attention to the *relationship* between himself and the one who sent him, so that we do not misunderstand

Pastoral Perspective

Awash in lengthening shadows as the dark hour of the Son of Man draws near, one imagines Jesus focusing intently on finding the right final words to impart to the "the great crowd" (v. 12) gathering in Jerusalem for Passover. Commonly subtitled a "Summary of Jesus' Teaching" (NRSV), this passage is considered a finale of Christ's public proclamation. As such, the import of such a momentous event offers an interesting opportunity for reflection. Before reading this pericope aloud, a preacher or teacher could pose a wondering question to listeners: What do you think Jesus would say as a theological summary? Drawing from his considerable body of astonishing signs and lessons, what might Christ himself identify as bottom-line and absolutely elemental? Surely Jesus would astonish the crowd with a gorgeous final sonnet on grace, or a last ardent pitch to love God and neighbor with abandon, or, at the very least, a concluding exhortation to live as compassionate beings on this earth. John's Jesus delivers a surprising curveball, though. Instead of an expected riff on the beauty of mercy, he "cried aloud" (v. 44) a vehement message about . . . judgment (v. 48).

Judgment is not a frequent sermon topic in many churches today. The unkempt wildness of sin is often domesticated within the friendly confines of the liturgical Prayer of Confession, or referred to

Exegetical Perspective

This scene concludes Jesus' public ministry and the Book of Signs (chaps. 1–12) and provides a transition into the Book of Glory (chaps. 13–21). The first conclusion (vv. 36b–43) employs three summary reports with two indirect discourses from the prophet Isaiah (Isa. 53:1 and 6:10, cited verbatim from the Septuagint) that serve as rationales for two types of unbelief: the crowd and some Jewish authorities. In this scene, the author uses Jesus' direct discourse to highlight and emphasize the divine relationship between God as Father and God as Son during the public ministry of Jesus. The author does not privilege the characters in the story world of the Fourth Gospel with the revelation of Jesus' divine nature in the prologue (1:1–18) that the reader enjoys. The author maintains that Jesus was not merely a human agent acting on his own behalf; rather, he was God incarnate sent on a mission by God the Father. Thus Jesus is portrayed as a divine agent (Son) with a divine source (Father). Therefore, all that Jesus represents is that which the Father desires and directs him to exemplify in his public ministry to the Jewish crowds and authorities.

Believing and Seeing (vv. 44–45). Like the previous scene (vv. 36b–43), this one lacks a spatial and temporal setting. Because Jesus is alone and in hiding

Homiletical Perspective

In the spirit of the prophets Elijah (1 Kgs. 18:21) and John the Baptist (1:23), and drawing upon the words of Malachi 3:1, Jesus speaks with passion and urgency in John 12:44. Where the Hebrew prophets point to God's promise of a coming messiah or messianic age, Jesus, knowing himself to be the Messiah, points to God, who has authorized his work and message. A preacher might ask how the ministry of the individual or collective community points beyond itself to God. How do ministries of direct services to meet human need, or actions for social justice, or the fellowship and worship of the gathered community, point beyond ourselves to God and God's reign?

In the Synoptic tradition, Jesus' authority (*exousia*) is specifically and directly noted by others with curiosity, but no recognition of the source of his authority is made plain (e.g., Mark 1:21–27). In other instances, the authority of Jesus is acknowledged, but its source is questioned (Matt. 21:23–27). Also in the Synoptics, Jesus evades or only indirectly answers questions about his authority (Luke 20:1–8). In his preresurrection discourses in John's Gospel, though, particularly 12:44–45 (cf. 5:26; 12:27; 17:2; 19:11), Jesus speaks plainly about the source of his authority: God is the source of his power to speak and to act.

In John 12:44–50, Jesus seems to respond to a challenge or question regarding the source of his

John 12:44–50

him as an independent source of life? In the first four centuries, there arose a bitter argument between those who saw Jesus as separate from and subordinate to the Father, and those who insisted that Jesus was so united with the Father that there could be no talk of division or hierarchy between them.

Of the early church teachers who described Jesus Christ, the Word of God, as subordinate to the eternal God, Arius of Alexandria is particularly important. He points out that, in passages like this one, Jesus talks about the Father as if he (Jesus) were of lesser status, receiving power from the Father. Being sent and receiving power establish Jesus the incarnate Word as a creature, not identical with God's own being. Arius also argues that if we speak of Jesus Christ as "of the same substance" with God the Father (as the Nicene tradition came to do), then "according to this view the Father is composite and divisible and changeable and corporeal, and accordingly the incorporeal God is both corporeal and capable of suffering."[1] Much is at stake here: Can God be divided? Can God change? Is God able to suffer? According to Arius, these are all clearly impossible assertions. So just as clearly, while Jesus is Word of God, bearer of light and life, he is not the same as God.

On the other hand, teachers such as Athanasius of Alexandria insisted that Jesus Christ is God incarnate, without qualification. An Athanasian reading of this passage would emphasize the identity implied in verse 45: "whoever sees me sees him who sent me." There is no gap, no difference of status, between the Sender and the Sent One; Jesus is simply the visible image of God, who came into the world for its salvation. The verb "sent," then, does not imply hierarchy but Jesus' unbreakable unity with the Father.[2]

Why does any of this matter today? Even if the ancient terms of debate no longer compel us, we profit from bringing the concerns of both Arius and Athanasius to the reading of John 12:44–50. To be sure, the position of Athanasius became orthodox, while the teaching of Arius was declared heretical; but this does not mean that every insight of Arius is false, or every impulse faithless. With Arius, we will notice the way that Jesus directs attention beyond himself, to the one God who sent him—and thus we may learn from Jesus' humility and his own utter devotion to God. With Athanasius, we will notice Jesus' affirmation that anyone who sees him sees the

safely in the abstract by pinning sin to larger systemic injustices of one sort or the other. Reasons for the heavy swing of the pendulum toward scot-free salvation seem clear enough, not least because we are now living in what has been deemed "the age of self-defense."[1] We moderns too often experience judgment as "judgmental," that deeply unhelpful shaming tactic that destabilizes self-esteem. Amid the wreckage of a historical human propensity to use religion as a weapon of mass condemnation, we must excavate the critical reality of God's parental stewardship of our free-will lives. UCC pastor Molly Baskette comments:

> Some might say that today's mainline Church just doesn't *do* judgment anymore. And you might feel that that is fine with you; there are plenty of other sects and denominations that have chosen it as their cottage industry. But without this shadow side of the God of Love, our religion loses a certain rigor, loses a certain structure; loses, I dare say, its wealth. Even if we shy from it, we know that our Christian practice demands that we regularly take a fearless moral inventory of ourselves, humbly admit our mistakes, and, as part of this, seriously entertain the idea that we will be judged for these failures.[2]

To be sure, Christ's message in John 12:44–50 is not a typical televangelist's screed, and there is no whiff of hell-smoke or simmering brimstone anywhere. Jesus, painted so gloriously by John as the great "light of the world," states plainly that he has come not to judge but to save (v. 47). Even though Jesus does not come to judge, neither does his coming eclipse the one true judge, God.

The parsing of roles is keen in this passage. In fact, Jesus takes such care in affirming his credentialed right to speak God's dictates that the passage might easily be subtitled, "Summary of Jesus' *Authority*." To see me, Jesus says, is to see the Creator. To hear me is to hear the very thoughts of God. Among the many incendiary teachings of Christ, his ideas of Trinitarian function must have been the hardest for his first-century Jewish contemporaries to fathom. However, there is nuance here, in that Jesus seems less interested in proclaiming his status of oneness with God than in the fact that his words matter because they are straight from YHWH: "For I have not spoken on my own, but the Father who sent me

---

1. Arius, confession of faith to Alexander of Alexandria, about 320 CE, quoted in Aloys Grillmeier, *Christ in Christian Tradition*, vol. 1: *From the Apostolic Age to Chalcedon (451)*, 2nd ed. (Atlanta: John Knox Press, 1975), 226.
2. For further reading on Athanasius, see his *On the Incarnation* (Crestwood, NY: St. Vladimir's Seminary Press, 1996).

1. Barbara Brown Taylor, "Manifold Sins and Wickedness: Preaching Repentance in an Age of Self-Defense," a lecture delivered in Washington, DC, at the College of Preachers, 1999.
2. Molly Phinney Baskette, www.firstchurchsomerville.org/sermons/castthe firststone.html.

(v. 36b), the author employs Jesus' direct discourse outside of the presence of any characters and in an unknown spatial location with no intended audience in the story world; he is alone, crying out only to the implied readers. The author's introduction of the direct discourse sets the tone of urgency to emphasize Jesus' mood: "Jesus cried aloud," as a result of the overall report provided in verses 36b–43. In verses 44–45, Jesus informs the reader that he is in fact a divine agent of God the Father; therefore, he mirrors the presence of God when people both believe and see.

This reference to believing and seeing refers directly to the situation of unbelief in verse 40, which is a quotation from Isaiah to indicate the author's remedy for unbelief. That is, for one to believe or see, one does not need signs or mighty works, or even the words of Jesus; one must believe in God by seeing and believing in Jesus as God. Moreover, the acts of believing and seeing are related, in that in order to see, one must believe, and if one believes, then seeing is possible (cf. 3:3, 12 and the story of the man born blind in chap. 9).

Believing and seeing represent similar activities in this Gospel. Similarly, if anyone believes in Jesus, his or her belief is not merely in Jesus but in the one (God the Father) who sent him. Moreover, if anyone sees Jesus, she or he sees the one (God) who sent him. In an allusion to the prologue (1:1–3), the author employs similar language for the Logos: "and the Word (*logos*) was toward (*pros*) God and was God" (my trans.), but here in verse 45, Jesus replaces the Word. So, in seeing Jesus, one sees the Logos who was the same as God. Thus, Jesus as the preexistent Logos is the same as God, and seeing Jesus (God incarnate) is one and the same as seeing God. This scene, then, forms closure (*inclusio*) with the prologue and thus forms a conclusion to this section of the Gospel.

Light versus Darkness; Salvation and Judgment (vv. 46–47). In another allusion to the prologue in the Book of Signs, the author equates Jesus with the metaphor of light coming into the world (this is also a reference to 3:17–21). Jesus exclaims that this light is provided to anyone who believes in him so that they would not remain in the darkness. In other words, without belief in Jesus, one would be spiritually blind, because he as the light would allow them to see (cf. 3:3). As a result, because of belief in Jesus, one would be subject to light and not remain in the darkness, evil, or spiritual blindness (see chap. 9, the story of the man blind from birth).

authority. In this instance, Jesus states unequivocally that God the Father is the source of his authority. The teacher may wish to consider issues in the life of the congregation about Christian authority to minister. How does a congregation know when it is being guided and inspired by God to speak and act? What are the dangers inherent in speaking and acting on God's behalf? What might be the dangers of not speaking or acting with a sense of God's guidance?

Jesus then introduces the issue of judgment or the day of reckoning. Jesus is not the judge (v. 47); rather, God is the judge (v. 48). One might consider Jesus' first reference to this theme in John 3:17, where *krinō* is used for "judge" (cf. 12:47, 48). Chapter 3 announces God's desire that people believe in God's love and have "eternal life" and not "perish" (3:16). Jesus is clear that his mission (and that of the church) is not to condemn (judge) but to make incarnate and proclaim God's saving love (3:17). Judgment (*krisis*) is God's work, not the community's.

The preacher might consider the tension evident in the text between the exhortation to the faithful actively to evangelize while not casting judgment upon the intended proselytes. In other words, how might the believer claim the power to be a witness of God in light of the frailty of human knowing and the risk of religious hubris? This question could give rise to a homiletical discourse on contemporary witnesses or methods of evangelization. One might reflect upon the theologian Karl Barth's assumption that it is God's desire to be "partners" with humanity (the church) in the mission of God. In this view, faithfulness requires claiming both the relationship and authority God offers. According to Barth, "God . . . wants [humanity] to be His partner. There is a *causa Dei* in the world. God wants light, not darkness . . . cosmos, not chaos . . . peace, not disorder. [God] wants humanity bound and pledged to Him rather than to any other authority."[1] Earlier in the same treatise, Barth puts the governing factor of our authorization squarely between our "partnership with God" and the guiding spirit of God's loving purpose: "This much is certain, that we have no theological right to set any sort of limits to the loving-kindness of God which has appeared in Jesus Christ."[2] This interpretation could be tied to a discussion about a theology of abundance, especially when contrasted with a theology of scarcity.

1. Karl Barth, *The Humanity of God* (Atlanta: John Knox Press, 1952), 80.
2. Ibid., 62.

John 12:44–50

Theological Perspective

one who sent him—and thus we may learn to see in Jesus' words and actions nothing other than God's own self-revelation.

Jesus' reference to judgment and the "last day" (v. 48) in this passage is the second theme that deserves attention. Many people in our day, as in John's, look for Christ's second coming as a violent disruption of world events, bringing a judgment day in which people are sharply divided between righteous and unrighteous, sheep and goats, wheat and tares. Some passages in the Gospels, including some of Jesus' own teachings, inform such depictions (e.g., Matt. 11:20–24; 25:31–46). John's portrait of judgment here, as elsewhere in the Fourth Gospel, is distinctive, always connected with the proclamation of Jesus as the light of God coming into the world.

Judgment is not a verdict that Jesus renders (v. 47). Rather, judgment now is the self-rendered conviction of those who reject the light. In the last day, the word of judgment will be what Jesus' words have always been: eternal life (vv. 48–50). As C. H. Dodd puts it, "the word of judgment on the 'Last Day' is no other than the revelation of life and light which Christ gave in his incarnation."[3] This portrait of judgment helpfully counterbalances popular images that have inspired and terrified Christians since the medieval era. Rather than Jesus seated on a throne sorting people left and right for damnation and salvation, John's judgment scene depicts Jesus simply as light shining in the darkness, throwing the shadowy corners of the world into sharp relief. The final judgment is this: the darkness will not overcome the light.

MARTHA MOORE-KEISH

Pastoral Perspective

has himself given me a commandment about what to say and what to speak" (v. 49). Jesus is God's incarnate mouth, a distinction that underscores the fact that the Creator remains the sole judge of creation.

Using his divine voice, Jesus sets down unmistakable boundaries in this text, pointing out that the "keeping" (v. 47) and "receiving" (v. 48) of his word—Christ's lessons on how to live—are of maximum consequence. It is a striking concept: the penultimate words uttered by the ultimate Word, the *Logos*, will themselves do the judging on behalf of God. One can almost imagine the syllables falling from Jesus' lips as small, shining mirrors in which we can see our own true reflection. In this way, Jesus again emphasizes his intermediary role, with one hand pointing heavenward to God and the other hand pointing directly to us. Christ is drawing all of humanity into the act of judgment by teaching us that we are not unwitting subjects dragged helplessly before a divine magistrate. Jesus wants to be a lamp unto our feet, to light our way along the trail leading to ultimate truth. If we decide to stray from this radiant path, then we ourselves are judging that Jesus is not a trustworthy guide.

So it is that as we judge, we will be judged. Even though recompense has long been thought to be the fires of a literal hell, many today point to the hellishness of cognitive dissonance that can bloom chokingly along the fault line between intention and inaction, or altruism and selfishness. Although we likely doubt judgment in the form of a fireball to the chest if we turn away from the words of Jesus, we risk the crushing realization of a life only partially lived.

The good news is that God does not abandon us to our often faulty judgment. Jesus' great life, death, and enduring wisdom proclaim the fact that our glorious judge is always speaking a word of eternal life (v. 50). Even though YHWH knows intimately the deficits and disappointments of our final measure, God loves us anyway.

SUZANNE WOOLSTON BOSSERT

---

3. C. H. Dodd, *The Interpretation of the Fourth Gospel* (Cambridge: Cambridge University Press, 1958), 211.

Rejection and Judgment (vv. 48–49). Here Jesus relates the rejection of himself and his words (*rhēmata*) to the one who judges (*krinonta*). In the last days, it is Jesus' word (*logos*) that will judge the one who rejects him and his words (*rhēmata*). This reality of being judged in the last days depicts both realized and futuristic eschatology. The former is indicated by the fact that the one who rejects Jesus is judged in the present, and the latter is reflected in the one who rejects Jesus and his words as the one who will be judged in the last days. Because of this rejection of Jesus and his words, the one who rejects will be judged not because of his or her deeds, but because of what she or he has rejected, which equates with judgment in the last or final days.

The Commandment Is Eternal Life (v. 50). Finally, Jesus exclaims, "I know" (*oida*) that God's command is eternal life (*zōē*, "simply the best for all eternity, including the present," my trans.). In this sense, in this Gospel the author reinterprets the Bible through the Christ event. That is, like Moses, Jesus knows that what God truly desires for humankind is abundant life (*zōē*; cf. John 10:10) rather than death. Jesus speaks only that which God commands, because Jesus is truly in touch with the ultimate plan of God and can claim a privileged knowledge of what God's divine plan entails. Thus, whatever Jesus says and reveals is exactly what the Father has directed him to say and reveal. He knows that God's plan is for all who believe in him to have and continue to experience abundant, full life throughout all eternity. Like Israel, for the author's audience to experience this life that God intended, they must adhere to the commandment of life (*zōē*) to live abundantly and fully (read, "authentically").

LARRY D. GEORGE

In verse 46 (and, by inference, v. 45—"whoever sees me"), the prevalent theme of light (belief) and darkness (unbelief) in the Gospel of John is again addressed. A different approach to this theme might be from the perspective of apophatic or negative theology. Medieval works like *The Dark Night of the Soul* by John of the Cross and the anonymous *The Cloud of Unknowing* and the twentieth-century work *Miracles* by C. S. Lewis exemplify discerning God from the negative (darkness, chaos, judgment, and doubt).

A helpful current writer on negative theology is Barbara Brown Taylor. In her essay "Redeeming the Darkness" she suggests that to walk by faith is to walk in the dark. The trust of faith in this heightened opaqueness allows us to discover another way of knowing God. She suggests that this can be a seeing, a knowing that can be deeper and more powerful than knowing God only through positive affirmations or experiences that might be described as light. Our trustful relationship with Jesus guides us into a deeper knowledge of and relationship with God the Father. Taylor, referring to 2 Corinthians 5:7, writes, "Plenty of us are walking by faith and not by sight. We are feeling our ways along here. A lot of our old landmarks are gone. A lot of our old bulbs have burned out. But while waiting . . . we could do worse than befriend this darkness that may be richer than it first appears."[3]

Perhaps we could consider experiences when we, by faith, find the light shining dimly in a darkness that seems overwhelming to us. How does faith help us to hope (or even witness) in the darkness of personal or community circumstances? How can we believe that the light, God's incarnate or spiritual presence, while seemingly "withdrawn from our world," is not overcome by the darkness? Perhaps it may be that we look for points of light, rather than the brilliance to which we once may have been accustomed; or, perhaps by spiritual openness we may discover the revelation of God's presence, incarnate or spiritual, in ways we have not previously perceived. In general, the preacher or teacher may ask the discerning question: "How do persons of faith deal with hope when life's circumstances demand disbelief?"

NATHAN D. BAXTER

3. Barbara Brown Taylor, "Redeeming the Darkness," *Christian Century*, November 28, 2011.

John 13:1–11

¹Now before the festival of the Passover, Jesus knew that his hour had come to depart from this world and go to the Father. Having loved his own who were in the world, he loved them to the end. ²The devil had already put it into the heart of Judas son of Simon Iscariot to betray him. And during supper ³Jesus, knowing that the Father had given all things into his hands, and that he had come from God and was going to God, ⁴got up from the table, took off his outer robe, and tied a towel around himself. ⁵Then he poured water into a basin and began to wash the disciples' feet and to wipe them with the towel that was tied around him. ⁶He came to Simon Peter, who said to him, "Lord, are you going to wash my feet?" ⁷Jesus answered, "You do not know now what I am doing, but later you will understand." ⁸Peter said to him, "You will never wash my feet." Jesus answered, "Unless I wash you, you have no share with me." ⁹Simon Peter said to him, "Lord, not my feet only but also my hands and my head!" ¹⁰Jesus said to him, "One who has bathed does not need to wash, except for the feet, but is entirely clean. And you are clean, though not all of you." ¹¹For he knew who was to betray him; for this reason he said, "Not all of you are clean."

Theological Perspective

The story of Jesus' washing his disciples' feet marks a significant turning point in the Gospel of John. After Jesus' self-revelation to the world through a series of signs as the One who comes from the Father, he now turns his gaze toward his return to God through the self-sacrificial act of the cross. The Gospel of John presents a Christology from above, in which Jesus acts with complete self-awareness and knowledge of God's plan (2:24). He is completely aware of the road that lies ahead and of its significance. This turning point in his journey on earth, the beginning of his return to the Father, is announced in the rather strange act of washing the feet of his disciples, his own whom he has loved in the world, and whom he loves "to the end" (v. 1).

Peter is approached first to have his feet washed, and he reacts incredulously: "Lord, are you going to wash my feet?" (v. 6). Peter's refusal suggests that the disciples (for there is no reason to presume that Peter is alone in his ignorance and surprise) did not share in Jesus' foreknowledge of the divine plan. Peter's reaction is natural and indeed, in a certain sense, just. After having revealed himself as the One who comes from the Father, as the One who is their Master, in this act Jesus chooses to do the work of a slave—very humble work that generally slaves of non-Jewish descent would perform. No wonder

Pastoral Perspective

With very few exceptions, we do not consider feet to be the most attractive parts of our bodies. For many of us, feet are functional. Feet are hardworking. Feet carry our weight, enable us to stand, point us in the direction we need to go. Feet allow us to walk, run, skip, hop, and jump. Because we use feet every day, all the time, they take quite a beating. We cram them into shoes that do not fit, stand on them for far too many hours at a time, and pound them into pavement in the quest for aerobic exercise. As a result, feet become disfigured with corns, calluses, and bunions. Feet are usually not a very pretty sight.

Yet feet are the object of wonder when a baby is born. "Look at that tiny foot!" we say, "Those tiny toenails!" When our eldest son was born, his feet made me think of a puppy. Just the size of them let me know that he was destined to be tall (not a big leap of faith, considering that my husband is 6'3"). It does not take long for feet to lose their charming qualities, though. Barefoot babies are adorable; barefoot adults, not so much.

We can know a lot about people from their feet, how they care for those feet, and even the type of shoes they wear. Are their toenails trimmed neatly, or uneven and ragged? Are there calluses, indicating long hours standing, or perhaps shoes that do not quite fit? What kind of shoes does a person wear?

Feasting on the Gospels

Exegetical Perspective

Scholars traditionally divide John's Gospel into two sections. Chapters 1–12 focus on Jesus' teachings and miracles and are often referred to as the Book of Signs. This first section opens with a prologue (1:1–18) that describes the entry of the Logos into the world and his rejection by his own people. The second part of this Gospel, chapters 13–21, is traditionally referred to as the Book of Glory. This Book of Glory begins with Jesus' farewell to his disciples (chaps. 13–17). Just as the Book of Signs opened with a prologue, so too the Book of Glory begins with a prologue (vv. 1–3). This prologue, in contrast to 1:1–18, focuses on the Word's departure from this world.

John 13:1 serves as an introductory statement, not only to the scene, but to the second half of the Fourth Gospel, by including several themes that will be central to the Book of Glory: Passover, Jesus' hour, Jesus' knowledge, Jesus' return to the Father, and Jesus' love for his disciples. The opening words set the scene in relation to the Jewish Passover; this takes place on the day of Preparation, just before the Passover festival, in contrast to the Synoptics, which have this Last Supper on the day of Passover. According to John, it was on this day of Preparation that "Jesus knew" that the hour of his departure had arrived. Several times in the Fourth Gospel, Jesus (or the narrator) notes that this hour has not yet come

Homiletical Perspective

John 13:1–11 is a tension-filled text. The tension is intense, palpable, and teeming with actions and expressions ripe for powerful proclamations. Tension arises on account of several notable expressions and happenings by Jesus and his disciples: (1) the expression that Jesus' "hour had come to depart from this world and go to the Father" signifies that his amply foreshadowed death is alarmingly close to coming to pass; (2) the devil himself (as opposed to other demons) has infiltrated Jesus' close-knit band of disciples by entering into Judas's heart, and Judas is soon to commit treason against the kingdom of heaven by betraying Jesus; (3) Jesus washes the feet of his disciples, making a complete break from the custom and authoritarian social structure of his day, initially horrifying Peter in the process of doing so; and (4) Jesus reveals that not only does he know that he will soon be betrayed; he also knows who among his disciples is going to betray him. In preaching this text, each point of tension is open for engagement through thoughtful exegesis.

Consider further the religious and cultural context of death that surrounds the Passover event from the passing over of the angel of death to the slaughtering of the Passover lamb (Exod. 12). The discussion of the nearness of Jesus' death in the context of the Passover symbolizes both the brutality and the

John 13:1–11

Theological Perspective

Peter responds as he does. Jesus' assurance that he will understand later does not satisfy Peter, who responds with an adamant, "You will never wash my feet" (v. 8). Given the humble nature of this service, Peter's refusal is the good and just response of a loyal follower of Jesus, an expression of his awareness of Jesus' authority and the respect of which he is worthy.

Jesus responds in a harsh manner, however: "Unless I wash you, you have no share with me" (v. 8). These words suggest that Peter's refusal, understandable as it might be from a human perspective, constitutes an obstacle to salvation. This is somewhat evocative of the Synoptic Jesus' strong rebuke, "Get behind me, Satan," in Matthew 16:23, when Peter refuses to accept the possibility of Jesus' death. Jesus' threatening response leads Peter to beg to have not only his feet washed but also his hands and head, but once again Peter gets it wrong. Jesus tells him that he is clean already and not in need of further washing, that indeed the disciples are all clean, except for one, a reference to the traitor Judas.

It seems obvious that their state of being clean here has nothing to do with the actual foot washing, but instead refers to a spiritual cleanliness that the betrayer does not share. There are textual and theological difficulties here, though. The shorter text, which does not have the phrase "except for the feet," clearly presents the foot washing as symbolic of the full bath, and hence of the spiritual washing of believers that will take place as a result of Jesus' death. Peter's request to have his hands and head washed as well thus appears to be simply foolish, indicating his lack of understanding about the complete and final cleansing that takes place in the blood of Jesus.

The longer (and current) text, however, has somewhat different theological implications. It counteracts a problematic tendency to assume spiritual perfection in the faithful by symbolizing the need for further spiritual cleansing even after the initial bath of salvation. A perfectionist soteriology would negate the need for the ethical teaching that follows in 13:12–20. Theologically, the longer text is to be preferred, as it is in line with the need for believers not only to receive grace from God but also to learn to live consistently in light of that grace. To put it in later theological terms, it leaves room for the teaching of sanctification that follows upon the justification brought by Christ.

More importantly, the text hints that this is indeed a turning point in Jesus' ministry: respect for the Jesus who had revealed himself as the One

Pastoral Perspective

Functional or fancy? Heels or high tops? Boots or Birkenstocks?

Only the Gospel of John tells the story of Jesus washing the disciples' feet at the Last Supper. The timing is strange, out of order. Jesus does not wash the disciples' feet when they first show up at the door. Instead, in the middle of that Passover feast, Jesus removes his cloak, wraps himself in a towel, pours water into a basin, and one by one washes the disciples' dirty feet. It catches them all off guard, as it does us, for the act of foot washing is not something we are expecting at this sacred supper.

How wonderful it is to have one's feet washed, after all that those feet have been through. Because the foot washing comes at an unexpected time, the disciples know immediately that this is something out of the ordinary. It is a remarkable act of tenderness at a point in time when the disciples need a little TLC. Like the woman who anoints and washes Jesus' feet, Jesus pauses at the cusp of his own anguish and tends to his flock. They will not soon forget what he does for them on that dark night.

Following the example of Jesus, we are called to tender acts, acts of servanthood, acts during which we focus on one person at a time and give that person our full attention. In her book *How to be a Friend to a Friend Who's Sick*, author Letty Cottin Pogrebin tells the tender story of Colette. Colette endured a grueling regimen of chemotherapy, during which time a cadre of fifteen faithful friends took her to and from appointments, sat with her, brought her meals, and provided care and comfort in whatever ways she needed. After her treatment concluded, Colette threw a buffet lunch to thank her friends. As everyone gathered with plates of food on their laps, Colette went around the room and gave a personal tribute to each friend, sharing how that friend had helped her in a particular way. "I found it so moving that she would choose to individualize her gratitude," Pogrebin writes, "when it would have been so much easier to just call us all together and say, 'Thanks, guys, for what you did.'"[1]

Colette's buffet lunch echoes the scene at the Last Supper. It is unexpected, tender, and empowering, all at the same time. One by one, Jesus knelt at the feet of each disciple and washed his feet. Did he speak individual words to each of the disciples, perhaps a whisper under his breath, a word or two of acknowledgment for the ways each had touched his

---

1. Letty Cottin Pogrebin, *How to be a Friend to a Friend Who's Sick* (New York: Public Affairs, 2013), 253.

(2:4; 7:30; 8:20). The arrival of this hour marks the end of Jesus' public ministry and the beginning of preparing for his departure.

The reference to Jesus' having loved his own "to the end" (*eis telos*, v. 1b) may be understood in two ways. First, *eis telos* may be a reference to the end of his life; thus, he loved his own all the way to his death. Second, this phrase may be translated "fully" or "to the utmost," which carries the sense of complete love. Elsewhere in the Fourth Gospel, the author seems to use double meanings to illustrate the multifaceted aspect of Jesus' teachings (e.g., 3:3–8). The same is likely true here, since by loving his own to his death, Jesus loves them fully. In contrast to this expression of love, though, verse 2 indicates that the opposite of love is also present in the room. The author indicates the active role of "the devil," who had put betraying Jesus into the heart of Judas, son of Simon Iscariot. Literally "to give over," *paradidōmi* refers to Judas's bringing a detachment of soldiers to the garden which Jesus frequented (18:1–3). This passing reference to betrayal and Judas prepares the reader for verses 10b–11, where cleanliness/membership in the Jesus community is connected with this betrayal.

Between these references to betrayal, however, Jesus, again "knowing" that his departure was drawing near, washes the disciples' feet. This act takes place "during the meal," which recalls an earlier meal at which Jesus' feet were anointed by Mary as preparation for his burial (12:1–8). Interestingly, at this earlier meal, Judas Iscariot is said to have challenged Mary's act; at that point the author notes that Judas was a thief and the one who was "about to betray" Jesus. Foot washing was an act of hospitality offered to guests at a meal, an act typically reserved for slaves or women, although on rare occasions it was done as an act of supreme love and devotion.[1] The verbs employed in verses 4–5 underscore the role of a slave. Jesus "got up" from the meal, "took off" his robe, "tied" a towel around himself, "poured water" into a basin, and "washed" the feet of his disciples.

Peter's challenge to Jesus in verse 6 illustrates that he does not understand this reversal of roles, perhaps thinking that he should be washing Jesus' feet. Jesus' response, that he would understand later, does not satisfy Peter, who intensifies his rejection in verse 8. Jesus' second response in verse 8b suggests this washing represents membership in the Jesus-following community. If Peter refuses to allow Jesus to wash his

---

1. John C. Thomas, *Footwashing in John 13 and the Johannine Community* (Sheffield, England: JSOT Press, 1991), 26–60.

purpose for the death that Jesus will soon experience. Jesus' humanity in this moment must not be overlooked during the preaching moment, as it is akin to the unshakable pain and sorrow that often accompany an anticipated and rapidly approaching death, something that many persons and families from all backgrounds and belief systems have had to experience, or may be presently experiencing, especially when faced with a terminal disease. That one need not suffer such an experience alone and that Jesus himself faced an inevitable, imminent death may prove comforting to those experiencing a similar reality.

Furthermore, regarding anticipated, unavoidable, and rapidly approaching death, a word of hope appears, in the text that Jesus "had come from God and was going [to return] to God" (v. 3b). This word can also provide hope for persons and families facing terminal illness or death in general. It does not explain away the pain or sorrow, but it inserts the hope of an eternity with God despite the pain and sorrow.

Betrayal, especially if enacted by someone whom one loves deeply, is a difficult pill to swallow. In reality, it is a pill many have to swallow. Thus the text provides a unique preaching moment to uplift all who have suffered from betrayal. Nothing in the betrayal or the impending death of Jesus can deny the fact that Jesus has come from God and is going to return to God. This too is a word of hope, for it notes that neither action by an evil spirit or humankind nor a threat against one's own life can reverse the truth of our creation by God or the final station of our eternal existence with God. The preacher can engage this text to restore hope in those who are having difficulty identifying hope in the midst of tragic occurrences that appear to be beyond their control.

Jesus is fairly consistent during his public ministry to challenge long-held social norms and mores. Here in this text, Jesus' action of washing the feet of his disciples challenges the widely held perceptions concerning power and authority. Jesus' action is a prophetic action that lends itself well to prophetic preaching. Those occupying positions of great power and influence over others were the most likely candidates to have their feet washed by their servants or their disciples. By washing the feet of his disciples, Jesus turns this expectation on its head, thus vividly modeling leadership as service to others. The preacher would do well to identify where Jesus' actions continue to challenge our present

John 13:1–11

Theological Perspective

coming from the Father can no longer be expressed simply in terms of humility toward him as their Master (as Peter does in verse 8); rather, it is expressed in terms of accepting the service he is about to render as he turns his gaze firmly toward the cross. It might be a bit of a stretch to interpret the waters of the foot washing here as directly referring to the waters of baptism (although the symbolic similarity is suggestive), but it is clear that the foot washing here symbolizes the salvation of the cross. This is indicated by Jesus' statement that unless Peter is washed by him, he will not have a share (inheritance) with him.

Jesus' humble service foreshadows the *kenōsis* (emptying) of the cross, where the one formerly revealed as the glorious One who comes from the Father will die a saving death. Indeed, a new reality is announced here, a reality in which human presuppositions about glory and power are turned on their head. The love that Jesus has for his followers leads to their incorporation into friendship with God. The Gospel writer introduces Jesus' act with a statement about the deep love he holds for his followers. His service to his disciples is neither the service of a slave to his master's guests, nor the condescending service of a master to his social inferiors as an act of charity; rather, it is the service of a friend.[1] It is an act of inclusion into an intimate friendship with God through his Son.

RACHEL SOPHIA BAARD

Pastoral Perspective

life? Perhaps no words were spoken, for just the act of washing each person's feet would have spoken volumes. There, on those feet, were the personal marks of that man's life; the calluses, corns, and bunions, the ragged toenails, the dirt of the day pressed deep into the cracked skin of feet that had walked mile upon mile over grassy hillsides and dry, dusty roads and the palm-strewn pathway into Jerusalem just a few short days before. Kneeling there and washing their feet, Jesus acknowledged in a very personal way how each of those men had walked with him, and the path that each was being asked to walk in the days and months and years ahead.

Jesus knew that all of those feet would head off in a variety of different directions. Some of the feet would walk away from him and straight to the authorities. Some of the feet would skedaddle off in terror at being associated with the one who was about to be crucified. Some of the feet would soon be treading saltwater, searching for fish. Some would go back out, barely touching the ground, to share the wonder of Easter morning.

Feet are not often beautiful, but on that night, twelve pairs of feet were treated with loving care. Twelve pairs of feet were pampered and scrubbed in an unexpected and remarkable way. Twelve pairs of feet were readied for the journey ahead.

One pair of feet was about to be pierced with nails.

KATHLEEN LONG BOSTROM

---

1. Sandra M. Schneiders, *Written That You May Believe: Encountering Jesus in the Fourth Gospel* (New York: Herder & Herder, 2003), 192–94.

feet, he has no "part" or "share" (*meros*, v. 8b) with Jesus. While *meros* seems to imply a sharing of the destiny of Jesus, including eternal life and possibly martyrdom,[2] at its very basic level, it implies that the one who rejects this washing is relegated to the status of an outsider, that is, no longer part of the group.

Once Peter understands that this washing is related to his membership and status in the group, he asks Jesus to wash his hands and head, which seems to imply a complete washing. Jesus responds that those who have already bathed do not need another washing, except for their feet. The two verbs in verse 10 (*louō* and *niptō*) imply two different types of washing, one a complete bath (*louō*) and the other a subsequent washing between full baths (*niptō*).[3] If this is the case, this foot washing represents a cleansing from postbaptismal sins (perhaps even the ones that the disciples are about to commit), thus maintaining one's membership in the Jesus community. In the section to follow (13:12–20), Jesus will instruct his disciples to offer this ceremony to others.

There is one, however, who has not been bathed and is thus not clean. This reminds the reader of the presence of the betrayer, who has not been cleansed. Being cleansed, that is, being a member of the community, involves loyalty. The one who betrays group loyalty is no longer a member of the community (cf. 1 John 2:19).

COLEMAN A. BAKER

notions of power and authority, as well as to propose new opportunities for the church to be in service to others.

This narrative is filled with actions of which the preacher must take notice. Jesus *gets up* from the table where he is seated with his disciples. Jesus *takes off* his outer robe. Jesus *ties* a towel around his frame. Jesus *pours* water into a basin. Jesus *washes* and *wipes* his disciples' feet. Every action in this text is taken by Jesus. Jesus' disciples are no more than beneficiaries of Jesus' actions. As it relates to being made clean, the actions necessary to achieve cleanliness are actions that are the sole possession of Jesus. That the work of salvation is solely the work of Jesus is worthy of being highlighted, through a focus on Jesus' bodily actions.

Peter's initial protest against Jesus' intention to wash his feet provides Jesus with the opportunity to respond with the claim and the promise of unity with his disciples. Yet another tension arises here, namely, the tension caused by misunderstanding another's intent. The text itself begins with a statement concerning the completeness of Jesus' love for those on the earth who are his own. This love is clearly manifested not only in Jesus' washing of his disciples' feet but also in his expressed desire to become one with his disciples, that his disciples may have a share of him. The preacher can engage the tension that may arise in not understanding what God is allowing to happen to one, even if what is happening is remarkably good, a tension to which many people can relate today.

This tension-filled text provides the preacher with seemingly innumerable opportunities to engage the pain and sorrow that can accompany the human experience related to betrayal and death, the Christian hope of unity, an eternity with Jesus on account of his selfless actions, and the opportunity to be like Jesus in prophetically challenging norms and mores that misguidedly support oppressive power structures. This narrative of a foot-washing Jesus in the context of Passover with death close at hand should provide for powerful preaching in all contexts.

MICHAEL W. WATERS

---

2. Ibid., 93–94.
3. See Thomas, *Footwashing*, 97–99. Thomas also notes that Seneca reports that early Romans washed only their arms and legs daily, because they got dirty in between their weekly full baths (*Moral Epistles to Lucilius* 86.12).

¹²After he had washed their feet, had put on his robe, and had returned to the table, he said to them, "Do you know what I have done to you? ¹³You call me Teacher and Lord—and you are right, for that is what I am. ¹⁴So if I, your Lord and Teacher, have washed your feet, you also ought to wash one another's feet. ¹⁵For I have set you an example, that you also should do as I have done to you. ¹⁶Very truly, I tell you, servants are not greater than their master, nor are messengers greater than the one who sent them. ¹⁷If you know these things, you are blessed if you do them. ¹⁸I am not speaking of all of you; I know whom I have chosen. But it is to fulfill the scripture, 'The one who ate my bread has lifted his heel against me.' ¹⁹I tell you this now, before it occurs, so that when it does occur, you may believe that I am he. ²⁰Very truly, I tell you, whoever receives one whom I send receives me; and whoever receives me receives him who sent me."

Theological Perspective

The second half of the story of Jesus' washing his disciples' feet is firmly ethical in tone, but it is important not to turn it into a mere moralistic tale of exhortation to engage in acts of charity. Having announced, through the symbolic act of foot washing, that a new reality is about to dawn, Jesus proceeds to teach his disciples what the practical aspects of this new reality are. He starts by testing them: "Do you know what I have done to you?" It is clear that far more than the physical act of cleaning their feet is the focus here; otherwise there would be no need for such an inquiry. Jesus' act foreshadows the atonement accomplished on the cross.

Although the humble act of foot washing in which Jesus had engaged just moments before hinted at the *kenōsis* (emptying) of the cross, the self-humiliation and indeed self-emptying of God in Jesus, he now reasserts his authority as their teacher and Lord. His ethical imperative lies precisely in that authority: if he, as their teacher and Lord, washes their feet, they also should wash each other's feet. After all, servants are not greater than their master, and if this action is not beneath him, then this action is certainly not beneath them. More significantly, the act of foot washing symbolizes the kind of community Jesus is establishing, the community that he wants to leave behind in the world

Pastoral Perspective

Has anyone ever washed your feet (since you became an adult, that is)? Washing a child's feet comes with the territory of parenting. Washing an adult's feet is caregiving of a very different sort. Having one's feet washed is by no means a usual occurrence for most people, unless one gets pedicures regularly. In fact, the best part about a pedicure might just be sinking our feet into warm, bubbling water and having someone take time to treat our feet with kindness.

Some illnesses, such as diabetes, require careful tending of the feet. Hip, knee, or leg surgery may make it impossible for a person to reach his or her own feet, thus necessitating help from another person in order to tend to one's extremities. Generally speaking, however, most people wash their own feet. It is doubtful that one's host or hostess greets one at a dinner party with a bowl of soapy water and a towel and asks one to kick off one's shoes and dip one's feet into said bowl. Most people in our North American culture would be horrified if that actually happened.

In Jesus' day, though, foot washing was common. It served as both a means of hygiene and an act of hospitality. Most travel was done on foot, sometimes with a pack animal. In the Middle East, where much of the landscape is rocky and dry, the journey literally kicked up a lot of dust. When guests arrived for a meal, the host offered water so visitors could wash

Exegetical Perspective

This passage is the continuation of the scene in 13:1–11, where Jesus gets up from the meal to perform a task typically reserved for slaves. The present passage is linked with 13:1–11, not only in reference to the washing of the disciples' feet but also in the emphasis on the betrayer (13:2, 10b–11, 18b–20), whose disloyalty to the group does not surprise Jesus. The betrayer's disloyalty stands in stark contrast to the loyalty of Jesus and the rest of the disciples, which is illustrated in humility and love.

Having just washed the disciples' feet and encountered resistance from Peter, Jesus uses the opportunity to elaborate upon his action, something he has done throughout the Fourth Gospel. Verses 12b–20, in the voice of Jesus, are presented as a brief explanatory discourse associated with the foot washing. With the foot washing complete, Jesus returns to his place at the table, an indication, perhaps, that the washing has taken place during the meal, rather than before it. As he returns to the table, Jesus asks rhetorically if they ("you" is second-person plural here) understand the significance of what he has just done to them. He has already said directly to Peter in verse 7 that Peter does not understand now but will at a later time.

His rhetorical question in verse 12 is followed by an explanation in verses 13–16. Jesus notes that

Homiletical Perspective

Jesus' actions and expressions while washing his disciples' feet possess deeper meaning for his disciples' calling and purpose. This deeper meaning is initially veiled from his disciples' understanding, and this lack of understanding creates an additional layer of tension in a setting already teeming with tension as the hour of Jesus' death draws near. Subsequently, after washing his disciples' feet, Jesus brings class into session to provide his disciples (and the readers of this text) greater clarity and understanding concerning his actions and expressions during the totality of the foot-washing event. These are important lessons that Jesus must teach, lessons that must be learned by his disciples and by Christian believers today. The preacher has an opportunity to impart a powerful word for his or her contemporary audience.

As is common with Jesus, his own actions provide the first lesson for his disciples. For lesson one, Jesus instructs his disciples to do as he has already done, to follow in the path of his own example. Jesus begins the lesson with an inquiry leveled at his disciples: "Do you know what I have done for you?" Of course the disciples do not know, and now Jesus must explain. Here we find evidence that God's actions at times are mysterious to us. Deeper or fuller understandings of God's actions sometimes come after the action has already been completed.

John 13:12–20

Theological Perspective

as he returns to the Father: a community of love and mutual service.

There seems to be a slight shift in meaning regarding foot washing here. Whereas Jesus' own act of washing his disciples' feet symbolizes the self-emptying and therefore the salvation that he will accomplish on the cross, he also presents it as an act of humility that should mark the life of the community he will leave behind in this world. The divine act becomes a human ethical imperative, but the kenotic element remains. The followers of a Master who acts in such a manner ought to have an ethos that differs from the kind of relationships one encounters in the world; they should have an ethos of self-emptying, of *kenōsis*, of regarding the other before oneself, of true mutual friendship and service. This is not the service of slaves to their masters, but the mutual service that friends lend one another (cf. 15:12–13).

The need for this ethical teaching is established in part by the addition of "except for the feet" in the longer version of verse 10, which suggests that those who have bathed already nevertheless need to wash their feet again. Although believers are endowed by the Spirit and are in no further need of redemption, due to the finality of Jesus' redemptive work, they still need further guidance in order to live the Christian life and to become increasingly more like their Master. The community of mutual love established by the cross ought to live a life of grateful and constant acceptance of that love. More than that, they are to emulate the love that Jesus has for his disciples in their actions toward one another.

Jesus' teaching of his disciples shifts in an ominous direction when Jesus excludes the betrayer from the mutual love of the new community. Jesus' foreknowledge is once again affirmed: he knows not only what is lying ahead for himself but also what role the betrayer will play in these events. Some commentators tend to focus on Peter's reaction to Jesus' act of service as symbolic of human resistance to love; but Peter, although bumbling and ignorant at times, is eager to be part of the community of love. The one who truly symbolizes resistance to love is Judas. Despite having journeyed through this world with the One who had come from the Father, he is the one who is about to betray Jesus, who is not clean, and who is therefore excluded from the community of love.

There is a hint of the concept of election in verse 18 when Jesus states that he does not speak of all of his disciples when he gives them his ethical teaching of love, for he knows whom he has chosen. One should tread carefully here, to avoid reading some

Pastoral Perspective

their own feet. If one had servants, it was their job to provide this service. Foot washing and hospitality went hand in hand (dare we say "foot in foot"?).

Jesus added a new dimension to this common act of hospitality. He provided the water and towels, but then, even though he was the host of the meal, he was the one to kneel before the disciples and to wash their filthy feet. Peter was appalled, but Jesus quickly dispelled his refusal to allow Jesus to wash his feet. "You may not understand," Jesus told him, "but trust me, this is not a luxury; it is a requirement."

After Jesus finished, he re-dressed, returned to the table, and then attempted to explain what he had done. This is the kind of service to which you are called, he told the disciples: you are not only fishermen but foot-washers. You are to follow my example and to be servants of those whom you serve in my name. In the washing of feet, in serving others as Jesus had served them, the disciples were drawn into an act of kindness that allowed them to share the fullness of Jesus' ministry. One who does not take the role of servant cannot truly be called a follower of Jesus.

Herb was a medical missionary in Africa for many years. He had all the necessary medical training it took to be a licensed physician, and he practiced medicine and healing both in Africa and then, later, in the United States. When Herb was working at a Chicago hospital and putting himself through medical school, he met a wonderful man, Chaplain Lily. Many of the people who came into the hospital were the poorest of the poor, so Pastor Lily carried his Bible in one hand and a pair of nail clippers in the other. As he made his daily rounds, he offered to clip the patients' toenails. Some of the people had not bathed in eons; some did not even own a pair of shoes; but no matter what state of disrepair their feet were in, Chaplain Lily offered to clip their toenails.

Moved by the chaplain's example, Herb started carrying a pair of nail clippers in his pocket wherever he went. When visiting a patient, Herb brought out his nail clippers. Many of the people he visited were older or infirm and could not tend to their own feet, so Herb did. Herb trimmed thousands and thousands of rough, ragged, thick, dirty toenails. He continued doing this in his retirement. For many people, it was the one act of kindness offered to them, a job even family members often hesitated to perform.

After he became critically ill himself, Herb clipped toenails until he could no longer do so. Then others stepped in. After Herb's death, his family gave out nail clippers to members of their church and

the disciples correctly refer to him as "teacher" (*didaskalos*) and "lord" (*kyrios*), titles that serve to highlight Jesus' authority and honor.[1] If Jesus, their Lord and teacher, has washed their feet, they should also offer this washing to one another. Given Jesus' interpretation of the washing in verse 10, namely, that this represents forgiveness for postbaptismal sins, perhaps the obligatory washing of one another's feet is, at least partially, meant to suggest forgiveness among those who follow Jesus. Jesus' action—washing the disciples' feet as a sign of forgiveness for postbaptismal sin—serves as an "example" (*hypodeigma*, v. 15a) of something that the disciples should now do for one another. The disciples are instructed to act in precisely the same manner that Jesus has just acted. While some have understood this to refer to foot washing in particular, the language of "example" and "as I have done for you" suggests that the disciples should follow Jesus' example in extending forgiveness to those within the community who have already been washed.[2]

Having given some explanation of the significance of the act he has just performed, Jesus illustrates why they should follow his example by citing two relational realities. Slaves are not greater than their masters, and messengers are not greater than those who send them. This is to say that slaves and messengers are not above doing the things that their masters and senders have done. If Jesus, their Master and sender, has subverted traditional social norms in an act of love and forgiveness, they, the slaves and messengers, must also.

Now that Jesus has provided an explanation about the significance of the act, the disciples should "know" what he did to them (v. 12). Now, if they know, they are expected to act. Just as in verse 8 membership (*meros*, NRSV "share") in the community is dependent upon receiving the foot washing, here being blessed (*makarios*, v. 17) is dependent upon the disciples' carrying out this foot washing for one another.

Following the exhortation to wash one another's feet, Jesus returns to a subject mentioned in the previous section, the betrayer (13:2, 10b–11). In 13:10–11, Jesus distinguishes between the disciples and the betrayer, Judas (13:2). "Not speaking of all of you" (v. 18a) refers directly to the "blessing" for

The preacher of this text might engage the mysteries of God as just that—mysteries—and in so doing, quell the fears or the feelings of spiritual inadequacy that often accompany not having a clear understanding of what God is doing or of what God is calling one to do. Even when one does not know what to do, doing what Jesus did is never a bad starting point.

For lesson two, Jesus affirms for his disciples what his actions have shown: that he is teacher and Lord. The foot-washing event serves as Jesus' final witness to his disciples before his death on the cross that he is equal to God and that he is the teacher of all because he possesses the knowledge of all (cf. 2:24). Here, the text presents the preacher with the opportunity likewise to affirm for the congregation how Jesus' actions and expressions continue to show today that Jesus is both teacher and Lord.

Lesson three is a lesson in servant leadership. Jesus places the foot-washing event in the context of a demonstration of who he is and who he is calling his disciples to be. Jesus instructs his disciples to do as he has done as teacher and Lord. As teacher and Lord, Jesus first humbles himself to wash their feet. The disciples are to humble themselves as Jesus did and wash each other's feet. The disciples are not greater than Jesus, for Jesus is their teacher and Jesus is Lord over all. If Jesus can humble himself, the disciples must certainly humble themselves as well, for humility in service is imperative for faithful service in the kingdom of heaven. The preacher would do well to emphasize that in the kingdom of heaven, the first are last, and the last are first, and that no one is greater in the kingdom of heaven than he or she who first serves others.

Jesus provides his disciples with a fourth lesson: possessing knowledge of what to do is of no value unless one endeavors to do what one knows, a knowledge based upon Jesus' example. Jesus extends this lesson by expressing to his disciples that if they actively put into practice the things that they know to do, guided by Jesus' own example, they will be blessed for doing so. This lesson is echoed throughout Scripture, from the instruction that "obedience is better than sacrifice" (1 Sam. 15:22) to the statement that "faith without works is dead" (Jas. 2:17). Here the preacher can emphasize that the greatest blessings from God come when endeavoring to follow Jesus' own example.

As a fifth lesson, Jesus instructs his disciples that whoever receives those whom Jesus sends actually receives Jesus himself, and those who receive Jesus receive the Father. This is an important lesson,

1. John C. Thomas, *Footwashing in John 13 and the Johannine Community* (Sheffield, England: JSOT Press, 1991), 108. Also see John Carlson Stube, *A Graeco-Roman Rhetorical Reading of the Farewell Discourse* (London: T. & T. Clark, 2006), 90.

2. Charles Talbert, *Reading John: A Literary and Theological Commentary on the Fourth Gospels and the Johannine Epistles* (New York: Crossroad, 1992), 194.

John 13:12–20

Theological Perspective

concept of double predestination into this passage. Jesus' words seem to be directed at his chosen disciples: he knows whom he has chosen to be his followers, which does not necessarily mean that Judas in turn is chosen to be the betrayer. Indeed, one should be careful not to read the doctrine of predestination into this passage at all. Rather, the text is emphasizing that even Judas's betrayal does not fall outside of the scope of Jesus' foreknowledge. Jesus knows his followers, and he knows exactly what is going on in their hearts and minds. He knows his community well.

The section ends with yet another shift in emphasis when Jesus assures his disciples that whoever receives those whom he has sent also receives him, and thereby receives the Father. Surprising and loosely connected as this verse might seem at first, it does underscore the fact that as Jesus prepares for his final earthly journey, he focuses on the community that he leaves behind. He makes them his own through his service on the cross, as symbolized by his act of humbly washing their feet, and commands them likewise to serve each other, since they are not, after all, more important than their Master. He also empowers them to be the ones who will bring others into the community of love, and thereby bring others into communion with the Father. In short, those whom he has chosen (excepting Judas, the one who chooses to exit the community of love through his betrayal) will now embody him in this world as he goes back to the Father. They become, indeed, the household of God.

RACHEL SOPHIA BAARD

Pastoral Perspective

other friends, along with a note sharing their father's story, and encouraged people to carry the clippers and continue Herb's ministry.

Coffee, conversation, clipping. A small act of kindness. A great example of being a foot-washer for Jesus.

The disciples would never forget what Jesus did for them on that dark and holy night. Washing their feet was an object lesson of the most profound sort. They may not have completely understood what Jesus was trying to tell them, but Jesus trusted that they would figure it out, once they were serving as his body in the world, once they were the hands and heart and voices—and feet—of their Savior.

How are you called to be a foot-washer for Jesus? How do you serve in the name of the servant? Perhaps you could volunteer your time on a busy weekday evening to work at the homeless shelter or spend one Saturday afternoon a month teaching literacy skills to adults who never had the chance to learn how to read and write. Get your own feet dirty by walking for arthritis, so people who cannot walk themselves have an advocate in their court. At the very least, you could buy a gift certificate for a pedicure from a local nail salon as a welcome-home present to give to an elderly person following a hospital stay, and then volunteer to drive that person and sit with him as he gets his feet tended to.

Perhaps we should all carry a pair of nail clippers in our pocket or purse.

KATHLEEN LONG BOSTROM

understanding and following Jesus' example of foot washing, but may also point back to the obligatory service in verses 14–15. If both the blessing and the exhortation from verses 14–15 are in view here, then Jesus' words, "I am not speaking of all of you," mean that the betrayer will not enjoy the blessing that results from obedience to Jesus' exhortation; nor is he included in the exhortation itself.

The betrayer, as indicated in verse 18b, will soon display ultimate disloyalty to Jesus and the group. Such disloyalty is expressed in the citation of Psalm 41:9, which can be taken to mean that a member of my group will utterly dishonor me.[3] In an ironic twist, one of the feet that Jesus has just washed is now pictured as having been raised against him. As is characteristic of Jesus in the Fourth Gospel, he is not taken by surprise by these actions (2:24). John's Jesus uses the "I am" sayings to connect himself with the presence of Israel's God (6:35–48; 8:12; 9:5; 10:7–9, 11–14; 11:25; 14:6; 15:1–5), which is further demonstrated here by Jesus' exposing the betrayer before the act of betrayal.

At first glance, verse 20 appears to interrupt the flow of thought from verse 19 to verse 21. There is a connection to verse 16, though, where the theme of being sent is first raised in this scene. This verse not only echoes the themes of mission and "being sent" from verse 16; it also prepares the audience for the continued theme of sending in the rest of the Fourth Gospel, which climaxes in 20:21: "Jesus said to them again, 'Peace be with you. As the Father has sent me, so I send you.'" This passage, then, ends by emphasizing Jesus' sending of the disciples on mission, to act in the same manner toward one another that he has just acted toward them.

COLEMAN A. BAKER

because soon Jesus will no longer be physically present with his disciples. His presence will still be made known through the Paraclete in his disciples' actions and expressions, though, especially in their service to others. Here in Jesus' expression, the unity between him and his disciples is made complete. Jesus' ultimate desire for both his ancient and his modern disciples is that we become one with him, even as he is one with the Father. Here the preacher has an opportunity to affirm not only Jesus' imperative that we follow his example, but also that in so doing we become unified with him.

Jesus again addresses his betrayal, but notes that there is a deeper meaning and purpose in the betrayal: that Scripture be fulfilled. This is the sixth and final lesson taught by Jesus to his disciples after the foot-washing event. Even in a betrayal, a betrayal enacted by the devil himself (13:2), Scripture will still be fulfilled. Jesus again affirms his lordship, but further still, Jesus affirms for his disciples that there is no action of opposition against the kingdom of heaven that can thwart the fulfillment of God's calling and purpose for Jesus or for those who are one with Jesus. The hope of the fulfillment of Scripture in the face of opposition invites the preacher's active proclamation to encourage and strengthen the faithful.

With Jesus, class is always in session. From the foot-washing action, expressions, and teachings of Jesus, Jesus' disciples emerge all the wiser. Jesus ensures that because of his humble example and his teachings, his disciples will possess a greater understanding of the meaning of his washing their feet and, as a result, they will possess a greater understanding of who Jesus is and of who Jesus has called his disciples to be.

MICHAEL W. WATERS

---

3. Bruce Malina and Richard Rohrbaugh, *Social-Science Commentary on the Gospel of John* (Minneapolis: Fortress Press, 1998), 224.

John 13:21–30

²¹After saying this Jesus was troubled in spirit, and declared, "Very truly, I tell you, one of you will betray me." ²²The disciples looked at one another, uncertain of whom he was speaking. ²³ One of his disciples—the one whom Jesus loved—was reclining next to him; ²⁴Simon Peter therefore motioned to him to ask Jesus of whom he was speaking. ²⁵So while reclining next to Jesus, he asked him, "Lord, who is it?" ²⁶Jesus answered, "It is the one to whom I give this piece of bread when I have dipped it in the dish." So when he had dipped the piece of bread, he gave it to Judas son of Simon Iscariot. ²⁷After he received the piece of bread, Satan entered into him. Jesus said to him, "Do quickly what you are going to do." ²⁸Now no one at the table knew why he said this to him. ²⁹Some thought that, because Judas had the common purse, Jesus was telling him, "Buy what we need for the festival"; or, that he should give something to the poor. ³⁰So, after receiving the piece of bread, he immediately went out. And it was night.

Theological Perspective

Theology has a way of juxtaposing realities we would rather not address. A case in point is this passage from John, where the theological tensions are persistent and palpable. Side by side are the disciple whom Jesus loved and the disciple who will betray Jesus. John 13:23 is the first introduction to the Beloved Disciple. He has never appeared in the Gospel before this point, yet he is abundantly loved by Jesus. Why here? Why now? The contrast between the two disciples, one who lies on the bosom of Jesus, and one who exits into the realm of darkness from the community he has known for three years, should be striking. This passage holds together the painful reality of abiding and abandonment, of dedication and departure, of relationship and reality.

The Beloved Disciple in the Gospel of John is not a stick figure who illustrates devotion to Jesus. The Beloved Disciple is each and every one of us. The Gospel of John insists, from the very beginning, that anyone who hears, reads, or encounters the stories narrated in this Gospel has the potential to be the disciple resting next to Jesus, reclining on him—an incredibly intimate image. At the same time, we all have the potential to be Judas too, the one who goes to the dark side, overtaken by unbelief. For John, this is a theological climax, a theological question, a theological moment of urgency. The Beloved

Pastoral Perspective

This passage portrays a community in crisis, a tableau of a family system, a fragile ecosystem, and perhaps a template for a congregation in transition.

The scene opens on the heels of Jesus' announcement that someone will "lift his heel" against him (13:18). Jesus is haunted by the presence of this "heel," who undoubtedly contributes to his troubled spirit. He faces the implosion of his network as the betrayer is exposed.

We all live in this tension at the table (the Lord's Table, the dinner table, the boardroom table) wondering, "Who will it be? Who will get caught? Who will transgress and not get caught?" In communities where a politician gets slapped on the wrist for corruption, a pastor leaves a church with a trail of misconduct behind, a corporation is bailed out, or an abusive spouse is reported, the system shivers as it adjusts to the betrayal of the common trust. One could preach at the table on this breath-holding that stymies our communities because we are wondering who the "heel" is. Because there is always a heel. Sometimes the heel is not the Judas next to us but the Judas within us.

One way to explore this passage is to enter the scene from different perspectives, as in an Ignatian reading of Scripture.[1] As one might study an

1. For an introduction to Ignatian reading of Scripture, see http://www.ignatianspirituality.com; accessed May 1, 2013.

Feasting on the Gospels

Exegetical Perspective

In the Last Supper Jesus washed the disciples' feet and foretold his betrayal (13:1–20). Then John 13:21–30 depicts the disciples' anxious reactions, featuring the Beloved Disciple and Judas.

This pericope begins, "After saying this Jesus was troubled in spirit" (v. 21). What did Jesus say earlier? While explaining to Peter why his feet needed washing, Jesus said to the disciples: "You are clean, though not all of you" (13:10), to which the narrator adds: "For he knew who was to betray him" (13:11). Again Jesus said: "I am not speaking of all of you; I know whom I have chosen. But it is to fulfill the scripture, 'The one who ate my bread has lifted his heel against me'" (13:18; quoting Ps. 41:9). Clearly, the betrayal by Judas weighs down Jesus' spirit. Judas was a disciple, close to him and trusted with the common purse. Nothing can be more hurtful than the back-stabbing by a loved one. No wonder Jesus felt distressed.

Why did Jesus tell his disciples about the traitor ahead of time? Four reasons are noteworthy. The first is to fulfill the prophecy of the Scripture (13:18) and prove that everything, even conspiracy, is under God's providence. The second is to fulfill Jesus' prophecy so that the disciples may believe Jesus is the Messiah when his words come true (13:19). The third is to show Jesus had prior knowledge but did

Homiletical Perspective

In the midst of shadows and light, basin and towel, food and drink, this passage is usually viewed through the narrow lens of the impending crucifixion. Although such a focus accurately reflects John's sober intent, it runs the risk of losing its sharp and demanding edge when we preach as if Jesus is already on the cross. He is not! Jesus is very much alive in this passage: troubled, testifying, and even offering food to his betrayer! In so doing, he offers us a radically different way to live and move in our tumultuous world. Jesus shows us how to love and serve in uncertain times, when the night has come.

As we invite congregants into the text, we first notice a troubled Jesus, who unabashedly declares (*martyreō*, "witness") that someone is about to betray him (v. 21). In the midst of mounting tension, Jesus does not shrink from truthful testifying. He does not rely on rigid stoicism, hoping that troubles will disintegrate if he keeps a stiff upper lip; neither does he demonstrate a languid trust, assuming that if he resolutely hopes for the best, then the best will surely come. Instead, Jesus clearly reveals that there are powers to be unmasked and truths to be unveiled in the midst of profound tension and tumult. If we choose to preach around this theme, we will do well to wonder aloud about how we can best serve as faithful witnesses in the midst of our own particular

Theological Perspective

Disciple and Judas illustrate in only nine verses the possible reactions to Jesus.

The theological difficulty in this passage is that Judas, a supposed insider, does not get it, yet even a cursory glance of the entirety of John's Gospel intimates that Judas's betrayal was known way before now (6:64). Is he just a pawn in God's Christology? Is the Gospel of John only an exercise in theological manipulation?

Theological interpretation of this passage demands a serious analysis of this juxtaposition. In only a few verses, John can hold together what discipleship looks like with what discipleship sorely lacks. The disciple whom Jesus loves here must be understood through the lens of the prologue to John's Gospel, specifically 1:18, where the one and only God, Jesus, rests on the bosom of the Father. The only other time in the entire Gospel of John that the term "bosom" is used is in 13:23. In other words, the relationship that has been described between Jesus and the Father is the very same relationship that exists between the believer and Jesus. It is this relationship, evidenced by the closeness between the disciple whom Jesus loved and Jesus, that is put in contrast with Judas. This is a critical point in determining what is at stake theologically in having these two characters side by side here in the Gospel.

Judas's betrayal will not be handing Jesus over to be arrested. Jesus will come out of the garden, thereby initiating his own arrest. To betray Jesus is, rather, to disbelieve. This correlation is made clearly the first time that Judas is introduced in the narrative: "'But among you there are some who do not believe.' For Jesus knew from the first who were the ones that did not believe, and who was the one that would betray him" (6:64). In the end, betrayal as unbelief is equivalent to not being in relationship with Jesus. This is at the heart of the comparison between the Beloved Disciple and Judas. The Beloved Disciple demonstrates what a relationship with Jesus looks like. In contrast, Judas's exit into the night highlights his separation and, ultimately, the profound absence of relationship.

There is little theological wiggle room here. Either you believe in Jesus, the light of the world, or you do not and find yourself on the dark side. Judas has crossed over, and there is no turning back. There will be no mention of Judas again until he accompanies the Roman soldiers and the police representing the chief priests and the Pharisees to the garden to arrest Jesus. Judas is now outside of the fold, no longer a disciple, no longer a sheep who knows the voice of

Pastoral Perspective

ecosystem by simulating and testing the interactions, reactions, and subsystems that form it, the Ignatian method invites testing the story by becoming a part of it and experimenting with the various parts of the system.

First, ask what it feels like to be Judas here. Feel sweat beading on your brow. Smell the other disciples' fear. Feel your heart racing. Touch your palms, imagining the heft of the coins of betrayal. Pierce your heart as you look one last time at Jesus.

What is it like to be Jesus in this family portrait? Sense the butterflies in your belly, as you alone know what lies ahead. Look at, and through, the disciples surrounding and astounding you with their ignorance. Taste the bitterness of betrayal and the gall of being misunderstood.

Now step into Simon Peter's shoes. Brush away cobwebs of self-doubt that make you think you might be the guilty one. Silence the voices that ask if your investment in these past years was worthwhile. Listen to the rustling as Satan enters one of your friends with a swift sleight of hand, turning Judas into a name that will always be associated with betrayal. Staunch the tide of tears rising to your eyes because you begin to see, dimly, in a mirror.

Putting ourselves into the scene holds a mirror up to us. The Ignatian method of entering the text makes this story not only about Jesus and his disciples but also about the conflict-ridden city council meeting or the contentious board or session meeting at church. Sensing the fear and betrayal in this system feels like a family meeting in the funeral home or the lawyer's office after the death of a loved one. Isolating Simon Peter's lack of awareness gives us a clue to ways the first world is oblivious to its betrayals of the rest of the planet through egregious economic policies, energy consumption, and elephantine debt. As the "butterfly effect" reveals the interconnectedness of every action on the planet, the butterflies in Jesus' belly forecast a series of life-changing, world-altering events. Consider the systems surrounding you, and analyze the various players, the impact of their actions, and the reaction of the whole ecosystem.

Much as a system does not change overnight but shows signs of change, the Gospel of John offers fair warning of betrayal. One could track this with the careful eye of a researcher (teaching a Bible study) or with the creativity of a youth group "treasure" hunt (guiding participants to the trail of breadcrumbs left by the Gospel storyteller) or in a sermon examining each step of the journey as a detective might

Exegetical Perspective

not dodge the betrayal, because the Son obeys the Father's will, even unto death. The fourth is to show that Jesus was in control of his destiny. He was not a political victim, nor was his death a mere accident. Rather, he embraced his death as glory, so that his believers can receive eternal life.

How did the disciples respond to Jesus' allegation? All of them felt perplexed (v. 22), because everyone was a suspect, and no one knew who it was. Peter was so anxious that he motioned to a disciple to ask Jesus. This anonymous disciple, dubbed "the one whom Jesus loved," appears so named for the first time (v. 23) and again in 19:26–27; 20:1–10; 21:7, 20–24. He must have had a close relationship with Jesus, because he reclined next to Jesus, able to lean back and talk to him. In a *triclinium*, a banquet hall with long tables along three sides of the room, the seat next to Jesus at the central table is a position of honor. The Greek for "reclining next to Jesus" literally means "leaning back against Jesus' chest." Even though there is no scholarly consensus concerning his identity (speculation includes son of Zebedee, John Mark, and Lazarus),[1] it is clear that he was a witness to Jesus' Last Supper, crucifixion, resurrection, and post-Easter appearances. While on the cross Jesus entrusted his mother to him. He outran Peter to the tomb and immediately believed. Jesus defended him while predicting Peter's martyrdom. He is the hero of faith and the source of tradition for the Johannine community.[2]

Answering his question, Jesus said that the one to whom he gave a piece of bread dipped in the dish was the traitor (v. 26). It is not clear whether the dipped bread is a symbol of Jesus' body stained with blood, but the Johannine community might associate it with the eucharistic bread. The thought that fellow believers who have shared the same body and blood of Jesus might succumb to temptations or pressures and betray their brothers and sisters to the Roman authorities would be a heavy burden to bear, as it was to Jesus. What happened to Judas might also serve as a warning that anyone could fall prey to Satan and become a traitor.

As treasurer Judas had to be well beloved and trusted by the disciples, so much so that, even though Jesus had identified him as the traitor, other disciples could not believe it (v. 28). They still thought the best of him, thinking that he might be

1. James Charlesworth, *The Beloved Disciple: Whose Witness Validates the Gospel of John?* (Valley Forge, PA: Trinity, 1995), 127–224.
2. Raymond Brown, *An Introduction to the Gospel of John*, ed. Francis Moloney (New York: Doubleday, 2003), 175–99.

Homiletical Perspective

tensions. A careful blend of prophetic courage and pastoral sensitivity will certainly be required!

Next, we notice that Jesus' testifying leads to a clarifying question by the Beloved Disciple: "Lord, who is it?" (v. 25). Truth-telling in all its forms ultimately leads to the searching of souls and the birthing of questions. What would our congregations look like if we began to grow more comfortable with— and committed to—asking rigorous questions from the pulpit? As we reflect on Peter's response, clarifying to be sure, but also borne of blame and fear, we may consider inviting our listeners to think carefully about how we can reframe our typical, reactive questions during moments of stress and fear into more reflective and action-oriented questions, such as the following:

> "How can we help?"
> "What can we do differently so the same result does not happen again?"
> "If we cannot change this situation, how can we learn from it while loving God and one another?"

Jesus' unambiguous response to the Beloved Disciple's question exposes truth and confronts evil: "It is the one to whom I give this piece of bread when I have dipped it in the dish" (v. 26). This is no neat dismantling of "the enemy," however. As Jesus makes his claim, he hands the carefully dipped bread to Judas as a definitive sign of both friendship and hospitality. Jesus, the bread of life, literally and figuratively feeds his betrayer. This subversive sharing turns our usual understandings of friend and enemy upside down. As Jesus' disciples, we cannot help but pay attention to these subtle acts and, whenever possible, emulate them with creativity, compassion, and boldness. "Preach the gospel at all times," the adage goes. "If necessary, use words."[1]

We would do well to invite listeners to notice that when Jesus boldly shares bread, Satan enters Judas. It is no longer Judas who acts, but Satan who acts in him. John's apt description of Satan's entry into Judas reminds us that evil makes us less ourselves, causing our God-given identities to diminish until we are mere shadows of what we could be, preferring the darkness to the light of day (see 3:19–20).

John's repeated delineation of good and evil throughout the text forces another question: are we to mirror his approach, drawing rigid lines in the sand in our own communities around membership

1. Although widely attributed to Francis of Assisi, this particular saying has not been found among his writings.

John 13:21–30

Theological Perspective

the Good Shepherd. This should create some significant theological angst. The theological ante is upped when we begin to ask the question "why?" when it comes to Judas.

Another character not to overlook is Satan. There seems to be a cosmological battle here between good and evil, between God and the devil, between life and death. The Fourth Evangelist seems to indicate that the reason for the betrayal of Judas is evil, simple as that; yet evil is not simple. It is a complex and complicated force, as difficult to understand, describe, or determine as God. The Gospel of John makes no attempt to clarify the presence, power, and potency of evil. Rather, after Judas comes to the garden, we never hear from him again, ever. There are no rationalizations, justifications, or explanations for Judas, nor are there any stories that narrate what happened to him as a result. We are left only with our questions and perhaps even our despair.

Theology is incredibly complicated, yet we allow texts and traditions to determine biblical and homiletical claims, regardless of real-life realities. To hold both Judas and the believers of John 13:21–30 in the same sermon or Bible study will necessitate a willingness to live with ambiguity, to accept that perhaps a response to God according to this text may really be the choice of the listener and could very well end up in a ministry to those who have become so placated by the gospel that there is nothing that motivates them going forward. A sermon or study that tends the theological complexities and incongruities of this passage will not endeavor to solve the discomfort for the congregation. Rather, it will tell the truth about what it means to believe in Jesus and call for a decision that some may not want to make.

KAROLINE M. LEWIS

Pastoral Perspective

affix note cards to a bulletin board (by tracing the clues that Judas—or Jesus or Simon Peter—gives us). Remember that earlier Judas complained about the costly perfume (12:4–5). Building the character of Judas as the one who would betray Jesus, the Gospel writer comments, "Not because he cared about the poor, but because he was a thief" (12:6). In the same way we witness Jesus' steady march toward Jerusalem, we see the inexorable march toward Judas's betrayal in John 12 and 13. Explore those clues.

A close reading of the text in a Bible study, a game of clues, or a sermon tracing betrayal can hone our ability to recognize warning signals: lake levels dropping, church attendance wavering, commitment flagging, fabric fraying in a family. Such practices can help us cultivate the spiritual discipline of mindfulness, wakeful attentiveness to the signs of crumbling—or signs of growth—among the disciples in our midst.

Using this Scripture as a template for our systems, learn from the crumbling relationships here. The infrastructure is breaking as trust is broken between Jesus and Judas. The web trembles as Judas races out the door and Peter clings to silken strands of hope. Be awake to the way your systems are telegraphing changes—negative and positive—and be ready to respond, improve, improvise, and heal. You will recognize the signs. Like your stomach rumbling at an 11:00 a.m. meeting, your church will make grumbling noises when it is hungry for spiritual nourishment. Like lightning flashes over a distant mesa when the sky overhead is still clear, signs of trouble in the family or community or the world tip us off to problems ahead. Like Simon Peter, we hear and see and feel something coming, but we just look away or believe what we want to believe.

Think how Jesus might have felt, knowing that one of his cohort would betray him. No wonder he tells Judas, "Do quickly what you are going to do" (v. 27). He is ready to rip the bandage off quickly, with minimal impact to the community! This strategy may work in your system too. The Gospel pericope ends with a sense of urgency: "And it was night."

Night is coming; pay attention to the signs.

LAURA A. LOVING

going out to buy things for the festival or to give alms to the poor, following a custom of the Passover (v. 29). It is not easy to admit that a good person can turn to evil, but only God knows the secrets of human hearts.

One verse concerning Judas is important to note: "Jesus said to Judas, 'Do quickly what you are going to do'" (v. 27b). It was used by some gnostics in later centuries as an evidence to argue that Judas followed Jesus' order to hand him over to the high priest, so that God's salvation could be carried out. In their revisionist view, Judas was Jesus' most trusted disciple, who had the esoteric knowledge of God's plan and was willing to bear the stigma of traitor for Jesus (*The Gospel of Judas* 56 reads, "But you will exceed all of them. For you will sacrifice the man that clothes me").[3] This view is totally debunked, however, by verse 27a, which reads, "After he received the piece of bread, Satan entered into him." Judas betrayed Jesus because of his association with Satan (see also 13:2). He became Satan's accomplice; he should take the blame.

It is no surprise that this pericope ends with "And it was night" (v. 30). In the Gospel of John, night is a symbol of darkness, ignorance, sin, and anything against God. "The light shines in the darkness, and the darkness did not overcome it" (1:5). Nicodemus visited Jesus at night; he did not understand Jesus' word about birth from above (3:2). In contrast, the Samaritan woman met Jesus at noon; she believed Jesus to be the Messiah and led the city of Sychar to confess him as Savior of the world (4:6). Judas's betrayal happened at night, but at dawn Jesus rose from the dead. Night will not prevail.

JOHN YIEH

requirements, theological viewpoints, and stewardship practices, to name just a few possibilities? Reflecting on the ways in which our current contexts both mirror John's Middle Eastern world and deviate from it will be a helpful practice as we find our unique voices. In an era of denominational bickering and congregational conflict, would our congregations and communities be better served by humility and honesty, acknowledging our tendency to demonize those with whom we disagree?

Finally, it may be helpful to remind our congregants that all of this testifying and questioning, sharing of bread, and betraying of trust occurs during a meal shared by Jesus' intimates. Although those gathered are his closest companions, they do not see what is happening before their very eyes! The disciples' confusion is obvious, and their interpretations run the gamut, some assuming that more grocery shopping is in order, while others assume that money is to be given to the poor. Jesus' intent is wholly missed.

What a powerful way to remind us that mealtime is messy! Whether our table is marked by argumentative chaos, unpleasant manners, the silent treatment, heated debate, or even betrayal, we understand implicitly the promise and the pain that envelops each secular or sacred meal we share.

As we invite congregants to the Lord's Supper, we can certainly draw upon the memories of our own sacred meals in quiet pews or at boisterous tables. Although Jesus' death is drawing quickly near, we invite our companions to remember these complicated moments of Jesus' *life*. Surely Jesus' invitation to us, in the midst of our own unsettled and uncertain lives, will draw us closer to him, to one another, and to the kingdom of heaven. In hopeful response, we "lift up our hearts," pointing to what Jesus says and what he does. At Table, we remember his life, through his word and his deeds. They are of one strand, pointing to the One who sent him and so sends us into a world ravenous for healing and hope.

DEBRA T. BIBLER

3. Rodolphe Kasser, ed., *The Gospel of Judas: from Codex Tchacos* (Washington, DC: National Geographic Society, 2006), 4, 53; Simon Gathercole, *The Gospel of Judas: Rewriting Early Christianity* (Oxford: Oxford University Press, 2007), 132–49.

John 13:31–35

³¹When he had gone out, Jesus said, "Now the Son of Man has been glorified, and God has been glorified in him. ³²If God has been glorified in him, God will also glorify him in himself and will glorify him at once. ³³Little children, I am with you only a little longer. You will look for me; and as I said to the Jews* so now I say to you, 'Where I am going, you cannot come.' ³⁴I give you a new commandment, that you love one another. Just as I have loved you, you also should love one another. ³⁵By this everyone will know that you are my disciples, if you have love for one another."

Theological Perspective

John 13:31 marks the official beginning of the Farewell Discourse in the Gospel, Jesus' final words to and prayers for his disciples before his arrest in chapter 18. This literary context calls attention to the theological impulse of this passage. By preparing the disciples for his departure, Jesus must somehow communicate that his absence does not mean abandonment. The relationship that has been possible with Jesus will continue even in his glory. The language about glory and love here must be interpreted against the backdrop of Jesus' clear love and concern for his followers.

A major theological issue up-front in this short passage is to identify the character referred to in the clause "when he had gone out" (v. 31). The exiting person is Judas, the one who would betray Jesus. Jesus has washed the disciples' feet, hosted a meal for them, shared bread with Judas, and Judas betrays Jesus, not by handing Jesus over—Jesus himself will do that when Judas returns with the cohort of soldiers to arrest Jesus—but by not believing in Jesus as the Word made flesh, the "I am," the very presence of God before him. The arrest scene has very little to do with Judas's betrayal. There will be no kiss to identify Jesus, no words of greeting to Jesus, no repentance

Pastoral Perspective

"I give you a new commandment, that you love one another" (v. 34). Churchgoers may have heard this mandate at Maundy Thursday services or have sung versions of it at camp or Vacation Bible School ("This is my commandment, that you love one another . . ."[1]). The simplicity of Jesus' commandment could cause us to dismiss it. We know we are supposed to love one another. The church has served this, like hot dishes and Jell-O salad, as standard fare for ages. However, the context of this advice and the urgency of the commandment offer additional food for thought in a congregation hungry for renewal.

Our pastoral challenge is to teach an old "new commandment" in a fresh way.

To engage those for whom this is not familiar, those for whom the word "commandment" is itself strange or archaic, one might frame it in three different ways. When one takes a picture to an art shop to be framed, the shopkeeper offers alternatives: a brushed nickel frame feels modern and industrial; a weathered barn board makes a rustic statement; a gilt frame sets the picture in your grandparents' parlor. We can offer different frameworks for Jesus' new commandment.

The first frame shows the rustic, sometimes chaotic, world where commandments ordered

---

* See "'The Jews' in the Fourth Gospel" on pp. xi–xiv.

1. A number of traditional folk tunes and lyrics are in circulation.

Exegetical Perspective

After Judas left the supper room, Jesus began his Farewell Discourse, which reminds us of the final testaments of Jacob and Moses (Gen. 49; Deut. 33), by announcing his imminent glorification and giving the disciples a new commandment to love one another.

Jesus said, "Now the Son of Man has been glorified; and God has been glorified in him" (v. 31). In Aramaic, the expression the "Son of Man" is used as a self-reference. It also refers to the judge of the world at the end of time in the Daniel tradition (Dan. 7:13–14). Jesus may claim here to be the eschatological judge who will render final justice on God's behalf. Because Jesus has done many wonders, such as turning water into wine (2:11) and raising Lazarus from the dead (11:40), both he and God have been glorified.

To be "glorified" has an additional meaning in the Fourth Gospel. Earlier in the story Jesus had said to the Greeks in Jerusalem, "The hour has come for the Son of Man to be glorified. Very truly, I tell you, unless a grain of wheat falls into the earth and dies, it remains just a single grain; but if it dies, it bears much fruit" (12:23–24). The metaphor of grain makes it clear that to be glorified means to die a death that will yield good results. On the same occasion, a heavenly voice also said that God would be glorified again when Jesus faced his hour of death (12:28–33). How

Homiletical Perspective

This passage begins Jesus' lengthy discourse to the disciples after he has washed their feet and they have shared a meal. Jesus' words of imminent departure, once viewed through the solitary lens of the crucifixion, are both enriched and expanded when experienced through the retrospective lens of the resurrection. As we invite congregants to walk *between* crucifixion and resurrection, dark and light, betrayal and love, we can certainly demonstrate the ways in which these two events inform one another and so deepen our experience of the living Christ. After all, our weekly resurrection proclamation runs the risk of becoming tinny and flat if not folded into a stark memory of an intimate's betrayal and a horrifying death. On the other hand, we run the risk of allowing the crucifixion to become the defining moment for us as Christians, rather than one of several, without the broad sweep—and corrective—of the entire liturgical narrative.

As preachers, we can certainly draw attention to the fact that Jesus' words to the disciples begin immediately upon Judas's hurried departure. Jesus is betrayed. Night has fallen. There is no hint of discouragement in Jesus' words, though. Jesus' repeated and intentional use of the word "glorify" brings this point closer to home. Jesus is not giving up his life, but rather deepening his life as one who has been

John 13:31–35

Theological Perspective

or remorse afterward. Instead, the arrest of Jesus will be another event that illustrates the glory of Jesus. The connection between Judas's departure and Jesus' glory is worth some theological probing. What is it that connects the two in the Fourth Evangelist's mind? How is Jesus glorified in the moment of Judas's abandonment? What does glory have to do with betrayal?

It is important to note that for John, Jesus' glory cannot be isolated to the event of the crucifixion alone. The cross is not the final or ultimate expression of the glory of Jesus, or the glory of God, for that matter. The entirety of the Word made flesh—the incarnation, crucifixion, resurrection, and ascension—indicates the glorification of God, the revelation of the very presence of God in Jesus. Jesus' talk about his departure does not simply mean a pastoral pat on the back, a "There, there" kind of expression. By devoting more than four chapters to the Farewell Discourse, the writer of the Fourth Gospel emphasizes not just the death of Jesus, but the life of Jesus as well. That which becomes human must die—of this there is no doubt—but here it is God who has become human, God who will die. The Gospel of John takes this very seriously, so that the full understanding of what it means that the Word became flesh is signaled in Jesus' reference to his departure.

With this in mind, the link between the disbelief of Judas and Jesus' glory highlights what is at stake in believing in Jesus as the Word made flesh. To believe in Jesus means to know the depth and breadth of God's decision to become human, a decision that has everything to do with just how close God wants to be with us. One cannot pick and choose parts of God's revelation in Jesus in which to believe, to trust, or to have hope. God revealing God's self in the person and ministry of Jesus demonstrates the lengths to which God will go to know us, love us, and be in relationship with us.

Perhaps Judas did not know what to do with such an abundant demonstration of intimacy. The disciples were invited into this intimate relationship with Jesus during his time on earth, but the pointing toward Jesus' exit from earth could be understood to mean that the relationship thus ends. Jesus must communicate that his leaving will in no way mean the termination of this relationship. Jesus' ascension, his homecoming with his Father suggested in these verses, expresses the fullness of the intimacy intended when it comes to believing in Jesus. Jesus will return to the Father, a place of extraordinary

Pastoral Perspective

community life and guided covenantal relationships with God. The new commandment acts as an appendix to the Mosaic code (not an amendment, which implies that the Hebrew mandates were somehow inadequate). Contrast this new commandment with the mandates of imperial Rome. Jesus offers a radical, even dangerous, alternative to the hegemony of Roman colonialism. The empire was not built on love for one another; it was building aqueducts and building up territories that made the emperor's heart sing.

The second frame could, with old-fashioned word studies of "commandment," guide learners to understand the language of faith and the eagerness of the early Christian church to instruct converts in the Way. The third frame could give a modern interpretation of the commandment as a model of "best practices,"[2] offering methods for following Jesus and benefiting the common good.

It is to Jesus the Way that this commandment leads us. The pastoral task of helping the congregation to meet this Jesus rests not only in framing the scene but in examining it in light of Jesus' imminent departure. The stage is set for Jesus' last days with intimations of suffering, but at this stage a scrim has dropped down, and we are separated from Jesus. We hear him talking about loving one another as he has loved the disciples, but a distance has crept into his voice. This is the moment of pastoral intersection with the text. Jesus is both intimate ("Little children, I am with you only a little longer") and off-putting ("Where I am going, you cannot come," v. 33) as he charts the landscape ahead. This is the teachable moment. Seeing Jesus behind this scrim separating him from mere mortals, we experience a moment of clarity.

This is a model for exploring "scrim moments" in our congregation. In the theatre, a scrim, the gauzy, translucent cloth that drops down as a screen or a backdrop on stage, appears opaque until it is lit from behind. Then the characters, set design, and props become clear. As we examine those "scrim moments" in our congregation, we help others to move through them by naming what is happening. For example, a daughter may have lived in the shadow of her mother's judgment and criticism her whole life long. Then one night, in the nursing home or hospital or the back bedroom, a light goes on and the mother says, "You know, I have always loved you." Instantly,

2. Mark Davis, "Commanding Love," Tuesday, April 23, 2013, http://leftbe hindandlovingit.blogspot.com/2013/04/commanding-love.html; accessed May 1, 2013: "I've come to see the 'commands' as articulations of 'best practices' for making sustainable community with God and others. In my mind, God's law is not something you follow because it is a law, but something that God makes a law because it is beneficial for life and community."

will Jesus die? He will be lifted up on the cross, and his love thus demonstrated will attract many people (v. 32). To say, "God will glorify him at once" (v. 32), means, therefore, that Jesus will die soon.

In view of his imminent "glorification," Jesus told the disciples he could stay with them only for a short while; he also said where he was going they could not go (v. 33). He had said the same thing to the Jews who tried to arrest him (7:34; 8:21). Obviously the disciples did not understand why Jesus had to leave them. It was shocking to some who might be fantasizing about Jesus' rise to power in Jerusalem. After three years of hard campaign for the kingdom of God and gathering a significant number of followers, they thought that Jesus might finally be ready to assert his messianic authority in the Holy City, so they were bewildered by the enigma of Jesus' departure and were wondering why they could not go with him.

Calling the disciples "little children" (v. 33), Jesus spoke tenderly like a loving father concerned about his children, who were vulnerable and disoriented. His first advice to the disciples was a new commandment to love one another (v. 34). In the context of his imminent departure, four points about the commandment are noteworthy.

First, the commandment to love one another is a wise counsel, intended to help the disciples cope with their grief over Jesus' death and their anxiety over separation. It is not simply another law to achieve righteousness. In Jesus' absence, mutual love will be absolutely crucial for sustaining their faith, hope, and love as a community.

Second, the commandment to love one another is a new commandment. What then are the old ones? For Pharisaic Jews, the written Torah traditionally contains 613 commandments based on the Ten Commandments that God gave Moses on Mount Sinai. Early Christians learned about two greatest commandments from a saying tradition of Jesus shared by Mark 12:28–31; Matthew 22:34–40; and Luke 10:25–28. While answering the question from a scribe, Jesus cited Deuteronomy 6:4–5 to say the first of all commandments is to "love the Lord your God with all your heart, and with all your soul, and with all your mind, and with all your strength" (Mark 12:30). He then added Leviticus 19:18 as the second greatest commandment: "You shall love your neighbor as yourself" (Mark 12:31). "On these two commandments hang all the law and the prophets" (Matt. 22:40). It is safe to assume that most early Christians, including the Johannine community, knew these two commandments.

glorified by God and will so glorify God in return (vv. 31–32). As Jesus testifies to the inseparable tie that binds him as the Son of Man to God, we sense only urgency and a deep awareness of who he is and what he is called to do. John Calvin in his *Institutes* boldly declared that

> without knowledge of self there is no knowledge of God. Our wisdom, in so far as it ought to be deemed true and solid wisdom, consists almost entirely of two parts: the knowledge of God and of ourselves. But as they are connected together by many ties, it is not easy to determine which of the two precedes and gives birth to the other.[1]

As we preach from this text, one of our most urgent tasks will be to invite our listeners to become more deeply aware of who we are and what we are called to do. Stories, poems, music, and even displayed art—which offer both a profound appreciation of divine presence in our lives and a humble recognition of our all–too-human and egocentric resistance to that presence—will certainly help listeners engage with honesty and depth.

Jesus' words provide further clues for our authentic following. His deliberate naming of the disciples as "little children" is a title used repeatedly in the first Johannine epistle to a conflicted church struggling to define itself after the resurrection (John 13:33; 1 John 2:1, 12, 28; 3:7, 18; 4:4; 5:21). Again, as preachers we can invite our listeners to draw compelling parallels with current issues of ego and conflict, as well as ongoing experiences of a divine love that claims us as beloved children.

Through tone and speech, Jesus makes the urgent claim that he will remain with the disciples for only a little while, causing them to engage the world differently. Although the disciples cannot follow him to where he is going, they can do something else: they can love one another. As Jesus deftly switches the focus and broadens the view with his "new commandment" or *novum mandatum* (for which our Maundy Thursday is named), he reveals that insider status as "little children" does not excuse one from certain responsibilities. In the context of the recent announcement of his betrayal and another one close around the corner, his command becomes all the more challenging, particularly as tensions build and conflict simmers.

For those of us in the pulpit, we might do well to confess that it is precisely within our tight circle of

---

1. John Calvin, *Institutes of the Christian Religion*, trans. F. L. Battles (Philadelphia: The Westminster Press, 1960), 35.

Theological Perspective

tenderness, closeness, and affection. Jesus is returning to the place where the whole story started, at the bosom of the Father (1:18). In doing so, however, he prepares an abiding place for his disciples, in the bosom of Jesus and God.

As a result, it is here that Jesus can then introduce the love commandment. Any other place, and it would have been misinterpreted and woefully underestimated in its significance. This is not just a pithy quotation that the disciples can hang in their kitchens by which to remember Jesus. It is more than significant that Jesus' commandment about love is located at this place, immediately after Judas's leaving and as further comment on his own departure. To "love one another, just as I have loved you" (v. 34) cannot be limited to the washing of feet. Love is not simply an expression of hospitality, as remarkable as it is between Jesus and his disciples, but representative of the very core of who God is in Jesus and who the disciples are because of Jesus.

The rest of the Farewell Discourse will unpack what this love looks like and feels like: in the promise of the Holy Spirit, the image of the vine and the branches, and the unity between God, Jesus, and the disciples. The call to love is an invitation to abide in a deep relationship with God and Jesus, a relationship that the disciples will actually act out with each other. Their love for each other will be the manifestation of the love between God and Jesus. This is no simple act of love but a life of love, a reality of love that imagines a fullness of communication and communion from beginning to end. Jesus' promise to his disciples is that by loving one another, they are embodying Jesus' love for and relationship with the disciples when he was with them.

KAROLINE M. LEWIS

Pastoral Perspective

the daughter has a clear picture, a different picture of this woman whom she could never please. Here the scrim separating generations falls away in a moment of grace.

Bittersweet clarity emerges just before the end. Jesus tells the disciples what is most important: to love one another. This is the kind of legacy we want to urge others to leave—a countercultural approach to inheritance. The good news, to leave a lasting legacy of love, is better advice than any financial advisor, money manager, or retirement planner could offer. When Jesus speaks, people listen, especially at the end of the journey, the end of the play, in Act V, when the scrim is backlit by the events about to unfold.

This announcement about love—whether to "love one another," or that "I have always loved you"—is the Christian categorical imperative that resets our priorities. Here Jesus does not give away the keys to the kingdom; instead, he tells the disciples that they cannot go where he is going—and then immediately tells them to love one another, as if the key is imbedded in his mandate. It makes us want to follow him wherever he is going.

Here are the missional and prophetic elements to the exposition. Loving as Jesus loves involves loving the unloved and the unlovable. Jesus models patience with recalcitrant children and courage to challenge systems that oppress widows and orphans. Loving as Jesus did means others will know you by your love. We can challenge our congregation to be the church that shows love for one another. Resurrect the folksy hymn, "They'll Know We are Christians by Our Love."[3] Garner a reputation for being a loving church, one that welcomes the stranger, opens the doors to the homeless, the outcast, the refugee, the least, the last, and the lost. We can reframe our church as a countercultural community that counts among its greatest assets the love of its people for one another. This fulfills the commandment: love locally; love globally; love extravagantly.

LAURA A. LOVING

3. Peter R. Scholtes, "They'll Know We Are Christians by Our Love" (F.E.L. Publications, 1966).

Exegetical Perspective

Why does Jesus add a new commandment? The disciples need it because it serves a special purpose. When they lose their master, they will feel orphaned and afraid, and they will need each other's love to safeguard their identity and goal as a group. For the Johannine community, suffering pressure from the synagogues of their time (9:18–34) and hostility from the world (15:18–25), mutual love was the best remedy for their fear of being besieged. This inward-looking and self-preserving rule of mutual love is indeed different from the grander and nobler commandment to love enemies in the Sermon on the Mount (Matt. 5:44), but there is no contradiction between the two. The commandment to love one another is context-specific, necessary for a minority group under stress. It is also the first step to the love of neighbors and the love of enemies. If they cannot love their own brothers and sisters, how can they love their enemies?

Third, the commandment to love one another sets a high standard. Disciples are required to love one another the same way Jesus loves them. Following Jesus in ministry, they have witnessed how Jesus loves all who come to him, in spite of their social standing and gender difference and in spite of his own hunger, fatigue, or risk of life. Jesus has called them, fed them, taught them, and prayed for them. Earlier in the night, Jesus has even washed their feet. Now they are commanded to imitate Jesus and do the same to one another. To love Jesus is to love fellow believers, and vice versa.

Fourth, the commandment to love one another is a mark of discipleship. If the disciples can practice Jesus' love for one another, people will recognize that they are his disciples. Mutual love is therefore the sign of genuine discipleship and important for evangelism. The commandment to love one another is not merely a strategy for survival, but also a way to build and expand the community of faith.

JOHN YIEH

Homiletical Perspective

believers, the established church community, that our love is often most sorely tested. As we enter our committee meetings, strategy teams, new initiatives, and planning circles, our conflicting personalities, blustering egos, and varied agendas may be the biggest stumbling block to our mission together as the sent people of God. It is precisely here, though, that some of our hardest and most essential work must be done if we are to bear witness with integrity and become known as vibrant disciples who "love one another." As preachers, perhaps one of our best hopes of engagement around this common reality may be humor. As G. K. Chesterton famously said, "Angels can fly because they take themselves lightly."[2] Humor can certainly be a powerful—and subversive—way to unmask illusions and lift up truth!

Certainly the truth is difficult to speak and to hear as we think about what it means to love one another in tense and troubled times. The hope of God's ever-expanding salvation story can be emphasized as we dance between crucifixion and resurrection, betrayal and forgiveness, fear and hope. Recognizing that we have restorative work to do in Jesus' name will be essential as we seek to bring Jesus' love into our skeptical neighborhoods. Acknowledging that we are part of a body—Christ's body no less!—that is too often marred by unnecessary and ego-bound conflict will be imperative as well.

A service of healing and wholeness with intentional space for confession, repentance, forgiveness, and renewal may be an interesting way to approach this passage and invite those who have been hurt by a congregation or a denomination into fresh conversation. In the spirit of resurrection power, we preach and pray, offering opportunities for light to blossom from darkness. We invite one another to live—and lead—with a Christ-focused urgency and clarity, so that places of disconnect and discord may bloom with fresh hope and the world will truly "know that we are Christians by our love"![3]

DEBRA T. BIBLER

2. *G. K. Chesterton's Christian Writings (unabridged): Everlasting Man, Orthodoxy, Heretics, St. Francis of Assisi, St. Thomas Aquinas and The Man Who Was Thursday* (1908; Oxford: Benediction Classics, 2012), 270.
3. Peter Scholtes, "They'll Know We Are Christians by Our Love" (F.E.L. Publications, 1966).

John 13:36–38

Theological Perspective

"Lord, where are you going?" (v. 36) is nothing short of a theological quagmire and is replete with possible answers. Where Jesus is going, particularly at this point in the Gospel, is a question that has multiple important meanings that the disciples have yet to grasp in any way. Jesus is going to be arrested. Jesus is going to be put on trial. Jesus is going to be crucified. He will die, be raised, and then will ascend to the Father. In other words, Peter has no idea what he is asking.

This brief scene has many theological foreshadowings for the rest of the Gospel. The exchange looks forward to 21:15–19, the conversation between Jesus and Peter on the shores of Galilee, Jesus' third resurrection appearance to the disciples. There, Peter will be asked to be the good shepherd when Jesus cannot be, because of his return to the Father. Jesus' last words to Peter will be, "Follow me" (21:22); and to follow Jesus will mean the entire reality of his life, death, resurrection, and ascension. Ironically, that Jesus will ask Peter to follow him in 21:19 has little to do with following and everything to do with a new definition of discipleship, being the "I am" in the world when Jesus is no longer here. To follow Jesus is to enter into his fully incarnated reality of God made flesh. No wonder Peter has no clue what is at stake when he asks his question.

Pastoral Perspective

Simon Peter asks Jesus, "Where are you going?" (v. 36). Is that a geographical or a spiritual query? People in helping professions learn to listen to questions carefully. What propels the question that a parishioner, a child, a senior citizen, or a confirmand asks? Listen for the anxiety, curiosity, doubt, indignation, alienation, justice-seeking, or attention-seeking within the question. Listen for the larger context. Here, Peter is the proverbial canary in the coalmine, warning with his questions that the air is being sucked out of the room, that their very Breath is on his last breath. Their leader is leaving.

Once a young girl tried to stave off her mother's departure (most likely to the store or library for sanity!). Mother desperately needed a break. The daughter cried, "Mommy, where are you going?" Her exasperated mother replied, "I'm going crazy!" The child piped, "Can I go with you?" One can imagine Jesus in this same situation with Peter. Peter's plea articulates the crazy, inchoate longings of children and adults alike: Please, let my world stay the same. Do not move my cheese.[1] "Do not . . . take not your Holy Spirit from me" (Ps. 51:11 NIV). Do not leave me. These feelings underlie the "acting out" of restless toddlers, defiant teenagers, demanding

1. Spencer Johnson, *Who Moved My Cheese?* (New York: Penguin, 1998).

Feasting on the Gospels

Exegetical Perspective

This pericope contains a dialogue about Jesus' destination and a prophecy about Peter's three denials of Jesus.

Jesus had just announced that he would stay with the disciples for only a little longer, and that where he was going they could not come (13:33). To Jesus' puzzling words, the impulsive Peter could not hold his tongue even for a moment. As usual he jumped at the first chance to ask Jesus where he was going. Jesus, however, avoided Peter's question regarding his destination and repeated his message that Peter (singular "you") could not follow him now (v. 36b). This statement was directed to Peter individually and concerned the present moment. Then Jesus added another statement that is just as perplexing: "but you [again singular "you," referring to Peter] will follow afterward" (v. 36b). There seems to be a question of timing in addition to destination. Wherever Jesus was going, Peter could not follow right away; however, he would at a later time. This bewildering statement, of course, drove the hotheaded Peter crazy, so he asked again, "Lord, why can I not follow you now? I will lay down my life for you" (v. 37).

Peter's dialogue with Jesus follows a typical pattern in Johannine narrative. In several conversations, Jesus' statement is misunderstood, which provokes his conversation partners to raise new questions.

Homiletical Perspective

We know about interruptions; they infiltrate our lives at every turn. Too often, we fight against them, fuming about lost plans and lost time. In our better moments, we embrace them, trusting that even the most trying of interruptions might be laden with holy possibilities. More often than not, we structure our days to avoid them, pretending that we have some small modicum of control—until the unavoidable interruption of tragedy explodes before our very eyes and we are forced to confront our false illusions.

This short but dense dialogue between Jesus and Peter clearly reveals the power and place of interruption. Most notably, this short-lived dialogue demands our attention because it is the only interruption in Jesus' lengthy monologue after he washes the disciples' feet (John 13:31–17:26). Especially because this passage never officially lands in the lectionary, it is a rich source that many preachers have rarely mined—and it can provide ample fodder for our preaching in a variety of contexts. We can certainly use this passage in connection with a Holy Week reading as the "last word" before Good Friday. The conspicuous gap between Jesus' call to the disciples to love one another as he has loved them (13:34) and the second denial by Peter (18:25–27) would certainly be an appropriate—and sobering—emphasis. On the other hand, if we preach this passage in conjunction with John

John 13:36–38

Theological Perspective

Peter's continued misunderstanding of what it means to follow Jesus is emphasized by his claim that he will lay down his life for Jesus. Only three chapters earlier, Jesus describes himself as the Good Shepherd, willing to lay down his life for the sheep. Jesus will lay down his life for the sheep by first exiting the safety of the garden to confront the more than six hundred soldiers and police outside, intent on his arrest. He will lay down his life by being crucified and buried. Little does Peter know that laying down one's life for Jesus will mean laying down one's life for one's friends, and for the sake of sheep that are not of this fold (10:16).

Jesus' reply to Peter's naiveté is the prediction of Peter's denial. While Jesus articulates Peter's denial as directed toward himself, to deny Jesus in the Fourth Gospel is simultaneously a denial of discipleship, where discipleship ends up doing "greater works than these" (14:12) and being the very presence of Jesus in his absence. As a result, in John, denial of Jesus is elevated to a theological level unlike that in any of the other Gospels. A careful reading of Peter's denial in John reveals that Peter does not deny Jesus; he denies his own discipleship. To reject Jesus is not simply to deny knowing him. It is to deny being his continuing presence in the world that God loves.

It is not often that we are invited into a place where Jesus' ministry and our ministry are so intimately linked. That Jesus relies on Peter, and that we are necessary for God to carry out God's promise of loving the world, is not our usual definition of discipleship. We are far more comfortable with following, tentative testimony, and safe expressions of faith. This passage allows no escape from or reasonable accountability for what it means to believe in Jesus. How we wish it could be different! This brief passage is pointed in its theological questioning and reasoning, which a sermon or Bible study should replicate. It is rare that we feel the urgency, the responsibility, and the integrity of what is at stake in embodying the love of God in and for the world.

Another angle of theological interpretation is the poignancy of Peter's question, "why can I not follow you now?" (v. 37). He cannot follow now because the Farewell Discourse has yet to happen. That is, in chapters 14–16 Jesus will indeed say good-bye, but he will also leave the disciples with hope in the Spirit, the Advocate who will be their comforter, helper, and intercessor in his absence. The Spirit is the Paraclete, literally, the one called alongside them for the sake of Jesus' ongoing ministry in the world.

Jesus will also offer a prayer for his disciples in chapter 17. This is not the prayer where Jesus

Pastoral Perspective

parishioners, and high-maintenance coworkers. This passage cuts to the heart of abandonment. A preacher could name these issues in an exposition of the text; a youth group leader could introduce this angst-y scenario as the start of building a skit; a confirmation class teacher could identify the issues of faith within this scene and help confirmands write a faith statement, first from Peter's perspective, and then from their own; a pastoral counselor could animate a therapy session with Peter's query as the backdrop for a client's anxiety.

Peter is often our stand-in in the Gospels, an ancient Everyman with contemporary counterparts in Everybodies who want to get it right. Here he promises to lay down his life for Jesus, an act of devotion and desperation. Jesus knows better. The promise rings hollow. Peter cannot help himself. As Jesus' right-hand man throughout their ministry together, he should be the one to "get it," but his own emotional needs push aside his sense of purpose and his collaboration with Jesus' ministry.

This conundrum gives us an opening for pastoral care in the congregation. Surprisingly, it may be the most active leaders, your "right-hand people," who are most in need in times of crisis, periods of transition, or galvanizing moments in the church's ministry. Recognize that active leaders need reassurance. Just because they lead the way, organizing the Mission Fair or representing the church in a protest or prayer vigil, they are not exempt from moments of crisis, from making hollow promises or feeling abandonment or fear. Sometimes marginal members of the congregation who present (to use a medical model) the most dramatic symptoms siphon our energy for pastoral ministry. Pay attention to your leaders. Who would have predicted that Peter would be the one to deny his Lord and mentor? Well, anyone who had witnessed Peter's earnest confessions crashing into his balkiness and uncertainties. Namely, Jesus, who knew his sheep.

Using this passage as a model for leadership, get to know your own flock. Jesus knows Peter, telling him kindly but firmly that he will not only not follow Jesus but will deny being a follower of Jesus. Think about this candor when you speak the truth in love to someone. Imitate Jesus' tender but tenacious insistence as you negotiate conversations with a burned-out church officer who needs to step down or with a rigid church-school teacher who has become a black-and-white thinker and cannot allow questions in the classroom. Hone your skills of observation and listening as you emulate this Christlike conversation.

Exegetical Perspective

His conversation partners become interested and curious, and their questions give Jesus a chance to clarify what he means to say. The continuous dialogue thus leads them to see Jesus' statement from a different perspective and reach a deeper understanding. Even when the characters in the story still miss it, the reader usually gets it. When Jesus said to Nicodemus, for instance, that no one could see the kingdom of God without being "born again," which also means "born from above" (3:3), Nicodemus misunderstood him and questioned how any grown person could possibly enter the mother's womb to be born again. It is of course a ridiculous proposition, but it is also a gross misunderstanding. How can Jesus mean to say something so absurd? The conversation continued. The attention was now focused on what it means to be born again or from above. Thus Jesus was able to rephrase his statement to say that only those who were born of water and Spirit can enter the kingdom of God (3:5). In other words, he was using the metaphor of birth in reference to a spiritual birth from God.

Another example is the Samaritan woman who spoke with Jesus about the "living water" that Jesus promised to her (4:10). The woman first misunderstood it to be drinking water and thought that she could be spared the sweaty labor of drawing water from the well. Obviously she misunderstood the kind of water Jesus was offering, but her misunderstanding provided Jesus a chance to say that he meant a spring of water in her that will gush up to eternal life (4:14), which the narrator later says is the Holy Spirit (7:38–39). In other words, the living water is supposed to be understood symbolically as the water of life. The same pattern of misunderstanding, questioning, and explaining can be found in Peter's dialogue with Jesus over Jesus' destination, where Peter would later join him.

When Jesus said Peter could not follow him where he was going until later, Peter became upset. Eager to show his loyalty, he protested and asked, why not now? In great passion he professed that he would follow Jesus wherever he was heading for, even if it meant he had to die for him (v. 37). Jesus knew Peter's sincerity, but he also knew his frailty; so he asked Peter a rhetorical question: "Will you lay down your life for me?" and went on to predict that Peter would deny him three times before the cock crowed (v. 38).

Where was Jesus going? As a character in the story, Peter did not know where Jesus was going, even though the narrator had indicated to the reader

Homiletical Perspective

20:19–25, we can speak in a way that allows this short, dialogical interruption to be reframed in the context of Jesus' postresurrection appearance.

However we choose to preach from this text, we will do well to pay attention to the ways in which Peter's poignant questions, born of confusion and sadness, mingle with Jesus' own bleak and predictive question in return. As preachers, we cannot gloss over these painful moments, hoping to spare our hearers. Our hearers, whether buoyant new believers or cynical and weary insiders, are generally much stronger and more resilient than we ever allow. We can remind one another that deep hope and healing can blossom out of these dark places of profound betrayal and personal blindness.

The normalcy and undeniable logic of Peter's initial question, "Lord, where are you going?" (v. 36), can certainly be another entry point for preaching. After all, there are many moments when, like Peter, we are tempted to wonder aloud about God's location in our lives. Songwriter and musician David Bailey has a powerful song entitled "Be Still" that begins, "When God seems far away, guess who moved?"[1] Bailey begins his song as an antidote to pointed fingers aimed at the Divine, one another, or even ourselves when life becomes increasingly complicated. Jesus offers his own antidote to this easy temptation, by refusing to be pigeonholed and ignoring Peter's initial question in verse 36. Instead, Jesus reframes Peter's question, setting in motion a trajectory for future discipleship by promising that he "will follow afterward" (v. 36).

Peter's ensuing question and bold claim in verse 37 reveal a profound missing of the mark. Peter confidently proclaims his willingness to "lay down [his] life," mirroring Jesus' self-descriptive language as the Good Shepherd in 10:11, 15. Peter's naive passion is all too familiar. This is certainly not the first time that Peter, staunchly clinging to his own preconceived notions (13:6–10), has misunderstood Jesus.

If one is preaching this text during the Easter season, it may be revealing to lay this dialogue beside Mary Magdalene's conversation with the risen Jesus at the empty tomb (20:15–17). Noting the ways in which both faithful believers are blinded by preconceived notions, in addition to overwhelming fear, sorrow, naiveté, and pride, may serve as another way for the scales to fall from our own eyes!

Jesus' ensuing question to Peter in 13:38—"Will you lay down your life for me?"—certainly does much

---

1. David M. Bailey, "Be Still," *Silent Conversations* (CD Baby, 2004).

Theological Perspective

disappears and tells the disciples to stay awake. Rather, the disciples hear every single word Jesus has to say about his entrusting them to the care of the Father, his love for them, and his promise that their abiding love and intimate relationship will continue. Moreover, Peter will not be able to follow Jesus until the gift of the Paraclete has actually been given. In John 20:19–31 Jesus appears to his disciples for the first time, as they sit behind closed doors, trying to protect themselves, in fear of the Jewish leaders casting them out of the synagogue for believing in Jesus. Jesus appears among them, a manifestation of what it means to claim "I am the door," and offers them peace.

It is extraordinary that Jesus' first words to his disciples after his resurrection have to do with peace, when his last words with them before his crucifixion, the Farewell Discourse, urged that their hearts not be troubled. Jesus then gives them the gift of the Holy Spirit. This is no ordinary dispensation of spiritual strength, though. In John, Jesus breathes *into* the disciples the Spirit, just as God breathed into Adam God's very breath of life (Gen. 2:7). Peter can only follow Jesus, and Jesus can only say to Peter, "Follow me," at the end of the Gospel, when God's breath, God's Spirit, has entered into him, the creative and life-giving presence that makes it possible to "do greater works than these." Jesus is right. Peter will be able to follow only afterward and that afterward is the profound Pentecost moment where the Spirit of truth is given to be with them forever.

KAROLINE M. LEWIS

Pastoral Perspective

In addition to proactive involvement with individuals, keep your finger on the pulse of the community as a whole. Recognize heightened anxiety in times of transition; be attentive to anniversary dates of a church fire, community tornado, or trauma. Beyond the congregation, test your political acumen by noticing, preaching about, or rallying around times of national or international events—those that are widely recognized, like the anniversary of 9/11 or Hiroshima Day, as well as some that may go unnoticed but contribute to communal unease or unnamed grief. Ask, "What's underneath this unrest?"

Lastly, ask Peter's question with mission in mind. Important questions to ask each day are: "Lord, where are you going?" and "Can I come too?" Jim Wallis, theologian and editor of *Sojourners Magazine,* writes about following Jesus into the midst of life at the Sojourners Neighborhood Meal Program, operating in Washington, D.C., just twenty blocks from the White House. He reflects:

> Just before the doors were opened and the people came in, all those who helped prepare the food and get it together would join hands and say a prayer. The prayer was often offered by Mary Glover. She was our best pray-er, a sixty-year-old African-American woman who knew what it meant to be poor and knew how to pray. She prayed like someone who knew to whom she was talking. . . . I'll never forget the words she always prayed: "Lord, we know that you'll be coming through this line today, so help us to treat you well."[2]

Where is Jesus going today? Into the boardroom where decisions about labor relations are made? Into the classroom where children too hungry to concentrate will be told they are "underperforming"? Into the nursing home where staff seek to offer dignity to patients on their final journey? Will Jesus be coming through the line at a soup kitchen near you? Our devotional lives, as well as our missional activities, would be radically readjusted if we daily asked Jesus where he was going and then tried to follow him.

Consider offering this devotional exercise: Start the day with a brief dialogue prayer. "Lord, where are you going?" to which Jesus responds, "Where are *you* going?" The answer creates a faith-filled itinerary for the day. This dialogue is also an excellent benediction for worship, sending people forth to follow Jesus after all.

LAURA A. LOVING

2. Jim Wallis, at http://sojo.net/blogs/2009/11/04/what-neighborhood-elder-taught-me-about-interfaith-prayer; accessed May 1, 2013.

Exegetical Perspective

that Jesus was going to die and rise from the dead in glory (12:23–24, 28–33). It is ironic, however, that Peter unwittingly answered his first question regarding Jesus' destination, when he swore to give up his life for Jesus. Jesus was facing death, and so would Peter. It was just not the time yet. Jesus knew Peter was not ready to die with him, and his prophecy came true, as Peter denied his relationship with Jesus three times when confronted in the high priest's courtyard (18:17, 25, 27).

Besides Jesus' foreknowledge, this dialogue tells us something about Peter as a disciple. Peter loved Jesus, so he anxiously tried to find out where Jesus was going. He eagerly swore his allegiance by his own life, even though, when threatened, he was too fearful to acknowledge Jesus. Sincerity was one of his virtues, but not courage. Later in his life, however, Peter would indeed face martyrdom for the sake of Jesus (21:18–19). After receiving the Holy Spirit from the risen Jesus and being rehabilitated with three commissions (20:22; 21:15–19), Peter would finally be able to follow his Lord where he went to face martyrdom (21:19). Peter was a flawed disciple, but he learned from his failures and emerged as an example of loyalty for all believers.

It is important to note that "follow" (akoloutheō), a word suggesting discipleship, is used three times in verses 36–37. Jesus loves people so much that he is willing to die for their sake. Following Jesus means, therefore, to lay down one's life for him in return. That is what Peter pledged, even though he would fail when his loyalty was tested. However, there is grace even in weakness. Understanding Peter's fear, Jesus reassured him and other disciples with the comforting words, "Do not let your hearts be troubled. Believe in God, believe also in me" (14:1).

Disciples will go wherever Jesus goes. They may be frail and fearful, but Jesus will keep good company with them.

JOHN YIEH

Homiletical Perspective

to expose Peter's own blindness. His use of "very truly" (as in v. 21) makes the connection between Judas's betrayal and Peter's denial all the more shocking. These "little children" (v. 33) have hardly embraced Jesus' command to love one another.

As Jesus' prediction becomes a sober reality in chapter 18, it also paves the way for Peter's future restoration in chapter 21. After a postresurrection appearance to the disciples and a cooked breakfast by the shore, Jesus and Peter begin a new conversation. Although this seaside chat is also marked with questions, it is designed to give Peter an opportunity to reframe his life in light of resurrection hope. "Do you love me?" Jesus asks repeatedly, until Peter is able to affirm his love over and against his betrayal (21:15–17). His threefold declaration of love frees him from the past. To bring the point home, Jesus commissions Peter to feed lambs and tend sheep in the very fashion of a good shepherd. Peter's identity is now lodged securely in the depths of Jesus' identity, which requires a "laying down" of one's life. Now Jesus' use of "very truly" in 21:18 points not to impending denial but, rather, to a martyr's death that will mirror Jesus' own self-offering.

Just as Jesus' identity rests in giving away his life, so it is with Peter, and so it is with us. Our ability to acknowledge that we are called to lay down our lives is a first step. Our brave confession that we falter is another. Our courageous commitment to reframe our betrayals and blindness in view of the resurrection will ensure that the world will be transformed.

A hopeful way to conclude a service of worship in which this text is preached might include the singing of "Open My Eyes," that our personal and public blindness might give way to divinely inspired illumination.[2] Our prayers in worship together might point to the way in which our actions as "little children" might become vivid and *positive* interruptions, testifying to the light and healing offered by Jesus. Even our silence in worship might serve as a form of countercultural interruption, reminding us that God's transformative love is never far away, if we have eyes to see and ears to hear.

DEBRA T, BIBLER

---

2. Clara H. Scott, "Open My Eyes, That I May See" (1895), in *The Hymnbook* (Richmond, Philadelphia, New York: Presbyterian Church in the United States, United Presbyterian Church in the U.S.A., Reformed Church in America, 1955), #390.

John 14:1–7

1"Do not let your hearts be troubled. Believe in God, believe also in me. 2In my Father's house there are many dwelling places. If it were not so, would I have told you that I go to prepare a place for you? 3And if I go and prepare a place for you, I will come again and will take you to myself, so that where I am, there you may be also. 4And you know the way to the place where I am going." 5Thomas said to him, "Lord, we do not know where you are going. How can we know the way?" 6Jesus said to him, "I am the way, and the truth, and the life. No one comes to the Father except through me. 7If you know me, you will know my Father also. From now on you do know him and have seen him."

Theological Perspective

The deep irony of John 14:1–7 is that words meant for comfort ("Do not let your hearts be troubled," v. 1) have been used recently for anything but. While they continue to be read as part of many funeral liturgies, they also crop up in many religious debates, especially those centered on the topic of who is in and who is out ("*No one* comes to the Father except through me," v. 6). What is Jesus trying to teach his disciples about the way forward and the nature of God, and how might we both benefit and be challenged by this?

The first point to make is to set this passage in context. The reader and teacher and preacher must remember that these are Jesus' parting words to his disciples. More specifically, Jesus has just told his followers that he is getting ready to go somewhere, the cross, where they cannot go, at least for now (13:36). So, naturally the disciples' hearts would be anxious regarding "the way." Like children about to be left by their parents, or students about to be abandoned by their instructor, the disciples need to be reassured that the future and *the way* to the future are still reliable, even after their leader leaves. This is *not* a passage exploring the possibility of other leaders and other paths. This is a passage for followers of Jesus who must now learn to trust in him, as they have all along been called to trust in God ("Believe in God,

Pastoral Perspective

In this wonderfully comforting passage in John, Jesus assures his disciples that God has a home for them being prepared for their future. Furthermore, Jesus reveals that he is going back to his heavenly home to work with God in preparing this special place that has room for all.

In today's world, "home" is big business. There are numerous television programs, books, magazines, and social media sites that focus on home design, home landscaping, home furnishings, home location, even vacation homes in exotic parts of the globe. A range of educational degrees and certificate programs prepares persons to design homes, to build homes ranging from the most modest of dwellings to those costing millions of dollars, to assist home owners in renovating their existing properties, and to guide home owners in decorating any and every room in the house. The exterior of the house and the land surrounding the home are now considered as important as the comfort, efficiency, and beauty of the home's interior, and of course the "location, location, location" of our homes is perhaps the key consideration in home ownership.

What does the word "home" mean to you? To many people, home goes beyond just a physical place. It has come to represent an environment of safety and security, a place that promotes creativity

Exegetical Perspective

John 14–17 comprises the Farewell Discourse, whose genre is testamentary literature. Recall the patriarchs on their deathbeds, bequeathing belongings and wisdom to their progeny (e.g., Isaac in Gen. 27 and Jacob in Gen. 48). Jesus has no material goods to dispense; instead, he gives his disciples peace (14:27) and the power to do even greater works than Jesus himself did during his earthly sojourn (14:12).

Using the second-person plural in 14:1, Jesus moves from personal conversation with one disciple (Peter, 13:36–38) to address the whole group. Notice, though, that they share only one heart: "Let not your [plural] heart [singular] be troubled" (the NRSV misleads here by incorrectly translating heart [*kardia*] in the plural). Like it or not, John insists that we are all in this together. The same sentence appears at 14:27b, forming a contained unit.

Why would their collective heart be troubled? Because, despite having heard Jesus repeatedly indicate that he was going to be lifted up on the cross (3:14; 8:28; and 12:32), the disciples cannot imagine life on earth without the earthly Jesus. They cannot, for the life of them or by the death of him, see how his departure could be good in any way. So Jesus says what he always does in John: "Trust me." Believe or trust language (*pisteuō*) occurs ninety-eight times in John, always as a verb, never as a noun (*pistis*).

Homiletical Perspective

Jesus' assurance to his disciples, as he prepares to leave them, is complicated because it includes two key statements (vv. 2–3, 6): one perhaps the most comforting, and the other perhaps the most controversial of all Jesus' sayings.

On the one hand, Jesus' promise—that his Father's house has many dwelling places, that he goes to prepare a place for us, and that he will come again and take us to himself so we may be where Jesus is—is the hope by which many commend themselves and their beloved dead to God's care and commit their bodies to the grave.

On the other hand, some Christians, fearful for the eternal salvation of people either not baptized or whom they deem to believe incorrectly, wield Jesus' declaration, "I am the way, and the truth, and the life. No one comes to the Father except through me" (v. 6), to subdue Jews, Muslims, and especially other Christians into theological submission. Other Christians, trusting God to use countless ways to disclose God's very self to all the people of the world, are embarrassed and even alarmed that Jesus made such an apparently exclusive claim.

Approaching this passage as a "farewell discourse" further complicates preaching when it leads the preacher to look for formal argumentation and reasoning. Rather than cognitive, linear logic, we find

John 14:1–7

Theological Perspective

believe also in me," v. 1). John 14 is no more meant to be a passage on religious pluralism than was Calvin's doctrine of predestination. This is a family conversation, a locker-room pep talk, a word of comfort and challenge for those who are *already following*.

Second, the main move Jesus makes is to remind the disciples that their future dwelling place is already here, *in his person*. This is the move the Johannine Jesus never tires of. Looking for water? I am here (John 4). Looking for bread? Here I am (John 6). Looking for a dwelling place, a mansion with room enough for all, maybe even a few who are not of this flock? Jesus is the way, the truth, and the life (v. 6). No one comes to the Father except through *me*, *me* right in front of you, *me* now talking to you, *me* who makes the Father and the future known to you. The constant move of Jesus in John is to recognize our fears regarding the *future*, then ask us to overcome those by abiding in Jesus' presence with us *now*. Martha, unlike Thomas, trusted in Jesus' power for resurrection *in the future* ("I know that he will rise again in the resurrection on the last day," 11:24). Both Martha and Thomas are challenged to trust this possibility *in the present*: "I am the resurrection and the life. . . . Do you believe this?" (11:25–26).

Third, and maybe most important, if the church would use this passage to talk about Jesus' relationship to those who do not explicitly claim him as "their way," the church must do so only on the basis of its own experience of the nature of Jesus' presence. As Jesus both comforts and challenges the disciples not to fear, but to trust, so the church should refrain from beginning its conversations by stoking rather than assuaging others' fears. As Jesus gives space and time for all who misunderstand his purpose and his promises, so the church must live out similar patience toward all with whom it comes in contact. As Jesus challenges the disciples to stop worrying about his absence *in the future* in order to experience his way and life and truth *in the present*, so the church should stop trying to judge who will be out and who will be in *in the future*, and comfort and challenge one another with signs of God's presence *now*.

This seems to me to be the wise and appropriate approach of two recent documents in the life of the denomination to which I belong. In response to a debate about Jesus as the "unique" versus "only" Savior of the world, the first says:

> Jesus Christ is the only Savior and Lord, and all people everywhere are called to place their faith,

Pastoral Perspective

and growth, that encourages the deepening of relationships, and that allows you to be your true self.

In the book *Spirit of the Home: How to Make Your Home a Sanctuary*, author Jane Alexander notes:

> This almost desperate interest in the external trappings of home—the newest colors, the latest furniture, the best cooker, the freshest curtains— disguises a more profound longing. In our hearts we want to come home to a real home. A real home is a place that nurtures us on every level. It gives us the creature comforts that make our bodies feel relaxed and comfortable. It provides the safety and serenity that allows our minds and emotions peace and security. Above all, it nourishes our soul.[1]

Think about your own home and what it means to you. Ask yourself if and how your home nourishes your soul.

We assume that the home being prepared by God and Jesus is a home for the spirit, a home that will nourish the soul. Do we have to wait until Jesus comes back for us to have a place where the soul can grow and mature? Can we design an earthly environment that also cares for body, mind, heart, and spirit? Jesus has told us that the kingdom of heaven can begin for us while we are still on earth. Let us start by thinking what our heavenly home might be like. Can we envision a home that offers warmth, safety, security, love, hospitality? Will our spirits be nourished by rest, serenity, joy, peace, gentleness, kindness, generosity, the overflowing of the presence of the Spirit? How can this vision of our heavenly home be translated to today as we live on earth? What can we do in our current lives to invite God to live with us and among us?

Spend some time in thought, meditation, and prayer concerning what you hope for in both your heavenly and earthly homes. What will allow your soul to grow and bring you to a closer relationship with God? What if God and Jesus took you in as a partner and consultant in designing the many rooms being prepared for all? What would be your contribution to the preparations? How would you design a space that would be uniquely yours, to reflect the special person God created you to be?

Alexander quotes psychotherapist Robert Sardello, who says, "The home is more than a box in which to live; it is a soul activity to be retrieved from the numbness of the world of modern objects. Each

---

1. Jane Alexander, *Spirit of the Home: How to Make Your Home a Sanctuary* (New York: Watson-Guptill Publications, 1999), 1.

Trusting is a dynamic process. Any of the following meanings is tenable for verse 1b:

1. Trust in God and trust in me (in this case Jesus issues a command).

2. You (already) trust in God; now trust in me also.

3. You (already) trust in God, and you (already) trust in me.

Not only do the disciples share *one* heart; they also share *one* home (*oikia*), God's home. *Oikia* (4:53; 8:35; 11:1; 12:3) and the related word *oikos* (2:16–17; 11:20) occur frequently and significantly in this Gospel. John routinely invokes the language of home, of family, of radical intimacy. In fact, every relationship humans consider primary is alluded to: parent (2:3); spouse (4:16); bride, groom, and friend of the bridegroom (3:29); sibling (11:1); friend (15:15); child (8:35); and teacher (13:13). There is *one* house.

The one house, however, has many "dwelling places," which is not surprising, since we have heard from the beginning that Jesus is the Savior of the whole cosmos (*kosmos*, 4:42) that he helped to create (1:3) and that his crucifixion was all-inclusive: "And I, when I am lifted up from the earth, will draw *all* people to myself" (12:32). All (Gk. *pas*), not some. That is a lot of people, requiring many "abiding places" (*monai*, v. 2). *Monai* is a noun from the verb *menō*, to abide, one of John's favorite words (used thirty-seven times, most famously in the vine and branches speech of chap. 15). Throughout the Gospel, John invites the reader to abide with Jesus and therefore have life, eternal life, true life, which begins now (20:31). John 14:23 reads: "Those who love me will keep my word, and my Father will love them, and we will come to them and make our abiding place [*monē*] with them" (my trans.).

Jesus prepares this "place" (*topos*) where we are all united in God's household by heading to the cross. There he births the church, God's home: "Then he said to the disciple, 'Here is your mother.' And from that hour the disciple took her into his own home" (19:27). After all, home is where the (singular) heart is. Church is a real place (*topos*), not a u-topia. Augustine proclaimed: "Our heart is restless until it finds rest in thee";[1] church is to be such a place.

Jesus comes and goes often in John. From the start, we know Jesus as "the one coming into the world" (1:9). His departure serves the goal of his eternal return whereby, thanks to the Paraclete, we

1. *Soliloquies*, 1.1.3 in *Augustine: Earlier Writings*, ed. J. H. S. Burleigh (London: SCM, 1953), 23.

circular thought and the repetition of important themes punctuated by key words—coming, going, believing, knowing, abiding, loving. This is not a systematic treatise but the weaving together of the important thoughts Jesus urgently wants his friends to understand, because he knows that his way of being with them is ending, since he is on his way to the cross. The closest I come to this kind of speech is the rambling I did when my wife and I dropped off our daughter at college. I imagine John 14–17 as a conversation soldiers might have over dinner and drinks the night before battle, or even as the surge of energy many people experience as they approach death, rather than as constructive theology.

The key to proclamation is the imperative, "Believe . . . believe" (v. 1b), with *pisteuete* best translated as "trust." Jesus says, "Trust me," and assures the disciples that they can. The sermon should likewise assure the hearers to such a degree that the sermon leaves them trusting Jesus. Jesus overwhelms us with reasons to trust him! Jesus is intimately connected to God, whom he calls Father. Jesus knows that God's provision, which he describes as a "house" with "many dwelling places," is abundant for all who trust Jesus and follow him as *the way*. Jesus has "come again" in the resurrection; his return announces that not even death can separate Jesus and his own from God. Jesus provides a permanent place of abiding with God for all who trust him.

Our future is secure—and already underway! Jesus is so trustworthy that we can embrace a way of life marked by abiding with God in this world today, because in Jesus we know the truth and have life. His reference to "my Father's house" is to more than a heavenly residence after we die; Jesus is speaking of the relationship of indwelling between God and Jesus; Jesus assures us that his return to his Father makes it possible for us to be included and participate in the relationship that he and his Father share.

Trusting Jesus, we will not let our hearts be troubled. Jesus is not telling us not to be sad. Jesus' heart is troubled when he sees Mary weeping at Lazarus's tomb (11:33), when he realizes his hour has come (12:27), and earlier that evening, when he declares that one of his own will betray him (13:21). These instances point to agitation and disturbance in the face of the power of evil and death, rather than sadness. Jesus does not rebuke the disciples for being saddened by (the prospect of) his death, or us for grieving over our own deaths or the deaths of loved ones.

Rather, Jesus tells the disciples and us that, even when evil and death surround us and are having

Theological Perspective

hope, and love in him. No one is saved by virtue of inherent goodness or admirable living, for "by grace you have been saved through faith, and this is not your own doing; it is the gift of God" (Eph. 2:8). . . . Yet we do not presume to limit the sovereign freedom of "God our Savior, who desires everyone to be saved and come to the knowledge of truth" (1 Tim. 2:4). Thus, we neither restrict the grace of God to those who profess explicit faith in Christ nor assume that all people are saved regardless of faith. Grace, love, and communion belong to God, and are not ours to determine.[1]

Or this from the Study Catechism:

Question 52. How should I treat non-Christians and people of other faith? **Answer:** As much as I can, I should meet friendship with friendship, hostility with kindness, generosity with gratitude, persecution with forbearance, truth with agreement, and error with truth. I should express my faith with humility and devotion as the occasion requires, whether silently or openly, boldly or meekly, by word or by deed. I should avoid compromising the truth on the one hand and being narrow-minded on the other. In short, I should always welcome and accept these others in a way that honors and reflects the Lord's welcome and acceptance of me.[2]

These two responses seem to have gotten both the letter and the spirit of John 14 right.

RICHARD N. BOYCE

Pastoral Perspective

place of the house, each room, hallway, closet, stair and alcove is a distinct structure that animates different aspects of soul."[2]

Clues that might help us design our heavenly and early homes are experiences in our lives that currently or formerly have enriched our bodies, minds, hearts, and souls. In a recent discussion concerning "what home means to you" a group of clergywomen shared the following list: the comfort and safety of Grandmother's house, watching Grandmother plait hair, the smell of pipe smoke, feeding the birds, the sight of an old rotary telephone, the taste of homemade biscuits, a place where you have to be taken in, the smell of bacon, finding your home within, a sense of contentment, the smell of Jergens lotion, having your own room that you could decorate any way you wanted to, enjoying art that feeds your spirit, a place to be creative, owning your own home, having a large garden, growing flowers, living with an extended family.

What would you add to this list? How can past memories, present realities, and future dreams help you design your own spiritual home? Involve the Holy Spirit in your quest. Ask the Spirit what the Spirit needs to be more a part of your living environment. Tour your home with an open heart and eye to what changes might be made to have a more "soulful" place. Your home may have some interesting suggestions.

Someone once said, "Dance like nobody's watching; love like you've never been hurt. Sing like nobody's listening; live like it's heaven on earth."[3] Living like it is heaven on earth may bring our spiritual homes in heaven and earth closer together.

KATHERINE E. AMOS

---

1. Office of Theology and Worship, "Hope in the Lord Jesus Christ" (Louisville, KY: Presbyterian Church (U.S.A.), 2002), 11–12.
2. *The Study Catechism* (Louisville, KY: Geneva Press, 1998), 12–13.

2. Alexander, *Spirit of the Home*, 8, citing Robert Sardello, *Facing the World with Soul* (New York: Lindisfarne Press, 1992).
3. Variously attributed to Mark Twain, Satchel Paige, William Purkey, Susanna Clark, and Richard Leigh. See http://quoteinvestigator .com/2014/02/02/dance/; accessed June 2, 2014.

will enjoy immediate, full, eternal unity with Jesus and, therefore, with God.

Enter Thomas, the Eeyore of the Fourth Gospel, who first appeared at 11:16 and who assumes the practical (veering toward the pessimistic) role and asks a fair question. On the heels of Jesus' grandiloquent locution about abiding places and enigmatic travel plans, Thomas, in a voice somewhat weary but not yet despairing, cuts to the chase: "We do not know and we do not even know *how* to know" (sense of v. 5). How often do Jesus' disciples plead either total or partial ignorance, such that they are excused from decision making or action? They are looking for seven habits, nine steps, or ten commandments, when the answer lies in intimate, if confusing and challenging relationships, the preeminent one being between Jesus and them. Jesus, for his part, is having none of it: "You know enough because you know *me*" (sense of v. 7). Train your eyes on me, and the path will always be true and life-giving. "I am the Way; that is, the truth and the life" (v. 6, my trans.). Here the words truth (*alētheia*) and life (*zōē*) are epexegetical, further describing the meaning of the Way, rather than introducing two more separate features of Jesus.

John 14:6 may raise questions about Christian exclusivism. Contemporary interpreters should be cautioned to attend first to the original context before moving to our own. First, John repeatedly insists on the universal scope of Christ's work (1:9; 4:42; 12:32); at 10:16 Jesus declares, somewhat enigmatically, that he has "other sheep that do not belong to this fold." To some, John is the most universalistic of the Gospels. To others, who contend that the original first-century Johannine community was forged in stressful, sectarian circumstances that led John to think in binary, exclusive, oppositional categories, John is the most sectarian of the Gospels. Second, those who see in 14:6 a verse to use to convince unbelievers that they had better become Christian or suffer eternal exclusion from the kingdom of God should note that the Farewell Discourse is addressed to those who are *already* Christian, encouraging them to eschew the excuses for inefficacy and, instead, trust that we know enough and are equipped enough to do greater works than Jesus himself did.

JAIME CLARK-SOLES

their way, we do not need to lose heart. Trusting that Jesus is intimately connected to God and doing God's work, we rejoice in the seemingly evil events of Jesus' hour as the completion of Jesus' work of driving out the ruler of this world and drawing all people to himself (12:31–32). Calling that Friday "Good," we trust that Jesus is present and working wherever evil and death hold sway, to the point that we participate in the work that Jesus is doing.

Jesus' "I am" statement in 14:6 describes who Jesus is for the faithful: a leader who is on the *way* to life and, in fact, is the *way* to *life* with his Father, because Jesus, Word-made-flesh, makes known the *truth* he received from his Father. Since our goal is to leave our hearers trusting Jesus, we dare not preach 14:6 as either a theological claim that people must accept or a declaration of Christianity's exclusive stance in relation to other religions. Jesus' life, glorification, death, resurrection, and return to the Father were to benefit the world by bringing us abundant life.

The church possesses and proclaims *particularity* rather than *exclusivity*. In Jesus, God's tangible presence in the world, we know and experience God in a particular way that Jesus calls "my Father." We know God through the way of Jesus' cross and resurrection. We come to the Father through Jesus and make Jesus known to all who will hear of him. We proclaim Jesus to any and all who will listen as the one way to God, in that he is the way we know and trust, even as we trust the God made known in Jesus to handle the future of all who have not heard, will not hear, or have heard of and embraced another way to God.

CRAIG A. SATTERLEE

John 14:8–14

8Philip said to him, "Lord, show us the Father, and we will be satisfied." 9Jesus said to him, "Have I been with you all this time, Philip, and you still do not know me? Whoever has seen me has seen the Father. How can you say, 'Show us the Father'? 10Do you not believe that I am in the Father and the Father is in me? The words that I say to you I do not speak on my own; but the Father who dwells in me does his works. 11Believe me that I am in the Father and the Father is in me; but if you do not, then believe me because of the works themselves. 12Very truly, I tell you, the one who believes in me will also do the works that I do and, in fact, will do greater works than these, because I am going to the Father. 13I will do whatever you ask in my name, so that the Father may be glorified in the Son. 14If in my name you ask me for anything, I will do it."

Theological Perspective

If Jesus' first words in chapter 14 assuage the disciples' concerns regarding "the way" forward (by pointing out that through the presence of "the Way" they are already there, 14:4–6), then this discovery of their "dwelling place" pushes on to the question of how God reveals Godself here and now. As Jesus concludes in verse 7: "If you know me, you will know my Father also. From now on you do know him and have seen him."

If there is one thing human beings can never get enough of, according to Scripture, it is knowledge of and deep relationship with God. This, Jesus has just made clear, is our true home, our ultimate "dwelling place." So Philip now follows Thomas with the obvious request: "Lord, show us the Father, and we will be satisfied" (v. 8). This is indeed a true statement, and speaks well of Philip's priorities and hopes for life. However, these words also reveal, once more, how out of touch and clueless he is with regard to the identity of the one with whom he is talking (another favorite theme in John's Gospel, from Nicodemus in chap. 3 on).

Jesus, as announced at the beginning, has come into the world so that the world may know God, the true life and light that enlightens everyone (1:9). Yes, in Jesus, God was in the world; yet the world, and his disciples, did not know him (1:10). Still, by chapter

Pastoral Perspective

In this New Testament passage, Jesus is clear about who he is and how he is related to the Father. He says that they are so close that seeing and being with Jesus is exactly the same as seeing and being with the Father. Jesus says, "Just believe that I am in the Father and the Father is in me. Or at least believe because of the work you have seen me do" (v. 11, my trans.).

In the Old Testament, while the Spirit of God led and protected the Jews, no human was allowed to get close enough to see the face of God. Only a few seem to have been allowed to communicate with God or develop a personal relationship. We have a much different concept of God through our experience with Jesus. Clearly, in this passage the disciples still have not understood the relationship between the Father and the Son or really gotten a clear picture of the Father as Jesus knows him. Jesus states emphatically that the Father and the Son are one. He explains to his disciples that his very words are not his own but are those of the Father, "who lives in me and does his work through me" (v. 10 NLT).

Jesus knew his Father in a most loving and intimate way. Jesus told of his own experiences with a loving and caring Father, and through stories and parables he described his Father as his own dear father. The love between the Father and the Son is wonderfully and beautifully expressed.

Exegetical Perspective

In the immediately preceding passage, Jesus declares that the disciples know the "way," but Thomas pleads ignorance, causing Jesus to provide a more extended explanation. This is a typical technique in the Fourth Gospel, which scholars have labeled "Johannine misunderstanding." The character is used as a setup so that John may convey necessary teaching to the audience through Jesus (cf. Nicodemus in 3:1–21; the disciples in 4:31–38; the religious authorities in 8:21–30).

Where Thomas lamented lack of knowledge, Philip now demonstrates lack of insight and vision. John 14:7 finds Jesus assuring both that through him, they have all the knowledge and vision they need in order to do greater works than Jesus himself did (v. 12). The multifarious verbs of knowing (*ginōskō, oida*) and seeing (*blepō, theōreō, horaō*) abound in the Fourth Gospel, and the goal of all of this knowing and seeing is, finally, trusting Jesus, in order to seize hold of life in its fullest sense (20:31).

Unlike the Synoptic Gospels, John considers Philip a main character; he is named twelve times (1:43, 44, 45, 46, 48; 6:5, 7; 12:21, 22), as opposed to once each in Matthew, Mark, and Luke. He appears at the beginning of Jesus' ministry; after the brothers Andrew and Peter, who were also from Bethsaida, Philip is the next one to follow. He is the

Homiletical Perspective

I imagine that the longer Jesus talks, the more the disciples feel evil and death hovering over the evening, waiting to pounce. The longer Jesus talks, the harder and harder it becomes to follow, let alone trust, all that Jesus is saying. Philip reaches his breaking point and, in light of the lofty claims that Jesus is making, asks a simple request: "Show us the Father, and we will be satisfied" (v. 8).

We can relate. Confronted by the powers of violence and death, we need more than words that are hard to follow and harder still to trust, even if those words come from Jesus. Finding it difficult not to let our hearts be troubled, we ask, "Where is God?" "What is God like?" "What, if anything, is God doing?" In other words, "Show us the Father, and we will be satisfied."

Jesus is a bit frustrated. "Have I been with you all this time, Philip," Jesus asks, "and you still do not know me?" (v. 9). Then, in no uncertain terms, Jesus points us to himself: "Whoever has seen me has seen the Father. How can you say, 'Show us the Father'? Do you not believe that I am in the Father and the Father is in me? The words that I say to you I do not speak on my own; but the Father who dwells in me does his works" (vv. 9–10). Jesus answers, "God is right here. Whoever sees and knows me has seen and known the Father." Jesus is in the Father, and the

Theological Perspective

14, we do not know him; so Jesus, with utmost patience and grace, attempts to explain. He does so with a threefold argument: through sight, and words, and works.

Sight. The first move is mostly a throwaway line. John's Gospel recognizes that the time for seeing God in Jesus is over. This was the gift of God to the apostles and all those blessed with seeing Jesus in the flesh. Jesus is now leaving the scene. Though his leaving allows another's coming (the Paraclete), the time for holding on to Jesus "in the flesh" is gone (see Jesus' words to Mary in the garden when she attempts to "hold on," 20:17). While Jesus is understandably perturbed by those who see him, yet fail to see the Father in him, the Gospel is written primarily, if not exclusively, for those who cannot see Jesus, except in the words and works of the church. "Have you believed [or not believed] because you have *seen* me?" Jesus asks Thomas later. "Blessed are those who have *not seen* and yet have come to believe" (20:29, emphasis added).

Words. It is impossible to hear Jesus' words regarding the source of his own words ("the words I say to you I do not speak on my own," v. 10) without hearing in them the reason for this Gospel and the teaching and preaching of the church that this Gospel will inspire. John writes this Gospel, and preachers preach the gospel, not so much to teach others about God, but in order by the Spirit to make God present. In the words of a recent Directory for Worship from my denomination, the sermon is "a proclamation of Scripture in the conviction that through the Holy Spirit Jesus Christ is present to the gathered people, offering grace and calling for obedience."[1]

Correctly understood, the words of preachers are not spoken "on our own," but proceed from the lips of him who is there in the Spirit. To hear these words, again with the Spirit's help, is to know God and, through this knowledge, to leave worship "satisfied." We are properly satisfied not with the wisdom or eloquence of the preacher, but with the presence of Christ these words convey. Worship, at its core, is not so much for education or entertainment or even evangelism, but for encounter. They would *hear* Jesus and, through this hearing, come to know the God who has sent him.

Works. James is not the only book that says faith without works is dead. Just as the signs Jesus

---

1. Directory for Worship, in *Book of Order, 2011/2013* (Louisville, KY: Presbyterian Church (U.S.A.), 2011), 89.

Pastoral Perspective

By examining Jesus' life as a model of God, we learn many things about God the Father:

- The Father's love for us is unyielding, magnificent, continual, unconditional, and beyond our knowledge and understanding.
- The Father accepts us as and where we are in life, rather than expecting us to be what we are not.
- The Father wants an intimate relationship with his sons and daughters and has given us that status. We are in the family of God.
- The Father considers all of creation good, sacred, and important.
- The Father wants us to be healthy and mature persons in mind, body, heart, and soul.
- The Father is a living spirit who has chosen to dwell with us in our earthly life.
- The Father provides for our needs and encourages physical, mental, emotional, and spiritual growth.
- The Father will go to any lengths, including the death of his Son, to convince us of his great love for us.
- The Father has provided the Holy Spirit to be active in our lives as a counselor, companion, advocate, and guide.
- The Father is just and gracious, loving us all equally.
- The Father rushes to meet us as we return to him and forgives us of our failures.
- It is the Father's intent that we should all be his children and live with him in this world and the next.

Jesus also explains that the work he has done while on earth has been done to glorify his Father. He further assures his disciples that they can also bring God glory: "I tell you the truth, anyone who believes in me will do the same works I have done and even greater works, because I am going to be with the Father. You can ask for anything in my name, and I will do it, so the Son can bring glory to the Father" (vv. 12–13 NLT).

This promise is made not only to the disciples but to anyone who believes in Jesus. We then are included in these mysterious words. Can we really do the work that Jesus did? Can we perform miracles in the lives of others and in our own life? What power do we have to heal, teach, preach the word of God, and bring others into the light and love of the Father and the Son?

We have varied and amazing gifts given to us by God to be used to glorify the Father. To begin with, each of us has the potential power to give healthy love to each other. The more we allow the Father and

first disciple to lead someone else (Nathanael) to Jesus and the second disciple to make a proclamation about Jesus: "We have found him about whom Moses in the law and also the prophets wrote" (1:45). That encounter ends with Jesus' announcing that he has replaced, in effect, Jacob's ladder (1:51). In chapter 6, Jesus "tests" Philip about feeding the crowds; Philip cannot see his way to the grandiosity of Jesus' works, but the work occurs anyway. Philip also participates in the crucial turning point in the Gospel. The Greeks (perhaps the sheep from another fold mentioned in 10:16) arrive and first consult Philip. After Philip (and Andrew) informs him about this development, Jesus declares: "The hour has come for the Son of Man to be glorified" (12:23). Presumably Philip remains on the scene to witness the exchange between Jesus and God (12:27–28).

While Thomas spoke as a representative of the group, and Jesus answered him as such (using second-person plural verbs), when Philip tries the same move, Jesus gets personal with him: "Have I been with you [plural] all this time, Philip, and you [singular] still do not know me? . . . How can you [singular] say, 'Show us the Father'?" (v. 9). Philip presses Jesus for more so that the disciples may be "satisfied" (*arkeō*, v. 8). This is important: the only other occurrence of this word appears in Jesus' exchange with Philip about feeding the crowd; there Philip again protests that what is available is not sufficient or satisfactory to complete God's work (*arkeō*, 6:7). Philip operates from a theology of scarcity as he stares blindly into the face of the Good Shepherd who makes our cup overflow (Ps. 23:5) and who came that we may have life and have it more abundantly (*perissōs*, 10:10). Philip demands "satisfaction" while Jesus is longing to gift him beyond measure.

How should Philip (and we) know that Jesus and God are unified? By attending to Jesus' words and works: "The words [*rhēma*] that I say to you [plural] I do not speak on my own; but the Father who dwells [*menō*] in me does his works [*ergon*]" (v. 10). Words and works are not two separate things for John, because, even as we know on our best days, words *are* works. John has numerous words for "words": *logos, rhēma, lalia, entolē*, not to mention verbs for speaking (*legō, laleō, apokrinomai*).[1]

Jesus' words are both authoritative and effective. His words are at least as authoritative as Scripture (2:22), if not more authoritative (5:39–47). Like

1. For a fuller treatment, see Jaime Clark-Soles, *Scripture Cannot Be Broken: The Social Function of the Use of Scripture in the Fourth Gospel* (Leiden: E. J. Brill, 2003), 294–310.

Father is in Jesus. We have Jesus'—no, the Father's—word on it.

Philip does not say anything further, but I wonder whether Philip is satisfied with Jesus' words. As a preacher, a Christian, and human being, I am not. I am not satisfied with Jesus' words during those seasons of life when I urgently need to know where God is and what God is like. I am certainly dissatisfied with words, even words of Jesus, during those seasons of life when death and evil rage unexpectedly and uncontrollably, and my community looks to me as someone who speaks for God, demanding to know where God is, what God is like, and what, if anything, God is doing. I know that accepting Jesus' word is the better way, but sometimes I need something a bit more concrete.

In response, Jesus points to his works, saying, "Believe me that I am in the Father and the Father is in me; but if you do not, then believe me because of the works themselves" (v. 11). The evidence of Jesus' intimate connection to the Father has been there for the first disciples to see—and for subsequent disciples to hear—throughout Jesus' public ministry. When words are too heady, distant, and theoretical, we can look to Jesus' works, because they reveal his intimate connection with the Father. Throughout his public ministry, Jesus repeatedly declares that the works he does are God's work and not his own (5:20, 36; 10:37–38; 14:10) and that his work is to complete God's work (4:34; 17:4). Thus, everything about Jesus—his words, works, and entire person—makes the Father known. More than God working through Jesus, Jesus dwells in God, and God dwells in Jesus and "does his works" (v. 10) in the world. Scripture does not say this about anyone other than Jesus. We have Jesus' works to confirm it.

In the sermon, the preacher might voice Jesus' words and then verify them with Jesus' works. Reviewing John's Book of Signs reminds us of Jesus' works: changing water into wine (2:1–11), healing the royal official's son (4:46–54), healing the paralyzed man at the pool of Bethesda (5:1–18), feeding five thousand with five barley loaves and two fish (6:5–14), walking on the water (6:16–24), restoring the sight of the man born blind (9:11–17), and calling Lazarus out of the tomb and raising him from the dead (11:1–45).

More than reminding us of his works, Jesus points us to where we might look when we find it hard to believe his words. Wherever joy and abundance replace embarrassment and scarcity, healing occurs unexpectedly, paralysis gives way to

John 14:8–14

Theological Perspective

performs are "starting point" reasons to believe for those for whom Jesus' presence and words are not enough, so the works that Jesus and the church perform are "starting point" reasons to believe for those for whom the church's presence and witness are insufficient. According to John's Gospel, the primary "work" of God is belief in the One whom God has sent (6:29). If this essential "work" is not possible, though, then belief based on the "works themselves" is a beginning. In the next passage (and indeed in the passages before, e.g., 13:35), we will explore the core works to which the church is called. (Hint: they all center in love; cf. 1 John 2:7–11.)

For now, the key, theologically, is to understand the proper function for all such works themselves. They do not secure God's love in Christ. Rather, they serve as proof that those who perform them are connected to Christ and, through Christ, to the Father. If the church can do nothing regarding "fruits" apart from the "vine," then if the church produces "fruit," it demonstrates its connection to the vine (15:5). The works do not establish the relationship; the works help foster belief that the relationship is already established. As the Heidelberg Catechism puts it, we who have been redeemed by grace through Christ must do good works "so that we ourselves may be assured of our faith by its fruits and by our reverent behavior may win our neighbors to Christ."[2] The fruits are a "sign" of a relationship, not the way to get the relationship going.

What we human beings most yearn for is knowledge of and a relationship with God and God's people. Ask after these things "in Jesus' name" (v. 14), and the Father will be glorified and we will be satisfied, no matter what else does or does not come our way.

RICHARD N. BOYCE

Pastoral Perspective

Son to live within us, the more this powerful love can grow and flow out to others. We can be focused and intentional about identifying, growing, and sharing the particular abilities we have to teach, educate, heal, affirm, and generously share material possessions and spiritual insights with those whom God brings into our lives. We can live with an open heart and mind to see what is given to us every day to do for the glorification of God.

A woman was once asked by a friend what she was doing in her retirement. Her reply was, "Oh, I am a handy woman for God. I do what he provides for me to do each day." If we are to be available to do God's work each day, we must be open to a partnership with God and pray continually for an intimate relationship so that we are constantly aware of the presence of God's Spirit.

Hafiz, the fourteenth-century Persian poet, was amazingly aware of a most intimate relationship with God. In his poem "The Seed Cracked Open" he writes:

> There are two of us housed
> In this body.[1]

Being open daily to the love and guidance of the Spirit allows us to use the power Jesus has promised us, so that we can partner with God to do the work that God has planned for us to accomplish in this world.

KATHERINE E. AMOS

---

2. Heidelberg Catechism, Question 86, in *The Book of Confessions* (Louisville, KY: The Office of the General Assembly, Presbyterian Church (U.S.A.), 2002), 43.

1. Hafiz, *The Gift: Poems by Hafiz, the Great Sufi Master*, trans. Daniel Ladinsky (New York: Penguin Compass, 1999), 35.

Exegetical Perspective

Scripture, Jesus' words are said to be fulfilled (*pleroō*) and are to be kept and observed (*tereō*) and believed or trusted (*pisteuō*). Jesus speaks efficaciously. At 4:50–51, he heals by a word, from a distance: "Jesus said to him, 'Go; your son will live.' The man believed the word [*logos*] that Jesus spoke to him and started on his way. As he was going down, his slaves met him and told him that his child was alive." At 5:8–9, "Jesus said, . . . 'Stand up, take your mat and walk.' At once the man was made well, and he took up his mat and began to walk."

The language of works (*ergazomai*; *ergon*) appears heavily in the Gospel, not to mention verbs of doing (*poieō*) and the occurrences of signs (*sēmeia*). The Father works and Jesus works, indistinguishably and vitally: "The Father loves the Son and shows him all that he himself is doing; he will show him [even] greater works than these [*kai megas toutōn*], so that you will be astonished" (5:20). Note how 14:12 parallels 5:20, using the same language. That is, as impressive as it may be for Jesus to do the very works of God, even more captivating is Jesus' claim that whoever trusts in Jesus will also do the very works (*ergon*) that Jesus and God do. Further, the one who trusts will do even *greater*[2] works than these (*kai megas toutōn*).

Astonishing indeed. Christians can do what Jesus did and more, and many have over these two thousand years (from the mundane to the miraculous). Whether we *will* do them is up to us; the fact that we *can* do them is due to the fact that Jesus completed the very work God sent him to do (19:30), such that if we ask *anything* (Gk. *ti*) in the name of Jesus, he will do it. Jesus appears to have left no room for his disciples to dream small.

JAIME CLARK-SOLES

Homiletical Perspective

movement, hungry people are fed and filled, calm overcomes a storm, someone receives new vision, and life triumphs over death, Jesus is still working. The preacher might name some of those places for the congregation, which means the preacher must be on the lookout for them. In the process, the preacher might find her or his own trust strengthened.

Do not stop with naming. The assurance is not so much in the works themselves, but in the powerful way trusting Jesus unlocks signs in a community that trusts Jesus' words. Jesus' departure means the disciples will continue God's work. Jesus' departure also means we get to continue God's work. Jesus' prediction of "greater works than these" (v. 12) is understood in terms of quantity rather than quality. Jesus' return to the Father makes possible all that could not be accomplished when Jesus was bound by his incarnation. Jesus withdraws so that God's work can expand. The faith community's works are also "greater" in that they point to the fullness of God's love for the world revealed in Jesus' death and resurrection.

That these are Jesus' own works, and not merely a faith community's efforts, is evident in Jesus' declaration, uttered twice, "I will do" (vv. 13–14). Jesus' continuing commitment and involvement in the faith community's works are guaranteed by his promise to do whatever is asked in his name, "so that the Father may be glorified in the Son" (vv. 13–14). Trusting in Jesus' word enough to ask in his name, the Christian community's power is immeasurable. Even more, struggling individuals within the community and people in the world that surrounds it will come to trust because of the works the community does in Jesus' name. The faith community's works are Jesus' works in the same way that Jesus' works are God's. More than ends in themselves, the works the faith community does in Jesus' name are part of Jesus' own work of making God known to the world. When you do not trust the words, look to the works. Jesus is there.

CRAIG A. SATTERLEE

---

2. It is, finally, immaterial whether the works are "greater" because Jesus was only one person confined to ministry in one land or because the disciples work in a new era of salvation history post-Easter.

John 14:15–17

15"If you love me, you will keep my commandments. ¹⁶And I will ask the Father, and he will give you another Advocate, to be with you forever. ¹⁷This is the Spirit of truth, whom the world cannot receive, because it neither sees him nor knows him. You know him, because he abides with you, and he will be in you."

Theological Perspective

There is a flow to John 14 that is easy to miss when you break it into portions. One statement leads to the next such that the passage feels almost stream of consciousness or free association. So it requires some attention to what precedes in order to understand what follows.

Jesus has just said that anything the disciples ask "in his name" he will do (14:14), and now he seems almost immediately to contradict himself. He tells the disciples that if they love him, they must keep his commandments. Love of Christ is necessarily demonstrated by obedience to Christ, especially in the willingness to love one another as Christ has loved us. Rather than simply confirming, "Ask me for this, and I will do it," though, Jesus says that he must ask the Father, who will send another to help this come true (v. 16). Anything else that is aligned with Jesus' purposes, Jesus will do.

This particular request is going to require a little teamwork, indeed, the promise of the constant and abiding presence of Jesus, and thereby of God. The one thing that Jesus asks, we cannot do—unless the Spirit abides with us, and sets up shop among us. As with the worry regarding the Way, and the desire to see the Father, the answer to all our questions about where, what, and how is *relational*. All of this requires that God be *with us*, as

Pastoral Perspective

Jesus promises a miraculous gift from God, the gift of the Holy Spirit: "I will ask the Father, and he will give you another advocate who will never leave you. He is the Holy Spirit who leads into all truth" (vv. 16–17 NLT). As we contemplate the abundance from God, including all of our material, intellectual, emotional, and spiritual gifts, we could never receive anything that compares to the gift of the living God dwelling in and among us. We know that the Spirit has been with Jesus during his earthly life and before, bringing counsel, power, peace, love, and joy. Now Jesus promises that the Holy Spirit will never leave us. This living Spirit of God knows us with great intimacy, will advocate for us in times of trouble and need, guide, educate, nurture, and counsel us, and listen intently to us and respond to our joys and sorrows. Nothing could give us more hope.

How can we trust that the Holy Spirit will be with us always and lead us into all truth? What evidence do we have in our own lives or see in the experiences of others that assures us the Spirit of God is alive and abides with us morning, noon, and night? In what ways have we seen the work of the Spirit throughout the world?

Think of what experiences you have had with the Holy Spirit and how the Spirit has nurtured and

Exegetical Perspective

Jesus continues the Farewell Discourse (chaps. 14–17), preparing his disciples for his departure and their receipt of the Holy Spirit. In this brief but powerful passage, Jesus reiterates his favorite theme (love); promises the Holy Spirit; and emphasizes the intimate unity of Jesus, God, the Spirit, and the believer.

The Fourth Evangelist uses love verbs (*agapaō*, *phileō*) fifty times, compared to Matthew's thirteen, Mark's six, and Luke's fifteen. The noun love (*agapē*) is used seven times; Matthew and Luke only use it once, and Mark never. Friend (*philos*) appears six times in John, while Matthew uses it once, Mark never, and Luke fifteen times. Unlike John, where Jesus uses *philos* in reference to his followers, Luke's Jesus uses it primarily in parables. Given the overwhelming prevalence of love language in the Fourth Gospel, we might accuse the author of preoccupation with a single issue. Why not? "For God so loved the world that he gave his only Son, so that everyone who believes in him may not perish but may have eternal life" (3:16).

In verse 15 Jesus declares that if his disciples love him, they will keep his commandments. The reader may ask, "What commandments?" Unlike Matthew, nowhere in John does Jesus command us to go the second mile, turn the other cheek, or render unto Caesar that which is Caesar's. Famously, Jesus issues a

Homiletical Perspective

We need to find a way around the apparent quid pro quo in this passage. "If you love me," Jesus says, "you will keep my commandments. And [if you keep my commandments,] I will ask the Father, and he will give you another Advocate, to be with you forever" (vv. 15–16). One commentator even asserts: "keeping Jesus' word or commandments is the condition of enjoying the Father's love and the abiding presence of the Father, Son, and Counselor-Spirit."[1] Does enjoying God's loving and abiding presence really depend upon my keeping Jesus' commandments? If it does, I have a problem, and I suspect that I am not alone.

Remembering John's Gospel helps me to get beyond the conditional. Jesus as "the way, the truth, and the life" (14:6) has nothing whatsoever to do with quid pro quo. Jesus' being lifted up from the earth and drawing all people to himself certainly does not depend on anything we do or fail to do. As he prepares to go to the cross and his glorification, Jesus is not laying down conditions. He is attempting to inspire trust among his disciples. These words are meant to assure, not to threaten.

Remembering that the word "condition" has multiple definitions also helps me. It is primarily

1. Gerard S. Sloyan, *John*, Interpretation: A Bible Commentary for Preaching and Teaching (Atlanta: John Knox Press, 1988), 181.

John 14:15–17

Theological Perspective

Christ was *with us*, in the flesh, face to face, person to person.

Here we come to the heart of a mystery that repeatedly trips us up in our worship, our service, and our prayers. Too often, the life of faith is described as a two-step shuffle where we receive the benefits of what God has done for us in Jesus Christ (justification), and then we respond to this initiative on God's part with our gratitude (sanctification). One is seen as a gift, the other our thank-you (just like the exodus from Egypt and our response of obedience in the Old Testament). One is *God's* work; the other is *ours*. Wrong!

Jesus in this passage tells the disciples that they can do greater works than he has done, except that *they* cannot. Indeed, *they* cannot even do the one thing necessary to show their love for him: obedience. The only way *they* can do this is if God abides in them and thereby works through or "participates" with them in all they say and do. It is like a vine and branches. Apart from me, you can do what? "Nothing!" (15:5).

Let us listen in on how some statements of the church attempt to put words to this profound paradox: "Human beings have no higher goal in life than to glorify and enjoy God now and forever, living in covenant fellowship with God and participating in God's mission." Humans cannot glorify God unless they are in fellowship with God and thereby participating in God's mission. We need the Spirit.

"God has put all things under the Lordship of Jesus Christ and has made Christ Head of the Church, which is his body. The Church's life and mission are a joyful participation in Christ's ongoing life and work."[1] The mission of the church flows from our relationship with Jesus through the Advocate. We need the Spirit.

"The Church is to be a community of witness, pointing beyond itself through word and work to the good news of God's transforming grace in Christ Jesus its Lord."[2] Though the world no longer sees Jesus, the world can see the works of the church and hear the words of the church and thereby know that God abides with the church and lives in the church. We and the world need the Spirit.

John 14 began with the disciples' anxiety as they were informed that Jesus was getting ready to leave them. How would they know "the way"? "I am the way," Jesus answered (14:6). How can they see and

Pastoral Perspective

guided you to be more Christlike. Do you open yourself daily to the presence and power of the Spirit? Are you open and willing to listen daily to the truth spoken to you by God's Spirit in you?

If we look for the Spirit to work in human ways, it is likely that we will be disappointed, because we will miss much of what the Spirit is saying and doing. Jesus warned that the world was not looking for the Holy Spirit and therefore would not recognize it, but that we could know the Spirit "because He lives with you now and later will be in you" (v. 17 NLT).

What personal environment within us offers the most productive home for God to work powerfully in our lives? We know that Jesus lived to bring glory to the Father. We too should work to bring glory to the Father, and then we can trust that the Spirit is living and working within us.

The gifts of the Spirit are love, joy, peace, patience, kindness, goodness, faithfulness, gentleness, and self-control (Gal. 5:22–23). Where these gifts flourish, the Spirit of God is present and working. However, we should be aware that God's Spirit can be active anywhere and in any circumstances, always devoted to hope, reconciliation, and freedom. The Spirit is mysterious and full of surprises. We do not control the work of the Spirit; we only pray that the Spirit will choose us as partners in God's mighty deeds.

In the Bible, the Holy Spirit appears in multiple forms, such as wind, flame, a dove, pillars of clouds and fire, and even as a "still small voice" (1 Kgs. 19:12 KJV). The Spirit hovered over Mary, descended in the form of a dove at Jesus' baptism, drove Jesus into the desert to be tempted, and appeared as flames to the disciples at Pentecost (Acts 2:3).

Today the Spirit manifests God in many ways in own lives. Lutheran pastor Laura Wind tells of the Holy Spirit appearing on a mission trip at a hot, humid location in the Caribbean. The only source of relief from the extreme heat, an oscillating fan, had ceased to work on the second day of the mission trip, and misery set in. The Spirit came in the form of a handyman who always accompanied church mission trips. Mike not only fixed the fan but also suggested a cold shower at bedtime and a wet wash cloth to use during the night, making the rest of the mission trip much more tolerable. To Pastor Wind, the Spirit was present in the handyman.[1]

The Rev. Dr. Karen Hudson, a Methodist minister, shares an experience with the Spirit when she took a

---

1. *Book of Order, 2013–2015* (Louisville, KY: The Office of the General Assembly, Presbyterian Church (U.S.A.), 2013), 1.
2. *Book of Order, 2013–15*, 2.

1. Laura Wind, personal communication.

single commandment in John; it occurs in the chapter just before ours: "I give you a new commandment, that you love one another. Just as I have loved you, you also should love one another. By this everyone will know that you are my disciples, if you have love for one another" (13:34–35). Furthermore, he reiterates this in the chapter immediately succeeding ours: "This is my commandment, that you love one another as I have loved you. No one has greater love than this, to lay down one's life for one's friends" (15:12–13).

The interpreter should resist the common but mistaken urge to distinguish between God's way of loving (*agapaō, agapē*) and human ways of loving (*phileō, philos*), with the former considered to be superior to the latter. The Gospel of John makes the *exact opposite* move, in fact. The Gospel uses the words interchangeably for God and people. God loves Jesus (5:20); God loves the followers (16:27); Jesus loves his followers (20:2); the followers love Jesus (16:27), and so forth, using the verb *phileō* as well as *agapaō*. This is a major theological claim for John: the so-called dividing line between divine and human love simply does not exist. Should this be surprising in a Gospel that insists so radically upon the incarnation?

Admittedly, John's pneumatology is unusual compared to other New Testament texts. All of the Gospels refer to the Holy Spirit descending upon Jesus like a dove. In contrast to Luke, however, who depicts the Holy Spirit as heavily active in the lives of characters from the beginning of his Gospel until the end of Acts, John insists that the Holy Spirit will become active for believers only after Jesus himself departs ("Now he said this about the Spirit, which believers in him were to receive; for as yet there was no Spirit, because Jesus was not yet glorified," 7:39). Why is this? A clue lies in Jesus' referring to the Holy Spirit not as *the* Paraclete, but rather as "*another [allon]* Paraclete" (v. 16). Jesus was the first; for the Spirit to be active among them while Jesus was there would have been redundant, since they each serve the same revelatory function.

What appeared to be bad news to the disciples, namely, Jesus' departure from them, turns out to be the best of news for both them and us. While Jesus walked the earth, his ministry was limited to one locale and one person, himself. Upon his departure, his disciples are given the Spirit and graduate from apprentices to full, mature revealers of God's love. The same holds true for all future disciples who never encountered the historical Jesus; contemporary believers have no disadvantage in comparison to the

defined as "something necessary," as in, it is necessary that you keep Jesus' commandments for Jesus to ask the Father to send the Advocate. However, it is also defined as "way of being." This definition is more in keeping with what John has in mind, since the way of being of one who loves Jesus is keeping Jesus' commandments, and the way of being of one who keeps Jesus' commandments is to love Jesus. Therefore, Jesus is saying, "After I am gone, I will ask the Father, and he will send another Advocate to you who love me and keep my commandments. The Advocate will help you by being with you forever."

In order to make clear that the Advocate is the Father's gift to the church and not anyone's personal possession, I remember that Jesus' words are not addressed to any "one" but to a community of disciples. As important as an individual's loving Jesus and keeping his commandments are, faith communities' loving Jesus and keeping his commandments are more important in two ways. First, the community that loves Jesus and keeps his commandments can support, admonish, forgive, exhort, and empower the individual and in so doing become the tangible expression of the Advocate. Second, this assertion—that keeping Jesus' word or commandments is the condition (both something necessary and a way of being) of enjoying the Father's love and the abiding presence of the Father, Son, and Counselor-Spirit—defines what the faith community is to be, how its members are to relate to one another, and what the faith community is to be about.

Since loving Jesus and keeping his commandments are necessary conditions for the Advocate to come to both congregation and individual, welcoming the Advocate involves more than beginning our meetings with a prayer for the Holy Spirit. If we stop loving Jesus and keeping his commandments, we ought not be surprised when we find that the Advocate has returned to the Father. Perhaps the audience for this sermon should not be the individual but the faith community.

Who is this "other Advocate" that Jesus will ask the Father to send? John 14:16–17 introduces the word "Paraclete," which the NRSV translates as "Advocate." The preacher might use this occasion to (re)introduce the Advocate to the church. My preference is to use the word "Paraclete," rather than settle on "Advocate" or any other English word as a means of unpacking all the dimensions of the Paraclete's work. "Paraclete" is often used to describe someone called to help in a law court. In the Jewish tradition, "paraclete" came to be used for angels, prophets,

John 14:15–17

Theological Perspective

know God, and thus be satisfied? By hearing the words and seeing the works that only he can produce (14:10–11). How then can they perform such works that lead to belief, their own and others? Only through receiving Christ through the Spirit, who will be with the church forever (v. 16).

Of course the kicker here is that while the means for obedience is "relational," the goal of obedience is also "relational." Back at the very beginning of this speech or consolation, Jesus reveals his new summary of the commandments: "I give you a new commandment, that you love one another" (13:34). Indeed, Jesus makes it clear that this is the way that others will know that the disciples are connected to him: "By this everyone will know that you are my disciples, if you have love for one another" (13:35).

Maybe, in some deep way, this is the reason that obedience to this commandment is the one thing that Jesus cannot simply do if we ask. As the Son asks the Father to give the Advocate who will be with us forever, so through, and only through, participation in this divine "family," the church becomes a "family" itself. Many commentators and theologians have observed on reading John that what at first glance seems easier (loving *one another*) proves harder in the long run ("Lord, just let me love *my enemies!*").[3] Nevertheless, just as in John's Gospel the intimate relationship between the members of the divine family serves as the basis for helping us know and trust God, so the intimate and persistent relationships among the members of the church family serve as a means for others to know and trust God—once Jesus is gone in the flesh. For a church that is ever prone to schism, this is not only a call to prayer but a summons to a "joyful participation in Christ's ongoing life and work," Father, Son, and Holy Spirit. This both requires and calls for *teamwork*—on God's part and our own.

RICHARD N. BOYCE

Pastoral Perspective

young girl on a shopping trip to a local department store. The child of an immigrant family sponsored by Rev. Hudson's congregation, she had been badly burned on her face and shoulder by hot liquid pulled from the stove in her home. The family had hesitated to take her to the doctor for financial reasons. When they finally sought medical care, they were told by doctors that there was nothing that could be done to remove the scarring from the burns. At the store, Rev. Hudson noticed a woman staring at the two of them. Finally the woman came up and said that the child needed to be healed. As the shocked pair stood in the store, the woman prayed for the child and then touched her face, saying that the child would be healed in the morning. The woman then disappeared.

Plans had been made for the little girl to spend the night at the Hudson home. Indeed, in the morning the burnt area on the child's face was completely healed. Dead skin was on the pillow that had cushioned the child's head the night before.[2]

As we think of the countless ways the Spirit works, we realize that the Spirit comes to us in the known and in the unknown. The more we are aware of the presence of the Spirit, the more we can see and be part of the glorious work of God.

Perhaps we need to approach the Spirit with the humility of a handyman or handywoman and just wait for the opportunity to be the love and healing presence of God in someone's life. The most exciting thing about the work of the Spirit is the mystery and surprise waiting for us in the work we do, as we partner in love and trust with our constant spiritual companion, a companion who never ceases to walk at our side.

KATHERINE E. AMOS

---

3. See Frances Taylor Gench, *Encounters with Jesus* (Louisville, KY: Westminster John Knox Press, 2007) 108–9.

2. Karen Hudson, personal communication.

first believers. Everything that they were taught and that they experienced is available to the same degree and with equally rich texture to us.

The word *paraklētos* presents notorious translation difficulty, because it has a range of meanings in the Greek, all of which the author signifies. English translations variously translate it "Comforter," "Advocate," "Counselor," and "Helper"; it might be best to keep it in its transliterated form, "Paraclete," so as to catch the attention of the hearer with the strangeness; after all, it is strange among biblical authors too. It appears only five times in the New Testament: four times in the Farewell Discourse (14:16, 26; 15:26; 16:7) and once in 1 John 2:1. Narrowing the Greek word to a single translation robs the author of rhetorical force and the listener of the chance to consider all the various functions of the Holy Spirit. The Holy Spirit is specifically said to do the following: teach, remind (14:26), abide (14:16), and testify about Jesus (15:26). Like Jesus, the Holy Spirit deals in truth. True to his word, the Word breathes (*emphysaō*) the Holy Spirit upon his disciples (20:22), making them one with God and Jesus.

Through the language of abiding (*menō*), love, being "in" (14:17, 20) and, later in the Discourse, an emphasis on "one-ness" (17:21–23), John insists that the intimate relationship that exists between him, God, and the Spirit also includes believers. The believer is a participant in the relationship, not a bystander. If the passage is read aloud and preached, the reading should go through verse 23, the pinnacle of the passage: "Jesus answered him, 'Those who love me will keep my word, and my Father will love them, and we will come to them and make our home with them.'" If God, Jesus, and the Spirit abide *en* (meaning both "in" and "among") us (14:17), have made their home with us (recall 1:14), how can we imagine there to be any distance between us and God? This, in turn, affects our eschatology.

Everything that matters—ultimate intimacy with God and Christ—is available *now*. Eternal life, abundant life, is here for the living—from this very moment into eternity.

JAIME CLARK-SOLES

and the just as advocates before God's court. The Paraclete exhorts and encourages, comforts and consoles, helps and makes appeals on our behalf. Contemplating the Paraclete leads me to remember various mentors, all with their own personalities and perspectives. I wonder how framing the Paraclete as our mentor would preach.

Jesus identifies his request to God as the source of God's gift of the Paraclete (v. 16). The use of the adjective "another" to modify Paraclete (v. 16) suggests that Jesus was himself a Paraclete and that the word is more than a synonym for the Holy Spirit. That the Paraclete has functions in common with Jesus and continues his own work is evident in Jesus' naming himself "the truth" (14:6) and calling the Paraclete "the Spirit of truth" (v. 17). The Spirit of truth dwells with communities of those who love Jesus and is within them, as someone they know in a way the world cannot.

The Paraclete makes it possible for those who love Jesus to live within Jesus' truth, because the Spirit of Jesus' truth is within them. Since the Paraclete "will be with you forever," "abides with you," and "will be in you," we can be assured that God's revelation in Jesus does not end with his death and return to God. In fact, more important than keeping the truth of Jesus present in the faith community, the Spirit of truth works to ensure that Jesus' truth is present to the world in the faith communities who love Jesus and keep his commandments.

God's gift of the Paraclete is the way around any quid pro quo that attempts to define our relationship with God. I suspect all the remembering I talk about—John's Gospel, the meanings of "condition," and that Jesus was speaking to a faith community— are not so much my doing as the work of the Spirit of truth. Perhaps the best thing the preacher can attempt is a sermon that allows the congregation to experience the Paraclete at work.

CRAIG A. SATTERLEE

John 14:18–24

¹⁸"I will not leave you orphaned; I am coming to you. ¹⁹In a little while the world will no longer see me, but you will see me; because I live, you also will live. ²⁰On that day you will know that I am in my Father, and you in me, and I in you. ²¹They who have my commandments and keep them are those who love me; and those who love me will be loved by my Father, and I will love them and reveal myself to them." ²²Judas (not Iscariot) said to him, "Lord, how is it that you will reveal yourself to us, and not to the world?" ²³Jesus answered him, "Those who love me will keep my word, and my Father will love them, and we will come to them and make our home with them. ²⁴Whoever does not love me does not keep my words; and the word that you hear is not mine, but is from the Father who sent me."

Theological Perspective

The Gospel of John stands out quite distinctly from its Synoptic cousins (Mark, Matthew, and Luke) in many ways, but particularly in its significance for Christian theology. Its view of Jesus proved formative for what became orthodox Christology, that is, what the church deemed the "right understanding" of Jesus' identity and significance. Today, Christians take Trinitarian theology (that Creator, Christ, and Holy Spirit are three-in-one and one-in-three) for granted, but that was not always so. Some two hundred years after this Gospel was written, Christians were conflicted over how to understand Jesus' relationship to God. All saw him as distinctively connected to God, but they disagreed over the nature of that connection. To say Jesus *was* God seemed to threaten God's nature as unchangeable, eternal, and indivisible. On the other hand, to deny Jesus' humanity and the reality of his death seemed to threaten our salvation. The Council of Nicaea (325 CE) thought it had resolved the issue. Jesus was not created but begotten; he was "from the same substance [*homoousios*] of the Father, God from God, Light from Light" *and* "was made man, suffered, and rose again on the third day."

Of course, it took another ecumenical council (Chalcedon in 451 CE) to work out the details of the "two natures" (divine and human) Christology,

Pastoral Perspective

Reading Gospel stories from the retrospective reality—twenty centuries after the fact—often dulls their impact to the point of seeming obvious. To the apostles hearing these words originally, and to the readers of John's account of them, these words were transformative. In the words preceding our passage (v. 16), Jesus introduces the apostles to the one who stands at the center of his succession plan. In so doing, he is raising the specter of another eschatological inbreaking of God, but in a form unlike the one that had occurred in Bethlehem a few decades before and quite different from Christ's return that will mark the end of the age.

This whole Gospel is written from an eschatological, God-inbreaking perspective. It is composed in large part to explain how Christ's coming prompted the launch, emergence, explosive growth, and persecution of the church post-Pentecost. It shows how these self-described Christians speak of Jesus as an ever-present reality, in spite of his apparent absence.

We in the church totally understand the reality that Jesus' incarnation was eschatological: he was conceived by the Holy Spirit, born of the Virgin Mary, named Jesus, for he shall save us from our sins, called Emmanuel—God with us.

This particular writer introduces Jesus' eschatological inbreaking not in homely family stories, as

Feasting on the Gospels

Exegetical Perspective

Harkening back to the initial and overarching theme of a farewell address to his disciples, in this passage Jesus reminds them that although the time of his departure has arrived, he will not leave them orphaned. Significantly, the adjective *orphanos* (v. 18) is used on only one other occasion in the New Testament (Jas. 1:27), although the verb *aporphanizō* occurs at 1 Thessalonians 2:17. Literally, the first phrase of John 14:18 can be translated as "I will not abandon you as orphans" (NLT). Following this key motif, the rest of the passage goes on to demonstrate how Jesus has made provisions for his disciples in preparation for his physical departure from them.

The second half of verse 18, however, also points to a key issue with regard to Jesus' departure and return. The verb *erchomai*, translated in the NRSV as "I am coming," points to the Parousia, the second coming of Christ. Although some commentators consider *erchomai* as indicative of Jesus' postresurrection appearances, it is more natural to understand *erchomai* as referring to the second coming of Jesus, as it is used already in the third verse of this chapter ("I will come again"; see also 14:28; 21:22–23).[1]

1. Leon Morris, *The Gospel according to John*, New International Commentary of the New Testament, rev. ed. (Grand Rapids: Eerdmans, 1995), 578; George R. Beasley-Murray, *John*, Word Biblical Commentary 36, 2nd ed., ed. David A. Hubbard and Glenn W. Barker (Dallas: Word Books, 1987), 258.

Homiletical Perspective

By now it should be apparent to the preacher that John likes to arrange the material in his Gospel into scenes. Throughout his testimony, John places the incarnate Word on the stage of his readers' and auditors' imaginations to make the Word as vivid and as compelling as possible. One such scene has been unfolding before our eyes when we come to this text. Jesus is speaking to his disciples near the end of his time on earth. He is at table with them for the last time.

Perhaps their feet are still damp from the washing Jesus has given them. Perhaps they are shocked at Judas's departure and alarmed at Jesus' foretelling of Peter's denial. Perhaps Jesus' "new commandment, that you love one another . . . as I have loved you" (13:34), strikes a dissonant chord between the sound of Judas's running off into the night and Peter's boast to be faithful unto death. The disciples have just witnessed a stunning act of service that signified their Master's entire ministry among them as the enfleshed Word of God, forgiving, cleansing, teaching, demonstrating loving obedience to the One who sent him.

What now? What happens after he is gone? Their fragile bond is already broken by betrayal and an unsettling prediction of denial, is it not? Is this a sign of things to come in their community? By

John 14:18–24

Theological Perspective

though only the Eastern Orthodox Church signed on with the Western church to that solution. (The other Eastern churches, including what we now know as the Coptic and Syrian churches, went their own way, bringing the vision of full "catholicity"—universality—to an end.)

This passage in John's Gospel reminds us that the roots of this controversy lie in the life of faith. "In a little while the world will no longer see me," Jesus says (v. 19), forecasting his own death to his disciples. He reassures them, though: "I will not leave you orphaned" (v. 18). Not only will you still (somehow) see me, but "because I live, you also will live" (v. 19). Although they cannot yet even imagine it, the disciples are about to lose the person who has become Light and Life to them. Jesus knows, as they do not yet, that his death could undo them. They are still neophytes on the road to the Way, the Truth, and the Life (14:6). Without the guide on whom they have come to rely, they will feel lost. Jesus goes on to describe an intimate connection between the disciples, himself, and God: "On that day you will know that I am in my Father, and you in me, and I in you" (v. 20).

Jesus' concern here is not with helping his followers think rightly about God—or himself, for that matter—but with helping them survive the loss to come, without losing their confidence in the Light and Life into which he has brought them. To that end, he goes on to elaborate on the nature of this intimate union as a triune connection, rooted and manifested in love: "Those who love me will keep my word, and my Father will love them, and we will come to them and make our home with them. Whoever does not love me does not keep my words" (vv. 23–24a).

That the followers of John's Jesus will need a dose of confidence is clear from the rest of the Gospel. This is a community unsteady, to say the least, about its place in "the world" (15:18–25). For the most part, it sees itself as at odds with the world, as simultaneously suspicious of it and suspected by it. Indeed, Jesus distinguishes between "the world," which "cannot receive" the "Spirit of truth" because it "neither sees him nor knows him," and "you," who "know him, because he abides with you, and he will be in you" (14:17).

In the immediacy of the initial loss, one can imagine Jesus' words in 14:18–24 serving their intended purpose. How are we to go on? What are we to do? Remember what Jesus said? We are to go on loving him by keeping to his words. If we do

Pastoral Perspective

did Luke and Matthew decades before, but in philosophical, mystical terms—the Word being with God, the Word being God, the Word becoming flesh and dwelling among us. The crucified Savior, risen Lord, ascended king somehow lives on in a movement that has exploded with growth far more after his disappearance than during his sojourn here.

Why? The answer is found in this successor to Jesus.

The coming of the Holy Spirit—the second God-inbreaking of the first century—took place on Pentecost (told in quick summary in John 20:22). Apart from the dramatic wind and fire of Pentecost morning fifty days after the crucifixion, the Spirit's presence could not be perceived by the regular senses. Nevertheless, that presence proved to be the seal of the Christ event. The crowds of Jesus' followers ebbed and flowed, often leaving him with his small circle of a dozen disciples. After his world-changing atoning death his own disciples went back to fishing. Even after his miraculous resurrection they went into hiding. Only after the Spirit's inbreaking did they go out and turn the world upside down. The trickle of loyal supporters who stuck with him through Jesus' precrucifixion ministry years morphed into a massive wave of followers.

So what of Jesus' Spirit successor? John quotes Jesus as he first introduces the believers to the third member of the Trinity as the one who will animate, empower, and guide these persons and this movement after he leaves them.

Right off, Jesus introduces the Spirit in metaphorical terms. The Greek word *paraklētos* means literally "the one called alongside." The NRSV translates it "Advocate." Other translations mostly use "Comforter" or "Counselor"—but a counselor who is more than a Rogerian, unconditional-positive-regard therapist, invaluable as that can be to one's clients. "Advocate" is also, and perhaps more tellingly, the defense attorney type of counselor—one who will stand up on your behalf, protect you from opponents, stand against injustice done to you, and instruct you, even telling you what to say, when to say it, and when to keep silent.

The church leader—whether operating as preacher or pastoral caregiver—bears a powerful word of affirmation and assurance when referring to this text. The church leader can attest: "A central function of the Holy Spirit is to advocate on your behalf. The Spirit is your defense lawyer, your public relations consultant, your defender."

Whereas Luke–Acts usually characterizes the Spirit's impact in miraculous terms, John's take is

Exegetical Perspective

In addition, the preceding verses (vv. 15–17) also point to a period after Jesus' departure when another comforter (i.e., the Holy Spirit) will be sent in his absence. Thus, instead of pointing to a brief separation and return in his postresurrection appearances, the force of being left orphaned suggests *erchomai* refers to the eventual but certain return of Jesus after his extended physical departure.

Continuing in the vein of preparing his disciples for his departure, Jesus reminds them that though *the world* will no longer see him because of his physical absence from it, *they* will see him (v. 19a). Although through death Jesus would be departing this world and therefore not physically visible, spiritually he would be seen by his disciples because he would be made alive through the resurrection (v. 19b). The clause "because I live, you also will live" suggests the spiritual awakening made possible "on that day"—that is, only after the resurrection of Jesus. As a direct consequence of this spiritual enlightenment, his disciples would come to the dual understanding of the indwelling of the Son in the Father, and the mutual indwelling of the Son and believers (v. 20).

Considering the often-repeated theme of the disciples' lack of understanding in John's Gospel (14:7–11), it is not surprising to read Jesus' reaffirmation of the importance of remaining in relationship with the Father through obedience and love. Just as the Son remained in the Father out of love and through obedience to his will, Jesus' disciples receive the love of the Father and of the Son by keeping the commandments given by the Son. Thus, the reciprocal relationship between the Father and the Son becomes the model for the continued relationship between the future departed Son and the seemingly orphaned believers. For this reason, one need not take the phrase "those who love me will be loved by my Father" as a merit- or works-based conditional statement, where the Father's love is contingent upon the believer's obedience and love of the Son. Instead, a purely relational bond is established with the Son that brings and keeps the believer connected to the Father's love. In other words, loving the Son leads believers to obey him, and naturally the Father loves them, because they have entered into a relationship of love with the Son.

It is to those who keep his commandments and love him that Jesus promises to reveal (*emphanizō*) himself (v. 21b). Again, emphasizing the disciples' inability to grasp the meaning of Jesus' words, Judas (emphatically not the betrayer Judas Iscariot) asks

Homiletical Perspective

what power will this "new commandment" to love one another become realized in the time after his departure? This is how John draws us in to the scene. There is plenty of room between the lines for our own questions to surface. How does one practice loving devotion to the teachings of one's faith in the midst of communities broken by betrayal, empty promises, or the deaths of leaders?

This text takes us right into the heart of the scene where Jesus' response to such questions is unfolding. We can catch in Jesus' words a glimpse of John's own vision of what knits a church together in the face of difficulty. Fractured by dissension, beset by fear, pressured by threats from without and within, fretting over those who have drifted away, John's fragile community worries about its future. Read the backstory of any church profile today, and you are likely to find resonances of these very concerns. The preacher can follow John's example here and draw on traditions received from the historical Jesus and craft an enduring image of church as a community of friends who act like a loving family.

You can take some time to distinguish between popular notions of friendship and what Jesus means by it. In our culture, one's friend can be someone you have known as an intimate for a very long time. Friendship can also describe a casual acquaintance. Someone who is "just a friend" might be on the margins of one's intimate relationships. Our social media allow us to "friend" someone that we once knew or barely know now. One can collect friends as one might collect commodities. Having a lot of friends is a sign of social success. When we call someone friend, what do we mean?

The text gives us the chance to probe the virtue of friendship more deeply by getting at what John means by it. Jo-Ann Brandt explains that while the greatest demonstration of friendship in John is "selflessness," at its heart is an "intimate mutual reliance," a healthy balance between altruism and self-interest.[1] Jesus needs his friends to complete his pattern of ministry.

John's vision of the new community that Jesus establishes is based on this view of friendship. It is not, however, a clique or closed society of like-minded individuals. John's vision of the community is one where strangers are welcomed into circles of friendship where people are loyal and devoted to one another, even in the face of great danger. In the

---

1. Jo-Ann A. Brandt, *John*, Paideia Commentaries on the New Testament (Grand Rapids: Baker Academic, 2011), 228.

Theological Perspective

that, we will be loved by God in return. Some two thousand years later, though, we know that the devil is in the details. Time and again, the Christian community has been ripped asunder by debates over precisely *what* "keep[ing] my words" entails. Time and again, the (always self-proclaimed) winners of such debates are tempted to position themselves as those beloved by God (and Jesus) made manifest in their hewing to his (their) words, his (their) commandments.

The early Christian controversies were no exception. The creed crafted by the council at Nicaea concludes by condemning those who might dissent from what the council was declaring Christian orthodoxy:"As for those who say that 'there was when [the Son] was not,' and 'before being born he was not,' and 'he came into existence out of nothing' . . . the catholic and apostolic church condemns these."[1] Today the debates that threaten unity take place over different issues, but they are no less fierce. It can be all too tempting to presume our place as those who know the words of Jesus and how to keep them.

In John 14:22, Judas ("not Iscariot," the text assures us!) asks, "Lord, how is it that you will reveal yourself to us, and not to the world?" Is Judas presuming a revelation to "us" that is deliberately concealed from "the world"? Is he presuming a revelation that somehow "we" see but "the world" does not? In other words, is the division between "us" and "the world" a triumph to be celebrated or a loss to be mourned? Jesus responds by simply repeating the link between love and word-keeping. As we attempt to live out that link, we would do well to remember that what binds us to Jesus and to God is, first and foremost, love. Whatever we determine to be involved in keeping Jesus' words or commandments, it must manifest love.

ELLEN T. ARMOUR

Pastoral Perspective

more relational: orphans being adopted; the disconnected becoming related and intertwined; the estranged becoming the beloved; the dead coming alive (the miraculous element not to be missed here); the unruly becoming godly. The church engaged in the *missio Dei* will seek to incarnate this work of the Spirit as fitting the body of Christ: caring for orphans, loving the marginalized, instructing in godliness.

Speaking of godliness, Jesus did say that those who love him will keep his commandments. In effect, *those who keep my commandments are those who love me.* Those words convey different meanings, depending upon how they are expressed. If expressed as rewards conditioned on prerequisites, or worse, as hortatory commands and threats, they become battering rams of shame for those struggling to follow the straight and narrow way. If a pastor, teacher, parent, or other leader expresses them as observations, though—in the indicative mood, as Jesus used it—then they simply state the obvious. If you love someone, you will want to please that person. Those who are pleasing you are most openly and naturally showing their love for you. It is in this spirit that Augustine could say famously, "Love and do what you will."[1]

Such a convergence of affection and performance manifests an internalization of God's work in the human soul, as suggested in Jeremiah's promise (Jer. 31:31–34) cited by the writer of Hebrews:

> This is the covenant that I will make with the house
> of Israel
> after those days, says the Lord:
> I will put my laws in their minds,
> and write them on their hearts,
> and I will be their God,
> and they shall be my people.
>
> *(Heb. 8:10)*

Of course, such an expectation begs the question, what commandments? John's Gospel outlines just two commandments: to love God and to love one another—specifically one's sisters and brothers in Christ. Then again, given that this Gospel is written decades after the Synoptics, one can assume that its readers were already familiar with Jesus' more detailed ethical teachings—and familiar with at least some of the other apostolic interpretations of his teachings, as found in the Epistles. So other elements of Christian teachings, morals, and practices probably are in John's mind, at least secondarily to his emphatic call to love.

JACK HABERER

1. "The Nicene Creed," *The Christian Theology Reader*, 2nd ed., ed. Alistair E. McGrath (Malden, MA: Blackwell Publishers, 2001), 11.

1. Augustine, *Tractates on the Gospel of John* 7.8, in *The Fathers of the Church*, vol. 5, trans. John Rettig (Washington, DC: Catholic University of America Press, 1995), 223.

a somewhat intriguing question: "Lord, how is it that you will reveal yourself to us, and not to the world?" (v. 22). The particular nuance Judas places on the question could be better understood if paraphrased as: "Lord, how will you reveal your glory (or your messiahship) only to us, and not to the whole world?" (See John 1:31 and 2:11 where, although using a different Greek verb [*phaneroō*], a similar declaration is made.) Furthermore, Jesus' response demonstrates his nurturing care toward them in that he takes the time to answer even what might seem like a misguided or unwarranted question. Indeed, his response signals the relational mode in which Jesus would continue to make himself manifest to believers after his departure.

Repeating the themes of love and obedience and the outpouring of the love of the Father, Jesus makes a promise to believers: "We will come to them and make our home with them" (v. 23). This promise directly relates to the interlude between Jesus' departure and his second coming, when believers are encouraged by the continued manifest presence of the Son and the Father, which is visualized in the communal idea of sharing a home (*mona*) together. Like the Father's celestial homes pictured earlier in verse 2 of this same chapter, which Jesus spoke of to comfort his disciples, he now envisages the spiritual indwelling of the Father and the Son in the life of the believer. Whereas at the beginning of the chapter a future hope is offered, the comfort believers are invited to in the interim period as they await the Parousia consists in the participatory communal experience with the Father and the Son, which is available to those who love and keep his commandments. Finally, as a reassurance of the validity of this promise, Jesus highlights the expectation of his and his Father's presence with believers by indicating these are not just his words; they carry the signature of the Father who sent him (v. 24). In this way, he reassures his followers they will not be left orphaned in his absence, for he promises to continue to be with them, just as the Father was with him during his earthly mission.

SAMMY G. ALFARO

world John knew, acknowledging one's fealty to Jesus might result in the breaking of a family tie, becoming an object of suspicion or even murderous rage. Friendship with Jesus and with those who followed him was no casual acquaintance. Maintaining such a relationship with One who appeared to be absent took courage.

You probably have friends who are "like family" to you. This is close to what John is describing here. Jesus embodies God's gesture of friendship toward all humanity. In his ministry we have seen signs of the transformative power that friendship with God affords. One such sign is a new community that befriends the world and one another in the same way that Jesus did.

All of which is fine, but what is one to make of a friend who departs, leaving one wondering how the friendship will continue? Has Jesus by his apparent absence demonstrated God's abandonment of those Jesus has befriended? Not a chance, says John. Jesus has not returned in the way John's church once imagined, but that does not mean Jesus has abandoned them, leaving them "orphaned" (v. 18). Neither does it mean that Jesus is not "coming" to them or to us, for that matter. In the text, Jesus is still present to his followers as enfleshed Word sent from God. In the afterlife of the text, we "see" Jesus differently from how the characters in the text see him. John is training the eyes of his community (and ours) to see one who may be hidden from the world, but who is alive in those who show their love for Jesus by keeping his commandments. To them, Jesus is "revealed."

The question of Judas (not Iscariot) in verse 22 gives John a chance to elaborate. In fact, Judas's question offers the preacher a point of departure. How does a church today reveal the One they follow and make him known to those who do not "see" him? How does one respond to God's generous gesture of friendship offered through Jesus? By keeping Jesus' word (v. 23). The preacher can help the congregation remember the times and occasions when Jesus kept his word. Now, how will we keep our word to him? After all, what are friends for?

RICHARD F. WARD

John 14:25–31

²⁵"I have said these things to you while I am still with you. ²⁶But the Advocate, the Holy Spirit, whom the Father will send in my name, will teach you everything, and remind you of all that I have said to you. ²⁷Peace I leave with you; my peace I give to you. I do not give to you as the world gives. Do not let your hearts be troubled, and do not let them be afraid. ²⁸You heard me say to you, 'I am going away, and I am coming to you.' If you loved me, you would rejoice that I am going to the Father, because the Father is greater than I. ²⁹And now I have told you this before it occurs, so that when it does occur, you may believe. ³⁰I will no longer talk much with you, for the ruler of this world is coming. He has no power over me; ³¹but I do as the Father has commanded me, so that the world may know that I love the Father. Rise, let us be on our way."

Theological Perspective

The Gospel of John is distinct in many ways from its Synoptic cousins Mark, Matthew, and Luke, but particularly in its significance for Christian trinitarianism—including pneumatology (the doctrine of the Holy Spirit), a too often neglected theological theme. Trinitarian theology was formalized primarily in response to controversies over the identity and significance of Jesus. As noted in the preceding essay (on 14:18–24), some two hundred years after the Gospel of John was written, Christians were conflicted about how to understand Jesus' relationship to God. All saw him as distinctively connected to God, but they disagreed over the nature of that connection. John's Gospel proved pivotal for both raising and resolving those controversies, in particular its understanding of Jesus as the Word (*logos*) of God that from the beginning was "with God" and "was God" and that served as that through which creation came into being (1:3–5).

The councils of Nicaea and Chalcedon drew on John's formula—elaborated through Greco-Roman philosophy—to resolve (at least, officially) the christological controversies of the day. The status of the Holy Spirit's relationship to God—and to Jesus, for that matter—was less contested, however, but not because it was patently obvious. Nicaea and Chalcedon established the limits of orthodox Christology

Pastoral Perspective

Here Jesus offers his disciples more details on his succession plan, stating that the Holy Spirit will come to them after he leaves. In the process he outlines the essential roles and tasks that the Spirit will exercise. In the process, he also hints at the kinds of tasks the Spirit-filled believers will be expected to carry out.

Keeping in mind what we said above (14:18–24) about the Advocate, it is clear here that the Advocate will first and foremost be advocating for Jesus. The Spirit "will teach you everything and remind you of all that I have said to you" (v. 26). The Spirit carried out that task when reminding this Gospel's writer, like the three Synoptic writers, of what Jesus had taught.

The Advocate acts similarly for believers today—and any church teaching ministry will do so as well. The first order of the day for Christian education is to teach about Christ Jesus, the only begotten Child of God. "We would see Jesus," said a group of Greeks to the apostle Philip (12:21). Indeed, the first order in worship is to point to Jesus, refreshing the memory of the congregants—marked especially by the recitation of creeds, the reading and proclamation of the Word of God, splashing in the waters to "remember your baptism," and, of course, serving the bread and wine "in remembrance" of him.

That teaching is an ongoing function, though. The Spirit not only brings to mind the things Jesus

Exegetical Perspective

Having encouraged his disciples with his promise not to leave them orphans (14:18), Jesus goes on to introduce them to the person who will be with them in his absence (vv. 25–26), and why it will be to their benefit that Jesus returns to the Father (vv. 27–31). Given the last sentence in this passage ("Rise, let us be on our way," v. 31b), this pericope brings to a close one of Jesus' discourses concerning his departure. In doing so, the passage retouches and expands on the main themes covered in Jesus' farewell address: the sending of the Spirit, the departure of the Son, and his return to the Father.

The Trinitarian framework developed in this conversation highlights the intra-Trinitarian relationships in a narrative form. First, the Holy Spirit, once again referred to as the Advocate (*paraklētos*, "helper" or "counselor," 14:16) is described as one whom the Father will send (*pempsei*) in the name (*onomati*) of Jesus (v. 26a). Significantly, the verb *pempō* is used synonymously in the New Testament with the verb *apostellō*, which frequently has the connotation of someone who is sent on a mission. Moreover, the mission on which the Spirit will be sent categorically parallels the mission of the Son who was sent by the Father as his representative (5:43).

Similarly, the Spirit is sent by the Father as a representative of the Son for the purpose of teaching

Homiletical Perspective

The preacher who is taking a congregation on a long, slow walk through the terrain of John's Farewell Discourse (13:31–17:26) has a chance now to pause and point to one of the great teachings of Christian faith: the promise of the Paraclete. It will be worth your while to linger here with your congregation. Many in your hearing may identify themselves as "spiritual but not religious." If so, the preacher can open the door to how this passage understands "Spirit" and what John's Gospel offers to those who claim its promises. Whenever preachers and teachers of the faith talk about "Holy Spirit," clouds of confusion are likely to gather. It might take more than one sermon to develop John's distinct perspective on matters that have puzzled most and even divided some Christian communities. In any case, the generosity of grace that God's incarnate Word is offering through this passage should not be overlooked.

Imagine a conference taking place outside the restraints of time and place. The theme of the conference is "Pentecost or Parousia? A Second Advent." The people who will be attending hold different impressions and understandings about the Paraclete or Holy Spirit. Some will be hoping to "get" the Holy Spirit and be able to return with the ability to speak in tongues or perhaps even interpret what others are saying "in the Spirit." Some are coming expecting

John 14:25–31

Theological Perspective

for much of Christendom (although many Eastern churches rejected Chalcedon's conclusions), but the limits of orthodox pneumatology remain officially undefined. Readers of the creed of Nicaea will find inserted, between what it affirms about Jesus and what it rejects, simply, "And we believe in the Holy Spirit." The confession of Chalcedon makes no mention of the Holy Spirit at all.

The roots of the concept of the Holy Spirit are multiple and variegated. They include passages from both New and Old Testaments, including John's Gospel, but extend beyond that into Greco-Roman philosophies. That theologians call this area of inquiry pneumatology reflects its Greek roots. The animating principle of life, *pneuma*, can be appropriately translated (depending on the context) as breath or spirit (as can the Latin *spiritus*). It has a Hebrew analogue, as well, in the word *ruach*. In Genesis 2:4b–3:24 (the second creation story), God brings the *adam* to life by breathing into it "the breath [*ruach*] of life" (Gen. 2:7). In a somewhat different but related key, the story of Pentecost envisions "a violent wind" that blows through the gathered crowd, followed by the descent of "tongues of fire" that inspire and enable those gathered to speak in every language (Acts 2:2–11). Here in the Gospel of John, Jesus speaks not in figures drawn from nature, but of an Advocate (v. 26) or helper, one who will be sent by God "in my name" to "teach you everything and remind you of all that I have said to you." This Advocate, "the Spirit of truth," will come in Jesus' absence and "be with you forever"; he will "abide with you" and "be in you" (14:15–17).

Like the other roots of Christian pneumatology, the coming of the Advocate is here associated with the giving of (new) life—both physical and spiritual. This passage is situated in the midst of Jesus' Farewell Discourse (13:31–16:33), a lengthy collection of sayings presented by the Gospel writer as offered by Jesus to prepare his disciples for his coming death. Clearly, they need preparation, like many of us, for facing the impending loss of a loved one. They do not want to know what is about to happen. They misunderstand Jesus' prediction of Judas Iscariot's impending betrayal as a trip out for groceries (13:27–29). Like the words of many of us trying to prepare others for our demise, the words Jesus chooses do not exactly communicate clearly. Speaking in euphemisms ("Where I am going, you cannot come," 13:33) may soften the blow, but it only confuses his listeners. Jesus responds, "I am going to prepare a place for you," so you can be sure I will come back for you, and

Pastoral Perspective

taught but also guides the application of Christian principles to new situations and questions. Such was the case as the Spirit guided the actions of the early church, as reported in the book of Acts, and inspired the writers of the Epistles and the Apocalypse. Today that inspiring and illuminating work of the Spirit shines light on the ongoing efforts of believers to discern the will of God for their lives. The preaching and teaching ministry of the church needs regularly to remind congregants that the Holy Spirit guides them through complicated situations and difficult decisions as they seek to discern God's will.

The Spirit does not simply serve as instructor. The Advocate serves as defense attorney, defending the believer against false accusations, serving as freedom rider in times of oppression, and as public relations specialist in times of humiliation. By implication, if the church is going to be aligned with the mission of God, then it in turn will be providing comfort, encouragement, advocacy, and defense for those falsely accused, those being oppressed, those suffering humiliation.

In this context Jesus speaks out the oft-quoted bequest, "Peace I leave with you; my peace I give to you. I do not give to you as the world gives. Do not let your hearts be troubled, and do not let them be afraid" (v. 27). This "peace that passes all understanding" (Phil. 4:7 RSV) converges an inner serenity with outward acts of beating of swords into plowshares. That peace can break through the chaotic swirl simply by providing a contemplative and spiritually evocative worship space. That peace can overcome trouble-mindedness as the liturgy walks the worshiper through the message of redemption and reconciliation. That peace also can be mediated through the pastoral care ministry as implemented both by one wearing a clerical collar and by another wearing jeans and a T-shirt, by teaching elder and deacon, by mother and by friend. Most certainly we cannot overstate how powerfully that peace can captivate via the power of lifting hearts and hands together to God in prayer.

In talking about the transition from Jesus' personal presence to that of the Holy Spirit, Jesus alludes to a downside of his story: the ruler of this world is coming for him. His passion, he says, will be precipitated by Satan, as Barrett says.[1] Then again, he reassures that the ruler of this world really has no power over him, as Witherington shows: "Jesus is acting as the Father commanded, not as Satan

---

1. C. K. Barrett, *The Gospel according to John* (London: SPCK, 1960), 392.

and reminding the disciples of that which Jesus had told them from the beginning. The verb "remind" (*hypomimnēskō*) used in verse 26 appears only here in the Gospel, but it occurs without the pre-fixed preposition *hypo* as *mimnēskomai*, meaning "remember," in John 2:17, 22 and 12:16. In both of these occasions the author inserts a post-Easter recollection the disciples have in connection to the earthly ministry of Jesus. These two insertions serve as examples of the post-Easter activity of the Spirit teaching and reminding the disciples of all the things Jesus had said to them.

Returning to the theme of reassuring his disciples as they prepare for his departure, Jesus guarantees them his peace (*eirēnē*), which is unlike anything this world has to offer. Peace here should be understood in the sense of the Hebrew *shalom*. Unlike the literal Greek equivalent *eirēnē*, which often negatively sig-nifies the absence of war, *shalom* positively refers to the blessing of the Lord that results in completeness, as in the priestly benediction of Numbers 6:24–26. The force of this declaration resides in the double pronouncement through which Jesus makes a pledge to give his peace to the disciples in such a way that it continues to be with them even after his depar-ture (v. 27a). For this reason, Jesus emphatically encourages them with two negative commands: not to be discouraged in their innermost being (*kardia*, "heart"), and not to be cowardly (v. 27b).

Then, in order to reaffirm his promise to his disci-ples, Jesus reminds them of what he has been trying to make them understand throughout this discourse: "I am going away, and I am coming to you" (v. 28a). The thought of his departure and absence should not sadden them, because in the interim period before his eventual return, he will be with the Father. In fact, Jesus expects his followers to rejoice if they truly love him, for his returning to the Father signals his return to glory. Whereas in hindsight this might seem like a simple concept to grasp, Jesus prepares his disciples by euphemistically speaking of his return to the Father in terms of a glorious exaltation, knowing full well his return to the Father would take place via his death on the cross, as the Gospel signals from the beginning. In short, the Son would return to the Father through his death on the cross, which would be the ultimate test for his disciples, who would grieve his departure, but then be reassured of his continual presence with the Father through his resurrection and ascension.

The last phrase in verse 28 undoubtedly presents a theologically challenging statement made by Jesus.

insights about how the world will end and in what manner Jesus will return. Still others may be won-dering if they have some sort of spiritual gift like teaching or healing. Some question whether there is any different between the *Holy* Spirit and a spirit that animates all forms of life. Many are coming hoping simply for a deeper experience of God.

The apostle Paul will be one of those invited to address the conference. He is expected to use his letter to the Corinthians as his text (1 Cor. 12:4–11). Those who believe that when the Holy Spirit does come, it is to bring gifts "for the common good" (1 Cor. 12:7) will be happy that Paul is there. Those who have been on an Emmaus walk[1] on a congrega-tional retreat will be happier perhaps to hear from Luke. There will be a concert of praise music before Luke speaks. The listeners will be eager to hear Luke expound on the happening he has written of in the second chapter of his Acts. Somehow the Spirit that animated and empowered Jesus' ministry came to an assembly of Jesus' followers to enable them to make the good news comprehensible in a pluralistic reli-gious culture. Is such a thing available today? If so, in what form might we expect it to become manifest?

Those who have come to the conference wearing detective hats will wonder why they cannot pick up clues from these presentations about Christ's coming at the end of time. For them, the coming of the Spirit and Christ's coming at some point in the future are sharply differentiated. They may leave the conference disappointed, especially after John speaks. John does not draw such a distinction. For John, God has come to dwell with us (v. 23), and in this particular pas-sage from John, Jesus lays out some of the ways God acts while dwelling with us through the agency of God's Spirit. Who is "us"? Jesus has made that clear in the previous passage. "Us" includes all those who are committed to showing God's love by demonstrat-ing what Jesus has taught them.

The first task of the Spirit, then, is to help us understand what we have been taught and learn to act upon it. The Spirit is present to us as one who will "teach [us] everything" when we are perplexed about how to act in loving obedience (v. 26). Those Aha! moments we have when we connect what we have been taught to some loving action we see in our experience are gifts of the Spirit. So are those moments when, while brooding over some question or ethical predicament, we start to remember times when a way opened up when there was no way in

1. http://emmaus.upperroom.org/; accessed January 18, 2014.

John 14:25–31

Theological Perspective

besides, "you know the way" (14:3–4). This prompts yet more confusion: "Lord, we do not know where you are going. How can we know the way?" Thomas asks (14:5). Not surprisingly, Jesus sometimes grows impatient with their inability to grasp the (not so?) obvious: "If you loved me, you would rejoice that I am going to the Father" (v. 28).

Jesus promises to leave them the gift of peace, something they will surely need as they grapple with his death and its significance for their (ongoing) lives: "Do not let your hearts be troubled, and do not let them be afraid," he says (v. 27). Tellingly, Jesus associates this gift with the coming of the Advocate, the helper who will link Jesus' survivors with their deceased beloved and with God. (The Holy Spirit is also often called the Comforter.)

We commonly refer to the three "persons" (*personae* in Latin) of the Trinity, but only God and Jesus are typically "personified" in obviously anthropomorphic ways. Throughout John's Gospel, Jesus refers to God as "Father" (and, by association, to himself as God's "Son"). This terminology was reflected in the creeds, liturgy, and hymnody of the church, almost exclusively so until the past few decades.

Feminist theologians like Sallie McFague have argued for expanding our theological vocabulary to include other significant personal relationships (she offers God as Mother, Lover, and Friend as examples).[1] Thinking of the Divine personified as an Advocate or Helper highlights important aspects of the relationship between divine and human that overreliance on familial and familiar metaphors can miss. In times of stress, loss, or grief, we can become aware of our need for an advocate, a helper, one who offers support when we most need it and least know where to find it, one who brings us peace—perhaps even the peace that "surpasses . . . understanding" (Phil. 4:7).

ELLEN T. ARMOUR

Pastoral Perspective

demanded."[2] Hence, Jesus quickly reports the upside of the story: he simply is obeying what the Father tells him to do.

The preaching and pastoral care ministries are potently informed by this, insofar as they allude to the central theme of the Apocalypse: things are not as they appear. When the Revelation of John is read as an apocalyptic commentary on the news, that is, a heavenly interpretation of the persecutions being suffered in John of Patmos's day, the overarching plot is not simply that of God-hating Roman rulers crushing the faithful, but of Christ's cosmic slaying of godless forces with the decisive victories having been guaranteed by the cross and resurrection. What Revelation portrays in vivid imagery, Jesus' words here in John 14:30 say in sum: you may think Satan is being victorious as you see me suffer, but it will actually be God who is winning out.

This dramatic narrative is summarized and applied to Christ's followers also in Hebrews: "let us run with perseverance the race that is set before us, looking to Jesus the pioneer and perfecter of our faith, who for the sake of the joy that was set before him endured the cross, disregarding its shame, and has taken his seat at the right hand of the throne of God" (12:1b–2). What a fresh word we carry to God's people: that we are called not just to follow Jesus through pain but to keep our eyes peeled to see the redemption and final victory that awaits their discovery!

In the process, it behooves us to remind one another that the love relationship Jesus enjoys with God the Father is one that also is deferential: "I do as the Father has commanded," he says (v. 31a). Indeed, it is that obedience that demonstrates how much Jesus loves the Father. The biblical themes of obedience and submission have fallen on hard times, given our sensitivity to the violations of power relationships that pervade the news. Nevertheless, the biblically informed teaching ministry still prods all of Christ's followers to seek to obey the holy God.

JACK HABERER

---

1. Sallie McFague, *Models of God: Theology for an Ecological, Nuclear Age* (Minneapolis: Fortress Press, 1987).

2. Ben Witherington, *John's Wisdom* (Louisville, KY: Westminster John Knox Press, 1995), 253.

Feasting on the Gospels

Exegetical Perspective

Taken on its own, Jesus' declaration that "the Father is greater than I" could be problematic for those who uphold Trinitarian beliefs, because it seems to subordinate the Son to the Father. In the context of the passage as well as in the rest of the Gospel, though, the reader must balance this saying with statements made by Jesus regarding his oneness with the Father (e.g., "the Father and I are one," 10:30). In addition, one must also consider the voluntary subordination of the Son to the Father during his earthly manifestation as seen in his complete obedience to and dependence on the Father in his earthly mission (4:34; 5:19; 8:29; 12:48–49). Thus the statement, "the Father is greater than I," could be unpacked as "in my earthly state the Father has greater authority than I do," thereby diffusing the potential problematic understanding that the Son is inferior in nature to the Father.

The last three verses of the passage continue on the theme of the Son's return to the Father, but clarify that despite the manner in which this return will take place (i.e., via the cross), the disciples must understand that everything is under the control of the Father. Understanding that the events leading to his crucifixion on the cross must soon take place, Jesus concretely informs his disciples that his Father is in charge. Though it may seem that "the ruler of this world" is in charge of his impending death, the disciples are forewarned of what will take place, in order that they may believe (v. 29). No matter how it may appear, they need to understand that what will take place in the days to come is not orchestrated by "the ruler of this world"; rather, it is the working out of the mission the Father commanded the Son to carry out (vv. 30–31). Thus Jesus valiantly tells his disciples to follow him as he takes the initiative and marches toward his death in complete, loving obedience to the Father.

SAMMY G. ALFARO

Homiletical Perspective

the experiences of Jesus and the host of others who have followed him. The Spirit that God has sent helps us to remember (v. 26) moments like that.

The tone of this brief selection is amplified throughout the entire text of Jesus' Farewell Discourse in John. It is a tone of comfort and assurance of God's presence, whatever the circumstances. Here it finds expression as a single word: "peace." It is the offering of peace to those who continue to act as Jesus' friends even though "the world" dangles—just out of the reach of many—a different kind of peace. Jesus' offering of peace does not include the assurance that one's life will be trouble-free. Neither is it offered simply to those who have the luxury of "getting away from it all" for some alone time with God. It is not offered to those who claim to have blueprints for the future course of events or who have been able to put the final touches on their own personal doctrinal fortresses. It is, however, offered to those who learn that whatever trouble we go through in our lives does not disprove God's presence or render impotent God's promise to dwell with us. As Fred Craddock has put it, "the peace of God is the confidence that God is God and neither our gains nor our losses are ultimate."[1]

So it is with Jesus' coming and going. John's message is clear: that the disciples' loss of the historical Jesus through his impending death is not ultimate. In fact, this apparent loss leads to an even greater experience of God-with-us, an active and holy presence of God that is not bound by time and space but is made manifest in the lives of those embody God's love.

RICHARD F. WARD

---

1. Fred B. Craddock, *John*, Knox Preaching Guides, ed. John. H. Hayes (Atlanta: John Knox Press, 1982), 111.

John 15:1–11

¹"I am the true vine, and my Father is the vinegrower. ²He removes every branch in me that bears no fruit. Every branch that bears fruit he prunes to make it bear more fruit. ³You have already been cleansed by the word that I have spoken to you. ⁴Abide in me as I abide in you. Just as the branch cannot bear fruit by itself unless it abides in the vine, neither can you unless you abide in me. ⁵I am the vine, you are the branches. Those who abide in me and I in them bear much fruit, because apart from me you can do nothing. ⁶Whoever does not abide in me is thrown away like a branch and withers; such branches are gathered, thrown into the fire, and burned. ⁷If you abide in me, and my words abide in you, ask for whatever you wish, and it will be done for you. ⁸My Father is glorified by this, that you bear much fruit and become my disciples. ⁹As the Father has loved me, so I have loved you; abide in my love. ¹⁰If you keep my commandments, you will abide in my love, just as I have kept my Father's commandments and abide in his love. ¹¹I have said these things to you so that my joy may be in you, and that your joy may be complete."

Theological Perspective

"I am the vine, you are the branches. Those who abide in me and I in them bear much fruit, because apart from me you can do nothing" (v. 5).

This section of text is a set of instructions for creating and sustaining the community of Jesus after he has died, part of the Farewell Discourse. He is speaking to the community that he believes can live out in the present, even in the midst of persecution, the qualities of peace and joy promised by belief in the Word. In this sense then, the eschatological promises are underway, realized in part in the present and to be fulfilled at the end of time. Two ideas warrant further theological attention in thinking about what the community of Christ looks like in the present, described in this passage through the metaphor of tending vines. First, the community of Christ is shaped by hardship as well as joy. Second, this community is the ground for anything else that can and should be done in the name of Christ.

With respect to the first point, John speaks very clearly, though metaphorically, about what it takes to be a part of the community of Jesus: expect to be pruned. "He removes every branch in me that bears no fruit. Every branch that bears fruit he prunes to make it bear more fruit" (v. 2). The difference between being left out of the community of Christ and being part of is *not* the difference between

Pastoral Perspective

What do we know about abiding? In our fast-paced world, what do we abide in or abide by?

Commonly, "abide" is used in reference to laws, rules, and traditions. We abide by the laws of the land; we abide by court decisions; we abide in the Reformed (or Baptist or Lutheran or Methodist or . . .) tradition. To abide, for most of us, means to obey by staying within an established system.

This understanding is not far from what Jesus' disciples would have heard. They too would have known that to abide means to stay, but their understanding would be stretched further. Jesus helps them grasp that to abide means to endure, dwell, or be present.

This understanding is different from simply keeping a law. When I choose to remain within the limits of a law, I am usually denying myself. For example, if I choose to stay within the speed limit, I will arrive at my destination later. I consciously make this choice because of a heightened awareness of the consequences of not abiding. I need to stay within the speed limit so as to not get pulled over, cause an accident, or model poor behavior to my teenager learning to drive.

This is not the tone that Jesus sets. He is not cautioning us to abide—or else. Jesus is not using the threat of consequences to coerce us into staying close.

Exegetical Perspective

This pericope immediately raises the question of genre and the possible literary connections with the Synoptic Gospels: is this a parable regarding fruit bearing, or is it, rather, a typical Johannine saying on spiritual growth? Regarding the question of genre, some interpreters argue that John 15:1–11 is a parable, based on the metaphoric nature of the language deployed, whereas most interpreters agree that the lack of a story line makes the pericope a poor candidate for the parabolic genre. Concerning the connection with the Synoptic Gospels, textual similarities and themes such as fruit bearing, spiritual growth, and harvesting (Matt. 7:15–20; Mark 4:1–9; Luke 6:43–45) have triggered debates on the literary relations between John and the rest of the Gospels. Here I contend that John 15:1–11 is better understood as a Johannine saying than as a parable, even if, as Richard Choi convincingly argues, the text sums up the topics of growth and fruit bearing, indiscriminate proliferation, and elimination as they are developed in the Synoptic Gospels.[1] Here I relate these questions to the topic of discipleship.

The passage begins with Jesus' proclaiming himself the true vine. Like other instances of metaphor

1. Richard P. Choi, "I Am the Vine: An Investigation of the Relations between John 15:1–6 and Some Parables of the Synoptic Gospels," *Biblical Research* 45 (2000): 51–75.

Homiletical Perspective

The image is crisp and clear and self-evident. Jesus is the true vine who is pruned by his Father so that healthy branches will produce abundant fruit. Disciples of this Jesus will be vital and thriving if they abide in him and do deeds of love. The metaphor is that of a thriving plant, reminding us of the righteous ones in Psalm 1:3, who "are like trees planted by streams of water, which yield their fruit in its season, and their leaves do not wither."

Undoubtedly, there is some judgment and some pain in the pruning, but the image is overwhelmingly positive and life-giving. Perhaps the sermon will be too! Where do you see the vitality of the ministry of your congregation bearing fruit and producing encouragement to others? Where have you encountered healthy vines and joyful obedience in your community of faith?

The memories may be literal. A farmer in a rural congregation in South Carolina once planted several acres of watermelons that he had presold to a grocer in New York City. When the truck arrived for the melons, though, there was a dispute over who was to harvest and load the crop. The deal fell through, the truck left empty, and the farmer gave all the watermelons to the local church youth group to sell at a roadside market for mission. The young people and their parents put on boots and gloves and went

John 15:1–11

Theological Perspective

experiencing only pain in the first and joy in the second. Rather, whether you are an unbeliever or a believer, you are going to be pruned by God. For the follower of Christ, this means that living in the promises of God will come with times when we experience the cutting away of what might have seemed to us to have been vital. Pruning involves taking off not only dead, lifeless branches but also those stems that still have life but that may nevertheless inhibit the overall strength and production of the larger vine.

Inherent in this passage is a troubling equation that is very often taken as a universal interpretation of theodicy: suffering brings growth, or worse, God makes suffering *necessary* for growth. We are dealing in metaphor here, a metaphor that attempts to make sense of the historical experience of suffering as a follower of Christ. The Gospel writer is challenged by the essential question of theodicy: How could it be that God would allow the faithful to suffer? Answer: It must be willed by God for the benefit of God's people. This is the meaning the author of the Gospel gives to the experiences of rejection suffered by the disciples. The meaning the writer makes should not automatically translate to a universal theological intent, though. That is, the meaning we make of difficult situations is simply the meaning that *we* make at a given time in our lives.

Conflating *our* meaning-making with *God's* intent runs the risk of idolatry. We can see the implications of eliding these two when we think about the things that get said to the grieving parents of a murdered child, or the person with a disabling condition: it must be God's will. Meaning is not causation, though.[1] What this means in practice is that when we face the suffering of others, it is incumbent on us not to impose *our* interpretations of their lives onto their own experiences, especially with the name of "God" attached. Suffering happens. God abides.

To the second point: "apart from me you can do nothing" (v. 5). This call from Christ is both a caution and a promise. It reminds the community that Christ's mission should be the centerpiece of what shapes them. No matter what pressures the world exerts, they should remain faithful to Christ. In that faith, they will never be alone in dealing with whatever may come. Christ is always there as the foundation of their lives. Christ abides. The lesson here for the contemporary church—both caution

1. Susan Wendell, *The Rejected Body: Feminist Philosophical Reflections on Disability* (New York: Routledge, 1996), 101.

Pastoral Perspective

Rather, Jesus is offering comfort, security, and a relational environment in which his disciples can thrive.

Sometimes this passage is interpreted in the former light. Indeed, if we focus on the second and sixth verses, we get the sense that some of us may be branches that are not bearing fruit and will therefore be cut away and cast into the fire. We draw the conclusion that abiding is equivalent to bearing fruit. Then, when we cannot see our lives bearing fruit, we worry that the jig is up. We have been revealed as flimsy followers and are in danger of being pruned.

That is not what Jesus is teaching here. Naturally, there is some warning to those who are truly dead to the ministrations of the gardener. The rest of us, though—those who are listening to Jesus and who, by that very act alone, are connected to the vine of Christ despite moments of doubt and fear about our faith—are comforted. The purpose of these verses is to demonstrate that we branches will be cared for by the divine vinegrower who knows just how to develop us, exactly when to prune, when to wait, and when to harvest. A skilled arborist, the vinegrower knows the difference between a dormant plant, which may need extra care and attention, and a dead one. This is a comfort and not a threat; those of us who have borne fruit will bear it again, in God's good time. Our job is to trust and abide.

On this final night, Jesus is preparing his disciples for the time when he will no longer be physically with them. "Abide," he counsels. Remain with me, as I remain with you. Continue with me, as I continue with you. Dwell with me, as I dwell with you. Endure with me, as I endure with you. Be present with me, as I am present with you.

This was Jesus' chance to say, "When I am gone, do not forget to talk about me and do the things we did together, like heal, serve the poor, and spread good news." Jesus' final words are not a to-do list, though. Instead, he says, "Abide." Stay. Remain. Dwell. Endure. Be present.

Of course, the disciples have other ideas. "What? There's so much to be done!" Current followers of Jesus can identify. We too experience great challenge when told to abide. We would rather go, work hard, and see evidence from our work. We think we should make time to take on a new spiritual discipline. We would sooner commit to scrubbing burned casserole off soup kitchen pans, planting dogwood trees, visiting lonely prisoners or hospitalized neighbors, or finally getting serious about prayer. That is not what Jesus is asking of us on this last, pivotal night.

in the Gospel, such as bread (6:35, 48), light (8:12; 9:5), door (10:7, 9), and shepherd (10:11, 14), the epithet refers to an everyday reality, seeking to offer an insight into a deeper dimension. The reference to God as the vinedresser (*geōrgos*) introduces the hermeneutical key by placing Jesus in hierarchical relationship to the Father. God's characterization as the head of the field is unique to John, although the term and the setting remind the reader of the parable of the Wicked Tenants (Mark 12:1–12 and parallels). Both pericopes share the emphasis on bearing fruit, but whereas the farmers in the Synoptic parable selfishly want to own the vine and its fruits, here the owner of the farm decides what counts as fruitful. The vinedresser's role in this text parallels the function of the lord of the vineyard in the Synoptic tradition (Mark 12:9). In Mark the vinedressers are intermediaries; here the farmer sits at the top of the hierarchy. God's role remains similar, though: in the Synoptic tradition God decides who is the owner of the vine; in this text God determines which branch shall continue to be attached to the vine.

The vine metaphor is powerful, both because it represents a fundamental material reality in an agrarian society and because it brings to mind important biblical echoes. In the Hebrew Bible, most prominently within the prophetic tradition, the vine is a symbol for Israel (Isa. 5:1–7; 27:2–6; Jer. 2:21; 6:9; 12:10–13; Ezek. 15:1–8; 17:5–10; 19:10–14; Hos. 10:1–2; 14:7). In Isaiah 5:1–7, for instance, God appears as a vinedresser who painstakingly cares for the vineyard, only to be rewarded with worthless grapes (Isa. 5:4). The song of the unfruitful vineyard, as it is commonly known, identifies Israel with a vineyard that is well taken care of by God and consequently is expected to bear abundant fruit. Instead of living up to God's plan, Israel promotes oppression, which results in God's punishment (Isa. 5:6).

In comparison with this prophetic tradition, John 15:1–11 shows a more existential tone that aims at exploring the relationship between the disciples and Jesus, offering the Father's love as the criterion of belonging. Here again, the action of the Father mines biblical motifs from the prophetic tradition. Those branches that do not abide in the Master dry up and are cast into the fire, where they are burned (v. 6). In Ezekiel 15 the prophet uses the metaphor of the wood of the vine thrown to the fire to refer to the inhabitants of Jerusalem who are delivered to judgment because of their unfaithfulness (Ezek. 15:8). In similar fashion, the fire here refers to God's judgment for the lack of fruitfulness.

out into the fields in search of the gift. They learned that some of the branches had separated from the vine, had turned brown, and probably had no fruit worth finding, but the green, living branches were still connected to the vine and likely had tasty watermelons under their leaves. Each such discovery brought great joy, a good sale, and money for mission in their church.

Sometimes the search for healthy vines in our ministry finds metaphors instead of melons. On Sundays of ordination and installation of officers in my denomination, the candidates for office kneel before the cross in the sanctuary, and teaching and ruling elders gather around them as all such elders present are invited to come forward to participate. Some of the elders lay hands directly on the candidates for ordination, and other elders place their hands on the shoulders of those elders as they stretch down the aisles in all directions. The configuration resembles living branches from the true vine, radiating from the cross of Jesus Christ, as we pray for the Holy Spirit to work through us in faith and in love. The joy in that service is the joy of being connected to Christ and to one another in ministry.

This connection of vine to branch and Christ to Christian is the key to the text and to the faithful life. It is not temporary, changing, or shallow; rather, the connection is abiding, enduring, and deep. The King James Version translates verse 4, "Abide in me, and I in you," and no one has improved upon it, except perhaps to emphasize it: "Abide in me as I abide in you" (NRSV). John loves this verb "to abide" and uses it more than any other New Testament writer to encourage us to abide in God's Word, and truth, and love. This steadfast connection to Christ reminds us constantly of God's presence with us and of the ministry of fruitful service always at hand.

Fred Craddock was once asked to share about the person who influenced him the most in his life and his call to ministry. He surprised the audience at the conference when he announced the name of someone that no one knew: Miss Emma Sloan. Fred explained that Emma Sloan was his Sunday school teacher throughout his childhood and youth. She gave him a Bible and taught him to memorize Scripture verses, though she never explained or interpreted them. She always told the children: "Just put it in your heart, just put it in your heart." Fred shared with the audience how Miss Emma taught them a Bible verse for each letter of the alphabet, and then ended with these words: "I can't think of anything, anything in all my life, that has made such

John 15:1–11

Theological Perspective

and promise—is the reminder that it is an extension of the mission of God, the *missio Dei,* and never an independent entity. While this is a clear enough statement of belief, the reality of worldly church existence is somewhat different.

At points in the church's life, there seems to be a tendency for congregations to become self-satisfied. One of the ways this can be seen is when congregations compare themselves to other congregations, denominations, or even other religions, and find that they are "doing better" (financially, in membership, in service, in welcoming the stranger, etc.) than others. While this is almost never openly asserted, it might be tacitly at work in the collective consciousness of the group. Faith communities that experience themselves as "doing better" may have come to see themselves as autonomous agents whose success is the result of their own actions or, equally as problematically, as persons more blessed by God than others because of what they are doing.

The comparison itself is misguided. We are one church, and we are not our own. Rather, whatever it is we accomplish as the church depends on being unified not stratified, and is possible only by the grace of God, the source of our mission and wellspring of our persistence. Keeping our dependence on God in the forefront of our thinking can help the church keep a handle on tendencies to self-satisfaction. The church that remembers that it exists only as an extension of the *missio Dei* will be vigilant in looking for ways it blocks or distorts the ongoing work of Christian unity and will find in that memory the promises of the abiding Christ.

EMILY ASKEW

Pastoral Perspective

Jesus knew we would have other ideas; so he gently addresses this tendency here. You are going to have to abide, he says. Not because the kingdom work is finished; not because everyone knows that I am the way, the truth, and the life; not because there is nothing else you could be doing—but because abiding is what is best for your relationship with me. This is the profoundly pastoral wisdom of the passage.

What did that mean for the disciples? Jesus knew they would struggle to abide, to dwell in his love and teaching. They would have a hard time remembering exactly what it was like to walk with him. They would want to leave. By giving them this illustration, Jesus allows them to see that sometimes fruit takes time to develop, and its ability to grow is in someone else's hands, specifically those of the vinegrower.

What does this mean for us? The struggles we have with abiding are different, but the words of encouragement are still true. No matter how tempted we are to be busy for God, John's Jesus does not leave us with a to-do list. He reminds us to abide. He calls us to reject the notion that constant activity gives us significance. He invites us to recognize that our salvation and position in Christ are a gift from God, cultivated and nurtured by the vinegrower, not the result of our own work. The branches do not bear fruit apart from the vine and vinegrower.

What if we truly lived as though this were our identity? Let it sink in that we are not gardeners but branches. We are not the creators or authors of our lives and ministries. We do not own or control the successes or failures. We are not responsible for knowing how everything is going to work out in the end. We are called first, and last, simply to abide.

LINDSAY P. ARMSTRONG

Exegetical Perspective

John 15:9 introduces the very Johannine theme of love, which is further qualified in the next verse by linking "love" and "commandments." God's love for Jesus is the example of Jesus' love for his disciples and the disciples' love for each other. According to John's theology (5:20; 17:24) Jesus' relationships with his disciples are molded after God's relationship to Jesus. In 12:49 Jesus refers his commandment back to the Father in order to legitimatize his authority, and in 13:34 Jesus gives the commandment to love one another as he has loved the disciples. John 14:15 explicitly establishes another connection between obedience to and love of Jesus that is later expanded to the Father's love for the disciples (14:21). John 15:10 condenses these links between the love commandment by once more making Jesus' obedience to the Father's commandment the paradigm of discipleship.

The Gospel deploys the image of the vine, which had traditionally been deployed in the prophetic tradition to portray a relationship between Israel and its God, and narrows it down to illustrate a relationship between the Master and his disciples. To put it briefly, a metaphor designed to express a national religious identity now identifies a sectarian community. Moreover, John's emphasis on binaries—for example, light and darkness, above and below, this world and the other world, love and hate—provides one hermeneutical key to understand some exclusivist notes behind the idea of discipleship expressed in the text, most explicitly in verses 5–6. In this case, discipleship is linked to remaining within the boundaries of the community. Outsiders (those who do not bear fruit) are likely to be identified as those belonging to "the world" (8:23). Bearing fruit as the main criterion for discipleship echoes the image of the grains of wheat in 12:24, where Jesus claims that it is necessary to die in order to bear "much fruit." The present text might offer comfort to endure the difficulties that follow from separating oneself from the world and entering a communal space where one's life is at risk, at least as it is perceived by the evangelist. Lastly, the text explicitly bestows the role of the judge on God (15:2), dismissing any attempt by leaders to discern who belongs and who is excluded from the congregation.

LUIS MENÉNDEZ-ANTUÑA

Homiletical Perspective

a radical difference as those verses. The Spirit of God brings them to mind time and time again."[1] Miss Emma Sloan was teaching little Fred Craddock what it means to abide in God's Word, to abide in Christ as the branch abides in the vine. Some things do not change throughout all our life; some things abide.

Dag Hammarskjöld, the well-respected secretary general of the United Nations until his death in a plane crash on September 18, 1961, was a man of faith. After his death his private journal was published under the title *Markings*. Two months before his death he included a prayerful petition that we might live in God:

> Give us a pure heart—that we may see Thee,
> A humble heart—that we may hear Thee,
> A heart of love—that we may serve Thee,
> A heart of faith—that we may live Thee.[2]

The prayer reminds us that abiding has to do with seeing, hearing, and serving God with deeds of love for others. We are to bear fruit and make a difference in our community because we are engrafted into Christ. The old quip is a little bit funny and a little bit true: a lot of church members who are singing "Standing on the Promises"[3] are just sitting on the premises! The two ends of this branch are really just one: to abide in the vine is to bear fruit for God.

The image is clear and crisp and self-evident: the vine, the branches, the fruit. The abiding mission of the church remains: to know Christ and to make him known in deeds of love.

ROBERT M. BREARLEY

1. Fred Craddock, *Craddock Stories*, ed. Mike Graves and Richard F. Ward (St. Louis: Chalice Press, 2001), 33–34.
2. Dag Hammarskjöld, *Markings* (New York: Alfred A. Knopf, 1964), 214.
3. R. Kelso Carter, "Standing on the Promises" (1886).

John 15:12–17

¹²"This is my commandment, that you love one another as I have loved you. ¹³No one has greater love than this, to lay down one's life for one's friends. ¹⁴You are my friends if you do what I command you. ¹⁵I do not call you servants any longer, because the servant does not know what the master is doing; but I have called you friends, because I have made known to you everything that I have heard from my Father. ¹⁶You did not choose me but I chose you. And I appointed you to go and bear fruit, fruit that will last, so that the Father will give you whatever you ask him in my name. ¹⁷I am giving you these commands so that you may love one another."

Theological Perspective

"No one has greater love than this, to lay down one's life for one's friends. You are my friends if you do what I command you" (vv. 13–14).

Love and friendship may seem self-explanatory for us in the twenty-first century. However, I want to suggest that we rethink what we understand about these two qualities in light of the way that the Gospel writer explains them and in light of what we know from the larger biblical text about how God loves. Love in this passage is not a psychological state, nor is it anywhere described as an internal quality. Love is an action—a really difficult action. The definition of love here is a radical willingness to die—not for your child or your spouse, but for a fellow follower of Christ. If we bring this down to the very mundane, if we look around the church, for whom would we die? For what reason would we die for a fellow follower of Christ? This is the definition of Jesus' expression of friendship: to give up everything for the other. For Jesus, in this text, friendship is obedient action, the obedience of Jesus to God first, and in response our obedience to Christ. "Do what I tell you," Jesus says, which is altogether different from what contemporary ears would hear in the offer of friendship.

Twenty-first-century readers cannot help but read the language of love and friendship psychologically.

Pastoral Perspective

On a trip to the north Georgia mountains, I was dutifully unloading groceries from my car while enjoying the mountain air and the bold stares of the surprisingly sociable deer forty feet away. After a few trips, I grabbed the last bag, locked the car, and went into the house, only to find three sixteen-year-old girls folding the now empty grocery bags and putting the last bottle of Perrier into the refrigerator. Surprised at the initiative, I expressed thanks, at which point one of my daughter's friends looked me straight in the eye, flipped her hair, struck a sassy pose, and announced, "That's what friends are for." Then they all three ran off, disappearing into the house, as only sixteen-year-old girls can do.

"That's what friends are for." It is a strange statement to hear from the mouth of a child's friend, even as it is provocative. Is that what friends are for? Certainly, friends do help us. Moreover, they are gifts given by a God who cleverly loves us in the ordinary settings and everyday people of our lives. Indeed, friends are one of life's greatest gifts. They accept us, care for us, make us laugh, challenge us, listen to us, steady us, help us pick up the pieces, and even inspire us to be better. They represent some of life's best relationships. Yet Jesus did not lightly say, "No one has greater love than this, to lay down one's life for one's friends. . . . I do not call you servants

Feasting on the Gospels

Exegetical Perspective

Scholars disagree on this text's limits. Whereas some commentators contend that the pericope starts in verse 7 (Stevick) or verse 9 (Neyrey),[1] most scholars choose to study 15:1–17 as one unit. The first option emphasizes the unit as an explanation of the vine metaphor; the second underscores "love" as the main topic; while studies that preserve the pericope as a whole contend that the text is structured following an *inclusio* scheme. By opting for a division that starts in verse 12, the emphasis is put on the question of the "commandment of love" from a horizontal perspective: Jesus claims that "laying down his life" (v. 13) is the ultimate criterion of love that his now-called "friends" ought to follow.

The previous pericope introduces a broad description of the reality of discipleship by using the vine as a metaphor. By posing God as the vinedresser and the disciples as the branches that bear fruit, John 15:1–11 emphasizes the vertical dimensions of the community. Starting in verse 12 the commandment centers on loving each other, posing Jesus' love as example and placing friendship at the core of the community structure. Jesus calls his disciples

1. Daniel B. Stevick, *Jesus and His Own: A Commentary on John 13–17* (Grand Rapids: Eerdmans, 2011), 200, and Jerome H. Neyrey, *The Gospel of John*, New Cambridge Bible Commentary (New York: Cambridge University Press, 2007), 255–60.

Homiletical Perspective

I hope that your congregation gets fan mail from time to time. Recently, our church received an encouraging e-mail from folks who stopped by to worship with us as they traveled from Ohio to Florida. They lifted the spirits of everyone: "We found your congregation to be warm and friendly and would definitely choose to worship with you again. . . . Thank you for your kindness." Somehow, by the working of the Spirit, they sensed they were in the presence of friends in Christ, and they could feel the love. Of course, that is not always the case, with our church or any church. Yet it remains our hope and our mission that people will know us by our love.

Our text, John 15:12–17, is not a narrative; rather, it reads like a string of aphorisms—each truth seemingly able to stand alone but then linking itself to the others in a more intimate relationship of love. So it is with the Christian community. The temptation is to pick our favorite truth and to stand alone in its light, but the invitation of Christ is to seek the intimacy of mutual love. The life of shared joy, shared sacrifice, shared obedience, shared friendship, and shared revelation bears fruit in loving one another. This up-close-and-personal love for our friends in Christ is the key to discipleship and witness.

Frances Taylor Gench makes a surprising observation when she comments that "nowhere in John are

John 15:12–17

Theological Perspective

We have been steeped in the language of individual psychology to such an extent that it is hard to imagine that there is any definition of love other than a personal warm and fuzzy feeling, or friendship as companionship and compatibility. In the era of Facebook, a friend may simply be someone who clicks "like" in response to a picture of someone we have never met. How very far away all of these are from the love Christ commands! Being a friend of Jesus' is neither a subjective state nor a disinterested glance. Love is radical action, and friendship is getting out into the world to "bear fruit" (v. 4), and "bearing fruit" in this first-century context is dangerous business—it can get you kicked out of the synagogue, persecuted, and even killed.

More difficult still for the modern mind is the notion that *God's love* for us through Christ is not a feeling, at least not a feeling to which we mere creatures can have access. The definition of God's love is God's actions. In the beginning, God does not think or feel; God creates. So it is with God's love: it is defined for us by what it does. "In the beginning was the Word, and the Word was with God, and the Word was God. . . . All things came into being through him" (1:1, 3). Even in God's internal life before history, we are not privy to God's feelings but, rather, Christ's role in creating the world. Does not God, in God's very being, feel tenderly toward us? We can anthropomorphize God's love and assume that it takes the form of what we want it to be, what we have come to call "love" in the present; but in reality, the definitions of God's love that we have access to are its results: it creates, redeems, bears fruit, lays down its life.

Psychologizing love and friendship can allow us to remain disengaged from one another, to identify as a community of Christ solely by profession of faith or physical proximity in a church building. If we believe that we have to cultivate internal states of being first, in order to manifest God's love, we may never get on with the business of bearing fruit. Preaching that is only therapeutic, rather than also always prophetic, can reinforce a kind of self-absorption that is unknown to the writer of this Gospel and ultimately at odds with what we read of God's love. This is not the love that compels me to lay down my life for you.

Let us be clear here: mandating death as the mark of love has a problematic and unevenly applied history, we now understand. The history of its misuse is well documented in theologies of liberation, among others. The idea may still present us with a

Pastoral Perspective

any longer, . . . but I have called you friends" (vv. 13, 15a). What is the purpose of friendship in the Christian life? What is the significance of Jesus, on his last night, no longer calling his disciples servants but calling them friends?

In 15:12–17, Jesus directs his disciples to "love one another as I have loved you." Indeed, the passage begins and ends with the instruction. While modern conversation about love and friendship can veer toward the cozy and sentimental, Jesus issues a radical call. It is perhaps the most radical call of the gospel, because his words indicate that the kind of love Jesus embodied is to be reproduced by Jesus' followers: "Love one another as I have loved you." This is love that goes all the way. It gives all things, hopes all things, and endures all things (1 Cor. 13:7). It does not necessarily go looking to lose one's life, but if that is what love requires, it does not falter. This is love in action and is not unique to Jesus, but is to be characteristic of all of Jesus' friends.

Often, when we think of friendship with Christ, we focus on how good a friend Jesus is to us. "What a friend we have in Jesus," we sing.[1] John 15 moves us rapidly to the flip side: to being a friend of Jesus and to the fruit that friendship with Christ bears.

Indeed, friendship is one of life's greatest gifts. Friendships go far beyond being a blessing and sign of how much God loves us, though. Friendships serve as training grounds. Our best friendships teach us how to love. Day by day and year after year, enduring friendships are places in which we practice patience, forgiveness, kindness, and justice. Friendships can be where we learn hospitality, mercy, generosity, and compassion. To be sure, not all friendships accomplish such lofty goals, but it is often through friendships that we learn to love and that we catch glimpses of what it means to radiate the goodness and holiness of God in the world.

In telling his disciples that he no longer calls them servants but friends, Jesus is suggesting that even as he leaves, relationships matter and friendship is a primary setting in which we love one another and grow in the skills needed to refresh the world with our way of life. Jesus as friend models the best of human love, even as his friendship becomes the source of disciples' capacity for friendship.

In the twenty-first century, there is anxiety about friendship. Once upon a time, friendships were a staple of American popular culture—but not so

---

1. Joseph Scriven, "What a Friend We Have in Jesus" (1855), in *Glory to God: The Presbyterian Hymnal* (Louisville, KY: Westminster John Knox Press, 2013), #465.

Exegetical Perspective

"friends" and grounds that relationship in the revelatory experience (v. 15). The commandment to love one another as Jesus loves the disciples first appears in 13:34–35; here it is qualified and broadened in scope by contrasting the figures of the "slave" and the "friend." The language of friendship is central to the message in this pericope (vv. 13, 14, 15) and calls for further explanation.

Friendship was a social institution in the Greco-Roman culture that encompassed a set of relationships similar to that of the patron-client. Consequently, friendship does not imply equal status or absolute reciprocity. When later in the Gospel the Jews cry out to Pilate that if he releases Jesus he is no longer "friend" of Caesar (19:12), they are implying not just a close relationship between the governor and the emperor but also a subordinate relationship of authority. Friendship, as Neyrey puts it, equals clientship, meaning that the patron (Jesus) offers protection in return for allegiance.[2] Within this frame, Jesus' words qualify the master-disciple relationship in terms of an exchange where he offers divine wisdom and goods (vv. 15, 16) and the disciples abide and bear fruit (v. 16). Furthermore, Jesus is himself a client of God, in that he keeps the Father's commandments in return for God's protection and love. Such dynamic relationship positions Jesus as a broker (15:9).

Although referring to the disciples as friends is not an uncommon practice in the Greco-Roman context, it is striking that Jesus insists that it is he who has chosen his followers (v. 16). It was customary practice that the pupils chose their master, not vice versa. Here John deploys the same conception of election we find in the rest of the Gospels, one that also runs through the whole Hebrew Bible, where God always takes the initiative in the relationship. We tend to think of friends as persons whom we freely choose to associate with in a mutual relation, whereas in verse 16 it is made clear that Jesus authoritatively "appoints" the disciples so they become fruitful. Our cultural conventions of friendship are thus challenged, because the disciples become friends if they are willing to do as Jesus commands (v. 14), and the initiative comes unilaterally from Jesus (v. 16).

Since we tend to think of love as a feeling that springs spontaneously out of someone's heart, it is surprising that love is here commanded: Jesus commands his followers to love one another. Rather than as an individual feeling of affection, love ought to

2. Neyrey, *Gospel of John*, 257.

Homiletical Perspective

disciples encouraged to turn the other cheek, walk the other mile, forgive those who trespass against them, give away possessions, or attend to the poor."[1] Other Gospels will invite us to love strangers, enemies, and foreigners, but John takes up the challenge of loving those near at hand, perhaps in the pew right beside us. Sometimes it is the most difficult task to love those we have known the longest in life and in church. Someone once remarked that when we get angry, we do not get hysterical, we get historical! The closeness of the community of faith is intended to be a blessing, but the proximity over time can be difficult.

One normally mild-mannered Christian pastor became so frustrated with the unkind thoughts and actions of the church staff that he stood up right in the middle of their meeting, declared that he had had enough of their bickering, and informed his fellow Christians that he was leaving their gathering. When they asked where he was going, he replied that he was going to lunch at the neighborhood hot-dog stand, where he could enjoy some pleasant company and perhaps some Christian fellowship!

Our text is bracketed with the command to love one another, and within those brackets we are given the resources of Christ to live out this mutual compassion. First, we are offered Christ the redeemer: "No one has greater love than this, to lay down one's life for one's friends" (v. 13). The preceding image of the vine and the branches emphasized the vital connection with Christ to remain alive and growing in the faith. Now it is in the dying to self for the sake of others that channels the love of Christ into our mission as church. Secondly, we are claimed by Christ the revealer: "I have called you friends, because I have made known to you everything that I have heard from my Father" (v. 15b). We do not love in our own understanding; we have been chosen. The love of Christ reveals the mercy of the heavenly Father, and that knowledge gives us confidence in loving one another.

For John, fulfilling this command to love one another has more to do with our consciousness of Christ than with our human determination. As tensions rise within the community of faith, it is Christ-mindedness rather than like-mindedness that will enable us to show compassion to our friends in the faith and to keep the peace from being shattered.

A seminary senior was visiting with a pastor nominating committee that asked, "What is the

1. Frances Taylor Gench, *Encounters with Jesus: Studies in the Gospel of John* (Louisville, KY: Westminster John Knox Press, 2007), 107.

Theological Perspective

respectable challenge, though. If we agree that the abusive parameters of this equation are unacceptable, what remains for us? Good news and bad news. The good news is that we do not have to feel any particular way to get on with the *practice* of friendship. This is good news, because if we were actually able to take the measure of the feelings of those who surround us in the congregation, we would find, I suspect, that we would have not regularly conjured up enough internal warmth to really suffer for me. The bad news is the same with a different emphasis: get on with the business of friendship without waiting to feel or expecting to feel anything in particular for another. If you follow Christ, you are ready to die for him, as God in Christ died for us. "If you keep my commandments, you will abide in my love, just as I have kept my Father's commandments and abide in his love" (15:10).

The love of God through Christ to us expresses again the generative nature of God's love: to reconcile us both to God and to one another. God's love is that which creates something new, restores what has been broken, completes what is unfinished, heals what has been hurt, and gives itself to the point of death. Certainly we can say that accepting the radical offering of grace offered by God should instill in us sense of well-being, of gratitude, of love. Those feelings can be complete, however, only when they are expressed in our actions toward one another. They are not precursors to action, but dependent on action for substance and endurance. This then is the fullness of salvation by grace alone. If we fully accept unmerited grace—accepting God's radical action of restoration by becoming one of us, suffering, and dying—we are compelled to respond. Our responses of gratitude to God are known by our actions toward others.

EMILY ASKEW

Pastoral Perspective

anymore. The late-twentieth-century bridge clubs, bowling leagues, and TV shows like *Friends* and *Seinfeld* have given way to slot machines, bowling alone,[2] and shows about modern angst, reality TV, and various contests to lose weight or become a millionaire. As workers log longer hours, as people relocate, and as technology changes the contours of relationships, friendship is often among the first things to be sacrificed. There are lonely people who live with feelings of failure when it comes to friendship. Others do not grasp what they are missing.

When it comes to living faithfully in today's world, Christianity focuses on words like love, justice, peace, forgiveness, and wholeness. Into this reality, John 15:12–17 places friendship at the center of what it means to live faithfully. Jesus calls us friends and not servants. He states that *he* chose *us*, not the other way around. Jesus then instructs that, as his friends, we are appointed to go and bear lasting fruit, blessing the world. *That* is what friends are for.

Most of us would accept help unpacking groceries any time, yet the riches of friendship with God go beyond the blessings we receive from each other. Being a friend of Jesus in relationship with other friends of Jesus provides the setting for teaching each other various practices of Christian love. We have been invited into a relationship. The most important aspect of Christianity is not the work we do, but the relationship we maintain and the surrounding influences, qualities, and relationships produced by that friendship. As he lay down his life for his friends, this is what Jesus asked us to give our attention to: growing resplendent in the love and goodness of God; able to astound others with our Christ-centered way of life; loving others as we have been loved.

LINDSAY P. ARMSTRONG

2. Robert Putnam, *Bowling Alone: The Collapse and Revival of American Community* (New York: Simon & Schuster, 2000).

Exegetical Perspective

be interpreted within the frame of the patron-client scheme previously described. In effect, love has to do with obedience, respect, and authority. Although the text disavows any identification between discipleship and slavery (v. 15), the boundaries between friends and slaves were occasionally blurred. In the Greco-Roman world, slaves were not simply limited to forced labor but, in many cases, were an integral part of the domestic unit; some of them remained very close to their owners, actively managing property, educating the children, or becoming authoritative experts in different matters. In fact, 15:20 identifies the disciples with servants in the context of persecution. It is well known that Paul deploys the figure of the slave in order to portray his relationship to the Lord (Rom. 1:1; Gal. 1:10), which proves that the lines dividing slave, friend, patron, and client were blurry.

The text no longer refers to the image of the vine but still invites the disciples to bear fruit (v. 16). As it abandons the metaphoric language, the message becomes more explicit: the pericope starts by making explicit the commandment that had been previously mentioned (15:10). Furthermore, the criterion for love is laid out in verse 13, which anticipates Jesus' destiny. There is no greater love than laying down one's life for one's friends. Previously Jesus introduced the new commandment (13:35), and Simon Peter answered by claiming he was able to abide with Jesus and follow him to the end, to the point of laying down his life for Jesus (13:37). Here Jesus' disciples are invited to act out this kind of love with each other, despite the fact that failure is anticipated, as the example of Simon Peter makes clear.

Rhetorically, the emphasis on love seeks to reinforce the group's boundaries in light of the hostile environment that is portrayed in the next pericope (15:18–25), making a dramatic contrast between the community and the world, the dynamic of love and hate, knowledge and ignorance. As Neyrey puts it, "love" functions in a series of binary opposites that reflect the social turmoil in which the community finds itself.[3] In this context, it is not surprising that the message has been previously introduced by an invitation to experience "joy" (15:11) as a consequence of abiding and bearing fruit, for, as the next pericope makes clear, that is a daunting task.

LUIS MENÉNDEZ-ANTUÑA

Homiletical Perspective

greatest need of our denomination?" The student responded without hesitation, "Our greatest need is for our churches to stay together and for Christians to love one another." John's Gospel joins us in hoping that the church called that seminarian to be their pastor, because his answer to that question was exactly right. To love one another is our greatest need. John wants to make sure that we do not forget to take our Christ-inspired love to church. We are to have compassion for our friends in the faith. The challenge is to love the near at hand, perhaps as near as the Christian beside you in worship.

Ann Weems imagines an unspoken dialogue of thoughts between two people seated beside each other in church, two people close in physical space yet far apart in what they are willing to share with each other. She titles the scene "You—Sitting in the Pew Next to Me." Each imagines what the other must be thinking, and each wonders if they will have the courage to risk getting to know one another. Near the end of the narrated yet unspoken dialogue, one worshiper thinks to himself:

> I'm scared when I look at myself. That's why I'm here—because I've heard there is a better way. I've heard that some take Christ seriously. . . . Could I talk to you about it? Would you laugh to think successful me needs you? Or would you be compassionate because you know I'm scared? Maybe you'll be the one to tell me. Or are you just another person in the pew that I'll never know?[2]

The command of Christ is to love one another in the church. It is not the easiest command, and it is not the easiest mission field. For John's Gospel, it matters the most. They out there will know us by our love in here. Loving the near at hand is our best witness.

ROBERT M. BREARLEY

---

3. Ibid., 256.

2. Ann Weems, *Reaching for Rainbows: Resources for Creative Worship* (Philadelphia: Westminster Press, 1980), 55.

John 15:18–25

18"If the world hates you, be aware that it hated me before it hated you. 19If you belonged to the world, the world would love you as its own. Because you do not belong to the world, but I have chosen you out of the world—therefore the world hates you. 20Remember the word that I said to you, 'Servants are not greater than their master.' If they persecuted me, they will persecute you; if they kept my word, they will keep yours also. 21But they will do all these things to you on account of my name, because they do not know him who sent me. 22If I had not come and spoken to them, they would not have sin; but now they have no excuse for their sin. 23Whoever hates me hates my Father also. 24If I had not done among them the works that no one else did, they would not have sin. But now they have seen and hated both me and my Father. 25It was to fulfill the word that is written in their law, 'They hated me without a cause.'"

Theological Perspective

So poignantly does this passage cast light upon the union of the divine Father and Son that we are opened up in new ways to the pathos of Jesus' suffering and love for the broken. In effect, we are led to ask why, for instance, would religious leaders turn their back upon the promised Messiah? Similarly, why would God allow his Son to become the object of derision, shame, and deathly opposition? Why does Jesus identify with the poor and the outcast? All of this leads us to ask after the nature of discipleship and friendship with Christ.

One of the interpretive keys to our passage is found in John's narrative of the events leading up to Passover. Just prior to the festival, the chief priests and Pharisees issue an order for his arrest. This disclosure is at once followed with the narrative of a dinner at the home of Lazarus (whom Jesus had raised from the dead). At this point Mary anoints Jesus with costly perfume, giving rise to Judas's disapproval and Jesus' retort: "Leave her alone. She bought it so that she might keep it for the day of my burial," to which he adds, "You always have the poor with you, but you do not always have me" (12:7–8). The juxtaposition of opposition to Jesus (an opposition that will eventually lead to his death), on the one hand, and his own life-giving ministry and

Pastoral Perspective

In the Farewell Discourse of Jesus (chaps. 14–17) the Fourth Evangelist tells his readers that "the hour" about which Jesus often talked has come. People must choose whether or not Christ is Lord. Immediately prior to our passage, Jesus reveals himself to be the "true vine." We, his followers, are "branches." In other words, Jesus is the source of our life-giving sustenance. Jesus also elevates the disciples to the more intimate level of friendship, because he has now taught them everything God has revealed to the Son. Jesus knows he will be depending upon his friends to be his hands and feet in the world. Their job will not be easy. "Because you do not belong to the world, but I have chosen you out of the world—therefore the world hates you" (v. 19b).

John uses dualism abundantly in his Gospel: light/darkness, truth/falsehood, love/hate, Christ's followers/the world; but he has no intention of reducing our level of understanding to clearly delineated categories of black-and-white thinking. Instead, he uses stark dualistic symbolism to articulate the radical difference a relationship with Jesus makes.

Life for Jesus' followers will not be easy. The early Christian community of which John was a part had clearly experienced alienation from the dominant political and religious powers. The "world" (Gk.

Feasting on the Gospels

Exegetical Perspective

Jesus' Farewell Discourse (14:1–16:33) takes a dramatic turn with this passage. Up to this point, Jesus' words have focused on the community and their relationship with him and with one another. Now he addresses the community's relationship with outsiders—named first as the "world" and then as "they." As is typical of farewell discourses, the hero warns his followers of difficulties they will experience after his departure. Whereas the preceding verses were marked by the themes of intimacy, abiding in love (15:1–11, the vine and branches), friendship, and the command to love as Jesus loved (15:12–17), the present passage is replete with the language of hatred, persecution, sin, and death. A dramatic turn indeed.

It is important to appreciate that this passage reflects the experience of the Johannine community. Jesus' words here about the hatred and persecution of the disciples do not reflect what happened during his life and ministry. This observation is a reminder of how the words of the Farewell Discourse, although placed on Jesus' lips on the night before he died, convey the words of the risen Jesus to his followers in a new context. Indeed, "by the time the Fourth Gospel was in its final form, persecution by the Romans and the expulsion of Jewish

Homiletical Perspective

This passage from the Fourth Gospel presents serious homiletical challenges. The sharp distinction between the community of Christ and "the world" could be taken as a demand that Christians withdraw into a sectarian enclave. We can be reminded how the early-twentieth-century German sociologist and theologian Ernst Troeltsch contrasted what he called the "sect-type" with the "church-type."[1] The pure sectarian draws a sharp distinction between the community of faith and the world outside. The ideal is purity of faith, without compromise. The sectarian goal is to maintain that purity while seeking to draw others into the community.

Christians must not accept or live by values and practices in the non-Christian "world." Taken literally, that is impossible for people who must, after all, live in that world. There is no zone of innocence into which Christians can retreat. Economically and politically, we are virtually compelled to live in accordance with secular standards. Even those Christian groups that have sought to withdraw into communes cannot do so in total isolation from the world, as the history of such enclaves abundantly illustrates. Even the more sectarian religious

1. Ernst Troeltsch, *The Social Teaching of the Christian Churches*, trans. Olive Wyon (orig. 1912; Louisville, KY: Westminster John Knox Press, 1992).

John 15:18–25

Theological Perspective

resurrection, on the other, sets the stage for our consideration of John 15:18–25.

This passage reveals the profound connection between resurrection, divine election, and discipleship. How else can one explain why people would follow Jesus in the wake of the knowledge that doing so inevitably draws you into danger? Certainly Jesus' prediction of his own suffering and death raises serious questions about the cost of discipleship. Doubtless many did raise such questions and, in spite of the danger, did choose the way of obedience. We would do well to consider why they did so.

Certainly, the key lies in seeing this passage from the perspective of the downcast or defenseless. For those who were powerless in society—as was no doubt the case with both Israel in bondage and the Christian communities to which John was written—Jesus' teaching about persecution and hatred would have resonated quite strongly with their everyday experience. Far from rising to the fever pitch of anxiety, Jesus' teaching about oppression would have, among such people, struck a very different chord. This is why, for example, Jesus' teaching "if the world hates you, be aware that it hated me before it hated you" (v. 18) does not frighten or alienate members of his audience. In fact, just the opposite is the case. By saying these things, Jesus is effectively declaring his solidarity with them. Indeed, Jesus says that those who turn against them because of their commitment to him also stand in fundamental opposition to the heavenly Father (vv. 21–22).

In short, the message of divine solidarity would have come as good news for those all too familiar with the malevolence of creaturely life. A particularly lucid account of divine solidarity is on display in Jesus' teaching: "you do not belong to the world, but I have chosen you out of the world—therefore the world hates you" (v. 19b). Not surprisingly then, Jesus' own ministry, mission, and election evoke a corresponding pattern of radical identification with the brokenness of the world. Two further elements of this cruciform existence and solidarity call for our attention.

First, John's Gospel cautions against the naive assumption that God's love for *all* equals a divine *approval* of all that we do. Jesus' life and death painfully reveal the wretched contours of creaturely rebellion: "If the world hates you, be aware that it hated me before it hated you" (v. 18). Jesus' teaching does away with any and all romantic depictions of the human condition. Surely no positive anthropology can explain Jesus' depiction of sinful rebellion.

Pastoral Perspective

kosmos) became so corrupted by the powers of darkness that God sent the Son, the light of the world, to save it. Yet many who had witnessed God incarnate, seen God's power through the signs of Jesus, and been exposed to the light chose to remain in darkness. They chose hatred rather than the abundance of God's love embodied in Jesus. They turned their backs on God's truth.

The language in this passage is intentionally strong. In John's Gospel, sin (*hamartia*) is the rejection of God's truth. When people have never been exposed to divine truth, they do not understand sin. That is not the case with those who have rejected Jesus (vv. 22, 24). They are culpable for their actions, because they have heard Jesus speak, seen his power, and witnessed his love. Yet they still oppose God's plan of salvation, despite the fact they have been eyewitnesses to its unfolding. They knowingly choose hatred and rejection as their response to the Messiah. They vehemently reject God's truth revealed through his Son.

Jesus warns his friends about not only his impending persecution but theirs as well. John closes this passage with Jesus' fulfillment of the law, in this case a general reference to the Old Testament Scriptures. "They hated me without a cause" quotes Psalms 35:19 and 69:4.

For many of us who live in privileged societies, it is easy to forget the urgency of choosing to stand with—or against—Jesus Christ. God has created humans with the gift of free will. More than anything else, God wants to have a loving relationship with us. Love can never be forced; it must be freely given. In Jesus, we see love in human form. We must respond. Will we choose to love God revealed in Jesus Christ, or will we turn away?

From its prologue, the Gospel of John has built the case for choosing Jesus as Lord. Jesus has demonstrated his power in and through miracles (called "signs" by John), including the resurrection of the dead (11:41–44). He has revealed himself and his life-giving love by using common metaphors (the door, the good shepherd). He has invited all to accept him as the long-awaited Messiah whom God has sent. Now is the moment of choice.

It is very difficult for contemporary Christians who live in countries where religious freedom is guaranteed to appreciate fully the worldly danger that those who choose Jesus in other contexts may face. The book of Acts reports the imprisonment of the apostles (5:17–18) and the martyrdom of Stephen (7:54–60). Early church historians reported

Christians from synagogues were already accomplished facts."[1]

A peculiar grammatical feature of this passage is the preponderance of conditional statements (i.e., sentences that begin with "if"). The first instance is found in 15:18, which expresses a real condition: "If the world hates you . . ." One consequence of the disciples' abiding in Jesus and being his "friends" (15:14) is that they share in the reaction of the "world" (*kosmos*) to him, a reaction marked by hatred. John employs the perfect tense of the verb *miseō* ("hate") in connection with Jesus to indicate that the hatred he encountered, which led to his being put to death on the cross, continues into the present in the experience of his followers. Intimacy with Jesus can and does entail opposition and suffering.

A second conditional statement appears in the following verse (v. 19): "If you belonged to the world . . ." This is a contrary-to-fact condition, because the community of Jesus' followers does *not* belong to the "world." Why? Because Jesus "has chosen" them "out of the world," which echoes what he said a few verses earlier: "You did not choose me but I chose you. And I appointed you to go and bear fruit, fruit that will last" (15:16). Notice how verse 19 is peppered with the word *kosmos*, which occurs five times. Here (and throughout this passage) the "world" denotes all that is opposed to God's revelation through Jesus. Elsewhere in John's Gospel, however, *kosmos* is that which God creates (e.g., 1:10) and is thus good. In fact, God so loved the *kosmos* that God sent his only Son that the world might be saved through him (3:16–17).

This multivalent sense of "world" assists in the interpretation of 15:20, where Jesus exhorts his disciples to recall what he said after humbly washing their feet: "Servants are not greater than their master" (13:16). That action, which symbolizes Jesus' self-giving love, the love fully manifested in his being lifted up (3:14; 8:28; 12:32; 13:1; 19:30), is the paradigm for his followers. While Jesus' earlier teaching centered on his disciples' washing one another's feet, the implication is that now—as Jesus' friends empowered to bear fruit—they are to play their part in the revelation of God's love in the world through lives of self-giving and service. Just as Jesus' revelation met with opposition, though, so too will the ministry of his followers. That is the force of the real condition, "If they persecuted me, they will persecute you" (v. 20).

communities, such as the Amish and the Hutterites, are made up of people who engage in ordinary economic activity and are subject to laws of all kinds. There just is not any escape from "the world"!

That said, the average congregation probably does not contain very many people who think of the church as a place of sectarian withdrawal. Even those who believe that being Christian should make a difference do not generally think of disengagement from responsibility in the real world. A congregation can be introduced to the eloquent words of the late-second-century *Epistle to Diognetus*,[2] which speaks of how Christians "live in their respective countries, but only as resident aliens. . . . They live on earth, but participate in the life of heaven" (6.5).

Moreover, most Christians in most countries are not subjected to the kind of persecution referred to in this passage. That does not mean, though, that this passage has nothing to say to us. While not persecuted, Christians often find their basic worldview and values disregarded in modern secular societies. Hostility to the way of Christ can be expressed by indifference as well as by violence. The way of Christ, rejected by such indifference, includes deep concern for the poor and the outcast, considering the marginalized people to be beloved by God.

Greed is encouraged by much popular culture, and the poor and marginalized are disregarded or even blamed for their condition. Christian concern is often taken to be soft. Such concern may be given sentimental lip service at Christmas, but it is not to be taken seriously by realistic people. Many American debates over health-care delivery emphasize costs, not the central point that a compassionate society will provide for universal delivery of health care.

Is that, in our time, "the world" rejecting Christ? Many people in American churches might find such thoughts offensive, and I can imagine that could lead to criticism of the preacher, if not out-and-out hostility. Such reactions can become an opportunity for more serious dialogue after the sermon. In such exchanges, Christians can be drawn into deeper thinking about the relationship between our views on contemporary issues and the mind of the Christ whom we are called to serve.

There have been times when American churches have helped to frame popular culture in accordance with deeper understandings of Christian faith. The

1. Raymond E. Brown, *The Gospel according to John XIII–XXI* (New York: Doubleday, 1970), 695.

2. *Epistle to Diognetus*, in *Apostolic Fathers: Volume II. Epistle of Barnabas, Papias and Quadratus, Epistle to Diognetus, The Shepherd of Hermas*, ed. and trans. Bart D. Ehrman, Loeb 25N (Cambridge, MA: Harvard University Press, 2003), 141.

John 15:18–25

Theological Perspective

It is here that we learn that creaturely opposition, persecution, and hatred of Jesus is in fact hatred of God. Those who persecute Jesus have not only failed to obey his teachings and repent of their sin but also fall victim to divine judgment. Key statements such as "I have chosen you out of the world" (v. 19b); "They do not know him who sent me" (v. 21b); "If I had not come and spoken to them, they would not have sin" (v. 22a); "Whoever hates me hates my Father also" (v. 23); and "But now they have seen and hated both me and my Father" (v. 24b) lay bare the fundamental truth of the divine unity. God the Father and Jesus are one. Opposition to and hatred of Jesus are, in fact, sinful rebellion against God.

Second, there is a message of abiding comfort in John's depiction of the divine unity of the Son and Father. Because Jesus and the Father are one, we ought to find considerable joy in the fact that divine election signals a fundamentally new identity. Jesus' solidarity with us is itself the promise of a life with God. Just as the psalmist teaches that "he is our God, and we are the people of his pasture, and the sheep of his hand" (Ps. 95:7), John reminds us that the Great Shepherd no longer calls us "servants" but instead calls us "friends" (15:15). To be hated by the world for Christ (v. 18) is to be marked as a friend of Jesus, one for whom he is willing to suffer and die (15:13).

In sum, far from conceiving of divine election as the gift of privilege or status, John reveals that election and discipleship constitute the basis for a cruciform life. Moreover, those familiar with brokenness and dispossession see, in Jesus' teaching and calling, a God of love, true friendship, and solidarity.

MARK HUSBANDS

Pastoral Perspective

the martyrdom of the disciples, including Peter and Paul around 64–65 CE. Tradition holds that Peter was crucified upside down at his own request, since he saw himself unworthy to be crucified in the same way as Jesus. Proclaiming the Christian faith carried huge risks for the early Christians. Falsely blamed by the Roman emperor Nero for a fire that destroyed parts of Rome in 64 CE, Christians were burned alive and fed to lions as crowds cheered.

People continue to be persecuted for their faith in some parts of the world. Terrorist attacks on Christians in parts of Africa, the Middle East, and Asia increase every year. In China, many Christians continue to practice their faith at their peril.[1] Many other countries make life very difficult, or even dangerous, for those who choose to follow Christ.

It is easy for those of us who do not face persecution when we proclaim our faith to forget about the price paid by so many throughout Christian history. Because there is little risk, we fail to summon the courage to proclaim our convictions. Unintentionally, we gradually trivialize the faith in Jesus Christ that should set us apart. We become complacent about weekly worship or daily prayer. We lack both the boldness and the joy of those whose faith in Jesus Christ is the ground on which all aspects of their lives are built.

John's harsh words are a powerful reminder to us that we are called to live as Christ's friends, his hands and feet in the world. We too are called to take up our crosses and follow Christ. Christians must commit to intentional discipleship, so we can remain faithful, no matter what happens in the future. Christ gave his life that we might live abundantly in the present and eternally in the future. Our response must be one of gratitude, commitment, and loyalty to Christ, no matter what the cost.

CATHY F. YOUNG

1. United States Commission on International Religious Freedom, Annual Report, 2013, 36; http://www.uscirf.gov/sites/default/files/resources/2013%20USCIRF%20Annual%20Report%20(2).pdf; accessed April 12, 2014.

The discourse contains a subtle shift in 15:20. The opposition to Jesus is described no longer as *kosmos*, "the world," but as "they." As will become clear (15:25; 16:1–4a), "they" refers to the Jewish leaders who oppose Jesus, and the chief problem, set forth in 15:21, is their failure to recognize that God is the one who sent Jesus.

The Johannine Jesus then uses two parallel contrary-to-fact conditional statements in 15:22 and 24. A key theme in the Fourth Gospel is that Jesus' words and works make God known (e.g., 10:38; 14:10–11), but it is precisely those words and works that "they" (i.e., the religious leaders) have refused to recognize as revelatory of God. Because "they" have heard and seen, there is "no excuse for their sin" (v. 22). Here we encounter John's understanding of sin (*hamartia*) as the rejection of God's revelation through Jesus. As 15:23 makes clear, the correlative of sin is hate. The refusal of the revelation of God's love in Jesus (3:16–17) leaves one in a condition marked by hatred, violence, and persecution. In John's worldview, rejection of Jesus is rejection of the Father.

The passage concludes in verse 25 with Jesus' citation of Scripture (named here as "law"): "They hated me without cause," a line that echoes both Psalm 35:19 and Psalm 69:4. The latter is likely the passage alluded to here, given that the Johannine Jesus has already cited words from Psalm 69:9 in 2:17 ("Zeal for your house will consume me"). In any event, Jesus uses Scripture to show how it bears witness against the religious leaders, a strategy he employed earlier (5:45–47), and which indicates that such hatred and opposition have been predicted far in advance (12:39–40).

The use of Psalm 69 in 15:25 may also serve another function. Typical of lament psalms—including those of the righteous sufferer—Psalm 69 includes an expression of trust in God's deliverance: "For God will save Zion and rebuild the cities of Judah; . . . and those who love his name shall live in it" (69:35a, 36b). Is this the hope that was foreshadowed by the hitherto uncommented-upon conditional statement at the end of 15:20: "if they kept my word, they will keep yours also"? If so, then a door is left open—to the *kosmos* and to "them"—for a positive response to Jesus.

THOMAS D. STEGMAN, SJ

American civil rights movement may be the most striking illustration. After centuries of slavery and generations of racial discrimination and official segregation, racism was deeply embedded in American culture. A handful of Christian leaders, mostly African American, confronted American racism as a profound deviation from the gospel of Jesus Christ. Even churches were largely segregated, especially but not exclusively in the South. So "the world" was not just opposed to the church; it was *in* the church! Racism and segregation were completely antithetical to Christ.

It may not stretch the truth too far to say that they expressed the kind of hatred of the real meaning of God referred to in this passage from John. Indeed, Christians who sought to change the culture were sometimes actively persecuted, even killed for their views. America, and later South Africa, were blessed by Christian leaders like Martin Luther King Jr. and Desmond Tutu who responded with loving firmness, overcoming hatred with love and thus bringing healing even to racial oppressors.

John 15:18–25 develops a sharp contrast between the way of Christ, who represents the love of God, and the way of the world. The contrast can be presented and illustrated clearly, but that does not mean that it comes down to a simple contrast between good people and bad people. Goodness and evil reside within the church as well as beyond the church, and they are present in all of us. Jesus is portrayed here as emphasizing that real sin is conscious, intentional rejection of God. We are all sinners, but there is a word here for us: do not turn away from the love of God we have experienced through Jesus Christ.

Perhaps there is also a word of encouragement for us. We must not become discouraged by the apparent victory of forces opposed to the loving justice of God. In the end, this is God's world, and our faithfulness will help to transform the world, bending it toward the goodness of God.

J. PHILIP WOGAMAN

John 15:26–16:4a

26"When the Advocate comes, whom I will send to you from the Father, the Spirit of truth who comes from the Father, he will testify on my behalf. 27You also are to testify because you have been with me from the beginning.

16:1"I have said these things to you to keep you from stumbling. 2They will put you out of the synagogues. Indeed, an hour is coming when those who kill you will think that by doing so they are offering worship to God. 3And they will do this because they have not known the Father or me. 4But I have said these things to you so that when their hour comes you may remember that I told you about them."

Theological Perspective

John 15:26–16:4a is of enduring significance for all who seek to bear witness to Christ in a complex and challenging world. In wonderfully compact prose, Jesus lays bare the transformative mission of the Holy Spirit, assuring his disciples that God will not abandon them in the midst of harrowing opposition. As we shall see, one of the principal reasons for John's teaching on the Spirit concerns apostasy. Not only this, but Jesus' teaching leads the reader to inquire about the kind of relationship that obtains between the work of the Spirit and the Son.

Jesus' announcement—"When the Advocate comes, whom I will send to you from the Father, the Spirit of truth who comes from the Father, he will testify on my behalf" (v. 26)—casts substantial light upon the symmetry and cooperation of the Son and Holy Spirit. The nature of this relationship has long been a subject of detailed theological reflection. As early as the second century, one finds the renowned bishop Irenaeus of Lyons focused upon the Spirit. Defending Christian belief against Gnosticism, Irenaeus explains the nature of the divine symmetry by insisting that God created all things through his "two hands," the divine Word and Spirit.[1] According to Irenaeus, the work of the Spirit is so closely tied to

1. Irenaeus of Lyons, *Against the Heresies*, trans. Dominic J. Unger (Mahwah, NJ: Newman Press, 1992), 4.20.1.

Pastoral Perspective

The time for Jesus' crucifixion has come. As Jesus' Farewell Discourse continues, he braces his disciples and followers for what lies ahead. "They will put you out of the synagogues. Indeed, an hour is coming when those who kill you will think that by doing so they are offering worship to God" (16:2).

Scholars believe the Gospel of John was written near the end of the first century CE.[1] During the first decades after Jesus' death and resurrection, the Christians were simply a sect within Judaism. Roman emperors who required their subjects to worship them as deities had exempted the Jews because of their strict monotheism. As the number of Christians grew, the Jews were increasingly worried about allowing Christians to worship or meet in their synagogues. Near the end of the first century, fearing that Christians might endanger this special Jewish exemption, the Jewish leaders expelled Christians from their synagogues. John's earliest readers were therefore worried about persecution, because they now lacked any protection from mandatory emperor worship.

That is why Jesus' assurance that he will not leave his disciples to face their trials alone is so important to John's readers. In this passage, Jesus promises to

1. Robert Kysar, *John, the Maverick Gospel* (Atlanta: John Knox Press, 1976), 20.

Exegetical Perspective

The Farewell Discourse of the Johannine Jesus (14:1–16:33) continues with warnings and encouragement to his disciples. The world's opposition to and hatred of Jesus' followers, introduced in the previous passage (15:18–25), is now given greater detail and specificity. Not only will the Johannine community experience expulsion from synagogues to which they previously belonged; Jesus also raises the possibility of martyrdom (16:1–4a). Sandwiched between these dire warnings is a promise of the Spirit, who will enable Jesus' followers to bear faithful witness to him (15:26–27).

Jesus' announcement of the coming of the "Advocate" (*Paraklētos*) in 15:26 is the third such notice in the Farewell Discourse. The *Paraklētos* was introduced in 14:16–17 as the Spirit whom the Father bestows to abide in the hearts of disciples. A bit later, in 14:26, the Johannine Jesus explained that the Father will send the *Paraklētos* to "teach you everything, and remind you of all that I have said to you." The Spirit will thus assist the community of believers to remember Jesus' words in such a way that they address their present circumstances.

Now, in 15:26–27, Jesus introduces another function of the *Paraklētos*: to "testify" on his behalf or, as the RSV renders it, to "bear witness" to him (the verb is *martyreō*). As "the Spirit of truth" (14:17)

Homiletical Perspective

The reference to the Advocate here is to the Holy Spirit. This is not an abstraction. Theological language about the Holy Spirit is often dry, sometimes more a verbal symbol than a living reality. Clearly that is not the intention of this passage, although someone reading about the Advocate coming from the Father may not immediately grasp the point. The task of preaching is somehow to breathe life into the language.

This living reality is what makes the presence of God most real in the consciousness of a professing Christian. It is partly a matter of emotional feeling, although not every emotional feeling is from God. Indeed, we are all aware of ecstatic outbursts that are directly opposed to what Christians believe about God. One thinks of the spirited rallies in Nazi-controlled Germany, with thousands of people caught up in something larger than themselves, but far lower than their true selves as understood through Christ. Christ, in this passage from John, defines the character of the Advocate. The Holy Spirit cannot be antithetical to the character of Christ. This means that, at bottom, it is the spirit of love, understood to be the love of God.

The Spirit can be present in the worship of a gathered congregation, insofar as the worship transcends self-centeredness and prejudices. Of course, much

Theological Perspective

the creative work of the Son that we *must* regard the Spirit as equally divine.

Put differently, rather than seeing the Spirit as an impersonal or instrumental force, Irenaeus insists that the Holy Spirit is to be believed and worshiped as the third person of the Trinity. Fully divine, the Spirit and the Son enact the Father's ongoing love, defense, and protection of all who have been born from above (Rom. 8:14–17; Gal. 4:5–7). This account of the relationship of the Son and Spirit enables us to grasp more clearly the significance of Jesus' teaching about the forensic work of the Spirit as the Advocate who will "testify" on Jesus' behalf (v. 26).

What does it mean for Jesus to speak of the Spirit as "the Spirit of truth who comes from the Father"? To answer this, let us return to the early church. In 375, the Cappadocian father Basil of Caesarea composed the very first theological treatise on the Holy Spirit. Fending off attacks from Arians and Pneumatomachi alike (the latter affirmed the divinity of the Son while refusing to grant the same of the Spirit), Basil insists that the Spirit is glorified through the communion that he shares with the Father and the Son. With considerable care and eloquence he crafts new ways of talking about the divine mystery of the triune God. In particular, he underscores the identity of the Spirit in terms of his action as the source of life, holiness, and truth: "He perfects others, but himself lacks nothing. He lives, but not because he has been restored to life; rather, he is the source of life." He adds that the Spirit is "the source of holiness, an intellectual light for every rational power's discovery of truth, supplying clarity, so to say, through himself."[2]

Although Basil would not live to see his work produce a rich harvest in the subsequent deliberations of the Council of Chalcedon (381 CE), he is rightly credited with furnishing Eastern Christianity with the necessary conceptual tools to express what it means to confess that the Spirit is God. So central to genuine worship and knowledge of God is the person and work of the Spirit that Basil declares: "In worship the Holy Spirit is inseparable from the Father and the Son. . . . For it is impossible to see the Image of the invisible God, except in the illumination of the Spirit, and it is impossible for him who fixes his eyes on the image to separate the light from the image."[3] Basil's work is in effect a perceptive and extended theological exposition of John 15:26.

2. Basil of Caesarea, *On the Holy Spirit*, trans. Stephen Hildebrand (New York: St. Vladimir's Press, 2011), 9.22.
3. Ibid., 26.64.

Pastoral Perspective

send the Advocate (the Paraklete) from God to help them. The Holy Spirit's function is to testify to the truth on Jesus' behalf. For Christians living in every age, the Holy Spirit functions as our divine guide. The Spirit confronts individuals and societies with the lordship of Christ, calling them to obedience to God's will.

Put more simply, the Holy Spirit keeps us on track so we can be true to God and to ourselves. The Spirit strengthens us in our faith, comforts us in times of affliction, and guides us as we seek to do God's will in our lives. God calls all of us into a relationship with the risen Christ, who then fills us with divine grace, forgiveness, and love. Our grateful response to these gifts motivates us to work for the fulfillment on earth of God's kingdom that Jesus inaugurated. We are called to work on behalf of peace, justice, and compassion for all.

Jesus called the disciples, just as he calls all of us, to testify on his behalf to the world. Because God loves variety, our individual calls will vary. It is the Holy Spirit who equips us for service in our world. The Spirit helps deepen our faith, strengthens our commitment to discipleship, and helps us discern our unique role in God's kingdom. In this text, Jesus reminds his disciples living in first-century Palestine that life will not be easy, but the Holy Spirit will give them all they need to stay faithful and bold.

The presence of the Holy Spirit in our lives can yield radical changes. A striking example of the power of the Spirit to transform lives can be seen in the story of Peter. Simon the fisherman was born in Bethsaida, a small fishing village on the Sea of Galilee. The first chapter of the Gospel of John records Jesus' call to Simon. Jesus must have seen very special qualities in that burly Galilean fisherman, for he said in 1:42 (my trans.), "So you are Simon the son of John? You shall be called *Cephas*" (Aramaic for "rock"). Peter began the long journey that slowly transformed him from a sometimes fearful man with a limited worldview into one of the boldest and best leaders the church has ever known.

At first, progress was slow. Peter, like the other disciples, questioned Jesus' ideas and actions. He avoided people whose nationality or religion was different from his own. At Caesarea Philippi, Peter knew the answer to Jesus' question about his identity, but then rebuked Jesus for saying that he would have to suffer many things (Mark 8:29–32). A suffering Messiah had no place in Peter's mind-set. He, like most other Jews of his day, expected a powerful and triumphant Messiah in the tradition of King David.

who "comes from the Father" (15:26), the *Paraklētos* bears witness to Jesus, who is "the way, and the truth, and the life" (14:6)—in other words, who is the revelation of God and of God's love in the world (1:14, 18; 3:16; 13:1). Moreover, it is through the indwelling of the Spirit that Jesus' followers can bear witness to this truth. They do so by proclaiming the gospel in word and deed, especially through their obedience to the commandment of love (13:34–35). The testimony of the disciples is therefore in continuity with what Jesus revealed in his life and ministry (which is the sense of the final clause in 15:27: "because you have been with me from the beginning").

The context of opposition and hostility hints at another connotation of bearing witness. This connotation is suggested by the NRSV's rendering of *Paraklētos* (literally, "one called to the side of") as "Advocate." The term presumes a forensic context, one the following verses (esp. 16:8–11) make explicit. Given the reference in 16:2 to opposition from synagogues, the Spirit as Advocate evokes the image of a legal defender. The Synoptic Gospels portray persecuted disciples' being given the Spirit's assistance in speaking at their trials (Mark 13:11; Matt. 19–20). Similarly, the Johannine Jesus here intimates that the Spirit as Advocate will empower disciples to bear witness in times of duress.

The next section is framed by Jesus' saying, "I have said these things to you . . ." (16:1, 4a). The phrase "these things" refers to what he has just said about the Advocate (15:26–27) and about the world's opposition and hatred (15:18–25). Jesus' purpose is then set forth at the end of 16:1: "to keep you from stumbling." The verb for "stumbling" is *skandalizō*, the same verb that appears in 6:61 (at the end of the "bread of life" discourse). A scandal is something that causes one to stumble and fall; more precisely for John, it is something that leads one to stop following Jesus (6:66). In his Farewell Discourse, the Johannine Jesus attempts to ward off such a disastrous decision, one made in the face of persecution.

What this persecution entails becomes clear in 16:2. First, Jesus declares, "They will put you out of the synagogues." This marks the third instance of *aposynagōgos* in John. In 9:22 and 12:42, the term—which refers to the expulsion of Jesus-believers from synagogues—appears in connection with the confession of him as the Messiah. Here is an example of how the Fourth Evangelist tells the story of Jesus from the vantage point of the Johannine community's traumatic experience of expulsion. Second, Jesus states that "those who kill you will think that

conventional worship combines references to God with nationalistic themes. A few decades ago, many Washington, D.C., churches combined the Doxology with a verse from the patriotic song "America," containing the words "Our fathers' God, to thee, author of liberty, to thee we sing; long may our land be bright with freedom's holy light; protect us by thy might, great God, our King."[1] Use of this kind of patriotic hymn may be appropriate in some worship contexts, but routine expression of unity of God and country, invoking as it does the power of God to defend one particular nation, hardly recognizes the love of God for the people of all nations. The glorification of liberty and freedom in that worship practice, without corresponding appreciation for justice and community, is hardly consistent with the deeper meaning of Christ.

One can similarly question the belting out of "God Bless America," although in the immediate aftermath of 9/11, its first verse was a suitable musical prayer: "God bless America, land that I love, stand beside her and guide her, through the night with the light from above."[2] Such love of country, combined with recognition of our need for divine guidance, does not seem inconsistent with the Holy Spirit. Still, that Spirit is much more, because God is so much more than any country—or any world, for that matter.

In this passage, Jesus is dependent upon the faithfulness of his followers. They who have been with him from the beginning know him and can represent him authentically. They have experienced his teaching and his love directly. They can testify on his behalf by the power of the Spirit.

Contemporary Christians, removed from the lifetime of Christ by two millennia, have not encountered him face to face. Still, we can pause over the fact that the chronological chain of witnesses has been unbroken from the beginning. Each of us has received the story, not only from written Scripture but from the testimony of the generation preceding our own, which in turn received it from its preceding generation, and so on back to the beginning—without a break.

This may understate the flaws along the way, not to mention the sin present in every generation, even within the church. Still, that thread of continuity is very important. It reminds all of us, in our own generation, that we are responsible for continuing the transmission. We are each links in a historical chain. It can

1. Samuel Francis Smith, "My Country, 'Tis of Thee" (1831).
2. Irving Berlin, "God Bless America" (1918).

John 15:26–16:4a

Theological Perspective

Having clarified the kind of relationship that our text indicates between the Son and the Spirit, we are still left wondering about the role that the Spirit plays among Christians facing persecution. This question is prompted by the connection Jesus draws between the *future indicative*: "When the *paraklētos* [translated variously as "helper," "advocate," or "mediator"] comes . . . he will testify" and the *imperative*: "you must testify also" (vv. 26–27). We should not miss the fact that in 16:1 Jesus explains why he has given us this teaching about the work and witness of the Spirit: "I have said these things to you to keep you from stumbling." Evidently, any hope we might have in resisting the temptation of apostasy (i.e., "stumbling") rests firmly upon the prior and constitutive work of the Spirit. The Spirit grants us not only saving knowledge of Christ but also life, holiness, and truth.

In the end, Jesus' teaching here makes one claim patently clear: in the face of inevitable persecution, followers of Jesus were called to bear public witness to the truth of Christ. Thus the crucial work of the Spirit here is the appointed means by which Jesus' disciples would be empowered to live faithful lives in the midst of persecution. In a world where our brothers and sisters in Christ continue to face persecution, imprisonment, and even death for their witness, John 15:26–16:4a represents a moving invitation to consider the profound depth of God's love and care for the vulnerable. Not only does this passage teach us about the fundamental symmetry between the identity of Son and the Spirit as God; it also leads us to place our confidence in the transformative power and presence of the Holy Spirit. The Spirit is the ground of hope in the midst of the most severe challenges to faith—so much so that only in the Spirit do we find the enduring source of life, strength, holiness, intellectual light, and empowerment for the work of heralding the glad tidings of the gospel.

MARK HUSBANDS

Pastoral Perspective

It was Peter who denied his Lord three times on the night of Jesus' arrest (18:15–27).

After Jesus' crucifixion and resurrection appearance to his disciples, who had returned to their original lives as fishermen, a powerful change took place in Peter. It was Peter who addressed thousands of Jewish pilgrims who had gathered in Jerusalem to observe Pentecost (Acts 2:14–36). It was Peter who healed a crippled beggar (Acts 3:1–10). Peter and John had such a profound impact on the people they encountered that both were dragged before the temple priests and council (Acts 4:1–12). The man who healed the sick, spoke with boldness, and refused to back down when confronted by the authorities was a far more mature and committed disciple than the one who denied his Lord three times. During the period of approximately fifteen years that is covered by the first twelve chapters of Acts, Peter was the dominant leader of the church. He spread the gospel in what is now Syria, Turkey, and Greece prior to his crucifixion in Rome.

With the help of the Holy Spirit, what happened to Peter can happen to us. Faith can transform our fears. Our self-protective stances can give way to openness, as we increasingly trust God's power. Selfishness can be replaced by love of others. God calls all of us to witness in our own way. Some are called to preach and teach, others to share their faith through music and the arts. Many help those struggling with questions of faith by sharing their personal experiences with the risen Christ. All are called to act lovingly, to pray faithfully, and to encourage others. Actions often speak louder than words. One of the most famous lines attributed to Francis of Assisi (1181–1226) is this: "Preach the gospel always. Use words if necessary." We proclaim Christ in the way we live our lives and the way we share, guided by the Holy Spirit, God's truth and love.

CATHY F. YOUNG

by doing so they are offering worship to God." He thereby raises the possibility that actual martyrdom is the witness some will bear on his behalf (recall the use of the verb *martyreō* in 15:26–27).

Indeed, it is no accident that the Johannine Jesus employs the notion of "hour" in 16:2 (as well as in 16:4a). The NRSV translates the Greek particle *hina* in 16:2 temporally—"the hour is coming *when*" (my emphasis). However, as Gail R. O'Day observes, *hina* usually indicates purpose, not time. Moreover, the formulation in 16:2 parallels what Jesus says about himself in 12:23: "The hour has come for [*hina*] the Son of Man to be glorified."[1] Jesus' "hour" refers to his being lifted up—that is, to his giving his life on the cross, as well as to his resurrection and exaltation. The use of "hour" in connection with the disciples in 16:2 points to their participation in the dynamics of the revelation of God's love (15:12–13).

A word of caution is in order. It is important to recall that John's Gospel was produced in the crucible of a heated intra-Jewish debate over the status of Jesus, an issue made explicit in 16:3. The sad history of violence between Christians and Jews, and of Christian anti-Semitism, should be warning enough about the dangers of polemical texts such as this one.

Finally, in 16:4a, Jesus repeats from 16:1: "I have said these things to you." Here he does so in conjunction with remembering. The point is that his followers' experience of suffering and opposition ought not to cause them to stumble and fall away from Jesus. He has already warned them about this. Jesus' words in 16:4a also circle back to 15:26–27, where he spoke of the Spirit. We have seen that one of the functions of the *Paraklētos* is to remind the Johannine community of all that Jesus has said and taught. The warning in 16:1–4a is an instance of such a reminder.

THOMAS D. STEGMAN, SJ

be said that the fate of the Christian church depends upon the faithful witness of each generation to the next. In saying that, we must not forget the presence of the Holy Spirit in inspiring and guiding us.

In this passage, as in the immediately preceding one, we are reminded that those who are faithful to Christ must expect opposition from those who "have not known the Father or me" (16:3). Even those who kill faithful Christians may think they are themselves the true worshipers of God, but because what they worship is less than the God we experience through Christ and the Holy Spirit, they are dreadfully misguided. Even short of violence, the act of excluding faithful Christians from places of worship ("they will put you out of the synagogues") is also a rejection of the God of love whose nature is revealed in Christ. In this passage, as elsewhere in John, there are evidences of serious conflict between early Christians and leaders of the Jewish community, in the context of internal Jewish rifts. Historically, such passages in John have given rise to anti-Semitism—ironic, because anti-Semitism itself is so alien to the divine spirit of love, and neglects the plain fact that Jesus and most of his earliest followers were Jews!

How are we to translate this passage into contemporary life? Partly, its words come as another reminder that we should not be surprised or discouraged when our witness for love in the world is opposed and when causes we believe in deeply are frustrated. We must be patient and take the long view. That may be part of the meaning of that last verse (16:4a): "I have said these things to you so that when their hour comes you may remember that I told you about them." Jesus had no illusions about the reality of opposition, nor should we. We may even be ostracized within the church!

There is so much religious fanaticism in the world today, present to some extent in most religions, and certainly present in Christianity. Fanatics always seem to be the most "religious" people around, yet their fanaticism gives rise to behavior and policies far removed from this "Spirit of truth who comes from the Father" (15:26). The true test remains whether our faith and witness are grounded in the love of God that we experience through Christ.

J. PHILIP WOGAMAN

1. Gail R. O'Day, "The Gospel of John: Introduction, Commentary, and Reflections," in *The New Interpreter's Bible*, ed. L. E. Keck et al. (Nashville: Abingdon Press, 1995), 9:765–66.

John 16:4b–15

^{4b}"I did not say these things to you from the beginning, because I was with you. ⁵But now I am going to him who sent me; yet none of you asks me, 'Where are you going?' ⁶But because I have said these things to you, sorrow has filled your hearts. ⁷Nevertheless I tell you the truth: it is to your advantage that I go away, for if I do not go away, the Advocate will not come to you; but if I go, I will send him to you. ⁸And when he comes, he will prove the world wrong about sin and righteousness and judgment: ⁹about sin, because they do not believe in me; ¹⁰about righteousness, because I am going to the Father and you will see me no longer; ¹¹about judgment, because the ruler of this world has been condemned.

¹²"I still have many things to say to you, but you cannot bear them now. ¹³When the Spirit of truth comes, he will guide you into all the truth; for he will not speak on his own, but will speak whatever he hears, and he will declare to you the things that are to come. ¹⁴He will glorify me, because he will take what is mine and declare it to you. ¹⁵All that the Father has is mine. For this reason I said that he will take what is mine and declare it to you."

Theological Perspective

Czeslaw Milosz's acutely perceptive "A Poem for the End of the Century" depicts a world "When everything was fine / and the notion of sin had vanished." Many of us inhabit such a world: where the story of Jesus' atoning death and sacrifice is "Totally enigmatic / Impossibly intricate." In such a context, the terms "sin" and "holiness" are so foreign that people are tempted, as Milosz writes, simply to "consume and rejoice / Without creeds and utopias."[1] In dramatic fashion, Milosz underscores the growing distance between the biblical narrative and the post-Christian West.

This loss of moral meaning noted by Milosz ought to lead Christians to wonder how indeed people may recover a true and abiding sense of the spiritual brokenness of our present moment. Perhaps on this score, things have never been easy—or at least, John's Gospel suggests as much. As we shall see, John 16:4b–15 leads us to place hope firmly in the presence and work of the Holy Spirit.

John 16:4b–15 is a crucial turning point in the biblical depiction of the mission of God. The key to interpretation lies in the discovery of an important

1. Czeslaw Milosz, "A Poem for the End of the Century," in *New and Collected Poems, 1931–2001* (New York: HarperCollins, 2003), 545–47.

Pastoral Perspective

It is devastating for Jesus' disciples to learn that their leader will soon leave them. Each one has left the only life he has known to follow Jesus. Without him, what will they do? Speaking to them, Jesus acknowledges that "sorrow has filled your hearts" (v. 6).

Anticipatory grief is a normal reaction to impending loss. It is devastating to learn that a loved one has a terminal illness. Anticipatory grief can also overwhelm us when we discover we need to move away from close family and friends with whom we have shared life for years. Any parent who has dreaded an empty nest deals with anticipatory grief as the youngest child prepares to leave home.

The disciples are too overcome to ask Jesus about any details. In verse 5 Jesus says, "But now I am going to him who sent me; yet none of you asks me, 'Where are you going?'" They are, however, beginning to understand that they are facing a drastically new landscape in their lives.

Therefore, Jesus comforts them by elaborating on the coming of the Holy Spirit (Advocate): "It is to your advantage that I go away, for if I do not go away, the Advocate will not come to you" (v. 7). These are Jesus' great words of hope for those gathered around him and for all who continue to worship him as Lord. The Holy Spirit has been with God's people since creation. The Spirit has been fully present in the

Exegetical Perspective

Beginning with 16:4b, Jesus' Farewell Discourse (14:1–16:33) revisits themes from its opening section (14:1–31): his return to the Father, the sorrow of the disciples, and the sending of the Advocate (*Paraklētos*). Jesus continues to speak uninterruptedly, as has been the case since 14:22. The present passage divides nicely into three parts of roughly equal length: (1) Jesus' departure and the gift of the *Paraklētos* (vv. 4b–7); (2) the *Paraklētos* vis-à-vis the "world" (vv. 8–11); and (3) the *Paraklētos* as the guide to all the truth (vv. 12–15).

The phrase "these things" in 16:4b refers to the hatred and persecution that Jesus' followers will inevitably encounter (15:18–16:4a). Jesus states that he did not discuss this topic "from the beginning"— that is, during his ministry—most likely because at that time he was the focus of opposition (e.g., 5:19–47; 8:13–59). The situation has changed "now" (v. 5), an allusion to the arrival of Jesus' "hour" (i.e., to his cross, resurrection, and ascension), when he will return to "him who sent me" (v. 5a). Before Jesus departs, he instructs his disciples about the suffering *they* will endure on his account. The end of 16:5 presents an interpretive challenge. There Jesus remarks that no one asks where he is going. Peter, however, had asked this very question in 13:36 (cf. 14:5). One solution is to read Jesus' observation of

Homiletical Perspective

Verse 13 is key to this passage: "When the Spirit of truth comes, he will guide you into all the truth." How are we to know the truth? Is it the same thing as fact? Most people in an average congregation will simply equate the two. Indeed, we should be suspicious of claims about truth that are directly opposed to observable evidence. Many centuries ago, most people thought of the earth as flat, but that is directly contrary to the clear evidence that the world is round. Similarly, five hundred years ago the Copernican revolution in astronomy was roundly condemned by both Protestant and Roman Catholic leaders as being inconsistent with the biblical view that the earth is the center of the universe. In our own time polls demonstrate that millions of Christians reject well-established theories of evolution. Such views, so directly contrary to scientific evidence, cannot be considered truth.

Still, truth is not the same thing as fact. A reporter covering a story can present facts accurately but do so in such a way that misleads readers. A televised event can convey a mistaken impression just because of a reporter's decision about what to show. The camera does not lie, but much depends on where the camera is pointed. On November 15, 1969, five hundred thousand citizens, mostly young people, gathered on Washington's Mall in a demonstration protesting U.S.

John 16:4b–15

narrative seam marking the transition from a predominantly christocentric view of God's work to one in which the Son and the Spirit have distinct (yet mutually affirming) roles to play in the ongoing life and witness of the people of God. Given that Jesus' imminent departure would appear to constitute a deep loss of authority, comfort, and guidance for the disciples, readers are led to ask how they would remain on course in the midst of the devastating news of Jesus' departure. How would they remain faithful when all of the opposition that had hitherto been directed toward Jesus would now turn toward them? Nevertheless, Jesus insists that it is to their advantage that he leave.

Far from abandoning them, leaving them to traverse the journey of faith alone, Jesus promises the mission and guidance of the Spirit. This is, in effect, a declaration that their sacrifice and obedience will be vindicated, that, in spite of appearances, the way of righteousness will be known. In the midst of their sorrow, the disciples learn that "when he [the Spirit] comes, he will prove the world wrong about sin and righteousness and judgment" (v. 8). In short, the Spirit will reveal the divine victory over sin and evil as he carries out the rule of Christ. Indeed, the Spirit glorifies the Son by taking what is his and making it known among his disciples.

John underscores the fact that God takes seriously human rebellion and unrighteousness: the Spirit will call to account all who in unbelief carry out acts of injustice and evil (unrighteousness). The significance of this is far-reaching indeed! Not only will the dispossessed have an ally in Jesus, but this ally is God. For this reason, Jesus insists that it is to their advantage that he return to the Father, for the Spirit's reproof of sin and judgment is crucial to Christ's proclamation of "deliverance to the captives." In short, the Spirit comes to judge, convict, reprove, and correct an unbelieving world by exposing the deep-seated causes of human pain, suffering, and death.

While the coming of the Spirit is a sign of decisive judgment upon the ongoing rebellion and human forgetting of God, it also constitutes the appointed means by which the disciples will be protected from the evil one and be sanctified "in the truth" (cf. 17:15–19).

As Milosz intimates, Jesus' disciples are not the only ones to face the enfeebling disaffection of being aliens in a strange land, silently bearing the weight of the radical discontinuity between the holiness of God and the false autonomy of creaturely rebellion. Now, as then, yearning for God's name to be truly

conception, birth, and life of Jesus. Jesus promises that after his death, God will send the Holy Spirit to dwell within and among all of his followers.

The role of the Holy Spirit in our lives cannot be overestimated. It is by the power of the Spirit that Jesus' followers learn that they are not abandoned, but sent to bear witness to the love of God. The depth of God's love is demonstrated most powerfully through Jesus' death on the cross. In that ultimate act of sacrifice, Jesus' crucifixion overcomes sin and death. People are freed to focus on love and grace rather than fear and guilt. Without the Spirit's help in sharing that good news, Christianity would have been extinguished centuries ago. Once they are empowered by the Spirit, a tiny band of followers of Jesus of Nazareth begins the movement that grows into a world religion that continues to take the gospel to the ends of the earth. We are called as powerfully as are the disciples to witness to God's love and Jesus' victory over sin and death.

The Greek word *paraklētos,* translated "Advocate," literally means "one called alongside." It carries with it a legal connotation, as in one called alongside as an attorney. In this passage, John is saying that in the eyes of the world Jesus will be judged, convicted, and killed. The Holy Spirit, however, will reverse the sentence. "When he comes, he will prove the world wrong about sin and righteousness and judgment" (v. 8).

In the verses that follow, Jesus refers to sin not in its moral context, but in terms of one's choice to accept him as Lord or turn away. He talks about righteousness in terms of his return to God. Righteousness refers to the fact that Jesus is about to finish all God sent him to do on earth. Judgment is directed toward the "ruler of this world" (v. 11), the powers of evil that Satan represents. The exaltation of Jesus will destroy Satan's grip on the world.

Jesus concludes with the promise that the Spirit of truth (the Paraclete) "will guide you into all the truth" (v. 13). That statement must be understood within its context. The Spirit reveals the lordship of Jesus Christ to the world, then and now. We claim that universal truth. The Spirit gives us new insights into past events and revelation, but God's truth is not something we can manipulate. God is both transcendent and immanent. God dwells within and among us through the Holy Spirit, but God is at the same time wholly other. We humans cannot grasp the mind of God.

Therefore, each of us as a committed Christian has some of God's truth, but none of us has all of it. God's truth as revealed through Jesus Christ and the

the disciples' silence as portending what follows in 16:6, where he notes that, with the news of his pending departure, sorrow has filled their hearts. Their silence results from the depth of their sadness.

Jesus then reassures and encourages the disciples in 16:7. It is to their advantage that he "go away," because he will then send them the Advocate. This is the fourth time (here, running through 16:15) in the Farewell Discourse that Jesus announces the gift of the *Paraklētos* (14:16–17; 14:26; 15:26–27). John carefully links the bestowal of the Spirit with the glorification of Jesus, which is to say that the *Paraklētos* is sent only after the completion of Jesus' "hour" (7:39; 20:17). According to the Fourth Evangelist, the *Paraklētos* takes the place of the glorified Jesus in being present to (because it is within) his followers.

The Johannine Jesus goes on to explain in 16:8–11 what the Spirit will do with respect to the "world" (*kosmos*). Whereas in 15:26–27 the *Paraklētos* acted as Advocate (the NRSV's consistent translation of the term) or defense attorney for Jesus' followers, now he takes on the role of prosecutor who "will prove the world wrong" (v. 8). The verb *elenchō* is best rendered "expose to light." Just as the coming of Jesus brought light into the world (1:9; 3:19–21), so now the *Paraklētos* will reveal the truth and bring to light all things. In doing so, the *Paraklētos* will show how the *kosmos* is wrong about "sin and righteousness and judgment."

First, the *Paraklētos* proves the world wrong in its failure to believe in Jesus (v. 9). Here we encounter the Johannine understanding of "sin" (*hamartia*) as the refusal to believe God's revelation through Jesus: "the light has come into the world, and people loved darkness rather than light" (3:19; cf. 12:37). The present tense verb ("do not believe") indicates that the issue now is the ongoing rejection of Jesus' revelation of God's love.

Second, the *kosmos* is shown to be wrong concerning "righteousness" (v. 10). The term *dikaiosynē*, so prominent in Paul's writings, appears only here in the Fourth Gospel. The key to interpreting John's meaning is Jesus' explanation: "because I am going to the Father." The one condemned as a blasphemer (5:18; 10:33, 36) God has vindicated as being truly righteous, by raising him from the dead and exalting him. God's glorification of Jesus is, in effect, the seal of approval of the latter's revelation of divine love.

Third, it follows that the *kosmos* is also wrong about "judgment" (v. 11). Jesus' victory over death is the definitive defeat of "the ruler of this world" (see 12:31; 14:30), that is, Satan, who is now "condemned"

Vietnam war policies. In the course of the demonstration, a small group of radicals called the Weathermen shouted anti-American slogans, confirming a popular stereotype that demonstrators were disloyal. Evening news, and the Nixon administration, focused on the hundred or so radicals, while largely ignoring the peaceful hundreds of thousands of others, many of whom carried small American flags. Was the media coverage factual? Yes, of course, but it conveyed an untruth to viewers.

Even well-established scientific theories such as the theory of evolution do not do justice to the deeper truth. For truth, ultimately, is more than the sum of observable fact. What is ultimately at the center of all reality?

John 16:13 makes a bold assertion: the "Spirit of truth" will guide us "into all the truth." The deepest truths are made evident through the Spirit. According to John, that Spirit comes from Christ. That is to say, Christ best discloses for us the deepest truths about God. Through Christ, we grasp the heart of the matter: the grace of God is the deepest truth. When we are, through Christ, open to that grace, we can experience in our own lives the power of the Spirit. That helps us to see the meaning of our lives and of the factual world into which we are born.

Reflection on this passage from John provides a good opportunity to remember that this Gospel itself illustrates the distinction between fact and truth. Most New Testament scholars have long concluded that the Fourth Gospel was not written by the disciple John and that much of its portrait of Jesus, including Jesus' long Farewell Discourse, cannot be taken as the literal words of the historical Jesus. Does that mean they are untrue?

John is best understood as a theological interpretation of the meaning of Christ; it was probably written toward the end of the first century CE, decades after the actual disciples were gone. It makes use of commonly accepted and transmitted stories about Jesus, but it goes further in exploring their meaning. Its truthfulness thus depends not upon literal fact but upon its coherence as a statement of Christian faith. In that respect, John must be respected not simply as adequate but as profound.

Other features of this passage provide fruitful entry points for a preacher. For example, verse 11 presents a contrast between the Holy Spirit and the "ruler of this world." We may be impressed by the power of those who control events in this world, but the reality of God transcends earthly power—and those who exercise it are accountable to God.

Theological Perspective

hallowed demands the comforting presence and truth of the Holy Spirit.

Like his early disciples, we would do well to remember Jesus' identification of the Spirit as the "Spirit of truth." Who among us at crucial stages of life's journey has *not* needed such a guide? Who among us, in the face of conflict, misunderstanding, false accusations, or covetous rumor-mongering, has not found ourselves yearning for vindication, crying "How long, O Lord?" Knowing in advance that his disciples would face opposition, hatred, and persecution, Jesus promises that the life-giving Spirit will come and "guide you into all the truth; for he will not speak on his own, but will . . . take what is mine and declare it to you" (vv. 13–14).

The theology of Basil the Great helps considerably to illustrate the central importance of this life-giving work of the Spirit:

> All that live virtuously desire him, as they are watered by his inspiration and assisted toward their proper and natural end. He perfects others, but himself lacks nothing. He lives, but not because he has been restored to life; rather, he is the source of life. He does not grow in strength gradually, but is complete all at once. He is established in himself and present everywhere. He is the source of holiness, an intellectual light for every rational power's discovery of truth, supplying clarity, so to say, through himself.[2]

Who could miss the striking contrast between Basil's compelling witness to the beauty, truth, and light of the Spirit and the tragic violence of crucifixion, or, for that matter, the radical forgetting of God and persecution of Christians in our own day? When "the notion of sin has vanished" such that "No power can abolish / The cause and the effect," we would do well more earnestly to pray, "Come, Holy Spirit!" For in this prayer lies the transformative power and conviction of the life-giving Spirit of truth. As Basil writes, echoing the witness of John, "He is the source of holiness, an intellectual light for every rational power's discovery of truth." Rather than falling victim to sorrow, may we who "have the first fruits of the Spirit" (Rom. 8:23) take comfort in the promise and work of the Spirit.

MARK HUSBANDS

Pastoral Perspective

Holy Spirit must be treated with respect and humility. Faithful Christians have differences of opinion. Those differences, as old as Scripture itself, must be handled with thoughtfulness and civility. In our country, faithful Christians have been on both sides of the issues of slavery and full rights for women. Currently, people of sound faith differ on the issues of homosexuality, climate change, and abortion. In each case, individuals have partial truth. Ultimately, we believe God's truth will be revealed through the Spirit, but it usually takes some time for that revelation to become widely understood.

There is another important role for the "one called alongside." The Holy Spirit as Comforter comes alongside all who suffer, face crises, experience persecution or discrimination, or are lonely and need comfort. The Spirit brings God's consolation to those in need, strength to the weary, and hope to those overcome with discouragement. The Holy Spirit also uses us, Christ's hands and feet in the world, to reach out to those who are suffering. When someone repeatedly comes to mind or we feel a deep urge to take a stand, the Holy Spirit is nudging us to act.

God's great gift to us did not end with Christ's death and resurrection. The Spirit continues to guide and embolden Christians in every place and time to live out their faith as followers of the Lord. Instead of striving to reach the illusion of perfection, we can live as grace-filled disciples who have already been saved. In grateful response for what God has already done for each of us, we can stretch out our arms to others as Jesus stretched his to invite all to believe in him.

CATHY F. YOUNG

---

2. Basil of Caesarea, *On the Holy Spirit,* trans. Stephen Hildebrand (Crestwood, NY: St. Vladimir's Seminary Press, 2011), 9.22.

(the perfect tense verb indicates a past action with ongoing effects). Notice it is "the ruler of this world" who stands condemned—not the *kosmos* itself. Indeed, as D. Moody Smith aptly points outs, "the world is not simply condemned to hopelessness and destruction, for God did not send the Son to condemn the world, but finally to save it. . . . the Spirit-inspired proclamation of Jesus condemns not the world, but the world's condemnation of Jesus. It is still a sign of hope to the world."[1]

Jesus' words in 16:12—"I still have many things to say to you, but you cannot bear them now"—are transitional, as he prepares a final instruction for the disciples about how the Spirit will assist them. In 16:13 he teaches that the *Paraklētos*, once more named "the Spirit of truth" (14:17; 15:26), "will guide" them "into all truth." The verb rendered "guide" is *hodēgeō*, which literally means "lead on the way." The reference to "truth" and the allusion to "way" recall 14:6, where Jesus presents himself as "the way, and the truth." The Johannine Jesus thus intimates that the Spirit will remind and illumine the disciples about what he did and taught during his earthly ministry (14:26; cf. 2:19–22). Moreover, *hodēgeō* connotes that the Spirit will empower Jesus' followers to conform their lives more and more to what Jesus taught.

The final clause in 16:13—"he [i.e., the Spirit] will declare to you the things that are to come"—has been the source of debate. While some commentators contend that the Johannine Jesus refers here to new revelation in the life of the church, John's meaning is that the Spirit will shed light on and unfold the implications of what Jesus taught—including through the events of the "hour"—in new and changing circumstances. Jesus is the definitive revelation of God (1:18). Like Jesus (7:16; 12:49–50), the *Paraklētos* declares only what he has heard (v. 13). Jesus' promise that the Spirit "will take what is mine and declare it to you" (v. 14, repeated in v. 15) assures the reliable continuation of the revelation of God's love through the generations.

THOMAS D. STEGMAN, SJ

A preacher may also usefully focus on the comments concerning sin. When the Advocate (Holy Spirit) comes, "he will prove the world wrong about sin" (v. 8), because its conceptions of sin are not framed in the light of Christ. This provides an important corrective to much conventional wisdom about sin, even within the church. Too often we portray sin as particular acts or the violation of particular rules. Important as rules and principles are, they do not convey the deeper reality. Sin is everything that stands between us and God, whose nature is best disclosed to us through Christ.

Consider: the grace of God is given to us despite our unworthiness. We can count on that love. There are actions and attitudes (and social institutions and policies), though, that make it more difficult for us to see and receive that grace. It is not that God is rewarding us for good behavior; it is that bad behavior prevents us from receiving the gift of God freely given. So when this or that is labeled sin, the key question is whether it does, in fact, stand as a barrier to God. On the other hand, things that facilitate receiving God's grace are to be applauded.

Here we confront the reality of how the institutional systems by which life is governed either support or hinder God's work in the world. The early-twentieth-century theologian Walter Rauschenbusch put it this way in his book *Christianizing the Social Order*: we may know an unchristian social order by whether it makes good people do bad things and a Christian social order by whether it makes bad people do good things.[1] That way of putting it is admittedly overly simple; nevertheless, it is a reminder that we can be led by social arrangements to be more open to the love of God or to be more closed.

Ultimately, all of this hinges upon how we understand this Christ whom John portrays. If Christ is God's love for us and for all people, then we can be led by the Advocate, the Holy Spirit, in a way that draws us home.

J. PHILIP WOGAMAN

---

1. D. Moody Smith, *John* (Nashville: Abingdon Press, 1999), 296.

1. Walter Rauschenbusch, *Christianizing the Social Order* (New York: Macmillan, 1923), 125–27, 156–65.

John 16:16–24

¹⁶"A little while, and you will no longer see me, and again a little while, and you will see me." ¹⁷Then some of his disciples said to one another, "What does he mean by saying to us, 'A little while, and you will no longer see me, and again a little while, and you will see me'; and 'Because I am going to the Father'?" ¹⁸They said, "What does he mean by this 'a little while'? We do not know what he is talking about." ¹⁹Jesus knew that they wanted to ask him, so he said to them, "Are you discussing among yourselves what I meant when I said, 'A little while, and you will no longer see me, and again a little while, and you will see me'? ²⁰Very truly, I tell you, you will weep and mourn, but the world will rejoice; you will have pain, but your pain will turn into joy. ²¹When a woman is in labor, she has pain, because her hour has come. But when her child is born, she no longer remembers the anguish because of the joy of having brought a human being into the world. ²²So you have pain now; but I will see you again, and your hearts will rejoice, and no one will take your joy from you. ²³On that day you will ask nothing of me. Very truly, I tell you, if you ask anything of the Father in my name, he will give it to you. ²⁴Until now you have not asked for anything in my name. Ask and you will receive, so that your joy may be complete."

Theological Perspective

At the end of his Farewell Discourse in John 13–16, Jesus uses vivid imagery to lift up contrasts between preresurrection and postresurrection life, between measured time and eternity, between the disciples' sorrow in the face of the world's rejoicing, and between knowledge about God acquired through the senses and direct experience of God in Jesus Christ. Jesus speaks pastorally to prepare the disciples to face coming events. He reminds them that humanity's visual and perceptual limitations often lead to false conclusions.

Two groups will witness the same event, Jesus' death on the cross: one group will see only tragedy, while the other group will see triumph. In seeing this way, both groups will let themselves be deceived by shortsightedness. What the former group perceives as loss of their beloved hero is instead verification of his heroism. The latter group believes they are watching their own victory, when in fact they expose their blindness to fulfillment of prophecy that is happening in plain sight.

Jesus' pastoral care of his disciples is simultaneously a theological interpretation of the import of his death, framed by the phrase "a little while." The phrase occurs three times in two contexts regarding Jesus' passion and worldly suffering, both of which will last for "a little while." After a short interval of

Pastoral Perspective

Khalil Gibran, the Lebanese poet, philosopher, and author of *The Prophet*, describes joy and sorrow:

> Some of you say, "Joy is greater than sorrow," and
> others say, "Nay, sorrow is the greater."
> But I say unto you, they are inseparable.
> Together they come, and when one sits alone with
> you at your board, remember that the other is
> asleep upon your bed.[1]

Joy and sorrow mingle in the room together. It is difficult to feel joy and sorrow at the same instant, yet they constantly merge. It seems that human life is suspended between these two poles, hanging like scales between sorrow and joy. Have you felt the sorrow of tragedy amid the joy of celebration? Have you ever felt joy in the midst of tragedy? It seems we are constantly balancing these two states of being.

In tragedy there are moments of great sorrow—finding out a loved one was present at the scene of an accident, injured, or maybe even killed; realizing that life (our lives) will no longer be the same; grieving the past and the way things once were. Tragedy can cause sorrow.

In tragedy there may also be moments of great joy—finding out a loved one was there at the scene

---

1. Khalil Gibran, *The Prophet* (orig. 1923; New York: Knopf, 2004), 30.

Exegetical Perspective

The literary context of this passage places the reader right in the middle of a conversation between Jesus and his disciples sitting around the table at the Last Supper. On this final night together, after washing their feet and dismissing Judas to betray him, Jesus has one last conversation with his disciples. Conversation, of course, might not be the best description, because Jesus has actually been talking, uninterrupted, for nearly three chapters now—but, honestly, who wants to interrupt Jesus?

A Little While. Foreshadowing his approaching death, Jesus tells his friends, "A little while, and you will no longer see me, and again a little while, and you will see me" (v. 16). The phrase "a little while" is clearly important to the author of the Gospel, as it is repeated seven times in the brief span of four verses. The Greek word *mikron* does carry the simple meaning of a short measure of time; however, like the English word "little," *mikron* can also imply that something is insignificant or unimportant. In an effort to plant a seed of hope before all that is about to transpire, might Jesus be telling his disciples that his approaching time away from them (three days in the tomb) pales in comparison to what is to follow (his resurrection)?

Jesus' discussion of this "little while" also had significant implications for the immediate audience

Homiletical Perspective

In just a few paragraphs, this text grapples with three major themes of Christian discipleship: fear, transformation, and joy. Drawing on the image of new birth, Jesus compares what lies ahead for the disciples to the experience of a woman going through labor.

Fear. For most women, the transition phase of labor is the most difficult part of the birth experience. Contractions grow longer, and the intervals between them grow shorter. The physical and emotional signs of labor grow more intense. A surge of adrenaline results in the desire to flee, fear sets in, and exhaustion peaks as the laboring mother has little opportunity to rest between contractions.

The transition phase of labor is often playfully depicted on television programs, when a laboring woman grabs her spouse and shouts some choice words, though the physical signs accompanying this phase are too graphic for the average show. Transition is the moment in the hospital room when the laboring woman threatens to leave and go home. Despite the parenting manuals, the prenatal classes, and the so-called birth plan, in a relatively short period of time the transition phase pushes the mother to her limits.

The events surrounding Jesus' death will push the disciples to their limits. Jesus will be ripped away

John 16:16–24   **201**

John 16:16–24

sorrow, the disciples will enjoy unprecedented, endless joy. Their lack of understanding will end in "a little while"; then they will no longer need Jesus to enlighten them but will enjoy a direct understanding of God that will last forever. Resurrection is the promise of the end to physical suffering as well as the end to human confusion about the apparent triumph of evil in a God-forsaken world.

In earlier verses, Jesus comforts the disciples by stating that after his departure, the Holy Spirit will continue to guide them. In this passage, Jesus expands that pastoral, pneumatological encouragement into a Trinitarian, soteriological understanding of how his temporal relationship with the disciples will, in a little while, become an everlasting relationship with the triune God. Jesus, now physically present, is soon to absent himself, but through the power of the Holy Spirit and the miracle of the resurrection, he will return to them in a Trinitarian presence of profound and enduring comfort. As he explains in verse 23, they will no longer speak in his name to the Creator, but will encounter their Creator directly.[1]

While providing the disciples with gentle words of hope to sustain them in future difficulties, Jesus invokes simple turns of phrase to signal the powerful change that is coming with and through their future suffering. In the three repetitions of Jesus' prediction of his absence, there is a distinct contrast between conditions of "not seeing" and "seeing." When Jesus says, "You will no longer see me" (v. 16), the Gospel author uses the verb *theōreō* to mean that the disciples will no longer be merely spectators of Jesus' human life. His earthly life, which lasted only a little while, will come to an end. Painful though that end will be, Jesus will soon be seen again (*opsesthe*, "you will see," v. 17). At that time Jesus will be visible not via the disciples' limited visual acuity, but through the resurrection and its fulfillment of the divine-human encounter.

Three repetitions of the contrasting phrases—about the disciples' not seeing Jesus for a short while and then Jesus' being visible for eternity—also indicate the coming perfection of the disciples' ability to see Jesus fully, much like Paul's contrasting of seeing through a glass dimly and seeing face to face (1 Cor. 13:12). By telling the disciples that God will make Jesus visible again to them in a short while, Jesus is explaining how his coming death and resurrection

unharmed, spared injury, and still alive; realizing that life will change, grow, and heal from the tragedy; giving thanks that life can be lived in the future.

Within tragedy there can be both sorrow and joy.

In celebration there are moments of great joy. My team has finally won. There was success in passing the test, in making it another year, in surrounding ourselves with people who care. I can be thankful for the wonderful things in my life.

In celebration there may also be moments of great sorrow. When my team wins, the other team loses. As I celebrate the wonderful things in my life, it may mean that others do not have those wonderful things (such as access to food, clothing, and housing). As I celebrate, it may be at the expense of those who mourn.

Within celebration there can be both joy and sorrow.

Perhaps this is what Jesus explains to his disciples in John 16:16–24. The disciples speak and express their bewilderment about what Jesus has just said in the preceding verses. They have been listening for quite a time and are now confused, asking, "What does he mean by saying to us, 'A little while, and you will no longer see me, and again a little while, and you will see me'; and 'Because I am going to the Father'?" (v. 17). Jesus anticipates the confusion and answers the disciples, not with a description of the time line and what "a little while" signifies, or with answers about the mystery of his departure and return, but with an exposition on what they may experience during this process. Jesus anticipates the effect his absence and subsequent presence will have on his followers. Jesus talks directly to them about their lament, mourning, and pain.

The pain that Jesus describes is akin to the intense pain of childbirth. The Greek term used here is *lypē* (v. 21), a word that signifies a physical or emotional pain, grief, sorrow, or distress.[2] Jesus attests that the disciples feel sorrow. The grief of the disciples is a present reality as they struggle with what Jesus has revealed to them about his leaving and his return. Jesus does not tell them to snap out of it, ignore the pain, or pretend their grief does not exist. Jesus says to them plainly, "You have grief [NRSV "pain"] now" (v. 22).

We must attend to our own grief and our own sorrow. In a world that produces countless stories of loss and anguish, it is easy to become overwhelmed

---

1. John Dominic Crossan, "Aphorism in Discourse and Narrative," *Semeia* 43 (1988): 132–33.

2. Richard Whitaker and John Kohlenberger, *The Analytical Concordance to the NRSV* (Grand Rapids: Eerdmans, 2000), 756.

of John's Gospel, living in the time after Jesus' ascension ("you will no longer see me") and still awaiting his promised return ("you will see me"). The author of the Gospel may be seeking to reassure those in his community who are confused by the delay in Jesus' return (Parousia) by describing this in-between time as *mikron*, that is, of lesser importance, compared with what is promised to follow. The author's framing of the in-between time as a "little while" or a "little thing" carries eschatological nuances worth exploring with present audiences as well.

Pain and Promises. Whatever Jesus' intent may be in discussing this "little while," the disciples are completely confused by his words. When he pauses to take a breath, the disciples finally get a word in, and it is one of the most honest expressions of truth that we hear out of their mouths. They say, "We do not know what he is talking about" (v. 18b). Within the narrative world of John's Gospel, the disciples have every reason to be confused at this point. How could they imagine beforehand the anguish of seeing their Master and friend put to such a cruel death? How could their minds ever conceive that such a horrible death on that Friday would be only the beginning to the weekend that would forever change the cosmos? Of course they did not know what he was talking about. How could they?

Jesus anticipates their confusion and gives them a bit more of an explanation, including a parable-like metaphor of labor and delivery that, in its own way, seeks to frame present suffering as less significant than the promise of future joy. To the disciples' questions, Jesus responds not with answers but with promises: "You will have pain, but your pain will turn into joy" (v. 20b). He does not say, "Your pain will be forgotten," or "Your pain will disappear." Rather, it will turn (*genēsetai*) into joy. The good news of Easter does not erase the suffering of the cross, but it does transform it, as it transforms all of creation. The resurrected Jesus still bears the scars on his hands and his side. Pain is a reality, but pain will be turned into joy.

Jesus continues to promise, "You have pain now; but I will see you again, and your hearts will rejoice, and no one will take your joy from you" (v. 22). It is not just the case that after Jesus is raised, the disciples will see him again, but also that *he* will see *them*.[1] He will see us. He will see us as we are

from them. They will question everything they have been doing since they answered his call. The disciples will witness just where following Jesus leads: to a cross. They will not know what to do with themselves during these life-altering events. They will find themselves unprepared, caught up short, their allegiances called into question.

The disciples are about to endure labor pains— short, swift, sudden pains. Jesus will leave them, and this causes them to butt up against their own limitations. Unable to see exactly what lies ahead, they become fearful. Anxiety and uncertainty set in, not unlike waiting for a child, especially in the ancient world, when infant and maternal mortality rates were significantly higher than in the United States today.

The preacher might play off the themes of fear and uncertainty that we face as followers of Jesus, both as individuals and as the community of faith. Where are the places where we come up against our own limitations? In what ways do we feel unprepared for the difficult things Jesus asks us to do? What aspects of following Jesus make us want to turn around and go home? What are the moments in which we are guilty of saying to one another, "We do not know what he is talking about," when it comes to Jesus' instruction, and we instead allow our confusion or ignorance to stand in the way of the difficult work of discernment and action?

Transformation. The trials that the disciples are about to endure will bring about transformation. Here the birth metaphor is also helpful. Childbirth involves terrible pain, seizing of muscles, fear; yet most mothers look forward to giving birth (and not just because they are anxious for pregnancy to be over). A mother already loves the child that she is bringing into the world; she has been looking forward to it for a long time, shaping her own life to welcome a new life. Even though the ordeal of labor will exhaust her, and in some cases even damage her body, when that baby is placed in her arms, she weeps tears of joy and wonder.

So too, prior to Jesus' death and resurrection, the disciples have already glimpsed something of what God is doing in him. They have been following him, witnessing signs and wonders, listening to his voice. Like expectant parents, they have not fully grasped the new birth that Jesus promises, but they have an inkling. We see this in verse 30, when they say, "We believe that you came from God."

Jesus promises the disciples that the pain that they are about to endure will result in something

1. Frederick Dale Bruner, *The Gospel of John: A Commentary* (Grand Rapids: Eerdmans, 2012), 947.

John 16:16–24

Theological Perspective

is the way that God will be fully revealed to them—through God's power, not their own.

When in verse 16 Jesus first tells them they will not see him, the disciples do not understand. In their confusion they repeat it to one another, trying to discern his meaning through their own powers of deduction. In verse 19, Jesus recognizes their desire for better understanding. He reassures them that true understanding is coming not through their own efforts but through God's making Godself known in the cross. His response is similar to those guarding the tomb at the resurrection, who ask the women disciples why they seek to solve the mystery by looking for an answer among themselves, in the limitations of human wisdom, rather than looking to God, the source of life, who in a little while will make all things clear (Luke 24:5).

Jesus then turns from discussing matters of the mind to the deeper cares of the heart. In a short while, indeed, the disciples' intellectual queries will be satisfied. More importantly, though, in an equally short while, their pain and sorrow will be ended and their heavenly Parent will bless them with a complete and everlasting joy. To illustrate that this promise is an existential reality, Jesus uses the parable about a woman's giving birth. Giving birth appears throughout the Bible as a symbol of the end of times, for example, in Isaiah 13:8, Micah 4:10, and Romans 8:22, where creation groans in waiting for the coming of new life. Jesus lifts up the pain and joy of childbirth as a sign of God's involvement in bringing new life into the world, compared to the superficial rejoicing that the world does as it causes Jesus and his disciples to suffer.

Like the experience of a pregnant woman, the suffering the disciples must undergo due to Jesus' perceived annihilation is not devoid of meaning but is the space and time needed for Jesus' rebirth and transformation from human to Trinitarian presence.[2] The temporal, self-congratulatory ascendancy of evil will be over in a little while, but sorrow's transformation to joy in the resurrection will last forever.

REBECCA BLAIR YOUNG

Pastoral Perspective

and saddened by the daily news. There are people starving for nourishment around the globe; there are societies begging for reconciliation and peace; there are children in our own neighborhoods who struggle to receive attention, love, and care. Perhaps we need to sit with grief for a while, a grief that belongs to us because it affects us directly or indirectly. Perhaps this is the only way we can expect to find healing.

In the metaphor that Jesus uses to describe this transformation from sorrow to joy, he explains that a woman in labor experiences pain. However, "when her child is born, she no longer remembers the anguish because of the joy" (v. 21). Jesus does not say that her pain was not real. Jesus asserts that she does not remember it because of the joy that comes afterward. Joy and sorrow mingle in the room together, but the joy will be final. In this way, the wisdom of Jesus differs from the wisdom of Khalil Gibran, who implies that not only are sorrow and joy "inseparable"; they are equally ultimate.

Jesus gives his disciples comfort by reminding them of their joy and promising them that they will rejoice. Jesus initiates their joy at his reappearance: "I will see you again, and your hearts will rejoice" (v. 22). When we make room for sorrow, we make room for joy. When we make room for Good Friday, we are making room for Easter. When we can rejoice, like the woman in childbirth, the pain and grief are not erased, but we do not remember them in the same way anymore.

Every sorrow in our lives helps illuminate something: a new journey, a different way to make meaning, an interesting sense of joy. This is not to say that we need to create hardship or wallow in our sorrow in order to experience joy. We need not dwell on grief until it makes us depressed, angry, and immobilized people. However, we do need to acknowledge it. We need to look for moments of hopeful elation while acknowledging the pain. We strive for joy while remembering our sorrow. We allow God's grace to remind us that, both in our joy and in our sorrow, God is with us.

S. VANCE GOODMAN

2. Anne Etienne, "Birth," *The Ecumenical Review* 34 (1982): 228–37.

truly meant to be seen, and no one will take this joy from us.

In My Name. Jesus follows this promise of future joy with a call for his disciples to do more than passive waiting during the "little while." He calls them to active hoping. He shares the promise of eventual unending joy and then charges them to be about the work of prayer. "Ask," he says, "and you will receive" (v. 24), so long as the asking is done "in my name" (vv. 23, 24, 26). This brief phrase, "in my name" (*en tō onomati mou*), which has been adopted as a liturgical pattern in the church throughout the centuries, has caused a good deal of confusion on the part of Christians whose prayers spoken "in the name of Jesus" do not seem to be answered. Is "the name of Jesus" a magical phrase that gives our prayers more weight? If so, why does this incantation so often seem not to work?

When the phrase is considered within the literary context of all that precedes it in this passage, a more nuanced meaning may emerge. Jesus' ministry is one that is soon to be characterized by intense suffering and death, which he foreshadows in his "little while" references. Allusion to his death is immediately followed by telling his disciples that they too will endure suffering and persecution on his account. Thus, given the larger context of this passage, the reference to petitioning "in my name" cannot be separated from participation in Jesus' suffering, life-giving pattern of ministry.

New Testament scholar Dale Bruner suggests that one could translate "in my name" as "in my mission."[2] Consider how differently that might sound: "I tell you, if you ask anything of the Father *in my mission*, he will give it to you. . . . Ask and you will receive" (vv. 23b, 24b). Instead of a formulaic ending to prayers, the phrase might become a means of directing our minds, our hearts, and our lives to the pattern of Jesus' own ministry, "so that your joy may be complete" (v. 24).

BUZ WILCOXON

joyful, fruitful, and enduring. The pain and persecution that the Johannine community is about to experience will be redeemed by what God is doing in Jesus, and in the relationship that Jesus' followers share, not only with him but also with the God who sent him.

The preacher might explore how we as followers of Jesus are involved in a transition moment, a moment of decision that results in transformation. In the life of faith, we will all experience moments where our faith is tested. Many among us have stories to share about how this testing led to personal or community transformation, a renewal of relationship with God and one another.

Joy. This is the term Jesus uses to describe the outcome of the events that are about to take place: not just fleeting happiness, but complete joy. As labor brings a mother to her physical and emotional limits, but results in the great gift of new life brought into the world, the disciples' labor pains will also lead to rejoicing, not only for a small band of followers but for the whole world. Jesus establishes a direct line between complete joy and intercession in Jesus' name. Jesus' oneness with the Father gives his followers immediate access to and intimacy with God.

Jesus introduces the topic of prayer in terms of the coming of a day when his disciples will ask nothing of him, where their joy will be complete, when all will be as it should be, and the followers of Jesus will want nothing more. "No one will take your joy from you," Jesus promises. This is a liberating claim in a world where competing interests threaten to render our happiness tenuous.

The preacher might invite the church community to explore how it makes decisions to follow Jesus, and how those decisions, those moments of transition and transformation, contribute to the rejoicing brought about by what God has accomplished in Jesus. What are the marks of a community marked by complete joy? Such an invitation could explore issues of prayer and justice, and the difference between making intercessions on behalf of those in need and working to bring about the healing and wholeness of the new birth ushered in by Jesus' resurrection.

APRIL BERENDS

2. Ibid., 948.

John 16:25–33

²⁵"I have said these things to you in figures of speech. The hour is coming when I will no longer speak to you in figures, but will tell you plainly of the Father. ²⁶On that day you will ask in my name. I do not say to you that I will ask the Father on your behalf; ²⁷for the Father himself loves you, because you have loved me and have believed that I came from God. ²⁸I came from the Father and have come into the world; again, I am leaving the world and am going to the Father."

²⁹His disciples said, "Yes, now you are speaking plainly, not in any figure of speech! ³⁰Now we know that you know all things, and do not need to have anyone question you; by this we believe that you came from God." ³¹Jesus answered them, "Do you now believe? ³²The hour is coming, indeed it has come, when you will be scattered, each one to his home, and you will leave me alone. Yet I am not alone because the Father is with me. ³³I have said this to you, so that in me you may have peace. In the world you face persecution. But take courage; I have conquered the world!"

Theological Perspective

These concluding verses from Jesus' Farewell Discourse to his disciples represent something of a distillation of the gospel message. In his final words, Jesus makes references to his preexistence, birth, death, resurrection, and ascension, and the resultant changes in the relationship between Jesus' followers and their heavenly Creator. Through a synopsis of his life on earth, Jesus highlights the key Johannine theme that he is sent from God in heaven and plans to return there soon. His speech follows the Johannine pattern in which a narrative about Jesus leads to a discourse on his life and its ultimate meaning. The evangelist's method for conveying theological lessons parallels God's method of proclaiming good news to the world: through narrative.

In the Gospel of John, the narrative of the human life of Jesus represents a theological treatise on God's life in Christ. God the Creator loves the world by living out the life of a creature, using the "plain speech" of love in action expressed in Jesus' own life story. When God speaks plainly to creation in and through Jesus' life, the creatures themselves enjoy unprecedented access to their Creator, no longer needing a mediator but having a direct connection to God in Jesus. At the end of his speech, Jesus invites the disciples to head to their new home with him, because

Pastoral Perspective

Our world is full—full of movement, full of noise, and full of energy. We have difficulty escaping it. The world comes at us constantly and is always pressing in upon us. As human beings, we are both part of the world and affected by the world all the time. Sit out on the beach without sunscreen, or drink water from a nonpotable spring, and you will feel the effects of the world. With the Internet, television, and other media, we are barraged by what the world has to offer. From sunburns and parasites to the latest in technology and news, the world is coming toward us. Even on remote islands, human beings have found a cell-phone signal and WiFi; the broadcasting continues to enter our every waking moment. Even if we calm our surroundings, our minds and hearts continue to be flooded with thoughts. Where, amid all of the fanfare and glitter, do we find a moment of silence and stillness?

A prayer attributed to Teresa of Avila begins by asking a question:

> How is it, God, that you have given me this hectic busy life when I have so little time to enjoy your presence? Throughout the day people are waiting to speak to me, and even at meals I have to continue talking to people about their needs and problems. During sleep itself I am still thinking and dreaming about the multitude of concerns

Exegetical Perspective

This section (16:25–33) serves as the closing argument for Jesus' series of instructions to his disciples around the table at the Last Supper. Though they will linger in the upper room a little longer, the chapter that follows (chap. 17) is in the form of a prayer; thus, Jesus' formal tutorial on discipleship ends here. The vocabulary and themes within this final statement clearly link it to all that was spoken beforehand in the discourse, for here Jesus takes the opportunity to address his disciples once more on important themes such as his death/departure, their confusion/comprehension, his relationship to the Father, and their mission performed in his name.

Actions Speak Plainer Than Words. Jesus begins his closing remarks by acknowledging that much of what he has said this night may be confusing to the disciples. Remember, it was just a few verses earlier that they responded, "We do not know what he is talking about" (16:18). Here Jesus promises that he will soon speak to them clearly—no longer in "figures of speech" but in "plain" talk (NRSV "plainly," v. 25). In this Gospel account, Jesus does not speak to the assembled group of disciples again until after the resurrection (chaps. 20 and 21), and his language in those discourses is not significantly different in terms of style or vocabulary. The timing of Jesus' promised

Homiletical Perspective

Building on the discourse of the first half of the chapter, Jesus continues to speak words of comfort to his anxious disciples. Persecution will soon come to Jesus' followers; indeed, it has already come to John's original hearers. This text, like the texts that surround it, is concerned with what happens after Jesus leaves his disciples. Given what the original audience already knew to be true—that the early church would suffer persecution—the fearfulness of the disciples must have seemed very real.

The disciples finally acknowledge that Jesus came from God, that he is the Messiah, the promised one. This acknowledgment brings joy, but it also brings fear to the hearts of the disciples, for the one who has come from God now says that he is going to leave them soon. The disciples have been following Jesus all this time, they see now that he is sent from God, and they cannot imagine life without him. The news about Jesus' leaving causes them to panic. What will their lives look like now? Whom will they follow?

Most of today's hearers in North America or Europe have not experienced persecution because of their faith. Though the concept of separation from Jesus is less immediate for us, we can in some ways relate to those early Christians when it comes to being afraid of separation from Jesus Christ. The fear of being left alone, left to our own devices,

John 16:25–33

Theological Perspective

he will establish a spiritual safe house in his new life in heaven with God.

As the passage opens in 16:25, the disciples hear that theology is not limited to verbal expression but is made more comprehensible through actions. Jesus winds up his discourse by acknowledging that he has intentionally used thought-provoking "figures of speech" to teach the disciples. He informs them that he will be making a major revision of his pedagogical style. At this point, the disciples declare that they finally understand him, but he ignores their claims and continues with his explanations. The hour is coming, he says, when he will speak plainly through actions rather than clever turns of phrase. The actions he refers to are his imminent death and resurrection, which will speak more plainly than words ever could. Through the stark message of the cross and the empty tomb, he will tell the world of the astonishing love of his (and our) heavenly Parent.

When that hour comes, it will occur on a day that the disciples "will ask in my name," according to Jesus' words in verse 26. The plain speaking of Jesus in that hour on the cross will inaugurate a day in which the disciples speak directly to their heavenly Parent to convey their needs. The disciples' asking (aiteō) is different from Jesus' asking (erōtaō) on their behalf. The disciples petition God for what they need as an inferior makes a request of a superior, whereas Jesus makes inquiries about the disciples to God "on such a footing of familiarity as lends authority to the request."[1] The King James Version, unlike the NRSV, reflects the difference by having disciples "ask" whereas Jesus "prays." In verse 27, Jesus reassures the disciples that he no longer has to inquire on their behalf, because God loves them in and through their relationship with Christ, which they can express in actions as well: by actively loving and believing in him.

In verse 29, the disciples echo Jesus' words of verse 25, expressing their delight that Jesus is using plain speech rather than perplexing discourse. The fact that they echo Jesus' words rather than rephrasing them suggests that they merely repeat what they think Jesus wants to hear.[2] Having quickly forgotten Jesus' reiterated phrase "a little while" from a few moments earlier (vv. 16, 19), they think that the hour in which they will experience God directly is here now. Furthermore, at the precise moment when

1. Richard C. Trench, *Synonyms of the New Testament* (New York: Cosimo, 2007), 144.
2. Gail R. O'Day, "Preaching as an Act of Friendship: Plain Speaking as a Sign of the Kingdom," *Journal for Preachers* 28 (2005): 14.

Pastoral Perspective

that surround me. . . . I know that you are constantly beside me, yet I am usually so busy that I ignore you.[1]

Poignantly, a saintly woman attests to the difficulty of finding rest. When we have deadlines, meetings, things to do, and schedules to keep, how do we find a moment of tranquility? How, in a world where there is injustice, hardship, and grief, do we find peace?

Jesus reminds the disciples that they can find peace in him while remaining in this world. In John 16:33, Jesus concludes his conversation with the disciples by explaining, "I have said this to you, so that in me you may have peace. In the world you face persecution. But take courage; I have conquered the world!" The world is neither ideal nor easy, and yet we are an integral part of it. Jesus understands that "if you belonged to the world, the world would love you as its own. Because you do not belong to the world, but I have chosen you out of the world—therefore the world hates you" (15:19). How can we be an integral part of something to which we do not belong and that hates us? We are given assurance that God is our peace: "Peace I leave with you; my peace I give to you. I do not give to you as the world gives" (14:27). Jesus does not deny that the world presents itself in distress and tribulation; at the same time, Jesus has declared peace for us, a peace that is available through him.

We have access to peace. Through the example of Jesus' life, ministry, and message, we are capable of recognizing God's love and peace. Jesus shares this news with the disciples: "You will ask in my name. I do not say to you that I will ask the Father on your behalf; for the Father himself loves you, because you have loved me and have believed that I came from God" (v. 26–27). Jesus describes a relationship with "the Father himself" that is grounded in God's love for us. We need no longer look for an intercessor, because, as Jesus says in 10:30, "The Father and I are one." Through the person of Jesus, we have been given a tangible glimpse of God's character.

Jesus took time to pray. We are offered a relationship with God through prayer. If we can calm our surroundings and our hearts, we take respite in prayer to revitalize our souls. We do this in order to deepen our spiritual journeys, but Jesus shows us that peace not only entails sitting still, calming the

1. Teresa of Avila, "Prayer for a Busy Life," in *Catholic School Chronicle*; accessed April 10, 2013; http://www.nicksenger.com/csc/prayer-for-a-busy-life-by-st-teresa-of-avila.

plain speech is described as occurring when "the hour" has come, which previously has been used to make reference to the impending events of his crucifixion and resurrection.

Might it be that these crucial events of Good Friday and Easter morning are what Jesus has in mind when he describes speaking plainly of the Father? Could it be that what the disciples will soon see and experience will reveal and make plain the promises that earlier have been too confusing to comprehend? It is through these events (more than any spoken words) that the disciples will learn "plainly" about the depth of God's sacrificial love.

Of the Father's Love Begotten. After Jesus explains these coming events and what they will reveal to his followers about God, he takes a moment to make certain that the disciples do not misunderstand the nature of their relationship with "the Father" (vv. 26–28). It is not the case that Jesus loves the disciples so much that he must die in order to change God's opinion of them, or to make God love them more. John here endeavors to avoid portraying Jesus as the loving one who saves his followers from an angry deity.[1] No, Jesus says, "The Father himself loves you" (v. 27a). Jesus' incarnate presence with them is physical proof of how vast is God's love for them in the first place. Remember, it is through God's love that Jesus has been sent to the world (3:16). The disciples' love of and faith in Jesus are what bring them into relationship with God (v. 27b). In other words, to love Jesus is to love God, and to be loved by Jesus is to be loved by God. Jesus recapitulates this unity of love by summarizing his mission as being sent from the Father and returning to the Father (v. 28). The love of the Sent One and the love of the Sender are one and the same.

Do You Now? After hearing Jesus speak about their love toward him, the disciples quickly insist, "Yes!" or literally, "You see!" (*ide*, v. 29). What follows is their rapid affirmation of what they know and believe about Jesus: "we know *that* you know all things," and "we believe *that* you came from God" (v. 30). However, their quick response to Jesus seems to be a little too quick, and too full of certainty. After having seemingly praised them for their love and belief (v. 27), Jesus now skeptically counters, "Do you now believe?" (v. 31).

---

1. A later version of this idea was propounded by the second-century Marcion. See Bart D. Ehrman, *Lost Christianities: The Battles for Scripture and the Faiths We Never Knew* (New York: Oxford University Press, 2003), 103–9.

is something we need not worry about if we take Jesus' words here as truth. The relationship of the Father to the Son, as well as the sending of the Spirit (14:16–17, 26) demonstrate that the nature of God is to be in community with God's own self. That very relationship is the means by which Jesus invites us to share in his own life.

In the face of persecution, Jesus would not be alone. He knew that God would be with him. Because Jesus was not alone, we are not alone. The very nature of God's oneness is togetherness. The same God who is Father, Son, and Spirit holds us in relationship—with God's own self and with one another.

In many ways our culture entices us with a worldview that encourages us to go it alone; perhaps the challenge of this passage to the postmodern hearer lies in the relational nature of God that it presents. We are accustomed to a society that promotes individualism, that presents barriers to authentic community, and that readily offers technological substitutes for intimacy with our neighbors. The preacher might explore the concept of relationship, tying this to the life of the church community. Do the ways in which we order our lives nurture relationships with God and our neighbors? Are there changes that we can make to strengthen these relationships? Are we afraid of being in relationship with God?

In this and the surrounding passages, Jesus makes clear that he has done what God has sent him to do. The disciples, though confessing that Jesus has come from God, have trouble believing that Jesus' work on earth can be accomplished if Jesus intends to leave them. This is a legitimate worry. It is worth noting that Jesus does not name a human successor. Instead he invites a community, a community marked by death and resurrection, the intimate relationship between Father, Son, and Spirit, and the promise of a joyous reign of everlasting peace. The preacher might invite the gathered community to consider how these characteristics manifest themselves in the lives of the church and its members today.

Jesus assures his followers that he has already conquered the world (v. 33). He has won and he is winning. John's Gospel tells us that he was present at the very beginning of the world, at the birth of creation. The testimony of the Gospel describes how he has brought healing to those who were broken. He has breathed new life into individuals who have died and into religious systems in need of reform. We see in him the continuing work of God's creation.

The amazing thing for those who seek to follow Jesus is that because God sent Jesus for this work,

Theological Perspective

they are hoping for Jesus' praise, Jesus reminds them that they will abandon him.[3] In verse 30, they assure Jesus of their awareness that he knows everything. Rather than verbally acknowledge they are right, he demonstrates it directly by showing that he can predict in advance their future abandonment of him at the crucial hour. His question in verse 31, "Do you now believe?" suggests a gently mocking tone. Jesus recognizes the weakness of their knowing and their believing and is fully aware that they will run and hide at the first sign of trouble.

In verse 32, Jesus tells the disciples that they will scatter and their fellowship will be shattered, as each one runs separately to his own home. Usually human beings headed for home are buoyed with hopes for a place of welcome and comfort, but when the disciples head home out of fear, their actions speak plainly about their lost hopes. Moreover, their abandonment of Jesus makes it clear that they neither know nor believe what he has told them. He reminds them that, for him, there is only one true home: with God. Jesus does not have to go anywhere to arrive at home, for he lives in God's promise that the divine home is wherever justice and peace reign.

Because Jesus lived a life of justice and compassion, God dwelt in and with him. For that reason, in John 16:32, Jesus can claim that he is never alone. God's dwelling place on earth is in the life of Jesus. As Jesus reminds the disciples, when we speak out our faith in clear terms by practicing justice and peace, the world will persecute us. We can take courage, knowing that their persecution of us will never destroy our life in Jesus Christ, because it is there that God chooses to dwell along with us, and together with God in Christ we enjoy safe and everlasting refuge.

REBECCA BLAIR YOUNG

Pastoral Perspective

mind, and meditating. Seeking peace does not mean that we block out the world, with its chaos, noise, and movement. As Thomas Merton explains, "To choose the world is to choose to do the work I am capable of doing, in collaboration with my brother, to make the world better, more free, more just."[2] Jesus engaged in the world and brought peace to people through justice seeking, goodwill, and healing. When we access the peace of God, we cannot help but share that peace. In seeking peace for ourselves, we may be empowered to embody peace by advocating for others. As integral parts of the world, perhaps a world that despises us, we are encouraged to enact the peace of God in the world by working toward reconciliation and justice.

How does peace manifest itself? This peace takes shape in Jesus' feeding five thousand hungry people (6:1–14), calming a storm (Mark 4:35–41), and walking on water amid rough winds (6:16–21). This peace looks like Mahatma Gandhi, who led India to independence by utilizing movements of nonviolent resistance in the face of oppression. This peace sounds like the "I Have a Dream" speech of Martin Luther King Jr. as he fought for African American civil rights amid violent and unequal segregation laws. This peace looks like Tawakkul Karman, who won the Nobel Peace Prize "for non-violent struggle for the safety of women and for women's rights to full participation in peace-building work."[3] Peace looks like a chaplain sitting with a family in the hospital, watching as their loved one takes her last breath. Jesus shows us peace as both contemplative and active. This peace looks like people holding hands and helping each other stand. Peace is engaged when people break bread together in the name of God's love for them.

S. VANCE GOODMAN

---

3. Ibid.

2. Thomas Merton, *Contemplation in a World of Action* (Notre Dame, IN: University of Notre Dame Press, 1998), 147.
3. "The Nobel Peace Prize 2011–Press Release," Nobelprize.org. 7 October 2011; retrieved April 13, 2013.

Exegetical Perspective

He asks rhetorically, for their actions will soon prove how little the disciples do believe at this point in the Gospel narrative. Because they have heard Jesus foreshadow what will soon befall them, they think they are prepared for it. Jesus' prediction that they will scatter and leave him (v. 32) serves as a sobering reminder that facts *about* him ("we know *that* . . . we believe *that*" in v. 30) are not enough to maintain their faith and unity in the face of what is to follow. They will abandon the one who has been sent for them. This quick transition from positive response to a humbling chastisement is reminiscent of the Synoptic Gospels' accounts of Peter's confession of faith at Caesarea Philippi, which is immediately followed by Jesus telling him, "Get behind me, Satan."[2] In both cases, it is truth about Jesus that the disciples are able to confess, rather than knowledge of him. Although their confession is true, it is not yet complete.

Parting Gifts. Jesus corrects the disciples' reliance on facts about him and instead describes a more personal assurance that comes through belief in him. He says, "In me you may have peace" (v. 33). In the events that will soon occur at Calvary, their factual knowledge about Jesus will fail. Instead, Jesus promises a personal knowledge that will bear them through the disappointment and pain of the coming days. In his person he gives them the gift of peace. In his last remark he bids them "take courage" amid their coming persecution by the world, for Jesus himself has "conquered the world" (v. 33). These two final gifts of peace and courage are given in concert with the previous gift of joy (v. 22). Having offered them all he has to give, Jesus concludes his remarks so that he may pray for his disciples and then lead them out to the garden. The hour is coming.

BUZ WILCOXON

Homiletical Perspective

Jesus has the ability, through the Spirit, to call us into this work. In following Jesus, we join him and we join God in the restoration of creation. The end result, what Jesus came to accomplish, is a deep and eternal peace, a peace that brings with it a depth of understanding not previously experienced.

This is good news for the persecuted Christians of the first century, and it is good news for us today. Most of us do not fear for our lives the way the saints of the early church did. We do know, however, what it is like to be isolated and what it means to be anxious and afraid. The preacher might invite listeners to name our fears and the things that stand in the way of our fullest relationship with God in Jesus Christ.

Jesus' heartening words to the disciples speak comfort, but they also hint at action, the involvement of the followers of Jesus Christ in God's ongoing acts of creation. When we consider that in Jesus we have direct access to God the Creator, we find that his prayers become our prayers, and our prayers become his. That should have implications for the ways in which we pray and the ways in which we live our lives. If we truly believe that Jesus prays to God along with us, does that change the nature of our intercessions? If we are drawn into God's family as a child to a father, when God sees Jesus Christ, then God sees us. This passage promises us that sort of intimacy, intimacy that is at the same time both a call to responsiveness and a generous gift.

APRIL BERENDS

---

2. See Matt. 16:13–23; Mark 8:27–33; Luke 9:18–27 (though Luke does not report Peter's negative response and chastisement).

John 17:1–5

¹After Jesus had spoken these words, he looked up to heaven and said, "Father, the hour has come; glorify your Son so that the Son may glorify you, ²since you have given him authority over all people, to give eternal life to all whom you have given him. ³And this is eternal life, that they may know you, the only true God, and Jesus Christ whom you have sent. ⁴I glorified you on earth by finishing the work that you gave me to do. ⁵So now, Father, glorify me in your own presence with the glory that I had in your presence before the world existed."

Theological Perspective

The seventeenth chapter of the Gospel of John begins with a prayer by Jesus to his heavenly Parent. The prayer describes his relationship with God as well as his relationship to the world into which God sends him. Jesus begins the prayer by looking up. The biblical view of the heaven is different from our view of the universe. Where our ancestors looked up and imagined a heavenly dwelling for the Divine, we see physical space extending billions of light years. Even in the age of science, though, it remains significant that Jesus looks up at this moment, because he is looking beyond worldly limits to a far greater, unlimited life. Jesus is looking in prayer beyond the cross to the resurrection.

Jesus indicates this by his words, "The hour has come" (v. 1). As readers, we know he refers to his impending death, just hours away. In spite of having this foreknowledge, Jesus never asks for the cup to be taken away from him, as he does in the three Synoptic Gospel narratives. Later, in 18:11, Jesus tells Peter that he must drink the cup that God has given him—quite different from his prayer as told in the Synoptics. The Christology of the Synoptics depicts Jesus as a man in sorrow on the eve of his death, sad to leave good friends, and somewhat reluctantly accepting his coming suffering, because it is God's will for him. John presents a Christology in which

Pastoral Perspective

In the children's book *Jellybeans* by Sylvia Van Ommen, a rabbit named George and a cat named Oscar meet in the park for jellybeans and hot chocolate. They share a snack together and begin a perceptive discussion about what might come after this life. "Do you think there's a heaven up there? A place you go when you're dead?" asks Oscar. "I don't know. I think so," answers George. They continue to speculate about what they might see and if they will recognize one another. George surmises, "But if we bump into each other and we don't recognize each other.... Then we can just become friends all over again.... Eat jellybeans together and stuff like that."[1] Oscar and George approach the future with hope—hope that they will see each other and eat jellybeans again eternally. This winsome conversation touches on one of the most daunting doctrines in the Christian tradition.

Eschatology, or "last things," is a baffling and humbling topic in Christian theology. We approach this subject with humility, knowing that "now we see in a mirror, dimly, but then we will see face to face" (1 Cor. 13:12). Can we ever be completely sure about the shape of future hope and the glory of

1 Sylvia Van Ommen, *Jellybeans* (Brookfield, CT: Roaring Book Press, 2002), 32–35.

Exegetical Perspective

For the previous four chapters (chaps. 13–16), John's narrative has provided an extended portrayal of Jesus' actions and teachings at the supper table on the eve of his crucifixion. With the start of chapter 17, the Last Supper begins to draw to a close in prayer. Before leading his disciples to the garden (18:1), where he will be betrayed and arrested, Jesus lingers for one final moment to pray for his followers, that they may be united in their mission to a hostile world. Before Jesus' divine conversation turns to focus on others, it begins with an address from the Son to the Father concerning his glory.

Father/Son Time. The introductory phrase, "he looked up to heaven," as well as Jesus' first word of the prayer addressing God as "Father," suggests a clear distinction between Jesus ("the Son") and God ("the Father"). A few verses later, however, Jesus seems to be hinting at a stronger degree of unity between "the only true God, and Jesus Christ whom you have sent," who are known together (v. 3). While later theologians would draw upon this text to discuss the interrelationship of the persons of the Trinity, it is worth noting exegetically that this dual language (alternating between emphasis on unity and emphasis on distinction) is consistent with the larger pattern of usage in John's Gospel.

Homiletical Perspective

We find in this passage the climax of Jesus' Farewell Discourse. Rather than offering instructions directed toward Jesus' disciples, this section begins a prayer addressed to God the Father. Jesus has just promised that his disciples have direct access to God through him, and here his promise comes full circle when he prays to be glorified with the glory that he possessed at the beginning of creation, an equal and shared glory bestowed by the Creator.

As Jesus' instruction in chapter 16 serves as a moment of transition and clarity for the disciples, so this prayer serves as a moment of transition for Jesus. For though the pivotal events of his trial, death, and resurrection will be described in subsequent chapters, chapter 17 communicates the sense that Jesus, while still in this world, is already joined with the Father. He has finished what God has sent him to do. He has glorified God by bringing God near, manifesting God's power, and revealing God's presence through signs of healing, forgiveness, and resurrection.

The preacher might want to call attention to the way the term "glory" is used in the context of worship. In many traditions, the word is used frequently without much explanation. What do we mean when we say this word? In the twenty-first century, when we use "glory" outside of religious contexts, it often

| Theological Perspective | Pastoral Perspective |

Jesus is already speaking triumphantly as he sees that his hour has come to its pinnacle of glory, with imminent union with God and union among the disciples in his name.[1]

The next verse explains why death on a cross is the moment of divine glory. In verse 2, Jesus asks for God to glorify him through this death on a cross because God has given Jesus "authority" over all people. In his actions, Jesus affirms and expresses the type of authority that God has given him over all people. In contradiction to worldly forms of authority, Jesus' authority is that of a human being willing to die for others. Worldly authority is the human power to take other people's livelihoods and lives in order to expand one's wealth and status. Divine authority is precisely the opposite, as we read in Philippians 2:6–11. In Christ, God shows that real authority—and thus real divinity—is the act of giving up all efforts to gain power. Real authority is not absolute power over others but absolute love of others, shown in the willingness to give up everything, including divine status itself, in order to express that love in perfect fulfillment.

The world wants to worship a god of absolute power. In Jesus Christ's crucifixion, God expresses the divine self as the God of absolute love. The first twelve chapters of the Gospel showed the glory of God through displays of power in the miracles, teaching, and life of Jesus, what the evangelist calls "signs." In Jesus' hour of glory on the cross, the evangelist recounts no miraculous displays of power as the Synoptics do when relating the same events. One commentator notes, "If the signs reveal God's glory by displaying divine power, the crucifixion reveals God's glory by conveying divine love."[2]

Continuing in the same vein, in verse 2, Jesus states that through his authority over all people, he has been granted the love to give eternal life to everyone. To give everyone eternal life through love, as opposed to using coercive power, means that we gain eternal life by being in love with God in Jesus Christ. In other words, eternal life as described and exemplified by Jesus in John's Gospel is a relationship of love and fellowship, rather than one of power and submission. We as Jesus' followers are not received into a heavenly afterlife as reward for subservience to a higher power. Eternal life takes place in the here

God? Although we cannot be definite, we are given hints of God's purpose for creation through the life and teaching of Jesus. After a long dialogue with his disciples, what scholars have called the Farewell Discourse, Jesus turns his attention to prayer. In John 17:1–5, Jesus prays for his disciples and defines eternal life within his prayer. Jesus says, "And this is eternal life, that they may know you, the only true God, and Jesus Christ whom you have sent" (v. 3). The knowledge of God is eternal life.

What does it mean to know God? The word Jesus uses to denote the verb "to know" is *ginōskō*, a term that means "coming to know, to be aware of, feel, or perceive." A second word used in the book of John to signify "know" is the Greek word *oida*, a term that means to "know, remember, or appreciate." This second term is definitive, representing a fullness of knowledge, whereas *ginōskō* refers to a progression in knowledge and implies the kind of knowledge that comes in building relationship with another.[2] We can know (*oida*) facts and figures. In knowing another person, the best we can do is to know (*ginōskō*) another by having an active relationship with her or him.

So it is with God. We can spend time learning facts about God, reading books, and studying theological ideas, and this can be helpful in our relationship with God. However, to know God, as Jesus is explaining, is to enter into a relationship of trust and hope, constantly learning and growing in connection with God. Knowing God in this way involves communication through prayer, Scripture reading, paying attention to God's work in our lives, and embodying God's love in the world. This kind of knowing is what Jesus refers to as "eternal life."

According to this description, eternal life is both a present reality and a future blessing. Jesus does not say of eternal life, "that [the disciples] may know [God and Jesus Christ] when they die" or "that they may know you when they are made perfect," relegating it to some distant future moment. Knowledge of God can happen now, in the present. Eternal life includes a present relationship with God through participating in a faithfully obedient life and communing with God's love and justice. Eternal life begins now because knowing God involves a process. Just as getting to know someone takes time and dedication, knowing God involves using our strength and energy to be in relationship with our Creator.

---

1. Brian P. Stoffregen, "John 17.1–11: 7th Sunday of Easter–Year A," Crossmarks Christian Resources, http://www.crossmarks.com/brian/john17x1.htm; accessed April 17, 2014.

2. Craig R. Koester, *The Word of Life: A Theology of John's Gospel* (Grand Rapids: Eerdmans, 2008), 122.

2. James Strong, *The New Strong's Exhaustive Concordance of the Bible* (Nashville: Thomas Nelson, 1995), 795.

Exegetical Perspective

After addressing God, Jesus acknowledges that "the hour has come" (v. 1). This phrase is used at the beginning of the Last Supper account (13:1) and is repeated five times throughout the preceding chapter (chap. 16) as a way of Jesus' alluding to his death. Thus, during this extended meal scene, the refrain of "the hour has come" serves as an increasingly foreboding reminder to the audience (think of the way that music in a film score can signal danger) that builds the suspense toward Jesus' impending betrayal and death. The phrase appears here at the beginning of the prayer, and its shadow is cast over all that will follow.

From Glory into Glory. Jesus proceeds in his prayer to offer his first petition, "glorify your Son so that the Son may glorify you" (v. 1). Of the seven petitions spoken within the prayer, this request to be glorified is the only one that is repeated (v. 5).[1] This reference to being glorified connects the audience to the theme of glory that has been running throughout the entire Gospel. John's consistent stress upon Jesus' glory has led Albert Winn to call the Fourth Gospel "a continuous transfiguration narrative."[2] The Greek word for glorify (*doxazō*) appears four times in these first five verses of the prayer and is accompanied by its noun form (*doxa*, "glory") as well. It is the linguistic root of our liturgical term "doxology" and means to honor or praise someone. To be glorified is to be lifted up in the opinion of others and figuratively put on a pedestal.

Thus, it is with holy and prophetic irony that on the eve of his crucifixion Jesus asks to be glorified, for he is about to be lifted up and put not on a pedestal but on a cross. He is soon to receive a most unglorified treatment, reserved only for criminals. With this foreshadowing (which has earlier appeared in 3:14; 8:28; 12:32, 34) John is making a claim about his understanding of Jesus' glory and how greatly it differs from that which the Greco-Roman world has to offer.

Eternal Knowing. As mentioned above, the request to be glorified is repeated in verse 5, and paying attention to this repetition leads us to see a small but significant pattern in the opening section of Jesus' prayer. With the "glorified" references serving as bookends and with the repetition of the word "given" between them (vv. 2, 4) a chiastic structure emerges:

1. Frederick Dale Bruner, *The Gospel of John: A Commentary* (Grand Rapids: Eerdmans, 2012), 960.
2. Albert Curry Winn, *A Sense of Mission: Guidance from the Gospel of John* (Philadelphia: Westminster Press, 1981), 36.

Homiletical Perspective

means something that individuals seek for themselves or take from other people. As it is used here, glory has less to do with status and accolades and more to do with how God is revealed in the world and to us. In the Gospel of John, glory is both reality and promise.

Jesus does not seek glory for himself; instead, he seeks glory for the one who sent him and for the people on whose behalf he has been sent. The disciples do not fully understand this glory, but in the previous passage Jesus assures them that they will know the fullness of joy that comes from what will be revealed in the future.

One potentially fruitful homiletical approach would be to situate this passage within the Gospel narrative, examining the way that God's glory manifests itself in Jesus throughout the entirety of John. The glory of God is all-encompassing, stretching back before the foundations of the earth. John's Gospel makes clear that not a corner of creation remains untouched by God's glory. It can show up anywhere: in Samaria, at a pool where desperate people seek healing, among adulterers, and in the midst of those who are hungry. Even the cross—especially the cross—reveals this glory. When Judas leaves to betray Jesus, Jesus says, "Now the Son of Man has been glorified, and God has been glorified in him" (13:31). God is glorified in love poured out for the world. When Jesus speaks of glory, he speaks of power and love bound up together. Such love is starkly revealed upon the cross, and just when we begin to think that God has done the ultimate loving thing in Jesus' death, we find that there is even more to this love than we dared hope. A stone is rolled away, and we discover that life in Christ does not end at the tomb, but rather makes a glorious new beginning.

Through Jesus, God displays this powerful, loving glory in relationship with humanity. Jesus prays that we might know him. Knowledge of God, Jesus says, is eternal life. God wants to know us and be known by us. Jesus wants to restore us to relationship with God. This is what he has come to do. At first glance, the glory to which Jesus refers seems rather esoteric and inaccessible, but Jesus has come to help us know it. Glory is not merely something that happens all around us; it is a dance into which we are swept. Because God wants to know us, we witness God's glory not as bystanders, but as participants

Jesus' prayer asks something of God, but it also asks something of us. If we believe that God is revealed in Jesus Christ, our lives should start to take

Theological Perspective

and now as we are embraced in absolute, gratuitous divine love.

Jesus explains eternal life in verse 3. He begins by saying that "this is eternal life," using the phrase in the present tense. Jesus shows us that eternal life is eternal because it is divine love that is freely available to all creatures, without limit and without regard to the creature's worldly status or situation. In addition, Jesus never says that eternal life is something we possess; rather, it is a form of knowing. More precisely, it is the knowledge of God found in Jesus Christ. Soteriologically, this type of knowing means that salvation is not based on intellectual knowledge about God, nor moral knowledge of right and wrong and how to shape one's actions to attain eternal life. The good news of our Lord Jesus Christ is that salvation is truly universal, in that everyone, whatever their intellectual or moral standing in the world's eyes, can gain salvation in the relationship freely offered to us by God in Jesus Christ.

In Indonesia, there are two words for "knowing" that can enhance our understanding of the meaning of eternal life. One can know information, *mengetahui sesuatu*, from the root word *tahu*, to know. One can also know another being, *mengenal seseorang*, from the root word *kenal*, which means to know in the sense of having a relationship with another. Similarly, we may know doctrines about who God is, but that knowledge has little to do with eternal life. The word *kenal*, on the other hand, is the key. When we have a loving relationship with God, we know God in a way that goes far beyond words and the accumulation of knowledge. We experience God through our personal relationship with Jesus Christ, who is one with us as a human being, while simultaneously eternally one with God. Jesus is the way that we truly know and experience our Creator, our Lover, as well as the one through whom we experience the gift of eternal life.

REBECCA BLAIR YOUNG

Pastoral Perspective

Eternal life is a gift for the present moment and in the future. As Christopher Morse describes, "there is both an 'already' and a 'not yet' frame of reference within the gospel message."[3] "Already" we can experience a relationship with God's love and grace by acknowledging our creation as children of God and by living lives after the example of Christ. The "not yet" refers to God's dominion over all forms of domination and injustice in our world, a future for each of us that has not yet arrived. This hopeful "not yet" in the future includes the progressive relationship with God that will continue to grow. When we know God, we experience eternal life, a quality of life that exceeds what the world can offer.

Eternal life in the present encourages a life of great worth through relationship with God, and this quality of life is a taste of what we might experience in the future. This is not to say that life is perfect or that things turn out perfectly, once we have decided to acknowledge God's pervasive love. Perhaps perfection is not the point of eternal life at all. The Gospel of John reminds us that eternal life, both the present and the future, are blessed by the promise of a relationship with God through Jesus Christ. We are promised God's presence with us, God's love for us, and we are assured that we will never be alone. We can be hopeful in a future that entails the consummation of God's presence and purpose for creation.

Just as Oscar and George were perplexed about the question of heaven, we do not know what precisely the life hereafter holds. Although we do not have definitive answers, however, we have been given a glimpse of what eternal life holds for us. Whether or not there are jellybeans, hot chocolate, and best friends, we are given the promise of a continual relationship with God, beginning now.

S. VANCE GOODMAN

---

3. Christopher Morse, *Not Every Spirit* (New York: Continuum Publishing, 2009), 327.

Exegetical Perspective

A Petition: The Son glorified (v. 1)
B Authority and people given to the Son (v. 2)
C Eternal life: Knowing God (v. 3a)
C' Eternal life: Knowing Jesus (v. 3b)
B' Work given to the Son (v. 4)
A' Petition: The Son glorified eternally (v. 5)

While the authority, people, and work given to Jesus are important concepts, full of rich christological significance, the primary purpose of the chiastic structure is to draw attention to the center of the text. Sandwiched between the "glorified" and "given" statements, Jesus offers a brief definition of the phrase "eternal life." Seemingly shifting from prayer back into instruction, Jesus states, "This is eternal life, that they may know you, the only true God, and Jesus Christ whom you have sent" (v. 3). Life that is eternal (literally "life of the ages") is nothing more and nothing less than knowing God and knowing Jesus Christ.

To know (*ginōskō*) can mean many things: to perceive, to understand, to recognize, to comprehend significance, even to come into very intimate personal relationship. John is utilizing the full breadth of the word's meanings when he has Jesus present this startling and brief definition of eternal life. The objects of this knowledge are twofold: the only true God and Jesus Christ, yet they are presented here together, as part of the same single act of knowing, as if knowing one is dependent on knowing the other, thus offering a thoroughly christocentric understanding of divine revelation.

This definition (which reads like a brief creed) appears to be inserted into the prayer and may be a clear sign of later editing.[3] Whether original to the text or not, its inclusion provides continuity between the two petitions for glory at the beginning of the prayer and the later petitions for Jesus' disciples that will soon follow (vv. 6–26). Thus, as Jesus is glorified through the cross and resurrection, he is revealing to his followers the glory of "the only true God," and in doing so, he is giving them the gift of eternal living.

BUZ WILCOXON

Homiletical Perspective

on the cruciform pattern of the life that he lived. In John's Gospel, Jesus takes the golden rule a step further than loving one's neighbors as oneself when he says, "Just as I have loved you, you also should love one another" (13:34). He advocates for a love of neighbor rooted in something much deeper than the human desire to be treated with fairness and respect. He tells his followers to love with everything that we are, even if it means risking our very lives. Our love will never be as perfect as the love present in Jesus at the birth of creation, or as wondrous as the love poured out on the cross, or as powerful as the love that triumphs over death, but this is the love set forth as our model. It is love that stretches beyond our wildest imaginings, beyond time itself into eternity.

Leading up to this passage, Jesus speaks of the pains and rewards of childbirth (16:21–22). He uses an ordinary yet dramatic metaphor to describe the newness of what he is doing. He is bringing about a new birth. He is making new. He is pulling us back into relationship with God and loving us back to life. It is a glorious thing, both temporal and cosmic, for Jesus is clear that he has finished what God sent him to do, and that the glory that follows is something much more complete than what his followers witnessed on earth.

The preacher might invite the congregation to pray this prayer out loud. What if we made this prayer our own prayer? What if we prayed, every day, for our lives to reveal God's glory in the world? What if we prayed, every day, for the glory of God to fill the cosmos? What if we prayed, every day, that we might behold this glory and that we might let it shape our lives?

APRIL BERENDS

---

3. Bruner, *Gospel of* John, 970, 981.

⁶"I have made your name known to those whom you gave me from the world. They were yours, and you gave them to me, and they have kept your word. ⁷Now they know that everything you have given me is from you; ⁸for the words that you gave to me I have given to them, and they have received them and know in truth that I came from you; and they have believed that you sent me. ⁹I am asking on their behalf; I am not asking on behalf of the world, but on behalf of those whom you gave me, because they are yours. ¹⁰All mine are yours, and yours are mine; and I have been glorified in them."

Theological Perspective

Prayer. From the perspective of liturgical theology, John 17 provides a poor model for intercessory prayer, especially for intercessory prayer in a congregational setting. It is entirely clear that the function of this prayer is primarily to inform the disciples (and through the disciples to instruct the readers) concerning right Johannine Christology and ecclesiology. This becomes especially clear in the verses preceding this section, where Jesus instructs his Father on the true meaning of eternal life, in much the same tone that he instructs Nicodemus in John 3.

This trickiness is in part a consequence of John's strong insistence on the unity of the Father and the Son.

In the Gethsemane scene in Mark, Matthew, and Luke, the distance between the Son and the Father, whose will Jesus both seeks and regrets, is entirely clear. In the crucifixion narrative for each of the Synoptic Gospels, there is a distance between the one who prays and the one to whom he prays. In the Synoptic crucifixion the distance between Father and Son is even clearer. In Luke the prayer bridges the distance; in Mark and Matthew the prayer decries the distance (Mark 15:34; Matt 27:46; Luke 23:46).

As we might guess from the closeness of Father and Son in the form of the prayer of John 17 and from the unity declared in our chapter's content,

Pastoral Perspective

Prayer is not always linear and organized—not even for Jesus! Biblical scholars disagree about how to categorize verses 6–8 of Jesus' famous final prayer. Is Jesus continuing to pray about his glorification as in the previous verses, or is he starting to pray for the church, as in the verses that follow? Exegetical interpretation probably needs to make a choice between these options, but pastorally, leaving the question unanswered may be more fruitful.

Whenever we pray for others, our activity necessarily involves three parties: God, the person or people for whom we are praying, and ourselves. While the primary thrust of this text is to emphasize the unity of God, Jesus, and believers, this unity is grounded in respectful particularity. When we pray, we experience both closeness and distance from both the subject and object of our prayer. It was no different for Jesus. If his desired unity was already complete, there would be no need to pray. In pouring out his heart to God, Jesus is expressing his desire to bring the three parties closer together.

Does prayer matter? Does it make a difference? Does it change reality? There are no simple answers to these questions, and this text testifies to the complexity of communication between the human and the Divine. When we pray, we have faith that God hears our prayer, but seldom do we believe that we

Exegetical Perspective

Jesus' sudden shift from discourse to prayer pairs "name" and "glory" and foreshadows John's portrait of the cross as revealing Jesus' glorification, instead of Mark's depiction of his God-forsakenness. The paired terms resound throughout this valedictory intercession (vv. 22, 26). "I have been glorified" (v. 10) parallels "I have made your name known" (v. 6), framing and focusing this passage to extend Jesus' initial petition to be glorified (vv. 1–5). The disciples overhear it at table, unlike Jesus' soliloquy on the Mount of Olives in the Synoptics. This intercession for Jesus' hearers, however, anticipates John's concern for his late-first-century messianic movement splitting from its sibling sect (John's antagonistic "Jews"). In sum, John champions the Word from God (1:1–14), claiming it had tangibly and knowingly come "by name" into the world only to be rejected, yet glorified.

That paradox was nothing new. Rescued Hebrews, tired of manna, grumbled in the wilderness (Exod. 32) against Moses, who knew God's name (Exod. 3:14) and saw the back of God's glory (Exod. 33) and, hence, a hope revealed for Israel. John's Gospel echoes and reassigns these same stories with its own remedy for vipers and waterless tracts during the wanderings (Num. 20–21 with John 3:14; 4:14; 6:41). Thus Jesus' prayer knowingly duplicates and, for John, trumps Moses' farewell to Israel (Deut. 31–33).

Homiletical Perspective

At the conclusion of chapter 16, Jesus teaches his disciples to anticipate his return to God, along with their own dispersion into the world after his passion. At the beginning of chapter 17, Jesus prays for himself (vv. 1–5), to glorify God and to be glorified by God. The way in which Jesus is glorified, however, appears strongly only when he turns attention to the disciples with verse 6. This commissioning prayer of sorts portrays the disciples as divine gifts to Jesus ("They were yours, and you gave them to me," v. 6b). The backdrop is the disciples' confession that they believe Jesus has come from God (16:29–30). Jesus admonishes the disciples that they will be scattered into a chaotic world (16:31–32). He clearly intercedes for the disciples here, since they need divine care. This prayer, however, does more than intercede. It empowers the disciples with a commissioned unity.

Preachers may consider the critical dialectics between intercessory prayer and commissioning prayer. The forms are not mutually exclusive, even in this text. Jesus recognizes that the world can be a perilous place (16:33), but it is important to note that in his prayer for the disciples Jesus does not pray against the world. Too often passages like this one end up in sermons that vilify the "world" as an evil arbiter of destruction. Clearly, humanity operates often in that capacity. Jesus' prayer, however, is not for the disciples

Theological Perspective

there is no recounting of the Gethsemane narrative in John's Gospel, and on the cross there is no cry of abandonment or even of intercession. There is only the cry of victory: "It is finished"—the work of the Father and of the Son, one work.

Christology. For the church's theological reflection, the great topic sentence of the Fourth Gospel is John 1:14: "The Word became flesh and dwelt among us" (RSV). The doctrine of incarnation, the mystery of incarnation, is anchored in this Gospel far more than in the Synoptics and perhaps even more consistently than it is in Paul.

Incarnation is manifest in this Gospel in a variety of ways, but in this passage the relationship between Father and Son is most clearly this: the words that the Son speaks are the words of the Father.

The claim, both that Jesus is "sent" and that the words he speaks are the words of the Father intended for the disciples, draws on an image that is also essential for Paul. For Paul, the "apostle" is the one who is sent (Gk. *apostolos*), and what the sent one is to do is to declare directly and exactly the words of the Sender. Paul's other word for this relationship is "ambassador" (2 Cor. 5:20). For John, Jesus is both the great apostle, sent by the Father to declare the Father's words, and the true ambassador, sent to represent the Father in the world.

In this passage the Word becomes words. What the incarnate Word declares is the message he has received and continues to receive from the Father.

Incarnation is in many ways the great mystery of our faith, but for many Christians or seekers, its more metaphysical dimensions can seem a mystery too great. To say that the words Jesus speaks are the very words of God is perhaps a first step toward the larger claim, that those who have seen him have seen the Father.

Ecclesiology/Election. The claim in this prayer that God has chosen some people to be separate from the world, to have life in Christ, is a major instance of two critical themes in John's Gospel.

First, those who believe have been chosen by God to be believers.

Second, those who believe have been chosen from, and over against, the "world."

The doctrine of election in the New Testament and in Christian theology should not be confused with the contemporary debate about determinism. Nor is it entirely clear that for John's Gospel "chosenness" is the opposite of "free will." Rudolf Bultmann,

Pastoral Perspective

are somehow changing God's mind or providing God with information that God lacks. The mystery is no less apparent when we consider the "results" for the one named in prayer. We hope for healing or restoration through intercession, but the details of how and when and why that happens are beyond our ken. Only one truth about prayer is apprehended directly: we know it changes *us.* We grow closer to God. We are bound more fully to one another.

In this remarkable prayer, Jesus understands himself in the light of God, but also in the light of his disciples in the upper room and those who will follow later. The parts cannot be isolated; they are all mixed together. He does not first establish his relationship to God, and then bless the church from this newly constructed higher elevation. Rather, he establishes his unity with God in the context of his unity with the church—with us.

Though we often undertake prayer in search of peace, Jesus here models quite the opposite. The sense of struggle—almost of thrashing around—within the text is not a Johannine lapse in style. John cannot lay it out neatly, because Jesus is struggling with his very incarnational identity. Nothing is orderly as Jesus articulates both his unity with God and his solidarity with us. As Karl Barth put it, Jesus is "immediately and directly affected by" our existence and achieves no "stoical calm or mystic rapture."[1]

Jesus' words in this chapter are notoriously confusing and complicated. A good teacher might unpack each phrase to bring some order and clarity, but a good pastor can take the disorientation itself as a starting point. This prayer is difficult because when we pray, we inhabit, in some small way, the precarious position that Jesus first holds—the contested territory between God and human community. When we pray, we are going where only Jesus can fully go, but, because he is the "pioneer and perfecter of our faith" (Heb. 12:2), we have a path to follow.

Giving voice to the disorderly nature of these verses yields some helpful doses of good news to the church today. First, we need not be ashamed if our own prayer life feels like it is in a shambles. Jesus shows us that prayer is messy. True prayer always tests the limits of language and shapes us as much when it "fails" as when it "succeeds." If we go through desert times when we feel neither God's presence nor our own transformation, we may be

---

1. "There is not in Him a kind of deep, inner, secret recess in which He is alone in Himself or with God, existing in stoical calm or mystic rapture apart from His fellows. . . . He is immediately and directly affected by the existence of His fellows" (Karl Barth, *Church Dogmatics,* III/2, ed. G. W. Bromiley and T. F. Torrance (London: T. & T. Clark, 1960), 211.

Exegetical Perspective

Between God's direct address to Moses about words once given to Israel and Moses' final song invoking "O heavens" (Deut. 32:1), Deuteronomy affirmed how the prophet had proclaimed YHWH's name, and how Israel should "ascribe greatness to our God" (Deut. 32:3). Read lyrically, this second stanza of Jesus' Passover Eve prayer likewise intends to magnify God's name and entrust revelatory words to his disciples and the later church.

John's Last Supper describes no meal, only foot washing and feasting on these extensive words of Jesus—including this prayer. Perhaps these "words" prefigure the later Eucharist's preparatory hymn lyrics and prayers invoking "God the Father," just as Jesus' words here point ahead to his bodily, bloody (uniquely John's) glorification in crucifixion. Verbs about sharing resonate. Disciples "received" (Gk. "took") his words (v. 8); Jesus "gave" God's words to them. Then Jesus prays, "I have made your name known." The RSV's "manifested" (*phaneroō*), as in "revealed," better catches the Greek nuance—a face-to-face disclosure of character. The parallel statement in verse 26, "I made known your name," however, does use "know" (*ginōskō*), so frequent throughout the Johannine literature. If Jesus intends to reveal God's name, though, he never says aloud, here or elsewhere, what this "name" is.

The unspoken name, of course, is that unpronounced name of the God of Israel: YHWH. Any name—this enigmatic name especially—is more than labeling. Encapsulating John's whole Gospel here, Jesus' prayer names the essential nature and manifest power of this world's author who so loves it, despite rejection, and asks disciples, also facing rejection, to keep revealing God's glory to the world as they love each other. The prayer's sixfold rhythmic giving of "name," "words," and "disciples" by God and by Jesus, and of followers' receiving "words" and "names" testify to the importance of that Word's being "kept," again suggesting later witnesses preserving Jesus' words, just as past and future followers confess Jesus as the God-given Word.

Biblically, "kept" connotes guarding, protecting, obeying, and observing. Yet what disciple ever received the words/Word and kept them/It? The Greek nuance, "kept and continuing to keep," transcends these Last Supper disciples to include John's latter-day believers. John's Jesus affirms here that he has "knowingly revealed" this unspoken name to the followers God gave to him—those already belonging to God. The lines blur between who possessed what and whom and when and how ("All mine are yours, and yours are

Homiletical Perspective

to conquer the world, a task that John's Gospel attributes directly to Jesus (16:33). The relationships of Jesus to God and Jesus to the world, therefore, are critical to understanding the commissioning character of Jesus' prayer for the disciples here.

As the prayer opens, we learn that Jesus views his earthly ministry as successful, even as he contemplates his passion. Actually, Jesus' success is not the submission of the world, but the glorification of God in his own mission to extend God's care for the world. This glory is not due to a militaristic heroism, but to an unrelenting desire to serve. Preachers would do well to underscore Jesus' unity with God here, to understand the character of his commissioning prayer for the disciples. The work of God in Jesus includes Jesus' teaching and witness to the disciples. In turn, he prays that the disciples embrace his witness as truth (vv. 6–8) and that they now share in his witness. Their commission is rooted in their unity with Jesus and his work. The unity of Jesus and God, therefore, is a defining resource to the disciples—and perhaps our own prayerful sermons.

Surprisingly, this prayer claims that the disciples have been faithful to the witness they have received. The faithfulness of the disciples is a challenging conclusion. On what grounds may we preach their faithfulness? The disciples' failure to live up to their calling is a prominent feature of the Gospel, yet Jesus' prayer underscores the faithfulness of their witness: "and I have been glorified in them" (v. 10). The sermon may anticipate the possible "how" questions of the readers or hearers. Glory comes to Jesus in our care for the world, which participates in the very unity that Jesus shares with God. The world will meet God/Jesus through the disciples' faithful work. As with Jesus' own glorification in his faithfulness to the caring mission of God (v. 4), the prayer calls attention to the faithfulness of the disciples; Jesus is glorified in them as they continue Jesus' mission in the world (v. 10).[1]

If we emphasize in Jesus' prayer that his glory will be manifest in the disciples, one may question if his prayer for the disciples' witness also seeks to vindicate his own mission. Since this passage is placed just before Jesus' passion, concern for vindication does seem fitting. The disciples' faithfulness to the mission of God's care would witness to the unity between Jesus and God. Therefore Jesus' unity with God extends into the disciples' faithful embrace of

---

1. D. G. Van der Merwe, "The Exposition of John 17:6–8: An Exegetical Exercise," *Hervormde Teologiese Studies* 59, no. 1 (2003): 169–70, 175–77.

John 17:6–10

Theological Perspective

the most influential interpreter of John's Gospel for the twentieth century, acknowledges that John's Gospel assumes a dualism between those who are chosen and those who are not, between those bound to the world and those called by Christ, but Bultmann says that what we find in John's Gospel is a "dualism of decision."[1] Every person is confronted by the choice whether or not to accept Christ as God's true ambassador. To accept Christ is to choose the light; to refuse Christ is to choose the darkness. Those who choose the light know that it was not by their own intellect, wisdom, or force of will that they came to Christ; it was sheer gift—though included in the gift was their decision.

The doctrine of election is in part the church's attempt to find words for the experience of Christian believers in the first century—and in the twenty-first as well. Of course we chose to be part of the believing community. Some of us remember the day. Most of us can talk about the process. Nevertheless, of course it is not our choosing that brought us to this community. "'Tis grace that taught our hearts to fear, and grace our fear relieved," and the very moment that we realize that we believe, we realize that it is not our belief that brought us here. John Newton surely knew John's Gospel.[2]

When John's Gospel distinguishes believers from "the world," John is not so much concerned with condemning the material or the ordinary or the mundane. He is distinguishing those who have been graced to believe in grace from those who have not—at least not yet.

The Epistles of John sometimes sound as if the world as such is not worth our attention, and the early Christian gnostics who read John's Gospel were quite clear on that. In John's Gospel, however, even when belief is set most starkly against unbelief, we are required to remember that other topic sentence: "For God so loved the *world* that he gave his only Son."

DAVID L. BARTLETT

Pastoral Perspective

learning something about the great gulf that God must overcome to reach us. Table graces, bedtime prayers, and prayers before meetings may feel perfunctory, yet these habits mold us subtly and gradually. Bumping into the mystery of prayer can help us apprehend the mystery of God.

Second, we are reminded that we do not pray alone. Jesus is right there with us at this scary intersection between the things of heaven and the things of earth. Jesus here exemplifies what Paul promises in Romans 8:26: "the Spirit helps us in our weakness; for we do not know how to pray as we ought, but that very Spirit intercedes with sighs too deep for words."

Third, we are reminded *again* that we do not pray alone. The words "those," "they," and "them" occur approximately a dozen times in these five verses. Always in view is the community of faith, the living body of Christ, the church. Christ's companionship finds us anew in the presence of our brothers and sisters, who journey with us. When we can no longer pray, they will continue. When we are weak, they will impart strength. When we feel far away from God, we may perhaps feel close to one of them.

We need not idealize the church to find hope in these verses. Whether Jesus was speaking about his disciples or the church of the future (our present), we know that neither outfit was perfect. A sectarian reading of this text might (mistakenly) contrast the pure church with the evil world, or the pristine church of the New Testament with the compromised church of today. We know this is not the case. Betrayal, denial, and obtuse confusion are part and parcel of any human community. The first disciples were no more perfect than the later ones. Somehow, though, Jesus has cast his lot with us all.

MICHAEL S. BENNETT

---

1. See the discussion in Rudolf Bultmann, *Theology of the New Testament*, trans. Kendrick Grobel (New York: Scribner's, 1955), 76–77.
2. John Newton, "Amazing Grace" (1772).

Feasting on the Gospels

mine," v. 10a). Words or disciples? Both? Semantically, God's words-given-to-Jesus parallel followers-given-to-Jesus, indicating, again, a later church determinedly "keeping" Jesus' words while being "kept" by Jesus' words from "out of the world," to repeat yet another motif in this chapter and John's Gospel.

"From out of the world" underscores John's testimony that this "world" is lightlessly, lifelessly ignorant. It ironically rejects the Word of life and light (1:4, 9) and hates those followers who received this unnamed name and the words of Jesus and him as God's tangible Word. Indeed, God's once-beloved world hates or, worse, does not want to know this Word, let alone be intimately known by it. John probably relies here on Psalms 22:22 and 9:10 and Isaiah 62:2, all of which speak of proclaiming and receiving a special name within the congregation or at some eschatological hour, as Hebrews 2:12 and Revelation 2:17 and 3:12 echo this "naming." In the religious politics of an apocalyptic day, that name famously marks the faithful in Revelation versus the mark of the beast—Christian against Antichrist in John's light-or-dark worldview. No wonder Jesus demurs "asking on behalf of the world" (v. 9b).

Throughout this Gospel, Jesus revealingly rekindled God's name in a shadowy world proclaiming "I am"—I am "the resurrection and life," "the way, and the truth, and the life" (11:25; 14:6)—re-sounding the original I AM WHO I AM revealed to Moses in a fiery bush (Exod. 3:14). Soon enough, in a dark garden, as soldiers carry torchlights and ask unknowingly for him, Jesus will again answer, "I am" (18:6). Down they fall, flattened seemingly by his words alone, as if by the sword of his mouth (Rev. 1:16). Was that unutterable name penultimately revealed there? John's ambiguous semantic equation indicates that Jesus is as God is together with disciples (and church) keeping alive the potency of this gloried name as Jesus' words. It bespeaks power.

Making "known" this vitality becomes more than sharing information with John's congregants. This prayer is dialogically mystical about giving and receiving Jesus' words and disciples as God's own and as God's Word in Jesus. It is a communing in and communication of glory. In anticipation of and participation in that glory and its naming that shape this prayer, John's church survives through a mysterious, relational force—love—drawing believers out of the world, while framing them within this world with a protective glory as ones specially "kept by" and "keeping" this Word's intercessory name.

RICHARD D. BLAKE

Jesus' witness and mission. Multiple levels of unity are woven together in this portrait of God's care. Preachers should resist the temptation to isolate the various threads of unity for too long. The prayer weaves together these concerns for vindication of Jesus' ministry, intercession for the disciples, and their commissioning.

It seems odd that verse 9 specifies that Jesus is not praying for the world here—the very world for which God cares enough to send him. Yet Jesus continues to pray for the disciples, because they are gifts from God, united to Jesus' own faithfulness (v. 6). God's care for the world, through Jesus, will continue in the disciples' faithful service and witness to the truth of God's care through Christ.[2] The disciples are God's gifts. The words that Jesus passes along to the disciples are God's gifts. The ultimate truth here is that Jesus is God's defining gift, a truth the disciples embrace.

If the church inherits the witness and mission of the disciples, we inherit the unity woven in God's gifts to humanity. Jesus prays for the disciples because God's care extends through unity in Christ and through the church of the disciples as an extension of that gift. Likewise, the ensuing passion of Jesus cannot be separated from his unity with God and God's gift of care for humanity. God's care and gifts are unified in humanity within the grace of Christ's own unity with God and humanity. It would be an easy mistake to preach a vindication that reflects a triumphalism for the sake of God's glory alone. This text does not bifurcate God's glory from God's care for this world. Jesus' glory emanates from his unity with God and God's character to care for humanity. It seems fitting that we struggle to understand whether the church's commission vindicates Christ's unity with God or is vindicated by Christ's glory in God's care for humanity.

DALE P. ANDREWS

---

2. John Riches, Susan Miller, and Karen Wenell, "Worship Resources: Contextual Bible Study Notes for May Lectionary Readings," *The Expository Times* 117, no. 7 (April 2006): 289; Van der Merwe, "Exposition of John 17:6–8," 187.

John 17:11–13

11"And now I am no longer in the world, but they are in the world, and I am coming to you. Holy Father, protect them in your name that you have given me, so that they may be one, as we are one. 12While I was with them, I protected them in your name that you have given me. I guarded them, and not one of them was lost except the one destined to be lost, so that the scripture might be fulfilled. 13But now I am coming to you, and I speak these things in the world so that they may have my joy made complete in themselves."

Theological Perspective

John 17, which is constructed as a prayer to God, is better understood as the climax of Jesus' final instructions to his disciples—his last testament—before he departs and returns to his Father. Through the disciples, Jesus and the evangelist also instruct believing readers of the first century and all the centuries since.

John 17 provides the opportunity for John's Gospel to elaborate on two great themes of John 1:1–18, the prologue. As the poem reflects on the creative and incarnate Word, now the Word made flesh reflects on himself, his own mission, and the mission of the church that follows him.

John 17:11–13 draws first on the theme of the unity of Father and Son at the beginning of the prologue and then on the great affirmation of incarnation in John 1:14: "The Word became flesh and dwelt among us."

The Name. In the preceding theological essay (on 17:6–10) we suggested that the unity between Father and Son consists in part of the words that they share—the message sent from the Father to the Son. In these verses the unity is manifest in the *name* that they share.

In John 1:1 the evangelist makes two claims about the relationship of the Word and the Father:

Pastoral Perspective

An early-twentieth-century sentimental hymn by E. M. Bartlett, "I Heard My Mother Call My Name in Prayer," might have been forgotten, had it not become a country gospel standard in the 1940s and 1950s. That era's rapid pace of industrialization, economic upheaval, and mobility from farm to city made "mother" and "home" solid selling themes in popular music. Add "prayer," and you had a winning combination that can still be heard at bluegrass festivals decades later.

The hymn pictures a mother kneeling by her bed. "She was talking there to Jesus . . . and I heard my mother call my name in prayer."[1] For all of our postmodern sophistication, there is still something profound about hearing someone else pray for us. To be known, to be remembered, to be held up to God by those we love—these are deep human longings. During worship in some churches, the "joys and concerns" time can go on nearly as long as the sermon. While it is moving to experience intercession directly, it can also be powerful to "overhear" someone praying who is unaware that you are listening.

A colleague had a daughter who was going through a very difficult time adjusting to college life and had to come home for some rest and treatment

1. E. M. Bartlett, "I Heard My Mother Call My Name in Prayer" (1923).

Exegetical Perspective

While superficially there seems little new in verses 11–13, intra-Gospel and interbiblical allusions add meaningful layers to John's usual spare vocabulary that may have given his church a better understanding of faith, hope, and communality. Two introductory particles ("and/but now") bind the seemingly disjointed motifs and rhythms in this third section of Jesus' prayer. The Greek negative element behind NRSV's "and [not] now" (v. 11) imprecisely matches verse 13's "but now." The rare vocative "Holy Father" (v. 11) expands the simpler "Father," above twice (vv. 1, 5), and below (vv. 21, 24), but approximates "Righteous Father" (v. 25). So, this short-short-long pattern invokes a liturgical emphasis in verses 11–13, anticipating the prayer's final sections that share these themes with this and earlier stanzas: name, glory, unity, being in or out of the world with its implied evil, and, especially, Jesus' intercession for the disciples. The grammar in this prayer's prior section also implied that John's future faithful church was "still keeping" Jesus' words, just as his original disciples overheard his words at table in verses 11–13. John continues that double audience.

This passage startles with a non sequitur: "I am *no longer in the world*," Jesus prays (v. 11). Then he says, in an archaic form in present tense suggesting repetitive oratory, "I *am speaking* these things *in the*

Homiletical Perspective

In church, we pray to God for all kinds of things: for the world, for family, for work and careers, for health and healing, for spiritual deliverance and for growth, even for finances and the bills that pile high. We pray for church growth and for church ministries, even as we question them. This passage, though, invites preachers to consider other critical questions. How does Jesus pray for his disciples? How might Jesus pray for us? Jesus just might not pray for the things we seek. When we engage this passage, sermons may ponder some of the difficult judgments at stake in how Jesus might pray for us.

The Gospel of John spends a lot of time trying to distinguish the beloved community from those outside. In our own identity politics, we often define ourselves by pointing out who we are and who we are not, to whom we belong and to whom we do not belong, whom we claim and whom we do not claim. John does not escape our shared capacity to establish the good we claim by seeing others in deleterious ways: nonbelievers and believers, those judged and those with eternal life. Like John, we seem to feel best about ourselves by pointing out others astray or askew. This Gospel writer sometimes even calls nonbelievers the children of Satan. For instance, Jesus tells the gathered "Jews" in 8:31–59 that they belong to the devil; and they return the blessing, charging

John 17:11–13

Theological Perspective

"The word was pressed right up against God" and "the word was God's own self" (my trans.). The two phrases hold together the tension between claiming that the Word was so close to God that you could not see any space between them, and the claim that the Word actually was God. That tension has permeated theological thinking to this day, and the clearest claim may also be the oddest one: the Son is to the Father both identical and beside.

The way in which our passage delineates the "identical" and "beside" is to talk about the "name" that belongs to the Father but that the Father has also shared with the Son. Looking to the whole narrative of John's Gospel, we suggest that the name is the phrase that Jesus uses again and again to refer to himself: "I am" (Gk. *egō eimi*). Jesus' continued use of the phrase calls the early readers, probably Jewish Christians, back to God's puzzling self-reference in Exodus 3:14: "God said to Moses, 'I AM WHO I AM.' He said further, 'Thus you shall say to the Israelites, I AM has sent me to you.'" The Hebrew letters in God's self description are YHWH, and when Jesus says to various Israelites that he is himself "I am," he claims God's name for himself. Names have power, and because Jesus can claim God's name, he can protect his people in the power of God. In traditional language, our passage reminds us that Jesus is both Lord and Savior.

Unity. In John's Gospel not only does the life of the Son reflect the life of the Father, but also the life of the church reflects the reciprocal relationship between Father and Son. As Father and Son dwell in community, in unity, so Jesus' prayer for the church is that they may be one, not by their own effort or authority, but by the preserving power of the Holy Name shared by Father and Son.

John Calvin catches the scope of the prayer:

> Christ shows the way that they shall be kept [in the power of God's name]: *that they may be one.* For those whom the heavenly Father has decreed to keep He collects into a holy unity of faith and the Spirit. But because it is not enough for men [*sic*] to agree in general, He adds the phrase, "Even as we are." Our unity will be truly happy when it bears the image of God the Father and of Christ, as the wax takes the form of the seal impressed on it.[1]

It may be that in presenting Jesus' prayer, the Gospel writer was hoping for unity between his

Pastoral Perspective

for depression. He mentioned it in passing at a theological meeting. Three weeks later he got an unexpected phone call from someone who had attended that meeting. An enthusiastic voice asked, "How's your daughter? I have three hundred pastors praying for her." Asking for prayer can be important, but receiving prayer without asking is pure grace.

In this text, we receive the grace of overhearing Jesus in prayer for us. He prays for his disciples because "they are in the world," even as Jesus is being reunited with God. This prayer is a gift for the church, as Jesus sets out three areas of concern. First, he prays that "they may be one, even as we are one" (v. 11). Unity in Christ is a theme that provides great latitude for pastoral exploration. A previous generation saw in this chapter a call to denominational relations and ecumenical cooperation. While a valid reading, Jesus' focus seems to be more on recreating within the church the love that exists between Father and Son. A sense of intimacy is suggested that goes beyond mere institutional cooperation.

In this prayer, we are called to overcome the forces that divide us within congregations: socioeconomic circumstances, race, education levels, even length of membership in the church. Church consultant Anthony B. Robinson has said that members of a vital and growing church seldom introduce themselves at meetings by saying, "My name is John, and I've been a member of First Church for twenty-three years."[2] Let us name what unites us, rather than those things that divide.

In today's divided culture this prayer also gives strength to our efforts to overcome barriers between types of Christians. "Progressives" and "evangelicals" share the prayer of our Lord "that they may be one," yet often we spend our time positioning one another as foils and enemies. Where might there be points of contact? When might pronouncements and disputes be put aside, in favor of simple fellowship and prayer? How might we seek to listen to one another, instead of immediately crafting clever responses to the words of the other? Jesus' prayer invites these questions.

Second, Jesus prays for the disciples'—and our—safety and protection. This petition is intermingled in verses 11–12 with the prayer for unity. This suggests perhaps that internal disunity is one of the greatest threats to the church's flourishing, but external threats are also very real. In a time when many congregations are experiencing membership decline, financial crisis, and cultural dislocation, Jesus offers

---

1. John Calvin, *New Testament Commentaries*, trans. David W. Torrance and Thomas F. Torrance (Grand Rapids: Eerdmans, 1961), 5:142.

2. Anthony Robinson, personal communication.

world" (v. 13), where he also presumes the disciples still are. Yet verse 6 declared them to have already been given to Jesus "from [lit. "out of"] the world." Certainly Jesus' ambiguous transcendence throughout John as "Word made flesh" resists any discord between being and not being in the world. It is both.

Jesus' phrasings pray rhythmically. The "in the world" (or "not") of Jesus and disciples anchors this threefold structure of verses 11–13, along with the repeated "I am coming to you." The central and triple "protect/protected/guarded" motif hinges verse 11 to its doubled emphasis in verse 12. The first petition to "protect them in your name" in the future, with slight alteration, extends Jesus' declaration, "I protected them in your name," in the past, and "I guarded them." ("Name" again echoes the "I am" detailed in verses 6–10.) Finally, these three verses crescendo with "so that" phrases suggesting the intended homiletic thrust of this supplication. Therefore, just as Jesus and God are one, the unity of the first disciples and future church approximates their having Jesus' "joy made complete in themselves." Certainly, this completed joy=oneness spoke fresh hope for John's church as these poetic parallels played out as prayer and preaching.

"Protect" (vv. 11–12) is the same word as "kept" in verse 6. The root meaning denotes guarding prisoners. Jesus' petition inverts the image: "May God safely enclose the faithful against this world's outside evils"—both temptations and persecution. John frequently uses "keep" as the Septuagint's Wisdom literature occasionally does; being wise includes staying ethical (John's *logos*, Word, may well link back to *Sophia*, Wisdom). Wisdom 10:5 once described how Wisdom "*kept* [Abraham] blameless . . . and *preserved* him resolute." Jesus prays with the same word pair "kept/preserved" (*tērein/phylassein*) for his disciples and claims to have "protected/guarded" them. Figuratively "keep" also connotes "obey." In the Septuagint, and occasionally in John, *phylassein* ("guarded") implies "fulfilling" commands by "keeping" scriptural requirements. At least semantically, again with verse 6, Jesus "kept" his disciples just as followers "keep" his words. John understands his later church's protected unity, then, as constituting this "keeping"—especially Jesus' commandment to love one another (13:34–35).

Another peculiarity occurs within the oneness of God-Jesus-disciples, where none are lost "*except* the one destined to be lost" (lit. "the child of lostness," as with the preeschatological figure in 2 Thess. 2:3). The RSV's "perdition," from Latin *perdere*, carries too much unhelpful *Inferno* imagery, as does any

that Jesus has a demon! We often preach such condemnations back and forth with the world.

When we engage texts like this one in John, we risk preaching a dualistic theology—all good or all bad, righteousness or unrighteousness, divine sanction or demonic possession. John builds community by differentiation in these ways; even from the prologue, John builds community by drawing stark contrasts between the children of light and looming darkness.[1] These contrasts should compel concern for community building in our preaching.

The prayer in chapter 17 appears to operate simultaneously as a prayer of vindication, a prayer of intercession, and a prayer for commissioning the disciples. A gospel of vindication would charge that Judas was condemned, never to escape the clutches of the devil. Even in Jesus' prayer taking care of the disciples, he considers the lost one as divinely "destined to be lost" (v. 12). Here is one of the more disturbing theological pieces of Scripture we face. Earlier, this Gospel writer underscores that some who were following Jesus turned away because the message was difficult to bear; more chillingly, John claims that Judas is the devil himself (6:60–71).[2]

One challenge for preaching is to ask whether the Gospel reconciles or resigns Judas to destruction. John's theological judgment is that Judas was "destined to be lost," but how does Jesus consign anyone to destruction? John's Gospel does not report Judas's response, but Matthew's Gospel conceives of his despair and repentance (Matt. 27:3–5). Can our Christology or God's sovereignty be so cavalier as to discard a lost one? Our Jesus leaves the ninety-nine to seek the one lost (Matt. 18:12–13; Luke 15:4–7). Why could not Jesus pray Judas back into the fold?

In Jesus' prayer we learn that the disciples are gifts (vv. 6, 11), as they receive the revelation of Christ. They are not of the world, nor are they like the lost one. Must it be that the community of believers could not stand if the sovereign God did not intend nonbelievers? What does Jesus pray when he prays for the lost, for the nonbeliever, even for one who turns away? What does Jesus pray when he prays for the world?

Are we really defined by what others do not believe? Does the community of believers pray in thanksgiving that at least we are not like "the publican" (cf. Luke 18:11), those people, that race, that

1. David M. Reis, "Jesus' Farewell Discourse, 'Otherness,' and the Construction of a Johannine Identity," *Studies in Religion/Sciences Religieuses* 32/1–2 (2003): 39–43.
2. B. J. Oropeza, "Judas' Death and Final Destiny in the Gospels and Earliest Christian Writings," *Neotestamentica* 44, no. 2 (2010): 353–54.

John 17:11–13

Theological Perspective

church and the other (more Petrine?) churches of his generation. It may be that he was simply praying that people would get along in the congregations of his own faith community. As is often the case with the history of biblical interpretation, new occasions teach new meanings, and the prayer for unity has become a prayer for Christian unity, a kind of appropriate watchword for the ecumenical movement of the twentieth and twenty-first centuries.

Destiny. In John 17:12 it seems likely that "the one destined to be lost" is Judas, though it is not impossible that it is a reference to Satan. What is clear here is that in this passage the claim about (pre)destination is in part a claim about how we read Scripture. If Scripture is the key to God's intentions, and if we find in Scripture the intimations of a future fulfilled in our own time, then the present time is not arbitrary or accidental. It was foretold and therefore foreknown.

Discussions of predestination are sometimes abstracted and confused by our tendency to separate the question of providential fulfillment from the question of scriptural interpretation, which was absolutely integral to its first-century meanings.

Joy. For much of the New Testament, as for much Christian interpretation since, Christian joy is primarily an eschatological category. In this world we live with sorrow and tribulation; in the world to come we shall dwell in the joyful presence of God. For John's Gospel eternal life is not just a category about life beyond death; resurrection is a present reality as well as a hoped-for future. So joy is not only a gift for the end of time; it is an eschatological gift in the midst of time.

Even as he prepares to enter into God's joy beyond the world, and to prepare a place for his followers there, Jesus leaves with them the eschatological, eternal gift of joy. Of course that does not mean that these Christians (or we) are spared suffering and tribulation. It does mean that in the unity of Father and Son and the unity of the church in their strong name, we can live, even now, in joy (v. 13).

DAVID L. BARTLETT

Pastoral Perspective

a promise of protecting presence. A candidate for ordination was once asked how she would reconcile possible church decline with her bright aspirations for ministry. "I don't believe God will let the church die," was her response. Our optimism for the church is not grounded in our own skills or powers, but in Jesus' promise.

Finally, Jesus prays that his followers may have his "joy made complete in themselves" (v. 13b). This third petition can be read as the natural culmination of the other two. If we are able to live in united community, rather than fractious discord, and if we experience the palpable sense of Christ's protection, then we are ready to live joyful lives. One of the strongest indictments of the church today may be its sense of duty-bound drudgery. We are not living as true disciples of Jesus if we are stoically preserving our buildings, grudgingly making our offerings, or dutifully serving on three committees just to fill slots.

This is a place where pastoral leadership and preaching can make a big difference. If life with Jesus means our joy is complete, then—at least occasionally—church should be fun. A friend runs a large and complicated genetics lab. When asked about the most important thing she has learned as she has progressed from being a solo researcher to a team leader, she cites one simple rule that she enforces strictly: "No misery!" What if we playfully and creatively started enforcing this rule in our congregations?

Just as Jesus watched over and formed the disciples during his earthly ministry, he promises to continue protecting and forming the church. Like the earnest, kneeling mother in the old gospel song, Jesus pours out his heart for his people. We benefit not only from the power of that prayer but from the precious opportunity to overhear it. It is a gift the value of which is impossible to overestimate.

MICHAEL S. BENNETT

(pre)destined Calvinism, which is simply not here in the Greek. Yes, Jesus did portend a betrayal (13:18). Clearly, for John, this is Judas as the lost sheep.

The "protect/guard" pairing suggests shepherding, as in the good shepherd of John 10. John's church, however, should not think of Luke's redeemable, singular lost sheep. Instead, John depicts the faithful flock that knows the shepherd's voice and his lying in the sheepfold portal, safeguarding those inside with his very body against outside evils ("the thief and bandit") entering to molest the obedient, kept sheep. If one chose to be lost outside, so be it (apparently). Pointedly, John calls Judas a thief (12:6), and Barabbas, only in John (18:40), is a bandit. Each factored into the double meaning of "laying down one's life" for insiders by this good shepherd and rejected keeper—God's Word.

Which Scripture, then, is "fulfilled" by verse 12? Matthew's mix of Jeremiah, Zechariah, and Deuteronomy, or the Psalm 69:26 allusion in Acts prooftexting Judas? Does "so that" modify, instead, "not one of them was lost," echoing Ezekiel 34:16's better shepherd? If so, then the "exception" phrase may be a later editor's emendation to demonize Judas, with John 13:18 already in hand as written "Scripture"— ironically, Jesus' own quotable words! Either way, his voice throughout this prayer resounds to overhearers and future readers who realize that his "joy is [still] made complete in them."

The tense of "complete" (v. 13) denotes "continuing to be made complete," sharing its root *plēroō* with "fulfill" (v. 12). It imagines as "contents"—literally, a vessel crammed full—scriptural words filled with the Word and disciples fully overjoyed. John's lexical climax suggests an ultimate semantic purpose. "Joy" here (*chara*) echoes God's own grace (*charis*) (1:14–17). Furthering the Baptizer's last words, "rejoic[ing] greatly at the bridegroom's voice" (3:29), Jesus' "joy" crescendos now in farewell speeches that disciples (and church) hear: 14:28, 15:10–11, and 16:16–24, where "none taking away your/my/our joy" parallels overcoming birth pangs by the mother's joy at a new birth. So, past and future disciples who "have pain now" can appreciate Jesus' dual meaning of "going to" God—impending death, while rejoicing in his/their/God's completeness. Such double-sided grace preached to his followers' own suffering in this world with Jesus' protective hope, whenever this prayer's liturgical rhythmic structure and words were "kept," would thus keep the church "in joy."

RICHARD D. BLAKE

color, that gender, that sexuality, those demoniacs? At least we are not like the one "destined to be lost"! Sermons wrestling with this passage from John's Gospel could be grossly misguiding if reduced to verse 12. Jesus does not appear to worry about God's losing face or losing power in the face of adversity or a world that may refuse to trust the gospel message. Nevertheless, the Gospels, including this prayer, suppose a divine design for the betrayal of Jesus by one doomed to destruction, in fulfillment of Scripture (Matt. 26:24; Mark 14:21; Luke 22:22; and John 17).[3]

Is it possible that God's sovereignty is not as fragile as our faith in God? Why do we need to protect God's sovereignty? We certainly cannot blame the Gospel writers alone. We make similar faith claims when life overwhelms us, saying, "You know, everything happens for a reason." Jesus' prayer for vindication and intercession does not displace God's care for the world through Christ. His prayer of protection for the disciples takes joy in them as they seek to serve his witness and mission.

God's care through Christ makes this departing prayer also a commission. Jesus prays for the gift of discipleship, for the emerging community of faith to know who they are and to what they are called. Jesus prays for the disciples as God's gifts to him. Jesus is glorified when we embrace the call to be a gift. A gift is not wrapped up in itself; a gift is wrapped up by the giver, to be opened in the joy of anticipation and embrace. Jesus prays that the disciples may know the joy of unity in Christ (v. 13). The witness of discipleship and the church is not a call to be a beacon on a hill in order for the world to remain in glorious envy of our glow. Jesus does not pray against the world for the risk the world poses to the disciples. Instead, his intercessory prayer actually commissions the disciples to undertake God's care and mission to the world, in unity with Christ, even when the world may not trust it.

DALE P. ANDREWS

3. Ibid., 348–49.

John 17:14–19

¹⁴"I have given them your word, and the world has hated them because they do not belong to the world, just as I do not belong to the world. ¹⁵I am not asking you to take them out of the world, but I ask you to protect them from the evil one. ¹⁶They do not belong to the world, just as I do not belong to the world. ¹⁷Sanctify them in the truth; your word is truth. ¹⁸As you have sent me into the world, so I have sent them into the world. ¹⁹And for their sakes I sanctify myself, so that they also may be sanctified in truth."

Theological Perspective

In the prayer of Jesus that comprises John 17, the evangelist attempts a grand theological framework for—well, for *everything*—by placing four parties in relation to each other: (1) the Father, (2) the Son, (3) believers, and (4) the world. Here in the prayer's middle portion, the focus is on the second and third: that is, on our relation to Christ.

The notion of our similarity with Christ has loomed large for interpreters of this passage. Especially since the fifth century, the great doctrinal question of how to speak simultaneously of Christ's humanity and divinity has occupied the attention of theologians who read these verses.

In those early centuries, interpreters puzzled over the meaning of the word *kathōs* ("just as" or "as"), which appears three times in these verses (vv. 14, 16, 18 and a total of seven times in the prayer as a whole). This term described the relationship between Christ and the disciples; but what is the nature of this relationship? According to John Chrysostom (d. 407), for instance, the saying that the disciples "are not of the world, just as I am not of the world" (v. 14), seemed, on the face of it, a false statement, since Christ's otherness from the world consists in his identity of nature with the Father, whereas in truth there is a great, even infinite difference between that divine nature and our human

Pastoral Perspective

Jesus is praying here for his disciples, whose association with him has put them at risk. In so doing, he frequently refers to "the world." In John's Gospel, this term means one of two things. Negatively, "the world" names the human realm that rejects God, oppresses the weak, and harms God's creation. Positively, "the world" simply names the human community and the created order. Jesus' entire ministry, culminating in the foot washing that has just occurred, witnesses to a truth at odds with the world order, negatively understood.

Jesus declares servant-love to be the reality at the heart of all things, as opposed to any political, economic, or social principle based on domination and exclusion. Simply to agree with Jesus here is itself unacceptable to the powers that be. Yet the risk goes deeper. Jesus says he is sending his disciples into the heart of darkness, just as the Father sent him to them. They are sent, like him, to witness to servant-love. So Jesus prays that they may be protected from harm. Finally, he asks that they be sanctified in truth, that is, that they be set apart by their knowledge of the truth and by the power of the servant-love that Jesus has made known.

In praying for his disciples, Jesus is also praying for the church nascent within them. That means he is praying for us too, who are also being sent into a

Feasting on the Gospels

Exegetical Perspective

John 17:14–19 is a continuation of the second peti-tion (vv. 6–13) of the discourse in John 17 usually called the high-priestly prayer. Many of the same words and themes found in verses 6–13 are found here: the preserving power of the Word (*logos*, vv. 14, 17), tension with the world (*kosmos*, vv. 14, 15, 16, 18), the prayer for protection (v. 15). Still, this lat-ter part of the petition for the disciples does bring new material and emphasizes previous themes in a new way. The prophesied tension between the dis-ciples and the world is intensified (vv. 14–16). The evangelist introduces the theme of sanctification or consecration (*hagiazō*) of both the disciples and Jesus for the task at hand (vv. 18, 19). Although the word "truth" (*alētheia*) is common elsewhere in the Gospel, it now appears for the first time in the high-priestly prayer (vv. 17, 19). Interpreters should use an unabridged concordance to aid in their analysis of particular words in this prayer, which are part of the larger theological tapestry of John. Particularly important is the context provided by the discourses that come after Jesus' foot washing (13:12–16:33).

John 17:14–16 clarifies the disciples' need for this prayer of protection: they have been hated (the aor-ist of *miseō*, "to hate," in v. 14 is here best translated as a perfect tense to show its continuing impact) by the world. The Gospel is very clear that reception

Homiletical Perspective

The desire to simplify the intricate structure of this text is understandable, but oversimplification risks depriving the listener of its depths. For instance, while this part of Jesus' prayer for the apostles has often been distilled into the popular aphorism according to which Christians are "in the world but not of it"—one thinks, for instance, of the image of "resident aliens" proposed by Stanley Hauerwas and William Willimon[1]—we should not expect such for-mulaic prepositional distinctions to do all the work. Not only is such a disposition difficult to maintain; it is impossible without the divine protection and sanc-tification invoked here.

Far more fruitful would be to mine the rich pos-sibilities that arise when one comes to appreciate the text's associative properties. For example, "Sanctify them in the truth; your word is truth" (v. 17) sug-gests that this Word of God, the all-encompassing Christ, is the very locale, the world *within* the world, so to speak, in which the process of sanctification takes place. Further, by this same series of metaphor-ical associations, this microcosm is both the body of Christ and the Word of God, Christ himself, which Jesus says is already in the possession of his disciples.

1. Stanley Hauerwas and William Willimon, *Resident Aliens: A Provocative Christian Assessment of Culture and Ministry for People Who Know That Some-thing Is Wrong* (Nashville: Abingdon Press, 1989).

John 17:14–19

Theological Perspective

nature—indeed an "abysmal difference."[1] So what could the term mean? For Chrysostom, the "just as" must be merely a rhetorical figure, a way of expressing love for the disciples, as though to say that he graciously regarded them as standing with him. So interpreted, it serves to emphasize their very difference from him, since it is only by his grace that any similarity can be spoken of.

John Calvin (d. 1564) shared Chrysostom's horror at any implication that we share Christ's divine nature, but he approached the problem of the "just as" in a different way. Christ, he said, though possessing both a divine and a human nature, is speaking here in neither nature specifically, but rather in his capacity as *mediator,* that is, as the one who, standing between God and humanity, has the functional "office" of bringing salvation to humanity. We as believers, particularly those in ordained ministry, are Christ's "tools" in the exercise of this office, through the proclamation of the Word. Thus the key "just as" statement in this passage, which helps to explain the others, is verse 18: "As you [the Father] have sent me into the world, so I have sent them into the world." Calvin takes this to mean that "he has the same calling in common with the apostles." Our similarity to Christ is therefore a matter not of our *essence* but rather of our *function* (as is suggested by the inanimate metaphor of being "tools"). It consists in what we are called to do in response to God's call.[2]

Calvin's explanation is characteristically clear and sensible. Yet one wonders if it might be too clear. For taken together, the three points of likeness between the believers and Christ—not belonging to the world (vv. 14, 16), being sent into the world (v. 18), and being sanctified (v. 19)—suggest something more than the mere instrumental function of believers. The words convey a sense that we not only do what he wants but actually are like him. How is this the case?

Augustine, in his treatment of this passage, manages to show us a way to talk about our likeness to Christ without losing Chrysostom's sense of our "abysmal difference" from him. Augustine's reading of the passage is an example of a *mimetic* understanding of our relationship to God, whereby, even given that abysmal difference between us and God, there is still a likeness or echo or imitation of God within us, present already in our creation. This likeness becomes known again as Christ uncovers it in

1. John Chrysostom, *Commentary on Saint John the Apostle and Evangelist: Homilies 48–88* (New York: Fathers of the Church, 1960), 388.
2. John Calvin, *Institutes of the Christian Religion*, trans. Ford Lewis Battles (Philadelphia: Westminster Press, 1960), 4.3; Calvin, *The Gospel according to St. John*, vol. 2, trans. T. H. Parker (Grand Rapids: Eerdmans, 1961), 146.

Pastoral Perspective

dangerous world. It is hard at first to understand this. We may have difficulty relating our own situation as Christians to the one Jesus describes. Jesus is praying for a community that is hated by the world (negatively understood) because it does not belong to the world. However, most of us do belong to the world, in one way or another, inasmuch as we profit from or acquiesce in systems that oppress some while lifting others up. Of course, there are Christians around the world who suffer for their faith, but this only increases our anxiety that when Jesus asks that his followers be protected, it is not us he has in mind.

If we have, however, incurred the world's hatred for the sake of Christ, it is still not immediately obvious what Jesus means about sending us into it. We may not belong to the world, but we are clearly already part of it. The only way we can be sent into the world is to go further in. What does that mean, and how do we do it? The key lies in the comparison Jesus makes between *our* being sent and *his* being sent: "As you have sent me into the world, so I have sent them into the world" (v. 18). We know what John means when he says Jesus was sent into the world: "The Word became flesh and lived among us" (1:14).

If we are sent as he was sent, then we are somehow to imitate his incarnation. This seems an odd idea at first, since we are surely already flesh and blood. When the Word became flesh, he did not simply enter into our condition. He embraced our embodiment as something good. In so doing he called the world—particularly the human part of it—back to its true nature as an interconnected whole, since this is what "world" (Gk. *kosmos*) means, and this in turn is what it means to be a body. We imitate Jesus' act by embracing our connection with the world Christ came to save.

This recapitulation of the incarnation is the true work of the church, which it can carry out only in and through the Holy Spirit. As a community of persons committed to more connection, not less, we subvert the fallen world's disordered attempts to escape connection or, worse yet, to exploit it for cruel ends. In so doing, we do not reject the world, but we act as a catalyst within it to restore it to its proper chemistry. In this sense we do belong to the world, but to the world as it has recovered its unity in the Word through whom all things were made.

This charge has profound implications for congregational life. "I have given them your word," says Jesus (v. 14a). This Word is, of course, Jesus himself, whose incarnate life is the energy at work in our midst, healing our own disconnections so that his

Feasting on the Gospels

of eternal life in Jesus Christ puts one at odds with the world. Jesus comes into the world, but the world prefers darkness to the light that he brings (3:17–21). Perhaps the best cross-reference for the hate that the world shows Jesus and his disciples is found in John 15:18–25. Followers of Jesus incur the same wrath from the world that Jesus did (15:18, 19). Those who hate the Father hate the Son (15:23, 24). Ultimately, the world's hatred is inexplicable: "They hated me without a cause" (15:25, echoing Ps. 35:19).

If Jesus' disciples do not belong to the world (vv. 14, 16) and are hated by the world, one might expect his prayer to be sectarian in intent, a request that they be removed from the world. Jesus specifically denies this, though: "I am not asking you to take them out of the world" (v. 15). Instead, Jesus asks the Father to protect his followers from the evil one (v. 15; cf. 17:11; see also similar statements in the Johannine Epistles, 1 John 2:13–14; 5:18–19), a petition very much like that in Matthew's version of the Lord's Prayer (Matt. 6:13).

In the theology of John, the world (*kosmos*) is a paradoxical place. Although it was created by the Word (*logos*, 1:10), and God's love for it is the reason he sent the Son (3:16), "the world" in John is primarily characterized by hostility to God. It has been under the control of "the ruler of this world" (16:11). Even so, Jesus does not pray that his followers be removed from this world; they have a ministry to it. As Jesus has been sent into the world by God, so he is sending his disciples into the world (v. 18). Their witness will have the same divisive effect that Jesus' did. Surely the message of eternal life will convince many that Jesus is God's Son ("so that the world may know that you have sent me," v. 23), but it will also prove that the world has been wrong about Jesus (16:8–11) and is liable for judgment (3:18).

The word that the NRSV translates as "sanctify" (*hagiazō*, vv. 17, 19) is probably better translated here as "consecrate." Jesus is praying that disciples be made holy (see the address "Holy Father" in v. 11) for the task of mission (v. 18), to be set apart for God's work. "Truth" (*alētheia*) is the agent of this consecration (v. 17). John loves the word "truth"; it is perhaps the broadest of the many terms he uses to describe the salvation we have in Christ. The incarnate Word displays God's glory, "full of grace and truth" (1:14). The truth liberates (8:32); it is the essential content of Jesus' message (5:33; 8:45). Jesus is "the way, and the truth, and the life" (14:6). In the parenthetical comment at the end of verse 17, John says that God's word is truth.

This Word is what both sets the disciples apart and operates for the sake of their sanctification.

What is striking about this prayer is not only Jesus' stark presupposition that having his Word and undergoing sanctification entails being hated by the world; it is also that Jesus does not pray for the resolution of the cosmic conflict at all. If anything, his petition appears to heighten the contrast between the disciples and the world, by invoking the protection of the very heavenly Father who is sanctifying the disciples.

True sanctification, of course, is no license for sanctimoniousness, and despite the emphasis often placed on being "set apart," the intent of sanctification is not so much segregation as holiness, holiness that bears with it godly power. Hence, this passage calls more for a willingness to persevere in the face of unresolved hostility than for a misplaced, if well-meaning, rush to peacemaking. Other texts summon the Christian to the hard work of reconciliation among friends, family, neighbors, and enemies, but this is not one of them. This is because the hostility Jesus has in view here is no mere matter for social mediation or political diplomacy in the human sphere; it is, rather, the primal conflict between the holy and the profane, between light and darkness, between God and the evil one, between the seed of the one and the brood of the other.

One can imagine any number of atomistic sermons that might home in on one of (or a combination of) these themes: the givenness of the Word (v. 14a); the hatred with which the world regards disciples of Jesus (v. 14b); the plea for protection from the evil one, which necessitates, of course, the recognition that the evil one actually exists and is bent on harming Jesus' followers (v. 15b); the petition for and the aim of sanctification, the anchoring of sanctification in the truth, and the identification of the Word with the truth (17:17, 19; cf. 14:6); the sending of the disciples "into the world" on the very mission of Christ himself and, strangely enough, from the same point of departure (v. 18)—yes, they and we are heaven sent!

Nevertheless, while we are faced with a number of possible focal points, a sermon that does justice to this text will at minimum recognize two things: (1) the given Word itself testifies to and endures the hostility of the cosmos (a fact that, in deference to John 3:16, we often overlook in our treatment of Johannine texts); (2) this same Word is the very truth in whom and by whom alone our sanctification

John 17:14–19

Theological Perspective

himself. In this sense we not only obey him or function as his instruments but also have a true likeness to him, even in his very divinity.

Thus for Augustine, both in Christ's case and in ours, the state of not being "of the world" (vv. 14, 16) is a function of being "born of the Holy Spirit." That is, the same movement or dynamic at work within God's very self is also at work in us to regenerate us and thus distinguish us from the world. Therefore, without in any way minimizing our distance from him as sinful creatures, the assertion of likeness here is anything but incidental or superficial.

Again, when Jesus in verse 17 asks the Father to sanctify the disciples, Augustine suggests that the disciples are already sanctified in being "not of the world"—that is, they are already confirmed in their likeness to the Father and Son—and this is but an "advancement" or amplification of that likeness, not something new. As Augustine's contemporary Cyril of Alexandria (d. 444) put it, Jesus here shows his desire for what "was in us at the first age of the world, and at the beginning of creation by gift of God, to be quickened anew into life."[3] Our salvation itself is based therefore in a movement of mimesis, which renews in us a divine resemblance that was already there.

JOHN W. COAKLEY

Pastoral Perspective

servant-love can flow freely among us. Therefore, whenever we gather, whether for worship, study, service, or social action, we are engaged in a process of formation, learning how to embrace connection without abusing it.

This is a dangerous discipline, since our life together as a community inevitably tempts us toward exclusivity and competition for power. It would seem spiritually safer for each of us to pursue a separate and private relationship with God than to risk becoming just one more instance of the fallen world. Yet our relationship with Jesus impels us toward one another within the framework of a redeemed worldliness. "I am not asking you to take them out of the world, but I ask you to protect them from the evil one" (v. 15). The "evil one" is the spirit of disembodiment and deceit that resists and rejects the incarnation. Secure in the promise that the Father will not let this evil infect our hearts, we pursue habits of friendship that help us to be more open to the stranger, more apt to forgive our enemies, less fearful of contamination or disempowerment by communities different from ours.

Such friendship cannot develop apart from truth. The moment we forget our individual and collective bias toward disconnection (which usually manifests itself in selective connection), our mutual love becomes collusion to exclude. We are right to think we fall short of the ideal Christian community evoked in this passage. However, as we know, the disciples in the upper room with Jesus fall short of it as well. The truth that sanctifies us and sets us free is the reality of God's love, which we experience both as judgment and release. This is why constant critical self-assessment and a joyful spirit go hand in hand in the Christian life, through him who, although he was already holy, became our holiness by becoming one of us.

THOMAS EDWARD BREIDENTHAL

3. Augustine, *Tractates on the Gospel of John* 55–111, trans. John W. Rettig (Washington, DC: Catholic University of America Press, 1994), 279–82 ; Cyril of Alexandria, *Commentary on John*, vol. 2, trans. T. Randell (London: Walter Smith, 1885), 535.

The Gospel also defines truth in terms of the consecrating power of the Holy Spirit. In the chapters preceding the high-priestly prayer, the Holy Spirit is twice called the "Spirit of truth" (15:26; 16:13), and he is sent by the departing Christ to testify to (15:26, 27; 16:12–15) and against the world (16:7–11). This is precisely the kind of empowerment that John is speaking about in 17:17, 18. Many find it puzzling that Jesus' high-priestly prayer does not mention the Holy Spirit: using "truth" as a veiled reference to the Spirit is entirely in keeping with the theological symbolism found elsewhere in the Gospel.

As part of this prayer of sending for the disciples, Jesus also consecrates himself (v. 19). The phrase "for them" or "for their sakes" (*hyper autōn*) is given an emphatic first position in the sentence. The author clearly wants us to notice that Jesus' consecration for us is part of his sacrifice on our behalf. Notice other places in John where the preposition "for" carries the meaning of offering or sacrifice (11:51; 15:13; cf. 10:17, 18). In the flow of the Johannine narrative, Jesus is making reference to his future sacrifice or glorification as his consecration that in turn consecrates his disciples.

Although exact definition of the setting of the Gospel of John is difficult, this part of Jesus' high-priestly prayer would surely have been a great comfort to those in the Johannine church. They would have applied Jesus' words to themselves as disciples. Jesus prayed for their empowerment in ministry. He understood their tension with the world, but he also gave them the means to persevere in ministry. Ultimately it is Jesus' own sacrifice that models their behavior in the world, and God's truth, whether that be the message of eternal life or the power of the Holy Spirit, sustains them in their missional task.

LYLE D. VANDER BROEK

occurs.[2] Thus sanctification, by definition, amounts to being set apart from the world (17:6) and conformed to Christ.

Whether the sermon aspires to assure those undergoing hot persecution in Africa or cold alienation amid American culture wars, whether it offers counsel to those bullied and harassed for their Christian profession or to whole congregations tempted to retreat from the changing demographics in their neighborhoods, the sermon should send the listeners out to engage in mission (1) with their eyes wide open to the dangers and (2) with their hearts assured of God's ultimate protection. We are to be alert, but not alarmed; awake, but not anxious. What the sermon should not do is to reinforce naive assumptions that the dark powers of the world will readily welcome the Word that has been entrusted to the disciples of Jesus. Nor should it substitute a commodity, an accommodation, a pragmatic solution, or a sociological ideology for Jesus. In short, this text calls for a sermon that reminds the church of Jesus' intercessory role (Rom. 8:34) in praying for his followers, and sends them out "like lambs into the midst of wolves" (Luke 10:3).

Liturgically speaking, this passage invites a prayer that either concludes or directly follows the sermon (as distinct from the usual prayers of the people). As a prayer, the high-priestly prayer is endlessly instructive and begs for frequent use, though with judicious adaptation. Assigned to the Seventh Sunday of Easter of the Revised Common Lectionary, many parts of this prayer invite far broader and more frequent utterance in the church's petitions, perhaps along these lines: "Thank you, Father, for your Word, Jesus Christ the truth, by whom and in whom we are sanctified. Having sent us into the world, as you sent him, protect us from the evil one, and give us perseverance in your mission whenever we face hostility or temptation of any kind."

TIMOTHY MATTHEW SLEMMONS

2. John Calvin, *Institutes of the Christian Religion*, ed. John McNeill, trans. Ford Lewis Battles (Philadelphia: Westminster Press, 1960), 2.5.12.

John 17:20–26

20"I ask not only on behalf of these, but also on behalf of those who will believe in me through their word, 21that they may all be one. As you, Father, are in me and I am in you, may they also be in us, so that the world may believe that you have sent me. 22The glory that you have given me I have given them, so that they may be one, as we are one, 23I in them and you in me, that they may become completely one, so that the world may know that you have sent me and have loved them even as you have loved me. 24Father, I desire that those also, whom you have given me, may be with me where I am, to see my glory, which you have given me because you loved me before the foundation of the world.

25"Righteous Father, the world does not know you, but I know you; and these know that you have sent me. 26I made your name known to them, and I will make it known, so that the love with which you have loved me may be in them, and I in them."

Theological Perspective

Here at the end of his great prayer Jesus speaks of believers, not just his present disciples but "those who will believe in me through their word" (v. 20). Although he projects his thought into the future, there is no suggestion of the movement of time here. He envisions the church as a timeless community of believers, seeing its meaning in terms of its unchanging relation to both God and the world.

With regard to the church's relation to God: this is a mimetic relation. The church mirrors or imitates God. The imitation consists specifically in its oneness, a oneness of a particular sort. It is not oneness in the sense of unanimity of belief (cf. Eph. 4:5), though that is the kind of oneness that would soon come to define the authoritative "catholicity" of the church (Christians came to understand "catholicity" as presented by Irenaeus of Lyons [d. ca. 202], as "one and the same vivifying faith"[1]). Nor is it oneness as opposed to plurality, as though obliterating meaningful distinctions of identity between constituent parties.

Rather, it is a oneness that coexists paradoxically with plurality, as is the case between the Father and the Son, who are one God yet also distinct "persons," as the later tradition came to put it. "I ask . . . that

1. Irenaeus of Lyons, *Against Heresies* 3.2.3, in *Ante-Nicene Fathers* (Grand Rapids: Eerdmans, 1981), 1:416.

Pastoral Perspective

With this passage we come to the conclusion of Jesus' last discourse before his arrest and crucifixion. In it he explicitly includes later generations of Christians in his prayer. We have been included all along, of course, but now, as Jesus introduces the theme of unity, we who have believed through the witness of others are especially mentioned (v. 20: "those who will believe in me through their word"). Probably John had in mind the church of his own day, already threatened by division, but we, who have never experienced an undivided church, can readily apply Jesus' prayer for unity to ourselves.

Jesus' reference to those who have believed the message of others anticipates Jesus' conversation with Thomas: "Blessed are those who have not seen and yet have come to believe" (20:29). The contrast here is between Thomas, who has not trusted the witness of Mary Magdalene and the other apostles, and later followers of Jesus, who depend on that witness. Why are these later followers more blessed than he? Because by believing the gospel based on trust in others, they have experienced Christian community as a vehicle of salvation. Trusting the witness of the apostles is no different from depending on one another for forgiveness, insight, and encouragement. Such dependence is a dimension of saving faith that is often overlooked. Jesus is implying that we, who stand at

Exegetical Perspective

Here we see the third of Jesus' petitions in his farewell prayer, addressing the situation of second-generation believers who believe in Jesus through the word proclaimed by his disciples. Christians in the Johannine church surely believed that Jesus' prayer for the disciples (17:6–19) applied to them and their situation, especially concerning the hostility they felt from the world (17:14, 15). Such application would have been even more obvious in 17:20–26, where Jesus clearly has the future church in mind. It is probably best to see verses 20–24 as the third petition and verses 25–26 as a conclusion to the larger prayer.

The first part of Jesus' prayer for the future church focuses on unity ("that they may all be one," vv. 21–23). As many scholars note, verses 21–23 have a complex and repetitive structure that emphasizes its importance. Notice the six "that" (*hina*) clauses in verses 21–23. Interjected into this series of requests are two "as" (*kathōs*) clauses (vv. 21b, 22c). These verses may be two structurally parallel units, each consisting of a *hina* clause, a *kathōs* clause, and two more *hina* clauses (vv. 21 and 22, 23). The *hina* clauses focus on the content of the petitions, while the *kathōs* clauses show the divine basis for the request.

Jesus' prayer in verse 21 is that the church be "one" (v. 21a) and be "in" (*en*) the Godhead (v. 21c), a relational oneness modeled upon and empowered

Homiletical Perspective

Readers of this passage are often immediately struck by and marvel at the strong pastoral assurance arising from the fact that Jesus prays well beyond the pages of the canon, for numberless generations of Christians to come, including contemporary preachers and listeners who will (or who have) come to believe in him through the testimony of the apostles. Such readers are not wrong to see a reference to themselves here, and there is no reason that preachers should balk at offering this promising assurance to the faithful.

Structurally speaking, what stands out is the remarkable series of causal statements indicating Jesus' reasons for praying as he does, as well as the Father's loving purpose for glorifying Jesus. These reasons present themselves as expository building blocks that could be arranged in a variety of ways. For instance, a sequential treatment would yield a more complex, layered structure, akin to that of the text, but would likely do little to penetrate the density of the textual fabric, while grouping Jesus' rationales together affords the possibility of a simpler organization.

Briefly, Jesus twice prays that his disciples may be one (vv. 21a, 22). He offers two other petitions with the aim "that the world may believe" (v. 21b) or "know" (v. 23) that the Father has sent Jesus.

John 17:20–26

Theological Perspective

they may all be one. As you, Father, are in me and I am in you" (v. 20–21a). Like the oneness of the divine persons, then, the oneness of believers has to do with the relation among them, described as the presence of each believer within each other believer in a divinelike harmony or concord.

To say that believers display harmony does not, however, fully express the sort of mimesis envisioned here. For such harmony could arise simply from believers' obedience to the divine command. To speak of the church imitating God here implies something more than that: the church indeed obeys God, but also is like God in some real way. For what underlies this notion of likeness is the idea of the incarnation. This becomes clear in the relationship between Jesus' words, "that they may be one, as we are one" (v. 22b), and the following parallel phrase, "I in them and you in me" (v. 23a). Here Jesus is saying not only that the Father is to the Son as the believers are to each other but also that the Father is to Son as the Son is to believers. The Son, in other words, has a material, and not simply analogous, relation to believers. He is "in" them, for, after all, he has "become flesh" (1:14). The analogy is thus more than an analogy, being rooted not in mere similarity, but somehow in a true presence.

That implied presence of Christ in believers suggests an ambiguity in the relation of Christ to the church. For if Christ is truly "in" the church and not simply reflected or imitated by the church, and if Christ is divine, then this can imply that the church is itself in some sense divine. Some interpreters have been concerned to guard against any such implication. John Calvin, for instance (with his characteristic care to keep Christ's humanity distinct from his divinity), says "we are one with Christ not because he transfuses His [divine] substance into us, but because by the power of His Spirit He communicates to us His life and all the blessings He has received from the Father." In other words, Christ conveys *benefits* to us, but language suggesting that we might share his "substance" is but a figure of speech.

Yet even Calvin's brilliant rationalizing does not quite dispel the ambiguity, or paradox, of the incarnation. The caution of Cyril of Alexandria (d. 444) in his commentary on these verses bears remembering, that the text is not "constructing the reality from the shadow"[2] (i.e., is not evoking a sense of the truth through figures of speech that are mere metaphors

Pastoral Perspective

several removes from the apostles, have the opportunity to receive their witness by way of one another, and so to grow in our faith, not only in God, but in the church as an anticipation of God's reign.

This dimension of faith helps us see what Jesus means by unity. Unity is a relationship of mutual dependence and trust, such that our primary access to God is by way of one another. This does not mean that we cannot have private encounters with God. We can and do have such encounters. As a long line of Christian mystics reminds us, though, these experiences are only to be trusted if they drive us back into community. It is our capacity for community that is the glory God has given us.

How might this approach to Christian unity shape our ongoing but often faltering efforts to overcome our many divisions? The ecumenical movement has never been about shortcuts to unity, but about painstaking identification of areas where there is actual agreement, combined with a steady exploration of ways in which legitimate disagreements can be sustained within the framework of a larger fellowship. We have perhaps been too focused on agreement as a measure of oneness. If the gospel comes to us circuitously through the witness of others, then the bonds formed between those who give testimony and those who receive it constitute the basic fabric of our life together as Christians.

Agreement in matters of theology, ethics, and polity is important, but it cannot be our first concern. Our first concern must be to make ourselves available to as broad and diverse a spectrum of believers as possible, so as to maximize our exposure to a multitude of witnesses. One might even say that disagreement goes hand in hand with Christian unity. On the one hand, it is the inevitable byproduct of our engagement with many points of view. On the other, when we refuse to let it divide us, disagreement can be the catalyst for a deeper, shared engagement with Christ.

Although they may be suspicious of the church, young people who love Jesus care deeply about the unity Jesus is praying for. Whether or not they self-identify as Christian, they understand that the possibility of unity with God, with the earth, and with one another is the fundamental question facing humankind as this new century progresses. Unity cannot be imposed; that leads to totalitarianism. However, if, as John's Gospel presupposes from beginning to end, a unity grounded in mutual love lies at the heart of all reality, then our own well-being depends on our availability to one another as brothers and sisters

---

2. John Calvin, *The Gospel according to St. John*, vol. 2, trans. T. H. Parker (Grand Rapids: Eerdmans, 1961), 148; Cyril of Alexandria, *Commentary on John*, vol. 2, trans. T. Randell (London: Walter Smith, 1885), 547.

by the unity between the Father and the Son (they are "in" [*en*] one another, v. 21b). It is possible that the final *hina* clause in this unit (v. 21c), "that the world may believe that you have sent me," is not a further petition but the consequence of a unified church. The second of the parallel paragraphs (vv. 22, 23) is almost a carbon copy. Jesus prays that the church be one or "completely one" (vv. 22b, 23b) based upon the oneness of Father and Son (v. 22c) and the fact that Jesus is "in" (*en*) believers and the Father is "in" (*en*) him (v. 23a). As in the first paragraph, the final *hina* clause (v. 23c) appears to describe the effect such unity will have: "so that the world may know that you have sent me."

As much as any other passage in the Gospel, verses 21–23 illustrate the theological and literary demands put upon the interpreter of John. This dense unit raises a host of questions, many of which can be answered only with reference to the larger narrative. What exactly would the oneness of the church be? Is Jesus praying for theological unity (recognition that he is God's Son and that eternal life comes only in him) or for communal unity (suggested, perhaps, by Jesus' desire that the church be "completely one," v. 23)? Is this prayer for unity an indication that the Johannine church was divided? What does it mean to be "in" God? Can it be equated with "abiding" (*menō*), as in the vine/branches metaphor (15:1–11), or is it simply shorthand for "love" (15:26)? How does the unification of the church convict the world of the fact that Jesus was sent by God (vv. 21c, 23c)? Does this desired result, the world's recognition that Jesus is God's Son, represent a hope for the world's conversion, or would it simply be further proof that it wrongly rejected Jesus (see v. 25; 15:8–11)?

Despite the questions raised by this petition, it is clear that Jesus seeks the unity of the church, and that the basis for this unity is the relationship between the Father and the Son. They are "one" (vv. 21, 22), and they are "in" each other (vv. 21, 23). Jesus has the glory of God (vv. 22, 24), has been sent with God's mission (vv. 21, 23), and is loved by God (vv. 23, 24). As much as any other paragraph in John, this petition is the basis upon which future Trinitarian definitions will be made. Only Matthew among the Gospels rivals John in terms of explicit reference to the future church (although the word *ekklēsia* is not used in John; see Matt. 16:18; 18:15–20; cf. John 20:22, 23). The church has its foundation in the words, activity, and relationships of Jesus!

The second part of Jesus' prayer for the future church comes in verse 24. Here Jesus "wills" or

Lastly, he asserts that the love (and, by inference, the glory) he has received from the Father has been and will continue to be his reason and purpose for revealing the name of God to his disciples (vv. 24, 26). This love (v. 26) and glory (v. 22) are to reside in the disciples, along with Christ himself, even as the disciples are to dwell within the Father and the Son (vv. 21, 23).

Several things are at stake here, all of which are reiterated in some fashion and thus acquire gravity by virtue of repetition: the unity of the church through the ages; the mutual indwelling between believers and the Lord Jesus, and between the Son and the Father; the shared love and glory that characterize what is elsewhere termed becoming "participants in the divine nature" (2 Pet. 1:4); and lastly, the evangelistic mission of the church itself as a witness in the world—a witness, that is, to Jesus' divine origins. The implication is that, when the world sees a truly united church, united not just in name but also in spirit, they will recognize the Son of God present in the world through those who belong to him.

While the unity of the church and its resultant testimony in the world are clearly linked in the text and are understandably the focus of many sermons on this text, one should not overlook Jesus' desire that his disciples might share eternal fellowship with him and see his glory (v. 24). This petition presents a wonderful, pregnant opportunity for doing justice to the doctrine of justice itself, that is, for recalibrating our understanding of justice—so often buffeted by the political, ideological, humanistic, ethical, and sociocultural winds—recalibrating it according to its essentially theological standard in Christ himself and the cross that awaits him (18:1–19:42).

As few other texts make clear (e.g., Isa. 53:8 makes the point negatively: "by a perversion of justice he was taken away"), true justice, that is, specifically theological and christological justice, begins with or, rather, is the worship, the adoration of the glory of Jesus Christ, the reversal of his rejection by the world and his humiliation on the cross, and the vindication of the name of the heavenly Father. Although justice itself is not mentioned as such, this petition represents the only time God is addressed as "*righteous* Father" (*pater dikaie*, v. 25). It is clear that the rectification Jesus asks of the Father is that the glory of the Son, hidden from the world that does not know God and that has rejected Jesus, may be revealed to those who do know that he is from God (v. 24). In short, all our political machinations gussied up as justice are a sham, if justice does not

John 17:20–26

Theological Perspective

taken from human experience). For it is not the human experience of harmony that creates the image of the divine Christ and places it within us. Rather, the reverse is true: the presence of the divine Christ within us creates our harmony.

Finally, with regard to the church's relation to the world, the passage describes the church's evangelistic work. Jesus says that people will become believers "through their [the apostles'] word" (v. 20), that is, only through encountering the gospel through the witness of the apostles who are present with Jesus as he is offering his prayer. In this sense the church is founded on the apostles. Augustine even noted that some believers (Joseph of Arimathea, for example, and the Virgin Mary) were not among the apostles at that moment and so were not included in the prayer, implying that even some who had become Jesus' followers "had not yet believed in him in such a way as he wanted himself to be believed in"[3] until they had heard the "word" of the apostles—a remarkable assertion of the apostles' importance in constituting the church.

Although the apostles' "word" is essential for belief, when Jesus imagines how people will come to such belief, he speaks not of the hearing of that word, but rather of the example of the apostles' oneness. Each of his two statements of desire for the believers to be "one" is followed by a result clause: "so that the world may believe [or know] that you have sent me" (vv. 21b, 23b). The spectacle of believers' oneness will itself bring others into their company. Evangelism, like the church itself, has mimesis at its heart.

JOHN W. COAKLEY

Pastoral Perspective

who cannot find life in isolation. If the love of the Father for the Son and of the Son for the Father is the cornerstone of the universe, then our love for one another in our various congregations and communities should be the flashpoint for passionate ecumenism.

For individual congregations, such ecumenism means a concerted effort to develop partnerships with nearby communities of faith—partnerships that actually bring congregants from different traditions into significant contact with one another. We need more opportunities for shared study, prayer, testimony, and reflection across congregational and denominational borders. There is no telling what such cross-pollination will produce. We may fear losing our denominational identity in the process—or worse yet, our claim on the truth.

As Jesus brings his prayer to a close, he addresses this fear: "Father, I desire that those also, whom you have given me, may be with me where I am, to see my glory" (v. 24). This statement contrasts with Jesus' statement earlier in the evening: "Where I am going you cannot come" (13:33). What Jesus means there is enigmatic, but at the very least he seems to say the disciples cannot follow him in the way of the cross or join him in his return to the Father.

Now he appears to be saying something different. He wants them and us to be with him all the way to the cross and beyond. What accounts for this shift? Perhaps it is simply the difference between a statement of fact ("where I am going you cannot come") and a wish ("I want those you have given me to be with me where I am"). The shift is probably more about the sea change that can occur when we dare to risk everything ecumenically. Such risk-taking is the necessary condition for being where Jesus is. When we cross that line, we join Jesus in his rejection of separation, and in so doing draw close to him in his death and in his resurrection.

THOMAS EDWARD BREIDENTHAL

---

3. Augustine, *Tractates on the Gospel of John 55–111*, trans. John W. Rettig (Washington, DC: Catholic University of America Press, 1994), 285.

Exegetical Perspective

"desires" (as opposed to "asking," vv. 9, 20) that his followers experience his postresurrection glory. "Glory" can mean various things in John. Jesus reflects God's glory in his earthly ministry and in his crucifixion (17:4, 5). Jesus imparts his glory to his disciples in their present life in this world (v. 22). Here Jesus appears to refer to a future glory. Although his disciples will not be removed from the world (17:15) and its trials, Jesus affirms that at some point they will be with him in his glory (v. 24b). Jesus does not leave the disciples without an advocate in this life: the Holy Spirit will empower them to testify (15:27) and discern the truth (16:7–11). They will experience the fullness of glory with Christ after this life: dwelling places are being prepared for them (14:1–7). Then they will know fully the God whom Jesus has revealed and be unified with the triune God in love (vv. 24b, 26b).

The last two verses in the high-priestly prayer are best seen as a conclusion to the entire prayer. God is addressed as "righteous Father" to a sinful world that does not know him (v. 25). Jesus again affirms those who recognize that he has been sent by God (17:3, 18, 21, 23), and he reemphasizes that he has revealed God's name (17:6, 11) and loves his disciples (vv. 23, 24). This farewell prayer of Jesus (chap. 17) would have been treasured by the Johannine church, as it has been by later generations of believers, because it defines the ministry of Jesus on their behalf (17:1–5), affirms Jesus' concern for his disciples in a hostile world (17:6–19), and shows his desire for a unified church (17:20–24), all spoken in the context of his loving relationship with the Father.

LYLE D. VANDER BROEK

Homiletical Perspective

first derive from and "do justice to" God, giving the Father and the Son the glory that is their due.

Thus, Jesus' petition to the righteous Father seeks the ultimate vindication: vindication of the Father's holiness and judgment of human sin; vindication of the Father's reputation as just and righteous; vindication of the Son's glory, in contrast to which his merciful condescension (Phil. 2:5–8) is made clear; and vindication of God's mercy, in that an intimate fellowship and an indwelling with human beings that was not previously possible is henceforth to be seen among the disciples. Jesus, of course, is asking for his original glory to be displayed not in blinding celestial light shows but, rather, in an earthly fellowship of mutual love and mercy that stands in stark contrast to a world that would crucify anyone, but especially the Son of God.

At the heart of this text, and of any sermon that would do justice to it, is the very dialectic between adoration and missional witness that so often finds itself short-circuited, either for pragmatic concerns or with the result that mission is unduly forestalled. Although one hesitates to say it in the face of so much enthusiasm for the missional church, any asymmetry in this tension, any predominance (at least insofar as it is informed by this text) must accrue in favor of adoration, since the knowledge and the belief that Jesus prays will dawn upon the dark and disbelieving world will arise by virtue of the love and the glory of his disciples' dwelling in God.

Adoration, communion, and love will have their evangelical effect. Such a glory, such a unity—one that abides and endures quite despite all the superficial, if controversial and even painful, evidence to the contrary—is divinely bound to be noticed by the world, and it is more than possible. Indeed, it is a providential certainty that this end will be better served by the prayer of Jesus to the Father of rectification, and by the church joining Jesus in that prayer, than by the church insisting to the world that it must be so.

TIMOTHY MATTHEW SLEMMONS

John 18:1–11

¹After Jesus had spoken these words, he went out with his disciples across the Kidron valley to a place where there was a garden, which he and his disciples entered. ²Now Judas, who betrayed him, also knew the place, because Jesus often met there with his disciples. ³So Judas brought a detachment of soldiers together with police from the chief priests and the Pharisees, and they came there with lanterns and torches and weapons. ⁴Then Jesus, knowing all that was to happen to him, came forward and asked them, "Whom are you looking for?" ⁵They answered, "Jesus of Nazareth." Jesus replied, "I am he." Judas, who betrayed him, was standing with them. ⁶When Jesus said to them, "I am he," they stepped back and fell to the ground. ⁷Again he asked them, "Whom are you looking for?" And they said, "Jesus of Nazareth." ⁸Jesus answered, "I told you that I am he. So if you are looking for me, let these men go." ⁹This was to fulfill the word that he had spoken, "I did not lose a single one of those whom you gave me." ¹⁰Then Simon Peter, who had a sword, drew it, struck the high priest's slave, and cut off his right ear. The slave's name was Malchus. ¹¹Jesus said to Peter, "Put your sword back into its sheath. Am I not to drink the cup the Father has given me?"

Theological Perspective

This passage of Scripture is the opening stanza in a narrative that builds to a confrontation between Jesus and the high priest of Israel. In this section, however, the narrative describes the encounter between Jesus and his betrayer, Judas. While at a literary level this passage is full of dramatic tension, a closer look can unlock one of the major theological insights of the text. Behind and beneath the action of the text, the reader is confronted with the meaning of revelation. This passage and the two that follow it draw the reader into a consideration of what it means to know Jesus.

The setting of the scene is a garden. Jesus and his disciples are in a garden, a garden associated with knowledge. The text is specific in mentioning that Judas knows the place. This scene draws the reader back, symbolically, to the garden of Eden, in which the action takes place regarding the tree of knowledge. In this instance, the garden is the locus of both knowledge and mystery, of the known and the unknown. Judas approaches, along with a detachment of soldiers and representatives of the religious establishment. They are carrying torches, lanterns, and weapons. These details suggest that a violent encounter with Jesus is anticipated. The forcible apprehension of Jesus has been carefully planned.

In his encounter with Judas and those who come to seize him, however, Jesus is the principal actor;

Pastoral Perspective

When Cowboy Stadium was built in Arlington, Texas, no expense was spared. It was designed to be state-of-the-art, maximizing the viewing experience (with the world's then largest television screen) while also maximizing capacity. This is why specific sections were built without seats. Yes, there are people who will pay money to stand, sometimes twenty to thirty people deep, to watch a football game in a confining gated space. When seeing these landings with people packed in like sardines, I was in awe that someone would want to experience a professional football game slammed against others, with beverages and food being spilled everywhere, with no relief in sight for almost three hours. If you happened onto a posh spot toward the front of the landing and you had to go to the bathroom or get another beverage, you inevitably lost your spot and returned to the back of the section. I, however, was thinking all of this from my comfortable seat at midfield when my father explained: "They are fans. They just want to be at the game. The view is not always what matters; sometimes it is the experience they want. They are willing to stand for their team."

There are several stands taken in this text from John. Judas takes the first stand. It is one of opposition. He has broken away from the twelve disciples and betrayed Jesus. He preys upon Jesus'

Feasting on the Gospels

Exegetical Perspective

The passage describes Jesus' arrest, shortly after his last meal with his disciples. The Johannine version of this scene differs in a number of ways from that of Mark. Most striking is Jesus' serenity and composure. Like the good shepherd, he will voluntarily sacrifice his life for his sheep (10:11–15, 18). Obedient to the great command of love, he is about to lay down his life for his friends (15:13).

The action takes place in a garden, though John does not give its name (it is Gethsemane in Mark 14:32 and Matt. 26:36). There is no agony in John's account (cf. Mark 14:32–42; Matt. 26:36–46; Luke 22:40–46). The closest the Johannine Jesus comes to worrying about his death is in 12:27, but the slight wobble quickly passes, as Jesus is immediately reassured by the voice of God in 12:28. Throughout the entirety of the passion narrative (chaps. 18–19), Jesus faces his approaching death with courage and divine majesty. It is no surprise, then, that here at his arrest Jesus takes the initiative and identifies himself to Judas and his companions.

We last saw Judas in chapter 13, slipping out into the night, shortly after Jesus announced that one of his closest disciples would betray him (13:21–30). Now he returns with two groups of people. One is the temple police, supplied by the Jewish chief priests and Pharisees. We are familiar with this group from

Homiletical Perspective

The scenes of this chapter surface questions that complicate the drama in the passion of our Lord. Each character heightens the tensions that punctuate the story of redemption. Close observation reveals how the lines assigned to Judas, Peter, and Jesus illuminate their characters and the action of the story.

Look first, if you will, at Judas, who defies easy description and comprehension. We are introduced to him in the scene before us as leading a detachment of troops and officers sent from the chief priests and Pharisees. The contingent comes with lanterns, torches, and weapons (v. 3). We see him elsewhere as the treasurer for the disciples, the one who keeps the money bag (13:29). It is clear from this scene that he knows where Jesus is. Indeed, nothing about this scene is hidden from public view. What is Judas's aim? What are his program and purpose?

The commonly held view is that he is greedy—that he sells his Lord for money—or that Satan enters his heart. Some interpreters would make the matter more complicated. The question can be asked whether he is a Zealot who believes that Jesus is the Messiah. If so, it would be reasonable to assume that if Jesus were forced to fight, God would come to his rescue; so his betrayal would force a showdown. Even though it contributes to

John 18:1–11

Theological Perspective

that is, Jesus goes out to them, rather than allowing them to come to him. Jesus is the interlocutor; he asks them who it is that they seek, rather than being interrogated by his captors. Jesus is actor rather than victim. This encounter provides the Christian reader with a significant insight into the meaning of revelation. As theologian Karl Barth often pointed out, divine revelation consists of God seeking us, God confronting us, God inquiring of us, rather than the reverse. In this passage Jesus is portrayed as the knower rather than the one who is known.

Verses 4–8 constitute the heart of this passage. Here Jesus, knowing all that is going to happen to him, asks his captors whom they are looking for. This phrase suggests that the seeking, confronting, and inquiring that constitutes divine revelation takes place in the context of the omniscience of God. To Jesus' question they reply, "Jesus of Nazareth." When Jesus confirms that he is the one they seek, they draw back and fall to the ground. This reaction to Jesus' self-revelation constitutes the central theological insight. We are not told precisely why they fall back. On this we are left to conjecture. This reaction does suggest that the confrontation is surprising and shocking. Jesus' self-identification is the revelation of the unfamiliar. He is not what they are expecting. This revelation of the unfamiliar is also at the heart of the Christian understanding of the incarnation. The Divine has taken on a form so common and human that we are knocked off balance.

The third insight into the meaning of revelation in this passage is that there is a definitive demarcation between God's action in the process of revelation and our response to that revelation. Verses 8–11 conclude this particular scene, and here the action involves the disciples, specifically Peter. Jesus tells his captors that if they are looking for him, they must let the disciples go. At this point, Jesus' revelation of himself marks the divergence of the work of atonement and the work of discipleship. This is the end of discipleship as the work of accompanying and observing the ministry of Jesus. The new mandate will not become visible to the disciples until Pentecost.

Peter's striking of the servant of the high priest is a tacit and inarticulate protest against the end of discipleship that has been disclosed by Jesus' self-revelation as atonement for the sins of the world. It is here that Jesus' self-revelation elicits an act of spontaneous violence. Throughout Jesus' ministry, his self-revelation has often elicited anger, condemnation, and acts of hostility. In cutting off the ear of

Pastoral Perspective

predictability and meets Jesus and the disciples in the garden. They are looking for a place of peace, rest, prayer, and solace. Judas meets them there with betrayal, accusation, evil, and death instead. Judas brings a collusion of temple and state to arrest Jesus, as if one of the two were not enough. He stands among Roman soldiers and police from the chief priests and the Pharisees. He stands among Jews and Gentiles. He stands in the dark and peaceful garden with lanterns, torches, and weapons looking for the Light of the world, the Prince of Peace. Judas stands for all that Jesus sought to free him from, and he stands in darkness with an army.

It would make sense then, that it would be Jesus' turn in the story to take his stand, to stand against evil and darkness and pronounce his power over Judas and the temple-state army before him. He makes his stand, though, with gentleness, peace, and truth, much as he has with Judas in their previous times together. If Judas knows Jesus so well as to be able to predict his location, should he not then be able to predict Jesus' response? Why then the army and weapons? Judas's stand is one of fear and cowardice. He mistakenly believes he needs numbers and might to accomplish his task.

Jesus takes his stand in confidence and self-awareness. He knows who he is and, most importantly, he knows whose he is. His confidence does not mean he wants or desires that which is to come, but he has accepted what the Father has put into motion and will "drink the cup" that is before him. Jesus takes a stand and takes control of what seems to be chaos in the dark and light, temple and state, peace and weapons, good and evil. Jesus steps out of the darkness and initiates his own arrest. Jesus' confidence in his own identity is so shockingly powerful and unfamiliar to those gathered that his words are literally earthshaking. With his words, "I am he," they fall to the ground.

The stands in the text are clear. Judas stands in opposition to Jesus. He chooses betrayal and money over loyalty and faith. The soldiers, police, and Pharisees stand in fidelity to the religious and political leaders giving the orders; thus they stand in fear and duty. Peter stands in faithfulness, yet it is a warped faithfulness, tinged with violence as he strikes the high priest's slave, cutting off his ear. Peter's stand is one that remains in question, as he will soon deny Jesus, as foretold by Jesus himself. Here, though, at least, he makes an effort to be loyal to his leader.

Finally, Jesus' stand is the one that is the most significant and the most shocking. This is the account of

Feasting on the Gospels

the Synoptic Gospels, but the insertion of the Pharisees here is strange. In the Synoptics, Jesus debates with the Pharisees throughout his ministry, but the arrest and execution is the work of the chief priests alone. Historically, there is much to recommend the Synoptic account; the Pharisees enjoyed debating problems of Jewish law, often quite vociferously, but there is no reason to think that they wanted Jesus executed. It was the Jewish priestly leaders who feared Roman reprisals if Jesus and his movement continued unchecked.

John's insertion of the Pharisees (both here and at 11:46–47) is probably a reflection of the troubled contemporary context of the evangelist. Writing in the late first century, when the Pharisees had emerged as the undisputed leaders of the Jewish faith, and at a time when relations between church and synagogue were difficult, it would be natural for John to insert his contemporary opponents, symbolized by the Pharisees, into the heart of his narrative.

A second group at the arrest is worthy of note. In John's presentation, Judas is also accompanied by Roman soldiers. All have come out with "lanterns and torches and weapons" (v. 3b). Clearly they mean business and are prepared for resistance. The word translated "detachment" in verse 3 is *speira*, a word that literally means "a body of two hundred men"; and the word used of their leader in verse 12, a *chiliarchos*, means "a tribune." Even if John is using these terms in a rather loose and imprecise manner, the scene he presents is of a relatively large-scale operation, already involving the prefect's auxiliary troops. It is not impossible, on a historical level, that Pilate did lend some aid to the arresting party. More probably, however, John's theological interests have led to the introduction of the Roman troops. The scene makes it clear that no one was able to arrest Jesus; it was only because he voluntarily gave himself over to his captors that they were able to seize him. John's insertion of Roman troops makes this all the more dramatic and foreshadows a theme that will occur again later in the trial narratives: that all the powers of Jesus' day—both Jewish and Roman—were unable to act against him.

The exchange between Jesus and the arresting party is highly dramatic. Twice Jesus asks them whom they seek, and when they reply, "Jesus of Nazareth," he identifies himself three times with "I am he" (twice in direct speech, and once in an authorial report). The phrase "I am he" is a translation of the Greek *egō eimi*, "I am." This is probably to be understood as one of this Gospel's famous "I am" sayings.

unfolding the will of the Father, there is no praise to be offered for Judas's deed.

Second, there is Peter; his behavior is equally complex and confusing. He has a sword. The Fourth Evangelist does not tell us where he got it, nor does he address the question of what he was doing with it, or why Jesus permitted him to keep it. Is this an isolated event? Do the disciples carry swords on other occasions?

What is clear is that Peter gets it wrong. He thinks he can fight his way out of this situation. Even though he follows Jesus, he thinks he knows the best way the mission should unfold. His position is that everything can be accomplished by the weapon you carry.

Seeing how Jesus is situated between Judas and Peter makes the message of the Messiah ever clearer. First, he goes to a garden and publicly enters it. When the troops come seeking him, he does not run or hide. Indeed, he goes to them and asks whom they are seeking. Jesus is not hiding; neither is he scared. Rather, what one sees in him is boldness about his mission. One can argue that he is far more confident than Peter, who is willing to fight.

He asks, "For whom are you looking?" When they say, "Jesus," he answers, "I am he." They fall back because of the power that is within him. He is taken only by his own consent. Those who come for him have no power except what he gives to them.

Peter takes the sword and cuts off the ear of the high priest's servant, but Jesus commands him to put away the sword (v. 11). He makes his mission utterly clear when he asks the question, "Am I not to drink the cup that the Father has given me?" (v. 11). The Lord Jesus has made peace with his mission. He has submitted to the Father's will.

Oh, the ways in which we can forsake the Father's will by chasing alternatives. In ever so many situations, the fulfillment of the mission, symbolized by the cup, offends us. Rejecting it, however, amounts to disobedience or to fashioning another mission.

One decision to be made for preaching this text is how much consideration to give to the fact that Galilee was a hotbed for revolution. There was general resentment of Roman occupation among the Jews. Deep resentment persisted for historic wrongs, for deportation under the Babylonians, domination by the Persians, and invasion by the Greeks. Hostility reached fever pitch with Roman occupation. Galileans were notorious for their noncooperation. Hints and traces are all over the Gospels, and the passion narrative in particular. It is to be noted that neither Barabbas, who was preferred over Jesus, nor the two thieves

John 18:1–11

Theological Perspective

the servant Malchus, Peter symbolizes his refusal "to hear" the words of Jesus, marking the end of their journey with them. Jesus instructs Peter to sheath his sword and then asks him rhetorically if Jesus could refuse to "drink the cup" that the Father has given him. Peter is portrayed as aware of, but unable to put into words, his fear and trepidation.

Here Malchus is not just an observer. The inclusion of his name has significance for our theme of revelation. The name Malchus means "counselor" or "king." It has majestic connotations. It is possible that Peter sees in this servant Malchus what he cannot see in Jesus. It is possible that Malchus sees in Jesus something that confirms his worth before God in spite of his lowly status. These are all potent possibilities. The text, like God's revelation, does not give us all of the answers.

In his encounter with his captors, there is no mention of Jesus' teachings. At this moment, Jesus' self-revelation is not to be found in doctrinal statements or creedal confessions. H. Richard Niebuhr, speaking of the revelatory moment, notes that "concepts and doctrines derived from the unique historical moment are important but less illuminating than the occasion itself. For what is revealed is not so much the mode of divine behavior as the divine self."[1] The reader is left to ponder these questions. What does it mean to experience the revelation of God? What are we to make of the fact that God often chooses to reveal Godself in surprising and unexpected ways? What is it about the revelation of God to a sinful world that elicits both spontaneous and planned violence? Indeed, the function of revelation is not to answer all of our human questions, but to fire our imaginations, to increase our desire to know more, and to show us what we have been unable to see.

JAMES H. EVANS JR.

Pastoral Perspective

his arrest, and he initiates it. The soldiers are looking for *him*, and yet *he* questions *them*. Their task is to arrest him, and he sets the parameters of his arrest, allowing for his disciples to go free. Peter takes his stand of violence, and even then Jesus maintains control. At every step of the drama unfolding in the garden, and even in the scenes to follow, Jesus stands confident, composed, and in control. Again, although this does not mean he wants what will happen or desires any of it, he has come to terms with the cup set before him, and he stands ready to drink the cup the Father has given him.

What is the cup set before your church? Your family? Your community? Are you clear in your sense of who you are and whose you are, such that it gives you a firm foundation upon which to stand when you are questioned? Are you brave enough to step out from the darkness and initiate that which needs to happen, in order to follow through with the plans God has for you and your future? Jesus' act of stepping out of the darkness goes against human instinct. Typically, when we are hunted, we hide. Jesus' divinity shines forth, though, teaching us more about how God's love can transform our hearts and our actions when we surrender to the cup God sets before each of us. What is the cup set before you? Are you willing to take a stand for it?

VICTORIA ATKINSON WHITE

---

1. H. Richard Niebuhr, *The Meaning of Revelation* (orig. 1941; Louisville, KY: Westminster John Knox Press, 2006), 68.

Exegetical Perspective

Often the phrase is used with a predicate (e.g., "I am the bread of life," 6:48), but sometimes, as here, the phrase can be used on its own (as in 6:20 and 8:58). The phrase calls to mind the name of God in Exodus 3:14, and also the characteristic manner of God's speech in Second Isaiah (a document with many echoes in John's Gospel).

The reaction of the onlookers suggests that Jesus' words are to be regarded as nothing less than a divine self-disclosure. Faced with Jesus, the arresting party have no power and fall to the ground. Jesus' threefold "I am" also contrasts with Peter's three-fold "I am not" later on (18:17, 25 and implicitly in 18:27). Jesus' words will save his disciples, even at the expense of his own life (v. 8); Peter, however, will save his own life at the expense of his loyalty to Jesus. The theme of preserving his "own" is an important one in John, and the evangelist describes the fulfillment of Jesus' earlier words (6:39 and 17:12) as if they were part of the Jewish Scriptures.

Finally, John recounts the story of the high priest's slave's ear (vv. 10–11). The story is also found in the Synoptic Gospels, where it appears to be less developed. In Mark's Gospel, it is an unnamed bystander who severs the ear (Mark 14:47); in Matthew it is one of Jesus' followers, though he is unnamed and is admonished by Jesus (Matt. 26:51–53); in Luke it is again one of Jesus' followers, but Jesus immediately heals the man's ear (Luke 22:50–51). John specifies that the disciple was Peter, gives the slave's name as Malchus, and also adds that it was his right ear. Within its immediate context, the incident allows Jesus to upbraid Peter and to express his readiness to "drink the cup" that his Father has given him, that is, to go to his death. Later on, this scene will be recalled when the third of Peter's questioners in the high priest's courtyard will be a relation of Malchus—a note that adds an extra urgency and danger to Peter's position (18:26).

HELEN K. BOND

Homiletical Perspective

between whom Jesus was crucified were mere common ordinary thieves. They were from a long line of rebels who reached back to the days of the Maccabees, and stretched forward to the Bar Kokhba rebellion.

Some strands can be found even in the Gospel traditions. The Lukan account has Jesus acknowledging two swords among his disciples (Luke 22:38). Following the resurrection and preaching of the early church, there is a scene before the Sanhedrin where explicit reference is made to Theudas and Judas, who were rebels from that region (Acts 5:36, 37).

The preacher will have to decide which of these matters to explore in the sermon and which will help the listener make sense of her or his own situation. What, the preacher might wonder, would be the value of probing these issues in detail? Which ones will help the purpose and movement of the sermon?

Building a homiletical thought from weighty passages like this one requires careful preparation. Key to building a compelling sermon from a text like this is that, when all is said and done, you want more than your own opinion; you want to listen to the text itself. Another key is present in the intimacy shown between the Son and the Father, and the utter insistence of Jesus that he is not acting on his own. This interdependence, so utterly crucial to the integrity of God's mission in the world, is promised to the followers of Jesus through the Paraclete, the Holy Spirit (chaps. 14–16).

The scene before us depicts options that are inconsistent with God's will. It will be helpful for the preacher to ponder with the congregation how the Spirit brings to remembrance the teaching of Jesus and the way of the Messiah in difficult moments where the will of God is not clear and must be discerned.

W. C. TURNER

John 18:12–18

¹²So the soldiers, their officer, and the Jewish police arrested Jesus and bound him. ¹³First they took him to Annas, who was the father-in-law of Caiaphas, the high priest that year. ¹⁴Caiaphas was the one who had advised the Jews* that it was better to have one person die for the people.

¹⁵Simon Peter and another disciple followed Jesus. Since that disciple was known to the high priest, he went with Jesus into the courtyard of the high priest, ¹⁶but Peter was standing outside at the gate. So the other disciple, who was known to the high priest, went out, spoke to the woman who guarded the gate, and brought Peter in. ¹⁷The woman said to Peter, "You are not also one of this man's disciples, are you?" He said, "I am not." ¹⁸Now the slaves and the police had made a charcoal fire because it was cold, and they were standing around it and warming themselves. Peter also was standing with them and warming himself.

Theological Perspective

This passage of Scripture is the second of three stanzas in a narrative that begins with the arrest of Jesus in the garden and builds to a confrontation between Jesus and the high priest of Israel. In the first section the issue is of the self-revelation of Jesus as the one who will redeem the world. In this section Jesus has already been arrested, and Peter has vented his frustration by striking the servant of the high priest and cutting off his ear. The significance of Jesus' impending sacrifice is already being recast by the religious leadership of the day as a matter of political expediency (v. 14). Because Jesus has informed Peter that he cannot take the path that Jesus is to take, the meaning of discipleship or following Jesus is radically changed.

It is in this light that we must understand the description of Peter in this passage as one who is following Jesus. It is not the act of following undertaken by the disciples for the past three years, a following centered on a communally held vision of the inbreaking of a new social and religious order. The act of following described here is broken, confused, tentative, and steeped in failure. Peter's act of following Jesus here is driven by a futility brought on by the image of a powerless Jesus, rather than the

* See "'The Jews' in the Fourth Gospel" on pp. xi–xiv.

Pastoral Perspective

Peter gets a bad rap in this text. There is no way around it. His epic failure, embarrassingly foretold by Jesus himself in 13:38, comes to pass and is retold by preachers and dissected by commentators for years to come. Peter is sometimes most often known for failure, namely, his denial of Jesus.

If timing is everything, Peter's denial of Jesus comes with the worst possible timing. In the previous verses Peter tried to show his loyalty to Jesus with an act of violence against the high priest's slave, and Jesus told him to stand down. This was Jesus' cup to drink. Peter mustered up all of his strength and confidence against an army of men with weapons, when he and Jesus were surrounded by only a handful of disciples. The odds were against him, but he still tried. Peter wanted to prove his fidelity to Jesus. He wanted to exert his pride in being a follower of Jesus. He did what he thought was good and noble, but Jesus rejected his act of violence. Peter failed.

Following Peter's ear-slicing incident in the garden, Jesus is arrested and put on trial. At this point, most of the other disciples have fled in fear. Jesus is left with two disciples and the army dispatched to detain him. The odds are not in Jesus' favor. This is the time when Jesus needs his friends the most, yet he is virtually alone. It is here that Peter's most

Exegetical Perspective

The passage continues the story of Jesus' arrest, describing events later that same night. Verse 12 simply rounds out the previous story, noting that the Roman soldiers and their officer, along with the Jewish temple police, bound Jesus and brought him first to the residence of Annas, the former high priest. With the exception of Peter's first denial, subsequent events in this passage, specifically the introduction at this point of Annas and the disciple "known to the high priest," have no Synoptic parallel.

John shows more interest in the high priesthood than any other evangelist. Caiaphas was already introduced in 11:49–50, where he advised the assembled council that Jesus must "die for the people." The ironic truth of his words was attributed to his high-priestly gift of prophecy (11:51–52). The reader is reminded of the earlier passage here in verse 14, where Caiaphas's advice/prophecy is repeated. In both passages, Caiaphas is said to have been high priest "that year" (v. 13b). Since the high priesthood was not an annual office (Caiaphas himself held the post for roughly nineteen years), the phrase probably means "that fateful year."

The new character here is Annas, who is introduced as Caiaphas's father-in-law. We know a certain amount about Annas from the Jewish historian Josephus. When Judea became a Roman province in 6

Homiletical Perspective

A detachment of troops is assigned to Judas to make the arrest of Jesus. They bind him. They assert their power. One can only imagine what they think when they fall back in his presence. Surely they know what might have been the case, had Jesus asserted the power that is in him, for the sake of preventing their deed.

The tensions within this scene increase by the moment. When Jesus is arrested, he is carried first to the house of Annas, the father-in-law of Caiaphas, who was the high priest that year. No explanation is given for why he is carried to Annas's house and not directly to the house of the high priest. We are told only that Caiaphas the high priest is the one who said concerning Jesus, after he raised Lazarus from the dead, that "it is better for you to have one man die for the people than to have the whole nation destroyed" (11:50), and the Fourth Evangelist labels Caiaphas's words prophecy (11:51).

Peter follows the detachment, and so does another disciple. He is not named, but we are led to conclude it is the Beloved Disciple. The details are vivid: Peter is standing outside the door at Annas's house. The other disciple, who is known to the high priest, asks for permission for Peter to enter. When this is granted, the servant girl asks Peter whether he

John 18:12–18

Theological Perspective

optimism inspired by the image of Jesus as miracle worker at Cana.

Nevertheless, Peter must follow Jesus, even at this moment. The arrest of Jesus in the garden reveals not only the true mission of Jesus but also something significant about Peter. Theologian H. Richard Niebuhr describes the significance of such a revelatory moment: "Revelation is like a classic drama which, through the events of one day and place, makes intelligible the course of a family history."[1] The arrest of Jesus on that one day in that one place redefines Peter's own inner history. At that moment, it becomes clear that he is not who he thinks he is. He has thought of himself as close to Jesus, but now he follows from a distance.

There is a second dimension to this text that must be addressed. In this passage a second character is introduced, described as "the other disciple." This other disciple is also described in Johannine scholarship as "the Beloved Disciple" or "the one whom Jesus loved." This other disciple is mentioned five times in the Gospel of John but is not mentioned in any of the other Gospels. While the issue is still debated among scholars, one school of thought is that "the other disciple" is the author of the Gospel of John. What is of interest for us here is that this other disciple is introduced as a contrasting persona to that of Peter. Our text states that this other disciple is known to the high priest and thus is allowed to enter into the courtyard of the high priest.

The theological point is that this other disciple is able to follow Jesus more closely than Peter. Peter has to wait outside until the other disciple returns and facilitates his entry into the courtyard. Peter, who is described in the other Gospels as Jesus' chief lieutenant, is here marginalized. Peter, who is described elsewhere in the New Testament as an insider, is here revealed to be an outsider. It is precisely this alienation, this status as outsider, that is revealed about Peter in the garden. Here we are reminded that divine revelation is always in some sense revelation of our sin and failures. Again Niebuhr observes that "the revelation which illuminates our sin prophesies our death, the death of the self and that of the community."[2] Jesus' self-revelation in the garden is also the painful revelation of the end of Peter's prior understanding of himself, as well as the end of the entire movement that Jesus led. While Peter's image in the subsequent tradition of the church is rescued,

1. H. Richard Niebuhr, *The Meaning of Revelation* (New York: The Macmillan Co., 1941), 94.
2. Ibid., 95.

Pastoral Perspective

memorable failure comes to light. Jesus is on trial for his life, and Peter denies their friendship the first of three times.

One should note, however, that Peter is the only disciple who is even given the opportunity to deny his relationship to Jesus. The others have fled in fear; they are nowhere to be found. At least Peter has stayed by Jesus' side up until this point. He has walked with Jesus and the army of soldiers. He has approached the looming gates standing between Jesus and the trial of a lifetime. Peter is there when no one else is. Peter may have failed, but at least he has shown up, at least he has tried.

It is ironic that verses 15–18, which tell the story of Peter's denial of Christ, are sandwiched in between the ongoing story of Christ's trials. It almost reads as an interruption—or does it? The Gospel writer John is recording the passion of Christ, the story of life triumphing over death, good conquering evil, and love outlasting hate. John is recording the story of God's eternal and overwhelming love for humanity, such that God would sacrifice God's own Son. God's interruptions in our paths of free will are what enable life to triumph over death and love to conquer hate. God's interruptions bear witness to God's love for us. The same is true with this interruption in the text.

In the middle of Jesus' trial stories is Peter's denial of his Lord. In the middle of what seems to be chaos and evil is the story of what could be read as Peter's demise. The good news, though, is that neither story ends here. The trial continues, and Jesus proceeds to "drink the cup" given to him by his Father (v. 11). We also know that eventually Peter becomes the one upon whom Christ builds his church. What seems to be Peter failing his Lord at the most inopportune moment is therefore only an interlude alluding to the message to come: in the end, good wins, love wins, life wins. Peter fails, yes, in this passage; but thanks be to God that God does not judge us on one, or even three, particular failures. God looks at the entire picture of our lives, not just the interruptions or failures of our faith and actions.

Certainly Peter is known as the father of the church, the rock upon whom the church was built (Matt. 16:18). What most often comes to mind at the mention of his name, though, is his denial of Christ. Is not the same true for each of us? Politicians are often remembered for their shortcomings, rather than the people they helped and the programs they initiated. Celebrities are even applauded and tracked for their dramatic antics, rather than upheld for their

Exegetical Perspective

CE, Rome took over the power of Herod I to appoint a high priest. Their first appointment was Annas (or Ananus I, as Josephus calls him). Although Annas held office for only nine years, he was clearly the head of an influential high-priestly dynasty. Not only did he act as high priest himself, but so too did five of his sons (Josephus, *Antiquities* 20.198). In the first phase of Roman occupation of Judea (6–41 CE), virtually all of the high priests were from this family (and the incumbencies of the two who were not were brief). The note that Annas was related by marriage to Caiaphas is attested only in John's Gospel, but it may well reflect historical fact. (Caiaphas himself seems to have come from an unknown priestly family, and his rise to eminence would make good sense if he had married into the foremost family of his day.[1]) The suggestion that Annas was involved in Jesus' death is similarly found only in John's Gospel, though again it would be quite natural on a historical level for Caiaphas to consult with his father-in-law, particularly if the latter had formerly occupied the high-priestly office.

Peter's entry into the high priest's courtyard is considerably expanded by John. While the other evangelists seem to imagine an open area into which people are free to enter at will, John portrays an enclosed courtyard with entry only through a gate watched by a female porter (similar perhaps to Rhoda in Acts 12:13). Peter does not follow Jesus alone in this Gospel (as in the Synoptics) but is accompanied by a disciple "known to the high priest." In fact, it is this other disciple who speaks to the gatekeeper and gets Peter into the courtyard. Who is this disciple? Is he simply an unknown Judean disciple brought into the narrative solely to help Peter gain entry? Is he more significant? A number of suggestions have been made by scholars. One possibility is that he was Judas. This would explain why he is known to the high priest, why he escapes questioning, and why the maid asks Peter if he is "also" a disciple.

More commonly, however, he is thought to be the Beloved Disciple. This is a character unique to John's Gospel, an idealized disciple (perhaps based on John, the son of Zebedee) who often appears in scenes with Peter, where he is portrayed in a slightly better light than Peter. This identification is not without its difficulties, though. The word for "known" here, *gnōstos*, suggests a level of friendship between

1. For further information regarding Caiaphas, see Helen K. Bond, *Caiaphas: Friend of Rome and Judge of Jesus?* (Louisville, KY: Westminster John Knox Press, 2004).

Homiletical Perspective

is one of Jesus' followers. In verse 17 we see the first denial.

How ironic that Peter denies that he was with Jesus. He is the one who drew the sword and showed willingness to fight. We see again this emphatic position taken by the Fourth Evangelist—namely, that there is no viable alternative to the Father's will. One cannot invent a greater service than what has been given. Put another way, such intervention would be inconsistent with what was spoken in the teaching concerning the good shepherd and the sheepfold: to come in any other way than Jesus' cross is to be a thief or a robber (10:1).

What is at stake here is obedience with integrity. Obedience is prescribed; it is ordained. Any alternative to the way of suffering is tainted with the works of Satan. The very taproot of temptation is to find another way, to avoid suffering. Such notions have their origin with the deceiver.

Peter, falling for the deception that there is an alternative to suffering, second-guesses Jesus, a leader who will not stand up and fight for himself. Fighting is the way Peter knows. Perhaps we see in Peter disgust over the form Jesus' obedience takes— namely, suffering, rather than standing up like a man and fighting back. "I was ready for the bold deed," Peter thinks, "but you would not release me to help you. I am from Galilee, and I know how it is done in that region."

The great temptation for the church has often been to defer to the powers of the magistrate, to find a path to obedience that makes more sense, that requires less suffering, that demands less cost, or that protects dignity in terms the world understands. What the evangelist exposes in these scenes are the many forms denial can take, and the serious consequences of the false options that are around us.

The scene shows Peter standing by the fire, by the coals. He is keeping warm. He has an opportunity to get back on track, to get it right. The servants and officers are by the fire as well. The servant girl presses him, but in the pressing, what is yielded is a second denial of Jesus. As Peter plunges deeper into anguish, his only hope is in the one he has denied.

What are some ever-present seductions that might lead to denial of Jesus? How might the preacher address them? First, dig into the anatomy of denial. One could say Peter is on trial here before the servant girl. Presumably, she is poised to make some decision about Jesus herself. How might one be similarly situated? There is a tendency in many circles of piety to cordon off matters of faith by circumscribing

Theological Perspective

redeemed, and rehabilitated, there is no question that in this text Peter comes face to face, in a sense, with his own demise.

The demise of the image of Peter as the chief disciple is confirmed by his denial of his status as a disciple of Christ. The servant girl in the text asks Peter if he is one of the disciples of Jesus. Peter replies that he is not. This simple exchange, which is repeated later in the Gospel of John, confirms Peter's identity as an outsider. While the tradition has Peter denying being a follower of Jesus three times, the point has been made in the first instance. Peter now sees himself as no longer a follower of Jesus.

Many sermons make a point of describing this denial as an act of infidelity to Jesus, a willful rejection of the Savior of the world, a rejection that is rectified only when the risen Christ asks Peter three times if he loves him (chap. 21). It is also possible to see Peter's response as the recognition of an important fact about himself. Because discipleship, as he has known it, has ended, he is no longer a disciple of Jesus.

Even in the bleakness of his situation, though, the work of revelation has not ceased for Peter. The scene closes with Peter warming himself by the fire with the servants and officials of the religious establishment, unaware of what is transpiring in the inner sanctum of the high priest's house. There may be something that is sustaining Peter at this moment, however. Perhaps "it is the possibility of the resurrection of a new and other self, of a new community, a reborn remnant."[3] It is this faint glimmer of the possible that prepares Peter to become the key guardian of the collective memory of a resurrected Christ.

JAMES H. EVANS JR.

Pastoral Perspective

God-given talents. At school reunions old faces and names are remembered for the mischief or trouble they caused, rather than the good they did or how smart or kind they were. The bad tends to stick with the mind longer than the good. To God, however, the opposite is true.

God sees our redeeming qualities and focuses on our efforts and potential. Peter showed up when Jesus needed him. He showed courage by staying with Jesus when all the others abandoned him. It was only through this courage that Peter had the opportunity to deny Christ. Yes, it was wrong and cowardly, but it was not so wrong that God wrote Peter off. This story's placement bears witness to God's continuous work in the world, even when it seems as if it is the worst moment in time.

What is it you are known for? What is your church known for? What is your community known for? Is it good or bad? Is it what you want, or do you want to change it? Undoubtedly Peter rolls over in his grave every time the story of his denial is recounted, because he did so many other good things for the world and for his Savior, yet he is remembered for this one thing. The Gospel writer John inserts this story in the middle of Jesus' trial to remind us of God's continuing work in this world, even through someone like Peter. How then is God working through you to redeem your failures into something amazing?

VICTORIA ATKINSON WHITE

3. Ibid., 96.

the unnamed disciple and the high priest that seems unlikely in the case of the Beloved Disciple. Furthermore, it is hardly a fair contest; the unnamed disciple is not questioned by the maid at all, and his loyalty is not put to the test. If, despite these difficulties, Peter's companion here *is* the Beloved Disciple, presumably the evangelist's point is that both disciples followed Jesus into the courtyard; while Peter denied Jesus, the Beloved Disciple did not, continuing to "follow" him as far as the cross (19:26–27).

Peter's entrance into the courtyard leads naturally onto the first of his denials. As in Mark's Gospel, the three denials frame Jesus' interrogation in front of the high priest (Mark 14:54, 66–72), and John will conclude the story in 18:25–27. There is a dramatic contrast here between Jesus, who at that very moment is being questioned by the high priest, a man of high status, power, and authority, and Peter, who is questioned by a serving maid, a lowly doorkeeper. Jesus maintains his sovereign demeanor, while Peter quickly crumbles. The maid's question here expects the answer "no" (it uses the little Greek word *mē*), and Peter easily conspires with her doubts: "I am not."

Verse 18 concludes this short scene by describing the setting in more detail, depicting the slaves and temple police warming themselves by the charcoal fire. For the moment the suspense is lightened, and Peter appears to have got away with his lie. The reader soon realizes, however, that this is merely the beginning of Peter's descent into complete denial. While Jesus' "I am" in the garden exposes him to danger and saves the lives of his friends, Peter's "I am not" sets him apart from his Master, a distance that will begin to be healed only in chapter 20, and even more thoroughly in 21:15–19 (a narrative that once again takes place by a charcoal fire, 21:9).

HELEN K. BOND

them to interior regions of private morality. Hazard some questions in your sermon: How is Jesus confessed or denied in our public spaces? What are some of the ethical and policy decisions made by Christian professionals? Consider decisions doctors make in the treatment of patients who are indigent, or who they know have little likelihood of recovery. What are some of the consequences for lawyers who know the guilt or innocence of their clients? What of bankers who have power to adjust rates, make foreclosures, and so on? What of youthful decisions in the face of bullying, or to maintain anonymity for perverse behaviors in cyberspace? How might such occasions for making decisions be narrated as a moment of trial for a Christian?

Are there examples—historical or from current events—that reveal clear opportunities to confess or deny faith? Imagine scenes in which one could have spoken, but retreated to the safe zone of comments like, "Nobody asked me; it was none of my business; it was someone else's responsibility." How does such retreat amount to denial?

Confront the hearer with the forfeited opportunities to say, "Yes, I am one of his . . . ," and face the consequences. What is the great proclamation of this text? Perhaps when all is said and done, there is no solace in the face of denial. Rather, good news comes in confessing Christ. Can Peter count on Jesus to come to him and sustain him regardless of his failures, or in the midst of his own suffering? It will not be until the end of John's Gospel, beside another charcoal fire, that Peter will learn the answer to that question (chap. 21).

W. C. TURNER

John 18:19–24

¹⁹Then the high priest questioned Jesus about his disciples and about his teaching. ²⁰Jesus answered, "I have spoken openly to the world; I have always taught in synagogues and in the temple, where all the Jews* come together. I have said nothing in secret. ²¹Why do you ask me? Ask those who heard what I said to them; they know what I said." ²²When he had said this, one of the police standing nearby struck Jesus on the face, saying, "Is that how you answer the high priest?" ²³Jesus answered, "If I have spoken wrongly, testify to the wrong. But if I have spoken rightly, why do you strike me?" ²⁴Then Annas sent him bound to Caiaphas the high priest.

Theological Perspective

This passage is the third stanza in a narrative of Jesus' arrest. In each stanza the progressive meaning of Jesus' self-revelation is further developed. When he is arrested in the garden, Jesus becomes the interlocutor, questioning those who have come to seize him. In the second stanza, Peter is questioned about Jesus, and the implications of Jesus' self-revelation for Peter are profound. In this brief third stanza, Jesus is interrogated by the high priest. It is important to note that while Jesus is questioned by the high priest, this questioning is not just a verbal struggle between two antagonists. It is a rhetorical performance in which two notions of revelation are locked in battle: revelation as the radical gift of God to everyone and revelation as the special possession of the few.

In the opening verses of this passage Jesus replies to the questioning by the high priest. His response indicates a revelation that is subversive and revolutionary. In verse 20, Jesus declares, "I have spoken openly to the world." This response emphasizes the Johannine notion of the world, as over against the provincialism of the ruling religious elite. It also echoes the prologue to John and its understanding of the cosmological significance of Christ's appearance.

* See "'The Jews' in the Fourth Gospel" on pp. xi–xiv.

Pastoral Perspective

What is your island? An organization was met with a crisis that was about to go public. The news was not good, and the potential for misinformation and rumors was high. Their reputation was at stake. The public relations director addressed the staff with a simple message. "Stay on your island," she said. She gave the staff a brief statement of the most pertinent information and instructed them to answer any questions with only the information in the statement. "If you stay on this island of information and do not go swimming for other answers, we will be fine." Her advice was sound and put the anxious staff at ease. When the story broke in the news, the message to the public was clear, concise, and consistent from everyone. They stayed on their island, and their reputation was spared.

In today's text, Annas the high priest's reputation precedes him. Few people despise Jesus as much as Annas does. One can imagine that Annas has been keeping a tally of the ways Jesus has disrupted his world, cost him money, and confronted his family's power in both the political and religious sectors. The high priest is salivating with revenge, having plotted Jesus' capture and death with his son-in-law Caiaphas. As Jesus stands before him, the odds are not in Jesus' favor. Every word that comes from Jesus' mouth could incriminate him. Annas is trying to

Exegetical Perspective

This passage describes Jesus' Jewish trial in John's Gospel. The passage is strikingly different from what we have in Mark: there is no formal gathering of a council ("Sanhedrin" is the word used in the Synoptic Gospels), no assembled chief priests, scribes, and elders, no witnesses, no charges, no accusation, and no verdict. Instead, Jesus is taken first to Annas, who questions him briefly regarding his disciples and his teaching, and is then led to Caiaphas. No account of any proceedings before Caiaphas is given (the narrative space is devoted instead to the second and third of Peter's denials, 18:25–27).

At first sight, it appears strange that a Gospel as notoriously antagonistic toward "the Jews" as John's should contain such a brief Jewish trial. Part of the reason for the evangelist's restraint here may be the fact that the Gospel presents most of Jesus' ministry as a trial in front of largely hostile Jewish opponents. Throughout the first twelve chapters, a variety of characters is brought on as witnesses, and Jesus continually debates his identity and mission with "the Jews." Moreover, many of the elements associated with the trial scene in Mark's Gospel have already appeared in John's narrative: the temple-destruction-and-reconstruction charge (2:19–22), Jesus' identity as Christ and Son of God, and the charge of blasphemy (10:24–39), Jesus' vision of the open heavens

Homiletical Perspective

What comes to the forefront in this passage is the contest between the high priest and Jesus. It is a matter of authority. Annas arrogates to himself the authority to quiz Jesus about his identity. Jesus speaks with boldness to say, "I have been public; I have nothing to hide; I have cut no corners." Rather than submitting to the priest's authority by answering his question, Jesus invites the priest to "ask those who heard what I said to them; they know what I said" (v. 21).

Take another look at this interaction. Do you see what happens to Annas's authority? It just is not there. Annas fears that the people have followed Jesus and esteem him as a prophet. We see this in verse 20. In verse 21 we see the testiness of Jesus; he stands his ground. In contrast to Annas, Jesus' confidence is clear. The Fourth Evangelist proceeds with subtle moves, but there can be no question that we see the test of authority when we view verse 22. The officer slaps Jesus with the palm of his hand. This is an act of insult; he feels that his superior has been insulted, and so he acts to put Jesus in his place. He is defending the priest. The question here is: Who is on trial? Who has the legitimate authority to pronounce judgment?

It is only after this scene that Jesus is sent to Caiaphas. All that has taken place has been not before the

John 18:19–24

Theological Perspective

Jesus continues in verse 20: "I always taught in synagogues and in the temple, where all the Jews come together. I have said nothing in secret." Jesus' response also emphasizes his ministry to the truly devout and his embrace of the deep traditions of popular Jewish piety, as over against the secretive and ritualistic religious practices of the ruling religious elite.

In verse 21 Jesus asks, "Why question me? Ask those who heard me. Surely they know what I said" (NIV). The asking and answering of this question emphasize the empowerment of the hearers of the word. They not only hear; they know. Revelation has come to them. Here revelation is clearly manifested as subversive speech. Not only does it undermine the barriers to true piety supported by the religious elite; it also undermines the social structures that have reinforced religious oppression. The undermining of the moorings of both religious and social oppression becomes clear in the next section of the narrative.

Verse 22 reads, "When Jesus said this, one of the officials nearby slapped him in the face. 'Is this the way you answer the high priest?' he demanded" (NIV). Here, as in the encounter in the garden, we note that Jesus' reply evokes a violent response. At this point it is clear that Jesus has, in the minds of the religious elite, and especially their representatives, engaged in subversive speech. It is possible that this official, whose anonymity is a testament to his lack of status within the ruling structures, has been struck by the testimony of Jesus.

Thus his assault of Jesus is, in reality, a response to being struck by the words of Jesus. Perhaps the words of Jesus revealed in him something that had long been hidden. Like Malchus in the first stanza of this narrative, the official is more than a minor character. He is an important part of the substructure of this narrative. Unlike Malchus, he is unnamed. Unlike Malchus, he is the perpetrator, not the recipient, of violence. This unnamed official has internalized the oppressive consciousness of the ruling religious elite to the extent that his own identity has been submerged. The subversive speech of Jesus addresses the official's inner struggle and calls forth his submerged identity.

At this point, it is clear that the action in this passage is now centered on Jesus and this unnamed official. This is crucial to understanding the response of Jesus in verse 23: "If I said something wrong, . . . testify as to what is wrong. But if I spoke the truth, why did you strike me?" (NIV). Jesus' reply is not to the high priest, but to this unnamed official. The

Pastoral Perspective

distract Jesus from his island as a means of bringing all of this to a swift and dramatic end.

Annas expects this to be quick and easy. According to Jewish tradition, Annas and his family controlled the markets outside the temple. Thus, when Jesus drove the money changers and the animal traders out of the temple (2:13–22), Annas took a big hit to the pocketbook during the busiest time of the year, Passover. This is his time for revenge. He wants to be rid of Jesus and his disciples.

Annas begins with questions about Jesus' disciples and what he is teaching. Jesus' answer is calm, thoughtful, honest, and controlled. Jesus stays on his island. He has been open, in public spaces, keeping nothing in secret. He has nothing to hide. He is even so bold as to invite Annas to call witnesses to his testimony. Jesus has been consistent in his message from the beginning. His teachings are about loving God and loving neighbor (Matt. 22:36–40). All of his sermons and parables have been a variation of the Great Commandment, as have his miracles and daily living. Jesus has no hidden agenda. He stays on his island.

On the contrary, the core of Annas's island is revealed, and it has changed. As high priest, his energy should focus on seeking the heart of God. He is a man of great power and responsibility, with significant duties within the temple. He should be drawing the people closer to God; instead, he enriches the elite under the guise of maintaining proper worship regulations. Annas has lost sight of the island of the temple, of the island of a true high priest in service to God. His island has become the preservation of tradition, rather than the worship of God.

Annas is not the only one to stray from his true calling, his island. How often do we too stray from our islands and become distracted with either worldly desires or trying to be something we are not? Churches can be guilty of the same thing. Some churches have gone to great lengths to try to be all things to all people. Sprawling church campuses with schools, daycare centers, coffee shops, cafes, libraries, self-help groups, and even singles' and seniors' groups can enable members to come to church for one-stop shopping. The churches appear lively and full of growth. The programs can be great for outreach, but often the members have all their needs met within the church walls, such that they never leave to be in community with others. The opposite can also be found in churches where people are there only out of a sense of tradition and social responsibility. Church is a duty more than an act of communal worship, fellowship, or accountability.

(1:51), a gathering of a council (11:47–53), and Caiaphas's verdict (11:49–50). There is thus no need in John's presentation for a lengthy Jewish trial, and Jesus' main trial will be before the Roman prefect (18:28–19:16).

In verse 19 the high priest begins his interrogation. Who specifically is the high priest in this scene? The flow of the narrative clearly suggests Annas (see 18:13), but we have been told several times that the "high priest that year" was Caiaphas (11:49; 18:13, 24). Some ancient manuscripts even altered the order of the verses here, inserting verse 24 after verse 13, so that the interrogation takes place before Caiaphas. On one level, John's attribution of the title high priest to Annas is quite straightforward: Annas (or Ananus I) held the high priesthood 6–15 CE, and previous incumbents seem to have continued to use the title "high priest" as an honorific even after their deposition (Josephus, *War* 2.441, *Antiquities* 20.205, *Life* 193). More subtly, however, John's lack of clarity may suggest that the precise incumbent was of less interest to him than the high-priestly office. The evangelist likes one-to-one encounters with Jesus, and this scene allows the evangelist to bring Jesus face to face with the high priest, the supreme representative of "the Jews."

The high priest's question appears a little banal until we realize that it reflects the categories of the false prophet in Deuteronomy 13:2–6; 18:20: that is, one who leads others astray (hence the reference to disciples) and falsely presumes to speak in God's name (hence the reference to teaching). Ironically, the scene takes place at the same time that Jesus' prophecy that Peter would deny him is being fulfilled (13:36–38). For John, Jesus is clearly no false prophet.

The scene may say something even more important about Jesus' identity. Throughout, Jesus speaks in a characteristically bold manner. He sums up his ministry (vv. 20–21), noting that everything has been done in public (a motif that emerged earlier in the Gospel; 7:4; 10:24). He speaks with dignity and majesty, his words echoing the voice of Wisdom (Prov. 8:2–3; 9:3; Wis. 6:14–16) and even the characteristic speech of God in Second Isaiah (Isa. 45:18–19; 48:16), reinforcing the unity between himself and the Father.

The high priest begins by taking charge, but seems to disappear as the narrative progresses. Despite his eminence, he relies on his attendant to speak up for him (and to slap the prisoner, probably drawing on Exod. 22:28), and in the end has nothing to say. As already noted, nothing is related of the

high priest, but before the father-in-law of the high priest. High priest, father-in-law, officer—anyone, it seemed, could play this game. Interrogate this prophet from Galilee, this rustic preacher, this miracle worker, this nobody without a pedigree. See if you can make him crack. He might have been someone special in Galilee, but now he is in Jerusalem. Intimidate! Interrogate! Show nothing but contempt. That is the order of the day.

On the other hand, Jesus in both his presence and his demeanor commands respect for his work, for his mission, for his obedience to God. Even more, he shows with great resolve what has been given him to do by the Father. He is preserving a threshold of honor and dignity for the work of God.

Jesus' challenge to his interrogator to ask the people who have received his ministry what he has said to them (v. 21b) brings other themes and scenes from the Fourth Gospel into view. Jesus insists that they know what he has said. The evangelist urges anyone who will to look at the work of Jesus through the eyes of those who gladly receive him. Who Jesus was and is, his life, his ministry, his testimony about the one who sent him—these are borne out in the witness of those Jesus healed. In John's Gospel, these are the ones who matter. Those to whom the Father sent him are the sons and daughters of Abraham.

To the priests, those people are pawns in a political chess game and not to be believed. However, the halt, the crippled, the blind, and the lame matter in the sight of God. In so many words Jesus is saying, "I care for them, even if you do not. To you they are only collateral in the lethal game you are playing with Caesar. I taught in the synagogues. Ask those who have heard me."

If asked, what would they say? One would speak as the man born blind (chap. 9). There the rulers of the people were confounded. They sought to put the man on trial, but he turned the tables on them, asking how a sinner could open his eyes. They sought to prove that Jesus was a not a prophet, because he healed on the Sabbath. The man responded by saying, in essence, "That is your problem; all I know is that, whereas I was blind, now I see." The result? Jesus charged the man's inquisitors with spiritual blindness. Jesus said, "If you admitted you were blind I could heal you. But because you say you see, I will seal you in your blindness" (the sense of 9:41). A similar sentence is being pronounced in this scene in chapter 18.

The ongoing conflict is about authority. It has reached the highest level. Jesus stands before the

John 18:19–24

Theological Perspective

high priest has receded into the background of this narrative, and this official, who is caught up in the rigid and unjust legalism of the religious ruling class, has moved to the center. The text here leaves us with the question of to whom the revelation of Jesus is given and for whom that revelation is most problematic. As a whole, the story does suggest that the ruling religious elite found the revelatory words of Jesus to be problematic in a legal and, perhaps, political sense.

However, a closer reading of the text also suggests that for those caught up in the legal and political snares of religious domination, the revelation of Jesus evokes a kind of existential crisis. It is this existential crisis that is at the heart of this stanza of the narrative. The crisis for this official is not that Jesus' words are "profane" (outside of the essence of Israel's religion) or that they are "secular" (opposed to the essence of Israel's religion). This is why Jesus challenges him to "testify to what is wrong" in his words. The crisis is rooted in the fact that Jesus' words are "the truth." It is possible that the revelation of Jesus as the truth is, in fact, meant for this official and not the religious ruling elite. An important clue to this reading is that the high priest never directly speaks in this narrative. The writer of John simply tells us that "he questioned Jesus" and that then "Annas sent him, still bound, to Caiaphas the high priest" (NIV).

This text challenges the reader to consider the meaning of the revelation of Jesus as shaped by his personal encounter with others. Jesus' revelation cannot be fully captured by setting it over against correct belief (orthodoxy) or correct ritual behavior (orthopraxy). A genuine understanding of this revelation must take into account what Jesus says, what Jesus does, and most importantly who Jesus is. This is why the Gospel of John emphasizes Jesus' revelation of his identity: "I am the good shepherd"; "I am the bread of life." It is the revelation of Jesus' identity that both evokes and resolves the existential crisis of humanity.

JAMES H. EVANS JR.

Pastoral Perspective

There is little vitality or growth. These are examples of churches that have lost sight of their islands. They have become distracted and need to reconnect.

Jesus' island is clear and consistent, just as he is with his answers on trial before Annas. Love God, love your neighbor, and everything else will fall into place. This should also be at the core of every church, every church family, every member, and every follower of Christ. He insists that he has been open and honest about all of his teachings. We should be as well. Annas wants to catch him doing something in secret. He wants to be able to convict him of wrongdoing, but there is none to be found. We too should be open and in community, sharing the love of God and offering love to our neighbors. When our churches are so big that all of our neighbors are also church members, we are spending too much time "in secret" and need to move beyond the church walls and reach out to others. Similarly, if we attend church only out of duty, we need to rekindle our passion for the church and revisit the island Christ left for us.

What is your island? Is it similar to that of Christ? Have you found yourself distracted or otherwise drawn to other islands like that of Annas? Holding to a clear and concise message of who we are and what we do because of what we believe offers a center to cling to when others put us on trial, question us, or try to tear us down because of insecurities in their own lives. Just because they are off course from their islands does not mean we should be. Jesus never wavered from his island, and in the end his message triumphed. Thanks be to God.

VICTORIA ATKINSON WHITE

Feasting on the Gospels

scene in front of Caiaphas, and neither high priest appears again in the narrative. This may be part of a motif in John's Gospel whereby Jesus is shown to be the replacement of Jewish feasts and institutions (purification processes in 2:1–11, the temple in 2:19–22, manna in the wilderness in 6:22–65, and of course the paschal lamb in 1:29, 35, and 19:14). In chapter 17 (often known as the high-priestly prayer), Jesus brought his offering to the Father and consecrated himself (17:19). For John's audience, of course, Jesus is the true high priest, the authentic conduit of God's revelation, the new mediator between God and humanity (see also 1 John 2:1–2).

On a purely historical level, many modern Jesus scholars are inclined to regard John's pared-down Jewish trial narrative as more historical than that found in the Synoptics. The very existence of a formal, fixed council known as *the* Sanhedrin has come under intense scholarly scrutiny lately (particularly the seventy-one-member body described in the Mishnah). It is more likely that the high priest summoned an ad hoc group of advisors, drawn from the priestly and lay aristocracy of Jerusalem, and composed of whichever people seemed appropriate to the matter in hand. John's account also avoids the difficulties of the Markan report of a nighttime trial on the very day of Passover (events in John take place a day earlier, on the day of Preparation, 19:14). In contrast to Mark, John's informal hearing before the high priest and one or two advisors has the air of verisimilitude. It is not really a trial at all, but a brief fact-finding investigation, once Jesus has been taken into police custody, a necessary preliminary to handing Jesus over to Pilate the next day. Even the implicit charge, that of being a false prophet, may well have a greater claim to historicity than the rather anachronistic-sounding charge of blasphemy found in Mark (see also *b. Sanh.* 43a, 107b[1]). Whether John was intentionally more historical at this point (perhaps because he had better traditions?) or his theological interests simply led him to present a scene with a greater level of verisimilitude, is difficult to know.

HELEN K. BOND

rulers of the people. Jesus stands his ground: "If I have spoken wrongly, testify to the wrong. But if I have spoken rightly, why do you strike me?" (v. 23).

The stakes have not changed. The battle for true authority still rages. Who speaks truth? Who is the rightful ruler? Whose acts manifest the works of God? The mask has been removed, even from priests who front for the princes of this world. Whether it is before Annas, Caiaphas, or Pilate—any throne, principality, dominion, or power—the Lord and those who speak in his name are never afforded the ease of surrender. The order is to prosecute all imposters. The verdict is simple and clear if you ask those who have been delivered.

Consider options for how to construct a sermon on this passage. Look, for example, at where trials of this sort are taking place at present. What are those whom God has sent being accused of? In what ways are they putting their accusers on trial?

Alternatively, take a close look at verse 19. The high priest is asking Jesus about "his disciples and his teaching," but those specific questions are not spelled out in this part of the story. What do you imagine those questions might have been? "Who exactly are your disciples? What difference is your teaching making in their lives, Jesus?"

The preacher standing before the congregation might be wondering the same thing: Where do I see Christian discipleship playing out in my world? Where is there evidence of Jesus' teaching making a difference?

Finally, consider this option: whenever you want to fling some query at Jesus, questioning his presence in the world or the relevance of his teaching today, remember his response to the high priest: "Why are you asking me? Ask those who heard, and felt, and believed what I said. They are the ones who know." They do indeed.

W. C. TURNER

---

1. On Jesus in the rabbinic tradition, see Robert E. van Voorst, *Jesus outside the New Testament: An Introduction to the Ancient Evidence* (Grand Rapids: Eerdmans, 2000), 104–22.

John 18:25–27

²⁵Now Simon Peter was standing and warming himself. They asked him, "You are not also one of his disciples, are you?" He denied it and said, "I am not." ²⁶One of the slaves of the high priest, a relative of the man whose ear Peter had cut off, asked, "Did I not see you in the garden with him?" ²⁷Again Peter denied it, and at that moment the cock crowed.

Theological Perspective

Along with all three Synoptic Gospels, John recounts Peter's denial of Jesus. He arranges the events rather differently, though, and distributes the details in a way that is almost the reverse of the other Gospels. For a start, John splits the denials and has Peter quizzed first at the gate to the high priest's court (18:17). Peter denies Jesus twice more after he has entered the courtyard, while he is warming himself at the fire made by "servants and officers" (18:18). Unlike Luke, who keeps the entire ordeal in the same place, Mark and Matthew both have Peter move from the courtyard to the "gate" (Mark) or "porch" (Matt.), presumably to get away from the first questioner. The suggestion that Peter wants to escape, or at least to avoid further attention, is absent from John, since Peter continues to go into the courtyard after his first denial.

The other details peculiar to John fill out the scene so as to shift, when compared with the Synoptic Gospels, the weight of the information that is given. John's account is more elaborate in regard to the questioners, but Peter receives notably less attention. The reader learns, therefore, that the servant girl serves as the gatekeeper and that the last challenger is a relative of the unfortunate Malchus, whose ear Peter lopped off when Jesus was arrested. The girl's occupation simply fills out the little scene

Pastoral Perspective

The extended passion narrative in John's Gospel includes the three denials by Peter that he is a disciple of Jesus. The story of Peter begins as a call to follow Jesus, and in time Peter becomes a member of Jesus' inner circle of disciples; this inclusion is most evident in the Synoptics' account of Jesus' Transfiguration (Mark 9:2–8; Matt. 17:1–9; Luke 9:28–36). At times Peter displays cluelessness about the character and mission of Jesus, illustrated most prominently at the Last Supper in John 13:6–10 and now in his three successive denials that he is a disciple of Jesus. It is significant that Peter is prominently displayed as a leader within a small group of disciples, yet at the same time he is not the object of emulation. Peter is utterly human, and nowhere is this more evident than in the three denials in the courtyard (18:17, 25, 27).

In most congregations, pastors have witnessed such denials—in either subtle or blatant forms—by those who do harm to the body of Christ, in what is done or left undone, and by those who choose conformity to the world, rather than the renewing of their minds (Rom. 12:2). It is true that this passage, rehearsed and performed in the worshiping community's journey toward the cross, is stark and unsettling in its finality and decisiveness. For that reason it can be an experience that we try to hold at a distance. We may find it difficult to imagine ourselves in such a

Exegetical Perspective

Many chapters ago, back in 13:38, Jesus foretold that Peter would deny him three times "before the cock crows," even though Peter had declared his willingness to lay down his life for Jesus. The text at hand, 18:25–27, recounts Peter's second and third denials of Jesus. Between 13:38 and 18:25, Jesus delivered a long discourse in chapters 14–16 that led to the prayer for the disciples in chapter 17. In 18:1 Jesus led his disciples to the garden (Gethsemane, according to Matthew and Mark) where Judas betrayed him to soldiers and officers from the chief priests and Pharisees. In response, Peter cut off the ear of Malchus, the high priest's slave, before being reprimanded by Jesus.

At this point in the narrative, the Gospel of John diverges in a few details from the other Gospels. Jesus is brought to the house of Annas (v. 13; in the other Gospels he is brought to the house of Caiaphas, the high priest) for questioning, and Simon Peter and "another disciple" follow along. This other disciple has connections with the high-priestly household, speaks to the woman guarding the gate, and brings Peter into the courtyard. She poses the first question to Peter, whether he was a disciple of Jesus, something Peter denies. Verse 18 leaves Peter standing with the soldiers and officers warming himself by a fire. The high priest questions Jesus in verses

Homiletical Perspective

Peter is the poster child for denial. It is easy to bash him. We are quick to judge him because of his inability to claim his discipleship in a tough situation. In this pericope, Peter is a liar three times over. Despite his lofty words to follow Jesus all the way to death, Peter is not up to the task. Even though he has a prominent role in John's Gospel, Peter exhibits questionable courage. His blatant denial of Jesus is legendary. Perhaps we judge Peter too harshly, though. Can the preacher tell Peter's story so that we glean important lessons about discipleship?

In nearly every instance where we see him, Peter has the right words to say, but he often falls short of walking the walk of discipleship (6:68–69; 13:6–9). In a poignant exchange, Peter declares his willingness to die for Jesus, but Jesus knows better (13:36–38). In the Gospels, Peter is the most outspoken, always ready with questions and opinions, impulsive, and adventurous to a fault. We have a portrait of a real human being, complex and layered. When we read all four Gospel accounts in relation to Peter, we find a person who is open to innovation and change, quick-tempered, impulsive, emotional, loyal, and brave—all the characteristics of a solid disciple.

In the courtyard of the high priest, Peter is alone, save for the unnamed disciple, in enemy territory surrounded by hundreds of police officers. Peter is

John 18:25–27

Theological Perspective

at the door; but why does John mention Malchus's family? The reference sets up a connection between Peter's denials and his actions in the garden. Jesus stops Peter's assault on the arresting officers because it is an attempt to prevent his death: "Am I not to drink the cup that the Father has given me?" (18:11). Failing to understand who Jesus is, Peter goes on to deny his discipleship altogether. The two events—the assault on Malchus and the denials—are of a piece: misunderstanding of the cross births the denial of Jesus and of discipleship. This is the trajectory of the disciple who does not yet understand Jesus' "glorification."

As far as Peter is concerned, though, John's version of this story is more clipped. Peter's words of denial do not vary: to the twice-asked question, "Are you not also one of this man's disciples?" he says simply, "I am not" (v. 25b). The third time, we are not given his answer and the fact of denial is simply reported (v. 27). More striking still, John omits all mention of Peter's reaction to the cockcrow. In each of the other Gospels, the story ends with Peter's grief, leaving him weeping at the enormity of his betrayal. John, however, closes with the cockcrow itself, which throws the emphasis on the denial as fulfilling Jesus' prophecy in 13:38: "Will you lay down your life for me? Very truly, I tell you, before the cock crows, you will have denied me three times." John does not remind the reader of this, though, but leaves the reader to draw the conclusion.

That John shows no interest in the story beyond the moment of cockcrow has prompted the argument that the evangelist has only a limited interest in this event. Beyond providing another example of Jesus' foreknowledge, the incident is not theologically significant.[1] Two considerations invite a richer theological reading, though, at least for the final version of the Gospel. The threefold denial is picked up again when, after his resurrection, Jesus appears to the disciples by the Sea of Tiberias (21:1–24). Following the breakfast, Jesus asks Peter three times, "Simon son of John, do you love me?" (vv. 15–17). The placing of this interrogation immediately after a meal may recall the occasion when Jesus predicted Peter's denial. This was provoked by the disciple's indignant, "Lord, why can I not follow you now? I will lay down my life for you" (13:37). That exchange occurs at the supper during which Jesus washes the disciples' feet and gives them the commandment to

---

1. Rudolf Bultmann, *The Gospel of John: A Commentary*, trans. G. R. Beasley-Murray (Philadelphia: Westminster Press, 1971), 648.

Pastoral Perspective

setting, called upon to answer such direct questions, or offering such a blunt rejection of the faith. Surely we would not succumb to such a temptation or speak falsely about something—namely, our faith—that is so central to who we are, would we?

The question posed to Peter on the way of the cross, however, may for most of us be framed in a language that is more subtle and nuanced and therefore open to temptation and self-deception. To claim one's identity as a disciple of Jesus, in Peter's experience, is to stand against the empire and the powers of this world. At this stage in his journey, he finds it to be too much, and thus there is a failure of witness. The brokenness of Christ's body, and the resulting guilt and isolation, is a sign of this failure in many of our congregations.

Clergy often observe such denials, but the honest preacher and pastor will confess that he or she has also walked in Peter's shoes. As clergy draw closer to the cross—the experiences of conflict, suffering, adversity, pain, and abandonment—they are also tempted to withdraw to places of safety and security. A prophetic voice becomes more silent; a sinful habit is ignored; a broken relationship is not mended. Leadership takes us to difficult, complex, and even dangerous places. It is true that the Peter of John 18 is not the Peter of Acts 2. In the latter text he is filled with the Holy Spirit; here he exemplifies a lack of courage with which any pastor or leader will identify somewhere along the journey. That pastor can only pray for inner strength and forgiveness. The Jesus Prayer seems relevant here, even if borrowed from another Gospel: "God, be merciful to me, a sinner" (Luke 18:13).

In many communities in the United States, the culture of a generation ago was one that reinforced faith, church participation, and the particular narrative related to Jesus' life, death, and resurrection. Perhaps you remember a time when being a member of a congregation or being a member of the clergy was respected and honored. Perhaps, instead, you came of age when the dominant culture was not so supportive of "church" as others experienced it. In any case, in our time, being a Christian means swimming against strong currents (the consumer culture that undergirds our economy, the popular and high culture that shapes our experiences) when we begin to take up the cross and follow Jesus.

To deny Jesus in our present cultural ethos is to be in alignment with postmodern culture and the empire of political loyalty. Again, the temptation may not always be obvious, but to be a disciple of

Feasting on the Gospels

Exegetical Perspective

19–24, but in verse 25 the attention returns to Peter, still standing and warming himself at the fire.

Again he is asked whether he is a disciple of Jesus, with basically the same question as before. In both instances the Greek indicates that the questioners are not overly suspicious and that they expect a negative answer. "You are not also one of his disciples, are you?" In each case, Peter replies simply, "I am not" (*ouk eimi*), a response that stands in contrast to Jesus' earlier affirmations in 18:5–6, 8: "I am he" (*egō eimi*). The connection with the arrest is further strengthened in 18:26, when another slave of the high priest, a relative of Malchus, whose ear Peter had cut off, questions somewhat more aggressively, "I saw you in the garden with him, didn't I?" (my trans.). Whereas in the other Gospels Peter denies with increasing vehemence (even curses and oaths in Matthew and Mark) that he knows Jesus, in John's Gospel Peter's third denial is simply reported, along with the cock's crowing immediately.

In the other Gospels, we are accustomed to the description of Peter weeping bitterly as he realizes what he has done. In John, no details at all of Peter's reaction are included, and we do not see him again until 20:2 and the footrace with the Beloved Disciple to the empty tomb. John does, however, feature Peter in chapter 21, where the miraculous catch of fish is followed by the breakfast on the beach. In 21:15–19 Jesus gives Peter the opportunity for a threefold confession of his love for Jesus, a threefold commission to care for Jesus' "sheep," and a pronouncement regarding his eventual martyrdom, a detail that harkens back to Peter's statement in 13:37 about his willingness to die for Jesus.

As part of a characteristic Johannine narrative strategy, the reader is helped to note all these connections being created among chapters 13, 18, and 21 and to see that Peter is a key figure linking them together. In contrast to his portrayal in the other Gospels, Peter plays only a small role in the first twelve chapters of John. Only his initial call in 1:40–42 and his memorable statement in 6:68 are reported. Starting in chapter 13, however, Peter figures prominently.

In the foot-washing incident in 13:1–20, Peter's reaction is highlighted. With the Beloved Disciple's help, he gets Jesus to identify his betrayer in 13:21–30. As the scene moves to Jesus' new command to love one another in 13:31–35, Peter responds in 13:36–38 with questions about *following* Jesus and a declaration of his willingness to lay down his life for Jesus. This statement prompts Jesus' announcement

Homiletical Perspective

clearly outnumbered and outarmed; that is, if he still has the sword he drew earlier when Jesus was arrested in the garden (18:10–11). All of Peter's cohort has fled into the night, and only he follows Jesus this far. He tries to keep a low profile in the courtyard. Peter's attempt to travel incognito, though, is not as successful as he thinks. He has been questioned and has denied being one of Jesus' disciples. When pressed by the relative of the man whose ear he chopped off, Peter denies that he was even in the garden during Jesus' arrest; this is his third denial. At that moment, the cock crows in the background; Jesus' prediction has come true to the letter. There is nothing left to say. Peter knows what has happened, and so do we.

Peter's denials are prudent, given the circumstances. He is afraid and with good reason. He is surrounded by a multitude of the enemy—Roman and temple police and officers—armed and prepared to shoot first and ask questions later. What would we do if we were in Peter's situation? Likely keep our mouths shut and hope for the best. Peter's actions are understandable.

Dr. Derrick Bell was the first tenured African American professor at Harvard Law School. He is best known for his decision to resign his post over the Law School's hiring practices when there were no African American women or other women of color on the faculty. He states that courage must be understood in context and with an acknowledgment of fear:

> Courage is a decision you make to act in a way that works through your own fear for the greater good as opposed to pure self-interest. Courage means putting at risk your immediate self-interest for what you believe is right. . . .
>
> Ethical living is an ongoing commitment, as we meet life's day-to-day challenges and opportunities, to assume risks in honor of self and all others.[1]

In the Fourth Gospel, the "enemy" is anyone who does not see what God is doing through the life and ministry of Jesus. How often do we find ourselves standing with the enemy? We may privately rail against institutions and leaders who care nothing for people. We are righteously indignant at the many acts of injustice we witness, but what do we do with our anger and frustration? We collude with our

---

1. Derrick Bell, *Ethical Ambition: Living a Life of Meaning and Worth* (New York: Bloomsbury, 2002), 39, 43.

Theological Perspective

"love one another." Peter's denial demonstrates the truth of Jesus' words, "you cannot follow me now."

Again it is Jesus' death, his laying down his life for the sheep as the fulfillment of the Father's will, that makes true discipleship a reality; before that, it is neither understandable nor possible. Jesus' three-fold questioning of Peter by the lakeside reverses the denials in a ritual of forgiveness and purification, and it commissions Peter to do what neither he nor the disciples could grasp at the time of the foot washing: follow the path of the good shepherd who "lays down his life for the sheep" (10:11). There is more to the denials, then, than a fulfilled prediction. Together with the questions on the lakeshore, they are an index of Jesus' work, of the passage from darkness to light.

The splitting of the denials between the gate and the courtyard provides another indication that this story has theological importance in John's Gospel. John puts the first denial immediately before Jesus' interrogation by Annas. He then returns to Peter, continuing the story with the particle *de*, which here has the force of "meanwhile."[2] In this way, John emphasizes that Peter is busy denying Jesus at the same time his Master is being questioned. Peter's encounters occur as a parallel interrogation and testing. The master is questioned among the "great ones," the disciple among the servants, though the latter does not necessarily mean that Peter is in less danger. While Jesus is denying nothing, however, Peter denies everything.

John's staging of these incidents thus both joins Peter and Jesus in their circumstances and distances them from each other with the distance between light and darkness, in terms of their responses. Jesus is the measure of the disciple, and the contrast is painfully clear, which is as it must be while the "ruler of this world" has his hour. That agony, however, is transformed on the other side of the Son's return to the Father, his glorification and resurrection. After that, the Spirit is given, the disciple commissioned, and life reborn "from above."

ALAN P. R. GREGORY

Pastoral Perspective

Jesus is to affirm his lordship, even in the midst of a pluralistic religious landscape and a consumerist culture of personal values. These are not often decisions we make rationally or intentionally; nevertheless, our lives are shaped by the culture in which we live, work, and play.

The three denials of Peter are often linked with the three questions that Jesus asks of Peter in John 21 ("Do you love me?"). The twenty-first chapter is often referred to as the epilogue to John's Gospel, and yet it is found in the earliest of the ancient manuscripts. Most scholars see the purpose of the questions addressed to Peter as his restoration as a leader in the early Christian movement. Jesus does not give up on Peter, even in the face of the denial and abandonment. This is reassuring to all followers of Jesus, for we have all denied him in some way.

The faithful teaching and preaching of this text will move from the judgment of Peter ("How could he deny Jesus?" "Why could he not be more courageous?") and the distancing of context ("When we will be asked to deny that we are Christians?") to the spiritual reflection that calls us to sense Peter's response as our own. Self-awareness about the ways we fail to display courage and resistance in the face of competing loyalties, and a reading of the culture that competes for our deepest loyalty and embrace will lead us to the realization that we are more like Peter than we may realize.

KENNETH H. CARTER

---

2. Raymond E. Brown, *The Gospel according to John XIII–XXI*, AB 30 (Garden City, NY: Doubleday, 1970), 827.

Exegetical Perspective

that Peter will deny him three times before the cock crows. In 18:15, Peter *follows* Jesus to the high priest's residence, where his denials occur. Peter will *follow* the other disciple to the empty tomb in 20:6. In 21:20–22, after Peter's threefold confession of love for Jesus, the Beloved Disciple is *following* Peter and Jesus, and specific reference is made back to 13:21–30, but the significance of it all is that Jesus tells Peter, "*Follow* me!" (21:19, 22).

These narrative threads hold the account together. They also provide a focus on the drama in 18:25–27 and highlight one of the larger concerns of the Gospel of John, namely, the increasingly hostile relationship between the Jewish Christians of John's community and the non-Christian Jews in the synagogue. In the Synoptic Gospels, Acts, and the Pauline letters, the tension between Jews who believed in Jesus as the Messiah and those who did not is evident, and the difficulties only increased after the destruction of the Jewish temple in 70 CE. As Judaism sought to define itself in light of that tragedy, Jesus became a polarizing figure. In John's community, it has come to the point that people who confess Jesus as the Messiah are being expelled from the synagogue (9:22; 12:42; 16:2). One goal of John's Gospel is to encourage Christians to make that confession. From the perspectives of both the Christian community and the Jewish synagogue, it is no longer possible to try to have it both ways. One can no longer be a Jewish Christian and participate in the Jewish synagogue.

Peter, therefore, becomes a critical figure for those who are struggling to decide whether to confess or to deny Jesus, to follow or to flee. The question posed to Peter is the same one faced by those in John's audience: "Are you a disciple of Jesus Christ?" The answer is either "I am" or "I am not." It truly is a matter of life and death.

MARK G. VITALIS HOFFMAN

Homiletical Perspective

enemies in the ways we shop, the way we vote, the way we turn a deaf ear and blind eye to what is happening in our communities, in our nation, and in our world. It is easier to go along to get along.

The preacher must remind us that we are all often in Peter's situation. We are confronted on a regular basis with opportunities to do the right thing for the right reason. Sometimes, we are effective, but more often we fail. Good intentions do not change the world. Peter is not the only one guilty of compromise, expediency, self-protection, and fear.

In the midst of failure, disappointment, and shame, however, this is not the end of Peter or his story. His failure sets the stage for a marvelous comeback. Peter emerges from the passion story with more fire and passion than ever—rightly directed, channeled, and empowered. Peter never gives up in the face of failure or shame. Peter always comes back for more. The next time may be his opportunity to embody true discipleship—hearing and doing the word, and engaging in acts of compassion and justice.

It is a fact that we deny Jesus in our daily walk. In what specific ways does your community deny or reject Jesus? We all have moments when we fall short of what we confess and what we say we believe. Like Peter, though, beneath the surface there is the faith and the will to do the right thing. There will be things to test our faith, commitment, and resolve. In any given moment, we may deny that we know Jesus and that we are his disciples. We do not love all the time or love completely; we pick and choose when and how we follow Jesus. We give in to the pressures of the culture: consumerism, justice for some but not all. We rely on electronics and social media for community, instead of being with people.

Peter denies his connection with Jesus while surrounded by his enemies. It is a life-and-death situation. Our situations may not be as dramatic, but they are just as crucial. The challenge and invitation is to determine how we will handle ourselves in a world that lulls us into complacency and compromise.

BARBARA J. ESSEX

John 18:28–38a

²⁸Then they took Jesus from Caiaphas to Pilate's headquarters. It was early in the morning. They themselves did not enter the headquarters, so as to avoid ritual defilement and to be able to eat the Passover. ²⁹So Pilate went out to them and said, "What accusation do you bring against this man?" ³⁰They answered, "If this man were not a criminal, we would not have handed him over to you." ³¹Pilate said to them, "Take him yourselves and judge him according to your law." The Jews* replied, "We are not permitted to put anyone to death." ³²(This was to fulfill what Jesus had said when he indicated the kind of death he was to die.)

³³Then Pilate entered the headquarters again, summoned Jesus, and asked him, "Are you the King of the Jews?" ³⁴Jesus answered, "Do you ask this on your own, or did others tell you about me?" ³⁵Pilate replied, "I am not a Jew, am I? Your own nation and the chief priests have handed you over to me. What have you done?" ³⁶Jesus answered, "My kingdom is not from this world. If my kingdom were from this world, my followers would be fighting to keep me from being handed over to the Jews. But as it is, my kingdom is not from here." ³⁷Pilate asked him, "So you are a king?" Jesus answered, "You say that I am a king. For this I was born, and for this I came into the world, to testify to the truth. Everyone who belongs to the truth listens to my voice." ³⁸Pilate asked him, "What is truth?"

Theological Perspective

After the seemingly brief and informal appearance before Annas, Jesus is taken to Pilate, where he is interrogated by the Roman governor, who is at the top level of the judicial process. At the theological level, however, Pilate is the one interrogated by his strange, disconcerting prisoner. Since Jesus' accusers do not enter the *praetorium*, "so as to avoid ritual defilement" (v. 28b), Pilate's interview is conducted shuffling to and from the *praetorium*, in which Jesus is being held. This gives John's account of the trial a distinctively dramatic movement in which Pilate's coming and going is a metaphor for his dilemma.

The suspense internal to this incident illustrates Pilate's reluctance to make a judgment, to do what his job calls him to do—a reluctance that puts him in an ironic counterpoint to Jesus. Though he is the prisoner, John's Jesus occupies throughout his trial, albeit hiddenly, the position of the true judge. At the beginning of this passage, Jesus is handed over by "the Jews," and in the end (19:16) Pilate returns him to "the Jews." This shows how they remain for John the principal agents of Jesus' death, even though it is the Romans who carry out the execution. Pilate's examination is nonetheless a theologically rich

Pastoral Perspective

In this passage we discover the political and religious authorities in tension. Jesus is a threat to the religious leaders, but they do not have the authority to put someone to death. The political leader Pilate senses that this is a religious matter, but finally intervenes. Still, there is an ambiguity, and this is addressed in Pilate's questions of Jesus: "Are you the King of the Jews?" (v. 33), "So you are a king?"(v. 37).

Jesus answers, simply and compellingly, "My kingdom is not from this world" (v. 36). It is an oversimplification to state that the Jewish people of Jesus' day wanted an earthly ruler or messiah. It is clear in the Gospel of John that the sin of blasphemy (Jesus' claim to be divine) was the point of contention within the Jewish community. It is also important to remember that all of the conversation is within the Jewish community. The Gentile mission has not yet occurred. At the same time, Jesus does pose some kind of threat to the political empire; so his statement, "My kingdom is not from this world," contrasts Jesus' mission with that of the empire that Pilate represents.

The followers of Jesus across the centuries have been tempted again and again to desire a kingdom that is very much from or aligned with this world. At times, Christians have wanted to fuse the

* See "'The Jews' in the Fourth Gospel" on pp. xi–xiv.

Exegetical Perspective

In John 18:12, Jesus was arrested and brought to Annas, formerly a high priest himself and now father-in-law of Caiaphas, the high priest. Peter's denials framed the initial interrogation of Jesus in 18:19–24, which established only that Jesus had spoken publicly and rightly. Jesus' transfer yet again that night to Caiaphas was followed by Peter's final denial. The text at hand, 18:28–38a, now resumes Jesus' trials with an early morning transfer to Pilate. According to Johannine chronology, the arrest occurred on Thursday night, and this trial before Pilate is on Friday morning. In contrast to the account in the Synoptic Gospels, however, this is not the day of Passover but the preceding "day of Preparation" (19:14, 31). This detail is important for John, because it means that Jesus will be crucified at the same time that the Passover lambs are being slaughtered.

This is John's first reference to Pilate, so it is assumed that the reader is aware that Pilate was the procurator (governor) of Judea. Pilate's usual residence (*praetorium*) was in Caesarea Maritima, but when in Jerusalem, he probably stayed either at the Antonia Fortress on the north side of the Temple Mount or at Herod's palace on the western side of the city. Whether or not he was anticipating problems during the Passover festival, he doubtless was

Homiletical Perspective

The Fourth Evangelist makes preaching the passion of Jesus easy. The Fourth Evangelist makes preaching the passion difficult. So go the reactions to the Fourth Gospel. Preachers either love it or they hate it. There is very little middle ground. The dramatic flair of the text brings realism and energy to the worship context. At the same time, the nuances of John's language and the theological twists of the narrative make the preaching task a challenge.

After his arrest, Jesus quickly moves toward his "hour," the culmination of his ministry and mission—his death, resurrection, and ascension. This pericope would be a great plotline for *Law & Order*;[1] as with the television show, the success of John's drama relies on an engaging cast of characters: Jesus, "the Jews," and Pilate.

The Jewish religious leaders, here called "the Jews," are not consistently named or identified. In this episode, though, they are the temple authorities and their cronies who oppose Jesus, his ministry and mission, and his followers. It is important that we do not use this passage and others in this Gospel to promote anti-Semitism. In the Fourth Gospel, those

1. *Law & Order* (NBC, 1990–2010), is a procedural drama. Each episode has two parts: the investigation of a crime and arrest of suspect(s) by the New York City Police Department, and the prosecution of the defendant(s) by the New York County District Attorney's Office.

Theological Perspective	Pastoral Perspective

Theological Perspective

moment, not least because of the way it raises the question of kingship.

As a theme, kingship is relatively undeveloped in John's Gospel, although there are important connections between the figure of the good shepherd and kingly rule.[1] Narrating Jesus' trial before Pilate, however, John presents kingship in relation to truth and judgment. Pilate asks Jesus directly, "Are you the King of the Jews?" (v. 33b). Jesus' reply, though, is to inquire about the relationship between this question and Pilate himself. Is this what the governor has heard, or is he asking on his own behalf?

Pilate, perhaps with some brusque contempt, denies he is a position to know any more than that the Jews have made Jesus his judicial problem. He asks Jesus the broad question, "What have you done?" (v. 35b), at which point Jesus returns to the first question about kingship. His words puzzle Pilate or perhaps strike his interrogator as evasive. "So you are a king, then!" (v. 37, NIRV). If this is an attempt to pin Jesus down, it fails. Instead of affirming or denying, Jesus tells Pilate that "king" is the governor's term, freighted with the governor's meaning. Then we have the connection between kingship and truth: "You say that I am a king. For this I was born, and for this I came into the world, to testify to the truth" (v. 37). To this, Pilate gives one of history's most famously enigmatic replies, "What is truth?"

Jesus' admission that kingship does indeed belong to him is qualified by the contrast with worldly kingship. This is not a simple contrast between "this world" and "another world," though, such that one might fairly draw from this a doctrine of Christian political quietism or indifference. "World" is caught up in John's play with "world" as location and "world" as condition. The world is this world as pitched in darkness, as the "night" in which the Son is betrayed (13:30) and where men and women react against the truth, thereby bringing themselves to judgment (8:44–46; 12:48). Under this condition of the world, subjects fight for their rulers.

Since their actions are overruled by the Father's will for the Son, Jesus' disciples (with the notable exception of Peter, 18:10–11) do not fight to prevent Jesus' arrest. Neither, of course, are they his "subjects"; rather, they are, as Jesus has told them, his "friends." In this world—as both place, the object of God's love (3:16), and condition—Christians must bear witness against the grip of the world's

Pastoral Perspective

commitments of worship, faith, and justice with a particular political agenda. This happens in the context of American Christianity in the politics of the left-wing and right-wing parties, with liberalism and conservatism. The issues differ, but the passions are similar. We quickly forget the statement of Jesus: "My kingdom is not from this world."

The encounter between Jesus and the civil government is inevitably an ambiguous one. The ambiguity lies in the government's tendency, in many instances, to claim our deepest commitment and loyalty. This can occur in times of warfare, or when laws impinge upon social issues that we care deeply about, or in so closely identifying our ethnic tradition with the faith that we cannot easily distinguish between them.

To say that the kingdom of God is not from this world is to practice the spiritual discipline of detachment. Our political processes are so intense and so polarized that they can often make a claim for our deepest and most intense engagement. To detach is to step aside and express a more fundamental conviction: that Jesus transcends political partisanship and religious division. To be sure, Jesus was an advocate for particular values (note his sermon in Luke 4, based on Isa. 61, as an example), but this cannot always be easily connected to a particular political movement.

A disciple of Jesus is called to detachment, yet detachment is never easy. We become easily attached to the kingdoms of this world for good reason: they provide power, security, and identity. The attachments shape us, individually and corporately. The kingdoms of this world are the very temptations placed before Jesus earlier in the Gospels (Matt. 4:1–11; Luke 4:1–13). These temptations, helpfully defined by Henri Nouwen in his classic *In The Name of Jesus*,[1] are to be relevant, to be spectacular, and to be powerful. To give in to temptation is to become attached to the kingdoms of the world; to resist temptation is to seek first the kingdom of God and God's righteousness (Matt. 6:33), knowing that in the midst of anxiety God will provide for all of our needs.

In the dialogue with Pilate and the questioning about his kingship and calling, Jesus states his mission clearly: "I came into the world to testify to the truth. Everyone who belongs to the truth listens to my voice" (v. 37). How do we listen to the voice of

1. For the references, see Raymond E. Brown, *The Gospel according to John I–XII*, AB 29 (Garden City, NY: Doubleday, 1966), 397.

1. Henri J. M. Nouwen, *In the Name of Jesus: Reflections on Christian Leadership* (New York: Crossroad, 1992).

Exegetical Perspective

making a point about Roman power by his presence in the city.

Though nothing specific has been charged against Jesus, the Jewish authorities vaguely present him as an evildoer or criminal. Pilate appears to recognize the flimsiness of their case and is ready to dismiss it as merely a Jewish matter, but the situation changes when it is made clear that the Jewish leaders are treating it as a capital offense. Though not explicitly declared, the Jewish charge against Jesus could be that of blasphemy, a charge that points back to Jesus' statements in 10:22–39 when he claimed, "The Father and I are one," and "I am God's Son." They took up stones to kill him at that point, but Jesus "escaped."

Later, in 11:45–53, the Jewish authorities indicated that they wanted Jesus killed, lest he attract a following among the people that would incite the Romans to come and destroy the temple and even the nation. Caiaphas the high priest "prophesied" that Jesus would die for the nation, and "from that day on they planned to put him to death" (11:53).

If the Jewish authorities have finally captured Jesus and are already prepared to kill him for blasphemy, why do they need to bring Jesus to Pilate now? This question has generated considerable scholarly commentary, with little consensus on contemporary Roman and Jewish judicial procedures and prerogatives. From the perspective of the narrative intent, however, the following observations can be made.

It is, of course, well known that Jesus was crucified. In John, this mode of death was anticipated by Jesus in 12:32–33, and the reader is reminded of that fact here in 18:32. Crucifixion was abhorrent to Jews and could be legitimately carried out only by the Romans, so Jesus needs to end up somehow under Roman jurisdiction.

While the Jewish authorities are portrayed as being eager to remove Jesus, they are not insensitive to his popularity among the people (11:48; 12:9–11, 18–19). It would be quite convenient for them, therefore, if responsibility for his death could be assigned to Pilate. While they work to avoid ritual defilement, they cannot avoid being involved in the messy business of Jesus' execution. The result in the narrative is that the authorities are portrayed as both craven and hypocritical.

Ultimately Jesus is crucified not for religious reasons but for a political one. This becomes clear in verses 33–38 when Pilate's interrogation focuses on whether Jesus is a king. Still, the Jewish authorities are targeted as the ones who "hand over" (the same

Homiletical Perspective

who follow Jesus, the recipients of his healings, and those to whom Jesus preaches are all Jews. Jesus himself is a Jew, a native of Nazareth. "The Jews" is used to describe the Jewish religious leadership, not all Jews. The leaders do not have the welfare of the people at heart. They enjoy a measure of freedom and power given by the Roman government. Furthermore, they benefit financially from their collusion with the oppressive empire. They impose and collect taxes related to the temple. They are as dreaded as the Romans, because they are in cahoots with the oppressor. Their mantra is, "It is all about us, and we mean to preserve and protect what is rightfully ours." In order to do this, they must get rid of Jesus, who not only criticizes them but threatens their power and status.

Then there is Pontius Pilate, the Roman prefect in Judea from 25 to 36 CE. His job was to maintain law and order. He had a military force of some three thousand troops at his command, and even more during pilgrimages like the Passover, which brought thousands to Jerusalem. During this period, Jerusalem was a hotbed of activity and increased resentment of the Romans. As judge and executioner, Pilate often had a full docket of cases with which to deal. Pilate felt no affection for the Jews. His disdain and contempt are evident in his dealings with Jesus and the religious leadership in this pericope.

This is an easy case for Pilate. The verdict has already been reached; his duty is simply to follow through with the execution (11:47–53). We should not expect Pilate to be an impartial judge in this scenario—he is no Judge Judy, Mathis, or Alex.[2] Pilate's loyalty is to Rome and not to the Jews. They are a nuisance and their intra-Jewish squabbles should have been handled in house, rather than placed on his doorstep. His animosity toward the leaders should not lead us to think that he sympathizes with Jesus.

Pilate knows the leaders have no power that Rome needs to respect. He toys with the Jewish leaders. His back-and-forth, inside–and–outside movements might suggest hesitancy on his part, but Pilate is in control of the situation. He calls the shots and can end the mockery of a trial whenever he wishes. His mantra is, "It is all about Rome and me. I intend to preserve and protect what is rightfully ours."

At the heart of the narrative is Jesus, who willingly gives his life for those whom he loves. At his arrest and preliminary hearings before Annas

---

2. *Judge Judy* (CBS, 1996–); *Judge Mathis* (Warner Brothers, 1998–); *Judge Alex* (Twentieth Century Fox, 2005–)

John 18:28–38a

Theological Perspective

calamitous darkness. That witness takes place in the world and is for the world, although it shall bring disciples persecution (15:20). In obeying the Son, though, Christians also hope, strain forward toward "another world," mediated by the kingship of Jesus, in which men and women are blessed in the excesses of God's goodness, "grace upon grace" (1:16).

Replying to Pilate, Jesus moves from kingship to truth, thus making the link between rule and judgment. The good king judges according to the truth: "may [the king] judge your people with righteousness," prays the psalmist (Ps. 72:2). The king must not be swayed by bribe or fear, by the to-and-fro of advantage; he must judge rightly and, therefore, in truth. Believing in Jesus means seeing the truth and also recognizing the divide, the judgment separating light and darkness, that the truth produces (3:19).

From the beginning of Pilate's examination, the subject of truth is in play. Is Jesus accused, or has he already been condemned? Who has the right to pass the death sentence? Is Jesus the king of the Jews? Does Pilate know what he is saying when he asks it? Pilate's retort to Jesus, "What is truth?" is hardly spoken with the wonder of a closet philosopher. It is exasperation and perhaps also reaction. Is he stung by the implication that he should judge rightly, that that is what is required of him?

John goes further than the other Gospels in presenting Pilate favorably, as a man caught between political danger and duty. From a theological perspective, though, there is no whitewashing of the Roman governor. Although he will admit to finding no crime in Jesus, he will not stand by that judgment and release him. When he declares, "I find no case against him" (v. 38b), he speaks correctly—and in the theological dimension, profoundly—but he does not speak truly, because he will not declare the right judgment.

Instead, he fumbles his way through the order to scourge, an abortive strategy for Jesus' release, an ineffectual refusal, even a desperate plea to Jesus himself, before finally handing Jesus over for crucifixion. Pilate's failure illustrates the unity of power and truth, rule and right judgment. Throughout, this Roman governor has himself been on trial, with his prisoner probing him to the core. Unwilling to live "according to the truth," Pilate the judge is judged wanting.

ALAN P. R. GREGORY

Pastoral Perspective

Jesus? In the first centuries, the desert fathers and mothers left the places of empire to find quiet and solitude. There they could separate truth from falsehood. In their activity, they were simply repeating the practice of Jesus, who would withdraw from the crowds to find time and space for contemplation. His ability to resist the temptations described in Matthew and Luke was grounded in his insight that we do not live by bread alone, but by every word that proceeds from the mouth of God.

How then do we listen to the voice of Jesus? We first acknowledge that his voice will always be at odds with the prevailing messages of the kingdoms of this world. In H. Richard Niebuhr's classic *Christ and Culture*, two of the most compelling models are Christ against culture and Christ transforming culture. Each model has within it the assumption that Christ and culture are not identical. In Niebuhr's framework, the culture is either at odds with Christianity or in need of transformation.[2] Some followers of Jesus are called to withdraw from the culture, establishing new traditions and alternative habits, and perhaps building new institutions. Other disciples are called to be in the world but not of it, living within the culture but working to transform it into an approximation of the kingdom of God.

It is clear that Jesus has little interest in serving as ruler of the kingdoms of the world. His approach to power is more clearly found in the hymn adopted by Paul in Philippians 2:1–11. Jesus' *kenōsis*, or self-emptying, is replicated in the actions of his disciples (with the notable exception of Peter, 18:10), who do not fight to keep him from being handed over for crucifixion. Paradoxically, his kingdom is based upon a power and an authority that flow from a radical trust in God, the source of his identity. He gives up this status, empties himself, and takes the form of a servant (Phil. 2:7). This is the ultimate form of detachment, and he is the outward and visible sign of a kingdom that is not from this world.

KENNETH H. CARTER

---

2. H. Richard Niebuhr, *Christ and Culture* (New York: Harper & Row, 1951).

Feasting on the Gospels

word is used consistently in reference to Judas at 6:64, 71; 12:4; 13:2, 11, 21; 21:20) Jesus to Pilate and thus are held most guilty (19:11b).

Pilate is described in a way that shows he is not sympathetic either to the Jews or to Jesus. In 18:28–38 he is portrayed as disdainful and impatient about the whole situation. Pilate is not impressed by Jesus. So in verse 33 it is perhaps better to phrase his question to Jesus, "*You* are the King of the Jews?" His disgust is expressed in verse 35 when he says, "I am not a Jew, am I?" His inability to understand is expressed in verse 37 as he tries to figure out who Jesus really is. By 19:16 Pilate—like Judas, who "handed over" Jesus to the Jewish authorities, who in turn "handed over" Jesus to Pilate—"hands over" Jesus to be crucified.

As depicted by the narrator, Jesus' trial before Pilate is a total travesty of justice. The Jewish authorities are hostile to Jesus, but have no legitimate charge against him. They are more concerned about their own survival and purity than they are for the truth. Pilate is depicted as a bored bureaucrat who does not really comprehend and who would prefer not to be bothered by this Jewish disturbance. Jesus is the only one who speaks the truth.

Throughout the Gospel, John writes history that is transparent and applicable to the experiences of his own community. It is particularly relevant in this scene. Just as Jesus here is in conflict with Jewish religious leaders, members of John's community are experiencing expulsion from the synagogue and even worse treatment from their fellow Jews (9:22; 12:42; 16:2). From the Roman side, Christians are potentially disruptive to the smooth flow of a pagan culture, and it is not understood that their allegiance is to one whose "kingdom is not from this world" (v. 36). Ultimately, the indictment of both Jewish and Roman authority is reflected in Pilate's classic question in verse 38, "What is truth?" Christian readers know that the truth is standing right in front of him ("I am . . . the truth," 14:6).

MARK G. VITALIS HOFFMAN

and Caiaphas and his final trial before Pilate, Jesus exudes a confidence that defies what we expect from one who is about to face death. His demeanor flips the script, and we know that it is not Jesus on trial but, rather, "the Jews," Pilate, and us! His mantra is, "Do not fence me in or try to limit what God is doing in this present age. It is all about God. What are you doing to preserve and protect all that is rightfully God's?"

The Fourth Evangelist gives us a portrait of Jesus as a "social prophet [who] criticized the elites (economic, political, and religious) of his time, [and] was an advocate of an alternative social vision, and was often in conflict with authorities."[3] Jesus is guilty of acts of compassion and justice, caring for people, and addressing the socioeconomic causes of their distress. His work was pastoral and political—a point that is often underdeveloped in our preaching. Jesus points to a realm (kingdom) where everyone has what is needed to survive; where none are superior based on status and privilege.

How do we react to Jesus? What interests do we seek to preserve and protect? What accusations do we level at Jesus as he peers into our hearts and minds? What defense do we offer for ourselves and our failings? In what ways are we like "the Jews"? Like Pilate? In our context, what is truth, as opposed to what is expedient, historical, scientific, consumable, predictable, provable?

The Fourth Evangelist portrays both "the Jews" and Pilate as those who have eyes but do not see and ears but do not hear. Jesus—the truth and light—stands before them, and they are so caught up in their own political fog that they are unable to see God's new thing in their midst. The Fourth Evangelist turns the questions back to us. In the end, we must all make a decision about Jesus—for or against. How we respond depends on whether we see and hear.

BARBARA J. ESSEX

3. Marcus J. Borg, *Meeting Jesus Again for the First Time: The Historical Jesus and the Heart of Contemporary Faith* (San Francisco: HarperSanFrancisco, 1995), 30.

John 18:38b–19:7

^{38b}After he had said this, he went out to the Jews* again and told them, "I find no case against him. ³⁹But you have a custom that I release someone for you at the Passover. Do you want me to release for you the King of the Jews?" ⁴⁰They shouted in reply, "Not this man, but Barabbas!" Now Barabbas was a bandit.

^{19:1}Then Pilate took Jesus and had him flogged. ²And the soldiers wove a crown of thorns and put it on his head, and they dressed him in a purple robe. ³They kept coming up to him, saying, "Hail, King of the Jews!" and striking him on the face. ⁴Pilate went out again and said to them, "Look, I am bringing him out to you to let you know that I find no case against him." ⁵So Jesus came out, wearing the crown of thorns and the purple robe. Pilate said to them, "Here is the man!" ⁶When the chief priests and the police saw him, they shouted, "Crucify him! Crucify him!" Pilate said to them, "Take him yourselves and crucify him; I find no case against him." ⁷The Jews answered him, "We have a law, and according to that law he ought to die because he has claimed to be the Son of God."

Theological Perspective

As Pilate's investigation proceeds, the governor's unwillingness to act, despite recognizing Jesus' innocence, undermines his rule. He knows the truth, but in seeking to control the situation in order to avoid judging rightly, his control unravels. With each ineffective ploy, Pilate becomes more desperate and, succumbing to fear, loses the initiative.

John's version of the Roman trial raises several historical problems. There is no extrabiblical witness for a "Passover amnesty," and scourging, as opposed to beating, was part of the very death sentence Pilate wants to avoid.[1] Embedded in John's telling, though, is a theological commentary that, though it raises interpretive questions of its own, may be discussed relatively independently of the historical problems—though not entirely, as shown by the question of Barabbas's crime.

The theme of kingship, specifically the kingship of Jesus, continues to dominate the theological dimension here. In the present passage, we have four moments, each of which contributes to John's representation of rule and power. These are the demand for Barabbas, the scourging and mockery

Pastoral Perspective

As the passion narrative continues, Pilate gives himself a problem: whether to release Barabbas or Jesus. Barabbas is a common criminal. For those who know the stories of the Gospels, Jesus is the logical person to set free, but the crowds demand that Barabbas be released. Pilate senses the wrongness of this action, but finally defers to the crowd's wish. The death sentence is pronounced against Jesus by an unlikely collaboration of political and religious authorities. The soldiers, servants of the empire, weave a crown of thorns and place it upon his head. The visual image is paradoxical: here is a king who suffers.

The passion narrative, in its essence, is a portrayal of the suffering God. In our congregations and in the culture we often reflect on the relationship between God and suffering. Some argue that God causes suffering; others assume that God is indifferent to suffering; still others imagine that God is powerless in the face of suffering. Within each of these very common perspectives is an image of God: the violent God, the distant God, and the weak God. None of these images is consistent with the wisdom of our best theological traditions, or helpful pastorally.

In contrast to each of these perspectives, John bears witness to a God who suffers. Jesus wears a crown of thorns. He is the (Passover) Lamb of God who takes away the sin of the world (1:29, 36). The

---

* See "'The Jews' in the Fourth Gospel" on pp. xi–xiv.

1. Raymond E. Brown, *The Gospel according to John XIII–XXI*, AB 30 (Garden City, NY: Doubleday, 1970), 870–74.

Feasting on the Gospels

Exegetical Perspective

John 18:38b–19:7 continues the trial proceedings of Jesus that began in 18:19. The high priest had not been able to lodge any conclusive charge against Jesus, nor had Pilate determined any fault, as he indicates in 18:38. The reader, however, is not being held in suspense, waiting to discover whether Jesus will be found guilty or released. Within the Gospel, Jesus has already indicated numerous times that he will die, and the discerning reader knows that it will be by crucifixion (3:14; 8:28; 11:50–57; 12:32–33). Even apart from these internal clues, it should be kept in mind that John's Gospel was written for a community who already knew quite well that Jesus had been crucified. What, then, is John accomplishing in narrating these scenes of interrogation and dispute between the Jewish leadership, Pilate, and Jesus?

First, this trial section serves to establish culpability for Jesus' death. In John, Jesus' most virulent antagonists are "the Jews." Does this mean John is anti-Semitic? No, and there are two matters to keep in mind.

It can be demonstrated that in John the term "the Jews" (*hoi Ioudaioi*) can refer variously to people living in Judea, that is, Judeans; people who are religiously Jewish; and a specific group of Jewish leaders and authorities. In this instance, it is clear that the ones accusing Jesus are the Jewish leaders,

Homiletical Perspective

The Fourth Evangelist continues to paint a picture that captivates us. The drama unfolds in layered textures. We will explore two preaching possibilities: revolutionaries and expectations.

Guilty as charged! We begin by looking at the two men accused of crimes against Rome: Jesus and Barabbas. Pilate continues to shuttle back and forth between "the Jews" and Jesus. Pilate declares that there is no case against Jesus. Due diligence requires him to release Jesus, but Pilate offers the Jewish leaders a choice. They choose Barabbas.

For the twenty-first-century believer, "bandit" conjures up images of Robin Hood, benignly taking from the rich and giving to the poor, but as we have seen throughout the Fourth Gospel, everything is political with a theological twist. The Greek word *lēstēs* points more to a revolutionary than a thief. Bandits in first-century Palestine resisted Roman oppression and often resorted to violence and murder. For the masses, bandits were heroes, because they took decisive action to overthrow Roman dominance. Their aim was liberation for the Jewish people, by any means necessary, in the here and now.

The Fourth Evangelist adds a twist: Jesus too is a revolutionary. His aim is the liberation of the Jewish masses, in the here and now. Jesus' actions speak to

Theological Perspective

by the soldiers, Pilate's presentation of Jesus, and the demand for crucifixion.

Having confirmed for the second time that Jesus is not guilty of a crime, Pilate offers to release Jesus under the terms of an annual Passover amnesty. If the governor is trying to secure Jesus' release at the crowd's request, his use of the inflammatory "King of the Jews" is puzzling. Here, however, theological drama may be decisive for John, as "the Jews" now make a clear choice between Jesus' kingship and the politics of Barabbas. Despite the suggestion that we have a shouting mob here, "the Jews" referred to are the chief priests and the officers of the temple.

Who, though, is Barabbas? Mark names him as a rebel and assassin, but John identifies him simply as a "bandit," though the political reading is possible, since this word is used elsewhere of insurrectionists.[2] The less specific identification, however, allows John an echo of Jesus' teaching about the good shepherd who "lays down his life," unlike the bandits who seek only to kill (10:1). A further resonance may also be the royal connotations of shepherd in the Old Testament. If John did understand Barabbas as a political rebel, then Barabbas becomes both a "wicked shepherd" and one of those who, unlike Jesus' disciples, fight for rule. This scene, therefore, presents again the contrast between his kingship and worldly kingship that Jesus explains to Pilate (18:36). The Jewish authorities reject Jesus' kingdom for the violence of worldly powers. They do so because they do not "belong to the truth" (18:37) and thus do not hear the shepherd's voice (10:4).

When the amnesty tactic fails, Pilate has Jesus scourged, the severity of which is rather contrary to his purpose, unless John intends a reference to Isaiah 1:6 or is confusing "scourging" with the milder "beating" (cf. Luke 23:16). Though the Roman soldiers deride Jesus, their mockery is an ironic witness to the truth and foreshadows the conversion of Gentiles. The reviling of Jesus also reveals the underside of worldly power. The soldiers exercise their hatred on a substitute, a mock-up of the rule to which they themselves submit. They strike back at the violence under which they suffer, venting their rage repeatedly upon Jesus. Brutality warps human beings, fostering the longing to destroy. The assault on Jesus comes from both sides of worldly rule: from above, the governor who sends him for the whipping, and from below, soldiers who make Jesus the stand-in for

Pastoral Perspective

suffering God identifies with us in our suffering. Suffering is not the outcome of our guilt before God; indeed, the One who takes our suffering upon himself is not guilty. Later, in 19:18, the suffering becomes a death sentence, as the suffering God becomes a sacrifice for the sins of humanity and a sign of God's reconciliation.

The death sentence is confirmed through the loud voices of the mob, who shout, "Crucify him! Crucify him!" to Pilate (v. 6). The experience of the mob is worthy of reflection. The movement of the Spirit is not always captured in the sentiment of the masses; at times, God is working from the opposite direction, and in hindsight we discover that we have missed the coming of God's kingdom. Popular opinion can indeed be wrong!

It would be easy to sit in judgment upon the crowds gathered in Jerusalem on that day, which was the day of Preparation for the Passover (19:14), but the loud voices of the mob also reside within each of us, particularly as we find ourselves at the intersection of weighty decisions. We are often tempted to add our voices to those of the mob; there is safety and security in anonymity, as we blend in with the harmony of an unjust or ill-considered decision.

The spiritual danger arises, however, in our inability to voice our convictions courageously. We may discover, with Pilate and the crowds, that we are on the wrong side of history. History does indeed repeat itself: a beginning sample might include first-century Jerusalem, the inquisitions, the genocide of the Jews in the Holocaust, the ongoing struggle in America against racial injustice. The movement toward greater access to freedom, justice, and human rights always passes through seasons of resistance, and speaking toward the resistance is always an act of courage and prophecy.

The passion narrative becomes a parable of a misguided mob mentality and the failure of leadership. The one who is innocent is found guilty. The one who is sinless is punished. The crowd wants and is granted a scapegoat. In the mysterious providence of God, though, we discover that the larger purposes of history are working themselves out. As we read in the narrative of Joseph and his brothers, "even though you intended to do harm to me, God intended it for good" (Gen. 50:20). God takes our human sinfulness and transforms it for redemptive purposes, which means that Pilate and the crowds are unlikely actors in a drama that moves toward salvation and redemption.

A final and deeper question related to the passion is our own complicity. How do we participate

2. C. K. Barrett, *The Gospel according to St. John*, 2nd ed. (Philadelphia: Westminster Press, 1978), 449.

and some English translations (e.g., The New English Translation, New Living Translation) even make this explicit. John is not, therefore, condemning Jews for the death of Jesus. He is criticizing the Jewish leadership for their persecution of Jesus and failure to recognize him as the Jewish Messiah.

It should also be remembered that John is a thoroughly Jewish Gospel in terms of its authorship and audience. Further, its final edition reflects a late-first-century-CE situation where Jewish Christians were being expelled from the synagogues and perhaps even killed (16:2). From John's perspective, therefore, what is happening to Jesus at the hands of the Jewish leadership anticipates the experience of the Jewish Christians in John's community.

Though "the Jews" are prosecuting Jesus, John does not exonerate Pilate or the Romans. Even though Pilate repeatedly (18:29–31, 38; 19:4, 6) claims not to find any case against Jesus, he is no friend of either Jesus or the Jews. The reader should discern Pilate's disdain when he uses an ethnic rather than a national title to refer to Jesus as "the King of the Jews." He also puts the Jewish leadership into conflicted positions—for example, making them choose between the "King of the Jews" and Barabbas—until they are forced into the nearly blasphemous statement in 19:15, "We have no king but the emperor." Pilate's malice and the Roman soldiers' hostility are also evident in their flogging and mocking of Jesus in 19:1–3. Pilate is not creating sympathy for the tortured Jesus when he presents him to the Jews in 19:4; rather, he is enjoying the spectacle of a pathetic "King of the Jews." Pilate ultimately does make the decision to deliver Jesus over to be crucified (19:16), but his ostensible power has been characterized by a failure to perceive the truth (18:38) and by fear (19:8).

Second, the trial section serves to establish Jesus' innocence. The Christian readers of this Gospel already believe this, but it is also important because John's community is part of the Roman Empire. When the person whom they confess as Lord and Savior is officially executed by the empire as a criminal, loyal citizens are likely to be suspicious of his followers. Pilate may be portrayed poorly by John, but Pilate does follow official protocol. In the end, it is clear that Jesus' death sentence is the result of the Jewish leadership's maneuverings, not because Jesus is guilty of a crime against the state. Pilate has noted that there is no case, Jesus has explained that his kingdom is not from this world (18:36), and Barabbas is also introduced as a foil to Jesus.

powers and principalities that control people and their destinies.

> If Jesus had had his way, the Roman Empire *and* the ruling elites among his own people . . . would no longer have held their positions of power. . . . An important goal of his ministry was to radically change the distribution of authority and power, goods and resources, so all people—particularly "the least of these," as Jesus called them—might have lives free of political repression, enforced hunger and poverty, and undue insecurity. It means that Jesus sought not only to heal people's pain but also to inspire and empower people to remove the unjust social and political structures that too often were the cause of their pain. It means that Jesus had a clear and unambiguous vision of the healthy world that God intended and that he addressed any issue—social, economic, or political—that violated that vision.[1]

The difference between Barabbas and Jesus was that Jesus waged his revolution without violence. He helped people change from the inside out, to claim their voice, to live their power, to assert their choices, to live with head and heart—in other words, to love God with their whole selves and to love their neighbors as themselves. Jesus' revolution does not resort to violence and mayhem, but is effective in shaking off the chains of oppression and domination. It results in a realm (kingdom) where all have what they need—a great reversal where the last will be first.

A second preaching possibility deals with expectations. Ours is a celebrity-driven society. We have high expectations of those we celebrate. We idolize tall, handsome men and shapely, gorgeous women. We expect them to live in palatial houses with open floor plans, granite countertops, stainless-steel kitchen appliances, walk-in closets, double sinks in the master bath, and large backyards for the dogs. We expect them to welcome the paparazzi, be impeccably dressed, wearing a smile, and ready to give the autograph or take a photo with passersby. We love our celebrities and watch their over-the-top reality shows. We wish we could be them.

We love them until they take a tumble from the pedestals we have built or head to rehab or get caught up in a sex scandal or commit a serious crime. We are deeply disappointed when the reality does not fit our expectation. We become

1. Obery M. Hendricks Jr., *The Politics of Jesus; Rediscovering the True Revolutionary Nature of Jesus' Teachings and How They Have Been Corrupted* (New York: Three Leaves Press, 2006), 5–6.

John 18:38b–19:7

Theological Perspective

their rage. To use the terms of a later theology, Jesus "takes our place" as the powers of this world exercise their fury. He stands his ground and reveals the glory of a different kingdom.

Jesus is brought out to the chief priests and the officers as the mocked king; but, instead of "Behold your king," Pilate announces, "Here is the man!" A straightforward reading of this would be the less theologically weighted: "Look at the (wretched) man."[3] Pilate is thus trying another tactic: Jesus is too pathetic to bother with any longer. The drama of Pilate's gesture and the abrupt introduction of "man" rather than "king"—which, used ironically, would have conveyed the absurdity just as well—lend support for a stronger reading. "The man," may either be a messianic reference deriving from Zechariah 6:12 or an allusion to myths of the "heavenly man." Especially in light of the demand for crucifixion that follows, the latter would resonate with Jesus' words, "as Moses lifted up the serpent in the wilderness, so must the Son of Man be lifted up, that whoever believes in him may have eternal life" (3:14). Whichever reading is preferred, the gulf between Jesus' kingship and worldly rule continues to widen.

Pilate's appeal meets with the enraged demand, "Crucify him!" Having failed yet again to shift the responsibility away from himself while also having Jesus released, the governor spits back an infuriated, "Crucify him yourselves," a permission both parties know is meaningless. Pilate pronounces Jesus innocent for the third and final time. His audience now produces a directly religious reason for Jesus' death: "he has claimed to be the Son of God" (v. 7b). At the theological level, the title "Son" is now brought into contact with the theme of kingship: in the scourged and ridiculed man appears both the manner of Jesus' rule and the depth of the Son's obedience.

Jesus' accusers thus disclose their root misunderstanding of Jesus' authority. Far from making himself Son of God, Jesus' sonship is characterized by obedience and commission. He is truly the Son of God and therefore does not speak or act on his own behalf. This will be revealed most fully when the demand of "the Jews" is fulfilled: "When you have lifted up the Son of Man, then you will realize that I am he, and that I do nothing on my own, but I speak these things as the Father instructed me" (8:28).

ALAN P. R. GREGORY

Pastoral Perspective

in the crucifixion of Jesus? Many have asked the question embedded in the hymn in the days leading to the passion: "Were you there when they crucified my Lord?"[1] Mature disciples of Jesus often have the sense that indeed they (we) were there; through our sins of omission or commission, we contributed to his harm or watched passively. The passion narrative continues to live and shape us as we look for the cross in our daily lives. We pray for the maturity to resist evil and injustice. We discern the winds of God's Spirit that are moving among us. We seek redemption in our own suffering and adversity. We look for the signs of God's providence even in the midst of tragedy and trauma.

To acknowledge that we were there at the crucifixion is to enter into dialogue with a God who suffers with us and for us. At the heart of our faith is a cross, "the emblem of suffering and shame," in the language of the old hymn.[2] We are asked, as disciples of Jesus, to take up the cross and follow him, and, in a more profound and mystical sense, our lives begin to take the shape of that cross. The apostle Paul writes, "I have been crucified with Christ; and it is no longer I who live, but it is Christ who lives in me. And the life I now live in the flesh I live by faith in the Son of God, who loved me and gave himself for me" (Gal. 2:19–20). The words from the crowd, "Crucify him! Crucify him," are ones that are spoken at times by us and, at times, if we are following Jesus, about us.

KENNETH H. CARTER

3. Rudolf Bultmann, *The Gospel of John: A Commentary*, trans. G. R. Beasley-Murray (Philadelphia: Westminster Press, 1971), 658–59.

1. "Were You There When They Crucified My Lord?" traditional African American spiritual, *Glory to God* (Louisville, KY: Westminster John Knox Press, 2013), #228.
2. George Bennard, "The Old Rugged Cross" (1913).

Exegetical Perspective

There is no extrabiblical record of a Roman custom of releasing a prisoner at Passover, but it is not an unreasonable gesture, and a similar detail is mentioned in Mark 15:6 and Matthew 27:15. (A better translation of John 18:39 might be, "It has become customary for you that I release . . .") John identifies Barabbas as a "bandit," a negative term for John (10:1, 8), which also characterizes the type of revolutionary—or "insurgent," in modern terms— who practices violent resistance to the state. This is the kind of person Rome regularly crucified. The term is used in Matthew 27:38, 44 and Mark 15:27 of those crucified with Jesus. When the Jewish leadership asks for Barabbas to be released instead of Jesus, John not only indicates their hostility to Jesus but also demonstrates that Rome should be suspicious of "the Jews," rather than the followers of Jesus. That John specifically records Barabbas's name also hints at an irony in the situation. Since Barabbas means "son of *abba*," that is, "son of the father," the choice is being made between a vicious character and the innocent "Son of the Father/God."

Third, the trials of Jesus establish his true identity as King of the Jews and Son of God. As noted above, "King of the Jews" is Pilate's ethnic and derogatory designation used in 18:33, 39. He will use it again, intentionally provoking controversy, in 19:19–21, as the charge posted on the inscription on the cross. The charge is true, though John would prefer the title "King of Israel," used in greeting Jesus as he enters Jerusalem in 12:13.

A new and also true charge is raised by the Jewish leaders in 19:7. Jesus' identity as the Son of God has been affirmed by the author (1:14, 18) and by John the Baptist (1:34) and asserted by Jesus throughout the Gospel (5:18; 10:36). For the alert reader, these two titles together here in the trial scene provide a match with the opening story of Nathanael, who in 1:49 declares to Jesus, "Rabbi, you are the Son of God! You are the King of Israel!" What Jesus then said to Nathanael applies as well here in chapter 19: "You will see greater things than these."

MARK G. VITALIS HOFFMAN

Homiletical Perspective

disillusioned and are quick to judge our fallen idols. We vow never to latch on to a celebrity again—until the next time, that is.

Jesus and his people lived in the shadow of the Roman Empire. There was no separation of church and state. The priests were religious leaders and peons for the Romans. The masses were poor, paying taxes to Rome and to the temple officials. The people mortgaged their land and their children in order to pay their taxes. The people resented the Romans and their own leaders. This is the backdrop against which Jesus stands trial before Pilate and the Jewish leaders.

In the ancient Near East, coronations were special events. Inaugurating a new ruler was a ritual signifying stability and political power. Again, the Fourth Evangelist paints a picture with a twist. Instead of anointing with oil, Jesus is anointed with the spit of the Roman soldiers. Instead of headgear made of gold and precious jewels, Jesus sports a crown of thorns stained with his blood. Instead of embroidered garments, Jesus is robed in purple cloth. Instead of shouts of adoration and trumpet blasts, Jesus' coming-out party is marred by shouts of "Crucify him! Crucify him!"

"Here is the man!" Pilate shows the leaders their would-be king, beaten and bruised in makeshift royal regalia. This is what Pilate thinks of the Jewish hope for a ruler. The people reject this man, for he does not meet their expectations. He is not the warrior to overthrow Roman domination. He is not powerful or rich. He has no army at his command. As a ruler, Jesus just does not fit the bill; yet there is something about him that will not let us go; we cannot look away.

The Fourth Evangelist got it right. "The Jews" and Pilate are challenged to open their eyes and see Jesus as God's anointed one. When we look at Jesus, what do we see: a fallen hero or a bold revolutionary? Do we see one who applauds our riches, or one who challenges us to sacrifice and work for justice?

The reality is that Jesus is exactly what the Jewish people needed. Jesus is exactly what we need. The preacher's challenge is to help us see Jesus—not as a superstar celebrity, but as the one who makes things right for all people, regardless of status, wealth, and privilege.

BARBARA J. ESSEX

John 19:8–16a

⁸Now when Pilate heard this, he was more afraid than ever. ⁹He entered his headquarters again and asked Jesus, "Where are you from?" But Jesus gave him no answer. ¹⁰Pilate therefore said to him, "Do you refuse to speak to me? Do you not know that I have power to release you, and power to crucify you?" ¹¹Jesus answered him, "You would have no power over me unless it had been given you from above; therefore the one who handed me over to you is guilty of a greater sin." ¹²From then on Pilate tried to release him, but the Jews* cried out, "If you release this man, you are no friend of the emperor. Everyone who claims to be a king sets himself against the emperor."

¹³When Pilate heard these words, he brought Jesus outside and sat on the judge's bench at a place called The Stone Pavement, or in Hebrew Gabbatha. ¹⁴Now it was the day of Preparation for the Passover; and it was about noon. He said to the Jews, "Here is your King!" ¹⁵They cried out, "Away with him! Away with him! Crucify him!" Pilate asked them, "Shall I crucify your King?" The chief priests answered, "We have no king but the emperor." ¹⁶Then he handed him over to them to be crucified.

Theological Perspective

The purpose of the Gospel of John is succinctly stated at the end of the book: "But these are written so that you may come to believe that Jesus is the Messiah, the Son of God, and that through believing you may have life in his name" (20:31). This Gospel is noted for its high Christology and central theological claims about Jesus' identity and mission as the sent one, God's Son and Messiah, for the purpose of manifesting the life-giving love of God for the redemption of the world. How might the text before us, part of the passion narrative of Jesus' arrest, trial, suffering, and execution, illuminate our understanding of who Jesus was for the purpose of helping us to believe and receive the kind of life, both now and in eternity, that God desires for us?

First, Jesus' teachings, ministry, and mission created controversies that are now coming to a climax. There were confrontations throughout this Gospel with religious leaders for whom Jesus' claim to be Son of God was blasphemy, a severe charge that in this environment warranted death. Political figures also took issue with Jesus' divine identification as a threat to the claims of kingship and power by Caesar and other leaders in the Roman Empire. The conflict over Jesus' identity and mission had

* See "'The Jews' in the Fourth Gospel" on pp. xi–xiv.

Pastoral Perspective

The author of the Gospel of John centers the story of Jesus' arrest on a series of conversations between Pontius Pilate and Jesus and between Pilate and the crowd. In this passage, we read of Jesus and Pilate's final conversation. As the nineteenth chapter of the Gospel of John unfolds, Pilate orders Jesus' flogging (v. 1), and the soldiers robe him in purple, crown him with thorns, and mock him. Intended to elicit Jesus' forced submission to the power of Rome, the beating and questioning instead clarify Jesus' kingship. He is a king, but not of this world, and not in any way that this world understands.

As the passage begins, Jesus stands before Pilate, who has already expressed his belief in Jesus' innocence but has yet to render his official judgment. At the heart of their final conversation is this issue of Jesus' identity as a king. Pilate keeps treating him as one, and the crowds keep calling him one. This issue of kingship forces Pilate's hand. If Jesus is a king of Israel, he is a threat to Pilate and the Roman Empire to which he belongs. If Jesus is not a king—for he has no army, no wealth, no power—he is surrounded by a crowd of people who say that he is, and they may believe it enough to rebel against the authorities. Pilate is left to choose between executing Jesus or inviting a possible armed rebellion. Either understanding of Jesus' identity as a king, whether

Feasting on the Gospels

Exegetical Perspective

These verses present the climactic closing scenes of the so-called trial of Jesus before Pilate (first introduced in 18:28). The trial is narrated through seven scenes in which Pilate is shuttling back and forth between the Judaic authorities outside the Roman *praetorium* (Pilate's headquarters within Jerusalem) and Jesus, who is inside the *praetorium*. Because the evangelist has foreshadowed Jesus' death (and resurrection) from early on in the narrative, there is no suspense about whether or not Jesus will be set free. Likewise as the trial unfolds, it becomes clear that this really is not the trial of Jesus; rather, it is the trial of Pilate. Thus the chief question is not the innocence or guilt of Jesus but, will Pilate choose to side himself with Jesus, who is the light of the world, or ally himself with the Judaic authorities who have chosen darkness?

The reference to Pilate's fear in 19:8 is rather ambiguous. While his fear is related to hearing those authorities report that Jesus ought to die according to Jewish law because he made himself Son of God (v. 7, alluding to Lev. 24:16), it is not clear why this should cause Pilate to fear. The matter is not helped by the NRSV translation, "he was more afraid than ever," which presumes that Pilate had previously been afraid. There is no reference or portrayal of Pilate's fear up to this point. A better translation

Homiletical Perspective

The unfolding passion narrative continues with the story of Jesus' arrest and trial before Pilate. At every turn of John's testimony, irony leaps from the text. The passage begins with a reference to Pilate's fear, a reaction to the hostility of the Jewish authorities to his conclusion that there is not much of a case against Jesus (vv. 6–7). John's observation that Pilate "was more afraid than ever" sets a dramatic tone for the exchange that follows. As a Roman official in his own praetorian palace, Pilate has all the trappings of power, yet it is he who is afraid and acts as though he is on trial. Jesus, mocked, beaten and draped in the now-bloody purple cloak, stands in silence, unmoved by Pilate's threatening presence and lack of understanding about where Jesus is "from." Silence speaks. As Bultmann suggests, who Jesus is "cannot be imparted through mere statement."[1] When Jesus does speak, it is a declaration of confidence and clarity about where true power resides. The roles of Jesus and Pilate are all but reversed.

For the preacher, the image of the powerless in the face of the powerful is a rich one to explore. There are few moments in Scripture that offer sustenance to the victimized and oppressed more clearly

1. Rudolf K. Bultmann, *The Gospel of John: A Commentary* (Philadelphia: Westminster Press, 1971), 661.

Theological Perspective

been escalating to its ultimate conflict with his opponents, who were now putting Jesus on trial for claiming to be the Son of God.

What this text reflects when one encounters Jesus is this: it is difficult to be indifferent to Jesus. His presence elicits powerful responses that can go one of two ways. The first is fear manifested in anger, hatred, and rejection of the claims Jesus is making and their implications for human lives and loyalties. The other is the kind of fear that the Scriptures describe as awe, a humble recognition of Jesus as the Christ, and willingness to hear and believe this one sent by God out of love for humanity.

Second, in his trial, Jesus shows us the clash between human and divine power. As a representative of the Roman Empire, Pilate had power that came with his position as a Roman governor. He occupied the headquarters of Roman officials; he had the authority to make judgments about who was to live and who was to die; and he had the right to execute his decisions by sheer fact of his positional authority as the prefect of Judea. Pilate also had the backing of force and coercion to exert his will. As Jesus is being handed over to his execution, it is ironically Pilate who is most afraid of what is transpiring in the swirling chaos. Pilate may be frightened about the impending wrongful execution of an innocent person. Perhaps he senses his own powerlessness to stop the horror that is happening as he is confronted by the angry crowd and threats from religious leaders calling into question Pilate's loyalty to Rome if he goes easy on Jesus (v. 12).

Whatever the reason, Pilate is "more afraid than ever" (v. 8). How telling, when it should be Jesus who is most afraid. In the face of his own powerlessness to persuade others to give Jesus a fair trial and in light of his failure to elicit a response from Jesus (vv. 8–9), Pilate appeals to the only source of power he has, his authority as a Roman prefect, which is the power either to release or execute Jesus (v. 10). Pilate may have authority, but he lacks the influence to direct these circumstances to a different outcome.

Jesus responds by reminding Pilate that whatever form of power Pilate possesses has been given him from above (v. 11). In Christ, we come to understand that God is the one with ultimate power, which relativizes all human claims to such. We see in this interaction a clash between the "powers and principalities," typified by Jesus, the Son of God, and Pilate, a son of Rome, a desperate political leader making claims to ultimate power over this one sent by God.[1]

Pastoral Perspective

confessed or professed, forces Pilate to see Jesus as a threat to his authority and power.

When he is faced with no real choice, Pilate conforms to the ways of the only world he knows. Power is in his hands. In his final attempt to understand Jesus' identity as a king, he gives voice to this power: "Do you not know that I have power to release you, and power to crucify you?" (v. 10). Pilate reverts to his inner sense of authority and proven habits of power, instead of discerning a new direction—perhaps even a nonviolent direction—toward rendering judgment.

As the author tells the story, Pilate takes his place on the Stone Pavement and calls Jesus to stand next to him. The timing of Pilate's judgment is an important detail. It is noon on the day of Preparation for the Passover (v. 14). The day of Preparation for Passover is an annual observance appointed in the Torah and tradition of the ancient Israelites. It is a day set apart for the preparation of all ritual and celebratory elements necessary for Passover's eight-day festival of salvation and liberation, of hearing and reenacting the sacred story of God's salvific act on behalf of the enslaved Israelites and leading them to freedom from Egyptian oppression.

This day of Preparation is full of cleaning and cooking and gathering and making ready for families to gather. This is the very day—in fact, it is in the very middle of this day—that Jesus is sentenced to death by Pontius Pilate. This is the day on which the crowds cry out, "Away with him! Away with him! Crucify him!" (v. 15). Pilate's power over life and death is woven into the religious remembrance of life from death and of liberation from oppression. In John's Gospel, Jesus becomes the paschal lamb being prepared for slaughter as an offering for salvation. Where is God's salvation now? This section of the Gospel closes with Pilate bending to the will and cry of the crowds as he orders the crucifixion of Jesus, the crucifixion of their king.

This passage invites us to wonder, what kind of king is Jesus, and what is the kingdom of God over which he reigns? When compared with Pilate, Jesus is a king without power and authority. He is a king without possessions, without army and support from the crowds. He is handed over by both his closest friends and the religious authorities to the political machinations of a Roman justice system that claims power over his life and death. He stands alone, judged as a criminal, sentenced to death. When our king is Christ—an innocent man of no wealth or power—are we willing in our own time and place to

would be "Pilate was rather afraid," evidently because he realizes that the stakes are getting higher.

In any case, this causes him to return inside, where he asks Jesus where he comes from (v. 9). There is significant irony in his question. On the one hand, Pilate is inquiring about the actual geography of Jesus' origin. On the other hand, the evangelist has already presented Jesus' origin as theological geography. He is from the realm "above" (3:3, 7, 31), that is, he is from God, and to God he will return. Pilate, however, is completely clueless about this, since he has already rejected Jesus' kingship (18:33–37a) and has refused to listen to the voice of the one who is the truth (18:37b–38, ironically recalling 14:6). Thus Jesus does not answer him.

This causes Pilate to point out to Jesus what would seem to be an obvious judicial fact. As Rome's agent, he has authority either to release or to crucify Jesus (v. 10). Jesus, however, counters by telling Pilate that he has no authority over Jesus unless it has been given to him from the realm "above" (v. 11a). Again, the narrative is laced with irony as the threefold use of the word "authority" (Gk. *exousia*) is playing off its twofold use in 10:17–18, where Jesus announces that as good shepherd he is the one who has authority from God to lay down his life for his sheep and authority to take it again. Thus Jesus is declaring that Pilate does not have authority over him, since he is the one who has been given authority over humanity (17:2) and is on God's authorized mission to bring true life through his own death. The only (ironic) authority Pilate has is to order Jesus' death, through which will come forgiveness and life.

Jesus' further comment in verse 11b, "therefore the one who handed me over to you is guilty of a greater sin," is significant for a number of reasons. First, these are Jesus' last words in the trial and thus present the final verdict of the true judge of the world. Second, the word "hand over" (Gk. *paradidōmi*) has been used to depict the actions of the devil (13:2), Judas (6:64, 71; 12:4; 13:2, 11, 21; 18:2, 5), and the religious authorities (18:35, 36). Because the devil instigates the handing over of Jesus, he is the one with the greater sin. Third, this does not exonerate either Judas or the religious authorities. The devil may have the "greater" sin, but the authorities are guilty of sin as well, for they have refused to see Jesus as the light of the world (9:40–41) and so have loved the darkness more, to their own condemnation (3:18–20).

Jesus' pronouncement of judgment motivates Pilate to seek a way to release him, yet at that very

than this scene. The full force of the powerful military government presses in on Jesus and threatens to end his life, but he says confidently, "You . . . have no power over me" (v. 11). When we feel overwhelmed, powerless, and vulnerable, it is easy to lose a sense of who we are. To recognize what is happening and to be able to draw upon our faith as a sustaining source of power when all else seems lost is a precious gift.

In the Gospel of John there is a constant contrast between two worlds, and in this scene the motif is poignantly elevated. John reminds us that throughout his ministry Jesus contrasted the ordinary with the eternal: table bread with the bread of life, ordinary water with life-giving water. Now, at the climax of the passion narrative, as Jesus stands before Pilate, the contrasts of power and powerlessness and of life and death play themselves out in high relief. This text also underscores an important message from Jesus about who is really in charge of his life. The scriptural references throughout the passion narrative make it clear that Pilate is but a pawn in a grander, more eternal drama of redemption and salvation.

Frustrated and trapped, not wanting to get caught in this Jewish tug of war, but at the same time not wanting to be blackmailed before the emperor for his indecision, Pilate takes Jesus out before the crowds. Ironically he assumes his place on the judgment seat, with the humiliated Jesus standing beside him. The concept of the "seat of judgment " or the "seat of power" can be fertile for preachers, particularly as one remembers the words of William Sloane Coffin, who liked to say that "those who are the farthest from the seats of power are often closest to the heart of things."[2]

The reference to the time and place of Jesus' trial underscores the symbolism of the moment of Israel's deliverance. John notes that it was the day of Preparation for the Passover (Heb. *Pesach*). There are many features to this ritual time; one is that all cooking of food must be done in advance. The day of Preparation remembers (Exod. 12:3) the sacrifice of a year-old lamb without blemish, which the Israelites offered during the night before their escape from Egypt. The blood of this sacrifice was wiped on the doorposts of the Israelites using a hyssop branch. It was to be a sign to the plague of death, so it would pass by the houses of the Israelites while on its way to slay the firstborn of the Egyptians (Exod.

2. Tessa Melvin, "'Town Meeting' Debates the Bomb," *New York Times*, November 21, 1982; http://www.nytimes.com/1982/11/21/nyregion/town -meeting-debates-the-bomb.html; accessed January 16, 2014.

John 19:8–16a

Theological Perspective

While Pilate's power may be delegated by God, this ought not to be seen as a moral or legitimate use of power, especially when that power is used for self-protection and to further injustice and wrongdoing.

Pilate represents for us the idolatrous futility of humans usurping the place of God by using power to secure our own ends. We witness a wonderful theological irony, typical in John's Gospel, in Pilate's encounter with Jesus. It is Pilate, the one with official power, who is afraid of Jesus. It is Pilate, the one with authority, who is swayed by the threats from others that he will be "no friend of the emperor" if he releases Jesus (v. 12). It is Jesus, the one confident of his identity and mission from God, who has the power and strength to face these circumstances.

Third, in another ironic theological twist, it is Jesus who is placed on the judge's bench by Pilate in an act of mockery (v. 13). Pilate now makes public what is true about Jesus Christ. The timing of Jesus' trial with the preparation for Passover cannot be ignored for its theological significance, in light of what we understand Jesus' mission to be. It is Jesus who is the paschal lamb of the impending Passover celebration, the one who will be sacrificed for the sins of the world. It is Jesus who is the king like no other, paradoxically denied such by the blasphemous confession of others who say they "have no king but the emperor" (v. 15). It is Jesus who sits in judgment of all human claims to ultimate power. "Written so that you may come to believe" (20:31) in Jesus the Christ, the Son of God, the one sent from God out of love for our sake.

WYNDY CORBIN REUSCHLING

Pastoral Perspective

stand with and speak for the innocent who are without wealth or power? Christians are called to live into this kingdom of God. What does that look like in our own day and time? Are we willing to stand alongside Jesus and open our eyes to see political and religious injustice destroying our human brothers and sisters?

Many examples in our daily living pose this challenge for us who are entrusted with living in this kingdom. We live in a society in which public policies related to those living in our communities without homes or who are food-insecure remain oppressive and unforgiving. What can we do, what can our churches do, to show the rest of our communities that living in the kingdom of God demands a generosity of our wisdom, our resources, and our love for those in need? Living in the kingdom of God also means that we acknowledge that we live in a global community where many, because of gender or generational hatred, are dehumanized by political and religious authorities. What can our churches do to stand with them, to be a voice for them, to see Christ in them? Do we recognize that when we stand with and speak for those treated unjustly in our world, we leave the crowds who cry out, "Crucify," and speak with compassion?

At the heart of John's telling of Jesus' crucifixion is his kingship. Christians worship a God whose kingdom breaks into this world through Jesus Christ. Its king is unlike any earthly king, for his power comes from his commandment to his followers to love one another (13:31–35).

AMY G. HELLER

---

1. See the following by Walter Wink: *Naming the Powers: The Language of Power in the New Testament* (Philadelphia: Fortress Press, 1984); *Unmasking the Powers: The Invisible Forces That Determine Human Existence* (Philadelphia: Fortress Press, 1985); and *Engaging the Powers: Discernment and Resistance in a World of Domination* (Philadelphia: Fortress Press, 1992).

Feasting on the Gospels

Exegetical Perspective

moment, Jesus' antagonists shout from outside that by releasing Jesus, Pilate will not be a friend of Caesar (v. 12). "Friend of Caesar" is a political claim that Caesar is one's royal patron, and if anyone makes himself a king or aligns himself with a would-be king, he becomes Caesar's enemy. Just as Caiaphas regarded Jesus' execution as a matter of supreme political expediency (11:47–53), now Caiaphas's allies are reminding Pilate of the supreme political implications of not executing Jesus. Ironically, Jesus used the term "friend" the night before to describe his relationship with his followers and to declare that the greatest love is to lay down one's life for one's friends (15:13–15).

The final scene of the trial (vv. 14–16a) establishes several theological points. First, the final verdict against Jesus (the true Passover lamb, 19:31–37) is made at the very time when thousands of Passover lambs are being slaughtered in the temple. Second, while both Pilate and Jesus' Judean antagonists reject any notion that Jesus is a king, he truly is king, and his glorious coronation is about to happen in his crucifixion. Third, the chief priests' declaration, "We have no king except Caesar" (my trans.), is ultimate blasphemy, as they are rejecting both God's covenant with David (2 Sam. 7) and God's reign as king of both Israel and the universe. Fourth, their claim becomes the motivation for Pilate to do exactly what they have wanted all along, to execute Jesus. Evidently Pilate is now quite willing to do their bidding, as he has been able to goad them into renouncing Israel's messianic hope and to swear their ultimate allegiance to his emperor. Fifth, by handing Jesus over (*paradidōmi*) to be crucified, Pilate has also sealed his own fate. He too has rejected the one sent to save the world, and in so doing he has allied himself with the devil, Judas, the religious authorities, and all who reject the light of the world. His trial is now over, as he has condemned himself.

RICHARD CARLSON

Homiletical Perspective

12:1–23). With the presence of Jesus standing before the crowds, with death looming in the air, John openly invites the sacrificial lamb imagery.

A word of caution and an important distinction: The concept of a sacrificial lamb has become a universal symbol that retains currency in contemporary culture, but the idea is often diminished and abused. In literature and film a "sacrificial lamb" is a common device used to advance the story. By and large, though, these are minor or throwaway characters. For the preacher these contemporary images of someone dying in a narrative do not get to the heart of the passion symbolism or provide a helpful insight to the more sophisticated theological concepts like atonement.

The passage ends with great theological irony, as Jesus is presented to the crowd for the last time. They shout, "Crucify him!" and Pilate responds, "Shall I crucify your King?" (v. 15). The final shout from the priests, who are symbols of the religious establishment, says, "We have no king but the emperor" (v. 15b). The words echo hauntingly in the days of Passover, with their declarations of the power of God over earthly powers. Preaching on this passage it would be important to note that one of the hymns of the *Hallel Nirtzah* portion of the Passover observance includes the line, "From the beginning to the end of the world You are Almighty G-d; and other than You we have no King, Redeemer and Savior who delivers, rescues, sustains, answers and is merciful in every time of trouble and distress; we have no King but You."[3] For the leaders of the religious community to make the confession they make to Pilate betrays the essential meaning of Passover and its message of liberation for those who remain faithful to YHWH alone.

NICK CARTER

---

3. Passover Haggadah, available at http://www.chabad.org/holidays/passover/pesach_cdo/aid/1739/jewish/Hallel-Nirtzah.htm; accessed January 18, 2014.

John 19:16b–25a

16bSo they took Jesus; 17and carrying the cross by himself, he went out to what is called The Place of the Skull, which in Hebrew is called Golgotha. 18There they crucified him, and with him two others, one on either side, with Jesus between them. 19Pilate also had an inscription written and put on the cross. It read, "Jesus of Nazareth, the King of the Jews." 20Many of the Jews* read this inscription, because the place where Jesus was crucified was near the city; and it was written in Hebrew, in Latin, and in Greek. 21Then the chief priests of the Jews said to Pilate, "Do not write, 'The King of the Jews,' but, 'This man said, I am King of the Jews.'" 22Pilate answered, "What I have written I have written."

Theological Perspective

The Nicene Creed (325 CE) is one of the most important statements about the essential beliefs of the Christian faith written and adopted by the church. For those of us who recite this creed in our various ecclesial contexts, part of what we affirm about Jesus Christ is this: "For our sake, he was crucified under Pontius Pilate." This is a broad statement that acknowledges Jesus was crucified for our sake, without giving specific details about what it is that Jesus' death accomplished "for our sake."

This is where various atonement theologies are used to interpret passages such as the one before us. Theological reflection fills in the lack of details by suggesting that Jesus' death and resurrection was God's victory over the power of death and destruction, or that Jesus' voluntary giving of his life for others offers us a profound and normative example of moral influence for the kind of loving sacrifice that should characterize our lives. Other atonement theologies suggest Jesus' death satisfied God's anger at human sin, or that he was punished vicariously and paid the "debt he did not owe for the debt we could not pay."[1]

This selection in John 19 tells us *how* Jesus died—by a brutal Roman crucifixion that brought about a

* See "'The Jews' in the Fourth Gospel" on pp. xi–xiv.
1. Ellis J. Crum, "He Paid a Debt He Did Not Owe" (Kendallville, IN: Sacred Selections R. E. Winsett, 1977).

Pastoral Perspective

The author of the Gospel of John describes Jesus' crucifixion through the lenses of two separate groups of people at the foot of the cross. It is as though the camera pans first to those responsible for his literal crucifixion—the governor, the religious authorities, and the soldiers. In the passage following this (19:25b–30), the camera will pan over to a second group of bystanders. Both of these groups reinforce the author's emphasis on the questions of kingdom and kingship. Within the context of a kingdom of this world, the kingdom of God is revealed. In this passage, the first group of witnesses is rooted in the kingdom of this world, its laws, and its understanding. In the passage to follow, the second group of bystanders is rooted in the kingdom of God.

In this passage, the execution of Jesus unfolds. The characters in the scene are Pilate, the chief priests, and the soldiers. Each of them is witness to Jesus' crucifixion. Pilate is the judge who literally inscribes the charge in the three languages of this part of the Roman Empire and posts them on the cross. The chief priests are the religious authorities who challenge the wording on the charge, so that their distance from this accused king of their nation is clear. The Roman soldiers are the executioners who crucify Jesus and gamble for his last possession, a seamless tunic. The author tells us only that

²³When the soldiers had crucified Jesus, they took his clothes and divided them into four parts, one for each soldier. They also took his tunic; now the tunic was seamless, woven in one piece from the top. ²⁴So they said to one another, "Let us not tear it, but cast lots for it to see who will get it." This was to fulfill what the scripture says,

"They divided my clothes among themselves,
and for my clothing they cast lots."
²⁵And that is what the soldiers did.

Exegetical Perspective

The four episodes narrated in this text are rooted in the very earliest traditions of Jesus' passion, as the Synoptic Gospels (Mark, Matthew, and Luke) and the Fourth Gospel all report on Jesus' journey from the trial to the place of execution (v. 16b); on the place of execution being named Golgotha, meaning Skull Place (v. 17); on Jesus being crucified with and in the middle of two others (v. 18); on an inscription being placed on the cross announcing Jesus as King of the Jews (v. 19); and on soldiers dividing Jesus' clothing by casting lots (vv. 23–25a). Likewise, some of these details were common features of actual Roman crucifixion scenes and so would be recognizable to a first-century audience. Nevertheless, the Fourth Evangelist narrates his own presentation of Jesus' death and gives distinctive theological insights into these events.

The trial narrative (18:28–19:16a) concluded when "Pilate handed over Jesus to them to be crucified" (19:16a). The very next line reports that "they took Jesus" (v. 16b). Within the immediate context, it is not completely clear to whom Pilate handed over Jesus or who took him. Not until 19:23 does it become clear that the (Roman) soldiers are the previously unidentified referents. Thus the same group of soldiers that performed the mock but ironic coronation of Jesus in 19:2–3 is now the group who crucify the ridiculed king of the Jews.

Homiletical Perspective

This is a remarkably brief account of an essential part of the Christian testimony. "We preach Christ crucified," says the apostle Paul (1 Cor. 1:23). The Synoptics have fuller accounts, and there is a temptation to fill in the blanks. While helpful in many places, to do so at first blush would rob John of his voice and perspective as a Gospel writer.

Unlike the stories of the nativity, the narrative of Jesus' crucifixion explores difficult themes of suffering, guilt, grief, and shame. The image of Jesus on the cross is arguably the most reproduced subject in the history of painting, and there are representations of it and allusions to it in countless other media, like film, sculpture, theater, music, and even comedy. Through the centuries great artists like Michelangelo, Rubens, El Greco, Delacroix, Grünewald, Velazquez, Gauguin, Dali, and Rouault have sought to express their perspectives on this brutal but sacred and enduring image. Like the individual Gospel writers, each has a different story to tell. Some paintings are detailed, explicit, and agonizing; others are soft and colorful. Some perspectives look up, others down. There are heroic and romantic, if not triumphant, depictions; still others show Jesus all but naked in humiliating defeat. It is important to observe that John, like these painters, has his unique perspective.

Theological Perspective

slow and agonizing death that many witnessed—but what do we know about *why* Jesus died? What are the theological possibilities in this crucifixion narrative that draw our attention to Jesus' execution that was "for our sake" and "because of us"?

Jesus carried the cross by himself to one of the most dreaded places, Golgotha, a hill that resembled a human skull outside the protective walls of Jerusalem (v. 17). Jesus the Christ, the one sent from God to reclaim a lost world, remained committed to this mission in spite of the cries for his death and the human actions that actually brought it about. This mission of reconciling love was something that only the Son of God could accomplish. Jesus truly was alone in this mission and in control when carrying his own cross. There was no one there to help him or do this for him. For our sake, Jesus willingly carried his cross, this instrument by which he would die so that we might live. The one did this alone because of the many.

Jesus died because of us. Throughout this narrative, we witness the human dynamics and various collusions that brought about Jesus' death. Jesus was sentenced to death by humans and handed over to political authorities for capital punishment, but even this was not enough. We see cruelty heaped upon cruelty as people mocked Jesus and disrobed him, exacerbating the shame of crucifixion. While Jesus acknowledged his death as fulfillment of the Scripture (v. 24), humans were the catalysts in bringing about Jesus' death by hatred, direct action, silent indifference, and cowardice. There are no indications that God punished Jesus or that God's wrath was appeased as reasons for Jesus' death. Jesus Christ died due to our human sinfulness, which is painfully portrayed in this text in many ways. We witness here the human capacity for evil and the deathly consequences of our actions, silences, cruelty, and complicities in bringing about someone's death. Yes, Jesus died because of our collective and representative sin. "Because of us" Jesus was killed.

We see again a powerful theological irony play out in this passage, a literary device used in John's Gospel that reveals who Jesus was and who he remains to this day. Jesus was charged with treason for his claim to be the Son of God. We do not know Pilate's reasons for having "Jesus of Nazareth, the King of the Jews," inscribed on the cross in the three primary languages of the day in Palestine: Hebrew, Latin, and Greek (vv. 19–20). Perhaps this was a form of mockery by Pilate, in light of Jesus' challenge to Pilate's own power and authority as a

Pastoral Perspective

Jesus carried his own cross and that he was crucified between two others. His execution was part of the legal business of that day when others judged for their crimes were also sentenced to death.

Nowhere in this passage is there any attention to Jesus' suffering and dying on the cross. The focus is on those responsible, who are tending to what they can gain from this execution—political power and maneuvering and a precious possession. Power, fear, and greed flow from Pilate to the chief priests to the soldiers. Jesus' human life and death are merely means to an end for this group.

What is at the heart of this issue over what is inscribed on the charge? Titles reflect power. For Jesus to be called a king of Israel is to give him a place in its history. As a king of Israel, he would be added to the long line of historic kings who tried to honor the covenants and commandments of the God. If Jesus were a king of this world, he would have possessions, but at the cross, Jesus' sole material item is taken away. The contrast between the written charge of being a king and the fact that he owns only a seamless tunic demonstrates the Gospel writer's emphasis on Jesus' kingship as a reversal of social norms. Jesus is king of the realm of God, a kingdom in which heaven and earth come together in him and through him. In this kingdom, power is not given because of birthright or title but, rather, through living by its commandment to love and to serve the outcast, the forgotten, the weak, the sick, and those otherwise silenced by society.

In our own time, cultural norms still elevate titles, social status, and material wealth as signs of power and significance. We are drawn to wealth and success and prosperity; some even see those as gifts from God, as though God would give to some and withhold from others and be fine with that. Living in a kingdom under the commandment of love is to be generous with the abundance that we have been given to those who are without. In this kingdom of God over which Christ reigns, as we love and serve others, we give and share what we have with those in need. In our culture, how hungry we are to know the personal stories of the rich and famous when they make mistakes. However, the stories about bringing goodness and justice into the world take a back page. The kingdom of God looks like a *People* magazine full of those who have, reaching out to those who have not, because the titles and the status and the wealth are not needed.

At the foot of the cross, this first group of people looks upon Jesus and sees him as a criminal and a

Exegetical Perspective

The report that Jesus carried his own cross (v. 17a) fits with Roman crucifixion practices in which the condemned would carry or drag their cross to the place of execution. Within the context of the Fourth Gospel, however, this is also a clear reminder that Jesus carries his own cross because he is in control of his death, so that as good shepherd he lays down his own life for his sheep (10:17–18). The reference to Skull Place (or Golgotha in Aramaic, v. 17b) is more than a remembrance of early Christian tradition (probably rooted in the actual events of Jesus' crucifixion). It connotes images of utter decay after death, of which Lazarus had experienced the earliest stages before Jesus raised him to life (11:39).

John 19:18 reports the crucifixion of Jesus very tersely. Nothing is reported about the crimes of the other two crucifixion victims. Nevertheless, the alert reader of this narrative fully understands that this is the hour for the royal lifting up/exaltation of Jesus that he prophesied in 3:14–15 and 12:32–33. He has been sent into the world for this very hour of his death, which will result in life going out abundantly to all who believe, for he is the Savior of the world (3:16–17; 4:42).

The theme of royalty comes to the narrative and theological forefront in 19:19–22. It was commonplace for the charges against the crucifixion victim to be hung from their necks or to be affixed to their crosses. In the previous trial scene, the issue of Jesus' purported kingship was central in most of its episodes (18:33–34, 36–37, 39–40; 19:2–3, 12–15). In their own ways, both the religious leaders and Pilate utterly rejected any notions of kingship regarding Jesus (Pilate because he understands kingship only via Roman imperial standards, the religious leaders because they reject any notion that Jesus is their ruler).

The inscription that Pilate has placed on the cross, "Jesus of Nazareth, King of the Jews" (v. 19), functions on different levels within the narrative. On the surface level it functions as the charge of royal sedition against Rome for which he has been crucified. Its threefold translation gives an inclusive warning: if any dare have royal designs over against Caesar, they will meet this same fate. Likewise it seems to identify the place of Jesus' origin as the Galilean village of Nazareth (recalling Pilate's inquiry about Jesus' origin in 19:9). Finally, with his refusal to change the inscription in the face of Judaic protest, Pilate is getting in one last humiliating dig at Rome's Jewish subjects and any messianic pretensions they might have.

Homiletical Perspective

John tells the story but, unlike Luke, does not dwell on the details or on the gruesomeness of the harsh reality. He tells the story of Jesus' crucifixion in barely two verses. Simon of Cyrene is not here, as he is in the Synoptics; so Jesus carries his cross (or the crossbar, which could weigh as much as 125 pounds) alone. Was this a decision on John's part to underscore Jesus' divine power over the events that are befalling him or to emphasize the unrelieved burden on the path to Golgotha that Jesus actively accepts as part of the redemption narrative?

This story is one that preachers usually address in Holy Week, regularly on Good Friday, but it is also the central question of the Christian life: what is it to take up the cross? In this query we address the heart of Christian discipleship. We can have no better guide to the subject than Dietrich Bonhoeffer, the German pastor and martyr. "In the Passion," says Bonhoeffer, "evil is overcome by divine love. . . . Evil becomes powerless when it is willingly borne."[1] This is the image that John craftily paints for us: of Jesus before the powerful Roman authorities and of the excruciating climax in these terse sentences reporting the crucifixion. It is this same insight of overcoming evil with divine love that is so critical to Martin Luther King's idea of redemptive suffering and nonviolent direct action. "This method," King said, "is directed against forces of evil rather than against persons who are caught in those forces. It is evil we are seeking to defeat, not the persons victimized by evil."[2] Many react to this line of thinking, saying that evil must be resisted, not borne. Bonhoeffer and King would disagree and point to the transforming power of the cross and its ability to disarm the forces of evil through love. It is for them the ultimate form of resistance to deny evil's power over you. John highlights this as no other Gospel writer. There are, of course, many other perspectives, but this is John's turn.

As the passage continues, we read of the inscription Pilate orders to be prepared for the title board or *titulus* on the cross: "Jesus of Nazareth, the King of the Jews." The title is disputed by the crowd, but Pilate says, "What I have written I have written" (v. 22). The preacher asks: What is Pilate thinking? Is he defensive or insecurely combative? John seems to suggest this is not the case, but that after his encounters with Jesus, Pilate thinks the title has some merit,

1. Dietrich Bonhoeffer, *Dietrich Bonhoeffer Works*, vol. 4, *Discipleship* (Minneapolis: Augsburg Fortress Press, 2001), 133, 136.
2. Martin Luther King Jr., "Nonviolence and Racial Justice," *Christian Century* 74, no. 6 (February 6, 1957): 166.

John 19:16b–25a

Theological Perspective

representative of Roman sovereignty. Maybe Pilate by now actually believed Jesus' claims to be the Son of God and Messiah.

The inscription ordered by Pilate certainly raised the ire of religious leaders, who asked him to edit the statement to read, "This man *said* [emphasis added], 'I am King of the Jews'" (v. 21). Pilate responded forcefully (v. 22), and the original inscription remained. The power of the irony is what the inscription reveals about what we have come to believe about Jesus. The very thing that brought a charge of sedition against Jesus becomes a public statement about Jesus' identity as "King of the Jews," the Savior and Messiah for whom we have been waiting. In the three languages of the day, Jesus is proclaimed as king in the public square, pushing against the territorial nature of kingship constrained by political boundaries and religious belief, in order to make known God's universal love and redemption for all humanity.

Jesus died because of us and for our sake. Jesus understood his death to be a fulfillment of the Scriptures, in which the soldiers dividing and casting lots for his clothing unknowingly took part (vv. 24–25a). Jesus' death occurred at the time of the Passover, embedding its sacrificial significance in a larger story, giving us a reminder of the presence of sin in human communities, and the provisions God has made for forgiveness and new beginnings. Many people, either unaware of their part or as active agents, contributed to Jesus' death.

It was human sin in its many forms that brought about Jesus' death. It was through this that God did something in Christ that only God could do in such horrible circumstances. Because of our sin and for our sake, Jesus voluntarily carried the cross to his own death, as a profound witness of sacrificial love in the face of human hatred and wrath. Jesus paid a penalty for what was done to him by us, resulting in his death on a cross. This is Jesus of Nazareth, the king for all people, for us in universal and sacrificial love.

WYNDY CORBIN REUSCHLING

Pastoral Perspective

traitor and sees his punishment as part of the daily job of being a Roman soldier. Their actions reflect their understanding. There will be other threats, other false messiahs, and other criminals to crucify. As we stand with them in reading this passage, what do we look upon? Do we see a king of everything who has nothing? If we see this king, do we know how to live into his kingdom? Can we in our congregations be stewards of all that God has given us, so that we are defined not by titles and status and wealth, but instead by generosity and being a blessing to others? What would it look like to be outward-looking in our lives? Imagine a church whose mission is to become aware of the needs of those in its community, and then pulls together its people to discern each person's God-given gifts to bring the kingdom of God beyond the church grounds and into the world. Do we instead stand like this first group at the foot of the cross, driven by our need to take care of our own needs, unable even to witness the suffering of those around us?

Although the evangelist says that Jesus' crucifixion is not witnessed by this first group alone, this passage confronts us with our own temptation as the church to be consumed by the inwardness of title, power, and wealth, instead of by the outwardness of God's kingdom.

AMY G. HELLER

On a deeper theological and narrative level, however, Jesus' origin is not Nazareth but the heavenly realm "above" (3:31), of which neither the religious leaders (18:2–8) nor Pilate (18:36–38) has any conception. Because Jesus is indeed king, it is here in his death that he is judging the world and its ruler(s), as well as overcoming the world and its antagonism (12:30–33; 14:30; 16:11, 33). The inscription, written in the language of the local populace, the language of the imperial court, and the empire's common language, is an ironic way in which Jesus' promise that he would draw all people to himself when he is lifted up (12:32) finds its fulfillment. Finally, in the Greek of 19:19, 22 the perfect verb tense is used three times to depict that what has been written will henceforth remain written, so that Jesus will always be identified for who he truly is, the crucified King of the Jews.

The soldiers' act of dividing Jesus' garments (vv. 23–25a) between them was standard operating procedure, as members of the execution squad confiscated the victims' few belongings as spoils. Not too surprisingly, the evangelist gives such a common detail significant theological meaning. Here the evangelist is drawing on the poetic parallelism of Psalm 22:18, which reads, "They divide my clothes among themselves, and for my clothing they cast lots." Whereas the psalm's parallelism meant that only one piece of clothing was being divided, the evangelist literalizes it so that two separate pieces of clothing are divided by the soldiers. More importantly, the evangelist clearly identifies their acts as the fulfillment of Scripture, so that even when the executioners divide the meager belongings of Jesus, God's plan is being fulfilled (v. 24).

The fact that Jesus' inner garment is described as woven whole and seamless from above (Gk. *anōthen* in v. 23b) recalls not only that Jesus' origin is "from above" (3:31; 18:36; 19:11) but also that Jesus' followers are the ones who are born "from above" (3:3, 7). In this way Jesus' inner garment, which does not get ripped apart (vv. 24–25a) but remains intact, points beyond itself to the lasting unity between Jesus and his followers, which is not rent asunder by his death but is solidified in his death and resurrection (15:1–11; 16:16–22; 17:1–26).

RICHARD CARLSON

albeit eerily so. Homiletically this invites us to reflect on several issues related to Jesus' titles, both those that are given to him and those he gives to himself.

We remember that the first time this title is used was in Matthew's Gospel when the magi seek the infant Jesus, and the last time in John's Gospel at the end of Jesus' life by Pilate. Both times it is used by Gentiles. On the other hand, Jesus himself qualifies the title in chapter 18 when he responds to Pilate's direct inquiry as to whether Jesus is in fact king of the Jews, saying, "My kingdom is not from this world." He says he has come only "to testify to the truth."

What title would we give Jesus? For theologians it is a christological question, but for those in the pew it is more simply, What does Jesus' suffering and death mean to me? What kind of king is crucified? What is royalty humbled? It is hard not to recall James Russell Lowell's nineteenth-century poem "The Present Crisis," which laments, "Truth forever on the scaffold, Wrong forever on the throne."[3] It is also an opportunity to reflect on what it means to be, in theological language, "a suffering servant" or, in more contemporary phrasing, a "servant leader."

A word should be said about the disposal of Jesus' clothes. The image of Jesus on the cross as the Roman soldiers gamble over his garments completes the epic tragedy. Here we can see that the imagery of the story has shifted from violence and suffering to shame and disgrace. It is interesting that the root of shame is an Indo-European word *(s)kam* meaning "to cover," thus giving rise to words like "sham" and "chemise." As the soldiers dispense with Jesus' coverings, John brings us back to this theme. In it lies the final irony: the cross, the ultimate symbol of shame, is to become the ultimate symbol of victory and eternal life.

NICK CARTER

---

3. James Russell Lowell, "The Present Crisis," in *Yale Book of American Verse*, ed. Thomas R. Lounsbury (New Haven, CT: Yale University Press, 1912), 275.

John 19:25b–30

25bMeanwhile, standing near the cross of Jesus were his mother, and his mother's sister, Mary the wife of Clopas, and Mary Magdalene. 26When Jesus saw his mother and the disciple whom he loved standing beside her, he said to his mother, "Woman, here is your son." 27Then he said to the disciple, "Here is your mother." And from that hour the disciple took her into his own home.

28After this, when Jesus knew that all was now finished, he said (in order to fulfill the scripture), "I am thirsty." 29A jar full of sour wine was standing there. So they put a sponge full of the wine on a branch of hyssop and held it to his mouth. 30When Jesus had received the wine, he said, "It is finished." Then he bowed his head and gave up his spirit.

Theological Perspective

One of the difficult theological questions posed by this text is, where was God when Jesus suffered and died? Renowned theologian Jürgen Moltmann suggests we must understand the death of Christ in a Trinitarian framework that maintains the relationship between God the Father and Jesus the Son.[1] The term "hypostasis," used by the Council at Chalcedon in 451, describes the union of the divine and human natures in Jesus Christ that cannot be separated. We cannot say it was the human Jesus who suffered, while his divine nature was immune from suffering. Because of the hypostatic union of the divine and human natures in the person of Christ, and the loving Trinitarian relationship between Father and Son, it was God in Christ who experienced suffering and rejection on the cross.

Both suffered for the sake of humanity, but they suffered in different ways. God the Father suffered by experiencing the loss of a Son, while Jesus suffered the physical pain and humiliation of the crucifixion. For Moltmann, this is the essence of God's love for the world, that God, through and in Christ, feels and shares in the suffering of humanity. While various theologies of the atonement seek to explain the cross

1. Jürgen Moltmann, *The Crucified God*, trans. R. A. Wilson and John Bowden (Minneapolis: Fortress Press, 1993).

Pastoral Perspective

The author of the Gospel of John describes Jesus' crucifixion through the lenses of two separate groups of people at the foot of the cross. The first group consists of Pilate, the chief priests, and the soldiers. In this portion of chapter 19 we find the second group, which includes Jesus' mother, his mother's sister, Mary the wife of Clopas, Mary Magdalene, and the disciple whom he loved. This scene is more intimate than the previous one. Instead of people talking about Jesus and who he is or is not, the people standing near the cross are being talked to by Jesus. They are the only friends present to look upon their son, nephew, friend, rabbi, king. They are examples to the reader of those who stand in the kingdom of God. Two elements emerge from this passage: what being a part of the kingdom of God involves and what that means for their lives—and for our lives—moving forward.

The first element of the kingdom of God revealed in this passage involves our recognition that the women and the Beloved Disciple are in the kingdom of God. Unlike the people in the preceding passage, this group has no one of power, authority, or wealth. What unites them is their relationship with Jesus. They are listed according to how he knew them, the women first and then the nameless Beloved Disciple. Unlike Jesus' other friends and disciples, this group

Feasting on the Gospels

Exegetical Perspective

These verses help form the climax of the entire Gospel. In his death Jesus has accomplished the salvific mission for which God has sent him, which includes saving the world from its captivity to sin under the demonic rule of the devil, as well as the inauguration of the family of faith.

John 19:25b–27 vividly narrates the latter point. This episode functions as performative speech; that is, that which Jesus pronounces happens, as a new family is birthed through his death. The Greek of verse 25b is intentionally constructed so that these four faithful women stand in contrast to the four malevolent male soldiers of verses 23–25a. The introduction of Jesus' mother (note that in John she is never named) recalls Jesus' first public ministerial act (2:1–11). At the wedding, Jesus had noted a rift between himself and his mother by telling her, "Woman, what concern is that to you and to me? My hour has not yet come" (2:4). Now, in the final act of Jesus' public ministry, he is healing that rift as his hour has now come, in crucifixion glory (on Jesus' hour, see also 12:23, 27; 13:1; 16:21, 32; 17:1).

Jesus' directive, "Woman, here is your son," moves in two directions. She is beholding her son, Jesus, on the cross; she is to behold her new son, the Beloved Disciple, who also stands by the cross. Jesus then says to the Beloved Disciple (the representative disciple,

Homiletical Perspective

The pathos at the foot of the cross now shifts from the cold image of soldiers gambling for Jesus' garments to the warm image of Jesus speaking his last words to those closest to him. With this transition in subject comes a corresponding change in tone from harsh to tender. Focusing on those who remain can be productive for some preachers, for instance, by attending to the fact that it was largely women who remained. Likewise, the disappearance of all but one of the disciples echoes hauntingly back to John 12:26: "Whoever serves me must follow me." What is perhaps most compelling, however, is the tenderness of the moment that John paints with the words Jesus addresses to his mother and the Beloved Disciple, the only one of the Twelve who remains faithful to the end.

Some commentators see this exchange as a metaphor for issues surrounding the competing authorities within the nascent church (Jewish vs. Gentile Christians), but there is another theme at work here. John proclaims that the love Jesus preaches (embodies) is, in addition to care for the world, a love of one's companions in ministry and a love shared within the Christian family (see 13:34–35). The extent of that love is boundless, and its centrality in the passion narrative only underscores the point. At the Last Supper, in a section absent from the other Gospels, Jesus washes the disciples' feet, and John

Theological Perspective

of Christ as the foundation of salvation, the cross of Christ reveals the pathos, the suffering of God. God is revealed in Christ on the cross. God is present in Christ on the cross. This is a doctrine of God according to Moltmann: a God who cannot suffer is a God who cannot love.[2] Jesus' death was not the defeat of life and love but, instead, their triumph. The cross of Christ reveals for us the extent and depth of God's love borne out in pain.

Perhaps the text before us also offers additional ways to respond to the question, where was God when Jesus suffered and died? At his loneliest of moments, fulfilling the mission he was sent to accomplish, Jesus had company at the foot of the cross. Save for the "disciple whom he loved" (v. 26), none of the original male disciples were with Jesus at the moment of his death. Three women were with Jesus when he died, however: his mother, his aunt named Mary, and Mary Magdalene (v. 25b). They were witnesses who saw and who stayed with Jesus during his crucifixion, offering solace while Jesus was dying. While humans were agents of Jesus' death, could humans also have been the conduits of God's presence and love during suffering and death? God was present along with and through the women who were also present in these difficult hours of pain, loneliness, alienation, and death. These women embody the pathos of God during Jesus' last moments.

By standing near the cross, these women offer a profound example of what it means to be present in difficult times, when everyone else has fled. While Jesus experienced the pain of crucifixion firsthand, these women experienced their own deep pain as they saw Jesus' suffering, yet they remained present to Jesus in these moments. By seeing and staying, the three women witnesses are reminders of God's presence during Jesus' trial and execution. Perhaps they were also the ones who acted to alleviate Jesus' thirst by offering him the "sponge full of wine" (v. 29), even though they knew Jesus would soon die. The presence of these witnesses near the cross provided a tangible reminder of God's loving and faithful presence in this darkest hour.

Jesus' mother, his aunt, and Mary Magdalene stayed, perhaps risking their own lives by this association with Jesus, who was killed as a blasphemer and common criminal. Because of this, the three women also offer us a model of faithful discipleship. When everyone else had fled, they remained steadfast at the foot of the cross. The women embody

2. Ibid., 222.

Pastoral Perspective

has stayed nearby as the tragic events have unfolded. Because Jesus is a king, and they are near him and bound to him by their relationships, they are in the kingdom of God over which he reigns.

Something new is revealed about this kingdom from Jesus as he speaks to his friends. Their relationships will be changed. He looks upon his mother and the disciple whom he loved and gives them a new relationship, one that the author tells us continues after they leave the foot of the cross. In the midst of his suffering, Jesus reminds them of their need to care for one another as a mother and a son. Blood and birthright do not matter in the kingdom of God, as they do in the kingdoms of this world. The love of a mother and son binds them together. Mary and the Beloved Disciple enter into a new relationship because Jesus speaks it into being.

The second element of the kingdom of God revealed in this passage involves having an awareness of and responding to human suffering and death. Unlike the first group, who ignore Jesus' suffering, who choose to gamble over his one seamless tunic instead of respond to his cries, these friends of Jesus pay attention to him. To be in the kingdom of God is to stand with the dying and, when one hears, "I am thirsty," to respond. The author tells us that sour wine is offered by them and received by Jesus. They tend to him in his agony. They literally reach out to him, closing the inhumane distance between sufferer and observer. Living in the kingdom of God is revealed by their movement toward their friend's pain and in their staying present until he said, "'It is finished' . . . [and] bowed his head and gave up his spirit" (v. 30).

What does it mean for us to live into the kingdom of God? It means that, because of Jesus, all our relationships are transformed. It means that we also have heard the voice of Jesus calling us into new relationships because of our life with him. The church is a community in which we are able to be brother and sister, mother and father together, not because of our birth, but because of Christ's call to us. This experience of being related to one another enables us to respond to those who are marginalized.

When we look beyond the walls of our physical churches and into the web of humanity, we too can create new relationships. Unlike a kingdom in which one is born into one's place, the kingdom of God is a place without rank or privilege, without those who are in or who are out, a community in which no one is isolated. As I write, there have been more and more shootings across the nation by persons isolated

whose faith is to be emulated by all disciples), "Here is your mother," so that a new familial reality is created among Jesus' followers (recalling previous family claims in 1:12; 3:3, 5; 11:51b–52; 16:21–22). The notation that the Beloved Disciple took his new mother into his own home at that hour presents the reversal of 16:32, where Jesus had told his disciples, "The hour is coming, indeed it has come, when you will be scattered, each one to his home."

John 19:28 opens by noting Jesus' knowledge (recalling previous notations of Jesus' omniscience in 2:24–25; 6:6, 64; 13:1, 3; 18:4) to signal that, although he appears to be the helpless victim, he understands exactly what is happening and is in full control of the action (recalling 10:17–18). The NRSV translation of the Greek *tetelestai* in 19:28, "was now finished," does not fully capture the evangelist's intent. First, this Greek word has more an understanding of accomplishment than of closure. Second, the verb is in the perfect tense, indicating an action that has happened but whose results or effects continue into the future. Thus the evangelist highlights that Jesus has accomplished God's mission in and through his crucifixion, and that its results will continue into the future, especially in the lives of those who will believe in Jesus apart from physically seeing him (20:29).

The scriptural passage that Jesus fulfills by saying, "I thirst," is Psalm 69:21, where the persecuted psalmist declares, "They gave me poison for food, and for my thirst they gave me vinegar to drink." The word translated "vinegar" (*oxos*) is actually the same word for sour wine used in 19:29. A number of things are being communicated in verses 28b–29. First, Jesus' death unfolds according to the divine plan rooted in Scripture. Second, in his death and in receiving the sour wine Jesus is drinking the cup that God has given him (as he noted to Peter in 18:11). Third, the one who offers living water unto eternal life now ironically thirsts (see 4:10, 13–14; 7:37–38). Fourth, whereas Jesus' first sign was to change more than one hundred gallons of water intended for purification into good wine (2:6–11), now at the end of his life he is offered merely a sponge soaked with sour wine. Fifth, placing the sponge on hyssop and then giving it to Jesus is a physical impossibility, because hyssop is a nonrigid stem that could not hold the weight of a wine-soaked sponge lifted to Jesus' mouth. Instead, the evangelist is introducing Passover imagery into the scene of Jesus' death, as hyssop was used to smear the Passover lamb's blood on the doorpost of a Hebrew household to save it

observes: "Jesus knew that his hour had come to depart from this world and go to the Father. Having loved his own who were in the world, he loved them to the end" (13:1).

The nature and dimension of God's love are also the marks of Jesus' intimate prayer in the upper room: "so that the world may know that you have sent me and have loved them even as you have loved me" (17:23). John wants his readers to know that this love was the central mission of the incarnation from beginning (3:16) to end (19:26–27), but the message of deep love among those within the membership of church family takes on special meaning when seen through this light. The last moments of Jesus' life are a testimony to his entire life, whether that is to those closest (within his family, among his disciples) or to those farthest, on the margins of life.

Jesus on the cross, close to death, is in control of the situation enough to address the care of his mother. On the one hand, this is a remarkable scene at the climax of the passion story; yet, for any pastor who has tended to the last moments of dying parishioners, the compelling need they express to care for those left behind is far from remarkable. Indeed, for caregivers it seems almost an expected last stage in readying oneself for the approaching end. That it appears here only underscores Jesus' humanity. What strikes the reader, however, is how Jesus entrusts the care of the Beloved Disciple to his mother and, in turn, entrusts her to the disciple's care. It is an act of care that is largely without parallel in the Bible.

It would be unwise to see it as merely an economic decision; it is far more a spiritual decision. It is Jesus' spiritual family that is of concern here. Homiletically, this exchange may provide an opportunity to explore ideas of what a dying person bequeaths besides wealth and property. A good example is an ethical will, which is an old Jewish custom of parents bequeathing to their children the values and wisdom of the family. It is something seen in Jacob's last words (Gen. 39), and one could easily argue that Jesus' words in John 13–17, immediately preceding the passion itself, are themselves an ethical will.

At the last Jesus says, "I am thirsty" (v. 28). The text says this request was "to fulfill the scripture," referring to Psalm 69:21. Some say the evangelist uses these passages to address the ways in which Jesus fulfills Hebrew Scripture and is a replacement of the temple. As theologically interesting as this may be, the content of the reference may be richer for the preacher. Jesus' humanity is painfully real,

John 19:25b–30

Theological Perspective

the essence of discipleship, which Jesus described as taking up and carrying the cross. Feminist theologians rightly raise questions about the dangers imposed upon women, who may be socialized into expectations that it is our role as women to submit and deny ourselves at any cost, opening us to exploitation and peril of all kinds. "Taking up one's cross" in these situations is used as an instrument of oppression, instead of as an avenue of experiencing God's sacrificial love for us.

The examples of the three women at the cross communicate something quite different. It is three women who have the strength of faith and a clear sense of what is happening at the moment of Jesus' death when they hear his final words, "It is finished" (v. 30). The male disciples flee the scene of the cross out of fear. The women disciples remain at the cross, due to their faith, strength, and courage. They remain at the cross by choice, having known Jesus in life, and now remaining with him in death. Hence, they provide us with a profound example of the rigors of Christian discipleship in difficult situations.

Those at the cross hear Jesus' final words, "It is finished" (v. 30). Because they remain, the women, along with the "disciple whom Jesus loved," are privileged to hear these final words, the summation of what Jesus was sent to do for humanity. Jesus' life led to this moment on the cross, and he finished what God had sent him to do. This was not a statement of resignation, but a proclamation of accomplishment of God's mission of redeeming love manifested on the cross.

After his proclamation, Jesus "bowed his head and handed over the Spirit" (v. 30b, my trans.). On one level, we may understand what happens at the moment of death when the life breath ceases. This certainly was the case with Jesus upon his death. Given the presence of symbolism and theological metaphors in John's Gospel, though, we may also see an anticipation of what is yet to come after Jesus' death: the giving of the Holy Spirit, who would empower disciples who remain to complete the mission that Jesus gave them to do, for the day they could say as well, "It is finished."

WYNDY CORBIN REUSCHLING

Pastoral Perspective

by their peers, their families, and their communities. The challenge for the church today is to seek out those marginalized in our society and invite them into this new relationship with us through Christ.

What does it mean for us to live into the kingdom of God? It means moving toward and being present with someone as his or her final breath is offered. Those who know this place of honor at the bedside of the dying know it is a place of holiness. The ministry of the church involves a willingness to be with and comfort those who suffer in body, mind, or spirit. In a society that values "feeling good" and "having a good time," what voice can the church add to the authentic human experience of suffering? How often is it easier to preach about what is good for us in the church, instead of what would be helpful to those in need? Do we offer more programs for people in our church, instead of going out into the community where those thirsty for love and compassion dwell? What happens to those who never feel good or for whom the feeling good ends? How can the church become that place of holiness where those who thirst and those who satisfy thirst come together?

Jesus' dying and death is another sign of the kingdom of God breaking into this world. In his suffering, Jesus was looked upon by his mother, his mother's sister Mary the wife of Clopas, Mary Magdalene, and the disciple he loved. He called them into new relationships and received their comfort. Living in the kingdom of God calls us into new relationships in response to the suffering of others.

AMY G. HELLER

Exegetical Perspective

as death spread over Egypt (Exod. 12:22–23). The image of blood and Passover will be expanded in 19:31–36 as Jesus, the good shepherd who lays down his life for his sheep, also dies as the Lamb of God whose blood gives life (recalling 1:29, 36; 6:53–56).

Jesus' final word (there is just one word denoting Jesus' speech in the Greek of 19:30) would be better translated, "It has been accomplished," rather than "It is finished" (the same Gk. word, *tetelestai*, as in 19:28), as the focus continues to be on accomplishment and its ongoing effects, rather than on closure.

Likewise the NRSV (and almost all other English translations) also fail to communicate what the evangelist actually wrote when they render 19:30b as, "Then he bowed his head and gave up his spirit." The word translated as "gave up" is the Greek word *paradidōmi*, the same word the evangelist intentionally and consistently used to depict the evil actions of the devil (13:2; 19:11), Judas (6:64, 71; 12:4; 13:11, 21; 18:2, 5, 36), the religious authorities (18:30, 35), and Pilate (19:16) in their treacherous, deadly opposition to Jesus.

These antagonists thought they had the power to hand over Jesus to accomplish their nefarious ends. In his death, however, Jesus trumps their handing-over activity by doing a handing-over action of his own, as he has always been in control of his own death (10:17–19). What did Jesus hand over in his death? The NRSV (and most English translations) read "his spirit." The problem is that there is no personal pronoun in the Greek of 19:30b. Instead, the Greek simply reads "the spirit." Here the reference is to the Holy Spirit, which in death Jesus hands over. This action at the end of his life forms a bookend with the descent of the Spirit into Jesus at the inauguration of his ministry (1:32–33; also cf. 7:37–39). Jesus' handing over of the Spirit also prepares the way for the crucified and risen Jesus to breathe the Spirit onto his disciples as he commissions them for the same divine mission for which he has been sent (20:21–23).

RICHARD CARLSON

Homiletical Perspective

and this request was probably common at crucifixions; hence the presence of the jar of sour wine and its being offered to Jesus. That Jesus is thirsty is "normal," but it presents a strange juxtaposition to his teaching in chapter 4 to the Samaritan woman at the well, when he declares that "those who drink of the water I give them will never be thirsty" (4:14). What is it that Jesus is thirsty for in his hour of testing? Righteousness? Could it be the sustaining spiritual relationship with a loving God that he has offered to others and must now draw upon himself?

This passage calls us to name and embrace the things that sustain us in our times of greatest challenge. Perhaps this should be seen as a spiritual lament, rather than a call for bodily sustenance. In this case the offering of the sour wine becomes an ironic final act of misunderstanding of what it is that Jesus truly seeks.

"It is finished." These are not words—as the world might hear them—of resignation and defeat, but of an exhausted yet prayerful declaration of accomplishment. In essence Jesus says to God, "I have done what you asked; I have given my all; the job is done." Sermons might revisit the words of John's Gospel (1:1–18; 4:14; 18:36–37) to explore why Jesus came into the world and what God expected Jesus to achieve. The question can then be asked, "What is it that God expects of us, and what are we prepared to give?" "What cross are we prepared to bear?" "For what would we give our lives?" It is with a heart oriented to the cross that Paul says in Romans 12:1, "I appeal to you therefore . . . to present your bodies as a living sacrifice, holy and acceptable to God, which is your spiritual worship."

NICK CARTER

³¹Since it was the day of Preparation, the Jews* did not want the bodies left on the cross during the sabbath, especially because that sabbath was a day of great solemnity. So they asked Pilate to have the legs of the crucified men broken and the bodies removed. ³²Then the soldiers came and broke the legs of the first and of the other who had been crucified with him. ³³But when they came to Jesus and saw that he was already dead, they did not break his legs. ³⁴Instead, one of the soldiers pierced his side with a spear, and at once blood and water came out. ³⁵(He who saw this has testified so that you also may believe. His testimony is true, and he knows that he tells the truth.) ³⁶These things occurred so that the scripture might be fulfilled, "None of his bones shall be broken." ³⁷And again another passage of scripture says, "They will look on the one whom they have pierced."

Theological Perspective

Unique to John's Gospel is the story of the breaking of legs and the piercing of Jesus' side. Alluding to Exodus 12:46 and Numbers 9:12, John identifies Jesus as the paschal lamb and reflects John the Baptist's testimony: "Look, the Lamb of God who takes away the sin of the world" (1:29, 36). He avoids the temptation to ignore the uglier parts of salvation history and demonstrates that even here God is at work.

"It was the Day of Preparation, and the next day was to be a special Sabbath" (v. 31 NIV). How is one Sabbath more special than another? This sacred space, divinely consecrated for restful attentiveness to God, is it not inherently "special"? Would not any Sabbath be just as important as every other Sabbath? The word is *megas* and can be translated "big" or "great." Thus, the upcoming day is no ordinarily sacred space. It is extraordinarily significant, for this Sabbath doubles as the beginning of the feast of Unleavened Bread. The urgency of Sabbath preparation heightens, and the Jews scramble to get things in order.[1]

Jewish law instructs that the body of an executed man be removed and buried the same day he dies,

* See "'The Jews' in the Fourth Gospel" on pp. xi–xiv.

1. A. T. Robertson, *Robertson's Word Pictures in the New Testament*, Electronic Database (Biblesoft, Inc., 2006); *Robertson's Word Pictures in the New Testament* (Nashville: Broadman Press, 1985). Robertson describes this as the "double reason . . . for wanting the bodies removed before sunset when the Sabbath began."

Pastoral Perspective

Some people seem to choose their moment to die. I have heard of many occasions when a family has kept a bedside vigil with a loved one, so anxious to be there at the end, and then something has taken them away. They have left the bedside, and in their absence their beloved died. The family feels guilty, of course, but they need reassurance. "No, she wanted it that way. She chose her moment."

Maybe Jesus chose his moment. He has put his affairs in order. Just a few verses previously he has looked down upon his mother Mary and the Beloved Disciple at the foot of the cross, entrusting them to one another's care (19:26–27). Knowing that they are now safe in each other's keeping, he is ready to go, and so we read on and come to the grisly, barbaric ritual that was part of this hideous means of execution. Jewish sensitivities have to be observed. Bodies writhing in agony on grim scaffolds cannot be left overnight to taint the Sabbath day. So the soldiers come to break the legs of the crucified ones. The mechanics of crucifixion need no elaboration; suffice it to say that when the legs are broken, the victims can no longer lift their weight to ease the pressure on their lungs and draw breath, and so they suffocate—a mercy of sorts, insofar as death is at least hastened. Jesus, however, will not die that way. The soldiers find him already dead. They will not have

Exegetical Perspective

This last scene at the cross offers another incident recorded only in this Gospel, and it adds a poignant touch to John's portrait of the death of Jesus. The scene also underscores the harsh reality of death by crucifixion. Victims often languished on the cross for a few days before finally expiring. Normally, the Romans approved of extending the victims' suffering, because they intended this cruel—but unfortunately not unusual—punishment as a warning to the populace at large. In this case, however, the Jewish authorities (the likely meaning of the term "the Jews" here) went to Pilate requesting that he have the victims killed and their bodies removed. Crucifixion fell under the regulation in the Mosaic Law whereby a criminal who had been hung on a tree was accursed, and his body could not be left exposed overnight (Deut. 21:22–23).

While it is not likely that the Romans regularly followed that rule, this execution was unusual, because a particularly holy day, a Sabbath falling on the Passover celebration, was about to begin. Pilate, apparently recognizing that to leave the bodies hanging on the crosses would enflame Jewish sensibilities, sent soldiers to carry out this gruesome task. The means employed was an iron bar, which the soldiers smashed against the leg bones. Called the *crurifragium*, the practice was sometimes used as a form of

Homiletical Perspective

The problem with proclaiming this text is that it reads like a scene from CSI "Whatever-city-you-live-in," where the graphic details of the subject's death are played out in the splendor of high-definition language. Poking and prodding into the details of how Jesus' body was treated by the soldiers has little benefit except to raise the Sunday gore factor. John's purpose in splattering these gruesome facts across the page is surely connected to his concerns about docetic claims that Jesus was a divine spirit without a real body—probably not a major concern in any local congregation today.

In John's day, however, there were apparently some who argued that Christ did not suffer on the cross but instead that he only seemed (*dokein*) to suffer. Pointing to his divinity, which the Fourth Gospel itself loudly proclaims, some questioned whether the Jesus who walked on water and through closed doors, could not be captured by his enemies, knew the innermost thoughts of others even before they spoke, and raised Lazarus after days in the grave could suffer in any way. Ultimately some even argued that Jesus' physical appearance was a mere illusion for human benefit. John's portrayal of Jesus' gruesome death connects his death with Hebrew Scripture and at the same time refutes the idea that his humanity was an illusion.

Theological Perspective

lest this "one who is hung on a tree" desecrate the land God has given (Deut. 21:22–23). At issue, however, in John's story is not so much the fact that the three on the cross may linger for the night. The issue is the Sabbath, that sacred space, and the picture he paints is one of people desperately scrambling to prevent the gravity of today's actions from seeping over into tomorrow. They do not want the bodies hanging there during the Sabbath (v. 31). Problem is, two of them are still alive! Deuteronomic law addresses the issue of burying dead criminals, but what about those who remain alive? What if those dangling from a cross cling to life and encroach upon the sacred space? Impossible! Break their legs! Hurry, do something! Time is running out!

As if the deeds of today have no bearing on tomorrow, they rush to contain the evidence of the execution, lest this symbol of their actions spoil the inaugural day of the feast. At least two cooperate, and the breaking of legs speeds their death, making way for an appropriate burial. As for the One they really trouble over, he is already dead, but to be certain, a soldier pierces his side, opening a flow of blood and water, leaving behind a stain that will live into many Sabbaths.

Too often we live such compartmentalized lives that we presume our decisions in the boardroom, conversations at the gym, or eraser marks on our tax returns bear no weight on who we are as mothers, fathers, husbands, wives, or even clergy. We presume that those "sacred spaces" stand alone and remain unstained by our actions in other places. In the text before us, the issue is capital punishment, and those arranging to remove the bodies aim desperately to fence off their Sabbath from the horror of the day before, effectively creating distance between their actions and their worship.

In the play *Twelve Angry Men*, jurors must determine the guilt or innocence of a young man charged with first-degree murder. The punishment is death. Upon entering the jury room, the guard mutters, "He doesn't stand a chance," and before deliberations begin, the jurors, anxious to be on their way, hastily take a vote. Anticipating a unanimous "guilty" verdict, all are surprised to see one juror voting "not guilty." Heavily criticized, the juror admits he is not certain of the young man's innocence, but he certainly believes the man deserves more—more of their time. "I want to talk for a while," he explains. "I think maybe we owe him a few words."[2] Aghast at

2. Reginald Rose, *Twelve Angry Men*, Stage Version by Sherman L. Sergel (Woodstock, IL: The Dramatic Publishing Co., 1983), 15.

Pastoral Perspective

the sadistic satisfaction of watching him struggle for breath until he expires. He has chosen his moment and is gone.

All this is entirely in keeping with the Jesus of John's Gospel. John is at pains to emphasize throughout that Jesus is in command of his own death. Back in chapter 10 Jesus spoke of himself as the good shepherd who lays down his life for the sheep, and he concluded, "I lay down my life, to receive it back again. No one takes it away from me; I am laying it down of my own free will. I have the right to lay it down, and I have the right to receive it back again" (10:17b, 18, my trans.). This is the Jesus who remains frustratingly aloof in his trial, so that Pilate, his interrogator with the power to release him, is the one who is painted into a corner, a prisoner of the crowd. This is the Jesus who carries his cross himself to his execution (19:17). This is the sovereign, regal Jesus of John's Gospel, who goes to his death in complete control of his destiny, whose cross is his throne and whose lifting up from the earth is an exaltation that draws people to him (3:14–15).

That evasive sovereignty, which has been such a feature of events leading up to Jesus' death in this Gospel, comes to a focus in what happens next: the centurion thrusts his spear into Jesus' side. There may be no need to break the legs of a corpse, but still the centurion cannot resist this gesture of contempt. We hear terrible accounts from war zones of dead bodies being mutilated as a final, degrading insult, and perhaps there is something of that here. Death is not enough, but must be finessed with humiliation. This soldier may have been cheated by the Jewish criminal out of the sadistic pleasure of finishing him off, but he will still violate his body and thus demonstrate his power over the crucified one—or so he thinks. Yet even in so doing, the soldier is being constrained by higher power, higher authority, higher purposes that are at work as he unwittingly fulfills ancient protocols and prophecies concerning sin offerings: "no bone of his shall be broken."

Then comes the final revelation. Out of the body comes a flow of blood and water. In the context of this most metaphorical of Gospels, these are evidently symbols of life. Elsewhere in this Gospel water symbolizes the Holy Spirit (e.g., 7:37–39), while blood denotes eternal life (6:53–56). It has been suggested too, plausibly, that the water and blood are references to the sacraments, to baptism and the Eucharist, to those sources of life and strength and renewal on the Christian journey.

execution itself. Here the purpose was either to cause massive bleeding due to blunt force or, by making victims hang only by their arms, to constrict their lungs and impede breathing.[1]

John tells us that the soldiers broke the legs of the other two, but they did not bother to shatter Jesus' legs, because he was already dead. Naturally, the soldiers appear disinterested in any deeper meaning of Jesus' death on the cross. They are simply doing what they have undoubtedly done many times before—getting rid of an undesirable person from a despised nation. Matthew has the centurion and some others exclaim that Jesus is the Son of God (Matt. 27:54), and in Luke a centurion declares that Jesus is innocent (Luke 23:47). In John the soldiers simply do their jobs.

Nevertheless, even in their inattention to the deeper meaning of this scene, these soldiers draw out a number of profound truths that John wishes to emphasize. First, the soldiers' action functions as a confirmation that Jesus controls his own death. Earlier in this chapter Jesus told Pilate that he had power over Jesus only because it was "given to him from above" (19:11). Then, after declaring on the cross, "It is finished," Jesus "gave up his spirit" (19:30). Such references imply that neither the Jewish authorities nor Pilate controlled Jesus' destiny. Now John makes the same point about the Roman soldiers. Jesus died by his own will, not because others wished to kill him.

The soldiers' action accomplishes a second function by fulfilling two Old Testament prophecies. At important points throughout this Gospel, John underscores the relation of scriptural passages to Jesus. For instance, in chapter 5 Jesus himself proclaims that the Scriptures "testify on my behalf" (5:39). Then he adds, "If [people] believed Moses," they would believe him too, because "he wrote about me" (5:46). By not breaking Jesus' legs, the soldiers fulfill a prophecy that "none of his bones shall be broken" (v. 36). The words do not match any specific Old Testament passage, but they suggest the requirement in Exodus 12:46 that no bone of the Passover lamb could be broken. Likewise, the words are reminders of Psalm 34:20, which praises the Lord for preserving the psalmist's life. In this context, the association with Passover is probably more central for John.

In verse 37, John quotes an additional prophecy from Zechariah 12:10: "They will look on the one whom they have pierced." Almost casually, one

1. Barnabas Lindars, *The Gospel of John*; New Century Bible Commentary (Grand Rapids: Eerdmans, 1972), 585.

The Jewish historian Josephus tells us that crucifixion was a slow process (*Life* 420–21). We also know that not everyone was nailed to crossbars; some were tied and they likely lasted longer. The quickness of Jesus' death is unusual. It may have been that the severity of his beating hastened his death. Whatever the cause, it was the case that Roman soldiers would sometimes break the leg bones of those being crucified to bring death more quickly. In Jesus' case it was unnecessary. That is the central point. The giver of life was already dead. It is with these kinds of images that John portrays the death of Jesus as a victorious event and not as any kind of defeat. Any who attempt to understand John reading individual passages rather than as an entire unit, a complete story, will miss the significance of this scene on the cross (and others).

For the followers of Jesus, the hours of Jesus' execution were excruciating. Having left their lives behind to follow their Lord, they were now watching, even if from a distance, as the life slowly drained from his body. The living water they were promised had seemed to run dry as Jesus himself cried out from the cross, "I am thirsty!" (19:28). In this scene everyone is parched; all are thirsty for a miracle that does not come. Jesus dies and on that day the disciples' hopes, dreams, and future evaporate too. There is little sense in trying to take your congregation back to feel the pain of that day.

Instead, invite them to remember their own thirst. Focus their attention on the day in which their own hopes dried out, spoke their last, and died. The sad truth is that all of us have watched or will one day watch some part of our future fade. Sooner or later we all stand in the sandals of the disciples on that terrible day. The good news is that Jesus' promise that "those who drink of the water that I will give them will never be thirsty" (4:14) is not invalidated in his death but inaugurated in his death and resurrection.

John's focus on the "blood and water" from Jesus' side has a historical connection with docetic concerns of that day and even the very real biology of being human, but John had ulterior motives too. Water in John's Gospel holds deep symbolic meaning. We can miss the intent in this passage if we do not listen carefully to the entirety of John's story. A central text is John 4:7–15, where Jesus and the woman at the well stir up the waters of interpretation over Jesus' meaning. John, however, dives into the water imagery in many other places as well: 1:31, 33; 2:6; 3:5; 5:2, 9:7; 13:5, and here in 19:28, 34. Interestingly the book of Revelation also picks up

Theological Perspective

his decision, the others angrily react, some even violently, and one juror aims to calm everyone down.

> We have a responsibility. This is a remarkable thing about democracy. That we are—what is the word? . . . Ah, notified! That we are notified by mail to come down to this place—and decide on the guilt or innocence of a man; of a man we have not known before. We have nothing to gain or lose by our verdict. This is one of the reasons why we are strong. We should not make it a personal thing.[3]

Trouble is, it *is* personal, and many things are both gained and lost. Ask anyone who has served on a jury for a capital crime. Though their task is officially completed when the verdict is read and the court dismisses them, they cannot fence off their decision from the rest of their lives, and rightly so. Lives are at stake. Theirs, yours, and mine. It does no good to fool ourselves into believing our decisions are not personal, for they affect us deeply and personally.

Something was at stake when "the Jews" (v. 31) in John 19 wished to rush the deaths of three men, including one for whom they served as jurors. They knew it was personal, and they scrambled to contain the consequences of their decision. As the Sabbath began, however, the flow from his side bled over into the sacred day, and the clear demarcation of one space from another proved impossible. With this smearing of blood, the story of salvation seeps into even the darkest of corners. Through the hasty actions of those attempting to get on with their lives, Jesus' blood spills, and it is both atoning and cleansing. It is sacrifice and baptism, a river of life carrying us from our worst of moments into the blessedness of Sabbath rest.

SEAN WHITE

Pastoral Perspective

The message is clear. We are here in the midst of death and at its mercy. We may sometimes choose the actual moment of our passing, but death wins nevertheless. We are profoundly vulnerable to all the powers of hell that may plunge us into despair at any moment, leaving us powerless and helpless. Yet with us is this Christ, this sovereign one who has mastered death and who is able even in its midst to constrain it to yield life and blessing and so to sustain us—just as a soldier's contemptuous brutality only succeeds in the gushing forth of life-giving water and blood.

The possible reference to the Eucharist in this passage brings to mind one famous description of the myriad contexts and occasions in which it has been celebrated, written by the great writer on liturgy, Dom Gregory Dix. In a long, meandering passage covering all kinds of circumstances, Dix says, "while the lions roared in the nearby amphitheatre; on the beach at Dunkirk . . . furtively, by an exiled bishop who had hewn timber all day in a prison camp near Murmansk. . . . And best of all, week by week and month by month, on a hundred thousand successive Sundays, faithfully, unfailingly, across all the parishes of Christendom, the pastors have done this just to make the *plebs sancta Dei*—the holy common people of God."[1] In such bleak and testing circumstances the Lord's Supper has been celebrated over and over again through the centuries, testifying endlessly that in the midst of death, brutality, and suffering there can usher forth streams of life from the one who is Sovereign and Savior—and we are sustained.

LANCE STONE

---

3. Ibid., 44, 45.

1. Dom Gregory Dix, *The Shape of the Liturgy* (London: Dacre Press, Adam and Charles Black. 1964), 744–45.

Exegetical Perspective

soldier jabs Jesus' side with a spear, resulting in water and blood flowing from the wound. At one level, John uses this incident as further confirmation that Jesus is really dead. The soldiers do not break Jesus' legs, but they do prod his side for any sign of lingering life. At a deeper level, this incident testifies to the salvation that Jesus is effecting for the world. Notice that the context of this verse in Zechariah 12 speaks of a "spirit of compassion" that God will pour out in Jerusalem (Zech. 12:10). Then the prophet promises that, "On that day there shall be a fountain opened for the house of David and the inhabitants of Jerusalem to cleanse them from sin and uncleanness" (Zech. 13:1 ESV).

The third function of the soldiers' action is to draw attention to two extremely significant concepts in the Gospel, "blood" and "water." This combination of blood and water also appears in 1 John 5:6–8, although in reverse order and further associated with the Spirit. For the Gospel writer, the blood recalls John the Baptist's proclamation that Jesus is "the Lamb of God who takes away the sin of the world" (1:29). Likewise, the water directs us back to the "living water" that Jesus promised earlier (4:10–15). For John and his readers these two elements would certainly carry sacramental significance: the gifts of baptism and Eucharist flow from the side of Jesus.

While there is considerable debate about whether this incident is to be taken as historical, it is generally agreed that, medically speaking, such a flow of blood and water is possible. John clearly intends this event to be taken at face value. He emphasizes that a trustworthy witness observed it (v. 35). While the identity of this witness is also the subject of debate, the purpose of the testimony is evident: "in order that you also may believe." This same aim appears in chapter 20, when John encourages faith in Jesus as "the Christ, the Son of God," in order that readers "may have life in his name."[2] The life readers will find is that signified in the blood and the water.

JAMES E. DAVISON

Homiletical Perspective

this theme as the "river of life" (Rev. 22:1) and has Jesus again saying, "Let everyone who is thirsty come. Let anyone who wishes take the water of life as a gift" (Rev. 22:17). Only in retrospect can anyone fully grasp the beauty of this symbolism: from death comes life flowing like a river.

There is also a dripping irony in this passage that allows a sermon to consider how our religious behavior can sometimes be hypocritical. While John is indiscriminate about who "the Jews" are in his story, here he is clearly talking about a small group of leaders threatened by Jesus. The role of those leaders in the death of Jesus should not open the door for any sermon to talk about Judaism or the Jewish people. People of any faith do not have to think long or hard about those within their own ranks who have done or said things with which we would not agree. Guilt by association is neither good theology nor good history. The earliest of Jesus' followers, and most of them for many years, were Jews.

In this instance, what we have is a small group of leaders who are more than willing to see Jesus falsely convicted, likely out of their anger toward him and fear of him, but who are also concerned about the religious propriety (see also 18:28) of leaving his corpse hanging during the Sabbath. This incongruent irony, in this case a willingness to deceive but not to offend, is not atypical of the faithful. In fact, Jesus was very clear that we must remove the log from our own eye before we go after a speck in the eye of our neighbor (Matt. 7:3). He understood all too well that we are inconsistent and that our motives and actions need constant scrutiny. Otherwise we too may well find ourselves calling profane what God has called sacred (see Acts 10:15).

VAUGHN CROWETIPTON

---

2. John 20:31. In both passages, some ancient manuscripts imply initial belief ("coming to faith"), while others indicate holding to already existing belief ("continuing in faith.") Unfortunately, no convincing argument can be made for one over the other.

John 19:38–42

³⁸After these things, Joseph of Arimathea, who was a disciple of Jesus, though a secret one because of his fear of the Jews,* asked Pilate to let him take away the body of Jesus. Pilate gave him permission; so he came and removed his body. ³⁹Nicodemus, who had at first come to Jesus by night, also came, bringing a mixture of myrrh and aloes, weighing about a hundred pounds. ⁴⁰They took the body of Jesus and wrapped it with the spices in linen cloths, according to the burial custom of the Jews. ⁴¹Now there was a garden in the place where he was crucified, and in the garden there was a new tomb in which no one had ever been laid. ⁴²And so, because it was the Jewish day of Preparation, and the tomb was nearby, they laid Jesus there.

Theological Perspective

"And now you know the *rest* of the story," Paul Harvey assured as he signed off his daily radio broadcast. I often wonder about the rest of the story, especially those stories told in the Gospels. I wonder what happened to the rich young ruler (Luke 18), Lazarus (John 11), or the centurion who acknowledged Jesus as Son of God (Mark 15). In this passage from John's Gospel, we learn the rest of the story about two somewhat mysterious characters, Nicodemus and Joseph of Arimathea.

The Bible has been described as a collection of stories that admonish the reader either to have faith or to have more faith, and along the way the writers paint pictures of what that faith looks like. In John 3, Jesus utters what has become a foundational verse in evangelical Christian circles: "For God so loved the world, that he gave his only begotten Son, that whosoever believeth in him should not perish, but have everlasting life" (3:16 KJV). Regrettably, the narrative around the promise has gotten lost, and many could not name the one who first heard those words of Jesus.

Some might even suggest it does not matter, that the players in the drama are incidental to the salvation story. At one level this may be true, for the story is God's story. From beginning to end, the

* See "'The Jews' in the Fourth Gospel" on pp. xi–xiv.

Pastoral Perspective

It is commonplace to talk about Jesus' death and resurrection, of Christ crucified and risen, of Good Friday and Easter Sunday, referring as they do to the humiliation and exaltation of Jesus of Nazareth. Such a pairing is, however, in danger of omitting the significance of a third moment in Jesus' journey through death: his burial in a tomb near where he was crucified. The faith of the church as it has been articulated through the centuries in the Apostles' Creed reminds us that Jesus was "crucified, dead, *and buried* . . . [and] the third day he rose again from the dead." So what value does Christ's burial have for us? How does the sealing of Jesus' corpse in the tomb contribute to our salvation?

We read that after Jesus has expired on the cross, Joseph of Arimathea and Nicodemus come to bury him. Both men, apparently, are frightened. Joseph, we are told, has been a follower of Jesus, though a secret one "because of his fear of the Jews" (v. 38). Nicodemus is a Pharisee and a member of the Jewish council whom we first meet in chapter 3, and the assumption is that he too is fearful, approaching Jesus furtively by night to avoid being seen.

Joseph and Nicodemus receive permission to remove Jesus' body for burial and two features of John's account stand out. The first is the extraordinary quantity of spices that they bring with them, about

Exegetical Perspective

This somber passage concludes the events that occurred at the cross of Jesus. After crucifixion, most victims were thrown into a common grave, although their families were sometimes allowed to give them a more decent burial. In contrast, John underlines the fact that Joseph of Arimathea and Nicodemus treated Jesus' body with reverence. They observed carefully the appropriate Jewish burial customs. Thus, although crucifixion itself implied a curse, there would be no further curse upon Jesus due to poor treatment of his remains.

Mark 15:43 and Luke 23:50 describe Joseph of Arimathea as a member of the council and a good man. Matthew does not mention the council, although he does call Joseph a rich man and a disciple of Jesus (Matt. 27:57). John agrees that Joseph was a disciple, but a secret one due to fear of the Jewish authorities (v. 38). Nicodemus is not mentioned in the other Gospels, but he has already appeared twice in John. He came to Jesus by night (chap. 3) and later, albeit rather cautiously, defended Jesus against accusations hurled at him in the council (7:51–52).

Earlier, in chapter 12, John judges secret faith severely. He comments that many of the authorities believed in Jesus but were afraid to admit this publicly: "for they loved human glory more than

Homiletical Perspective

When you look around my home, there are photographs everywhere. We love pictures, and as a photographer I love to take them. What you never see in the smiling faces of our family and friends in places we love, however, is the story of the picture itself. Snapshots are just that, moments frozen in time that all too easily lose their context. We laugh at some of our photographs, because leading up to the happy grins and warm hugs are some family battles over taking "one more picture" or angst over being late because of yet another photograph. Other pictures have stories of when this event happened or that time we went on that trip. Every picture tends to spill out of the frame.

John's picture of Jesus' burial is no different. The snapshot we get includes two characters, Joseph of Arimathea and Nicodemus. The scene is a garden, and it includes the lifeless body of Jesus, linen wraps, spices, and a deal to get the body for burial. Each of these elements raises more questions than the snapshot itself can or will answer, but like any good photograph it allows for creative speculation that can fertilize a sermon and allow it to grow.

Joseph of Arimathea (see also Mark 15:43, 45; Matt. 27:57, 59; Luke 23:50–51) and Nicodemus (3:1–21; 7:50) represent in this text an unlikely pair. Neither is part of the inner circle of Jesus' closest

John 19:38–42

divine pursuit of sinful humans takes center stage. At the same time, salvation happens only in the dance of grace and response, revelation and reception. Though the main character is God, salvation history unfolds in the lives of people, specific people, people like Abraham, Esther, Mary, and an unnamed Roman centurion.

In John 3, Jesus promises life to an influential man named Nicodemus, who gains enough courage to visit the rabbi only after dark. Though John withholds a detailed explanation for his visit to Jesus, their conversation begins with his understanding of Jesus' connection to God. Jesus then speaks of being born again (or from above). In his confusion, Nicodemus asks three brief questions, each amounting to "How can this be?" Then it is over. The narrative rapidly whisks Jesus away, leaving Nicodemus on the precipice of faith and the reader to imagine the *rest* of the story. Later he resurfaces, distancing himself from Pharisaic zealotry that aims to have Jesus arrested, but still with no indication of discipleship (7:50–51). Not until Jesus' death does the reader get a sense of Nicodemus's journey of faith.

In the Johannine narrative, the thread that runs throughout is the refrain of Jesus' love for the one telling the story. As if doxologically inspired, the evangelist recalls, "I am the one Jesus loved!" Time and again, he is reminded and cannot help but rejoice! Though he appears only a few times, Nicodemus is also curiously woven into the fabric of the text. He is not one of the Twelve, and neither walks on water nor declares his undying loyalty to Jesus. Rather, he is a member of the Sanhedrin, the very court that declares Jesus worthy of death. He also admits his doubts, challenges his colleagues, and ultimately accompanies Jesus to a place no one else apparently wants to go. At one point, Jesus assures the Twelve that he has sheep beyond the fold of their intimate circle (10:16), and the Spirit blows into those places as well (3:8).

Though the Gospel narrative focuses on Jesus' journey with the disciples, the Nicodemus stories weave a redemptive thread through it to a most unlikely place. Following a Roman crucifixion, the bodies of the crucified were often either left as prey for wild animals or buried anonymously in a common grave. Jewish burial custom required that those "hung on a tree" be buried the day they died (Deut. 21:22–23), and one might expect Jesus' relatives or closest friends to claim and prepare his body. Surprisingly, none show up, and out of the dark shadows of injustice and betrayal emerge two characters who

a hundred pounds of myrrh and aloes, a staggering amount. The second feature is that this tomb has never been used (v. 41). The usual practice in Jesus' time was to bury a body in a tomb, the corpse well wrapped with spices to mask the smell of putrefaction; eventually, when the flesh had decomposed, the bones would be put into a box known as an ossuary. In this way there could be several burials in one tomb. Jesus' tomb, however, had never been used by anyone.

These two features point to the burial of a king. Only a king would receive such treatment, and this is of course entirely in keeping with John's narrative of the arrest, trial, and execution of Jesus. The Jesus portrayed here is the sovereign Lord who lays down his life of his own free will. This is the Jesus whose cross is his throne as he is raised in exaltation upon it. So what particular insights does Jesus' sovereign lordship bring to his burial? What does it mean for us that it is the majestic, regal Christ who is buried?

Karl Barth, commenting on the phrase in the Apostles' Creed, "crucified, dead, and buried," speaks movingly of our burials. He writes, "Some day a company of men [*sic*] will process out to a churchyard and lower a coffin and everyone will go home; but one will not come back, and that will be me." Burial reminds us of the finality of death, giving it "the character of passing away and decay and to human existence the character of transitoriness and corruptibility."[1]

On the Scottish Island of Iona there is a burial ground with the grave of a Christian minister, Bruce Kenrick. "Here lies all that could die of Bruce Kenrick," reads the inscription. There is a commendable defiance about that, yet there is an element too of denial—the illusion that something of us cannot be buried but lives on. To quote Barth again, "Perhaps a memory will remain, so long as there are [people] who like to remember us. But some day they too will die and then this memory too will pass away. There is no great name in human history which will not some day or other have become a forgotten name."[2] That, for Barth, is the significance of burial. It means forgottenness. The grave is where every last trace of us returns to dust.

The irony, however, is that while the grave consigns to oblivion that which we might wish would live on, burial also speaks of that which we might wish to consign to oblivion but that keeps returning. Psychology and psychiatry have revealed only too

1. Karl Barth, *Dogmatics in Outline* (London: SCM Press Ltd., 1966), 118.
2. Ibid.

the glory that comes from God" (12:42–43). Here at the cross, however, John presents two underground disciples who made their faith known. Their motives are not explained. Either their fear had been transformed into a sturdy proclamation of trust in Jesus, or they believed in his message sufficiently to recognize the injustice of the proceedings against him. Whatever their exact motives, and even if somewhat discreetly, Joseph and Nicodemus set themselves in opposition to both the Jewish council and to the authority of the Roman Empire. This display of courage would certainly permit John to include them in his comment at the end of the first episode where Nicodemus appears: "But those who do what is true come to the light, so that it may be clearly seen that their deeds have been done in God" (3:21).

Joseph's and Nicodemus's actions in burying Jesus highlight a primary theological motif for John. This Gospel points out quite clearly that Jesus was condemned for claiming to be "king of the Jews." Not only does that claim make up the substance of the discussion between Jesus and Pilate in chapter 18, but it is also confirmed by the title that Pilate placed over the cross: "Jesus of Nazareth, the King of the Jews" (19:19–20). Pilate undoubtedly intended the inscription sarcastically, but in this burial scene John wishes to stress the truth of the claim. Further, the fact that the title was written in Hebrew, Latin, and Greek suggests that John takes Pilate's inscription to refer far beyond Jesus' own people: he is in fact king of all nations.

For this reason, John emphasizes the preparation of Jesus' body for burial. In the Synoptic Gospels, Joseph interred Jesus quickly, and the women waited until after the Sabbath to come with burial spices. Here, in contrast, Nicodemus has already brought valuable spices for the burial. Myrrh is known from other sources as a spice used in interments. Aloe is not mentioned elsewhere for burial purposes, but it does occur occasionally as an expensive spice used to anoint bodies. The spices themselves were expensive, and John relates that Nicodemus procured a large quantity of them—weighing approximately seventy-five American pounds in all. Now the rabbis report that a certain Onkelos burned some sixty pounds of spices at the death of Gamaliel, explaining that he was "far better than a hundred kings."[1] By suggesting that Nicodemus brought such

followers, and neither plays a significant role in the larger story, which makes their behavior all the more curious. Just as interesting is why the inner circle or Jesus' own family do not participate in the retrieval of his body and burial. While the text gives us no clear answer, it is fair enough to speculate that fear, shock, and disappointment were all part of the mix that kept his closest followers away.

A sermon might explore the things that keep us away from Jesus too. Preachers should be careful, however, not to overly generalize. It is rare for any of us to have a clear, unmixed motive for anything. While the sermon might explore several ideas (e.g., fear, embarrassment, doubt), the reality is that most of us are a mix of all of those things. That may be the most powerful of images to explore. We have no idea which emotion kept the "close" followers away or what brought the "far" followers close. What we do see in this story is that those things do happen to both the faithful and the just-barely faithful.

Another route for the sermon is more confrontational. This sermon takes to task the kind of faith James rails against in his letter: faith without works (2:14–26). In a more colloquial but similar form, my uncle used to say, "Anyone can talk a good fight." The reality is that in the moment of confrontation and need, the two disciples that cared for Jesus in his death were the last two anyone might have expected. While a congregation may not enjoy the confrontation, the reality is that there are many of us who will say and believe all the right things but fail to stand when the hour demands it.

For all of Peter's bravado, James and John's desire to sit on the left and right hand of Jesus, and discussion about who was the greatest in the kingdom of heaven, it is two unknowns who claim the body of Jesus and offer him a burial fit for a king. It is true that just a week or so before his death Mary had anointed Jesus with myrrh (12:1–3), an important act no doubt. At his burial, however, Nicodemus brought about a hundred pounds of it—a kingly amount for sure. According to Matthew 27:59–60, Joseph gave his unused tomb, a rarity in that world—unless you were wealthy or royalty.

We will all do well to remember that the tension played out between these two caretakers and the rest of the disciples can be palpable. While Nicodemus and Joseph may have been uneasy followers out of fear, on this day they did what no one else would since the disciples were huddled behind closed doors out of "fear" (20:19). That is the nature of our obedience and discipleship. We must take care in our

---

1. George R. Beasley-Murray, *John*, Word Biblical Commentary 36 (Nashville: Thomas Nelson, 1999), 359.

John 19:38–42

Theological Perspective

fill the gap left by those who presumably love him the most.

In each of the canonical Gospels, Joseph, a member of the Sanhedrin, approaches Pilate and asks for Jesus' body (Matt. 27:58; Mark 15:43; Luke 23:52; John 19:38). Variously, the writers describe him as a disciple, courageous, righteous, and one who disagreed with the decision of his colleagues on the Sanhedrin. Twice, he is described as a man who looked for the kingdom of God (Mark 15:43; Luke 23:51), and here in John at the foot of the cross he is accompanied by Nicodemus, the man "who had . . . come to Jesus by night" (19:39).

Earlier in Jesus' ministry, Nicodemus heard about the kingdom and the newness that accompanies those who see it. One wonders what he did with that insight. Did he share it with others on the council? What we do know is that two kingdom seekers, at great risk to their careers if not their very lives, now publicly identify with Jesus and carry his body to a resting place. Carefully, they follow the custom of washing, wrapping, and anointing, and before nightfall they place him in a tomb. Faithful ones outside the inner circle have opened their hearts and gone where only the Spirit could have led.

Forever a part of salvation history, Nicodemus and Joseph remind us there is always more to the story. Through their lives we discern that the Holy Spirit claims hearts even behind enemy lines. We hear in their witness salvation's rhythm beating in a surprising place. Maybe there are "fearful" and "secret" disciples all around us, and in his time the Lord Jesus will use them too in profound ways. Until then, let us prayerfully and humbly await the rest of the story.

SEAN WHITE

Pastoral Perspective

clearly how the past lives on in us, buried and yet often radically harmful, gnawing at the root of our personality. Here lies the truth of William Faulkner's maxim, "The past is never dead. It's not even past."[3] Bad parenting, abuse, trauma, guilt, distress—all these can lie buried but active in the graves of our psyches, continuing to prey upon our lives. The smell of the decomposing corpse may be masked by a hundred pounds of spices, but no amount can stifle the stench of such toxic relics. In Jesus' day it was believed to be important to bury a corpse properly, for otherwise there was the fear that its restless ghost might return. Far too many lives are haunted by ghosts that have not been properly laid to rest.

Here is where we find the saving value of Christ's burial. Historically, this has often been associated with his visit to hell to proclaim release to captives imprisoned there before his coming (1 Pet. 3:19), a journey into the past. In our day we might rethink Christ's burial as a journey into the underworld of our personalities, where lie forces and powers that continue to hold us captive. Here is Christ the Lord, John's Sovereign One, tunneling deep into the past to shine a light and to banish the dark shadows that lurk there. Christ's burial is the starting point for the healing of the past with its deadly potency.

The story of Jesus' burial involves two journeys: one into the dark and one into the light. The tomb closes upon Jesus, and there is deep darkness. He lies among the buried, in order that the buried might truly die with him and release their hold upon us. Joseph and Nicodemus are stepping out into the light, out of the tomb of fear that has held them for too long. The burial of the sovereign Lord of John's Gospel invites us to step out with them.

LANCE STONE

3. William Faulkner, *Requiem for a Nun* (orig. 1950; New York: Vintage, 2011), 73.

a superabundance of spices, John also implies that Jesus deserves royal honor.

Joseph and Nicodemus wrapped Jesus' body in cloth strips, possibly made of linen, placing the spices within the wrappings. The procedure, John notes, was in accord with traditional Jewish burial practices. It was consistent too with the manner in which the friend of Jesus, Lazarus, was buried; he too was wrapped with strips of cloth (11:44). Their attentive preparations for Jesus' burial demonstrated their great respect for him. Still, their actions also implied that they did not cherish any expectation that Jesus would rise from the dead.

John's narrative continues with the comment that, once the preparations were complete, Joseph and Nicodemus laid the body in a tomb. Mark says nothing about what sort of tomb Joseph used. Matthew says that the tomb was new and, further, that it belonged to Joseph himself (Matt. 27:60). Luke describes it as unused, a tomb in which "no one had ever been laid" (Luke 23:53). John says nothing about ownership of the tomb, but he does affirm Matthew's description that the tomb was new. Also, in agreement with Luke, John says that "no one had ever been laid" in the tomb (19:41). Once again, this emphasis in John's account suggests strong reverence and high regard for the deceased.

John provides one final note to the burial that is not mentioned in the other Gospels. The tomb, he says, was located in a nearby garden. There is some evidence of a garden in the vicinity of the probable location of Golgotha, near the north wall of Jerusalem, where there was a gate named the Garden Gate.[2] Burial in a garden would certainly imply high status, and, in fact, 2 Kings 21:18 happens to mention a garden in connection with the burial of King Manasseh of Judah. Thus John presents Jesus, in this lowest point of his humiliation, as the object of reverent care by two leading citizens of Jerusalem. They prepared the body for burial with an extravagance of spices and placed it in a high-class grave site. It was a somber close to the crucifixion, but it also suggested a burial appropriate to a royal personage.

JAMES E. DAVISON

labeling and characterization of others in the faith. In every life there are days that cause us to fear, to huddle behind closed doors and in the shadows. There are, however, also those days when our faith connects with the Spirit, and we stand when no others will. Both are true for all of us. This kind of sermon can remind a congregation not to count anyone out, that unlikely followers come from different places and in varied ways.

It would not be fair to think that Joseph and Nicodemus continued to work only in the background, quietly going to Pilate and secretly carrying Jesus' body off for burial. The unlikely two cease being "secret" followers in this episode. Typically in cases of notoriety there would be more reason to leave a body at the place of execution. Nothing says, "Do not follow this example," like a rotting corpse. Many times, even public mourning of the executed could be prohibited, to ensure no martyrs were created in the process (see Josephus, *Antiquities* 9.104). In this instance, however, Pilate seemed never to have taken the charge of insurrection seriously.

Nevertheless, Joseph risked his public stature by being associated with the followers of Jesus. Guilt by association was the rule of that day. In this instance, these two were the model of courageous disciples, offering to Jesus what no other follower would. The irony here, which John loves to highlight, is that the dedicated followers of Jesus faded into the shadows, hoping to keep their identity secret, while the secret followers came out into the light of day to serve their Lord. Perhaps the best sermon on these ideas rests neither on chiding the doubters nor praising the followers completely, but on reminding us all that both faith and doubt remain with us always.

VAUGHN CROWETIPTON

---

2. Raymond E. Brown, *The Gospel according to John (xiii–xxi)*, Anchor Bible (Garden City, NY: Doubleday & Co., 1970), 943.

John 20:1–10

Theological Perspective

Before they became the Bible, the stories of Scripture were lived. Unfortunately, that seems lost on many of us. Once they became cemented within the canon, they no longer smelled of the real world. The dust of ancient walking paths settled, and the sweat of an early morning run evaporated. No longer do people like Mary Magdalene, Peter, and the Beloved Disciple look anything like us, and we peer back through the pages of Scripture and see saintly figures assessing a scene with which we have become all too familiar. On the other hand, when they do resemble us, we vest them with a measure of faith that even the writers themselves insist they did not have. John tells the story of that first resurrection morning, and the portrait he paints, not unlike the works of Norman Rockwell, invites the reader to feel at home with people a lot like us.

Early in the morning, Mary of Magdala returns to the cemetery. I am reminded of words I have heard numerous times following an interment: "It will take us about an hour, and after that you are welcome to come back." In other words, the sexton will see to it that the casket is buried, the grave covered, and the flowers neatly arranged. Protecting the family from such a painful task, he invites them to return after the scene is tidied up. In the closing verses of chapter 19, John identifies Joseph of Arimathea and

Pastoral Perspective

John's account of the discovery of Jesus' resurrection introduces us to a number of people, some named and some unnamed. All in their own way play their parts. Our concern here, firstly, is with two participants who are not actually present in these verses, who are removed from the garden in which the events take place, but whose influence extends over everyone else.

Our attention turns first to a reference made by Mary Magdalene in her exclamation to Peter and the disciple whom Jesus loved after she has run to them from the empty tomb. "They have taken the Lord out of the tomb," says Mary, "and we do not know where they have laid him" (v. 2b). This statement introduces us to "they," the people who have taken him and have apparently laid him we know not where. Who are these nameless "they," these anonymous people who so trouble Mary, even though they are physically absent from the proceedings? Are they grave robbers, who were prevalent in these times? Are they the Jewish authorities, who have heard claims that this Jesus of Nazareth would rise from the dead and have maybe taken the precaution of removing his body? Might they be the Roman authorities with concerns about the body of an insurgent, crucified because he was a threat to law and order? Who knows? Despite their influence, their identity is

Exegetical Perspective

From the heartrending events of the crucifixion and burial on Friday, John turns to the arrival of Mary Magdalene at the tomb on Sunday morning. The other three Gospels also state that Mary came to the tomb, but in each of them she is accompanied by other women. John focuses entirely on Mary, describing her early morning arrival in the darkness. As elsewhere in John, "darkness" suggests lack of understanding and unbelief. In the preceding section, John has just reminded readers that Nicodemus was the person who originally came to Jesus *by night*, a reference to unbelief and the need for light (19:39; 3:19–21). That light, of course, is Jesus himself, the "light of the world," and those who follow him "will never walk in darkness" (8:12).

Clearly, John understands Mary Magdalene's arrival in darkness as a sign that she did not yet understand that Jesus was to rise from the dead. She discovered that the stone had been rolled away, but whether or not she looked into the tomb is not stated. Openings to tombs were only about three feet high, and Mary would have had to stoop and crawl to get inside. Probably, in the darkness, the removal of the stone was sufficient for her to conclude that Jesus' body had been stolen—a likely assumption, since grave robbery was frequent—or Jesus' enemies had removed the body. Whatever

Homiletical Perspective

On the highest and holiest day of the church year—which is when we most frequently preach on this passage—the problem is that we have already preached it so many times. What congregant has not heard this text? Even those who come just on Easter day! What preacher has not at least thought, this year I will proclaim the resurrection from the perspective of the stone or the linen wrappings? "Familiarity breeds contempt," goes the old saying. In this case, familiarity can breed daydreaming or naps on the part of the congregation. It is not that the text is not powerful; it is. It is not that the text has nothing to say, because it does. It is that the text itself calls us to do more than just believe certain things. This text calls us to become a particular kind of people.

Years ago, when I was coaching my son's baseball team, there was a young man on that team who really struggled with the game. His throws were wild. He could never hit the ball. Catching anything was out of the question. I tried to work with him on skills, confidence, and strategy. Nothing worked. His parents loved to see him out there trying, but he was losing heart fast. The other kids tried, but over time they became less than kind. One afternoon at practice one of the kids yelled at this young man, "What's the matter with you? Can't you see?!" Suddenly it dawned on me: he cannot see. After a conversation

Theological Perspective

Nicodemus as the ones who buried Jesus and tended to his body.

Mystery shrouds the absence of Jesus' closest friends, and I wonder how Mary felt when she learned who claimed his body. No doubt, Mary's own suspicions are roused as word of them spreads. The Sanhedrin? Pilate released Jesus' body to members of the Sanhedrin? Now, upon her return, some of her worst fears are confirmed.

As Mary approaches the tomb, nothing is tidied up. In fact, the seal has been broken and the stone rolled back, but Jesus is nowhere to be found. "They!" she exclaims. "They have taken the Lord out of the tomb!" (v. 2b). Among the people "they" may suggest, surely Nicodemus and Joseph top the list. The Sanhedrin, the very ones who wanted Jesus dead, took "responsibility" for giving him a dignified burial. They saw that his body would neither fall prey to wild animals nor be lost among the nameless others buried by the Roman guard. They saw to it, all right! He is gone! She has no idea where!

Though Jesus prepared the disciples for this moment by prophesying his death and resurrection, it looks different at the mouth of an empty tomb. The disciples never imagined abandoning Jesus. Some even vowed to die with him, and they surely never dreamed of the enemy taking possession of his body, to do with as they pleased. A fundamental trust has been violated, and Mary rushes for help.

Upon hearing the news, the Beloved Disciple and Peter race to the tomb to confirm Mary's horrible story, and in the process of inspiration, the Holy Spirit has retained some very human elements. On occasion, the reader has overheard the disciples discussing who is the greatest, and it echoed at least a measure of kingdom concerns. Here, though, the Beloved Disciple describes the ferocious dash, and he assures the reader that *he* got there first! Unashamedly, he highlights his athletic prowess three times, twice in verse 4 and again in verse 8. Unbelievable! Yet, thanks be to God!

A chasm develops between the reader and biblical characters when one forgets that Jesus alone is the incarnate God. Though we know better, for all practical purposes, we elevate other faithful people to similar status. While the earliest disciples serve as matriarchs and patriarchs of Christian faith and form the foundational layer of the "spiritual household," they, along with every other believer, are "living stones" among other living stones. They are not the "cornerstone" (1 Pet. 2:5–6), and the divine power that stirs them enlivens every other believer as well.

Pastoral Perspective

vague, their profile blurred. The "they" are necessarily ill-defined and obscure, pitted against the helpless "we," who do not know where he has been laid (v. 2).

The philosopher Martin Heidegger writes of what he calls "the They" in his discussion of what he calls "inauthentic existence," by which he means living that is diminished by anxiety and by an unwillingness to take personal responsibility for our lives.[1] For Heidegger, "the They" represent the faceless, impersonal powers at work in the world that dictate and constrain human life by robbing us of initiative and decision. So we might say that "they have closed the road for repairs," and we are not quite sure exactly who has closed the road, but we have a vague sense of influential powers that impinge upon our world. We might say, "They have to put an end to gun crime!" placing responsibility for stopping this evil onto some unnamed authority out there.

It was "the They" who were at work in Jesus' trial and death, stirring up public opinion against him, and now it is "the They" who have apparently decreed that Jesus' body must be removed for whatever reason. A world dominated by "the They" is one in which we are forever at the mercy of powers and authorities beyond us—often colluding with them—and never in full control of our own destiny. We encounter "the They" in the novels of Franz Kafka and in George Orwell's *1984*. In this passage "the They" are casting their influence over Mary and doubtless the other disciples too.

At the opposite extreme, however, is someone else who is very much present, but only in his absence— at least for now. This is Jesus. We are drawn to verses 6–7, where Peter enters the tomb and finds only the linen wrappings and the napkin for Jesus' head neatly rolled up. The contrast here is with Lazarus, who in John 11 emerges from his tomb still wrapped in his graveclothes, the trappings of death still binding him. He has cheated death only for a spell; it will return in due course to reclaim him.

Jesus, however, is gloriously free from the grave. The discarded graveclothes and folded napkin signify not only that his body has not been stolen by grave robbers but that he is utterly sovereign over death. The trappings of death are tidied and put in their place. This is completely consistent with John's portrayal of Jesus throughout his death, burial, and resurrection. This is the regal Jesus, in total command of his destiny, imperial and in total opposition to "the They." "They" will not consign him to a tomb.

1. Martin Heidegger, *Being and Time* (Oxford: Blackwell, 1962), 163.

she thought, she rushed back to tell the disciples of her discovery.

John intensifies the narrative by switching from past to present tense here. Mary literally "comes to the tomb," "sees the stone," and "runs and comes to Peter and the Beloved Disciple." Use of the present tense serves to heighten the sense of urgency as Mary Magdalene hurries to share her grief and anxiety with the disciples. Her outcry, "*We* do not know" where the body has been laid (v. 2), is a reminder of John's use of earlier sources in the composition of this Gospel. Mary also calls Jesus "the Lord," the first time this title occurs in John. It will be used frequently in the remainder of the Gospel. After making her report, Mary drops out of sight as John turns his attention to Peter and the Beloved Disciple. She will reappear in the next section, when John records her meeting with the risen Lord.

In Peter's last appearance in this Gospel, he was denying Jesus in the high priest's courtyard (18:15–18, 25–27). Now he resurfaces in the narrative, along with "the disciple whom Jesus loved." Without doubt this is John, the one to whom this entire Gospel is attributed. John does not say whether any other disciples were present. Rather, as with Mary Magdalene and as in other accounts in the Gospel, John focuses entirely on the person of interest. In this case, his attention focuses on two: Peter and the Beloved Disciple.

By the time this Gospel was written, early Christian communities acknowledged Peter as the leader of the apostles. Still, the Johannine community also revered John, and their loyalty surfaces in the description of these events. The Beloved Disciple outran Peter, but then hesitated, waiting outside the tomb. Then Peter arrived, "following him" (v. 6). The term "follow," as a call to faith and discipleship, is often significant in John (e.g., 8:12), and it is sometimes suggested that here the term aims to give precedence to the Beloved Disciple. It seems just as likely, though, that the term simply turns attention to the arrival of Peter, who in typical fashion rushed right into the tomb.

The Beloved Disciple had already noticed the graveclothes when he peered into the tomb, but now Peter saw that the body wrappings were still in place, with the head covering lying separately. While Peter considered the meaning of this, the Beloved Disciple also entered the tomb. John says matter-of-factly that "he saw and believed." Apparently recognizing that robbers would not waste time removing the graveclothes, the Beloved Disciple concluded that Jesus had risen from the dead.

with his parents, one where we all owned up to our embarrassment that we had missed the obvious signs, his parents took him to get glasses. That was the day everything changed. Suddenly, or at least in a short amount of time, nothing got by him. His throws were dead on target. He could hit the ball. Being able to see matters.

Resurrection is so many things, and it also cures myopia of the soul. It is only with the perspective of the resurrection correcting our marred vision that we can see the kind of kingdom God has in mind. Anyone who has really read the stories of our faith has thought this is crazy. Those who have never had that thought have never weighed the implications of Jesus' teachings, his parables, his resurrection. Perhaps it would help if we started our worship and Scripture reading with the words, "I know this sounds crazy, but . . ."

Telling in our passage is the second last verse: "for as yet they did not understand" (v. 9a). Not one of the disciples came to the tomb expecting resurrection. No one was giddy with excitement to see if Jesus was "still" there, if it had happened yet or not. Their assumption upon seeing the stone was that an assault from the outside had happened; someone had stolen the body. Even when the disciples arrived, their vision was so out of focus that for whatever reason they did not even recognize Jesus himself! Consider the participants in the story.

Mary Magdalene is not portrayed as looking inside the tomb. With the stone rolled away, she made what would be a typical assumption. Someone else had rolled the stone away to do something with the body of Jesus. That Jesus was buried was in and of itself no small thing. Vandals and others who were crucified were not always buried, in order to warn others not to commit similar acts. Jesus and his followers had no means to purchase a space, so the fact that Joseph and Nicodemus came forward to care for the body was a miracle in itself. In the midst of her own grief Mary made the mistake of assuming the worst. For her, resurrection was the last thing on her mind.

Simon Peter learned the tomb was empty from Mary. For Jesus' entire ministry Peter had been the one to make the brash claims, to speak for the other disciples, but not in this case. Mary informed him of what she had seen, probably describing her worst fears come true. Running to the tomb, Peter was outrun by another disciple but was the first to enter the tomb itself. Perhaps he was speechless. In this instance we get no proclamation from Peter. Only silence.

John 20:1–10

Theological Perspective

As trivial as this emphasis on the footrace between the Beloved Disciple and Peter may seem, the profundity of its inclusion in Scripture levels the ground upon which disciples in every age travel the way of faith.

This story is about the resurrection, but even the biblical witness is seasoned with somewhat embarrassing human concerns. Take note, and by no means explain it away. Faith happens here, amid the honorable and the dishonorable. Does it matter who arrived first? Maybe not, but the God-breathed witness includes the Beloved Disciple's adolescent ambitions and now invites the reader to wonder: If him, why not me? If those who first experienced Jesus' love behaved like this and, even proudly, asserted themselves over against others, maybe the Way can find me as well. Though a disciple would wish otherwise, humiliating actions and attitudes creep out, and some even find their way to the pages of Scripture. Nonetheless, the Holy Spirit apparently is not repulsed, but continues the redemptive program precisely in the midst of such humanness.

Finally, though, the Beloved Disciple arrived at the tomb first; he and Peter both personally confirmed what Mary had been saying. Jesus was gone! The large stone had been rolled away, as if to display the contents. Strips of linen, a burial cloth, but no corpse. As if someone really had taken his body, the cave stood empty, shouting a message no one seemed to understand (v. 9). What the text does say is that the Beloved Disciple "saw and believed" (v. 9). Maybe he believed Mary, nothing more, nothing less. "They have taken the Lord!" she shouted, and now with his own eyes he saw and believed. The tomb was empty, and no one knew where he was. Is this not, though, where faith begins: at the empty tomb? Come and see for yourselves, and listen closely to the message it proclaims.

SEAN WHITE

Pastoral Perspective

"They" will not constrain him with grave wrappings. "They" will not prevent his rising, for he is in control. Jesus defies "the They."

At opposite extremes in this narrative we have "the They" and Jesus, both present in their absence. What of the other participants in the story? What of Mary, Peter, and the Beloved Disciple? They are betwixt and between. Look at them running: Mary running to Peter and the other disciple, and Peter and the Beloved Disciple then running to the tomb. What kind of running is this? These disciples are stirred by what they have heard and seen, and this is the running of confusion, of bewilderment, of hope, of fear, of desperation, of longing. Above all, this is running away from "the They" and toward Jesus.

As we watch, we see that these disciples are in different places. Mary is bewildered, grief-stricken, as the verses that follow will further demonstrate. Peter is inquisitive, entering the tomb first, impulsive, searching. The Beloved Disciple sees and believes, even though he cannot yet understand. They are at different stages of faith, but all of them will feature in the remainder of John's Gospel, each in his or her own way being commissioned for service and testimony, each being entrusted with responsibility and initiative. Their running is muddled and uncertain, but it is taking them from inauthentic living dominated by "the They" to the new, risen life with Jesus.

So to today. In our contemporary, secular, post-Christian world, God is evidently a delusion. Religion is a symptom of humanity's infancy that must be discarded. The church has had its day and is finished. Science has disproved and displaced religion. The resurrection could not possibly have happened. Some things can never change. So "they" say. We Christians are sometimes confused, sometimes uncertain, sometimes believing, and sometimes struggling. We too are betwixt and between, like these disciples. The summons to faith, however, means defiance of "the They," as we are drawn to the sovereign, regal, risen Christ.

LANCE STONE

Exegetical Perspective

John comments that the disciples had not yet understood that Scripture foretold the necessity of the resurrection. Already in chapter 2, John had observed that the disciples would comprehend this event only after Jesus rose; then they would believe "the scripture and the word that Jesus had spoken" (2:22). Now John reports that the Beloved Disciple was first to recognize this momentous event. Although the Gospel never questions that Peter was the de facto leader of the apostles, it certainly highlights John's membership in the inner circle of disciples and his privileged position as the Beloved Disciple. To the degree that rivalries may have existed among the various Christian communities, we can imagine how significant John's being the first to believe would have been for the Johannine community.

The conjunction of "seeing and believing" will return in the appearance to Thomas, when Jesus states, "Blessed are those who have not seen and yet have come to believe" (20:29). It is sometimes suggested that this statement includes a backward glance to the Beloved Disciple, since he too believed without seeing, but the phrases are used quite distinctly—"seeing and believing" versus "not having seen and having come to belief." Moreover, the saying to Thomas suggests seeing the risen Lord rather than seeing the empty tomb. Thus, most likely John is not thinking of the Beloved Disciple in this statement to Thomas. In general, throughout John, the disciples display various levels of belief. For instance, in 6:69, Peter acknowledges that the disciples have "come to believe and know that [Jesus is] the Holy One of God." In fact, the Gospel implies that their faith and understanding will grow gradually, coming to completion only after he has departed and they have received the Holy Spirit, who will "guide [them] into all the truth" (16:13).

John uses this scene as the prelude for the remaining accounts in the Gospel, which narrate the appearances of the risen Christ, first to Mary Magdalene and then to others. Thus, in a rather muted conclusion John records merely that Peter and the Beloved Disciple returned home.

JAMES E. DAVISON

Homiletical Perspective

The Beloved Disciple (perhaps John himself?) entered the tomb last. He saw the linens and was credited as having "believed" once he saw. We should be careful here. The final statement of this section and the following narratives do not indicate that the Beloved Disciple believed in the resurrection at this moment. What is more likely indicated here is that this disciple began to believe the news Mary had reported: the body was indeed gone. After seeing these things, the disciples went home, and nothing more is said about their reporting to others that Jesus had risen. Only after Jesus appeared to them in the locked room and showed them his hands and side did the disciples come to firm belief in his resurrection (20:20).

The stories of these three can mirror our own. We may know about the resurrection but struggle to believe it when we see it. Our tendency is to place it in the past, as one of those hard to fathom yet somehow essential parts of the faith. At the same time, when we see resurrection in our own lives, it is as if we are Mary in the garden, staring Jesus in the face but not recognizing him. Perhaps the best sermon will challenge the congregation to see both the resurrected Christ, but also the effects of resurrection in our own lives. Through the corrective lens of resurrection faith, we can see why it is true that when Jesus tells us to leave behind the things that hold us captive, to love our neighbor (whoever that is), to pray for our enemies, to turn the other cheek, all so that we can follow him, our own lives are resurrected. Resurrection corrects our vision of ourselves, our community, and our connection to God.

VAUGHN CROWETIPTON

John 20:11–18

[11]But Mary stood weeping outside the tomb. As she wept, she bent over to look into the tomb; [12]and she saw two angels in white, sitting where the body of Jesus had been lying, one at the head and the other at the feet. [13]They said to her, "Woman, why are you weeping?" She said to them, "They have taken away my Lord, and I do not know where they have laid him." [14]When she had said this, she turned around and saw Jesus standing there, but she did not know that it was Jesus. [15]Jesus said to her, "Woman, why are you weeping? Whom are you looking for?" Supposing him to be the gardener, she said to him, "Sir, if you have carried him away, tell me where you have laid him, and I will take him away." [16]Jesus said to her, "Mary!" She turned and said to him in Hebrew, "Rabbouni!" (which means Teacher). [17]Jesus said to her, "Do not hold on to me, because I have not yet ascended to the Father. But go to my brothers and say to them, 'I am ascending to my Father and your Father, to my God and your God.'" [18]Mary Magdalene went and announced to the disciples, "I have seen the Lord"; and she told them that he had said these things to her.

Theological Perspective

One of Elisabeth Schüssler Fiorenza's best-known books is entitled *In Memory of Her*. It refers to a story that is found in all four Gospels, the story of Jesus being anointed with a jar of costly oil by a woman who is named only in the Gospel of John. In both Mark's and Matthew's accounts of the story, Jesus tells the disciples that "wherever the gospel is preached in the whole world, what she has done will be told in memory of her" (Matt. 26:13; Mark 14:9 RSV). The title of the book is ironic, however, because, in fact, this story is rarely told as a central part of Jesus' passion; and even the woman's name is lost to us. Schüssler Fiorenza writes, "The name of the betrayer is remembered, but the name of the faithful disciple is forgotten because she was a woman."[1] Still today, the church struggles with the role of women—both in Scripture and in the tradition.

While some might argue otherwise, the church should not make the mistake of assuming that it no longer needs to talk about women: about their value, the equal image of God that they bear, and their ability to serve as professional ministers in the church. Many people think that surely we must be beyond that by now: we live in the twenty-first century, after all. Women head corporations, attend college in

Pastoral Perspective

As in the Synoptics, Mary Magdalene goes to the tomb "early on the first day of the week, while it was still dark" (20:1), but in John she goes alone. Her purpose is not clear. Since Joseph of Arimathea and Nicodemus have already anointed Jesus' body (rather lavishly!) for burial, perhaps she comes only to mourn. John specifies that she is weeping (v. 11). Mary encounters not one angel, as in Mark 16:5; Matthew 28:2, but two, as in Luke 24:4. In John, though, the heavenly messengers say nothing about Jesus. They merely ask Mary why she is crying. Her answer, that Jesus' body is missing and must therefore have been taken by someone, demonstrates that she does not understand what is happening, despite Jesus' earlier assurance that he is "the resurrection and the life" (11:25). As Gail O'Day notes, "The world cannot make sense of an empty tomb with any theory except grave robbing."[1]

In the midst of death and mourning, who can understand anything? The Duchess of Yeovil, a houseguest at Downton Abbey, commiserates with young Tom Branson, the widowed son-in-law of Lord Grantham. "Grief is hard, Tom," she says. "When the Duke died, it made me clumsy. I kept

---

1. Elisabeth Schüssler Fiorenza, *In Memory of Her: A Feminist Theological Reconstruction of Christian Origins* (New York: Crossroad, 1985), xiii.

1. Gail R. O'Day, "Gospel of John," in *Women's Bible Commentary*, 3rd ed., ed. Carol A. Newsom, Sharon H. Ringe, and Jacqueline E. Lapsley (Louisville, KY: Westminster John Knox Press, 2012), 527.

Exegetical Perspective

The main characters in this first Johannine appearance of Jesus after his resurrection are Mary Magdalene and Jesus. The two men who preceded Mary to the tomb, Peter and the other disciple, are offstage at this point; they reappear only at the end of the passage, along with the rest of the disciples who hear Mary's announcement that Jesus is alive.

Indeed, in all the Gospels women are the closest witnesses of both the crucifixion (Matt. 27:56; Mark 15:40; Luke 23:49 speaks only of "the women") and the resurrection (Mark 16:1; Matt. 28:1; Luke 24:10). In John's Gospel, only Mary Magdalene meets Jesus at the empty tomb. She is a mysterious figure, having first appeared at the foot of the cross, along with Mary the mother of Jesus, and Mary the wife of Clopas, also identified as the sister of Jesus' mother (19:25). Her surname indicates that she came from the town of Magdala, a fishing village on the northwest shore of the Sea of Galilee.

Only Luke 8:2 provides any additional information. There Mary Magdalene is identified as a woman from whom Jesus cast out seven demons, and as one of several women who traveled with the disciples and Jesus, providing material support from their own possessions. Despite legends and rumors about Mary Magdalene (she was a prostitute; she should be identified with the woman who anointed Jesus'

Homiletical Perspective

When the other Gospels speak of the empty tomb, they variously describe the women's perplexity, excitement, or terror. Only John depicts grief. The Fourth Gospel alone seems to understand that the absence of Jesus' body is occasion for great sorrow. Mary Magdalene weeps, and any preaching of this text should pay close attention to her tears. John refers to them no fewer than four times.

The angels ask her why she is crying; then Jesus, unrecognizable to her, poses the same question. Her answer pertains not to his death but to the disappearance of his corpse. Beyond his dying, it is the loss of his body that crushes her. Preachers may be tempted to sentimentalize her grief, reducing it to personal, emotional attachment, an assumption that not only sells Mary short but permits listeners to hear the story from a safe distance.

A better course is to credit her with understanding that the absence of his body is catastrophic. There is nothing even residual of him, no touchstone of remembrance, no vestige of actual presence, no place that is not empty of him. The powers of darkness have not only killed him, they have wiped out all trace of him. His tomb is gutted. Its horribly open mouth taunts Mary with news not just of death but of nothingness. The evidence is that the claims and promises of Jesus were, like his tomb, empty.

Theological Perspective

numbers equal to, if not greater than, men, and have great control over their own reproductive choices and marital status. What is the need of feminist discourse anymore—either inside the church or outside of it?

There is no denying the advances women have made in the past few decades, in both secular and sacred contexts. For example, since the 1970s, most mainline Protestant denominations in the United States have ordained women; and currently in most mainline Protestant seminaries there are near-equal numbers of men and women. When you include Catholic and evangelical seminaries, however, men outnumber women more than two to one; Catholic and Orthodox churches continue to bar women from ordained ministry, and many Protestant church bodies do not support women in church leadership.

At the same time, both locally and globally, rape and domestic violence continue to touch the lives of millions of women, who often bear the brunt of both the burden and the blame of sexual assault. As we have seen, even in the twenty-first century, a young woman still can be shot in the head for advocating education for girls (Malala Yousafzai), and a woman still can be pulled off a bus and brutally gang-raped such that she dies from her injuries (Jyoti Singh Pandey). Just when we think it is finally safe to assume that the equality of men and women is both recognized and celebrated, some such event occurs to remind us of women's continued vulnerability and marginalization both in the church and in society at large.

This text in particular, then, is of central importance for women and men who seek both to highlight the role women had in the life and ministry of Jesus and to refute the idea that there were no female disciples, simply because no woman was named as one of the twelve apostles. Contrary to that notion, here, in this text, we see clear evidence of Jesus' intimate, loving, trusting relationship with Mary Magdalene, the disciple he chose as the first witness of the resurrection and the first to proclaim the good news that he was not dead, but alive.

It is one of the most tender scenes in Scripture. In the predawn darkness of that first Easter morning, Mary, who previous verses note was first to arrive at the tomb, discovers that the stone is rolled away. She immediately runs to tell the other disciples, because she is afraid that Jesus' body has been stolen. Peter and the disciple Jesus loved then go to the tomb themselves to confirm what she has seen; however, they do not seem to understand what has happened, and so they turn around and go back home.

Pastoral Perspective

dropping things and breaking them. It was because it felt disloyal to manage anything properly without him. Do you see?" "But you could manage?" Tom asks. "Yes," she replies, "I could. And so can you." "I wonder," says Tom.[2]

Many people who experience the death of a loved one wonder in the same way. They wonder how life can ever be the same again. They wonder how the sun can dare to rise again after the world has been irreparably damaged by death. They know the disorientation and disruption of our bodies as well as of our hearts that the Duchess describes. Mary Magdalene is so disoriented that she does not even notice that she is speaking with angels.

"They have taken away my Lord, and I do not know where they have laid him," she says (v. 13). She does not seem aware that she has made something like a statement of faith when she speaks of Jesus as "my Lord." She still thinks he is dead, though. When the angels say nothing in response, Mary turns around and sees a man she presumes to be the gardener. He asks her the same question the angels asked: "Woman, why are you weeping?" (v. 13, cf. v. 15), and she answers with similar words: "Sir, if you have carried him away, tell me where you have laid him, and I will take him away." Perhaps there is some irony intended for the reader in Mary's addressing Jesus as *kyrie*, since the word translated "sir" can also be "lord." She clearly does not recognize him, though.

Jesus then calls her by name: "Mary!" (v. 16). He said in 10:3, "The gatekeeper opens the gate for [the good shepherd], and the sheep hear his voice. He calls his own sheep by name and leads them out." Just as he called Lazarus by name and summoned him from his tomb—"Lazarus, come out!" (11:43)—so, when he calls Mary by name in the garden on Easter morning, she hears his voice and recognizes him, and he leads her out of her grief and misunderstanding. Just as Jesus began his ministry by asking the disciples of John the Baptist, "What are you looking for?" (1:38), so here at the end he asks Mary, "Whom are you looking for?" (20:15). What it means to be a disciple is to look for Jesus, to find him—or rather, to be found by him—and to hear him call us by name.

"Do not hold on to me," says Jesus, "because I have not yet ascended to the Father" (v. 17). "Do not hold" is a present imperative, so it means "do not keep holding on to me," which suggests that Mary has already embraced him, a perfectly

2. Season 4, episode 2, *Downton Abbey* (British Broadcasting Company, 2013).

feet with her hair; she was Jesus' lover), there is nothing beyond these sparse references in the New Testament to identify her. Yet her appearance at the crucial events of Jesus' cross and resurrection in all four Gospels testifies to her importance in the early church.

If we attend to the immediately preceding verses in John 20:1–7, we find that Mary has a double encounter at the tomb, first with Jesus' absence, and then with Jesus himself as the living Lord. This double encounter leads to two contrasting announcements to the disciples, which in turn frame this first resurrection narrative: "They have taken the Lord out of the tomb, and we do not know where they have laid him" (20:2) and "I have seen the Lord" (v. 18)—surely one of the most astounding statements in all of Scripture.

This movement from absence to presence, from bewilderment and loss to a vision of Christ, also shapes Mary's intensely personal experience at the tomb. Weeping, she repeats her narrative of loss twice, first to the two angels in the tomb, and then to Jesus himself. The angels sit where Jesus' body had lain, indicating a divine presence yet also an absence (vv. 12–13). Mary's weeping reminds us that Jesus also wept after the death of Lazarus (11:35). When Jesus repeats the angels' question: "Woman, why are you weeping?" (vv. 13, 15), with supreme irony she asks him where Jesus' body is. The scene is charged with emotion, drama, and paradox as Mary's increasingly anguished search for Jesus' body yields to her climactic recognition when he speaks her name (v. 16).

The emphasis on Jesus' absence in this passage suggests very strongly the hiddenness of the risen Christ in the world. There is a mode or kind of knowledge at work here that is different from that which is readily available to human effort. This hiddenness of Christ is a central theme in John, highlighted in 12:36, when Jesus departs and hides himself from the crowd. His true identity can be known only by those to whom God reveals it. Thus both belief and unbelief fall under God's gracious reign (12:39–40, citing Isa. 6:10).

Mary supposes Jesus to be the gardener. This theme of Jesus' unrecognizability recurs implicitly in 20:20, where the proof of his identity is his pierced hands and feet, and in 21:4. In each instance, recognition happens differently. Here, in a particularly poignant way, Mary knows Jesus when he says her name. In 20:20 his wounds testify to his identity; in 21:5–7 the great catch of fish tells the disciples that Jesus is the one standing on the beach.

If preachers are to convey the tremendous reversals and newness accomplished in the resurrection, the world's real horrors should be in view. Mary's weeping is a testament to the darkness and opens a crucial door for our facing of it, and perhaps for our naming of the fact that Jesus is lost to us in ways we may wish he were not.

Then her lament is interrupted. Two strangers, sitting in the emptiness, say, "Woman, why are you weeping?" Are they smiling? She blurts out her answer, then turns away, only to find another stranger in front of her, doubtless the gardener. The tomb is in a garden, and he must be the one who tends it. "Woman, why are you crying? Who are you looking for?" (v. 15; NRSV has "Whom," but this is a gardener, not a grammarian). These are, in John's Gospel, the first words spoken by the risen Christ: he comes asking about the meaning of our tears.

She reaches for the desperate possibility that he has relocated the corpse, and begs him to tell her where it is, so that she can put it in a better place. Does he smile at these ironies—that she is talking to the one she is looking for, that she will take charge of reburying him, that she means to shield from the world the one who has overcome it, that she wants the living Jesus to give back the dead one?

To all of it, Mary is oblivious. She cannot see who the strangers are, because there are tears in her eyes. She cannot recognize the voice of Jesus for the roar of injustice in her ears. Is it possible that we in our grief or anger or shame have been stumbling over angels? The people who are most eligible for Easter may not be able to see it when it comes.

She has no idea and is walking away, when Jesus simply calls her name: "*Mary.*" It stops her in her tracks; the truth breaks through; she turns, and the risen Christ fills her vision. In John's Gospel, this is the moment when the resurrection is declared. No angels have announced that Jesus is risen. His calling of her name *is* that announcement. This announcement is made not by telling her who he is, but by his appeal to who she is.

There is tremendous power in the speaking of a name. Your name is a sound, but more than a sound: it is you. To be called by the wrong name is to be misidentified, not rightly known. Then there is the matter of how your name is spoken: indifferently or appreciatively, roughly or tenderly, as if you are a stranger or as if you are understood. It is not Jesus' voice that Mary recognizes (she had not recognized it the moment before), but the sound of her name from that voice, as one who comprehends

John 20:11–18

Theological Perspective

Mary, however, remains, weeping and overcome with grief. It is in this moment of utter despair and hopelessness, when Mary is completely alone, that we see how much Mary means to Jesus. It is to her and her alone that the angels speak, and to her and her alone that Jesus himself appears—apparently even delaying his ascension into heaven to speak to her and console her. She recognizes him as he speaks her name, and at his request, she runs back to the disciples and is the first to proclaim, "I have seen the Lord."

Unfortunately, Mary fades from view after this moment, not only in the Gospel of John but in the further accounts of the disciples recorded in Acts as well as in the Epistles. To add insult to injury, in the Western Christian tradition, Mary Magdalene consistently has been misidentified as a reformed prostitute, usually depicted with long red hair and often with bare breasts. In this way, her apostolic authority is voided, as is any argument for the equal inclusion of women in the early church—and sometimes today, too.

This text, though (as well as its Gospel parallels), stands as an enduring reminder of Mary's status as *apostola apostolorum* ("the apostle of the apostles")—a title conferred upon her at least by the third century[2]—and refutes the notion that Jesus did not "call" any women to be his disciples. Clearly, Mary was called by Jesus; and if Mary Magdalene, so Mary Smith, Mary Yousafzai, Mary Singh Pandey, and any other Mary, born in any other country, in any other time. The name of Mary Magdalene, at least, has not been forgotten; and she lives as an enduring witness to the teaching and preaching role women always have had in the life and mission of the church, the role they should continue to be able to have in the church universal today.

KRISTIN JOHNSTON LARGEN

Pastoral Perspective

understandable response to the shocking insight that the stranger is not a gardener but Jesus himself.

In the first few years after our son Chris died, I often dreamed about him. He was invariably on the other side of a window from me, across a room, at the end of a long hallway. Despite my nearly irresistible urge to hold on to what was precious, he inevitably slipped away. How much harder for Mary, who finally understands that Jesus has been raised, to hear that he will leave. His repeated promise to send the Paraclete (14:15–17; 15:26; 16:7) and his assurance that "I will not leave you orphaned" (14:18), addressed to the disciples in the upper room (and to the reader), are surely meant for Mary too.

This suggests one of the more daunting challenges of Christian faith: that we are not in control. Jesus must return to the Father who sent him (14:12; 16:5), and Mary cannot prevent that. Even as we know him to be raised from the dead, he is not here. Jesus' prohibition, though, is paired with a command: "go to my brothers and say to them, 'I am ascending to my Father and your Father, to my God and your God.'"

As in all the earliest Easter accounts, Mary is the first to preach the gospel that Jesus has been raised. She tells the disciples, "I have seen the Lord," and reports her conversation with Jesus (v. 18). While much of Christian tradition since the sixth century has described Mary Magdalene as a penitent prostitute (a picture that the New Testament does not support), the early church remembered her as the first preacher of the gospel, the first person Jesus led from grief to faith, from mourning to proclamation.[3]

E. ELIZABETH JOHNSON

2. Ann Graham Brock, *Mary Magdalene, The First Apostle: The Struggle for Authority*, Harvard Theological Studies 51 (Cambridge, MA: Harvard University Press, 2003), 161.

3. See Brittany E. Wilson, "Mary Magdalene and Her Interpreters," in *Women's Bible Commentary*, 3rd ed., 531–35.

Exegetical Perspective

As readers we are invited to ask ourselves if we ever are talking to the risen Christ unawares, even when we think he is not to be found. The sense of Christ's absence is compressed with the fact of his presence, suggesting, at the least, hope in God who is present in the midst of absence.

In Mary's encounter with Jesus, the main theological point is not her recognition of Christ, but his knowledge of her (cf. Gal. 4:8–9). In both John's Gospel and the letters of Paul, there is no direct, unmediated knowledge of the truth of Christ; such understanding comes through God's knowledge of us. Similarly, in Luke's account of the road to Emmaus, the disciples do not recognize Jesus, because their eyes are kept from recognizing him (Luke 24:16). No matter how much time they, like Mary, have spent with Jesus, it is only by God's action that they are able truly to see and know him.

One further theme comes to light here: the mystery and elusiveness of Jesus' postresurrection body. Jesus' words, "Do not hold me," suggest that is just what Mary wants to do. The meaning of the Greek term ranges from "touch" (e.g., Luke 7:14; 22:51) to "cling," to sexual relations (1 Cor. 7:1). The personal closeness is noteworthy, yet simultaneously we realize that we cannot control Jesus' presence or absence. God in Christ exceeds our grasp.

John's Gospel sometimes is thought to present a very spiritualized and otherworldly picture of Jesus, yet the resurrection narratives combine superhuman qualities and very human touches. Jesus' body here is untouchable; but in the upper room he says, "Put your finger here. . . . Reach out your hand and put it in my side" (20:27). Similarly, in the appearance by the Sea of Tiberius, Jesus' command leads to a miraculous catch of fish (21:6), and then he cooks breakfast for the disciples (21:12). Here embodied encounter and transcendent divinity coalesce into miraculous presence.

SUSAN GROVE EASTMAN

Homiletical Perspective

her completely and in deepest friendship. For her, as perhaps for us, this is the turning point. The world seems without meaning until divine love grants meaning to us, and all is changed. The risen Christ awakens with our names on his lips.

"My teacher," she cries, and reaches for him. "Do not hold on to me," he says (vv. 16b, 17a). There can be no clinging to what was. Everything is new. Notably for Mary, this newness includes a new vocation. Quite the opposite of holding to him, she is sent by him. It turns out that the calling of her name is ultimately to commission her. He crowns her life with purpose: "Go and tell my brothers."

One should like to think that before she leaves, it has dawned on her that she is standing with him in a garden, and that he really is the gardener, and that he has called her to himself to live and love in this new creation. "You go and tell the others," he says, and makes her voice the first to sing of a re-created world.

Her commission is to be, as the early church said of her, "the apostle to the apostles."[1] Before conveying Christ's message to them all, she declares, "I have seen the Lord!" in ringing and authoritative testimony (v. 18). It is striking that the one who has seen him through the prism of tears is the first who can say, "I have seen the Lord." She speaks with the authority of a grief overturned by the living Christ—as we may also do, we who, like Mary, discern our own names called and our own voices summoned to declare that Christ is risen and the world is new.

PAUL SIMPSON DUKE

---

1. Ann Graham Brock, *Mary Magdalene, The First Apostle: The Struggle for Authority*, Harvard Theological Studies 51 (Cambridge, MA: Harvard University Press, 2003), 161.

John 20:19–23

¹⁹When it was evening on that day, the first day of the week, and the doors of the house where the disciples had met were locked for fear of the Jews,* Jesus came and stood among them and said, "Peace be with you." ²⁰After he said this, he showed them his hands and his side. Then the disciples rejoiced when they saw the Lord. ²¹Jesus said to them again, "Peace be with you. As the Father has sent me, so I send you." ²²When he had said this, he breathed on them and said to them, "Receive the Holy Spirit. ²³If you forgive the sins of any, they are forgiven them; if you retain the sins of any, they are retained."

Theological Perspective

One of the great strengths of the gospel message is that it speaks to all people, in all times and places. Christians throughout history have sought both to see themselves in Scripture and also to see Jesus in their own contexts. Neither one of these activities is inherently problematic, although both can be, if the end result is a Jesus familiar and congenial to us, and a gospel message that simply rubber-stamps our own outlook on life and comfortable way of being. Christians always must be on guard against this temptation to use Jesus to justify our own thoughts and actions, our own complacency and conceit.

In this passage, this particular danger surfaces around the simple word "peace." Some theological work is required to avoid the mistake of assuming that our favored definition of the word—the absence of conflict, the presence of quiet and rest, everyone agreeing and getting along—is what Jesus has in mind when he offers his disciples peace. In fact, the connection is not nearly as straightforward as we might think, especially when we connect Jesus' declaration of peace to his impressing upon them the wounds of his crucifixion, his announcement of his intention to send his disciples in the same way that he was sent by his Father, and the gift of the

* See "'The Jews' in the Fourth Gospel" on pp. xi–xiv.

Pastoral Perspective

This first of three appearances of the risen Jesus to his disciples (the other two are at 20:24–31 and 21:1–22) reprises four notable themes in the Fourth Gospel: "fear of the Jews" (v. 19), Jesus' bestowal of peace (vv. 19, 21), sending and being sent (v. 21), and the gift of the Holy Spirit (v. 22).

Several other times John says that someone acts out of fear. At 7:13, "no one would speak openly about [Jesus] for fear of the Jews"; at 19:38, Joseph of Arimathea is described as a "secret [disciple] because of his fear of the Jews"; and the parents of the man born blind are afraid of being excluded from the synagogue at 9:22 (cf. 12:42). "The Jews" in these passages refers to the specific religious authorities who arrest, try, and hand Jesus over to be executed, not the whole of the people of God. In chapter 20, the disciples huddle behind closed doors, because they are afraid of being convicted of guilt by association. Recall that Thomas has already—presciently—said, "Let us also go, that we may die with him" (11:16), as Jesus prepared to raise Lazarus from the dead and bring down the wrath of the authorities on his head. The disciples' fears are realistic. The collusion between the religious authorities and the Roman Empire has destroyed Jesus, and they have every reason to expect that they too are on the list of the usual suspects.

Exegetical Perspective

The first thing we note about this second resurrection story is the timing; it is the evening of the day of resurrection. The doors are shut, implying that the disciples have not believed Mary's report and have not gone looking for Jesus, but are still in hiding. Would they have believed Peter and the other disciple if they had returned with the announcement, "We have seen the Lord"? We do not know. None of the disciples is named in this scene, and we do not know whether the women are present. The absence of the first witness, Mary Magdalene, and the silence of Peter and the other disciple are notable. In any case, the disciples are still dominated by fear. No wonder. They have seen their leader brutally crucified; so what will happen to his followers?

The doors are shut because of fear. How very human. The fear and the closed doors are no barrier to the resurrected Christ, however, whose body miraculously overcomes all human obstacles. Jesus' first words are "Peace be with you," and he repeats this assurance, as if the disciples are in particular need of peace. Indeed, they are barricaded in a closed room, paralyzed by a warranted fear of the authorities, having just witnessed the extreme violence and oppression of a Roman crucifixion, and knowing that there is every reason for them to be next. They live in a violent society. The *Pax Romana*

Homiletical Perspective

The big challenge for preaching this text is its density. Into five little verses is packed a great jumble of themes: Jesus comes to us, though fears have locked the door; he keeps his promises, bringing peace and joy; he discloses his wounds; he sends us as he was sent; he breathes on us the Holy Spirit; he declares our power to forgive or not to forgive sins. This is a crowded room.

How do we choose what part(s) to preach and what to set aside? One measure of this text's complication is the lectionary's placement of it not only on the Second Sunday of Easter (every year) but also on Pentecost Sunday (Year B). Whatever our inclination to be thematically selective, the text has an essential unity. A coherent logic binds the elements of the narrative, which can be preached as an integrated whole.

It begins with fear. We are struck by the oddness of it. On the very day of joyous new life, the disciples huddle in a bolted room, afraid of the authorities. Have they simply dismissed Mary Magdalene's report and the Beloved Disciple's faith? Is their situation perhaps more analogous to ours? Hearing the Easter story, even perhaps believing it, does not necessarily banish fear. A preacher may wish to take sympathetic notice of how Christians singing fervent alleluias may retain their anxieties, not realizing the full implications of their song.

John 20:19–23

Theological Perspective

Holy Spirit. Taken together, we can conclude that the peace Jesus offers has nothing to do with tranquility, harmony, and affability. Instead, in this passage, Jesus invites his disciples into the same activity of peacemaking that characterized his own life and mission, the same activity that led him to the cross, an activity possible for us in the here and now only through the power of the Holy Spirit.

First, even a cursory glance through any one of the Gospels demonstrates clearly that the peace Jesus' ministry announces is nothing like the peace either the religious leaders or the political authorities desired. The Father did not send the Son into the world merely to confirm the status quo. Instead, Jesus' peace is the sort that brings back into the fold the outcast and the marginalized, and turns upside down the societal conventions of first and last, blessed and cursed, rich and poor. Jesus' peace invites the lion to see the lamb as neighbor and friend, the Jew to speak with the Samaritan, and the prostitute to dine with the Pharisee. Such actions show, to those with eyes to see, a new way of being in the world, a vision inspired by the inbreaking of the kingdom of God present in Jesus' very existence.

It is this peacemaking work, in no small part, that got Jesus killed. In this way, we can say that Jesus' unwavering commitment to the work for which he was sent, the work of reconciliation and renewal, the work of feeding and healing—the transformation of society he was engendering—led to a final showdown with the authorities that he could not avoid without abandoning the very people he came to save. Jesus' crucifixion thus cannot be fully understood and appreciated without a complementary understanding of his peacemaking activity.

This, then, is the second point: those of us who wish to call ourselves Jesus' disciples must be equally willing to commit ourselves to Jesus' type of peacemaking, an activity that surely also will be costly and challenging today, just as it was two thousand years ago. The radical vision of the kingdom of God is no less threatening to society today than it was in Jesus' time, and those who work for the inclusion of the ostracized, the love of enemies, and justice for the oppressed should be prepared for rejection and harassment.

Dietrich Bonhoeffer put it bluntly: "When Christ calls a [person], he bids him come and die."[1] The apostles found this out in the decades after Jesus'

---

1. Dietrich Bonhoeffer, *The Cost of Discipleship*, trans. R. H. Fuller (orig. 1937; New York: Touchstone, 1995), 89.

Pastoral Perspective

There are Christians today who also hide behind closed doors in fear. Egyptian Christians routinely experience violence from their neighbors, as do Christians in Iraq. Although most people in North America do not live in fear of religious authorities or reprisals from outsiders for their Christian confessions, there are other fears that haunt them. Some preachers fear telling what they believe to be the truth about ecclesiastical or social controversies because they have reason to think their congregations would fire them. Some church people fear the loss of close friends or family if they do the same. Others fear discovery of their sexual orientations or political or social or theological convictions.

In response to the disciples' fears, Jesus bestows peace. This is not the first time he has done so. In the Farewell Discourse he twice refers to peace. "Peace I leave with you; my peace I give to you. I do not give to you as the world gives. Do not let your hearts be troubled, and do not let them be afraid" (14:27). "I have said this to you, so that in me you may have peace. In the world you face persecution. But take courage; I have conquered the world!" (16:33).

This is also not the last time Jesus will give such a benediction. He will say a second time, "Peace be with you" (v. 21) in this paragraph and a third time in the next, "Peace be with you" (20:26). The word "peace" can mean simply "hello," although surely in this context it is intended to be a benediction, a blessing that carries the very *shalom* of God. The disciples rejoice when they see the Lord and hear his greeting of peace. The Elder may think that "perfect love casts out fear" (1 John 4:18), but the Fourth Evangelist thinks peace does.

"As the Father has sent me, so I send you," Jesus says (v. 21). He has already said more than sixty times in John's Gospel that God has "sent" him. John the Baptist too was "sent" by God (1:6, 33; 3:28), and the disciples themselves have previously been sent by Jesus (4:38). The good news of Easter is never simply the assurance that God has conquered death. It is always also a statement about mission. Jesus' resurrection implicates us in mission, by drawing us into the orbit of God's love for the world and empowering us by the Spirit to love as God loves.

At verse 22 Jesus says, "Receive the Holy Spirit." Although the Spirit has appeared at numerous points in John's Gospel, it is primarily in the Farewell Discourse that Jesus promises to send the Paraclete when he returns to the Father (14:16, 26). What Luke serializes—first Good Friday, then Easter, then Pentecost—John collapses into the single moment of Jesus' death,

was maintained by brutal oppression, particularly of those who claimed allegiance to anyone other than Caesar. Here comes Jesus into the midst of this fear and hiding, proclaiming insistently, "Peace be with you." Clearly he brings a peace that originates from an enigmatic source beyond the status quo of the Roman Empire.

Interwoven with Jesus' double proclamation of peace is a double affirmation of his identity. In the first instance, the marks on Jesus' resurrected and transcendent body show that he is the very same beloved leader who was nailed to a cross. On one level, these marks demonstrate the continuity between the risen Christ and the historical Jesus. On another level, they discredit any proclamation of Jesus apart from his very real physical suffering and death on the cross. This theme of Jesus' humanity and death, paradoxically joined with his divinity and resurrection, is central for John's community: "By this you know the Spirit of God: every spirit that confesses that Jesus Christ has come in the flesh is from God" (1 John 4:2). Pastorally, this means that we know Jesus through his suffering and death with and for us. He has entered into and overcome the depths of our dereliction, and we meet him there, just as the disciples met him in their hiding place.

The first experience of the peace that Christ brings comes through this assurance of the presence of Christ with and for us. The second experience of peace introduces and grounds Jesus' challenging words: "As the Father has sent me, so I send you" (v. 21). Remember that he speaks these words to a ragtag group of outcasts cowering behind locked doors. No longer secret, now they are to become public witnesses, even as they remember that Jesus also warned them, "They will put you out of the synagogues. Indeed, an hour is coming when those who kill you will think that by doing so they are offering worship to God" (16:2). It is likely that the community of John's Gospel experienced such excommunication and knew personally the challenge of public witness and the fear of persecution. Jesus' words are to us as well as to them.

Jesus does not ask the disciples to conquer their fear on their own; he "breathes" on them the Holy Spirit (v. 22), recalling the creative action of God in breathing into the first human being the breath of life (Gen. 2:7). Jesus does what God the Father does: he sends out the disciples and breathes the life-giving Spirit into them. This gift fulfills the promise Jesus made to his friends in the Farewell Discourse regarding the coming of the Holy Spirit: "But the Advocate,

Still, the living Christ comes to us, unhindered by our fears, unblocked by our defenses. If a shut tomb cannot hold him in, a shut church cannot keep him out. He does not rebuke their anxiety, but says simply, "Peace," anxiety's antidote. By this greeting, he keeps his promise to give them peace, but not as the world gives (14:27).

The showing of his wounds may be an extension of that gift. The wounds bear witness to the worst that the world can do, and disclose the truth that the worst is overcome. For the risen Christ to show the disciples his wounds is to ask, What remains to be feared? What will prevail but peace?

At this, they rejoice—another of his promises fulfilled. "I will see you again, and your hearts will rejoice" (16:22). Is it significant that their rejoicing does not follow instantly on his appearing, but on their seeing his wounds? Is it possible that life-giving joy will elude us who feel threatened by the world, until we know Christ as the bearer of terrible wounds, entirely overcome? When after this he says for a second time, "Peace," there is deeper resonance in the word.

A great deal more is needed, though, and here the text takes its decisive turn: the turn from Christ's new life to ours. It begins with his declaration that his disciples are to be *sent*. We can hardly be much surprised by this, since in all four Gospels the resurrection is accompanied by words of commission. In fact, this connection has already occurred with Mary Magdalene (20:17). Two factors make this commissioning different from the others. The first is its full parallel with God's sending of Jesus into the world. Precisely as Jesus was sent, so are we. Meaning what? That we too become the Word made flesh? That we too lay down our lives? To be assigned by the risen Christ a set of evangelizing tasks is one thing (Matt. 28:19–20). To be shown his wounds and then sent into the world as he was sent has the feel of a more encompassing and riskier enterprise.

This difference leads to the other. Only in John are the disciples empowered immediately, and so intimately, and by Jesus himself. To be sent as he was sent means that their spirit must now be his Spirit. He *breathes* on them. He says, "Receive the Holy Spirit." Again he is keeping a promise (14:16; 16:7), but who would expect it to take the form of his very breath on their faces?

There can be little doubt of what is being signified. As God in the primordial garden breathes into the nostrils of inanimate human-shaped clay to make it a living soul, so Jesus, having taken up his

John 20:19–23

Theological Perspective

resurrection, as all faced persecution, and many faced a martyr's death as well. While few Christians in the global north face death for their discipleship today, the fact remains that following Christ and engaging in his peacemaking activity continue to bring one into conflict with many public policies, laws, and social norms—and this conflict is not without its own cost.

If one takes this call and its consequences seriously, it should be clear that, by ourselves, humans are not capable of following Jesus: the power of sin is simply too great. By ourselves, we want to fit in, we want to maintain our social status, we want to preserve our privilege and good name—all of which are threatened by Jesus' peacemaking activity. In one of the most powerful aspects of this Gospel text, though, Christians are reminded that we do not stand alone in our attempts to follow Jesus. Instead, in the same way that the resurrected Jesus came and stood among the disciples and breathed upon them the Holy Spirit—transforming them from a motley band of followers into an indefatigable troop of missionaries that have transformed the world—the Holy Spirit continues to abide with us and dwell with us, making the impossible possible with the power of God.

It is not easy to be a peacemaker in a world marked by war in every corner. It is not easy to be a peacemaker in a society that incarcerates a vast number of men and women and then forgets about them. It is not easy to be a peacemaker in a country where guns are prevalent and too many children's lives are marred by violence at home, at school, and at play. Nevertheless, in the power of the Holy Spirit, Christians can and do follow Jesus in this radical peacemaking work, trusting that Christ is working in us, and that the glimpses of peace we are afforded continue to provide leaven to a needy society, transforming it in fits and starts, until the day when Christ will come again to perfect his work and inaugurate the fullness of his peace.

KRISTIN JOHNSTON LARGEN

Pastoral Perspective

for this is not the first time in the Fourth Gospel that Jesus has given the Spirit. As he dies in John 19:30, the NRSV says Jesus "gave up his spirit." However, there is no personal pronoun "his" in the Greek. The verb can indeed mean "gave up," but it more frequently means "handed over" (18:30, 35; 19:16), which would mean that Jesus "handed over the Spirit" at his death, rather than "gave up his spirit."

The church's authority to forgive or retain sin, which Jesus grants in verse 23, presents a real pastoral challenge to some. It is discussed also at Matthew 16:19; 18:18; and 1 Corinthians 5:1–13, where specific instructions are offered. The original function of church discipline was to maintain the integrity of Christian fellowship and urge offenders toward repentance and reconciliation ("you have regained your brother or sister," Matt. 18:15, my trans.). In the sixteenth century, though, Martin Luther criticized what he called the church's abuse of such authority in its pursuit of political and ecclesiastical control, and throughout the history of Protestantism disputes have arisen about the proper conduct of church discipline.[1]

The challenge to exercising anything like discipline among twenty-first-century North American Protestants is the proliferation of churches and the resulting "pluralistic game of religious free enterprise," as Peter Berger calls it.[2] Once there are multiple churches for people to join, the notion that any given community might discipline members loses much of its meaning, although Jesus' Easter words to the disciples ought at least to give us cause to reflect on the integrity of our own communities.

E. ELIZABETH JOHNSON

---

1. See Martin Luther, "Sermon on the Ban" (1519), in *Luther's Works*, ed. Jaroslav Pelikan (St. Louis: Concordia, 1955), 39:7–22, and Justo L. González, *The Story of Christianity*, vol. 2, *The Reformation to the Present Day*, 2nd ed. (New York: HarperOne, 2010), 232–33.

2. Peter L. Berger, *The Sacred Canopy: Elements of a Sociological Theory of Religion* (New York: Anchor, 1967), 153.

Feasting on the Gospels

the Holy Spirit, whom the Father will send in my name, will teach you everything, and remind you of all that I have said to you. Peace I leave with you; my peace I give to you. I do not give to you as the world gives. Do not let your hearts be troubled, and do not let them be afraid" (14:26–27; cf. 7:39; 14:16). The gift of the Holy Spirit, who is the presence of Christ after Christ departs, is both the guide to truth and the guarantor of peace. Both the guidance and the peace will be essential for the disciples as they open the locked doors and go out into a hostile world.

Finally, Jesus links the gift of the Spirit with discernment about forgiveness of sins. The sudden appearance of the theme of forgiveness seems odd, and is reminiscent of Matthew 18:18. The word translated "forgive" also can mean to "let go, release, leave alone," and this is its meaning in every other instance in John's Gospel. As the saying goes, "let it go." The word translated "retain" means to "seize, grasp," even "arrest." If we attend to these connotations of the words, we get a picture of the Spirit's guidance in leading the community to discern how to deal with sins in specific instances.

When, as the contemporary saying has it, should we "let it go," and when should we insist on a serious reckoning with a particular sin? Such an interpretation attends to the role of the Spirit as the Spirit of truth (14:17) that guards the unity of the community. Furthermore, the perfect passive form of the verbs, "they are forgiven" and "they are retained," implies that God is the one who has forgiven or retained sins, and the disciples' actions, guided by the Spirit, simply enact what God alone can do.

SUSAN GROVE EASTMAN

life again from a tomb in a garden, and having been perceived by Mary to be the gardener, now bends to breathe into his disciples the breath of life. They are created. He has made them living souls, the first children of God alive in this new world. This is the gift to all who "receive him" (1:12). How else could we be sent as he was sent?

The disciples are sent in particular to forgive sins. This final word may seem out of place to us. It feels too particular, too narrow a slice of what our being sent should mean—and too presumptuous and judgmental, since Jesus names the disciples' power to "retain" the sins of others as well as to forgive them. In fact, though, he is summing up what it means to be sent into the world as God sent him. The first witness to Jesus given in this Gospel comes from John the baptizer, who declares him to be "the Lamb of God who takes away the sin of the world" (1:29). That mission of Jesus is now the ongoing mission of his friends. To the extent that his friends refuse the mission, the sins of others remain. To the extent that his breath is breathing in them, the sins of the world are taken away.

The whole scene is about Jesus rising into the life of the community. Into their entombment he enters. Their fear gives way to his peace. In them, his joy rises. His being sent lives in their being sent. His breath is now breathing in them. His bearing away the sin of the world will now be expressed in their bearing away of sin. He rises into the rising of his church. Easter and Pentecost dance together. Those who know this will get up and go to the door and unlock it.

PAUL SIMPSON DUKE

John 20:24–31

²⁴But Thomas (who was called the Twin), one of the twelve, was not with them when Jesus came. ²⁵So the other disciples told him, "We have seen the Lord." But he said to them, "Unless I see the mark of the nails in his hands, and put my finger in the mark of the nails and my hand in his side, I will not believe."

²⁶A week later his disciples were again in the house, and Thomas was with them. Although the doors were shut, Jesus came and stood among them and said, "Peace be with you." ²⁷Then he said to Thomas, "Put your finger here and see my hands. Reach out your hand and put it in my side. Do not doubt but believe." ²⁸Thomas answered him, "My Lord and my God!" ²⁹Jesus said to him, "Have you believed because you have seen me? Blessed are those who have not seen and yet have come to believe."

³⁰Now Jesus did many other signs in the presence of his disciples, which are not written in this book. ³¹But these are written so that you may come to believe that Jesus is the Messiah, the Son of God, and that through believing you may have life in his name.

Theological Perspective

Pericope titles, like sermon titles, are double-edged swords. On the one hand, they help the reader zero in on what is central in the passage, but on the other hand, they can blind the reader to other important aspects of the gospel in the text. In my view, it is this "other hand" that we must deal with in the pericope before us—known almost universally as the "doubting Thomas" text. This text has been stuck with this title far too long, with the consequence that the familiar reader hardly even bothers to skim the text itself, presuming to know the message by the title alone: "Thomas doubts, and refuses to believe until he sees Jesus with his own eyes. Better that we believe without seeing."

The main problem here is that this title focuses all of our attention on Thomas and his actions, rather than the one who is, of course, at the center of the story: Jesus. So, while there certainly may be some advantages to looking at Thomas in this story and thinking about his need to see and to touch Jesus—and what that says about us and our faith today—much can be gained by turning our attention from Thomas to the resurrected Jesus—and not just Jesus in general, but the body of Jesus in particular, the physical body that bears the scars of his crucifixion, even in his resurrected glory. When we do that, an obvious theological question comes to the

Pastoral Perspective

We are not told why Thomas misses the first resurrection appearance in 20:19–23. The occasion, though, provides the motivation for the second scene. Thomas's response to the testimony of the others—"We have seen the Lord" (v. 25, echoing Mary Magdalene's proclamation in v. 18)—is to resist its implications: "Unless I see the mark of the nails in his hands, and put my finger in the mark of the nails and my hand in his side, I will not believe" (v. 25). Surely the good news is too good to be true, he thinks.

We often think the same thing, although for different reasons. Thomas is not likely to be skeptical about a resurrection appearance the way a modern person might reject claims of the miraculous. He is more likely to be asking for proof that it is really Jesus of Nazareth, rather than some other heavenly being, who has appeared. The stark evidence of how Jesus died is what Thomas needs to persuade him that Jesus has been raised. What is at stake is not a miracle or a wonder or even the power of God. What is at stake for Thomas is continuity between the Jesus they have known and this one standing before them. The question is not so much "Has Jesus been *raised*?" but "Has *Jesus* been raised?"

How could it be that this one who had disappointed their hopes, this one who had been so

Exegetical Perspective

With considerable pastoral wisdom, lectionaries usually place the reading of this story of "doubting Thomas" on the first Sunday after Easter. Thomas was not the last or only follower of Jesus to doubt the reality of the resurrection; his encounter with the living Lord speaks to all doubters since that time.

We do not know much about Thomas, apart from one revealing vignette earlier in John's Gospel. Jesus is on his way to Bethany, where his friend Lazarus has just died. Bethany is near Jerusalem, and by this time in the Gospel we know that Jerusalem is not a safe place for Jesus. The authorities are looking for him and plotting to arrest him. In fact, after Jesus raises Lazarus from the dead, the chief priests and Pharisees take counsel on how to put him to death (11:53). Thomas is the disciple who has an inkling of what is in store; when Jesus announces his plan to go to Bethany to console Lazarus's sisters Mary and Martha, Thomas says to the other disciples, "Let us also go, that we may die with him" (11:16). Immediately after this, when Jesus meets Mary the sister of Lazarus, he tells her, "I am the resurrection and the life. Those who believe in me, even though they die, will live" (11:25), and Mary confesses her faith in Jesus as the Messiah, the Son of God (11:27; cf. 20:31).

Of all the disciples, Thomas is perhaps the least surprised by Jesus' arrest and execution. He expects

Homiletical Perspective

We can do no justice to this text without taking Thomas seriously. We do not preach from above him but from beside him. He is our big brother and a fair theologian, with something crucial to teach us. The risen Jesus does not dismiss his wishes but grants them, reason enough to regard Thomas with respect and perhaps with a certain admiration.

Why? To begin with, he will not give himself over to someone else's religious enthusiasm. He will not surrender his mind to secondhand news. His bright-eyed fellow disciples tell of a living Jesus who appeared to them, spoke to them, and breathed on them. Thomas will not believe it, having not been there. Where had he been? Getting supplies for them, gathering news, looking in on others, taking a break from his overanxious friends? Give him this: he had not stayed hidden inside the room into which they had fearfully locked themselves.

The moniker "doubting Thomas" has the ring of a character in some tut-tutting morality play, but the consistent portrayal of Thomas in John's Gospel is of a solid realist, and a brave one at that. When Lazarus dies and Jesus heads for Judea to raise him, a mission that will end in his own death, Thomas grimly declares, "Let us also go, that we may die with him" (11:16). When Jesus, on the verge of his crucifixion, tells the disciples that they know where

John 20:24–31

Theological Perspective

fore immediately: what does it mean for us today, we who will be raised in a body like his, that Jesus' resurrected body carries scars? I argue that this fact has three important theological ramifications, all of which are worthy of further consideration.

The first is the most obvious: the importance of the resurrection of the physical body itself. This text provides an essential reminder that in the resurrection our bodies are not going to be "left behind." Contrary to what we sometimes assume, human beings are not simply souls trapped in temporary bodysuits that will be discarded at the resurrection. Instead, human beings are bodies, we are flesh: we have been created enfleshed, and we will live forever enfleshed. So whatever Paul means by a "spiritual body" (1 Cor. 15:44), it certainly does not mean "dis-embodied." God created our bodies and called them good, and good they remain, even in the resurrection.

The second point is that whatever we expect of "perfection" in heaven, whatever we expect about the "perfection" of the body, it does not and will not necessarily include removal of the scars we bear—both internally and externally—of the events that have wounded us. If we are going to be resurrected in a body like that of Jesus, then we must at least consider the possibility that our bodies too are going to bear the marks of the experiences we have had—even the tragic, painful experiences—that have made us who we are. We will not become someone entirely new and different in the resurrection; instead, our resurrected bodies will evince continuity with the people we have been on earth. (This also raises interesting theological questions about disabilities: must we necessarily assume that everything that is considered a dis-ability or even a defect on earth will be eradicated in heaven? Perhaps we might instead think about heavenly perfection not as something we each bear individually in our bodies, but rather as a heavenly community that functions perfectly together.)

This, then, leads to the third point, which is the most radical, the most troubling, and the most hopeful: heaven is not a place of forgetfulness, but of remembrance. Somehow, if Jesus carries the scars and thus also, one assumes, the memory of the crucifixion, we can also assume that both that terrible event and its memory must also have been taken up and transformed in the resurrection somehow. If so for Jesus, then for us as well.

I recognize that we do not typically think about heaven this way. Many, if not most Christians, might well agree with Dante, who positioned the

Pastoral Perspective

grotesquely repudiated, this one who had been executed for crimes against the state—how could this one be the one God had raised? They had to make sure that the vision before them was not just some divine wonder or magical marvel, but really Jesus of Nazareth. That is the point of John's story about Thomas, and that is the scandal of the gospel.

Jesus invites Thomas, "Put your finger here and see my hands. Reach out your hand and put it in my side. Do not doubt but believe" (v. 27b). His response is the archetypal Johannine confession of faith: "My Lord and my God!" Jesus then speaks directly to all of us who in the millennia since have made the same confession: "Blessed are those who have not seen and yet have come to believe" (v. 29b).

An American televangelist was once interviewed on the BBC about what he thought of Jesus. "Jesus was the most successful religious figure of all time," he said. And the interviewer came back with, "But I thought he ended up on a cross." "Oh no!" he replied, "He overcame the cross and put all that behind him."[1] That is precisely the opposite of what John thinks Thomas's encounter with Jesus is about. The one who is raised really *is* the one who is crucified, which means that Jesus sends us to do what God sent him to do—to give ourselves for the world, as he gave himself for the world.

People are waiting to see the marks. They are not looking for the marks in Jesus' hands and side anymore. They wait instead to see the marks of the church—the wounds in our hands and our sides—the evidence that we are really connected to the Jesus who was crucified and raised. For all that we hear about the sophistication of modern people, they are much more willing to believe that Jesus was raised from the dead than that his death and resurrection mean anything for their lives.

It is the church's calling to testify to that very thing. "As the Father has sent me, so I send you," says Jesus (v. 21b). The marks that matter today are not the ones in Jesus' hands and side, but the ones in our communities. Is there anything authentic and empowered about our worshiping communities that bears witness to Jesus' death and resurrection? Is there any legitimacy to our claim that we exercise authority on his behalf (v. 23)? So many of the stories we hear of people without faith include their disillusionment with the church as we know it, our failure to make real what we profess.

1. Quoted in Charles B. Cousar, *A Theology of the Cross: The Death of Jesus in the Pauline Letters* (Minneapolis: Fortress Press, 1990), 88.

it. He is perhaps more ready to face death than to accept life. Nevertheless, his own meeting with the resurrected Christ in some ways parallels that of Mary after Lazarus's death; both are in mourning and despair, and both come to believe in the identity of Jesus as the Lord who gives life from the dead. His story also somewhat parallels that of Mary Magdalene at the tomb. The Magdalene is consumed by grief and loss, so much so that she cannot recognize Jesus until he calls her name. Thomas is not persuaded by others' testimony and cannot recognize Jesus until he touches the wounds of Jesus. Each has a need, a potential barrier to faith, and in each case the risen Lord gives them the attention that will heal their faithlessness. Similarly, when Peter finally reappears in the narrative at the Sea of Galilee (21:1–19), Jesus brings Peter back into the relationship that was broken by Peter's denial. Each character enacts ways in which we, as subsequent followers of Christ, may be unable of ourselves to recognize and trust him.

Thomas himself replays the initial encounter between Jesus and the disciples, but in an intensified way. Jesus' arrival in the room behind locked doors is exactly parallel: he simply arrives among the disciples and announces, "Peace be with you" (20:26); but then the Lord immediately singles out Thomas and gives him exactly what he demanded— the chance to put his finger in the nail holes, and his hand in the spear wound in Jesus' side. As for all the disciples, and for all of John's subsequent readers, the proof of Jesus' divine identity as Lord and God is precisely the proof of his human suffering and death. Note how exquisitely this proof addresses the root causes of doubt, as it brings God's presence into the very suffering and ultimate losses that tempt us to mistrust God's goodness and power. Because Jesus Christ has tasted death for all of us, as Hebrews says (2:9), we can trust in God to bring life out of death and hope out of despair.

The theme of vision threads through the resurrection narratives: "I have seen the Lord," says Mary Magdalene (20:18); "We have seen the Lord," the disciples tell Thomas (v. 25). These statements bring to a climax the theme of sight and blindness in the Gospel as a whole. Through the miraculous signs that Jesus performs, beginning with the wedding at Cana (2:1–11), his glory is openly manifested and his divine identity proclaimed. Nonetheless, not everyone can see this identity—only those like the man born blind (9:35–41) whose eyes are opened. After Greeks come to the disciples and say, "We wish to see Jesus" (12:21), Jesus hides himself from public view

he going, Thomas is straightforward enough to say that, in fact, they do not (14:5). He is by no means a person of unsteady conviction or of a predisposition to doubt, but someone who is willing to face and to name the evident difficult facts.

His resistance to the Easter claims of his friends is stated in terms of the wounds of Jesus. His requirement on hearing their glad report is not that he see Jesus, but that he see the mark of the nails; and he does not require touching the risen Jesus in some general way, but putting his finger in the mark of the nails and his hand into the spear wound. His demand could not be more particular or more ghastly. For him, the only test of the resurrection is the wounds—not a vision of wounds, but an actual probing of real, torn flesh.

This narrative, in other words, is not about resurrection faith in some general sense; it is about resurrection's being real or not—*mattering* or not— depending on its relation to the violence borne by Jesus. Any claim that God obliterates such horrors is an illusion. Thomas seems to know that anxious people can fall into a collective wish-dream, that his friends could be subject to a shared, gleaming projection of an undamaged Christ. He will not tolerate a vision; he will not stand for resurrection as metaphor. The Word-made-flesh must remain—however differently—solidly real, bearing real witness to mortal brutalities. Easter jubilation is false if it forgets the grotesque and denies the ongoing, grim realities of the powers of death, which are transformed only insofar as the risen Christ is still bearing them.

Does God take evil with such awful seriousness, bearing it to these depths? Can the world's redemption be so real if the divine wounding is not so deep? The text invites sermons that point to what Thomas understands about the importance of the wounds to the resurrection. His refusal to believe his friends is the fruit not of intellectual skepticism but of absolute anguish. The world's evil is monstrous, and if the Christ whom it killed is not scarred by it and bearing it in newness, nothing matters.

Jesus honors Thomas's request. He does not do so, however, in private, but among the gathered disciples. The encounter presupposes community, and strengthens it. As before, Jesus speaks peace to the group; then he turns to Thomas and invites him to do exactly what he had said he required in order to believe: to see the wounds and to probe them. Go on, says Jesus, do it. Then, with simple directness, Jesus tells him not to be disbelieving but to believe. It is an appeal worth noticing. A sermon on Thomas

John 20:24–31

Theological Perspective

River Lethe at the boundary between purgatory and heaven, thereby asserting that an essential part of the ascension into heaven is the forgetting of one's sins and a solidifying of one's good deeds. Certainly, there is a way in which that makes sense. Why not enter into heaven with only the good parts of our lives intact, and the bad parts washed away into oblivion behind us? Obviously, however, our lives do not so easily separate out into good and bad. Instead, in the complex, interrelated reality that is human experience, the good and the bad are inextricably woven together; and it is never a simple matter of getting rid of the latter and preserving the former. Thus, I argue that this image of a "wounded" resurrected Jesus suggests something bolder, something more holistic, and, in the end, something more satisfying and integral than a straightforward parsing out of the good and bad in our lives.

This image of Jesus suggests that, in the resurrection, God is capable of taking even the worst of human experiences into God's own arms in such a way that they are transformed, and we are healed and made whole—not only each of us individually but the whole human family, indeed, the whole creation. In this way, we may finally be enabled to forgive ourselves and forgive others; and maybe, just maybe, in the service of God's justice, those who gave us our scars may see clearly the horror that they caused and be empowered genuinely to repent and ask for forgiveness, so that all might be reconciled.

After all, it is only because Jesus remembers the crucifixion and the events leading up to it that, in the resurrection, he is able to seek out Peter and offer him the threefold chance to declare his love for Jesus and atone for his threefold denial. This poignant moment of reconciliation could not have happened without the memory. Perhaps such experiences of reconciliation await us too, somehow, in the resurrection. The wounded body of Christ suggests it could be so.

KRISTIN JOHNSTON LARGEN

Pastoral Perspective

What people are looking for, at heart, is some legitimate and trustworthy connection with the Divine. They look to New-Age mysticism or self-help or even doing good deeds. John says, instead, that we find it in the wounded body of Jesus. Because it is really the crucified who is raised, God has made Jesus' cross, and nothing else, the clue to authentic human life and our trustworthy connection with the Divine.

Verses 30–31 sound for all the world as though it ought to be the end of John's book, although it is not. There remains yet another crucial chapter in which Jesus serves breakfast on the beach, he and Peter are reconciled after Peter's calamitous fall from grace in 18:15–18, 25–27, and the destinies of Peter and the Beloved Disciple are discussed. The real end of the book has the narrator say, "This is the disciple who is testifying to these things and has written them, and we know that his testimony is true. But there are also many other things that Jesus did; if every one of them were written down, I suppose that the world itself could not contain the books that would be written" (21:24–25). What then are we to make of this "first ending" in chapter 20?

Jesus has just done his most extraordinary of all the signs in this Gospel, and it is perfectly natural that the narrator should say of the resurrection, "Now Jesus did many *other* signs in the presence of his disciples, which are not written in this book. But these are written so that you may come to believe that Jesus is the Messiah, the Son of God, and that through believing you may have life in his name" (vv. 30–31, emphasis added). The faith of contemporary disciples in Jesus continues because the story that evokes and sustains it has been written and thus can be heard again and again.

E. ELIZABETH JOHNSON

Exegetical Perspective

and reveals himself only to the disciples (12:36b). After his resurrection, his appearances are elusive and sporadic, and the emphasis on his wounds suggests that if we do not see Jesus on the cross as well as in resurrected glory, we will not see him at all.

How can we see Jesus at all, given our distance in time and space from his bodily presence on earth? The emphasis on Jesus' body throughout the resurrection narratives in John leaves us, the readers, with this question. The Gospel itself turns to address our need, though, beginning indirectly with Jesus' surprising words to Thomas, and then directly speaking to us, the readers. Jesus says to Thomas, "Blessed are those who have not seen and yet have come to believe" (v. 29). How can this be? The larger shape of John's Gospel clarifies the mystery. Physical sight is no guarantee of understanding, as is abundantly clear in the unbelief that meets Jesus' public signs throughout the Gospel. Because "no one can come to me unless it is granted by the Father" (6:65), belief is not dependent on physical sight or presence; it is a gift of God. Those who have not seen Jesus in the flesh are in a position to know the grace of belief and trust, which we cannot generate from our own resources but receive from God.

Hence the closing verses of this passage, written for us, the readers, surely with a prayer that God use the book of John's Gospel to inspire and strengthen our trust in the mighty and life-giving name of Jesus, Son of God, incarnate, crucified, risen from the dead, life-giver.

SUSAN GROVE EASTMAN

Homiletical Perspective

should grant positive space for anguished doubt, but should also remember that Jesus comes to Thomas, urging him to believe.

"My Lord and my God!" Is it a gasp? A cry? A sob? Regardless, Thomas's need to touch the wounds has left him. Perhaps the wounds are even more terrible than he has imagined, and perhaps the risen Christ is more real than Thomas is to himself, and perhaps his word to Thomas is irresistibly resonant with life. All we know is that Thomas now utters the highest confession of faith in the Gospels.

Jesus shifts immediately to the subject of what such faith is grounded in: "Have you believed because you have seen?" Given the appearances of Jesus to his other friends, the question would not seem to be much of a criticism, but it does set up the pivot that Jesus now makes toward the rest of us. He seems to turn from Thomas to address *us*, pronouncing blessing on those who believe without having seen. As directly as the visible Jesus has urged Thomas, the unseen Jesus now urges us to believe—and perhaps to celebrate how the community's witness over time has led us into its blessed membership.

The whole Gospel, in fact, we are now told, was written for this very reason: so that we will believe in Jesus and "have life in his name." The story of Thomas has featured a man who thought the final truth was death. Jesus, bearing wounds, has made clear to him that the final truth is life. With that, the curtain rings down, and the author of the play walks onstage to tell us that every bit of it was written so that we might have this very life—or, to put it another way, that we would all, from our distance in space and time, learn to say and keep saying with Thomas, "My Lord and my God!" and so live an ongoing Easter.

PAUL SIMPSON DUKE

John 21:1–8

¹After these things Jesus showed himself again to the disciples by the Sea of Tiberias; and he showed himself in this way. ²Gathered there together were Simon Peter, Thomas called the Twin, Nathanael of Cana in Galilee, the sons of Zebedee, and two others of his disciples. ³Simon Peter said to them, "I am going fishing." They said to him, "We will go with you." They went out and got into the boat, but that night they caught nothing.

⁴Just after daybreak, Jesus stood on the beach; but the disciples did not know that it was Jesus. ⁵Jesus said to them, "Children, you have no fish, have you?" They answered him, "No." ⁶He said to them, "Cast the net to the right side of the boat, and you will find some." So they cast it, and now they were not able to haul it in because there were so many fish. ⁷That disciple whom Jesus loved said to Peter, "It is the Lord!" When Simon Peter heard that it was the Lord, he put on some clothes, for he was naked, and jumped into the sea. ⁸But the other disciples came in the boat, dragging the net full of fish, for they were not far from the land, only about a hundred yards off.

Theological Perspective

Repetition brings revelation and fellowship not only to the disciples but also to all those "who have not seen and yet have come to believe" (20:29) in Jesus as Lord.

Again, the resurrected Jesus appears.

Again darkness is barren, while light brings life.

Again Jesus commands, and the catch is abundant.

Again Peter charges headlong toward what the Beloved Disciple is first to understand and believe.

Whether viewed as an addendum or not, John 21 functions as a thematic restatement about the path to knowing God through the risen Jesus. Recalling the pattern of creation, light follows the darkness, and understanding follows confusion. Jesus initially appears to Mary Magdalene and the disciples in both literal and internal darkness (chap. 20). How striking that, in a Gospel characterized by insiders who recognize Jesus' origins and mission (e.g., Nathanael's exclamation, "You are the Son of God!" 1:49), the disciples fumble after the resurrection. The Gospel looks to assure those who will "come to believe" and "have life in [Jesus'] name" (20:31) without the benefit of such appearances as Jesus' disciples had (20:29). Seeing is not always believing.

After the Jerusalem appearances of Jesus, the disciples cling to each other, but without a strong sense

Pastoral Perspective

Because chapter 21 is an epilogue likely penned by a writer other than the evangelist, there are certain inconsistencies in language, sequence of events, and the flow of its narrative. Oceans of ink have been devoted to these details, but it might be helpful to think of chapter 21 in terms of general contours, not specific shapes. Impressionist painting provides a good analogy. Impressionism was a nineteenth-century art movement that violated accepted rules of painting by using texture, dabs of color, and visual effects rather than tightly drawn realistic forms (think Monet or Renoir vs. Rembrandt). Impressionists left their studios to paint outside in nature, where light, colors, and movement came to life on their canvases.

Likewise, chapter 21 has the feel of an impressionist work. The focus is on recognizing the risen Christ and how he transforms and enriches human life. The power of the narrative is larger than the sum of its parts, though; it derives from the whole story—the passion, the movement, and the changing moods of the characters. If the preacher or teacher chooses to focus on details (Peter's wet clothes or 153 fish), then the overall picture can get lost. Focus instead on the splashes of color, undertones, and themes that give texture to this narrative. Identifying some of these can help us move from ancient text to present context.

Exegetical Perspective

The general consensus among New Testament scholars is that chapter 21 is an appendix or epilogue added on to the Gospel. For those who consider chapter 21 an appendix, most likely added by someone after the composition of the Gospel, the book ends with 20:30–31, as it concludes with the purpose of the Gospel: "These are written so that you may come to believe that Jesus is the Messiah, the Son of God, and that through believing you may have life in his name." This ending verse has come after Thomas's admirable confession of the risen Jesus, "My Lord and my God!" (20:28), and Jesus' declaration of blessing, "Blessed are those who have not seen and yet have come to believe" (20:29). The opening verse in chapter 21 then would point to a conscious addition, where the Gospel turns to the traditions that may have been circulated in the early churches and later brought to their present position by an editor.

For those who consider chapter 21 an epilogue, however, this view only produces more riddles, rather than solving the problems. To begin with, if this section is an appendix, a discrete piece added to the original edition of the author, it seems difficult to explain how this later section is found in the most ancient manuscripts of the Fourth Gospel. Moreover, it would seem that the extended episode in chapter 21 stands essentially for the whole Gospel, especially

Homiletical Perspective

Before Easter is a theological doctrine, it is an experienced reality. In John's Gospel, each of the resurrection accounts is tailor-made for the recipient, a visit more than a spectacle. John is careful to list who was in attendance, and here the list of witnesses is not so much proof of the testimony as it is an explanation of why Christ showed up in this way. Jesus does not just appear in the sky for anyone to see; he "shows himself to his disciples." There is a pastoral intimacy inherent in each of the Easter stories in John, as Jesus feeds his followers both spiritually and physically, and there is a lesson here for all believers in how Christ makes himself known.

Effective preaching on this text will include exploration of the minds and hearts of the disciples in this post-Easter phase of their faith. Jesus does not make appointments; rather, he interrupts daily life. So there is no telling where he will show up next. The disciples were confused enough when Jesus was physically present to answer—or at least entertain—their questions on a daily basis. Now they have all of the same confusion, without the consistency of his presence. They have seen him risen, but what are they supposed to do now? They have spent years seeing him every day, but now, like us, they wait for unscheduled break-ins of the Divine.

Theological Perspective

of purpose. Some commentators argue that going fishing back home in Galilee indicates a lack of faith. They had already received the Holy Spirit and were commissioned to forgive sins (20:23). Furthermore, readers of John should recall how nighttime activities reflect ignorance and confusion about the light. If the best Nicodemus can muster about Jesus' origins in God is asking how he might fit into his mother's womb (3:4), readers should not expect much to be accomplished when the disciples fish at night. Read canonically with the miraculous catch in Luke 5:1–11, this episode emphasizes that only Jesus' intervention will produce results, not what the disciples attempt on their own. As long as they fish in doubt and apart from following the Lord's commands, the net remains empty. They have returned to their old lives when they are called to something new.

A different approach focuses on the necessity for believers to wait for the Lord in community. They were "together" (v. 2), marked as the branches whose life depends upon abiding in the vine, Jesus, in order to bear the fruit of love (15:1–17). No longer hiding behind locked doors, they traveled together back to Galilee and stayed together when Peter suggested going fishing (v. 3). John Chrysostom applauded how the disciples "put their leisure to good use," which is echoed by Augustine's observation that working for a living and being an apostle are not mutually exclusive.[1]

At dawn and for the third time, the disciples travel the path from ignorance to knowledge, belief, and fellowship with the Lord. Believers yet to come will share this path, despite their geographical and chronological distance from the disciples' experience. At first Jesus is seen, but not known; the disciples hear him, but do not know the voice of their shepherd—yet (10:27). Chrysostom noted that although this unknowing is related to the disciples' weariness, it does not rest entirely on the disciples' own inadequacies. Jesus himself chooses when and to whom he grants recognition. Jesus "showed himself" (v. 1), and the showing is much more than simply being visible; it points toward the larger terrain of relational knowledge, that is, really knowing someone. Chrysostom reasoned that Jesus refrains from manifesting his identity in order to facilitate interaction, which might be stifled with too

1. John Chrysostom, Homily 87 (3), in *Commentary on Saint John the Apostle and Evangelist*, trans. Sr. Thomas Aquinas Goggin, Fathers of the Church 41 (New York: Fathers of the Church, 1960), 463. Augustine, Tractate 122.3, in *Tractates on the Gospel of John 112-124. Tractates on the First Epistle of John*, trans. John W. Rettig, Fathers of the Church 92 (Washington, DC: Catholic University of America Press, 1995), 63–65.

Pastoral Perspective

A major theme is suggested by the geographical location of this postresurrection appearance by the Sea of Tiberias. Surely we are meant to associate this miracle with the one in John 6, where Jesus fed the five thousand by the Sea of Tiberias. The substance of that meal was also bread and fish, and though the boy's five barley loaves and two fish were not sufficient to feed the crowd, the disciples discovered that Jesus can transform insufficiency into abundance. Likewise we see that Jesus turns the disciples' insufficient (non-existent) catch into an abundant one in 21:6.

It is indeed a miracle when inadequacy becomes adequacy, when failure turns into success, or when scarcity is replaced by abundance. At deep levels, we worry about being inadequate as students, spouses, providers, friends, professionals, or parents. We fear failure in every aspect of life. We dread scarcity and what it means for us and those we love. Ask anyone who has been downsized, frustrated by a job search, or forced to retire early. The risen Jesus is in the life-changing business. It would be powerful to include contemporary examples of how life can change when Jesus' presence calms fears and his fullness transforms emptiness.

When we look closely at the fishermen in this story, we gain other insights. Only three of the seven men have names: Simon Peter, Thomas called the Twin, and Nathanael of Cana in Galilee. Readers of the Gospel are familiar with Peter and Thomas, but Nathanael is hardly a central character in Jesus' band of disciples. So there is likely a reason that Nathanael is named here. Recall that in chapter 1 Philip invited Nathanael to meet Jesus, saying, "We have found him about whom Moses in the law and also the prophets wrote, Jesus son of Joseph from Nazareth" (1:45). Despite Nathanael's cynical comment, "Can anything good come out of Nazareth?" (1:46), he decides to check Jesus out. As he approaches the man from Nazareth, Nathanael hears Jesus address him, "Here is truly an Israelite in whom there is no deceit!" (1:47).

Nathanael is stunned. Jesus is a complete stranger, yet Nathanael is known by him—fully and deeply known, right down to the deepest recesses of his heart. This prompts Nathanael to confess, "Rabbi, you are the Son of God! You are the King of Israel!" (1:49).

Nathanael's experience shows that while it is possible not to know Jesus oneself, it is impossible not to be fully known by him. In Nathanael's case (as with Mary Magdalene outside the empty tomb in 20:16) recognition *by* Jesus leads to recognition *of* Jesus. Similarly, the disciples do not recognize Jesus

with regard to the relationships involving Jesus, Peter, and the Beloved Disciple. Their relationships would be left hanging, were it not for the restoration recounted here. In the preceding chapters, for example, Peter and the Beloved Disciples were in conflict and rivalry. The last scene where they are together, in 20:1–10, shows no explicit resolution to their relationship.

Furthermore, the one who makes the remarkable confession of the risen Jesus in chapter 20 is Thomas, not Peter or the Beloved Disciple, who play the prominent role in the Gospel of John (13:21–30; 20:1–10). If the Gospel ends with the return of Peter and the Beloved Disciple to their homes (20:10) without restoration, one may surmise that they are considered to be apostates. This point of view contradicts the whole perspective of the Gospel of John. The development of the relationships between and among Jesus, Peter, and the Beloved Disciple has been expected in John's narrative, and this serves as a core motif in chapter 21.

The narrative in chapter 21 records the postresurrection appearance of Jesus to his disciples. The account of 21:1–14 begins and ends with the word "appeared" (twice in v. 1, once in v. 14) and thereby informs the reader that the account is a complete section in itself. This section contains two stories: verses 1–8, where Jesus orchestrates the miraculous catch of fish, and verses 9–14, where Jesus prepares a eucharistic meal with his disciples.

In verse 1, Jesus appears to the disciples at the Sea of Tiberias, also known as the Sea of Galilee (6:1). The phrase "after this" connects this appearance to the previous postresurrection appearances, 20:19–23 and 20:24–29. Seven of the disciples are listed, three by name: "Simon Peter, Thomas called the Twin, Nathanael of Cana in Galilee, the sons of Zebedee, and two others of his disciples" (v. 2). Peter is mentioned first and most frequently in this chapter (cf. 6:67–69; 13:6–9; 20:2–7). The sons of Zebedee (Mark 1:19–20; 3:17; 10:35–45) are not mentioned elsewhere in the whole Gospel. The identification of Thomas as "the Twin" (v. 2) refers back to the account of Jesus' appearance in 20:24. Nathanael is mentioned only in John (1:46–49); he is not considered one of the Twelve according to the Synoptic tradition. Two unnamed disciples appear at the beginning (1:35) and at the end (21:2) of the Gospel. The list of seven disciples, although not comprehensive, has a symbolic representation and points to the whole body of disciples.

In verse 3 Simon Peter takes a leadership role in the fishing excursion (cf. 6:66–71; 11:16; 13:4–20;

They have finally left the upper room, having evidently been convinced by Jesus' second visit that it was OK to do so—but where do they go? Peter announces that he is going fishing (presumably alone), only to have six other friends jump on board. Is Peter just filling time? Is he attempting to go back to his previous vocation, now that Jesus is not around in the same way? Whatever the reason for this spontaneous expedition on the Sea of Tiberias, one sees in Peter's actions both uncertainty and grief. The opening scene holds more in common with the days after a funeral than the celebratory trumpets of an Easter celebration.

As one hour drags on and then another, without catching a single fish, this attempt at passing time proves fruitless, in more ways than one. Then a voice interrupts their silence, telling them the fish are on the other side of the boat. John records no objection from the disciples, but it is worth considering what this advice from an unqualified source sounds like after an entire night of catching nothing. It would be one thing if the stranger on the shore had proposed some radical new technique for fishing, but the answer is so painfully simple that it seems to have no chance for success.

Given the parallels made in the Gospels between fishing and sharing the gospel, it might be particularly fruitful to spend some time asking if this congregation is the kind of church that will take advice from outsiders on "how to fish." The story of disciples who have not caught anything in recent memory bears a number of frightening parallels with the modern church, though our pride often keeps us from heeding the advice of those outside our walls.

Prouder folks might never have heeded the stranger's words, but the disciples have heard the same advice before (Luke 5:4). So, against their better judgment, they cast their nets on the other side. Their obedience pays off, and their net is suddenly full of fish. One of the ideas worth exploring in a sermon is the critical nature of humble listening to the work of discipleship.

The real miracle of the story is not the 153 fish that are hauled into the boat. It is the restlessness of Peter, once he learns who it is that stands on the shore. The disciple whom Jesus loved looks at their catch and makes a declaration of faith: "It is the Lord!" Here again is another word for the contemporary church: *Jesus does not show up wearing a name tag.* This is communal revelation at its finest, as fellow disciples help one another see what they might otherwise have missed.

Theological Perspective

forthright an appearance.[2] In effect, the resurrected Jesus' muted presence in the world might encourage human response to his call before the caller is even identified. At the very least, the disciples' ignorance gives comfort to future believers, who have good company in their own struggles to recognize and know Jesus.

Jesus calls to us in our darkness and the barrenness of our own efforts, echoing the Lord's call to the furtive Adam and Eve (Gen. 3:9). In both cases, God's people are given an opportunity to demonstrate trust and obedience, despite their failures. Jesus appears with the dawn as the "light [that] shines in the darkness, and the darkness did not overcome it" (1:5). This light recalls the base melody around which this Gospel proclaims Jesus to be the Word who is both creator and re-creator. The Word is the light before there was light, and "without him not one thing came into being" (1:3).

Resonating with the tones of Genesis, we think back to how God's word commanded "the waters [to] bring forth swarms of living creatures" (Gen. 1:20). Likewise, through the Word's command, fishes swarm into the obediently cast net. Cyril of Alexandria discerned the night labors as the befogged efforts of humanity trying to perceive God prior to the incarnation. However, "when early morning came, that is, when the mist of the devil was dispersed, and the true light dawned, that is Christ," then the disciples and their successors can obey Christ's command and haul in believers, whose numbers "seem in truth to surpass, and be out of all proportion to the strength of the holy Apostles."[3]

Through the abundance and the community, recognition ensues. Repeating the pattern at the tomb, the Beloved Disciple recognizes and shares his discovery with Peter (v. 7). Receiving this proclamation, Peter at once girds himself for action, as can the believing community from this point. Those who have not seen may yet believe in the signs of abundant life within a community that point to the Lord.

LISA D. MAUGANS DRIVER

Pastoral Perspective

standing on the shore, but when he addresses them, using a term of endearment ("children"), and when their empty nets strain with an extraordinary catch, recognition follows. There is a certain abundant grace that flows from being fully known by another. How is this grace magnified when we recognize that we are fully known by God?

This passage can also speak a word of grace to anyone presently on an emotional or spiritual roller-coaster ride. Certainly this was the situation in which the fishermen found themselves. Many of these men (at the very least Peter and the sons of Zebedee) had left their families, jobs, and hometowns to follow Jesus—who was dead and miraculously raised but, for all they knew, permanently gone. Jesus was the compass in their lives. Now they had no direction.

What do you do when your future is suddenly up for grabs? At times like this, most people feel decentered, adrift, "at sea." Those who mourn the loss of a loved one, experience the pain of a failed marriage, work hard but have no financial security, or whose emotional or physical health is declining, know this feeling well.

What did the seven do? They took comfort in familiar routines. They went back to what they knew: fishing. Were they trying to run away from their troubles by taking up their nets? Were they merely responding to the practical obligations of life at home? Either way, Jesus appears in the midst of their ordinary activities. He meets them where they are—physically, emotionally, and spiritually—and he points the way to bounty and fullness, to thriving, not just surviving. His appearance is an instance of pure grace, with no strings attached. Note that the men haul in their catch *before* they recognize Jesus; they do not *earn* it by first declaring him Lord. Instead, their blessings are literally beyond belief. Despite their doubts, their fatigue, their failure, they follow the directions of the stranger on the beach. Live-giving abundance flows.

LOUISE LAWSON JOHNSON

2. John Chrysostom, Homily 87, 463.
3. Cyril of Alexandria, *Commentary on the Gospel according to S. John*, Book XII.I, vol. 2, ed. and trans. T. Randell (London: W. Smith [late Mozley], 1885) 697–98.

Exegetical Perspective

14:5; 20:24–29). Fishing may have been a part of their living, an old occupation. The disciples go out at night to fish, but are unsuccessful (cf. Luke 5:5). Then the risen Jesus appears to them on the shore, but none of the disciples recognize him (v. 4). Just as he revealed his identity to Mary Magdalene by calling her name, "Mary" (20:16), so the risen Jesus reveals himself to the disciples by calling them "children" (v. 5; cf. 13:33; 1 John 2:1, 12, 14, 18, 28).

Jesus asks them about the fish (v. 5), and this question leads to his remarkable advice (v. 6): "Cast the net to the right side of the boat, and you will find some." Following directions from the risen Lord, the disciples catch a large school of fish. They are not even able to haul the net into the boat because of the great and surprising quantity of fish (v. 6). The number of fish—153—is given in verse 11.

This narrative has a recognizable parallel in Luke 5:1–11, where Luke describes the call of the first disciples. If both stories derive from a common tradition, what is peculiar in John is the role of the Beloved Disciple to recognize the risen Jesus (v. 7). Just as he reaches the empty tomb first (20:1–10), the Beloved Disciple is the first to recognize Jesus, this time as the Lord, a typical designation of the risen Jesus (v. 7; cf. 20:18, 20, 25, 28). Peter takes his witness and responds to it with typical impetuosity. He jumps into the water, putting on his garment, presumably out of respect for the risen Lord. The author apparently shows how the Beloved Disciple enlightens Peter. In the Gospel of John, the Beloved Disciple is the one who is closest physically to Jesus and understands his intention (13:22–25; 19:35). Now, unlike Peter, the other disciples come ashore, dragging the net full of fish (v. 8).

ROHUN PARK

Homiletical Perspective

In the Gospels, as in our churches, there is a variety of reactions to Jesus. The norm in my own denominational tradition is a rather buttoned-up, well-behaved affair in which we sing the selected hymns, sit politely during the sermon, and walk in orderly fashion out of the building when it is all over. In Jesus' own time, there were plenty of folks who could meet him and not behave erratically for having come in contact with the Son of God

There were and are others who meet Christ, though, and cannot be the same on the other side of their encounter. Like the woman at Bethany, Zacchaeus in the tree, and countless others who ignore social decorum in the presence of Jesus, Peter makes a fool of himself. The one who denied Christ dives out of the boat. From earlier stories about failed attempts to walk on water, we know that Peter is not the strongest swimmer in the group, but that does not stop him from trying. He barely gets an arm through his shirt before he is dog-paddling his way to Jesus.

There is a time for decorum, and there is a time for the raw sort of desperation that is on display in Peter's swim. Those who know their need of a Savior behave differently from those who do not, but it is important to note that the Fourth Gospel does not pass judgment on those who stay in the boat. They are the ones who bring back the catch that Jesus made possible, and considering Peter's swimming abilities, they may have made it to the shore faster than he did.

Peter was not thinking practically; he was hardly thinking at all. If given the chance, he would do it again a million times over.

S. BRIAN ERICKSON

John 21:9–14

⁹When they had gone ashore, they saw a charcoal fire there, with fish on it, and bread. ¹⁰Jesus said to them, "Bring some of the fish that you have just caught." ¹¹So Simon Peter went aboard and hauled the net ashore, full of large fish, a hundred fifty-three of them; and though there were so many, the net was not torn. ¹²Jesus said to them, "Come and have breakfast." Now none of the disciples dared to ask him, "Who are you?" because they knew it was the Lord. ¹³Jesus came and took the bread and gave it to them, and did the same with the fish. ¹⁴This was now the third time that Jesus appeared to the disciples after he was raised from the dead.

Theological Perspective

A curt dialectic ricochets between Jesus and the disciples. Jesus beckons the fishermen to bring some fish, and Peter does. While Jesus invites them to break their fast, the disciples struggle with their doubts. Met with silence and immobility, Jesus comes to them and feeds them. Drawn in by Jesus themselves, the disciples move toward the shore, toward recognition and communion with the Lord.

John's Gospel concludes by reestablishing Peter's place among the disciples. At the beach, an ominous charcoal fire burns (v. 9). The air is thick with unspoken recriminations. Peter has denied his Lord around such a fire. The others will soon choke back questions about Jesus' identity. Peter jumps at the chance both to reach Jesus first and to act on Jesus' request for some of the catch (v. 10). Peter clearly wants to make amends with actions rather than words; words will come painfully in the next pericope. Larger than life, Peter hauls the net to shore (v. 11) which earlier the disciples had been unable to haul into the boat (21:6). Peter may simply have rejoined his comrades to finish the job he had abandoned. In which case, we see John's concern to show how the disciples stayed together after the resurrection and needed one another to take on the task of fishing—soon, fishing for believers.

Pastoral Perspective

Whereas the emphasis in 21:1–8 is on recognizing Jesus as the risen Christ, the focus in 21:9–14 is on fellowship with Jesus. The spotlight moves from the actions of the fishermen on the water to the actions of Jesus on dry land. While the disciples may fish, it is Jesus who feeds.

These six verses contain many enigmatic details (a charcoal fire, a catch of 153 fish, a pristine net, an unexpressed question about Jesus' identity, a comment that this is the third post-Easter "revelation" of Jesus). Each of these might capture the attention of the preacher, but far more important is the unfolding testimony of fellowship with the risen Christ. It is the living presence of Jesus that must occupy center stage, because all Christian ministry, then and now, flows from that single source.

Three themes dominate this passage: the meal, the miracle, and the ongoing mission of the disciples. Verses 9, 12–13 set up the meal; verses 10–11 emphasize the miraculous nature of the catch; and verses 11–14 have the mission of the early church in mind.[1]

It is easy to picture this meal. A modest charcoal fire is burning, fish are cooking over the coals, fresh bread is laid out nearby. Jesus invites the disciples

---

1. Gail O'Day's analysis is extremely valuable in *The New Interpreter's Bible*, ed. Leander E. Keck (Nashville: Abingdon Press, 1995), 9:858.

Exegetical Perspective

John 21:1–14 contains two stories, the miraculous catch of fish (vv. 1–8) and Jesus' eucharistic meal with his disciples (vv. 9–14). The connection that exists between the two stories is the appearance of the risen Jesus by the Sea of Tiberias. The meal narrative in verses 9–14 in particular is reminiscent of the revelation of the risen Jesus to the Emmaus disciples in Luke 24:13–35.

On their arrival at the shore after their fishing adventure, the disciples see a charcoal fire lying on the ground: "When they had gone ashore, they saw a charcoal fire there, with fish on it, and bread" (v. 9). Attention is immediately drawn to the charcoal fire, because Peter was alienated from the Lord as he denied him by a charcoal fire (18:18, 25). In this way the author prepares the reader for Peter's restoration. Now Simon Peter encounters the risen Lord by another charcoal fire.

In verse 9 the meal Jesus has prepared is the same as in 6:1–14, the loaves and fishes, thereby pointing to the other traditions of Jesus feeding the multitude (6:1–15). Just as Jesus fed the crowd, he will now feed the disciples. Similarly, Peter will be called to feed the sheep, thereby becoming a provider of food and shepherd of the flock (vv. 15–19). In verse 10, when the disciples are instructed to bring some of the fish they have caught, Peter takes the lead and

Homiletical Perspective

This story is remarkable in its stark simplicity. The circumstances seem to beg for more—a radical teaching from Christ, or a more spectacular miracle. After all, this is Easter we are talking about, and the disciples have just laid eyes on the risen Christ. Moments before, Peter has made his way to the seashore in the most dramatic fashion possible, hurling himself over the side of a boat. The disciples drag in the catch of the year, having heeded Jesus' fishing advice. John tells us this was only the third time Jesus had appeared to them—in other words, the stage is set for something big.

In the first two resurrection appearances, Jesus appears inside locked doors and shows off wounds. But this time, soaking-wet Peter and his exhausted fellow disciples come ashore to discover that the resurrected Christ has thrown together a little breakfast. John is careful to point out that it is not even a holy fire Jesus is cooking on, just regular old charcoal.

If this story took place before Good Friday, it would seem almost not worth the telling, but told on this side of Easter, it sounds downright odd. A little too domestic. We expect more dramatic action from a risen Savior than breakfast preparation and beachside hospitality. It seems the disciples feel the same way, as they are left speechless, perhaps waiting for something else to happen. However, Jesus carries

John 21:9–14

Theological Perspective

By grace, the net was "full of large fish" and "was not torn" (v. 11). Jesus is the primary worker in gathering people to himself, while the disciples need only haul in what Jesus has caught. Recalling how unity so occupies this Gospel's vision of salvation, a net strained to the point of breaking evokes the community's own struggles. Threats of division (*schisma*, 7:43; 9:16; 10:19)[1] are countered by Christ's will to preserve the believers as one. Both Jesus' seamless garment (19:23) and the net remain intact (v. 11, "was not torn," a form of *schizō*), despite threats to their integrity. Furthermore, through Jesus, believers are united with both the Father and fellow sheep (or branches of the vine) in a way that no one will "snatch" them from Jesus' and the Father's hold (10:28–29).

While the specific number of the catch (153) may indicate a mundane sum, early commentators shared the premodern understanding that numbers are more than counters. For example, Augustine pondered the significance of 153 being a triangular number, the sum of the arithmetic sequence 1+2+3+4 . . . +17. Those "fishes," he surmised, could signify a message of hope that the mass of believers will be brought safely to the resurrection. That is possible only when the law (ten for the Decalogue) is fulfilled by the Spirit's sanctifying grace (seven associated with the Spirit, e.g., the seven gifts of the Spirit in Isa. 11:2–3). For "what is commanded by the letter is fulfilled by the help of the Spirit," lest any be deceived about their own power to reach the resurrection.[2] What Jesus provides to fulfill the law nourishes us for eternity.

In chapter 6 Jesus had provided a miraculous meal of fish and bread by the sea, but this time the meal appears ex nihilo, before the disciples bring any of the catch to Jesus. The Word who created in the beginning (1:1–3) has "food to eat that [the disciples] do not know about" (4:32). This first breakfast of the new creation directs us toward Jesus' claim, "I am the living bread that came down from heaven. Whoever eats of this bread will live forever; and the bread that I will give for the life of the world is my flesh" (6:51). For this reason many commentators connected the fish and bread to Jesus "roasted" by his passion so that he might feed others with his life.[3] The disciples hesitated to partake of the meal, though, or even to speak to Jesus.

1. Craig R. Koester, *Symbolism in the Fourth Gospel: Meaning, Mystery, Community* (Minneapolis: Fortress Press, 2003), 135.
2. Augustine, Tractate 122.8, in *Tractates on the Gospel of John 112–24; Tractates on the First Epistle of John*, trans. John W. Rettig (Washington, DC: Catholic University of America Press, 1995), 69–71.
3. For example, Augustine, Tractate 123; Peter Chrysologus, Sermon 55.5; Thomas Aquinas, *Commentary on the Gospel of John*, Ch. 21, Lecture 1, §2599.

Pastoral Perspective

to contribute some of their catch to the meal. Once they do so, he invites them to come and eat. We might imagine them sitting in a circle, with Jesus acting as the meal's host. It could be a scene from a Hallmark card, but of course there is more beneath the surface. The last time we encountered a charcoal fire was in 18:18, when Peter denied Jesus three times as he warmed himself in the courtyard of the high priest. Are we meant to remember this? Is Peter's denial around the first charcoal fire forgiven when Jesus invites him to break bread around this second charcoal fire? Recall that eating and drinking are metaphors for salvation through Christ (6:53–59). It is safe to say that there is more going on here than a simple meal.

Another striking feature of this meal is how little dialogue there is. Whatever questions the disciples still harbor about Jesus' identity (v. 12) are eventually answered by Jesus' actions. Jesus takes bread and gives it to them; he takes fish and gives it to them. Remember that these same men previously sat by the Sea of Tiberias and watched Jesus distribute bread and fish to some five thousand people. Now it is they who are filled. How can they miss the connection? Jesus' actions here speak as loudly as words, but this should not be surprising. Our simplest gestures can communicate powerful meanings: a smile, a wink, a hug, the squeeze of a hand, a thumbs-up across a crowded room, an exchange of rings. In some way the disciples' experience of the risen Christ opens their eyes, and eyesight becomes insight. Jesus' identity is revealed anew.

Verses 10–11 reiterate the miraculous features of the catch. It is easy to focus on the fish rather than on the act of fishing. The enormity of this miracle is described in three ways in verse 11: the net was "full of large fish," "a hundred fifty-three of them," and "there were so many." Abundance, fullness brimming over, extraordinary bounty.

While the theme of abundance is clear, what is not so obvious is that the verb in verse 11, "to haul or to draw," carries special meaning. John uses this verb to describe God's agency in calling people to faith in 6:44 ("No one can come to me unless *drawn* by the Father who sent me"). In 12:32 the verb is used to link the cross with salvation ("And I, when I am lifted up from the earth, will *draw* all people to myself"). When Peter *draws* the net ashore, his efforts function as an acted parable. Just as God is at work drawing people to Christ, so Christ's disciples are called by God to be fishers of people, drawing them into the fellowship of faith. Further, we learn

---

Feasting on the Gospels

Exegetical Perspective

climbs back on board (v. 11). Previously, the disciples could not drag in the net full of fish by themselves (v. 6), but Peter pulls the net with the 153 large fish ashore by himself without tearing it (v. 11).

Readers have been so interested in the number of fish. Why is it so specific, neither rounded nor obviously symbolic? It may simply be that "there were hundreds of fish" or just "there were so many fish." If the number signifies more than the abundance of fish caught, does it have a special meaning? Many scholars have speculated on this, providing various interpretations of the number 153. Such speculations cannot be verified, though, and the meaning of the number remains unclear. Be that as it may, the quantity of fish serves to underscore that the appearance of Jesus at the seashore is real and that the story of the author is trustworthy.

Next, Jesus invites the disciples to eat the meal he has prepared: "Come and have breakfast" (v. 12). Now they all recognize the presence of the risen Lord. The risen Jesus has appeared on the shore at dawn where the disciples are striving to catch fish, but not one of them has recognized him immediately. Even when they miraculously catch the fish on Jesus' advice, they cannot, apart from the Beloved Disciple, recognize Jesus. Of course, the sea at dawn (21:4) may be foggy, and since it is before sunrise, it may be difficult to distinguish a person precisely.

The contact between Mary Magdalene and the risen Jesus at the empty tomb was also early, as day was breaking (20:1). She also could not recognize him at first (20:15). Their failure to recognize the risen Jesus, though, has nothing to do with the weather conditions on the Sea of Tiberias or their own eyesight. In John's narrative, the failure to "see" relates to the contrast between "not aware" (v. 4, NRSV "did not know") and "aware" (v. 12, NRSV "knew"). It is the Beloved Disciple who comes to know and enlightens Peter as well as the others.

The disciples are in awe of the risen Lord and too frightened before him. None of them dares to ask him his identity, of which they are already "aware" (v. 12) in any case. Henceforth, the narrative brings the risen Jesus back into the lives of the disciples. While the disciples go about their everyday affairs, going out for a normal fishing trip, the risen Lord has broken into their lives. The fellowship that Jesus shares with his disciples unfolds in a similar, yet distinct, way.

Now, with the miraculous catch of fish, a ritual occurs. Jesus distributes the bread and fish among the disciples: "Jesus came and took the bread and

Homiletical Perspective

on with all the pomp and circumstance of a pancake supper, cooking for his friends as if this is the most normal thing in the world.

When Jesus asks for some of the fresh catch, it is eager Peter, unsurprisingly, who pulls the net onto the shore. Perhaps Jesus will multiply them tenfold, or teach them a lesson about the kingdom. Not quite. The net should break, John implies, but there is not a single tear. Those longing for miracles will have to settle for unbroken nets.

As the disciples stand around looking at one another for clues as to what to do next, Jesus issues the simplest of invitations: "Come and eat breakfast" (v. 12). So they do, receiving the sacramental meal in silence, directly from the hand of their Master and friend. The question they all want to ask is "Who are you?" but no one has the guts to ask it, because they already know the answer. If Jesus showed up in a more obvious way, perhaps they would not need to ask the question at all.

Sandwiched between Peter's desperate swimming and Christ's instructions, "Feed my sheep," this moment is usually lost in transition. It offers, however, a profound reflection on the nature of the holy in the midst of daily life. Jesus behaves as if this is just another day at the office, while the disciples are left speechless in their stupor and uncertainty. For many of us, this is the way God shows up—not in lightning-filled explosions of clarity and wonder, but in awkward moments of inexplicable holiness.

Too often our hearers have been trained to associate only the glorious with God's presence, but the Easter accounts are almost miracle-less. Instead, they are full of things like bread and fish and table fellowship. Jesus shows up to be with his disciples. This is what Easter looks like, John tells us. Sometimes life with Christ looks like the dead raised, mountains of transfiguring light, and the feeding of five thousand with last night's leftovers. More often than not, though, it is as simple as breakfast by the sea. It is the mundane mingled with miracle, charcoal fires, and unbroken nets. It is the pastor's rehearsed call to the communion table that she has given a thousand times before, not a burning bush or a thundering cloud, that draws us into Christ's holy presence.

Just as something in us wishes for spectacular encounters of faith—moments that wash away all doubt with their perfect clarity—it is always easier to preach on the spectacular, because it seems to make for more entertaining and engaging sermons. It is much easier to sell an impressive God. Perhaps what

John 21:9–14

Theological Perspective

Jesus' power did not always provoke silence. For example, when he had quieted the storm, his astounded but relieved disciples wondered aloud who he could possibly be (Matt. 8:27; Mark 4:41; Luke 8:25). While the disciples' ignorance of Jesus' identity is a pattern within the Synoptics, it is much less so in John's Gospel. The disciples already abide in the light and rarely experience such misunderstanding until Jesus' death and resurrection.

There are other instances where Jesus' words and actions did lead to stunned silence. His adversaries were silenced and "dared not" ask further questions, because Jesus had answered so well as to leave no graceful way to proceed with their opposition (e.g., testing Jesus during his last public teaching, Matt. 22:46; Luke 20:40). Following Jesus' transfiguration, Peter, James, and John needed no counsel to keep the experience to themselves (Matt. 17:9; Mark 9:9). In fact, the disciples were bewildered as much by Jesus talking about his own resurrection as they were about what they just witnessed (Mark 9:10; Luke 9:36). Thus encounters with divine dimensions of Jesus' identity could provoke apophatic space for reassessing who he might be and what this would mean for their lives.

Faced with obvious signs, the disciples chose silence. Who among them wished to be publicly chided about their doubts the way Thomas had been at Jesus' prior appearance? In their silence, and evidently in their hesitation to enjoy the meal, Jesus came to them in a ritual of taking the food and giving it to the disciples (v. 13), the same actions that ushered the feeding of the five thousand (6:11). In believers' silence before the mystery of the incarnation, the cross, and the resurrection, Jesus still comes to nourish and unite "those who have not seen and yet have come to believe" (20:29). At the altar of fellowship in his flesh and blood, partakers are strengthened and may then, like Peter, undertake Jesus' call, "Follow me" (21:19, 22).

LISA D. MAUGANS DRIVER

Pastoral Perspective

that God's net is secure, unfailing, and capable of holding all of the fish we can ever hope to catch.

One evening this passage was the topic of a small group Bible study. After the text was read out loud, one participant said candidly, "I am a pretty good fisherman myself, and here is what I know for a fact. When you haul in a net like that, you have lots of losers in there, along with the good fish. I am surprised that Peter and his bunch didn't weed out the bad ones." Life experiences like this can be a springboard to explore what grace is and is not; what forgiveness is and is not; what it means that Peter (the one who denied Jesus) is the one who hauls in the net; what it means when we feel undeserving of God's goodness—or conversely, what it means when we think we are the "keepers," and others need to be thrown back!

The mission of the early church is in view in the final verses of this pericope. Jesus initiates this breakfast on the beach from start to finish. He has already made preparations for the meal, he asks the men to contribute to it from the bounty that God has provided, and then he issues a simple invitation, "Come and have breakfast" (v. 12). Is this not the good news of the gospel in a nutshell? Salvation is initiated by God, made real through Jesus Christ, and made available by gracious invitation. It is offered to those who fail and come up empty; it is offered to those who are confused; it is offered to those who see and believe; it is offered to those who are fools for Christ and jump into the water with their clothes on; it is offered to those who have yet to discover whose fool they are. It is offered to everyone—keepers and losers alike—because the net of divine grace is big enough for all of us.

LOUISE LAWSON JOHNSON

gave it to them, and did the same with the fish" (v. 13). Jesus serves as host at the meal, which means that the episode has eucharistic overtones, as does the similar Emmaus scene in Luke: "he took bread, blessed and broke it, and gave it to them. Then their eyes were opened, and they recognized him" (Luke 24:30b–31a). If this account points to the life of the community, the size of the fish caught not only points to the great abundance of Jesus' gifts but also symbolizes the expansion of the church.

In John 21:14, the narrator announces that the risen Jesus reveals himself here for the third time to the disciples. Apparently "the disciples" designates the group, that is, the gathered disciples, not a single individual, because this listing of appearances excludes the appearance to Mary Magdalene (20:1, 11–18). The preceding appearances take place in Jerusalem, while this "third" appearance is by the Sea of Tiberias (Matt. 28:16–20; Mark 16:17; cf. John 6:1, also resurrection appearances in Galilee).

Given this, one might ask how else this appearance is different from the previous appearances. What purpose does this appearance intend to serve? How does this appearance supplement the two previous appearances? Does the author wish to provide explicit evidence that Jesus has been raised with a body, so as to have a meal with his disciples? Does he intend to say something about the two competing disciples, Peter and the Beloved Disciple, whose stories do not end at the empty tomb event in 20:1–10?

The reader can only conjecture. The account of 21:1–14, which begins and ends with the word "appeared" (twice in v. 1 and once in v. 14), presents the appearance of Jesus to the gathered disciples after his resurrection and a miracle of plenty. It also tells of Simon Peter and the Beloved Disciple, the two leading disciples in the Gospel. However, no special duty is assigned to them, as their rivalry has not yet ended. The commission and full restoration for them will soon follow (21:15–19).

ROHUN PARK

believers most desperately need to hear, though, is a word about the ordinary things of life in Christ.

The disciples are speechless, because they know that this is no common meal, and certainly no ordinary Host, and one would pray for the same unspeakable awe in every one of us who dares approach the sacramental mystery of daily living—a keen awareness of the extraordinary stirring just below the surface. To any passerby on the beach that day, this is simply fish and bread and friends, but in the arithmetic of Jesus it adds up to much, much more.

In our hurried world of deadlines and church strategies and mission statements, it is both refreshing and befuddling to serve the God who sometimes shows up just to show up. We live in an age where everything that has value must have some clearly defined purpose, where we are lost without roles and responsibilities. We squeeze all that we can out of our days, and still feel inadequate at their close. Too often, we put the same expectations on God, wanting the Holy One of Israel to fulfill a function in our lives, rather than being the source of our life. In the midst of our many distractions Jesus shows up, just as he appeared to the disciples to make sure they did not miss the most important meal of the day. It is maternal and kind and unnecessary in the way only grace can manage.

Perhaps the most faithful sermon on this passage is not one that tries to squeeze symbolic significance out of the number of fish caught, or uses homiletic gymnastics to make this moment more than it is. Preaching this text will require the pastor to be at home enough in his or her skin to accept that sometimes Jesus shows up just because. The best we can do is sit down, eat the meal that has been prepared, and trust that our questions are best left for another time.

S. BRIAN ERICKSON

John 21:15–19

¹⁵When they had finished breakfast, Jesus said to Simon Peter, "Simon son of John, do you love me more than these?" He said to him, "Yes, Lord; you know that I love you." Jesus said to him, "Feed my lambs." ¹⁶A second time he said to him, "Simon son of John, do you love me?" He said to him, "Yes, Lord; you know that I love you." Jesus said to him, "Tend my sheep." ¹⁷He said to him the third time, "Simon son of John, do you love me?" Peter felt hurt because he said to him the third time, "Do you love me?" And he said to him, "Lord, you know everything; you know that I love you." Jesus said to him, "Feed my sheep. ¹⁸Very truly, I tell you, when you were younger, you used to fasten your own belt and to go wherever you wished. But when you grow old, you will stretch out your hands, and someone else will fasten a belt around you and take you where you do not wish to go." ¹⁹(He said this to indicate the kind of death by which he would glorify God.) After this he said to him, "Follow me."

Theological Perspective

This text is considered by some to be part of the end of an appendix to the Gospel. Jesus appears to Simon Peter and inquires three times, "Do you love me?" This threefold inquiry of Jesus mirrors the threefold denial of Jesus by Simon Peter in chapter 18. Jesus takes initiative to engage Peter and entrusts him with the task of feeding the sheep. The teacher or preacher may explore the ways that being entrusted with a task after failure is about second and third chances. Encounter with Jesus makes possible the way to forgiveness and new beginnings. This conversation with Jesus opens the way to new possibilities for serving the other, for seeking the welfare of the other, for seeking the common good in the midst of the ambiguity of present circumstances.

The preacher or teacher may develop the theme of the way that Jesus' encounter with Peter demonstrates the power of forgiveness and freedom. Because Jesus loved Peter into new possibilities and forgave him, Peter is free to express the love of Jesus in concrete ways for the flourishing of the gospel. Forgiveness makes possible the freedom to dwell in new ways in a place to which one is called.

Love is lifted up as the basic qualification for Christian service. Love is rooted in Christ's forgiveness of the one who is called to love. The passage resonates with Peter's denial and is an invitation for

Pastoral Perspective

In the final encounter of John's Gospel, Jesus moves face to face with Peter, initiating this pericope's breathtakingly intimate exchange. From the communal story of fishing and dawn, recognition and fire and meal, Jesus now addresses Peter alone, asking, "Do you love me?" It is a real question, painful precisely for its reality: Peter had denied Jesus publicly, shouting—at the point of Jesus' greatest need—that he did not even know him. A less courageous leader facing one who had acted in this way might slide past this excruciating memory, pretend it never happened. Instead, Jesus faces Peter and asks this personal, vulnerable question. It could not be more freighted, nor more simple. It is also the only question that matters.

Even in asking, Jesus is risking further rejection, and perhaps for this reason he returns his relationship with Peter to a greater degree of formality. Instead of using the nickname he had bestowed when he first saw Andrew's brother (1:42)—Cephas/Peter, the Rock—Jesus addresses him now by his given name: "Simon son of John." He presumes nothing: no "Peter," signaling their friendship all these years. This dialogue returns Simon to his identity prior to that first encounter, *before* he became Peter, to consider anew his relation to this endlessly surprising stranger. Here at the close of this book he

Exegetical Perspective

John 21 is considered by many to be an epilogue to the Gospel that comes to a natural conclusion at 20:31. The complex intertextuality of the epilogue with the rest of the Gospel, however, indicates that it was crafted by hands well versed in the theological and exegetical trajectory of the Johannine school. The inclusion of chapter 21 is attested in all the early manuscripts of John, suggesting that it was integral to the canonical shape of the Gospel from an early date.

The epilogue includes the resurrection appearance by Jesus at the Sea of Tiberias (Sea of Galilee), through which the risen Christ facilitates the miraculous catch of 153 fish by seven disciples (Peter, Thomas, Nathanael, the sons of Zebedee, and two others unnamed), after being directed by Jesus to "cast the net to the right" (21:6). Then follows the bread-and-fish breakfast on the beach (cf. 6:9–13).

The next two sections occur within the same setting, as Jesus engages Peter in conversation. The first portion of the dialogue focuses on Peter's future tasks as one who draws people rather than fish to Christ, as well as the manner of his death (vv. 15–19). The conversation then moves on to focus on the vocation and destiny of the Beloved Disciple (21:20–25). In doing so, two different examples of how the work of Jesus is to be continued in the post-Easter community are given: one through

Homiletical Perspective

The Lord has welcomed the disciples to a surprise breakfast, and fish are on the grill. He takes the bread and fish and gives it to them, Jesus feeding his friends once more. Then the scene quickly becomes more serious, as Jesus' attention turns exclusively to "Simon son of John." No longer calling him by the friendly "Peter," the Lord asks him, "Do you love me more than these?" (v. 15). We have no idea to whom "these" refers, though we preachers are very tempted to imagine who "these" could be. Surely many sermons have been crafted around Peter's love for Jesus compared to his love for [fill in the blank] or their love for Jesus.

The point does not seem to make much difference in the text, though, as Jesus twice repeats simply, "Do you love me?" The questioning is intense, so much so that Peter is hurt by it. For the reader, and perhaps for Peter, the moment recalls earlier events. In John 13, Peter boasts that he will lay down his life for Jesus, but Jesus tells him instead that he will deny him three times. In John 18, the prophecy is bitterly fulfilled as the rooster crows. To whatever extent these events are in the background of Jesus' questioning, this conversation by the Sea of Tiberias is the restoration of a man who has failed himself and his Lord.

At first, Peter's response to Jesus' questioning seems evasive. He does not respond, "I love you,"

John 21:15–19

Theological Perspective

Peter to embrace Christ's forgiveness of him, despite his failure to bear witness to Jesus when it really mattered.

To hear the strong call of God's Word that one is forgiven and free makes it possible to settle into a place. To dwell is to root oneself in God's word and to be shaped by daily prayer for ministry and the people for whom one is bound to pray.

The preacher or teacher may explore the journey of the congregation or the wider community to learn something about what it is to dwell in a place. To dwell in a place and to live in the freedom of forgiveness empowers one to exercise hospitality, to think first of the other rather than oneself, to put down roots, to learn the stories of joy and struggle of those who come.

What does it mean to be invested in the stories of others? Hearing the stories of others expands the horizons of one's own social location and cultural experiences. What does it mean to learn something from the stories of others about how God is at work in the world? This wisdom opens the capacity for the astonishment of the gospel, to be surprised by God's presence and work in unfamiliar conditions and circumstances.

What does it mean live together as a community of God's people? The community shares God's blessings in the midst of the joys and sorrows that face the community, incarnating the freedom and forgiveness overflowing for the love of the world.

Jesus' instruction to Peter is, "Tend my sheep." This is a reminder that ministry is not simply about putting down roots and dwelling in a place and being hospitable when people come into the congregation. The tension between being rooted and being sent to be ambassadors and servants of Christ is always present. The cries of the suffering from beyond the parish are deafening. We are called to speak a word of the cross of Christ to the world. This is not illusory hope, but hope rooted in the sure promise that Christ has defeated the final power of sin and death. Death no longer has the last word. Stepping out and responding to God's call may prompt one to go in unanticipated directions for which one feels totally unprepared. Being rooted in God's word and in prayer and being courageous in discerning God's call to go out to the world do not make one immune from the vicissitudes of life or weariness of heart.

"Feed my sheep" is Jesus' third command to Peter. That seems a fitting charge to any pastor. Feed the flock to whom you have been called, and see them as

Pastoral Perspective

is returned to its beginning, invited to begin again: "Simon son of John, do you love me more than these?" (v. 15).

Human hearts testing love, suspended across this threefold questioning—does Simon remember that other charcoal fire before he answers? "Yes, Lord, you know that I love you." Again, and again, "Do you love me, Formal Name? Do you love me?" (vv. 16, 17). The persistence and radical vulnerability of this divine question is the very heart of this pericope, addressing the stony facade all Christians wear in denying our Lord. The forces of such denial are strong in our world and in the privileged West, including its churches: denial of the costs of our economic system and our complicity in it; denial of our responsibility to demand fundamental ecological reorientation; denial of sisters and brothers—creatures and ecosystems of all kinds—with claims to our love. We deny them, and we cower with petrified hearts. To this denial comes the face of God, facing us, seeing us, naming us personally, and asking in all simplicity, "Do you love me?" What does it truly mean to love Jesus? The voices of orphans starving in slums; the voices of countless plants, animals, and life-forms sharing our planet; the voices of future generations whose Earth we are wrecking: can these be *God-in-flesh* pleading, searching, "*Do you love me?*"

What does it mean to love Jesus? "Feed my lambs. Tend my sheep. Feed my sheep." What if they are human lambs *and* other-than-human, these sheep? What if they are literal animal lambs and the clean waters and green pastures that nourish them, the microbes thick in every crumb of healthy soil? What does it mean to love the Logos in whom all things are made and have their being (1:1–5), who speaks in the weakest and most voiceless members of the human circle and the broader biotic community?

If—deniers and betrayers of Love as it is crucified—we come face to face with this Love risen and strange and dear, personally addressing us in exquisite humility, restoring us to speak aloud in turn the love that is our home,[1] and opening our stony hearts to feed those whom this Logos shepherds, then we may think that is surely enough. Precisely here, though, Jesus issues a confounding word: "Very truly, I tell you, when you were younger, you used to fasten your own belt and to go wherever you wished. But when you grow old, you will stretch out your hands, and someone else will fasten a belt around

---

1. In John, Jesus speaks often of "abiding" in him (6:56; 15:4–10), which is the verb form of the noun used in 14:2, "dwelling places" or "homes."

the discipleship of Peter, the other through that of the Beloved Disciple. Both bear "witness [*martyria*] to the light" (1:7), though in different ways. Peter is charged to become a pastor to the community and will die the death of a martyr. The Beloved Disciple will provide the basis and the shaping of the written testimony (*martyria*) that we know of as the Gospel of John (21:24). Also, in contrast to Peter, the Beloved Disciple will die a natural death.

The first clause of verse 15 ("When they had finished breakfast") provides the bridge from the initial scene of the epilogue (21:1–14) to the risen Lord's questioning and commission of Peter. The name used—"Simon son of John"—links this episode with Jesus' initial engagement of Peter (1:40–42), as well as with 10:3: "The gatekeeper opens the gate for him, and the sheep hear his voice. He calls his own sheep by name and leads them out." Jesus is calling Peter out, not from the security of the sheepfold, but from the self-imposed exile resulting from his betrayal, so that he might live into a new life of service to the people of God.

Behind the threefold questioning of Peter, "Do you love me?" exegetes have long discerned the threefold denial of Peter during the heart of Jesus' passion as the cause of the repeated inquiry (13:38; 18:17, 25–27). The descriptive detail of the "charcoal fire" links the denial of Jesus with the setting of chapter 21 in a very concrete way (18:18; 21:9). The rehabilitation of Peter to the ministry of the gospel after his betrayal is facilitated in the command, also repeated three times, to "feed/tend" Jesus' "lambs/sheep." This articulates a basic Johannine theological commitment, that love of God/Jesus cannot be separated from the love of neighbor (e.g., 13:34; 15:12). In fact, love of Jesus is witnessed to by means of one's care of the neighbor. Much has been made of the different Greek words for "love" used in this exchange between the risen Christ and Peter (*agapaō* and *phileō*), although they function largely as synonyms in Johannine literature. Jesus, the "good shepherd," here designates Peter to continue in the role of "pastor" (i.e., "shepherd" in Latin) among those entrusted into Jesus' care (cf. 18:9).

Chapter 10 of John (the good shepherd discourse) stands in the background of this conversation, especially Jesus' revelation of 10:11: "I am the good shepherd. The good shepherd lays down his life for the sheep." This too will be the fate of Peter. The description of his death as cruciform (21:18–19; 13:36) is verified by church tradition that indicates that Peter died a martyr's death ("you will stretch out your

but only, "*You know* that I love you." You may find a message of grace for your congregation in this response. When a person has boasted of their fidelity and love and then failed in it, it is a shameful and fearful thing to profess that love again. Our knowledge of ourselves is limited and distorted—indeed, we see this most clearly in the light of our failures—and even our most fervent commitments are made in hope. As the congregation hears this question directed to Peter in the reading of the text, they also hear it directed to themselves: "Do you love me?" For us, as for Peter, that question is put into a context that includes both failures and doubts. We too have failed our Lord and ourselves in countless ways, and some in your congregation may doubt their love for Christ.

When this question is put to us, perhaps the most certain response we can make to God is not "I love you," but "*You know* that I love you." In that confession we rely not on our knowledge of ourselves, but on God's knowledge of us. We rest not in our own capacity to love but in the grace of God, whose Spirit calls forth and sustains our faithfulness and love. Whatever Peter knows of himself, the Lord does indeed know that Peter loves him. He knows all things, including Peter's faithfulness unto death.

As each question is asked and answered, Jesus gives Peter a charge: feed my lambs, tend my sheep, feed my sheep. Here Jesus connects Peter's love for him to his love and care for others. Peter is charged to live out his love for Jesus by caring for the sheep of God's pasture. This connection is not accidental, but is deeply woven into Johannine literature. It is integral to a life of discipleship: love for the other is the outworking of God's love within us. You might think here of connections to the new commandment in John 13 and the classic lines of 1 John 4. There the epistle writer says, "The commandment we have from him is this: those who love God must love their brothers and sisters also" (1 John 4:21). God's love for us and our love for God necessarily lead into love for neighbor.

If you focus your sermon on this aspect of the dialogue, you could call the congregation to their missional vocation. Your congregation is called to join God in God's redeeming work and to bear witness to their love for Christ and Christ's love for them by caring for God's people. As followers of Jesus we are not given the option of professing our love for God without also hearing the call to love one another. As part of the Christian community we receive many blessings from God, but these gifts are

Theological Perspective

if they are the entire world. Nourish them with Word and sacraments and see them as if they are only a small part of the world. Give attention to the concerns of the world as if they are rooted in the parish.

God's strong message to each one today is that one is forgiven and free. Settle into the place where God has called. God has promised God's presence in the midst of uncertainty. Take courage in moving forward. Whatever lies ahead, do not grow weary. Wherever one is being called, Jesus is already there.

Another theological approach is to explore faith as following Jesus wherever that may lead. Following Jesus manifests itself in observable behavior. Following Jesus does not simply bring a future promise of eternity with God. Following Jesus is made manifest in the present circumstances of attentiveness to the neighbor. The Christian community that claims to follow Jesus is engaged in responsible action with and for others.

Jesus' forgiveness of Peter opens the way for Peter to try again to be a faithful follower of Jesus. He certainly knows he failed in the moment of crisis. Now Peter is given another chance. He is forgiven by Jesus and invited anew into the gospel mission. Freedom comes as grace when one knows that she has erred, has failed to do the just and right thing in the moment of crisis, and is given another chance to try again.

This freedom that comes from Jesus as a gift to Peter at the end of the Gospel opens the way to living in new ways that bear witness to Jesus in concrete ways. When one has been given another chance to get it right, the sense of time and privilege is intensified. It is as though Peter has been to the edge of the abyss and seen the consequences of his earlier denial of Jesus, and in this text he is given a chance for renewed life.

ROBIN J. STEINKE

Pastoral Perspective

you and take you where you do not wish to go" (v. 18). It is a costly grace, this mercy of loving Jesus. It will soften us and open us and toughen us and fire us, and it will lead us in ways we cannot foresee and may not wish.

Jesus' pronouncement echoes on at least two levels pastorally: first, it names the shared human reality—avoided only by those who die young—of aging. Few passages of Scripture trace as hauntingly the contrast between the vigor and free agency of youth, going wherever one wishes in a mind and body able to act freely, and the increasing debility and helplessness of age, being led against one's will and at others' mercy. Yet verse 19 tells us that Jesus said these words, not because Peter was going to live into feeble old age, but "to indicate the kind of death by which he would glorify God"—that is, foretelling Peter's martyrdom. It appears, that is, that Jesus is using the image of old age so vividly evoked here as a *metaphor* for the equivalent helplessness in the maturity of the martyr's vocation, similarly falling into the hands of others and at their mercy, for the sake of the fullest possible witness to Christ.

Thus, the second level to which these last two verses of the pericope point is this calling to martyrdom. The Greek word for martyrdom (*martyria*) means "witness," a witness not even death can silence, and a vocation open to all who give testimony to this Logos who permeates all. Ultimately martyrdom means not just witnessing to one's faith, nor even just dying for it. Additionally, it means that level of complete and ongoing and unfolding *availability* to the call of Christ, no matter what, that will indeed take us to places—and loves and conversions and courage—we can scarcely imagine. Thus the passage ends with precisely this call, as simple (and life-changing) as Jesus' question to Peter had been. With Peter, we are returned anew to the very beginning. All of it—the love, the feeding, the wild availability— is held in this call of a lifetime: "Follow me."

LISA E. DAHILL

hands"). Some of the details of the text may seem somewhat removed from the spectacle of crucifixion (e.g., "someone else will fasten a belt around you"); yet the figure need not make sense of such details, in that it is also making a comparison to Peter's youth ("you used to fasten your own belt"). Still, the gruesome tradition of leading a victim by a tether, with arms already tied to the horizontal crossbar (*patibulum*), to the place of crucifixion has been proposed as one way of reading the details in harmony with ancient crucifixion practices.

In the apocryphal *Acts of Peter*, Peter is crucified upside down. That is, Peter dies a death patterned by that of Jesus, but not imitative of it. In John, Jesus' death is that of "the Lamb of God who takes away the sin of the world" (1:29). Peter's death is clearly not for the remission of sin, yet does, as did Jesus' own, "glorify God" (v. 19). Peter's death does so because it is the ultimate expression of love: "No one has greater love than this, to lay down one's life for one's friends" (15:13).

The pericope ends with the risen Christ's invitation, "Follow me" (21:19b; cf. 10:4). The statement leads one back to the initial "Come and see" of 1:39 and Jesus' call to Philip in 1:43, which is worded as the same simple command, "Follow me." Much of the Gospel of John is a narration of what such discipleship entails, including the pitfalls of such a path. For Peter, the newly commissioned pastor, following Jesus will mean the ongoing care of those who have been marked by the cross and resurrection of Christ and fed by the miraculous feeding (21:12) where Jesus himself is host as well as meal (6:51). Also, for Peter, in contrast to the Beloved Disciple (21:22), this shepherding will lead to a martyr's death for the profession of his belief in the one sent from God so that the world might have life, "and have it abundantly" (10:10).

ERIK M. HEEN

given to us so that others may be blessed through us. As for Peter, so for us: the restoration to discipleship is simultaneously a commissioning to apostleship.

The character and shape of apostleship is patterned after Jesus, as Jesus instructs Peter, "Follow me." The leadership that Peter will offer as a shepherd of God's flock must be patterned after the Good Shepherd. It must be leadership as discipleship, and here you may find inspiration for a sermon on Christian leadership, both in the church and the wider society. Insights about leadership are both popular and much needed, and the Christian preacher can make a distinctive contribution by framing leadership in the context of faithful discipleship. Peter's commissioning to ecclesial leadership comes immediately following his restoration from failure; it is a demonstration of God's grace and indicates no special worthiness on Peter's part. His charge to lead is shaped by the image of a shepherd who knows his flock by name and gives his life so that their lives may flourish. Indeed, by linking the prophecy of his death to the call, "Follow me," Jesus indicates that the character of Peter's leadership will be the denial of self to the glory of God, and not a path to his own prosperity.

There are many possible sermon options within this brief and intense exchange, and much depends on the particular aspect of the dialogue that captures your homiletical attention. All the options, though, reflect in some measure the intensity and personal seriousness of Jesus' conversation with "Simon son of John."

PATRICK W. T. JOHNSON

John 21:20–25

²⁰Peter turned and saw the disciple whom Jesus loved following them; he was the one who had reclined next to Jesus at the supper and had said, "Lord, who is it that is going to betray you?" ²¹When Peter saw him, he said to Jesus, "Lord, what about him?" ²²Jesus said to him, "If it is my will that he remain until I come, what is that to you? Follow me!" ²³So the rumor spread in the community that this disciple would not die. Yet Jesus did not say to him that he would not die, but, "If it is my will that he remain until I come, what is that to you?"

²⁴This is the disciple who is testifying to these things and has written them, and we know that his testimony is true. ²⁵But there are also many other things that Jesus did; if every one of them were written down, I suppose that the world itself could not contain the books that would be written.

Theological Perspective

This text includes the second of only two references to Jesus' coming again in the entire Gospel of John (14:3). What are we to make of this reference? One consideration is to explore the way that the Gospel of John has invited the hearer into glimpsing the end of the story. It is a bit like reading the last chapter of a mystery novel first. If you know how the story ends, it changes the way you become invested in the characters as they are introduced and developed along the way. One could use this metaphor to suggest that Jesus lets the hearers in on the end of the story. The end of the story is that life has the last word, not death. The end of the story is that love has the last word, not hate. The end of the story is that forgiveness and grace have the last word, not judgment and retribution.

In this way, the world cannot contain the fullness of this testimony. The end of the story is that God's final future is hope and not despair, reconciliation not recrimination, self-offering not self-interest. Following Jesus does not push these promises into the final future of God but invites response to Jesus' invitation, "Follow me!" This imperative suggests that the community has something to do now to bring to fruition the fullness of God's promised future. One dare not sit idly by, assured that one's own future

Pastoral Perspective

This final pericope of the Gospel of John continues Jesus' conversation with Peter, picking up after Peter hears Jesus' call: "Follow me." Peter immediately turns and points to that other disciple, the nameless one who keeps appearing next to him throughout these resurrection chapters in John, and asks, "What about him?"

His question echoes ancient human emotions: insecurity, envy, resentment. From Cain jealous of Abel, to Martha and Mary's negotiation of roles, we have seen competition before. Here it flashes forth in the tension between two original leaders in the Jesus movement: the Beloved Disciple leading the Johannine community, and Peter the head of what became the dominant tradition. In whatever form, the question is the same: "Lord, what about him? What are you going to do about her?" Three things bear notice: first, Peter—like Martha in Luke 10:40—brings his complaint into *prayer*, rather than acting out his jealousy against its target. He shows Jesus his raw need, opening himself, just as he is, to God in the flesh. Expressing emotion directly in prayer is profoundly honest, and such uncensored prayer is proof of the love Peter has just professed for Jesus: he is willing to open his real self to this Lord.

Feasting on the Gospels

Exegetical Perspective

This final pericope in the Gospel of John constitutes the third episode of the epilogue to the Gospel. The first episode, which begins with the resurrection appearance of Jesus at the Sea of Tiberias (Sea of Galilee), includes the miraculous catch of 153 fish and breakfast on the beach (21:1–14). The two following sections of the epilogue occur within the same setting, as the risen Jesus engages Peter in conversation about Peter's future ministry as pastor, as well as his cruciform death (21:15–19). The conversation then turns to the enigmatic Beloved Disciple's role as "witness" and engages the subject of his death, the timing of which causes controversy because it seems to contradict a saying of Jesus that he would "remain" until Jesus returned (vv. 20–25).

The Beloved Disciple, a figure unique to the Johannine community, gains in prominence only in the later portions of the Gospel. This is in contrast to Peter, who is introduced at the beginning (1:40–42), is explicitly named "Cephas" by Jesus in 1:42, and remains a significant figure throughout the narrative. The unnamed Beloved Disciple is explicitly introduced only in the context of the Last Supper (13:23). There he is reclining at the side of Jesus, a sign of favored status. Given Peter's own future betrayal,

Homiletical Perspective

Like many of our sermons, John's Gospel again seems to arrive at an ending, only to continue the story. After telling Peter how he will die to the glory of God, the Lord's last words to him in verse 19 are, "Follow me." The Gospel could have ended there. It is a dramatic note of call and commissioning to discipleship, and in the context of John's Gospel it is the first time Peter is instructed to follow. Still, there is always more to the disciple's story than the first, dramatic calling.

Peter's commissioning has comprised this entire chapter, and at the high point of receiving the call to discipleship Peter turns, looks at the Beloved Disciple, and asks, "Lord, what about him?" For the exegete, it is tempting to wonder, why does the Beloved Disciple now enter a narrative that has been tightly focused on Peter and Jesus? The possible reasons for this probably mean more to the first community of hearers than to the contemporary community. For the creative preacher it is even more tempting to imagine the many reasons that Peter asked about the future of his friend. Indeed, these musings have no doubt fueled many sermons on this text. Jesus rebukes Peter for his question about the Beloved Disciple, though, and turns the focus back to Peter. Essentially, the future of this other disciple is not

Theological Perspective

is secure; rather, one is called to respond actively, knowing that Jesus' invitation is to follow.

Again, why only a single reference, when the other Gospels repeatedly talk about the impending reign of God and return of Jesus in glory? Although it is not explicitly stated, the entire Gospel of John depicts the *present* shape of God's future promise for the flourishing of the world. John's emphasis on the incarnation of the Word is his way of describing God's ongoing project for the world. Far from being a picture of some distant final future, John's witness describes God deeply embedded in the present messiness and the life of the world.

God's future breaks into the present and pulls the community forward into active love for the neighbor. Active love is contextually concrete: feeding the hungry in a local soup kitchen, staffing a homeless shelter, sending cards to the nursing home, mentoring at-risk children and youth, taking a meal to a bereaved neighbor, babysitting for a single mom, offering a scholarship for a child to attend camp, praying for victims of natural disaster, phoning a homebound person.

Jesus could have said a lot of things, but the last words to Peter are "follow me." Jesus could have ended with "Love me" or "I am the good shepherd, the bread of life, the light of the world, the gate for the sheep, or the true vine." Jesus could have reminded Peter that "I am the way, the truth, the life, or the resurrection and the life." Instead, Jesus tells Peter, "Follow me."

The preacher or teacher may explore the ways that a community leans into what it means to hear the call of Jesus to "follow me." What does it mean to unleash the wisdom, creativity, love, and light of a community of faith? What does it mean to engage deeply with the suffering, marginalized, and ignored people and circumstances in one's neighborhood and the world? Following the great "I am" as the hands and feet of Jesus is an adventure that stretches the imagination of preconceived ideas of God's work in the world. Following Jesus opens the way for the flourishing of the whole creation.

Another possibility we may explore is the way that the text opens a window into the ways we worry about our own places in the world. One can ask what is fair, what is just, what is right. Peter asks Jesus about the place of the Beloved Disciple, who is never named in the Fourth Gospel. Perhaps Peter is jockeying for position in the reign of God that is to come. Jesus calls him out, because the generosity of God is not constrained by human assumptions about

Pastoral Perspective

Significant as well, second, is how Jesus responds to Peter's anxious question: he directs Peter's focus right back to his own discipleship, interrupting the scrutiny of others that creates crippling comparisons: Is she or he a better disciple than I am, receiving more applause, better loved, more hip? Am I superior, on this measure or that? How does our congregation compare to those others? It is a relief to hear Jesus break though this distracting self-evaluation, returning us to his own voice as the only reality worth paying attention to: "If I am calling this other person or community to a vocation different from yours, what is that to you? Follow me!"

Third, we see that differences in forms of discipleship are real. The evangelist draws the distinction clearly between these two apostles: Peter is the one *who loves Jesus* (21:15–19), indeed, whose relationship with Jesus is restored precisely on the basis of his threefold attested love. In contrast, this other apostle is the one *whom Jesus loves*, one who has no other name or identity except that of the beloved of Jesus, the one given the place of greatest intimacy at Jesus' last meal before his crucifixion (13:23–25; 21:20).

In 1940 Dietrich Bonhoeffer wrote a meditation on the figure of the Beloved Disciple. Without question Bonhoeffer is a model of one who loves Jesus actively, heroically—all the way to martyrdom, like Peter. Yet hear how he speaks of this other, more hidden disciple: "In this Gospel his name is not mentioned even once! . . . It does not read, 'the disciple who loved the Lord'; even that would be too much of himself." This one is—solely—the one whom Jesus loves. Thus this nameless figure

> becomes a witness of the experienced love of Jesus, of the most intimate proximity and communion with him. . . . Martyrdom is foretold for Peter, but [this disciple] abides with Jesus and his form disappears in communion with Jesus. All that lingers is a rumor among the people: this disciple will not die.[1]

Surely the church needs both Peter and the Beloved Disciple—the lover and the beloved of Jesus—as models of the life of faith. Surely, in fact, the fullest vision of discipleship includes both of them in one: a noncompetitive loving-and-being-loved that flow into one another without anxiety or comparative hierarchies of gifts—communities

1. *Dietrich Bonhoeffer Works*, vol. 16, *Conspiracy and Imprisonment: 1940–1945*, ed. Mark S. Brocker, trans. Lisa E. Dahill (Minneapolis: Fortress Press, 2005), 314–15.

Peter then ironically asks the Beloved Disciple to ask of Jesus the identity of the betrayer (13:23–25).

The tensive relationship established here between Peter and the Beloved Disciple is variously developed in the Gospel. The Beloved Disciple may well be the "other disciple" of 18:15–16, who does not betray Jesus in the courtyard of the high priest as Peter does, but rather follows him to the foot of the cross. There he and Mary are commissioned by Jesus to be as mother and son in the new family of God (19:25–27), a family Peter will join only after his rehabilitation (21:14–19).

Similarly, although Mary Magdalene is the first to witness the empty tomb in John, Peter and the Beloved Disciple have a footrace to it in response to her report, a race the latter wins (20:4). Though Peter steps first into the empty tomb, it is the Beloved Disciple who "saw and believed" (20:8). In the fishing episode that begins chapter 21, it is the Beloved Disciple who recognizes that the mysterious figure on the beach is Jesus, though Peter dons clothes and jumps into the sea in order to greet him. Peter is, therefore, a highly visible, named public figure. He is impulsive and passionate, yet proves unreliable during the passion. In contrast, the unnamed Beloved Disciple, though largely hidden from view, enjoys Jesus' intimate confidence. He is faithful throughout the passion, is given the care of Jesus' own mother, and is entrusted with the theological tradition that has its source in the *logos* of God (1:1).

In fact, the concept of "following" provides the bridge between the second and the final pericopes. The section that deals with Peter's future vocation (21:15–19) ends with, "*Follow* me." The final pericope (vv. 20–25) begins with Peter noticing that "the disciple whom Jesus loved was *following* them." The Beloved Disciple never wavers in his faith as does Peter.

In response to Jesus' question about the Beloved Disciple's future ministry, Jesus says, "If it is my will that he remain until I come, what is that to you?" (v. 23b). At the point of the final redaction of the Gospel of John, which includes the epilogue, the Beloved Disciple has died. Verse 23 is clear that the problem was not with Jesus' saying, but that the all-important "*If it is my will*" was missing from the saying that circulated in the wider Johannine community.

Jesus' abrupt rejoinder to Peter in verse 22—"What is it to you?"—repeated in verse 23, suggests that a comparison between the two disciples, something the Gospel itself encouraged, is now

Peter's concern. "Follow me!" Jesus replies, and these are the last words the Lord speaks to his disciple.

As we live out our daily discipleship, there are many opportunities to "look over our shoulder." Why must my road be steep and rocky, when another person's seems flat and smooth? Why does my journey lead into ever more suffering and loss? Perhaps, simply, why is this path of discipleship so challenging—I thought it was supposed to be easier? These questions come so naturally, yet the answers are hidden in the mysterious will of God. As a preacher, you have the opportunity to name these questions for your congregation. Such naming helps us to be honest about the challenges we face in discipleship, and this honesty also helps us to hear Christ's call anew. It is important to notice in this text that Jesus repeats his call to Peter. "Follow me!" he says a second time. The first, dramatic calling may have long faded, and perhaps some in your congregation need to hear this call again, for a second, third, or hundredth time. Through your sermon Christ may repeat his call to you, as well as to your hearers.

Turning now to verses 24–25, these lines both conclude the testimony of the Gospel and propel us into our own testimonies. Verse 24 sounds like the signature of a witness on a legal document, affirming that the Beloved Disciple has testified to these things. The word "testimony" is important because it tells us about the character of the whole Gospel. A testimony is not simply a recitation of events, but also points to their significance. When we bear witness or give testimony, we tell not only what we have experienced but also what we believe about it. We stake our lives on the truth of our testimony.

In these pages the beloved disciple has told what he experienced and what he believes about it. It is his confession of faith made to his community. Moreover, his testimony has credibility within the community. Not all testimonies are judged as true, but the scribes of this Gospel make the note that "we know that his testimony is true." How do they know? Presumably they know because of the person of the witness—his life among them, his integrity and faithfulness, his trustworthiness. He has staked his life on his confession, and they believe the testimony because they know the witness.

In one sense, this kind of signature may raise the credibility of the Gospel for the contemporary hearer, and your sermon on this text may encourage the congregation in their faith. It is heartening to know that the Christian story is based from the beginning on the testimony of witnesses and that

John 21:20–25

Theological Perspective

fairness and one's place in the world. If Jesus can offer living water to a Samaritan woman, all notions of what establishes one's proper place in the world are reimagined.

Throughout history, the world has endured disasters, calamities, ecological devastation, and human tragedy. Every Christian has dealt with the grieving loved one in the emergency room who asks, why me? In the wake of denial and doubt, Jesus invites Peter to do something, to take action, to step out in faith, knowing only that God is faithful to God's promises. Since we know that the end of the story is life, followers of Jesus are freed from the fear that death is the ultimate power. Since we know that the end of the story is love, followers of Jesus are free to be conduits of God's overflowing love that overcomes pervasive petty hatreds. Since we know that the end of the story is forgiveness and grace, followers of Jesus are free to dare and risk ways of interaction that abandon judgment and retribution.

Following Jesus is risky business. Jesus concludes the encounter with Simon Peter by telling him to "follow me." Perhaps this is a reminder that when one seeks to know the living God, life can unfold in unpredictable ways. God has surprises in store. Following Jesus can transform the way we interact in the workplace, in the gym, in gatherings with friends, in social media. Following Jesus calls us to engage courageously persons we may otherwise dismiss. Following Jesus calls for active advocacy to address social structures and systemic injustices.

The last few verses teach us something about the importance of witness and testimony. Every telling of every story is selective. Every person who tells a story is also an interpreter of that story. Part of participating in God's ongoing work in the world involves bearing witness to God's actions so that all may have abundant life.

ROBIN J. STEINKE

Pastoral Perspective

and leaders grateful for the way Jesus' call uniquely invites each person to live in love with him over time. Surely all of this acting and abiding in love reflects the unconditional *availability to Jesus* that is foretold for Peter in his martyrdom (21:18–19) *and* is embodied by the Beloved Disciple in "remaining" in Jesus forever (vv. 22, 23). Such whole-life availability to the divine call is what allows wildly diverse disciples to live in their own vocations without apology or jealousy of others—free to offer their best gifts for the life of the world, the shining forth of the love of Jesus in their own bodies' speech.

Hear again that great witness to this love, Dietrich Bonhoeffer:

> The all-encompassing nature of Jesus' love (John 3:16!) must become evident against every pietistic narrowing, and yet this is the very place where the utterly personal must also be expressed, that we too belong to those whom Jesus loved and loves and will love, that Jesus' love is not a private affair but is the center of the world. . . . To be content in Jesus' love—I would see that as the conclusion and significance of everything that is to be said about [the beloved disciple]. . . . What does it mean to recline at the breast of Jesus (John 13:23)? To be sheltered in him, guarded by him, protected from temptation and fall, held, drawn into trust? To be allowed to question him [John 21:20], to receive an answer, to lie at the heart of God?[2]

Jesus' response to Peter's anxious question releases us too to stop comparing ourselves to others and instead to listen, forever, to what our own call really is. This listening requires the gifts of self-awareness (personal and communal), reading well the signs of the times, and wise discernment of the living Word among us. The voice of this Word will never cease to address us, again and again calling us to follow (21:19, 22).

In fact, this living Word overflows even the pages of Scripture (v. 25) to address us everywhere in creation, crying out for our attention in strangers and enemies and loved ones, in the poor in every land and in the most vulnerable of many species today. In every place, every beleaguered ecosystem and community, the One in whom all things were made continues to work for abundance of life for all that is (10:10). To live in this abundance—wherever it calls us—is the love of Jesus.

LISA E. DAHILL

2. Ibid., 315.

inappropriate. Though Peter and the Beloved Disciple would have different vocations in the church, they would be equally significant. Peter, rehabilitated from his threefold denial, is commissioned as a shepherd/pastor and would die a *martyr*'s death. The Beloved Disciple's future role would continue to provide a faithful witness (*martyria*, NRSV "testimony") to Jesus by means of his preservation and interpretation of a theological tradition that stemmed from Jesus and became the Gospel of John (v. 24), a process intimately guided by the Paraclete (*paraklētos*, NRSV "Advocate"). His future role would be different from Peter's, not only because he was a scriptural theologian and not a pastor but because he would not die a martyr's death. There is in John more than one model of discipleship.

One might wonder, who is the "we" of verse 24: "*We* know that his witness [NRSV "testimony"] is true"? It is, perhaps, the "we" of 1:14–18, that of the postresurrection confessing community, a community that is being guided in all truth by the Advocate/ Paraclete. In 14:26 Jesus tells the disciples, "The Advocate, the Holy Spirit, whom the Father will send in my name, will *teach* you everything, and *remind* you of all that I have said to you." From the perspective of the epilogue, this same Holy Spirit continues to lead the community in all truth. As a confessing witness to Christ, the Gospel is a many-layered memory of Jesus' ministry brought alive through ongoing teaching in the new contexts in which the Johannine community discovered itself.

In the commentary literature, the received interpretation of the final verse of the epilogue, that "the world itself could not contain the books that would be written" about all that Jesus did, is an example of the tendency toward the hyperbole of ancient rhetoric. That may be. Perhaps, though, it is simply the witnessing community recognizing that under the ongoing guidance of the Holy Spirit, the Word of God continues to "remind" and "teach" the church of the salvation that is in Christ (4:42; 12:47) in ever new situations. Because of the changed situations that the gospel speaks itself into, it shall be ever rewritten in the lives of those who confess that "the Word became flesh and lived among us" (1:14). If so, then "the world itself could not contain the books that would be written."

ERIK M. HEEN

their testimony has been faithfully handed down. Especially for congregations who wrestle with the credibility of Christian claims, in a culture that values scientific evidence, this text may open the way for an apologetic sermon.

In a different and more personal sense, this verse may also draw us into our own testimony and signature. The Spirit Jesus breathed on his disciples is still working among and within God's people. God's redeeming love is at work in our world and in our neighborhoods, and we all have our own gospel accounts. The works of God in the day-to-day lives of the Christian community are signs that confirm the truth that the preacher proclaims. How does a watching world come to believe that what the preacher says is true? Because they have seen the gospel alive in a community that is empowered by God's Spirit.

In preparation for a sermon on this text, you could reflect on your own testimony and testimonies you have heard in your community, and your sermon could invite the congregation to consider their testimonies. How have they experienced God's work in their lives? What do they believe about it? How are they staking their lives on it? A follow-up to the sermon could be a time of exploring and sharing testimonies, perhaps through personal journaling or in small groups. Perhaps your sermon could incorporate the testimony of someone in your congregation or community.

In verse 25, it is as if the Beloved Disciple offers one last, wistful, and lovely thought to the scribes: There are so many more stories he could tell, but if he tried to tell the full significance of Jesus Christ, the universe could not contain the books. When we as preachers attend closely to the living testimonies present in our congregations, I think we will find these words are true indeed. The cosmos could not contain the books!

PATRICK W. T. JOHNSON

Contributors

P. Mark Achtemeier, Pastor, Presbyterian Church (U.S.A.), Dubuque, Iowa

Samuel L. Adams, Associate Professor of Old Testament Studies, Union Presbyterian Seminary, Richmond, Virginia

Sammy G. Alfaro, Assistant Professor of Christian Studies, College of Theology, Grand Canyon University, Phoenix, Arizona

Katherine E. Amos, Resident Professor of Spirituality and the Arts, Wake Forest Divinity School, Winston-Salem, North Carolina

Dale P. Andrews, Distinguished Professor of Homiletics, Social Justice, and Practical Theology, Divinity School of Vanderbilt University, Nashville, Tennessee

Ellen T. Armour, E. Rhodes and Leona B. Carpenter Chair in Feminist Theology and Director of the Carpenter Program in Religion, Gender, and Sexuality, Divinity School of Vanderbilt University, Nashville, Tennessee

Lindsay P. Armstrong, Executive Director, New Church Development, Presbytery of Greater Atlanta, Atlanta, Georgia

Emily Askew, Associate Professor of Systematic Theology, Lexington Theological Seminary, Lexington, Kentucky

Rachel Sophia Baard, Lawrence C. Gallen Fellow in the Humanities, Villanova University, Villanova, Pennsylvania

Coleman A. Baker, Program Manager, Brite Divinity School, Soul Repair Center, and Adjunct Professor, Texas Christian University, Fort Worth, Texas

Lee C. Barrett, Professor of Systematic Theology, Lancaster Theological Seminary, Lancaster, Pennsylvania

David L. Bartlett, Professor Emeritus of New Testament, Columbia Theological Seminary, Decatur, Georgia

Paul Barton, Associate Professor in the History of American Christianity and Missiology and Director of Hispanic Church Studies, Seminary of the Southwest, Austin, Texas

Stephen P. Bauman, Senior Minister, Christ Church United Methodist, New York, New York

Nathan D. Baxter, Retired Bishop, Diocese of Central Pennsylvania (Episcopal), Harrisburg, Pennsylvania

Michael S. Bennett, Pastor, First Parish Church, Congregational-United Church of Christ, Dover, New Hampshire

April Berends, Episcopal Priest, Sewanee, Tennessee

Debra T. Bibler, Associate Executive Presbyter, Flint River Presbytery, Albany, Georgia

Richard D. Blake, Professor and Graduate Studies Librarian, Waynesburg University, Waynesburg, Pennsylvania

Helen K. Bond, Senior Lecturer of New Testament, School of Divinity, University of Edinburgh, Edinburgh, Scotland

Suzanne Woolston Bossert, Minister, United Church of Christ, Boston, Massachusetts

Kathleen Long Bostrom, Retired Pastor, Presbyterian Church (U.S.A.), Wildwood, Illinois

Richard N. Boyce, Academic Dean and Associate Professor of Preaching and Pastoral Leadership, Union Presbyterian Seminary, Charlotte, North Carolina

Robert M. Brearley, Pastor, St. Simons Presbyterian Church, St. Simons Island, Georgia

Thomas Edward Breidenthal, Bishop, Diocese of Southern Ohio (Episcopal), Cincinnati, Ohio

Richard Carlson, Glatfelter Professor of Biblical Studies, Director of Internship, and Coordinator of Post-Internship Candidacy, Lutheran Theological Seminary at Gettysburg, Gettysburg, Pennsylvania

Kenneth H. Carter, Bishop, Florida Conference of the United Methodist Church, Lakeland, Florida

Nick Carter, President Emeritus, Andover Newton School of Theology, Newton Centre, Massachusetts

Christine Chakoian, Pastor, First Presbyterian Church of Lake Forest, Lake Forest, Illinois

Jaime Clark-Soles, Associate Professor of New Testament and Altshuler Distinguished Teaching Professor, Perkins School of Theology, Southern Methodist University, Dallas, Texas

John W. Coakley, L. Russell Feakes Memorial Professor of Church History, New Brunswick Seminary, New Brunswick, New Jersey

Colleen M. Conway, Professor of Religious Studies, Department of Religion, Seton Hall University, South Orange, New Jersey

Wyndy Corbin Reuschling, Professor of Ethics and Theology, Ashland Theological Seminary, Ashland, Ohio

Vaughn CroweTipton, Associate Vice President for Spiritual Life, University Chaplain, and Associate Professor of Religion, Furman University, Greenville, South Carolina

Lisa E. Dahill, Associate Professor of Worship and Christian Spirituality, Trinity Lutheran Seminary, Columbus, Ohio

James E. Davison, Retired Director of Continuing Education and Lecturer in Greek Language and Exegesis, Pittsburgh Theological Seminary, Pittsburgh, Pennsylvania

Joseph Prabhakar Dayam, Associate Professor and Chair of the Department of Theology and Ethics, Gurukul Lutheran Theological College and Research Institute, Chennai, India

Lisa D. Maugans Driver, Associate Professor of Theology and Program Director of Mentoring for the Center for Church Vocations, Department of Theology, Valparaiso University, Valparaiso, Indiana

Paul Simpson Duke, Co-Pastor, First Baptist Church of Ann Arbor, Ann Arbor, Michigan

Susan Grove Eastman, Associate Research Professor of New Testament and Director of the Doctor of Theology Program, Duke Divinity School, Durham, North Carolina

S. Brian Erickson, Senior Pastor, Trinity United Methodist Church, Birmingham, Alabama

Barbara J. Essex, Executive Director, United Protestant Campus Ministries, Cleveland, Ohio

James H. Evans Jr., Robert K. Davies Professor of Systematic Theology, Colgate Rochester Crozer Divinity School, Rochester, New York

Lincoln E. Galloway, K. Morgan Edwards Associate Professor of Homiletics, Claremont School of Theology, Claremont, California

Larry D. George, Associate Professor of New Testament Interpretation, Gardner Webb University, School of Divinity, Boiling Springs, North Carolina

S. Vance Goodman, Staff Chaplain and Bereavement Coordinator, Children's Medical Center, Dallas, Texas

Alan P. R. Gregory, Principal, South East Institute for Theological Education, London, United Kingdom

Jack Haberer, Pastor and Head of Staff, Vanderbilt Presbyterian Church, Naples, Florida

Erik M. Heen, The John H. P. Reumann Professor in Biblical Studies, Lutheran Theological Seminary at Philadelphia, Philadelphia, Pennsylvania

Amy G. Heller, Sunday Assistant, Episcopal Church of the Transfiguration, Dallas, Texas

Mark G. Vitalis Hoffman, Professor of Biblical Studies, Lutheran Theological Seminary at Gettysburg, Gettysburg, Pennsylvania

Mark Husbands, Leonard and Marjorie Maas Associate Professor of Reformed Theology, Hope College, Holland, Michigan

Susan E. Hylen, Associate Research Professor of New Testament, Candler School of Theology at Emory University, Atlanta, Georgia

E. Elizabeth Johnson, J. Davison Philips Professor of New Testament, Columbia Theological Seminary, Decatur, Georgia

Louise Lawson Johnson, Associate Pastor for Congregational Life, The Presbyterian Church of Lawrenceville, Lawrenceville, New Jersey

Patrick W. T. Johnson, Pastor, Frenchtown Presbyterian Church, Frenchtown, New Jersey

Michael S. Koppel, Howard Chandler Robbins Professor of Pastoral Theology and Congregational Care, Associate Dean for Academic Affairs, Wesley Theological Seminary, Washington, D.C.

Kristin Johnston Largen, Interim Dean and Associate Professor of Systematic Theology, Lutheran Theological Seminary at Gettysburg, Gettysburg, Pennsylvania

Karoline M. Lewis, Associate Professor of Biblical Preaching and The Alvin N. Rogness Chair of Homiletics, Luther Seminary, St. Paul, Minnesota

Laura A. Loving, Associate Pastor, Wauwatosa Presbyterian Church, Wauwatosa, Wisconsin

David Lower, Senior Pastor, Winnetka Presbyterian Church, Winnetka, Illinois

Bert Marshall, New England Regional Director, Church World Service, Plainfield, Massachusetts

Denise McLain Massey, Associate Professor of Pastoral Care and Counseling, McAfee School of Theology, Mercer University, Atlanta, Georgia

Judith M. McDaniel, Howard Chandler Robbins Professor of Homiletics Emerita, Virginia Theological Seminary, Alexandria, Virginia

Luis Menéndez-Antuña, Student, Graduate Department of Religion, Vanderbilt University, Nashville, Tennessee

Martha Moore-Keish, Associate Professor of Theology, Columbia Theological Seminary, Decatur, Georgia

Richard Newton, Assistant Professor of Religious Studies, Elizabethtown College, Elizabethtown, Pennsylvannia

Kay Lynn Northcutt, Fred B. Craddock Associate Professor of Preaching and Worship, Phillips Theological Seminary, Tulsa, Oklahoma

Rohun Park, Chaplain and Assistant Professor of New Testament, Yonsei University, Seoul, South Korea

G. J. Riley, Professor of New Testament, Claremont School of Theology, Claremont, California

Craig A. Satterlee, Bishop, North/West Lower Michigan Synod, Evangelical Lutheran Church in America, Lansing, Michigan

Timothy Matthew Slemmons, Associate Professor of Homiletics and Worship, University of Dubuque Theological Seminary, Dubuque, Iowa

Thomas D. Stegman, SJ, Chair of Ecclesiastical Faculty and Associate Professor of New Testament, Boston College School of Theology and Ministry, Chestnut Hill, Massachusetts

Robin J. Steinke, President, Luther Seminary, St. Paul, Minnesota

Lance Stone, Minister, English Reformed Church, Amsterdam, Netherlands

Sharon M. Tan, Vice President for Academic Affairs and Dean of the Seminary, United Theological Seminary of the Twin Cities, New Brighton, Minnesota

W. C. Turner, Professor of the Practice of Homiletics, Duke Divinity School, Durham, North Carolina

Lyle D. Vander Broek, Professor of New Testament, University of Dubuque Theological Seminary, Dubuque, Iowa

Richard F. Ward, Fred B. Craddock Professor of Homiletics and Worship, Phillips Theological Seminary, Tulsa, Oklahoma

Michael W. Waters, Founding Pastor, Joy Tabernacle African Methodist Episcopal Church, Dallas, Texas

Andy Watts, Associate Professor of Religion, College of Theology and Christian Ministry, Belmont University, Nashville, Tennessee

Sean White, Pastor, Eastminster Presbyterian Church, Knoxville, Tennessee

Victoria Atkinson White, Chaplain, Westminister Canterbury Richmond, Richmond, Virginia

Buz Wilcoxon, Pastor, Spring Hill Presbyterian Church, Mobile, Alabama

Alexander Wimberly, Presbyterian Church (U.S.A.) Minister and Doctoral Student, University of Notre Dame, Notre Dame, Indiana

John W. Wimberly Jr., Pastor Emeritus, Western Presbyterian Church, Washington, D.C.

J. Philip Wogaman, Professor Emeritus of Christian Ethics, Wesley Theological Seminary, Washington, D.C.

Arthur M. Wright Jr., Affiliate Professor of New Testament, Baptist Theological Seminary at Richmond, Richmond, Virginia

John Yieh, The Molly Laird Downs Professor of New Testament, Virginia Theological Seminary, Alexandria, Virginia

Cathy F. Young, Retired Pastor, Presbyterian Church (U.S.A.), Part-time Hospice Chaplain, Waterloo, Iowa

Rebecca Blair Young, Professor of Contemporary Systematic Theology, Jakarta Theological Seminary, Jakarta, Indonesia

Karen-Marie Yust, Professor of Christian Education, Union Presbyterian Seminary, Richmond, Virginia

Author Index

Nick Carter	John 19:8–16a HP; 19:16b–25a HP; 19:25b–30 HP	Larry D. George	John 12:36a–43 EP; 12:44–50 EP
Christine Chakoian	John 11:17–27 PP; 11:28–37 PP	S. Vance Goodman	John 16:16–24 PP; 16:25–33 PP; 17:1–5 PP
Jaime Clark-Soles	"The Jews" in the Fourth Gospel, xi–xiv; John 14:1–7 EP; 14:8–14 EP; 14:15–17 EP	Alan P. R. Gregory	John 18:25–27 TP; 18:28–38a TP; 18:38b–19:7 TP
		Jack Haberer	John 14:18–24 PP; 14:25–31 PP
John W. Coakley	John 17:14–19 TP; 17:20–26 TP	Erik M. Heen	John 21:15–19 EP; 21:20–25 EP
Colleen M. Conway	John 11:38–44 EP; 11:45–54 EP; 11:55–12:11 EP	Amy G. Heller	John 19:8–16a PP; 19:16b–25a PP; 19:25b–30 PP
Wyndy Corbin Reuschling	John 19:8–16a TP; 19:16b–25a TP; 19:25b–30 TP	Mark G. Vitalis Hoffman	John 18:25–27 EP; 18:28–38a EP; 18:38b–19:7 EP
Vaughn CroweTipton	John 19:31–37 HP; 19:38–42 HP; 20:1–10 HP	Mark Husbands	John 15:18–25 TP; 15:26–16:4a TP; 16:4b–15 TP
Lisa E. Dahill	John 21:15–19 PP; 21:20–25 PP	Susan E. Hylen	John 10:1–6 EP; 10:7–10 EP; 10:11–18 EP
James E. Davison	John 19:31–37 EP; 19:38–42 EP; 20:1–10 EP	E. Elizabeth Johnson	John 20:11–18 PP; 20:19–23 PP; 20:24–31 PP
Joseph Prabhakar Dayam	John 11:1–6 TP; 11:7–16 TP	Louise Lawson Johnson	John 21:1–8 PP; 21:9–14 PP
Lisa D. Maugans Driver	John 21:1–8 TP; 21:9–14 TP	Patrick W. T. Johnson	John 21:15–19 HP; 21:20–25 HP
Paul Simpson Duke	John 20:11–18 HP; 20:19–23 HP; 20:24–31 HP	Michael S. Koppel	John 11:38–44 PP; 11:45–54 PP; 11:55–12:11 PP
Susan Grove Eastman	John 20:11–18 EP; 20:19–23 EP; 20:24–31 EP	Kristin Johnston Largen	John 20:11–18 TP; 20:19–23 TP; 20:24–31 TP
S. Brian Erickson	John 21:1–8 HP; 21:9–14 HP	Karoline M. Lewis	John 13:21–30 TP; 13:31–35 TP; 13:36–38 TP
Barbara J. Essex	John 18:25–27 HP; 18:28–38a HP; 18:38b–19:7 HP	Laura A. Loving	John 13:21–30 PP; 13:31–35 PP; 13:36–38 PP
James H. Evans Jr.	John 18:1–11 TP; 18:12–18 TP; 18:19–24 TP	David Lower	John 10:1–6 HP; 10:7–10 HP; 10:11–18 HP
Lincoln E. Galloway	John 11:1–6 HP; 11:7–16 HP		